The Appraisal of Real Estate

The Appraisal of Real Estate

Eleventh Edition

**APPRAISAL
INSTITUTE®**

875 North Michigan Avenue
Chicago, Illinois 60611-1980

Acknowledgments
Senior Vice President, Communications: Christopher Bettin
Manager, Book Development: Michael R. Milgrim, PhD
Senior Editor/Writer: Stephanie Shea-Joyce
Manager, Design/Production: Julie B. Beich

For Educational Purposes Only
The opinions set forth herein reflect the viewpoint of the Appraisal Institute at the time of publication but do not necessarily reflect the viewpoint of each individual member. While a great deal of care has been taken to provide accurate and current information, neither the Appraisal Institute nor its editors and staff assume responsibility for the accuracy of the data contained herein. Further, the general principles and conclusions presented in this text are subject to local, state, and federal laws and regulations, court cases, and any revisions of the same. This publication is sold for educational purposes with the understanding that the publisher is not engaged in rendering legal, accounting, or other professional service.

Nondiscrimination Policy
The Appraisal Institute advocates equal employment and nondiscrimination in the appraisal profession and conducts its activities without regard to race, color, sex, religion, national origin, or handicap status.

Printed in the United States of America

99   98   4   3

The photos appearing in this text were supplied by H. Armstrong Roberts, Inc. and HISTORICAL PICTURES/STOCK MONTAGE.

Library of Congress Cataloging-in-Publication Data
The appraisal of real estate.— 11th ed.
       p.   cm.
    Includes bibliographical references and index.
    ISBN 0-922154-35-X
    1. Real property—Valuation.   2. Personal property—Valuation.
I. Appraisal Institute (U.S.)
HD1387.A663   1996
333.33'2—dc20   96-41019
                                                       CIP

Table of Contents

Appendices

Foreword

A s a new century approaches, the accelerating pace of change in technology, regulatory legislation, valuation methods, and value concepts has and will continue to play a significant role in shaping appraisal practice. Markets and business procedures are also being transformed. Securitization has fundamentally altered the character of capital markets which generate investment in real estate. The globalization of real estate and financial markets has greatly expanded the number of arenas in which American appraisers can offer their services. Electronic commerce has dramatically shortened the loan approval process and the time lenders expend on decision making. Although the rapidity of these changes may seem daunting, the time-tested principles and procedures that have long been the basis for appraisal practice are proving remarkably resilient and adaptable to contemporary conditions. The eleventh edition of *The Appraisal of Real Estate* has endeavored, therefore, to keep abreast of the innovations sweeping the field while preserving the best of the traditional body of appraisal knowledge.

This edition provides expanded coverage of evolving technologies such as GIS and EDI and introduces two new topics, securitization and international valuation. Updated areas include standards-related issues, reporting requirements, and regulatory legislation. Revisiting the three approaches to value, the text presents new applications to illustrate the combination of quantitative and qualitative analyses in sales comparison, provides new ways to estimate depreciation in the cost approach, and explores specialized appraisals of income-producing properties involving partial interests and business enterprise value as well as proposed and problem properties. Readers will find many other useful additions reflecting contemporary practice, e.g., the discussions of effective rent, rent loss during lease-up, and the terminal capitalization rate.

The Appraisal Institute would especially like to acknowledge the dedicated work of Thomas A. Motta, MAI, SRA, chair of the Publications Committee, and Frank E. Harrison, MAI, SRA, Publications Committee member. Both of these individuals reviewed the final manuscript and helped guide the decision-making process. I would also like to thank the many other developers, reviewers, and resource persons who contributed to the project over the two and a half years that the eleventh edition of *The Appraisal of Real Estate* was in development: Charles B. Akerson, MAI; Norman R. Benedict, MAI; David M. Bradley, MAI, SRA; James C. Burge, MAI, SRA; Robert C. Cantwell IV, MAI; M. Rebecca Carr, MAI; David W. Childers, MAI; Winfield L. Cooper, SRA; Robert David Domini, MAI; John D. Dorchester, Jr., MAI; Robert W. Dunham, MAI, SRA; Larry O. Dybvig, MAI; James D. Eaton, MAI, SRA; William A. Elgie III, SRA; Donald R. Epley, MAI, SRA, PhD; W. West Foster, MAI; Mark R. Freitag, SRA; George Garthoeffner, MAI, SRA; Howard C. Gelbtuch, MAI; James E. Gibbons, MAI, SRA; Diane M. Gilbert, MAI, SRA; Margaret A. Hambleton, SRA; Woodward S. Hanson, MAI; Bruce H. Harding, MAI; Jeffrey A. Johnson, MAI; Hugh Kelly; Peter F. Korpacz, MAI; Louann Hayden Lang, J.D.; David J. Lau, MAI; David C. Lennhoff, MAI, SRA; Mark Lee Levine, MAI, PhD; George Raymond Mann, MAI, SRA; Richard Marchitelli, MAI; James J. Mason, MAI; C. David Matthews, MAI, SRA; J. Virginia Messick, MAI; Arlen C. Mills, MAI, SRA; Nancy M. Mueller, MAI; Bill Mundy, MAI, PhD; Robert L. Parson, MAI; David A. Pearson, MAI; Joseph Rabianski, PhD; Anthony Reynolds, MAI; Stephen D. Roach, MAI; Mark I. Roth; Alan F. Simmons, SRPA; Lee B. Smith, MAI; Richard C. Sorenson, MAI; Norman B. Steinberg, MAI; Eugene W. Stunard, MAI, SRA; Gary P. Taylor, MAI, SRA; Gerald A. Teel, MAI, SRA; Roger E. Tegenkamp, MAI, SRA; Paula O. Thoreen, MAI; William T. Van Court, MAI; James D. Vernor, MAI, PhD; and Lee H. Waronker, MAI, SRA.

C. Spencer Powell, MAI
1996 President
Appraisal Institute

The Appraisal of Real Estate

Eleventh Edition

CHAPTER ONE

Real Property and Its Appraisal

L and provides the foundation for the social and economic activities of people and is both a commodity and a source of wealth. Because land is essential to life and society, it is important to many disciplines, including law, economics, sociology, and geography. Each of these disciplines may employ a somewhat different concept of real property.

Within the vast domain of the law, issues such as the ownership and the use of land are considered. In economics, land is regarded as one of the four agents of production, along with labor, capital, and entrepreneurship. Land provides many of the natural elements that contribute to a nation's wealth. Sociology focuses on the dual nature of land: as a resource to be shared by all people and as a commodity that can be owned, traded, and used by individuals. Geography focuses on describing the physical elements of land and the activities of the people who use it.

Land value is an economic concept. Lawyers, economists, sociologists, and geographers have a common understanding of the attributes of land.

- Each parcel of land is unique in its location and composition.
- Land is physically immobile.
- Land is durable.
- The supply of land is finite.
- Land is useful to people.

Real estate appraisers view these attributes as the foundation of real estate's value. They recognize the concepts of land used in other disciplines, but are most concerned with market measures of value, not theoretical concepts. Markets reflect the attitudes and actions of people in response to social and economic forces.

Concepts of Land

Governmental and Legal

Land use derives from the mandates of organized society. In countries where the ownership and marketability of land are not free, government often dictates the use of land. In free market economies, land use is regulated within a framework of laws. To understand how the various forces affecting land operate, the basic role of law must be recognized.

The cultural, political, governmental, and economic attitudes of a society are reflected in its laws. The legal profession does not focus on the physical characteristics of land, but on the rights and obligations associated with various interests in land. In the United States, the right of individuals to own and use land for material gain is maintained, while the right of all people to use the land is protected. In other words, the law recognizes the possible conflict between private ownership and public use.

"Whose is the land, his it is, to the sky and the depths." This ancient maxim is the basis of the following legal definition:

> Land includes not only the ground, or soil, but everything that is attached to the earth, whether by course of nature, as are trees and herbage, or by the hand of man, as are houses and other buildings. It includes not only the surface of the earth, but everything under it and over it. Thus, in legal theory, a tract of land consists not only of the portion on the surface of the earth, but is an inverted pyramid having its tip, or apex, at the center of the earth, extending outward through the surface of the earth at the boundary lines of the tract, and continuing on upward to the heavens.[1]

This definition suggests that land ownership includes complete possession of land from the center of the earth to the ends of the universe. In practice, however, ownership is limited. The U.S. Congress has declared that the federal government has complete and exclusive sovereignty over the nation's airspace and that every citizen has "a public right to freedom of transit in air commerce through the navigable air space of the United States."[2] Because land ownership can be limited, ownership rights are the subject of law; the value of these rights is the focus of real estate appraisal.

The laws that govern the use and development of land in the United States give landowners great freedom in deciding how to use their land. However, this freedom is not without restrictions. The basic concept of private ownership calls for unrestricted use so long as such use does not unreasonably harm the rights of others. In the past, the test of harm focused on owners of adjacent properties. The concept of harm has recently been expanded to encompass broader social and geographic concerns. The definition of *reasonable use* has been argued in many court cases.

Legal matters of particular concern to appraisers include easements, access regulations, use restrictions, and the recording and conveyance of titles. Because real estate appraising involves the valuation of real property rights, appraisers must be familiar with local and state laws, which have primary jurisdiction over land.

Economic

Land is a physical entity with inherent ownership rights that can be legally limited for the good of society. Land is also a major source of wealth which, in economic terms, can be measured in money or exchange value. Land and its products have economic value only when they are converted into goods or services that are useful, desirable, and paid for by consumers. The economic concept of land as a source of wealth and an object of value is central to appraisal theory.

---

1. Robert Kratovil and Raymond J. Werner, *Real Estate Law*, 8th ed. (Englewood Cliffs, N.J.: Prentice-Hall, Inc., 1983), 6.
2. The Air Commerce Act of 1926 (formerly 49 USC 171 *et seq.*); the Civil Aeronautics Act of 1938 (formerly 49 USC 401 *et seq.*); and the Federal Aviation Act of 1958 (see 49 USC 401).

The economic concept of land reflects a long history of thought on the sources and bases of value, which is referred to as *value theory*.[3] Value theory contributes to the value definitions used in appraisal reports and appraisal literature, and it is an important part of the philosophy on which professional appraisal practice is founded. The development of value theory and its relationship to other systems of thought are discussed in Chapter 2.

Social

Modern society has become increasingly concerned with how land is used and how rights are distributed. The supply of land is fixed, so increased demand for land exerts pressure for land to be used more intensively. Conflicts often arise between groups that hold different views on proper land use. Those who believe that land is a resource to be shared by all want to preserve the land's scenic beauty and important ecological functions. Others view land primarily as a marketable commodity. They believe society is best served by private, unrestricted ownership. Because land is both a resource and a commodity, there are no clear-cut solutions to this conflict.[4]

Both points of view have legal support. As a resource, land is protected for the good of society. As a marketable commodity, the ownership, use, and disposal of land are regulated so that individual rights are not violated.

In 1876 the U.S. Supreme Court established government's right to regulate "the manner in which [a citizen] shall own his own property when such regulation becomes necessary for the public good." The court quoted the words of England's Lord Chief Justice Hale: "When private property is 'affected with a public interest,' it ceases to be *juris privati* only."[5] Throughout American history, land ownership has been recognized as fundamental. John Adams wrote, "If the multitude is possessed of real estate, the multitude will take care of the liberty, virtue, and interest of the multitude in all acts of government."[6]

All laws and operations of government are intended to serve the public. Thus, in the public interest, society may impose building restrictions, zoning and building ordinances, development and subdivision regulations, and other land use controls. These controls affect what may be developed, where development may occur, and what activities may be permitted subsequent to development. In recent decades, the U.S. government has increased its efforts to regulate the air and water emissions from manufacturing processes and to reduce pollution caused by dirt, chemicals, and noise. Protective controls over land use extend to wetlands, beaches, and navigable waters, and to the preservation of endangered species. Acting on the perception that regulatory powers have occasionally been abused by governmental bodies, some property owners have filed inverse condemnation claims seeking compensation for loss in property value.

3. Paul F. Wendt, *Real Estate Appraisal: Review and Outlook* (Athens: University of Georgia Press, 1974), 17.
4. Richard N. L. Andrews, *Land in America* (Lexington, Mass.: D.C. Heath and Company, 1979), ix.
5. 94 U.S. 113 (1896). Quoted in "Land as a Commodity Affected with a Public Interest'" by Richard F. Babcock and Duane A. Feurer in Richard N. L. Andrews' *Land in America* (Lexington, Mass: D.C. Heath and Company, 1979), 110.
6. Ibid., 31.

Amendment V

Provisions concerning Prosecution, Trial and Punishment—Private Property Not to Be Taken for Public Use, Without Compensation.

No person shall be held to answer for a capital or other infamous crime unless on a presentment or indictment of a Grand Jury, except in cases arising in the land or naval forces, or in the militia, when in actual service, in time of war or public danger; nor shall any person be subject for the same offense to be twice put in jeopardy of life or limb; nor shall be compelled in any criminal case to be a witness against himself, nor be deprived of life, liberty, or property, without due process of law; nor shall private property be taken for public use without just compensation.

The Fifth Amendment to the U.S. Constitution requires the payment of just compensation whenever private property is taken for public use.

As the nature and extent of land use controls change, so do the nature and extent of private land ownership. Such changes impact markets and ultimately real estate values. Consequently, real estate appraisers must be familiar with the regulations and restrictions that apply to land use and understand how these regulations affect a specific property.

Geographic and Environmental

The study of land includes consideration of its diverse physical characteristics and how these characteristics combine in a particular area. Each land parcel is unique, and location is a very important attribute. The utility of land and the highest and best use to which land can be put are significantly affected by the physical and locational characteristics of the land and other related considerations, broadly referred to as *geography*.

Land is affected by a number of processes. Ongoing physical and chemical processes modify the land's surface, biological processes determine the distribution of life forms, and socioeconomic processes direct human habitation and activity on the land. Together, these processes influence the characteristics of land use.

Land can be used for many purposes, including agriculture, commerce, industry, habitation, and recreation. Land use decisions may be influenced by climate, topography, and the distribution of natural resources, population centers, and industry. Land use is also affected by trends in economics, population, technology, and culture. The influence of each of these factors varies.

Geographic considerations are particularly significant to appraisers. The importance of physical characteristics such as topography, soils, water, and vegetation is obvious, but the distribution of population, facilities, and services and the movement of people and goods are equally important. The geographic concept of land, which emphasizes natural resources, the location of industry, and actual and potential markets, provides much of the background knowledge required in real estate appraisal.

The Discipline of Appraisal

Land and everything attached to the land constitute real estate. Appraisers study the value of physical real estate plus its accompanying ownership rights, recognizing that real estate exists within the context of our society as a whole. Because the potential uses of land are influenced by legal, economic, social, and geographic factors, these considerations form the background against which appraisal activities are conducted.

Real Estate, Real Property, and Personal Property

In real estate appraisal, an important distinction is made between the terms *real estate* and *real property*. Although these concepts are different, some state laws and court decisions treat them as synonymous.

Real estate is the physical land and appurtenances affixed to the land, e.g., structures.[7] Real estate is immobile and tangible. The legal definition of real estate includes land and all things that are a natural part of land (e.g., trees, minerals) as well as all things that are attached to it by people (e.g., buildings, site improvements). All permanent building attachments (e.g., plumbing, electrical wiring, heating systems) as well as built-in items (e.g., cabinets, elevators) are usually considered part of the real estate. Real estate includes all attachments, both below and above the ground.

Real property includes all interests, benefits, and rights inherent in the ownership of physical real estate. A right or interest in real estate is also referred to as an *estate*. Specifically, *an estate in land is the degree, nature, or extent of interest that a person has in it.*

Interests in property vary, so real property is said to include the "bundle of rights" inherent in the ownership of real estate. Ownership rights include the right to use real estate, to sell it, to lease it, to enter it, to give it away, or to choose to exercise all or none of these rights. The bundle of rights is often compared to a bundle of sticks, with each stick representing a distinct and separate right or interest. Private enjoyment of these rights is guaranteed by the U.S. Constitution subject to certain limitations and restrictions, which are discussed below.

It is possible to own all or only some of the rights in a parcel of real estate. The extent of ownership determines the kind of interest, or estate, that is held. A person who owns all the property rights is said to have *fee simple title. A fee simple estate implies absolute ownership unencumbered by any other interest or estate.* An appraisal assignment may call for the appraisal of a fee simple estate or a partial interest. Partial interests in real estate are created by selling, leasing, or otherwise limiting the bundle of rights in a fee simple estate. Partial estates include leased fee and leasehold estates.

A leased fee estate is an ownership interest held by a landlord with the right of use and occupancy conveyed by lease to others; the rights of the lessor (the leased fee owner) and the lessee (leaseholder) are specified by contract terms contained

---

7. The definitions of real estate and real property used in the Uniform Standards of Professional Appraisal Practice (USPAP) promulgated by The Appraisal Foundation can be found in Appendix A.

within the lease. In the appraisal of income-producing property, the leased fee estate is the most frequently valued real property interest. *A leasehold estate, which is held by a lessee (the tenant and renter), conveys the right of use and occupancy for a stated term under certain conditions.* (A detailed discussion of the valuation of partial interests is presented in Chapter 7.)

All estates in real property are subject to, and limited by, the four powers of government: taxation, eminent domain, police power, and escheat.

Taxation is the right of government to raise revenue through assessments on goods, products, and rights. Because the U.S. Constitution effectively precludes the federal government from taxing real property directly, the right to tax property is reserved for state and local governments.

Eminent domain is the right of government to take private property for public use upon the payment of just compensation. This right can be exercised by a government agency or by an entity acting under governmental authority such as a housing authority, school district, park district, or right-of-way agency. *Condemnation is the act or process of enforcing the right of eminent domain—i.e., the taking of private property for public use.*

Police power is the right of government under which property is regulated to protect public safety, health, morals, and general welfare. Zoning ordinances, use restrictions, building codes, air and land traffic regulations, and health regulations are based on police power. The government also controls overflight, the air space over a property through which aircraft may pass so long as the property's occupants suffer no inconvenience beyond established standards.

Escheat is the right of government that gives the state or a local government (e.g., township or county) titular ownership of a property when its owner dies without a will or any statutory heirs.

In addition to government restrictions on property, private legal agreements may also impose limitations. One type of agreement is a restriction inserted in a deed. Private restrictions can limit the use or manner of development and even the manner in which ownership can be conveyed. The purchaser of a property may be obligated to use the property subject to a private restriction such as an easement, right-of-way, or party-wall agreement.

The individual rights in the bundle of rights can be sold, leased, transferred, or otherwise disposed of separately, subject to government limitations and private restrictions. Owners of certain parcels of land have a number of options. For example, one property owner could sell or lease the mineral rights to his property and retain the rights to use the surface area. Another owner could lease the property's surface rights to one party and the subsurface rights to another. Owners can also sell or lease the air rights to a property for construction of a building or for avigation (i.e., air traffic control). Thus, certain rights can be severed from the ownership of a property and be sold, leased, or given to others.

Appraisers not only distinguish between real estate and real property, they also differentiate between real estate, personal property, and trade fixtures. *Personal property includes movable items of property that are not permanently affixed to, or part of, the real estate.* Personal property is not endowed with the rights of real property ownership.[8] Items of personal property include furniture and furnishings that are not built into the structure, such as refrigerators and freestanding shelves. Under specific lease terms, items such as bookshelves and window treatments installed by the tenant may remain personal property and be removed at the termination of the lease.

It is sometimes difficult to determine whether an item should be considered personal property or real estate. Often the courts must resolve such conflicts. *A fixture is an article that was once personal property, but has since been installed or attached to the land or building in a rather permanent manner; it is regarded in law as part of the real estate.* Thus, a fixture is endowed with the rights of real property ownership and is part of the real estate. All real estate improvements were once personal property; when attached to the land, they become real estate.

Although fixtures are real estate, trade fixtures are not. *A trade fixture, also called a chattel fixture, is an article that is owned and attached to a rented space or building by a tenant and used in conducting a business.* Trade fixtures are not real estate endowed with the rights of real property ownership. They are personal property regardless of how they are affixed.

Some examples of trade fixtures are restaurant booths, gasoline station pumps and storage tanks, and the fitness equipment in a health club. In industrial real estate, the term can be used to refer to fixed building equipment installed for human comfort (e.g., plumbing, lighting, heating, air-conditioning) and to industrial equipment (e.g., air hoses, water pipelines, craneways, bus ducts). A trade fixture is to be removed by the tenant when the lease expires unless this right has been surrendered in the lease.

To decide whether an item is personal property or a fixture, and therefore part of the real estate, courts often use the following criteria.

1. The manner in which the item is affixed. Generally, an item is considered personal property if it can be removed without serious injury to the real estate or to itself. There are exceptions to this rule.

2. The character of the item and its adaptation to the real estate. Items that are specifically constructed for use in a particular building or installed to carry out the purpose for which the building was erected are generally considered permanent parts of the building.

3. The intention of the party who attached the item. Frequently, the terms of the lease reveal whether the item is permanent or is to be removed at some future time.[9]

Appraisers must know whether an item is personal property or a fixture to determine whether it will be included in the property value indication. If an item is classified as a fixture, it is part of the real estate, and its contribution to value is included in the value estimate. It is sometimes not possible, however, to exclude personal property

---

8. Although personal property generally consists of tangible items, called *chattels personal*, intangible personal property rights, or *chattels real*, may be created by a lease. Historically, ownership rights to real estate for a fixed number of years (e.g., a tenant's interest) were considered personal property. These rights were called *chattels real* to distinguish them from movable personal objects, or *chattels personal*. Today it is more common to refer to a lessee's interest as an interest in, or right to, real estate.

9. Kratovil and Werner, 18-23.

from a value estimate. Because the distinction between fixtures and personal property is not always obvious, appraisers should read leases carefully and know how these items are treated in their areas. Personal property that is related to real estate and is to be included in the value estimate should be identified and described in the appraisal.

Appraisal Practice

In our complex society, the words *appraiser* and *appraisal* can take on many meanings. It is important to use these terms correctly and to distinguish among the individuals involved in the appraisal process.

Buyers and sellers purchase and sell real estate and make financial decisions relating to prices and other real estate matters. They often have little or no background in real estate and must rely on others to make their decisions. The only "appraisal" they make is an evaluation of conditions they observe or facts that are made known to them.

Real estate salespeople are licensed to sell real estate. They have special training in their field and may or may not have extensive appraisal training. They are generally familiar with properties in a given locale and have access to historical market information. Some may develop appraisal expertise. As a group, real estate salespeople evaluate specific properties, but they do not consider all the factors that professional appraisers do.

Real estate financial officers and executives include loan officers, closing agents, title companies, relocation officers and agents, and others. This group also encompasses government officials who deal with land or land values in the private marketplace. These professionals vary in their ability to understand market forces in a given locale, develop value estimates, and apply appraisal concepts. Real estate investment advisors may have extensive training in understanding appraisals even if they do not develop appraisals themselves. Members of this group work with or review appraisals developed by others. While they are knowledgeable about appraisals, they are rarely trained appraisers.

Licensed and certified real estate appraisers meet minimum state testing and experience requirements and can perform appraisals in a given jurisdiction. Their competence may be limited to residential appraising or they may be able to handle general real estate appraisal assignments. They may work as appraisers full- or part-time, and may or may not have extensive training and experience. Licensed and certified real estate appraisers are required to meet continuing minimum education standards and must adhere to generally accepted appraisal standards; otherwise they may face censure or loss of license.

Full-time professional real estate appraisers are often licensed and certified in more than one state and spend the majority of their time appraising. These individuals have extensive training and experience and are committed to the profession. This group includes those who perform and review real estate appraisals. Appraisers are bound to strict compliance with regulatory requirements, and many are members of appraisal organizations such as the Appraisal Institute, which fosters participation in professional activities and educational development. Members agree to subject questions involving their ethical conduct or work performance to peer review, which reflects their strong commitment to professionalism.

In many parts of the world, real estate appraisers are called *valuers*. In North and South America, the term *appraiser* is more common. Professional real estate appraisers perform a variety of services, estimating several types of defined value, advising clients, and participating in real estate decision making. According to the Uniform Standards of Professional Appraisal Practice (USPAP), the current standards of the appraisal profession, *appraisal practice* encompasses appraisal, consulting, and review.

Appraisal is defined as the act or process of estimating value.[10] Appraisers perform analyses and render opinions or conclusions relating to the nature, quality, value, or utility of specified interests in, or aspects of, identified real estate. Real estate appraisal involves selective research into appropriate market areas; the assemblage of pertinent data; the use of appropriate analytical techniques; and the application of knowledge, experience, and professional judgment to develop an appropriate solution to an appraisal problem.

The nature of the real estate problem will indicate whether the task is an appraisal (valuation) or a consulting assignment (analysis or counseling). The value estimated may be market value, insurable value, investment value, or some other properly defined value of an identified interest in real estate as of a given date. Valuation assignments may produce market value estimates of fee simple estates, leasehold estates, preservation easements, and many other interests.

Consulting is the act or process of providing information, analysis of real estate data, and recommendations or conclusions on diversified problems in real estate, other than estimating value.[11] Consulting assignments include land utilization studies, supply and demand studies, economic feasibility studies, highest and best use analyses, and marketability or investment considerations that relate to proposed or existing developments.

In an appraisal assignment, the appraiser provides the client with an estimate of real property value which reflects all pertinent market evidence. In a consulting assignment, current market activity and evidence are studied to form a conclusion which may not focus on a specific value indication. In both types of assignments, conclusions are derived from appropriate data analysis performed in conformance with accepted standards of professional practice.

The application of appraisal procedures and the report that communicates the appraiser's conclusions are guided by the nature of the assignment. To avoid misunderstandings, it is important that the client and the appraiser determine at the outset whether the assignment is an appraisal or a consulting assignment.

A third type of service that appraisers perform is *a review, the act or process of critically studying a report prepared by another.*[12]

10. The Appraisal Foundation, *Uniform Standards of Professional Appraisal Practice,* "Definitions" section.
11. Ibid.
12. Ibid.

Appraisal Assignments and Reporting Formats

Although appraisal concepts are reasonably uniform and appraisers in many countries observe international standards, the application of basic concepts will differ.[13] Appraisers must understand and employ the concepts and procedures applied in the jurisdiction where their appraisals will be used.

The Uniform Standards of Professional Appraisal Practice (USPAP) distinguish between complete appraisals and limited appraisals. These two types of appraisal assignments are differentiated on the basis of whether or not the appraiser invokes the Departure Provision of the Uniform Standards. *Complete appraisals* are performed without invoking the Departure Provision of the Uniform Standards; *limited appraisals* are estimates of value performed under the Departure Provision. The Departure Provision states that an appraiser may enter into an agreement to perform an assignment that calls for something less than, or different from, the work that would otherwise be required by the specific guidelines, provided that prior to entering into such an agreement, 1) the appraiser has determined that the service to be performed is not so limited in scope that the resulting assignment would tend to mislead or confuse the client and the intended users of the report; 2) the appraiser has advised the client that the assignment calls for something less than, or different from, the work required by the specific guidelines and that the report will identify and explain the departure(s); and 3) the client has agreed that performance of a limited appraisal or consulting service would be appropriate.

Appraisal reports that communicate complete or limited appraisals may be presented in three formats: self-contained reports, summary reports, and restricted reports. A *self-contained appraisal report* fully describes the data and analyses used in the assignment. All appropriate information is contained within the report and not referenced to the appraiser's files. A *summary appraisal report* summarizes the data and analyses used in the assignment. A *restricted appraisal report* simply states the conclusions of the appraisal. A *form report* may be a summary or restricted appraisal report. The appraisal file for a summary or restricted appraisal report must contain all of the data and analyses that would be presented in a self-contained appraisal report. Further information on appraisal assignments and reporting formats is included in Chapter 26.

Purpose and Use of an Appraisal

The purpose of an appraisal is the stated reason and scope of an appraisal assignment, i.e., to estimate a defined value of any real property interest or to conduct an analysis or consulting assignment pertaining to real property decisions.[14] The

---

13. International appraisal standards are established by the International Valuation Standards Committee, 18 Deslisle Avenue, Toronto, Canada M4V 1S8. This group represents more than 40 countries and is recognized by the United Nations, the World Bank, and many other international organizations. The standards may be obtained by writing to the above address or by phoning (416) 922-3999.
14. Specific legal definitions of the terms *appraisal* and *assignment* are cited in the Code of Professional Ethics and the Standards of Professional Appraisal Practice of the Appraisal Institute. Members of the Appraisal Institute should be familiar with these definitions.

purpose of an appraisal is established by the client. It points to the information that the client needs to answer specific questions pertaining to real property. If the client's questions are clearly understood, the purpose of the appraisal can be described in terms of the information requested.

When an estimate of value is required in an appraisal, the type of value sought must be defined at the outset. The defined value may be market value, insurable value, going-concern value, assessed value, use value, investment value, or another type of value. Distinctions among these terms are discussed in Chapter 2.

The purpose of the appraisal establishes the foundation for the final value conclusion, which does not change to accommodate the use of the appraisal. The structure of an appraisal report may be adapted to the intended use of the value estimate, but the estimate itself will not change. For example, the appraisal of a single-family property might be reported on a form to facilitate a sale or mortgage financing, in a restricted report for rehabilitation decisions, or in a self-contained report for use in litigation. Whatever the circumstances, the dollar figure or figures associated with the defined value will be the same.

The use or function of an appraisal is the manner in which a client employs the information contained in the appraisal report. The use or function of an appraisal is determined by the client's needs. For example, a client may want to know the market value of a residence to avoid paying too much for it or accepting too little for it in a sale. Corporate clients may need to ascertain the rent levels or demographic trends in an area to determine the advisability of relocating there. Insurance companies and private citizens may wish to know the insurable value of buildings, and a developer may need to understand the supply and demand factors at work in a community before constructing an apartment complex.

Because an appraisal provides a basis for a decision concerning real property, the use of an appraisal depends on the decision the client wishes to make. In defining the appraisal problem, the appraiser should consider the client's requirements and reach an understanding that is acceptable to both parties and consistent with accepted standards of professional practice.

An appraisal may be requested in a number of situations. The following list does not reflect all possible uses for appraisals, but it does provide a broad sampling of professional appraisal activities.

Transfer of ownership

- To help prospective buyers set offering prices
- To help prospective sellers determine acceptable selling prices
- To establish a basis for real property exchanges
- To establish a basis for reorganizing or merging the ownership of multiple properties
- To determine the terms of a sale price for a proposed transaction

Financing and credit

- To estimate the value of the security offered for a proposed mortgage loan
- To provide an investor with a sound basis for deciding whether to purchase real estate mortgages, bonds, or other types of securities

- To establish a basis for a decision to insure or underwrite a loan on real property

Litigation

Eminent domain proceedings

- To estimate the market value of a property as a whole—i.e., before a taking
- To estimate the market value of the remainder after a taking
- To estimate the damages to a property created by a taking

Property divisions

- To estimate the market value of a property in contract disputes
- To estimate the market value of real estate as part of a portfolio
- To estimate the market value of partnership interests

Environmental litigation

- To estimate damages created by environmental violations
- To estimate damages created by environmental accidents

Tax matters

- To estimate assessed value
- To separate assets into depreciable (or capital recapture) items such as buildings and nondepreciable items such as land, and to estimate applicable depreciation (or capital recapture) rates
- To estimate the value of the real estate component of an estate plan which represents the foundation for future capital gains and inheritance taxes
- To determine gift or inheritance taxes

Investment counseling and decision making

- To set rent schedules and lease provisions
- To determine the feasibility of a construction or renovation program
- To help corporations or third parties purchase homes for transferred employees
- To serve the needs of insurers, adjusters, and policyholders
- To facilitate corporate mergers, the issuance of stock, or the revision of book value
- To estimate liquidation value for forced sale or auction proceedings
- To counsel clients by considering their investment goals, alternatives, resources, and constraints and the timing of their activities
- To advise zoning boards, courts, and planners, among others, on the probable effects of proposed actions
- To arbitrate between adversaries
- To determine supply and demand trends in a market
- To ascertain the status of real estate markets

Licensing and Certification

Since 1991 the United States has had a program of state licensing or certification of real estate appraisers. This program also provides for the establishment of national appraisal standards and examination procedures. Although the requirements do not as yet apply to all appraisers in all appraisal situations, state licensing and certification programs have become increasingly important. Appraisers who perform assignments for federally regulated agencies often must be licensed or certified by the state in which the appraisal property is located.

State licensing and certification programs were the result of two important developments.

1. Passage of the Financial Institutions Reform, Recovery, and Enforcement Act (FIRREA), Title XI, in 1989. This act brought the appraisal industry under federal regulation and mandated states to license and certify appraisers.[15]

2. Issuance by the Office of Management and Budget (OMB) in 1988 of Circular A-129, which became effective July 1, 1991. This circular mandates the use of state certified or licensed appraisers by federal agencies under the OMB's jurisdiction.[16]

Because the system is relatively new, there are notable differences among the states. For example, some federal agencies make it a policy to use the services of state licensed or certified appraisers, but on occasion they may select other appraisers who have special experience or skills. It is believed that, over time, the public interest will be furthered by ensuring that appraisers meet training and experience qualifications and perform appraisals in compliance with accepted professional standards.

Appraiser Liability

As the appraisal industry strives for greater professionalism, the scope of appraiser responsibility and potential liability grows. Appraisers may be held liable for negligence, misrepresentation, fraud, breach of contract, or lack of compliance with the standards imposed by government agencies, The Appraisal Foundation, and the Appraisal Institute. Areas of potential exposure include matters involving privity of contract,[17] disclosure, and litigation (discovery proceedings, interrogatories, and depositions).

Appraisers are advised to take measures to safeguard themselves from unintentional or involuntary malpractice. Ensuring competency through continuing education, the use of checklists and backup reviews, and strict adherence to the Uniform Standards of Professional Appraisal Practice can help reduce an appraiser's exposure to civil action.[18] Professional liability insurance is available and required by many lenders. Appraisers are advised to review all exclusions and retroactive dates in their insurance policies and to take normal precautions in their business practices.

---

15. For further information on licensing and certification, see the chart titled "Federal Legislation Affecting the Appraisal Profession" in Appendix A.
16. FIRREA mandated that each federal financial institutions regulatory agency (FFIRA) establish its own *de minimis* requirement— i.e., specified value threshold. For appraisals of properties above this threshold, the federal agency must retain state certified appraisers. The FFIRAs have set this amount at $250,000. Business loans of $1 million or less are exempt from this requirement, provided the primary source of repayment of the loan is not the sale of, or rental income derived from, real estate. The required use of state certified appraisers for federally related transactions took effect December 31, 1992.
17. Privity of contract concerns the relationship between two parties, e.g., an appraiser who has entered into an agreement to perform an assignment and a client such as a bank or accounting firm. The client may allege that the appraiser acted improperly and, as a result, a third party (an investor) was harmed.
18. For more information on appraiser liability, see *Real Estate Appraisers' Liability* by Mark Lee Levine (New York: Clark Boardman Callaghan, 1995). The bibliography of this text contains useful articles on areas of potential exposure for appraisers.

Contested value estimates may result from rapid changes in market conditions, the presence of contaminated materials on appraised properties, enforcement of environmental and preservation easements, and changes in legal and regulatory guidelines. The proliferation of legal proceedings suggests that litigation will continue to increase in the appraisal field as it has in other professions.

Key Concepts

- Land is a subject of investigation in a variety of disciplines, e.g., government, the law, economics, geography, and environmental studies.
- The distinction between real estate and real property is fundamental to appraisal.
- Ownership interests in real property may be held in a fee simple or leased fee estate. The right of use and occupancy is held in a leasehold estate.
- All estates in real property are subject to the four powers of government: taxation, eminent domain, police power, and escheat.
- Distinguishing between real estate, personal property, and trade fixtures is very important in an appraisal assignment.
- Various parties and professionals make use of appraisals.
- Appraisal practice includes appraisal, consulting, and appraisal review.
- The Uniform Standards of Professional Appraisal Practice (USPAP) define two types of appraisal assignments and three reporting formats.
- The purpose and the use of an appraisal are related, but distinct, concepts.
- Appraisals are required in situations involving the transfer of ownership, financing and credit, litigation, taxation, and investment counseling and in other business decision making.
- Federal legislation mandates that certain assignments for federally regulated agencies be performed by state licensed or certified appraisers.
- Appraisers may be held liable for professional violations.

Terms

appraisal

bundle of rights

complete appraisal

condemnation

consulting

eminent domain

escheat

fee simple estate

FIRREA

four powers of government

leased fee estate

leasehold estate

liability

limited appraisal

personal property

police power

purpose of an appraisal

real estate

real property

restricted appraisal report

review appraisal

self-contained appraisal report

state licensing and certification

summary appraisal report

taxation

trade fixture

Uniform Standards of Professional
Appraisal Practice

use of an appraisal

CHAPTER TWO

The Nature of Value

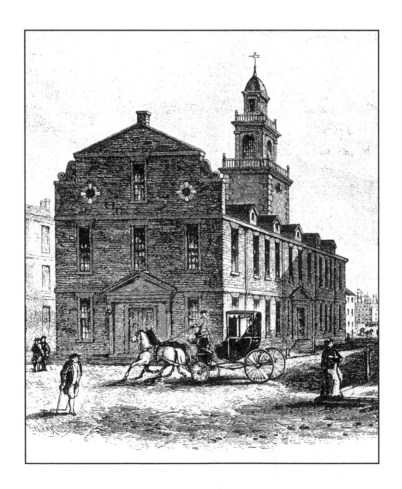

V alue considerations are a central concern in a broad range of real estate activities. The term *value* is often used imprecisely in common speech, but in economics it has a specific meaning which distinguishes it from the related concepts of price, market, and cost.

Distinctions Among Price, Market, Cost, and Value

Appraisers make careful distinctions among the terms *price, market, cost,* and *value.* The term *price* usually refers to a sale or transaction price and implies an exchange; a price is an accomplished fact. *A price, once finalized, represents the amount a particular purchaser agrees to pay and a particular seller agrees to accept under the circumstances surrounding their transaction.*

Generally the circumstances of a transaction reflect conditions within one or several markets. *A market is a set of arrangements in which buyers and sellers are brought together through the price mechanism.* A market may be defined in terms of geography, products or product features, the number of available buyers and sellers, or some other arrangement of circumstance.

A real estate market is the interaction of individuals who exchange real property rights for other assets, such as money. Specific real estate markets are defined on the basis of property type, location, income-producing potential, typical investor characteristics, typical tenant characteristics, or other attributes recognized by those participating in the exchange of real property. The market for new, single-family residences selling for $150,000 and the market for older apartment buildings located near the central business district and available for renovation are examples of specific real estate markets.

The term *cost* is used by appraisers in relation to production, not exchange; cost may be either an accomplished fact or a current estimate. (Appraisers distinguish between direct costs and indirect costs. For definitions of these terms, see Chapter 16.)

Costs may be identified with the project phase to which they pertain—i.e., either actual construction cost or overall development cost. *Construction cost, or contractor's bid price, normally includes the direct costs of labor and materials plus the contractor's indirect costs. Development cost is the cost to create a property, including the land, and bring it to an efficient operating state, as distinguished from the cost to construct the improvements.* Development cost includes the profit required to compensate the developer or entrepreneur for the time and risk involved in creating the project.

Real estate-related expenditures are directly linked to the price of goods and services in competitive markets. For example, the costs of roofing materials, masonry, architectural plans, and rented scaffolding are determined by the interaction of supply and demand in specific areas and are subject to the influence of social, economic, governmental, and environmental forces.

Price, market, and cost relationships also incorporate concepts of value. Value can have many meanings in real estate appraisal; the applicable definition depends on the context and usage.[1] In the marketplace, value is commonly perceived as the anticipation of benefits to be obtained in the future. Because value changes over time, an appraisal reflects value at a particular moment. *Value as of a given time represents the monetary worth of property, goods, or services to buyers and sellers*. To avoid confusion, appraisers do not use the word *value* alone; instead they refer to "market value," "use value," "investment value," "assessed value," and other specific kinds of value. Market value is the focus of most real property appraisal assignments and its estimation is the purpose of most appraisals.

Market Value, Use Value, and Other Values

Market Value

The concept of market value is of paramount importance to business and real estate communities. Vast sums of debt and equity capital are committed each year to real estate investments and mortgage loans, which are based on market value estimates. Real estate taxation, litigation, and legislation also reflect an ongoing, active concern with market value issues. In virtually every aspect of the real estate industry and its regulation at local, state, and federal levels, market value considerations are of vital importance and essential to economic stability.

The definition of market value used by appraisers and the clients they serve must be clearly understood and communicated. However, the definitions of market value used in real estate appraisal can and do represent different beliefs and assumptions about the marketplace and the nature of value. Market value is inherently a simple concept. It is an objective value created by the collective patterns of the market. The definition of market value, however, is controversial. Debate on the subject continues and often centers on rather fine distinctions.

Current definitions of market value reflect different schools of thought on five key points, which are enumerated below and discussed in the following pages.

1. Cash/cash equivalent versus non-cash equivalent
2. Real property rights versus real estate
3. Price versus highest price
4. Most probable price versus highest price
5. Equilibrium value versus market price

---

1. See Halbert C. Smith, "Value Concepts as a Source of Disparity Among Appraisals," *The Appraisal Journal* (April 1977).

Cash/cash equivalent versus non-cash equivalent

Some appraisers subscribe to the belief that market value is best measured in terms of all cash. This idea originated in the first half of the twentieth century when economic conditions were remarkably stable. During this period mortgage rates remained nearly level, real estate prices rose slowly, and the value of a fee simple interest was the subject of most appraisals. Because of these static conditions, financing terms were not of great importance and market value in appraisals usually implied all-cash transactions.

A second school of thought emerged in the latter part of the twentieth century when changes in real estate markets and financing created increasingly complex real property interests. Today long-term, fixed-rate loans are increasingly supplemented or replaced with more complicated financing instruments. Many clients now request estimates of the market value of a property subject to mortgages. Therefore, real estate analysts have focused their attention on the relationship between debt and equity interests.

Financing terms, which may or may not be equivalent to cash, affect value. Value affected by financing or leases can be market value because it is created by the activity of the collective market. However, when a comparable sale price is used to derive a value indication for the subject property, the sale generally should reflect typical market terms, or be adjusted to reflect a cash equivalent price.

Real property versus real estate

A market value appraisal is a valuation of specified rights in the subject property, not the physical real estate. The specified property rights can be the fee simple estate subject to a mortgage, a leased fee estate, or some other interest in the real estate.

Price versus highest price

General dictionaries define market value as "a price at which both buyers and sellers are willing to do business" and "what a property can be sold for on the open market."[2] Professional appraisers recognize that in general commerce the amount of this price depends on custom, encumbrances, and conditions; in legal use, price may depend on regulations, statutes, or an appellate court decision.

Most probable price versus highest price

Although there is logic and simplicity in defining market value as the most probable selling price, this definition does not exclude duress. If duress is present, it will be reflected in the transaction price and this price may not be market value.

The concept of market value as the highest price under a set of specific conditions, as opposed to market value as a central tendency under the same conditions, is also controversial. For a market to exist, there must be enough buyers, sellers, and product to provide competition; out of this competition a central tendency, a highest tendency, and a lowest tendency will develop. The notion of the highest price was originally rooted in the idea that market value should be the highest possible price represented by the central

---

2. *Webster's Collegiate Dictionary,* tenth edition (Springfield, Mass.: Merriam-Webster Inc., 1993) and *Random House Dictionary of the English Language,* unabr. ed. (New York: Random House, 1987).

tendency; it was not thought to be the highest possible price obtainable. Any definition that includes the word *highest* may be subject to misinterpretation.

Equilibrium value versus market price

A market in which the forces of supply and demand are in balance will result in prices significantly different from those produced by a market in which supply and demand are out of equilibrium. During the Depression, for example, values fell dramatically and many people believed, or wanted to believe, that property had intrinsic value although it was not then obtainable in the market. When the market is extremely active, prices rise above the level some people believe to be normal or intrinsic. In all cases, however, market value is the price that is available in the market. Intrinsic value is regarded by some practitioners and theorists as meaningless in relation to market value.

Despite differing opinions on individual aspects of the market value definition, it is generally agreed that market value results from the collective value judgments of market participants, not from isolated judgments. A market value estimate must be based on objective observation of the collective actions of the market. Because the standard measure of these activities is cash, the increments or diminutions in market value caused by financing and other terms are measured against an all-cash value.

The definition that follows incorporates the concepts that are most widely accepted, such as willing, able, and knowledgeable buyers and sellers who act prudently, and gives the appraiser a choice among three bases: all cash, terms equivalent to cash, or other precisely revealed terms. It also requires increments or diminutions from the all-cash market value to be quantified in terms of cash.

> The most probable price, as of a specified date, in cash, or in terms equivalent to cash, or in other precisely revealed terms, for which the specified property rights should sell after reasonable exposure in a competitive market under all conditions requisite to a fair sale, with the buyer and seller each acting prudently, knowledgeably, and for self-interest, and assuming that neither is under undue duress.

Some appraisers cite this definition verbatim in their appraisal reports and state separately that the value is stated in cash, in terms equivalent to cash, or in other terms. Other appraisers simply change one phrase in the value definition—i.e., they may substitute "in cash," with "in terms arithmetically equivalent to cash" or "in terms precisely revealed below" as appropriate.

The Uniform Standards of Professional Appraisal Practice of The Appraisal Foundation require that the following items directly related to the market value definition be included in every appraisal report.

1. Identification of the specific property rights to be appraised.
2. Statement of the effective date of the value opinion.
3. Specification as to whether cash, terms equivalent to cash, or other precisely described financing terms are assumed as the basis of the appraisal.
4. If the appraisal is conditioned upon financing or other terms, specification as to whether the financing or terms are at, below, or above market interest rates and/or

contain unusual conditions or incentives. The terms of above- or below-market interest rates and/or other special incentives must be clearly set forth; their contribution to, or negative influence on, value must be described and estimated; and the market data supporting the value estimate must be described and explained.

Although this definition includes non-cash equivalent financing terms within the scope of the market value of appraised property rights, these rights are valued in relation to cash. Increments or diminutions in market value attributable to financing terms are measured against an all-cash standard, and the dollar amount of variance from the cash standard must be reported.

The following definition of market value is used by agencies that regulate federal financial institutions in the United States.

The most probable price which a property should bring in a competitive and open market under all conditions requisite to a fair sale, the buyer and seller each acting prudently and knowledgeably, and assuming the price is not affected by undue stimulus. Implicit in this definition is the consummation of a sale as of a specified date and the passing of title from seller to buyer under conditions whereby:

1. buyer and seller are typically motivated;
2. both parties are well informed or well advised, and acting in what they consider their best interests;
3. a reasonable time is allowed for exposure in the open market;
4. payment is made in terms of cash in United States dollars or in terms of financial arrangements comparable thereto; and
5. the price represents the normal consideration for the property sold unaffected by special or creative financing or sales concessions granted by anyone associated with the sale.[3]

This federal definition is compatible with the definition of market value cited in *The Dictionary of Real Estate Appraisal*. The federal definition requires that the effect on property value of any special or creative financing or sales concessions be determined and that the value estimate reflect cash equivalent terms. Special financing or sales concessions often characterize transactions in depressed markets. This definition, therefore, addresses select categories of appraisal assignments in a real estate market characterized by unique circumstances.

In 1993 the Appraisal Institute adopted the following definition of market value, which had been developed by the Appraisal Institute Special Task Force on Value Definitions in an attempt to clarify distinctions among market value, disposition value, and liquidation value.

---

3. *Federal Register*, vol. 55, no. 163, August 22, 1990, pages 34228 and 34229; also quoted in the Definitions section of the *Uniform Standards of Professional Appraisal Practice*, 1996 ed.

The most probable price which a specified interest in real property is likely to bring under all the following conditions:

1. Consummation of a sale occurs as of a specified date.
2. An open and competitive market exists for the property interest appraised.
3. The buyer and seller are each acting prudently and knowledgeably.
4. The price is not affected by undue stimulus.
5. The buyer and seller are typically motivated.
6. Both parties are acting in what they consider their best interest.
7. Marketing efforts were adequate and a reasonable time was allowed for exposure in the open market.
8. Payment was made in cash in U.S. dollars or in terms of financial arrangements comparable thereto.
9. The price represents the normal consideration for the property sold, unaffected by special or creative financing or sales concessions granted by anyone associated with the sale.

This definition can be modified to provide for valuation with specified financing terms.

Market value definitions can be found in a variety of sources, including appraisal texts, real estate dictionaries, and court decisions. The Uniform Standards caution appraisers to use the exact definition of market value that applies in the jurisdiction in which the services are being performed. Government and regulatory agencies redefine or reinterpret market value from time to time, so individuals performing appraisal services for these agencies or for institutions under their control must be sure to use the applicable definition. (See Appendix A for a summary of federal legislation affecting appraisers.)

Use Value

The realities of current real estate practice require appraisers frequently to consider other types of value in addition to market value. One of these types, use value, is a concept based on the productivity of an economic good. *Use value is the value a specific property has for a specific use.* In estimating use value, the appraiser focuses on the value the real estate contributes to the enterprise of which it is a part, without regard to the property's highest and best use or the monetary amount that might be realized from its sale. Use value may vary depending on the management of the property and external conditions such as changes in business operations. For example, a manufacturing plant designed around a particular assembly process may have one use value before a major change in assembly technology and another use value afterward.

Real property may have a use value *and* a market value. An older factory that is still used by the original firm may have considerable use value to that firm, but only a nominal market value for another use.

Use value appraisal assignments may be performed to value assets, including real property, for mergers, acquisitions, or security issues. This type of assignment is sometimes encountered in appraising industrial real estate when the existing business enterprises include real property.

Court decisions and specific statutes may also create the need for use value appraisals. For instance, many states require agricultural use appraisals of farmland for property tax purposes rather than value estimates based on highest and best use. The current IRS regulation on estate taxes allows land under an interim agricultural use to be valued according to this alternative use even though the land has development potential.[4]

When appraising a type of property that is not commonly exchanged or rented, it may be difficult to determine whether an estimate of market value or use value is appropriate. Such limited-market properties can cause special problems for appraisers. *A limited-market property is a property that has relatively few potential buyers at a particular time.* It may be a limited-market property because of unique design features or changing market conditions. Large manufacturing plants, railroad sidings, and research and development properties are examples of limited-market properties that typically appeal to relatively few potential purchasers. However, this is not to imply that they have no market value.

Many limited-market properties include structures with unique designs, special construction materials, or layouts that restrict their utility to the use for which they were originally built. These properties usually have limited conversion potential and, consequently, are often called *special-purpose* or *special-design properties.* Examples of such properties include houses of worship, museums, schools, public buildings, and clubhouses.

Limited-market properties may be appraised for market value based on their current use or the most likely alternative use. Due to the relatively small markets and lengthy market exposure needed to sell such properties, there may be little evidence to support a market value estimate based on their current use. There is not generally a clear distinction between market properties and limited-market properties. If a market exists for a limited-market property, the appraiser must search diligently for whatever evidence of market value is available.

If a property's current use is so specialized that there is no demonstrable market for it, but the use is viable and likely to continue, the appraiser may render an estimate of use value.[5] Such an estimate should not be confused with a market value estimate. If no market can be demonstrated, or if data are not available, the appraiser cannot estimate a market value and should state so in the appraisal report. It is sometimes necessary to estimate market value in these situations for legal purposes, however. In these cases, the

---

4. The section on special use valuation in *Federal Estate and Gift Tax* (IRS Publication No. 448) states: "As the executor of an estate, you may elect to value qualified real property that is included in the decedent's estate and that is devoted to farming or used in a closely held business on the basis of its actual use for these purposes rather than its fair market value determined on any other basis."

5. Some practitioners effectively argue that, in certain situations, it is possible to estimate two or more market values depending on how the market is defined. For example, an appraiser is called to value a home that is specially designed for a person who uses a wheelchair. The property is attractive to the limited market of other wheelchair users who would probably be willing to pay more for it. An estimate of the home's market value based on this limited market would therefore be higher than the market value based on the broader market of home buyers for whom the special design features would have no appeal and would likely represent a penalty.

appraiser must comply with the legal requirement, relying on judgment rather than direct market evidence.

Investment Value

While use value focuses on the specific use of a property, investment value represents the value of a specific investment to a particular investor. As used in appraisal assignments, *investment value is the value of an investment to a particular investor based on his or her investment requirements*. In contrast to market value, investment value is value to an individual, not necessarily value in the marketplace.

Investment value reflects the subjective relationship between a particular investor and a given investment. It differs in concept from market value, although investment value and market value indications may be similar. If the investor's requirements are typical of the market, investment value may be the same as market value.

When measured in dollars, investment value is the price an investor would pay for an investment in light of its perceived capacity to satisfy his or her desires, needs, or investment goals. To estimate investment value, specific investment criteria must be known. Criteria to evaluate a real estate investment are not necessarily set down by the individual investor; they may be established by an expert on real estate and its value, i.e., an appraiser.

An investment value appraisal may be sought by the potential purchaser of an existing investment or income-producing property or by the developer of a new property.

Going-Concern Value

Going-concern value is the value of a proven property operation. It includes the incremental value associated with the business concern, which is distinct from the value of the real estate. Going-concern value includes an intangible enhancement of the value of the operating business enterprise, which is produced by the assemblage of the land, buildings, labor, equipment, and the marketing operation. This assemblage creates an economically viable business that is expected to continue. Going-concern value refers to the total value of a property, including both real property and intangible personal property attributed to business value.

Going-concern appraisals are commonly conducted for hotels and motels, restaurants, bowling alleys, industrial enterprises, retail stores, shopping centers, and similar properties. For these properties, the physical real estate assets are integral parts of an ongoing business. It may be difficult to separate the market value of the land and the building from the total value of the business, but such a division of realty and nonrealty components of value is possible and often required by federal regulations. Only qualified practitioners should undertake this kind of assignment, which must comply with appropriate USPAP standards.

Public Interest Value

Public interest value[6] is a general term covering a family of value concepts that relate the highest and best use of property to noneconomic uses such as conservation or preservation. The term originated in the 1970s in federal legislation relating to federal lands (i.e., private-public exchanges of federal lands deemed to be in the public interest) and federal income taxes (i.e., tax deductions for certain types of donations or dedications of private land for public purposes). The issue of public interest value has also come up in determining the just compensation required in land acquisitions by federal agencies.

Public interest appraisals have generally been characterized by 1) the use of comparables from other public transactions, 2) the most likely purchaser being a public agency, and 3) the land being treated as the basis for the entire compensation to the exclusion of other considerations, e.g., location. Huge amounts of public funds are at stake over what has become a highly controversial issue. Proponents of the public interest value concept recommend a redefinition of highest and best use and market value (to recognize preservation or conservation as a highest and best use), extension of the market concept to include public agencies and conservation groups, and adoption of alternative valuation models. Opponents contend that since noneconomic uses are not responsive to market forces, such uses cannot give rise to market value, the basis of which can only be economic highest and best use. They argue that the application of public interest value concepts invariably results in value estimates that exceed those derived from economic highest and best use analyses. Opponents further point out that government is a different type of player, not constrained to follow market economic rules.

The Appraisal Institute position can be summarized as follows: 1) if the purpose of an appraisal assignment is to estimate market value, then the highest and best use of the property to be appraised must be an economic use; and 2) preservation and conservation are not recognized as an alternative to be considered in highest and best use analysis.

Insurable Value

Insurable value is based on the replacement and/or reproduction cost of physical items that are subject to loss from hazards. *Insurable value is the portion of the value of an asset or asset group that is acknowledged or recognized under the provisions of an applicable loss insurance policy.* This value is often controlled by state law and varies from state to state.

Assessed Value

Assessed value applies in ad valorem taxation and refers to the value of a property according to the tax rolls. Assessed value may not conform to market value, but it is usually calculated in relation to a market value base.

---

6. This discussion is based on an article by Woodward S. Hanson, "Public Interest Value and Non-Economic Highest and Best Use: The Appraisal Institute's Position," *in Valuation Insights and Perspectives* (Spring 1996).

Factors of Value

Value is extrinsic to the commodity, good, or service to which it is ascribed; it is created in the minds of the individuals who constitute the market. The relationships that create value are complex, and values change when the factors that influence value change. Typically, four interdependent economic factors create value: utility, scarcity, desire, and effective purchasing power. All four factors must be present for a property to have value.

Utility

Utility is the ability of a product to satisfy a human want, need, or desire. All properties must have utility to tenants, owner-investors, or owner-occupants. Residential properties satisfy the need for shelter. Commercial properties may have design features that enhance their attractiveness. The benefits of these properties are called *amenities.* The value of amenities is related to their desirability and utility to an owner-occupant or tenant-occupant. The value to a tenant can be converted into income in the form of rent. The benefits derived from income-producing properties can usually be measured in terms of cash flow. The influence of utility on value depends on the characteristics of the property. Size utility, design utility, location utility, and other specific forms of utility can significantly influence property value.

The benefits of real property ownership are derived from the bundle of rights that an owner possesses. Restrictions on ownership rights may inhibit the flow of benefits and, therefore, lower the property's value. Similarly, a property can only achieve its highest value if it can legally perform its most useful function. Environmental regulations, zoning regulations, deed restrictions, and other limitations on the rights of ownership can enhance or detract from a property's utility and value.

Scarcity

Scarcity is the present or anticipated supply of an item relative to the demand for it. In general, if demand is constant, the scarcity of a commodity makes it more valuable. Land, for example, is still generally abundant, but useful, desirable land is relatively scarce and, therefore, has greater value. No object, including real property, can have value unless scarcity is coupled with utility. Air, which has a high level of utility, has no definable economic value because it is abundant.

Desire

Desire is a purchaser's wish for an item to satisfy human needs (e.g., shelter, clothing, food, companionship) or individual wants beyond the essentials required to support life. Desire, along with utility and scarcity, is considered in relation to purchasing power.

Effective Purchasing Power

Effective purchasing power is the ability of an individual or group to participate in a market—that is, to acquire goods and services with cash or its equivalent. A valid estimate of the value of a property includes an accurate assessment of the market's ability to pay for the property.

Supply and Demand

The complex interaction of the four factors that create value is reflected in the basic economic principle of supply and demand. The utility of a commodity, its scarcity or abundance, the intensity of the human desire to acquire it, and the effective power to purchase it all affect the supply of and demand for the commodity in any given situation.

Demand for a commodity is created by its utility and affected by its scarcity. Demand is also influenced by desire and the forces that create and stimulate desire. Although human longing for things may be unlimited, desire is restrained by effective purchasing power. Thus, the inability to buy expensive things affects demand.

Similarly, the supply of a commodity is influenced by its utility and limited by its scarcity. The availability of a commodity is affected by its desirability. Land is a limited commodity, and the land in an area that is suitable for a specific use will be in especially short supply if the perceived need for it is great. Sluggish purchasing power keeps the pressure on supply in check. If purchasing power expands, the supply of a relatively fixed commodity will dwindle and create a market-driven demand to increase the supply.

The History of Value Theory

The development of modern value theory began in the eighteenth and nineteenth centuries when economic thinkers of the classical school first identified the four agents of production—labor, capital, coordination, and land—and examined the relationships between the basic factors that create value and supply and demand. Classical theory was largely based on the contributions of the Physiocrats, whose ideas were put forth in reaction to the mercantilist doctrines that dominated earlier economic thought.

Mercantilism focused on wealth as a means of enhancing a nation's power. National wealth was equated with an influx of bullion into the national treasury. Mercantilists sought to maintain a favorable balance of trade by selling goods to accumulate gold, the chief medium of exchange. Between the fifteenth and eighteenth centuries, economic activity in western Europe was associated with overseas exploration, colonization, and commerce. Mercantilist doctrine promoted strong, central economic controls to maintain monopolies in foreign trade and ensure the economic dependency of colonies.

Physiocratic thinkers of the mid-eighteenth century objected to the commercial and national emphasis of mercantilism. They stressed other considerations in formulating a theory of value. Agricultural productivity, not gold, was identified as the source of wealth, and land was cited as the fundamental productive agent. The Physiocrats also identified the importance of factors such as utility and scarcity in determining value.[7]

---

7. Francois Quesnay (1694-1774) and Anne Robert Turgot (1727-1781) put forth an individualistic, agrarian-based concept of economic behavior without centralized state control. They popularized the phrase *laissez-faire*, "to let people do as they choose," which underscores their individualistic approach. See Eric Roll, *A History of Economic Thought*, 3d ed. (Englewood Cliffs, N.J.: Prentice-Hall, Inc., 1964), 134.

The Classical School

The classical school expanded and refined the tenets of Physiocratic thought, formulating a value theory that attributed value to the cost of production. The Scottish economic thinker, Adam Smith (1721-1790), suggested that capital, in addition to land and labor, constituted a primary agent of production. Smith acknowledged the role of coordination in production, but did not study its function as a primary agent. He believed that value was created when the agents of production were brought together to produce a useful item.

In *The Wealth of Nations* (1776), the first systematic treatment of economics, Adam Smith considered value as an objective phenomenon. By virtue of its existence, an item was assumed to possess utility. Scarcity also imparted exchange value to goods. The "natural price" of an object generally reflected how much the item cost to produce. In contemporary appraisal practice, the classical theory of value has influenced the cost approach.

Later economic thinkers who are regarded as members of the classical school offered theoretical refinements on the cost of production theory of value, but none contested its basic premises. David Ricardo (1772-1823) developed a theory of rent based on the concept of marginal land and the law of diminishing returns. Land residual returns were referred to as *rent*. Ricardo's theory has contributed significantly to the concept of highest and best use and the land residual technique used in the income capitalization approach to value.

John Stuart Mill (1806-1873) reworked Adam Smith's ideas in *The Principles of Political Economy* (1848), which became the leading economic text of its time. Mill defined the relationship between interest and value in use, which he referred to as "capital value"; the role of risk in determining interest; and the inequities of "unearned increments" accruing to land.[8] Confident in his analysis of the cost of production theory, John Stuart Mill asserted, "Happily, nothing in the laws of value remains for the present or any future writer to clear up; the theory of the subject is complete."

Challenges to the Classical Theory

In the second half of the nineteenth century, two serious challenges to classical value theory were put forward. One was the labor theory of value, an extreme position zealously espoused by Karl Marx (1818-1883). Marx claimed that all value is the direct result of labor and that increased wages to labor would lower capitalistic profits. Marx envisioned an inevitable struggle between the social classes which would eventually result in a violent political upheaval.

The other challenge was presented by the marginal utility, or Austrian, school, which was critical of both the classical and Marxian theories. The central concept of marginal utility links value to the utility of, and demand for, the marginal, or additional, unit of an item. Thus, if one more unit than is needed or demanded appears in a given market, the market becomes diluted and the cost of production becomes irrelevant. Value

---

8. For further discussion of value theory, see James H. Burton, *Evolution of the Income Approach* (Chicago: American Institute of Real Estate Appraisers, 1982).

Classical economists associated rent with land residual and the law of diminishing returns.
(HISTORICAL PICTURES/STOCK MONTAGE)

is regarded as a function of demand, with utility as its fundamental precept.[9] Marginal utility is the theoretical basis for the concept of contribution.

The Neoclassical Synthesis

These formidable challenges to the classical theory of value inspired economists to reconsider the problem. In the late nineteenth and early twentieth centuries, the neoclassical school successfully merged the supply-cost considerations of the classicists with the demand-price theory of marginal utility. Alfred Marshall (1842-1924) is credited with this synthesis, which forms the basis for contemporary value theory.[10]

Marshall compared supply and demand to the blades of a pair of scissors because neither concept could ever be separated from the determination of value. He stressed the importance of time in working out an adjustment between the two principles. Marshall maintained that market forces tend toward an equilibrium where prices and production costs meet. Utility-demand considerations operate in the limited span of a given market. In the short term, supply is relatively fixed and value is a function of demand. Cost-supply considerations, however, extend over a broader period, during which production flows and patterns are subject to change. Marshall believed that a perfect economic market would eventually result and that price, cost, and value would all be equal.[11]

9. Eugen von Boehm-Bawerk (1835-1882) defined value as "the significance a good acquires by contributing utility toward the well-being of an individual." William Stanley Jevons (1835-1882), a founder of modern statistics and a principal proponent of marginal utility, wrote "Labor once spent has no influence on the future value of any article: it is gone and lost forever." W. Stanley Jevons, *The Theory of Political Economy*, 5th ed. (New York: Augustus M. Kelley, 1965), 164; Burton, 17.

10. In 1890, Marshall published *Principles of Economics*, which succeeded Mill's *Principles of Political Economy* as the authoritative text on economic thought. In this book, Marshall advocated a dynamic theory of value to explain real world events. See Alfred Marshall, *Principles of Economics*, 8th ed. (London: MacMillan and Company, 1920); reprint (Philadelphia: Porcupine Press, 1982), 288-290, 664-669.

11. See Robert L. Heilbroner, *The Worldly Philosophers*, rev. ed. (New York: Simon and Schuster, 1964), 178-179 and Paul F. Wendt, *Real Estate Appraisal: Review and Outlook* (Athens: University of Georgia Press, 1974), 18-19.

Marshall was the first major economist to consider the techniques of valuation, specifically the valuation of real estate. In this regard, his writings and the writings of those who built upon his work are the source of the distinction between value theory and valuation theory—i.e., the method of estimating, measuring, or predicting a defined value. (The development of valuation theory and the three approaches applied in the valuation process are discussed in Chapter 5.)

Key Concepts

- The terms *price, value,* and *cost* are used and defined carefully by appraisers.
- A real estate market is the interaction of individuals who exchange real property rights for other assets such as money.
- Cost pertains to production rather than exchange; costs can be divided into direct (hard) costs, indirect (soft) costs, and construction and development costs.
- Value represents the monetary worth of property, goods, or services to buyers and sellers.
- Current definitions of market value reflect divergent thinking on five key points: financing terms, specified property rights, price versus highest price, most probable price versus highest price, and equilibrium value versus market value.
- The Uniform Standards of Professional Appraisal Practice (USPAP) include requirements for appraisal reports.
- Various definitions of market value exist, e.g., the nine-criterion definition of the Appraisal Institute, the definition used by agencies that regulate federal financial institutions.
- Values other than market value are also estimated, e.g. use value, investment value, going-concern value, insurable value, and assessed value.
- Four interdependent factors create value, e.g., utility, scarcity, desire, and effective purchasing power; utility and scarcity are supply factors; desire and effective purchasing power are demand factors.
- Various schools of economic thought have contributed to the development of modern value theory.

Terms

assessed value

cash equivalent price

construction costs

cost

demand

desire

development costs

direct, or hard, costs

effective purchasing power

going-concern value

indirect, or soft, costs

insurable value

investment value

limited-market properties

market

market value

price

public interest value

real estate market

scarcity

special-purpose properties

supply

use value

utility

value

CHAPTER THREE

Foundations of Appraisal

R eal property is the focus of appraisal activity. Because real property has value, the possession and successful management of real property create opportunities for individuals to achieve economic goals that are generally perceived to be desirable by society. In recent years, real estate markets have been turbulent. Lax underwriting in the 1980s contributed to an abundance of distressed properties and brought on federal intervention. Public controls have often been perceived by developers as excessive, and some property owners decry the taking of private property rights. Nevertheless, real estate markets remain an important investment vehicle and generator of economic activity.

In determining their level of participation in the real estate market, individuals consider their wants and needs as well as the choices available to them at different times. These choices represent the variety of options available and help support a free market economy in which both individual and collective decisions contribute to the nation's economic success. Similarly, the production of goods, services, and income depends on the combined effects of several essential economic ingredients. These ingredients are the agents of production: land, labor, capital, and entrepreneurship.

The human actions that collectively shape the operations of the market reflect the pursuit of economic goals. To analyze the many dynamic and interactive factors that influence people's attitudes and beliefs about value, the fundamental principles of anticipation and change must be addressed.

Anticipation

Value is created by the anticipation of benefits to be derived in the future. In the real estate market, the current value of a property is usually not based on its historical prices or the cost of its creation; rather, value is based on market participants' perceptions of the future benefits of acquisition.

The value of owner-occupied residential property is based primarily on the expected future advantages, amenities, and pleasures of ownership and occupancy. The value of income-producing real estate is based on the income it will produce in the future. Therefore, real property appraisers must be aware of local, regional, and national real estate trends that affect the perceptions of buyers and sellers and their anticipations of the future. Historical data on a property or a market are relevant only insofar as they help interpret current market anticipations.

Change

The dynamic nature of the social, economic, governmental, and environmental forces that influence real property value accounts for change. Although change is inevitable and continuous, the process may be gradual and not easily discernible. In active markets, change may occur rapidly, with new properties put up for sale and others sold on a daily basis. Abrupt changes may be precipitated by plant or military base closures, tax law revisions, or the start of new construction. The pervasiveness of change is evident in the real estate market, where the social, economic, governmental, and environmental forces that affect real estate are in constant transition. Changes in these forces influence the demand for and supply of realty and, therefore, individual property values. Appraisers attempt to identify current and anticipated changes in the market that could affect current property values, but because change is not always predictable, value estimates may be valid only for a relatively brief period after the date specified in the appraisal report.

Change is also evidenced by shifts in market preferences. Real estate is not readily adaptable to new consumer preferences and thus often suffers obsolescence. The physical, functional, and economic impairments observed in buildings as they age result in *depreciation, defined as a loss in property value from any cause.* Depreciation may be seen as the difference between the cost to reproduce or replace a property and its present value. In general, losses in property value are caused by deterioration or obsolescence. Because obsolescence can begin in the design phase, and deterioration may start while a building or improvement is still being constructed, the different types of deterioration and obsolescence found in a property have unique implications in appraisal. (A detailed discussion of deterioration and obsolescence is presented in Chapter 16.)

The appraisal principles of supply and demand, substitution, balance, and externalities, which are founded in general economics, can be applied to the unique physical and legal characteristics of a particular parcel of real property. When these principles are in proper accord, they indicate highest and best use, which has great significance in real property appraisal.

Supply and Demand

In economic theory, the principle of supply and demand states that the price of a commodity, good, or service varies directly, but not necessarily proportionately, with demand, and inversely, but not necessarily proportionately, with supply. In a real estate context, the appraisal principle of supply and demand states that the price of real property varies directly, but not necessarily proportionately, with demand, and inversely, but not necessarily proportionately, with supply. Thus, an increase in the supply of an item or a decrease in the demand for an item tends to reduce the equilibrium price; the opposite conditions produce an opposite effect. The relationship between supply and demand may not be directly proportional, but the interaction of

these forces is fundamental to economic theory. The interaction of suppliers and de-
manders, or sellers and buyers, constitutes a market.[1]

Usually property values vary directly with changes in supply. If properties for a
particular use become more abundant than they were relative to demand in the past,
their equilibrium value declines; by contrast, if properties become more scarce and
supply declines relative to demand, the equilibrium price of the properties increases. The
supply of and demand for commodities always tend toward equilibrium. At this theoretical point (which virtually never occurs), market value, price, and cost are equal.

*In real estate, supply is the amount of a type of real estate available for sale or
lease at various prices in a given market at a given period of time, assuming
production costs remain constant.* Typically, more of an item will be supplied at a
higher price and less at a lower price. Therefore, the supply of an item at a particular
price, at a particular time, and in a particular place indicates that item's relative *scarcity*,
which is a basic factor of value.

Figure 3.1	**Shift in Demand**

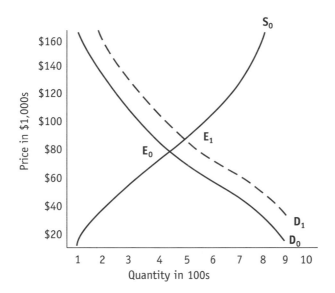

A shift in equilibrium price may result from unilateral changes in either the supply of or demand for a type of property. In
Figure 3.1, demand for a stable supply (S_0) of properties had increased from D_0 to D_1. The equilibrium price rose from
$80,000 ($E_0$) to $90,000 ($E_1$).

---

1. This discussion describes the operation of supply and demand in a free market. These forces do not operate freely when the
   market is dominated by the state and centralized planning is imposed on a command economy. For example, in formerly
   communist countries and in some developing nations, apartment blocks built, managed, and leased by the state remained in
   state ownership. Neither the quantity nor the quality of apartment units was directly responsive to the demand for those units.
   Rents did not reflect the demand situation either. With the growing popularity of free market economics, state-owned
   apartment properties are being "condominiumized" in former East Bloc countries and some developing nations.
       Analogous situations can also be found in the West where public housing is still largely owned and managed by
   government agencies. Mixed markets characterize the economic programs of the socialist and labor governments of some
   European countries.

Figure 3.2 | **Shift in Supply**

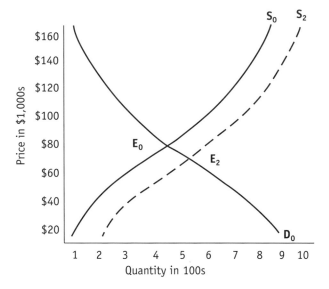

In Figure 3.2, the supply of properties increased from S_0 to S_2, while demand (D_0) remained stationary. The equilibrium price fell from $80,000 ($E_0$) to $70,000 ($E_2$).

Figure 3.3 | **Proportionate Shifts in Supply and Demand**

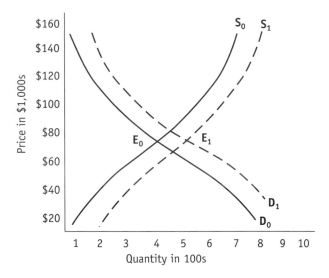

Proportionate shifts in supply and demand occur when the rate of increase in the demand for a type of property is the same as the rate of increase in the supply of the property. The equilibrium price remains at the same level, but the number of properties sold at the equilibrium price increases. In Figure 3.3, the increase in supply from S_0 to S_1 and the increase in demand from D_0 to D_1 were proportionate. The equilibrium price of $80,000 ($E_1$) remained the same, but the number of properties sold at the equilibrium price increased from 400 to 500. If supply and demand had decreased at a proportionate rate, the equilibrium price would remain the same but the number of properties sold would decrease.

Figure 3.4 | **Disproportionate Shifts in Supply and Demand**

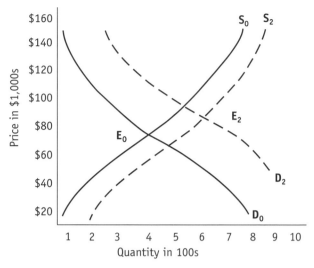

Disproportionate shifts in supply and demand occur when the rate of increase in the demand for a type of property is different from the rate of increase in the supply of the property. Disproportionate shifts in supply and demand produce changes in both the equilibrium price and the number of properties sold at that price. In Figure 3.4, the increase in demand from D_0 to D_2 outpaced the increase in supply from S_0 to S_2. The equilibrium price (E_2) rose from $80,000 to $90,000 for the 200 additional properties (400 to 600) sold at the equilibrium price. If supply and demand had decreased at disproportionate rates, both the equilibrium price and the number of properties sold at that price would decline.

The supply of real estate is dependent on the costs of the four agents of production, which are brought together to produce a product that is offered for sale. When demand in a particular market increases, property values are driven up and the quantity of new properties offered for sale generally increases. When the supply of the agents in production declines, property values again tend to rise. On the other hand, increases in the productivity of labor, greater technological efficiency, improvements in capital goods, or the utilization of more capital goods per worker tend to reduce development costs. A building boom set in motion by rising expectations of profit on the part of developers may result in an oversupply of properties.

Because real property is both a physical commodity and a service, the supply of real estate refers to the amount of service, or the usability of the space, as well as the quantity of physical space. Consequently, those involved in real estate are primarily concerned with the supply of land suitable for a specific use, not the total number of acres available. The supply of real estate incorporates both the quality and quantity of service space provided. Proper comparisons can be made only between properties that are similar both qualitatively and quantitatively. The quality of space may affect property value even more than its quantity. Quality is a function of the tangible attributes of a property, such as its condition, and its intangible attributes or amenities, such as its design. The supply of a specific property type may be inventoried to reflect existing improvements on the resale market and new construction entering the market.

Generally the quantity of space supplied for a given use is slow to adjust to changes in price levels. The length of time needed to build new structures, the large amount of capital required, and government regulations often hamper a supplier's ability to meet changes in the market. The quality of space, however, can change more rapidly because suppliers can convert nonproductive space to alternative uses, cure deferred maintenance, and partition existing space into smaller units.

Demand is the desire and ability to purchase or lease goods and services. In real estate, demand is the amount of a type of real estate desired for purchase or rent at various prices in a given market for a given period of time, other factors such as population, income, future prices, and consumer preferences remaining constant. Typically less of an item will be demanded at a higher price, and more will be demanded at a lower price.

Because it is difficult to augment the supply of real property for a specific use in a short time, values are strongly affected by current demand. Demand, like supply, can be characterized in terms of both quantity and quality. For example, demand in a residential market may be defined by the number of households in the market area and the household incomes as well as the size and characteristics of the households and specific housing preferences.[2] *Demand that is supported by purchasing power results in effective demand, which is the type of demand considered by the market.* Appraisers must interpret market behavior to ascertain the existing relationship between the supply of, and the demand for, the type of property being appraised.

The change in the amount of demand for real estate in response to a change in price is called the *elasticity of demand*. The elasticity of demand is measured by dividing the percentage change in the quantity demanded by the percentage change in the price per unit. Figures 3.5 and 3.6 illustrate elastic demand and inelastic demand. Similarly, the responsiveness of the quantity of real estate supplied to change in price is called the *elasticity of supply*, which is measured by dividing the percentage change in the quantity supplied by the percentage change in the price per unit. Figures 3.7 and 3.8 illustrate elastic supply and inelastic supply. Because the quantity of a real estate product offered for sale is slow to increase, supply is generally considered more inelastic than demand.

---

2. Residential demand reflects the number of households in the market area and their household incomes. Long-term trends indicate a continuing decline in average household size, which suggests a shift in demand from larger to smaller living units. In the short term, residential demand is strengthened by declining mortgage interest rates.

   Residential mortgage rates declined dramatically in the early 1990s, in some markets reaching their lowest levels in many years. Lower interest costs and a growing population of potential home buyers stimulated a gradual rise in home sales and housing starts. Federal discount rate increases in 1994, instituted by the Federal Reserve Board to counteract inflationary pressures, resulted in higher mortgage rates, which contributed to a decline in home sales and single-family development.

Figure 3.5 **Elastic Demand**

Figure 3.6 **Inelastic Demand**

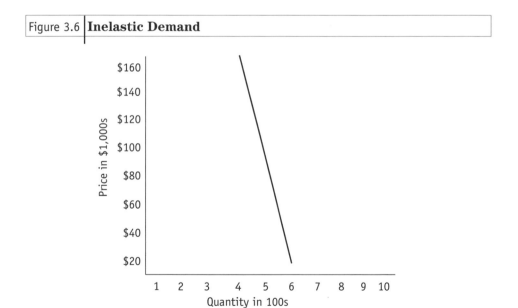

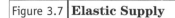

Figure 3.7 **Elastic Supply**

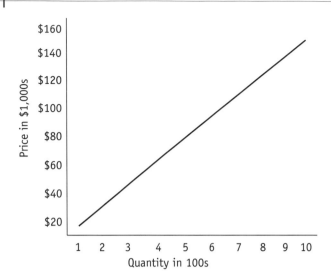

Figure 3.8 **Inelastic Supply**

Competition

Competition between buyers or tenants represents the interactive efforts of two or more potential buyers or tenants to make a purchase or secure a lease. Between sellers or landlords, competition represents the interactive efforts of two or more potential sellers or landlords to effect a sale or lease. Competition is fundamental to the dynamics of supply and demand in a free enterprise, profit-maximizing economic system.

Buyers and sellers of real property operate in a competitive market setting; in essence, each property competes with all other properties suitable for the same use in the particular market segment and often with properties from other market segments. For example, a profitable motel faces competition from newer motels nearby; existing residential subdivisions compete with new subdivisions; and downtown retail properties compete with suburban shopping centers.

Over time, competitive market forces tend to reduce unusually high profits. Profit encourages competition, but excess profits tend to breed ruinous competition. For example, the first retail store to open in a new and expanding area may generate more profit than is considered typical for that type of enterprise. If no barriers to entry exist, owners of similar retail enterprises will likely gravitate to the area to compete for the surplus profits. Eventually there may not be enough business to support all the retailers. A few stores may profit, but others will fail. The effects of competition and market trends on profit levels are especially evident to appraisers making income projections as part of the income capitalization approach to value.

Substitution

The principle of substitution states that when several similar or commensurate commodities, goods, or services are available, the one with the lowest price attracts the greatest demand and widest distribution. This principle assumes rational, prudent market behavior with no undue cost due to delay. According to the principle of substitution, a buyer will not pay more for one property than for another that is equally desirable.

Property values tend to be set by the price of acquiring an equally desirable substitute property. The principle of substitution recognizes that buyers and sellers of real property have options, i.e., other properties are available for similar uses. The substitution of one property for another may be considered in terms of use, structural design, or earnings. The cost of acquisition may be the cost to purchase a similar site and construct a building of equivalent utility, assuming no undue cost due to delay; this is the basis of the cost approach. On the other hand, the cost of acquisition may be the price of acquiring an existing property of equal utility, again assuming no undue cost due to delay; this is the basis of the sales comparison approach.

The principle of substitution is equally applicable to properties such as houses, which are purchased for their amenity-producing attributes, and properties purchased for their income-producing capabilities. The amenity-producing attributes of residential properties include excellence of design, quality of workmanship, or superior construction materials. In regard to income-producing property, an equally desirable substitute might be an alternative investment property that produces equivalent investment returns with equivalent risk. The limits of property prices, rents, and rates tend to be set by the prevailing prices, rents, and rates of equally desirable substitutes. The principle of substitution is fundamental to all three traditional approaches to value—sales comparison, cost, and income capitalization.

Although the principle of substitution applies in most situations, sometimes the characteristics of a product are perceived by the market to be unique. The demand generated for such products may result in unique pricing.

Opportunity Cost

Opportunity cost is the net cost of opportunities not chosen or options forgone, denied, or lost. An investor who selects one investment forgoes the opportunity to invest in other available investments. An investor will select the investment that best meets his or her investment objectives. Some investors look for the highest rate of return at the lowest risk, while others seek the assurance of long-term growth at a more conservative rate of return. In addition to the illiquidity the investor endures over the term of the investment, there is a potential for opportunity cost if alternative investments at comparable levels of risk outperform the investment chosen.

Opportunity cost may be incurred in a variety of forms. The owner of a property adjacent to a contaminated property may not be able to sell or borrow on the property because of the nearby contamination. The owner is thus denied some of his or her ownership rights and incurs an opportunity cost.

Opportunity cost is related to the principle of substitution, and is particularly significant in estimating the rates of return necessary to attract capital. By analyzing and comparing the prospective rates of return offered by alternative investment opportunities, an appraiser can estimate the required rate of return for the property being appraised. Interviews with investors regarding their yield expectations and assumptions about inflation and market growth may provide support for estimated property yield rates. Actual investor projections for properties recently acquired lend further credence to estimates of property yield.

Balance

The principle of balance holds that real property value is created and sustained when contrasting, opposing, or interacting elements are in a state of equilibrium. This principle applies to relationships among various property components as well as the relationship between the costs of production and the property's productivity. Land, labor, capital, and entrepeneurship are the agents of production, but for most real property the critical combination is the land and the improvements. Economic balance is achieved when the combination of land and improvements is optimal—i.e., when no marginal benefit or utility is achieved by adding another unit of capital. *The law of increasing returns* holds that increments in the agents of production added to a parcel of property produce greater net income up to a certain point. At this point, *the point of decreasing or diminishing returns*, maximum value is achieved. Any additional expenditures will not produce a return commensurate with the additional investment, according to *the law of decreasing returns*. At the point of decreasing returns, further increments in the agents of production will cause productivity to decline proportionally. This principle is also known as the *principle of diminishing marginal productivity* or *law of diminishing returns.*

The fertilization of farmland provides a simple example. Applying fertilizer to a land parcel increases crop yield only up to a point, beyond which the additional fertilizer will produce no further increase in the marginal output of the acreage. The optimum amount of fertilization is achieved when the value of the increment in yield resulting from the last unit of fertilizer equals the additional expenditure on fertilizer. This is the point of balance.

As a further illustration, consider a developer who is determining how many bedrooms to include in a single-family house being developed for sale on the residential market. The typical single-family house in this residential market has three bedrooms. It may be uneconomic to include a fourth bedroom if the cost to build exceeds the value added to the property.

The principle of balance also applies to the relationship between a property and its environment. A proper mix of various types and locations of land uses in an area creates and sustains value. A residence near other residences has much more market appeal than a residence next to a landfill.

The principle of balance and the principles of contribution, surplus productivity, and conformity are interdependent and crucial in highest and best use analyses and market value estimation. These concepts form the theoretical foundation for estimating all forms of depreciation in the cost approach, making adjustments in the sales comparison approach, and calculating expected earnings in the income capitalization approach.

Contribution

The principle of contribution states that the value of a particular component is measured in terms of its contribution to the value of the whole property, or as the amount that its absence would detract from the value of the whole. The cost of an item does not necessarily equal its value. A swimming pool that costs $10,000 to install does not necessarily increase the value of a residential property by $10,000. Rather, the pool's dollar contribution to value is measured in terms of how valuable its benefit or utility is in the market. Its contribution to value may be lower or higher than its cost. Thus, in some cases, a property's market value may not increase even though the real estate has undergone alteration, modification, or rehabilitation.

The contribution of existing improvements may not be in proper balance with the total property. Especially in areas of rapid transition, a property's present use may underutilize the land. Nevertheless, an existing, less-than-optimal use, called an *interim use*, will continue until it is economically feasible for a developer to absorb the costs of converting the property by either razing and replacing or rehabilitating the existing improvements.

Surplus Productivity

Surplus productivity is the net income to the land remaining after the costs of the other agents of production have been paid. The classical economists identified the surplus with land rent, which they understood to account for land value. Traditionally, the principle of surplus productivity has provided the basis for the residual concept of land returns and residual valuation techniques. The principles of surplus productivity and residual returns to the land are useful in establishing the highest and best use of land and in analyzing which option among alternative land use options will yield the highest value. Some twentieth-century economists argue that surplus productivity should be ascribed to a different agent of production, i.e., the entrepreneurship required to combine the land, labor, and capital into a complete real estate product.

Conformity

Conformity holds that real property value is created and sustained when the characteristics of a property conform to the demands of its market. The styles and uses of the properties in a given area may conform for several reasons, including economic pressures and the shared preferences of owners for certain types of structures, amenities, and services. The imposition and enforcement of zoning ordinances and plans by local governments to regulate land use may also contribute to conformity. Standards of conformity set by the market are subject to change. Zoning codes, which tend to establish conformity in basic property characteristics such as size, style, and design, are often difficult to change and may hasten the pace of obsolescence.

Individual markets also set standards of conformity, especially in terms of price. According to the *principle of progression*, a lower-priced property will be worth more in a high-priced neighborhood than it would in a neighborhood of comparable properties. Under the *principle of regression*, a higher-priced property will be worth less in a low-priced neighborhood than it would in a neighborhood of comparable properties. Of course, there are exceptions to these principles. The seasonal cottages and luxurious vacation homes that line a popular recreational lake may exert no effect, either positive or negative, on the value of one another.

Externalities

The principle of externalities states that factors external to a property can have a positive effect on its value or a negative effect on its value. When an essential product or service affects a great number of people, it is often provided by government. Bridges and highways, police and fire protection, and a host of other essential services are positive externalities provided most efficiently through common purchase by the government. Negative externalities result when inconveniences are imposed on property owners by the actions of others. For example, a firm that violates environmental law by dumping hazardous waste and manages to evade responsibility imposes the cleanup costs on others.

Real estate is affected by externalities perhaps more strongly than any other economic good, service, or commodity. Because it is physically immobile, real estate is subject to many types of external influences. Externalities may refer to the use or physical attributes of properties located near the subject property or to the economic conditions that affect the market in which the subject property competes. For example, an increase in the purchasing power of the households that constitute the trade area for a retail facility will likely have a positive effect on the sales (income-producing) potential of the property. External influences may be international or national in origin or they may emanate from the region, community, or neighborhood. Externalities may be as general as international currency and gold prices or as specific as a neighbor's standard of property maintenance. Appraisers observe and analyze how external influences affect the real estate being appraised.

At the international and national levels, manufacturing efficiency, interest rates, and socioeconomic priorities affect real estate values. National trade policy influences the demand for real estate in regional markets. Growing foreign commerce increases the gross domestic product and strengthens regional demand for real estate. In Texas and on the West coast, real estate markets often benefit from the stimulus of trade with Mexico and the Far East.

National fiscal policy also plays a vital role in the economy. The Tax Reform Act of 1986 eliminated many of the tax advantages of investing in income-producing property. This change had a far-reaching effect on the value of investment-grade properties. Due in part to the tax advantages available prior to the 1986 act, some real estate markets had been overbuilt. After the tax law was changed, the oversupply was recognized and values in these markets declined significantly.

An overabundance of capital investment in office building development combined with an international recession beginning in 1988 resulted in a severe oversupply of office space in the United States. Many companies leasing office space reacted to the economic decline by downsizing office staff or reducing the ratio of floor area per office worker. These trends significantly decreased the demand for office space. Office buildings under construction before the recession hit were often unable to obtain tenants upon completion, and many were forced into foreclosure. At the end of the 1980s and beginning of the 1990s, many office markets were dominated by sales of distressed properties and little new development occurred.

During this recessionary period, demand for loans decreased and interest rates declined. In the early 1990s, low interest rates stimulated a gradual economic recovery and sales of new and existing homes picked up. As business activity rebounded, the oversupply of office and industrial properties from the late 1980s was gradually absorbed. In 1994 the Federal Reserve raised interest rates to slow inflationary pressures and help keep rates of return on United States securities attractive to foreign investors.

On the regional level, the economic slowdown of the late 1980s had varying effects in different areas of the country. The Midwest, which has a diversified economy based on service, high-tech, and smokestack industries, did not experience as severe a recession as New England and California did. (The West Coast suffered the brunt of defense industry cutbacks.) Texas, which had been especially hard hit by the decline in oil production during the mid 1980s, began to diversify its economic base and was on the rebound by the early 1990s.

At the community and neighborhood levels, property values are affected by local laws, local government policies and administration, property taxes, economic growth, and social attitudes. Different property value trends can be found in communities in the same region and among neighborhoods in the same community. Appraisers should be familiar with external events at all levels that can have an impact on property values.

Forces That Influence Real Property Values

The value of real property reflects and is affected by the interaction of four basic forces that influence human activity: *social* trends, *economic* circumstances, *governmental* controls and regulations, and *environmental* conditions. The forces are interactive; they exert pressure on human activities and are, in turn, affected by these activities. The interaction of these forces influences the value of every parcel of real estate in the market.

To estimate value an appraiser investigates how the market views a particular property, and the scope of this investigation is not limited to static, current conditions. Rather, the appraiser analyzes trends in the forces that influence value to determine the direction, speed, duration, strength, and limits of these trends.

Social Forces

The social forces studied by appraisers primarily relate to population characteristics. Because the demographic composition of the population reveals the potential demand for real estate, proper analysis and interpretation of demographic trends are required. Real property values are affected not only by population changes and characteristics, but also by the entire spectrum of human activity. The total population, its composition by age and gender, and the rate of household formation and dissolution strongly influence real property values. Social forces are also manifest in attitudes toward education, law and order, and lifestyle options.

Economic Forces

Economic forces are also significant to real property value. Appraisers analyze the fundamental relationships between current and anticipated supply and demand and the economic ability of the population to satisfy its wants and needs demands through its purchasing power. Many specific market characteristics are considered in the analysis of economic forces—e.g., employment, wage levels, industrial expansion, the economic base of the region and the community, price levels, and the cost and availability of mortgage credit. The stock of available vacant and improved properties, new development under construction or in the planning stage, occupancy rates, the rental and price patterns of existing properties, and construction costs are also investigated. Other economic trends and considerations may be studied as the appraiser's analysis focuses on successively smaller geographic areas.

Governmental Forces

Governmental, political, and legal activities at all levels can have a great impact on property values. The legal climate at a particular time or in a particular place may overshadow the natural market forces of supply and demand. As mentioned previously, the government provides many necessary facilities and services that affect land-use patterns. Therefore, appraisers must diligently identify and examine how the following factors could influence property values:

- Public services such as fire and police protection, utilities, refuse collection, and transportation networks
- Local zoning, building codes, and health codes, especially those that obstruct or support land use
- National, state, and local fiscal policies
- Special legislation that influences general property values (e.g., rent control laws, statutory redemption laws, restrictions on forms of ownership such as those imposed on condominiums and timeshare arrangements, homestead exemption laws, environmental legislation regulating new developments and wetlands as well as the control of hazardous or toxic materials, and legislation affecting the types of loans, loan terms, and investment powers of mortgage lending institutions)

Environmental Forces

Both natural and man-made environmental forces influence real property values. Environmental forces that may be analyzed for real estate appraisal purposes include climatic conditions such as snowfall, rainfall, temperature, and humidity; topography and soil; toxic contaminants such as asbestos, radon, and PCBs; natural barriers to future development such as rivers, mountains, lakes, and oceans; primary transportation systems, including federal and state highway systems, railroads, airports, and navigable waterways; and the nature and desirability of the immediate area surrounding a property. All of these factors are environmental, although market participants usually associate the term with issues involving the conservation of natural resources (e.g., wildlife, timberlands, wetlands) and the regulation of man-made pollution. (The treatment of hazardous substances in real estate appraisal is discussed in Chapters 9 and 10.)

The environmental forces that affect the value of a specific real property may be understood in relation to the property's location. *Location considers time-distance relationships, or linkages, between a property or neighborhood and all possible origins and destinations of residents coming to or going from the property or neighborhood.* Location has both an environmental and an economic character. Time and distance are measures of relative access, which may be considered in terms of site ingress/egress, the characteristics of the neighborhoods through which traffic to and from the site passes, and transportation costs to and from the site.

To analyze the value influence of location, the linkages between the property and important points or places outside the property are identified, and the distance and time required to cover those distances by the most commonly used types of transportation are measured. Depending on the area and the property type, the appraiser may investigate the property's access to public transportation, schools, stores, service establishments, parks, recreational and cultural facilities, places of worship, sources of employment, product markets, suppliers of production needs, and processors of raw materials.

An understanding of value-influencing forces is fundamental to the appraisal of real property. Although the four forces are discussed separately here, they work together to affect property values. These forces provide the background against which appraisers view every parcel of real property. (Value influences are discussed in detail in Chapters 8 and 9.)

Highest and Best Use

By identifying and interpreting the local and regional market forces that affect a specific property, the appraiser determines the property's highest and best use. Highest and best use is fundamental to real estate appraisal because it focuses market analysis on the subject property and the feasibility of alternative land uses, allowing the appraiser to identify the property's optimum use in light of market conditions on a specific date.

Highest and best use reflects a basic assumption about real estate market behavior—that the price a buyer will pay or a seller will accept for a property is based on his or her conclusions about the most profitable use of the site or property. Therefore, sites and improved properties tend to be put to their highest and best use. However, the determination of a property's highest and best use set forth in an appraisal may or may not conform with the existing use. The determination of highest and best use must be based on careful consideration of prevailing market conditions, trends affecting market participation and change, and the existing use of the subject property.

Highest and best use may be defined as

> The reasonably probable and legal use of vacant land or improved property, which is physically possible, appropriately supported, financially feasible, and that results in the highest value.

Because the use of land can be limited by the presence of improvements, highest and best use is determined separately for the land or site as though vacant and available to be put to its highest and best use and for the property as improved.

The first determination (highest and best use of land as though vacant) reflects the fact that land value is derived from potential land use. Land has limited value unless there is a present or anticipated use for it; its value depends on the nature of the land's anticipated use, according to the principle of surplus productivity. *Among all reasonable, alternative uses, the use that yields the highest present land value, after payments are made for labor, capital, and coordination, is generally regarded as the highest and best use of the land as though vacant.* In other words, the highest and best use of land as though vacant is the use that brings the highest return to the land after the three other agents of production have been compensated.

To determine the highest and best use of the land as though vacant, the appraiser assumes that the parcel of land in question has no improvements. Even a site with a large building on it can be made vacant by demolishing the building. The question to be answered is: If the land were vacant, what use would result in the highest present land value?

The second determination (highest and best use of property as improved) refers to the optimum use that could be made of the property considering the existing structures. *Analysis of the highest and the best use of a property as improved implies that the existing improvement should be renovated or retained as is so long as it continues to contribute to the total market value of the property, or until the return from a new improvement would more than offset the cost of demolishing the existing building and constructing a new one.*

For example, a large, old house could continue to be used as a single-family residence, or it could be converted into apartments or offices. The decision depends on the rents or prices that could be charged for the existing property under the alternative uses and how these amounts compare with the costs of conversion. Although the existing improvement does not represent the highest and best use of the site as though vacant, it should not necessarily be demolished. Demolition is indicated when the value of the land as though vacant, less the cost of tearing down the existing improvement(s), exceeds the value of the parcel as presently improved.

Determining the highest and best use of land as though vacant is useful for land or site valuation. Determining the highest and best use of an improved property facilitates a decision as to whether 1) the use should continue and the improvements be maintained, 2) something should be done with the improvements (e.g., rehabilitation, modernization, remodeling, renovation), or 3) improvements should be demolished.

The relationship between the supply of, and demand for, land adaptable to a particular use is significant in determining highest and best use. A site or improved property may be put to an interim use until demand is sufficient to support its highest and best use. Thus, a more profitable use must sometimes be delayed due to insufficient present demand. In these situations, the interim use will continue until the value of the land as though vacant, minus the cost of demolishing the existing improvements, exceeds the total value of the improved property under its current use.

When properties are put to temporary, interim uses, the principle of consistent use must be addressed. *Consistent use is the principle that land cannot be valued on the basis of one use while the improvements are valued on the basis of another.* Improvements must contribute to land value to have any value themselves. Improvements that do not represent the land's highest and best use, but have substantial remaining physical lives, may have an interim use that temporarily supports value or they may have no value at all. In fact, the improvements could even have negative value if substantial costs would be incurred to remove them or if contamination affects the improvements and the costs of remediation would exceed the property value. (Highest and best use is discussed in detail in Chapter 13.)

The principle of consistent use also applies to the collection and selection of data. Market data applied in the approaches to value must be gathered from properties that have a highest and best use consistent with that of the subject.

Key Concepts

- Value is created by the anticipation of future benefits.
- The principles of anticipation, change, supply and demand, competition, substitution, and opportunity cost are fundamental to understanding the dynamics of value.
- The principles of balance, increasing and decreasing returns, contribution, surplus productivity, and conformity explain how the integration of property components affects property value.
- Factors outside a property, or externalities, exert an influence on the property's value.
- An appraiser must study the interaction of the social, economic, governmental, and environmental forces that affect property value.
- Understanding the highest and best use of a property is the cornerstone to the property's appraisal.

Terms

anticipation	interim use
balance	law of increasing and
change	decreasing returns
competition	location
conformity	opportunity cost
consistent use	point of decreasing returns
contribution	principle of progression
elasticity of demand	principle of regression
externalities	substitution
highest and best use	supply and demand
highest and best use of land as though vacant	surplus productivity
highest and best use of property as improved	

CHAPTER FOUR

Real Estate Markets and Market Analysis

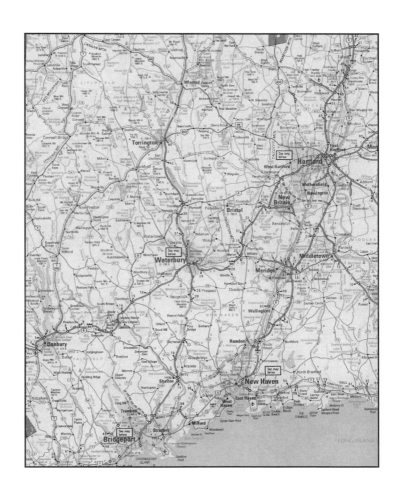

A ppraisers consider value in the context of real estate markets, so delineating real estate markets and submarkets is an essential part of appraisal. In valuation assignments, particularly in estimations of market value, an appraiser's understanding of the market for a specific property provides the criteria with which to research, select, and interpret the comparability of other properties. To arrive at an estimate of market value, the appraiser must identify and analyze the market or markets that influence the subject property.

Consulting assignments in which a value estimate is not necessarily required are often conducted to determine and interpret the characteristics of markets for investors and developers. For example, a feasibility study may focus on the profitability of a specific real estate undertaking in terms of the criteria of the specific market. To provide credible conclusions to such studies, real estate appraisers must thoroughly understand the real estate market or markets that are relevant to the assignment.

Real Estate Markets

Buyers and sellers of different types of property interact in different areas for different reasons. Thus, real estate markets are divided into categories based on the differences among property types and their appeal to different market participants. The markets for various categories of real estate are further divided into submarkets, which correspond to the preferences of buyers and sellers. Differentiating real estate markets facilitates their study.

All real estate markets are influenced by the attitudes, motivations, and interactions of buyers and sellers of real property, which in turn are subject to many social, economic, governmental, and environmental influences. Real estate markets may be studied in terms of their geographic, competitive, and supply-and-demand characteristics, which relate to overall real estate market conditions.

The identification and interpretation of real estate markets are analytical processes. Appraisers analyze the utility and scarcity of property, as well as the desires and effective purchasing power of those who seek to acquire property rights, to answer questions about real estate markets and submarkets.

Characteristics of Real Estate Markets

Real estate markets do not possess the same economic characteristics as markets for other goods and services, which are more efficient. The efficiency of a market is based on assumptions about the behavior of buyers and sellers as well as the characteristics of the products traded.

The goods or services traded in an efficient market are essentially homogeneous items that can be readily substituted for one another. In contrast, each parcel of real estate is unique and its location is fixed. No two parcels of real estate are physically identical. Although some parcels may be economically similar and could be substituted for one another, they differ geographically. The inherent features of real estate preclude its diverse markets from being highly efficient.

In an efficient market there is a large number of buyers and sellers who create a competitive, free market, and none of these participants has a large enough share of the market to have a direct and measurable influence on price. In real estate markets, only a few buyers and sellers may act at one time, within one price range, and at one location for any type of property. The high relative value of real estate requires great purchasing power, so real estate markets are very sensitive to changes in broad economic indicators such as wage levels, the stability of income, and the number of individuals employed. Construction costs, housing costs, and rent levels are all affected by market participants' ability to pay.

In an efficient market, prices are relatively uniform and stable. They are often the primary consideration in purchase or sale decisions because quality tends to be uniform at a set price. In real estate markets, prices are relatively high and very few purchasers have enough money to pay for property in cash. Therefore, the types of financing offered, the amount of mortgage money available, interest rates, down payment requirements, and typical loan duration affect the decision to purchase real estate. If a property cannot be financed favorably, it usually will not be bought. When a lender is less likely to extend a loan, the probability of a buyer being able to purchase the property declines.

An efficient market is self-regulating. Open and free competition is subject to few restrictions. Real estate markets, on the other hand, are not self-regulating. Federal, state, county, and local regulations govern the ownership and transfer of real estate; contract and deed restrictions further regulate the sale and purchase of property. A deed restriction, for example, may require that houses in a subdivision contain at least 2,000 square feet of area.

Supply and demand are never far out of balance in an efficient market because the market tends to move toward balance through the effects of competition. Although the supply of, and demand for, real estate also tend toward equilibrium, this point is theoretical and seldom achieved. The supply of real estate suitable for a specific use is slow to adjust to market demand, unlike the supply of less durable commodities. Furthermore, shifts in demand may occur while new real estate units are being constructed, so an oversupply, rather than market equilibrium, may result.

Units of real estate that are comparable in size and quality tend to sell at comparable prices; if supply and demand are in relative balance, real estate prices tend to be stable. But if the demand for real estate increases suddenly, an additional supply cannot be provided quickly. Similarly, if demand declines suddenly, the excess supply cannot be quickly removed from the market.

In real estate markets, supply and demand are considered causal factors and price is the result of their interaction. Price changes usually are preceded by changes in market activity. Often, supply or demand may shift suddenly in a period of no activity or increased activity.

Buyers and sellers in an efficient market are knowledgeable and fully informed about market conditions, the behavior of others, past market activity, product quality, and product substitutability. Any information needed on bids, offers, and sales is readily available. Buyers and sellers of real estate may not be well informed. Most people do not buy and sell real estate frequently, so they are not very familiar with the procedure or knowledgeable about how to judge a property. Information on bids, offers, and sales of a particular property or similar properties may not be readily available to buyers and sellers since some do not require disclosure.

Buyers and sellers in an efficient market are brought together by an organized market mechanism, such as the New York Stock Exchange, and it is relatively easy for sellers to enter into or to exit from the market in response to market demand. In real estate markets, however, entry and exit are not easy; they are complex and time-consuming. Furthermore, demand may be volatile due to sudden shifts in population. A sudden influx of population in an area may result in high prices because it will take months or years to construct new buildings and increase development to meet the demand. A sudden out-migration due to unfavorable economic conditions can result in an oversupply and lower prices.

Finally, in an efficient market, goods are readily consumed, quickly supplied, and easily transported. Real estate is a durable product and, as an investment, it may be relatively unmarketable and illiquid. Real estate is not usually sold quickly because its sale involves large sums of money and the appropriate financing may not always be readily secured. The supply of real estate is relatively inelastic; because property is fixed in location, the supply cannot be adjusted quickly in any market.

Real estate markets are not efficient and, due to imperfections such as a lack of product standardization and the time required to produce a new supply, it is difficult to predict their behavior accurately. Recognizing that real estate markets do not operate like the markets for other commodities, appraisers must analyze the significant aspects of market activity that make real estate markets inefficient. Real estate market analysis focuses on the motivations, attitudes, and interaction of market participants as they respond to the particular characteristics of real estate and to external influences that affect its value. This focus underscores the need for objective real estate appraisal in a free market economy and the responsibility of appraisers to the communities they serve.

Types of Real Estate Markets

Different real estate markets are created by the needs, desires, motivations, locations, and ages of market participants and the types, locations, designs, and zoning restrictions of property.

Five real estate markets can be identified to correspond to five broad categories of property.

1. Residential (detached single-family homes; attached single-family homes or duplexes; multitenanted apartment buildings)
2. Commercial (office buildings, service industry and professional centers, retail malls, wholesale marts, hotels and motels)

3. Industrial (manufacturing plants, warehouses, research and development build-ings)

4. Agricultural (cropland, orchards, pastureland, livestock operations, timberland) and extractive (mines, oilfields)

5. Special-purpose (properties with unique design or construction features which restrict their utility to the use for which they were built—e.g., schools, public buildings, airports, convention facilities, amusement/theme parks, golf courses)

Each market for a particular type of property can be subdivided into smaller, more specialized markets called *submarkets*. Submarkets for urban, suburban, and rural residential property can be further divided in terms of the purchasers' preference for high-, medium-, or low-priced properties. Multitenanted apartment buildings, which are income-producing residential properties, and offices, stores, loft buildings, parking garages, motels, hotels, and shopping centers, which are commercial properties, typically appeal to different groups of investors. Industrial properties include factories, ware-houses, and business parks. The market for agricultural properties can be divided into markets for pastureland, livestock operations, timberland, cropland, orchards, and ranchlands. Special-purpose properties include parks, cemeteries, houses of worship, clubs, golf courses, historic or recreational government properties, and public utilities.

The process of identifying and analyzing submarkets within a larger market is called market segmentation. Segmentation usually applies to groupings of consum-ers, differentiating the potential users of a subject property from the general population by their characteristics. *Disaggregation* is a related term that applies to the property. Disaggregation differentiates the subject property from other properties by creating subclassifications with differing product characteristics.[1] These terms are discussed in more detail in a subsequent section of this chapter.

A submarket can be created by changes in the demand side of the market; for example, a certain type of property may be in demand by a particular group. Families looking for homes and companies in need of warehouses may be considered real estate markets. The properties within these large markets are heterogeneous because resi-dences and warehouses can be large or small, old or new, well designed or poorly designed. A market is divided into a number of smaller, more homogeneous submarkets by recognizing the different product preferences of buyers and sellers. These preferences may relate to building size and design, price range, property location, or other factors.

Real estate appraisers identify and study market segments by considering locational, demographic, socioeconomic, psychological, and product-related characteris-tics. They may use survey research techniques to discover, quantify, analyze, and form conclusions about the composition of particular submarkets.

Market Analysis

Market analysis is the identification and study of the market for a particular economic good or service. The market analysis component of an appraisal must

---

1. Neil Carn, Joseph Rabianski, Ronald Racster, and Maury Seldin, *Real Estate Market Analysis* (Englewood Cliffs, N.J.: Prentice-Hall, 1988).

specifically relate market conditions to the property under investigation. It must show how the interaction of supply and demand affects the value of the subject property. Appraisers use market analysis to determine whether there is appropriate market support for an existing property under a specified use or evidence that there will be market support for a proposed use of a site at some time in the foreseeable future. If current market conditions do not indicate adequate demand for a proposed development, market analysis may identify the point in time when adequate demand for the project will likely emerge. Thus, market analysis informs the appraiser as to the timing of a proposed improvement and the amount of demand anticipated in a particular period of time.

Market analysis provides a basis for determining the *highest and best use* of a property. An existing or proposed improvement under a specified use may be put to the test of maximum productivity only after it has been demonstrated that an appropriate level of market support exists for that use. In-depth market analyses go much further in specifying the character of that support. Such studies may determine key marketing strategies for an existing or proposed property, address the design characteristics of a proposed development, or provide estimates of the share of the market the property is likely to capture and its probable absorption rate.

To measure the market support for a specified property use, the analyst must identify the relationship between demand and competitive supply in the subject real estate market—both now and in the future. This relationship indicates the degree of *equilibrium* or *disequilibrium* that characterizes the present market and the conditions likely to characterize the market over the forecast period.

The market value of a property is largely determined by its competitive position in its market. Familiarity with the characteristics and attributes of the subject property will enhance the appraiser's ability to identify competitive properties (supply) and to understand the comparative advantages and disadvantages that the subject offers potential buyers or renters (demand). With an understanding of economic conditions, their effect on real estate markets, and the momentum of these markets, an appraiser can better appreciate the externalities affecting the property. In its broadest sense, therefore, market analysis provides vital information needed to apply the three approaches to value.

In the sales comparison approach, market analysis helps the appraiser identify competitive properties and determine their exact degree of comparability with the subject. With a thorough understanding of current market conditions gained through market analysis, the appraiser can adjust the sale prices of comparable properties for changes in market conditions that may have occurred since the sales were transacted.

Market analysis also provides an appraiser with information about current building costs and market conditions for use in the cost approach. This information helps the appraiser estimate the profit an entrepreneur will expect (or, for an owner-built property, the intangibles associated with owner occupancy) and any economic advantage or obsolescence the property may have suffered since its construction.

In the market analysis process, an appraiser also collects data on vacancy and absorption rates, market rents, current and anticipated rates of return, and the competitive position of the subject property in its specific market. In the income capitalization approach, this information is used to determine the anticipated lease-up or sell-out rate for the subject, the share of the market that the subject is likely to capture, the future income stream it is likely to enjoy, and an appropriate discount rate or capitalization rate to apply to the income stream projection or annualized income expectancy.

The principles of market analysis seem simple, but the techniques and procedures applied by market analysts can be extremely sophisticated. Market studies can be developed into elaborate analyses. The levels of market analysis that can be performed reflect a spectrum of increasingly complicated methodologies.[2]

Estimates of demand are formulated differently depending on the level of analysis. In some cases, demand may simply be inferred from current market conditions or rates of change may be used to develop projections. Because of shortcomings in this simple approach, caution is advised. To perform an in-depth analysis of forecast (fundamental) demand, the analyst must gather and segment extensive data and apply sound judgment to make projections. The analyst refines the forecast demand estimate by considering the perceptions of market participants and assessing the likelihood that current trends will continue.

Two Approaches

There is no universally accepted set of steps or procedures to be applied in market analysis because each assignment depends on the specific needs of the client and these needs vary. Moreover, appraisers do not always agree on the best way for the market analysis component of an appraisal to be integrated with the determination of highest and best use. It is possible, however, to identify two schools of market analysts (see Figure 4.1). Many practitioners proceed from the general economy to the specific property; other practitioners begin with the specific property and then consider the general economy. It is important to note that regardless of the procedure employed, each approach considers a full complement of factors.

Appraisers approaching real estate market analysis as market researchers generally tend to emphasize the need to begin the analysis with an economic overview of the community in which the subject property is located. Their first concern is the local or regional economic base, its linkages to the national and even global economy, and the broad dynamics of supply and demand which determine prices and absorption rates in real estate markets. Depending on the type of study required, critical items in this economic overview can include population, employment, income, major industries, principal retail centers, areawide housing, overall urban growth trends, and the status of rural areas (agricultural land and wilderness).

---

2. For a comprehensive discussion of the various levels of market analysis, see Stephen F. Fanning and Jody Winslow "Guidelines for Defining the Scope of Market Analysis in Appraisals," *The Appraisal Journal* (October 1988), 466-476, and *Market Analysis for Valuation Appraisals* by Stephen F. Fanning, Terry V. Grissom, and Thomas D. Pearson (Chicago: Appraisal Institute, 1994).

Figure 4.1 | **Two Approaches to Market Analysis**

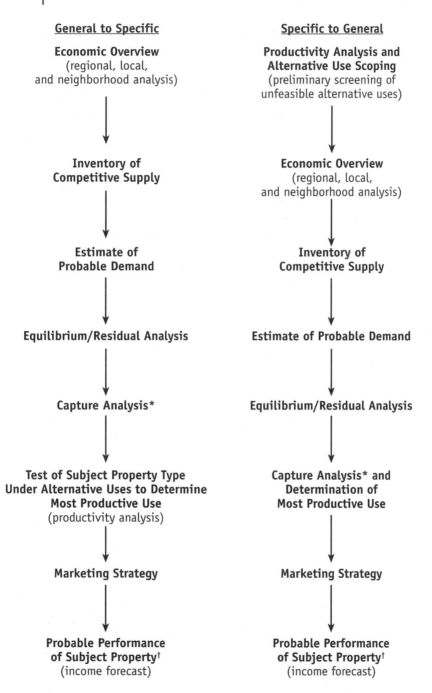

General to Specific

Economic Overview
(regional, local,
and neighborhood analysis)

↓

**Inventory of
Competitive Supply**

↓

**Estimate of
Probable Demand**

↓

Equilibrium/Residual Analysis

↓

Capture Analysis*

↓

**Test of Subject Property Type
Under Alternative Uses to Determine
Most Productive Use**
(productivity analysis)

↓

Marketing Strategy

↓

**Probable Performance
of Subject Property†**
(income forecast)

Specific to General

**Productivity Analysis and
Alternative Use Scoping**
(preliminary screening of
unfeasible alternative uses)

↓

Economic Overview
(regional, local,
and neighborhood analysis)

↓

**Inventory of
Competitive Supply**

↓

Estimate of Probable Demand

↓

Equilibrium/Residual Analysis

↓

**Capture Analysis* and
Determination of
Most Productive Use**

↓

Marketing Strategy

↓

**Probable Performance
of Subject Property†**
(income forecast)

* Market capture may be analyzed in terms of short-run absorption and long-run market share.

† A schematic representation of the interrelationship of market, feasibility, and highest and best use analyses is illustrated in Figure 13.1.

Analysts of this first school start by examining the market. Population, employment, and income data serve as indicators of *area demand*; data on the amount of space currently available (obtained from occupancy or vacancy rates) and space under construction or proposed for development provide a measure of competitive supply. *Comparing* demand and competitive supply identifies the extent of present and prospective equilibrium or disequilibrium in the market.

After supply and demand analysis, these market analysts study the probable alternative uses of the property and estimate the market support for and values associated with these uses. They consider the physical, legal or regulatory, and locational attributes of the subject property and ultimately arrive at a conclusion regarding its highest and best use.

A second school of practitioners contend that demand and supply are both embodied in the real estate product.[3] They believe that the best way to begin market analysis is to examine the characteristics or attributes that contribute to the productivity of the subject property and assess the subject's competitive position in its specific market. These analysts believe that understanding the physical, legal or regulatory, and locational attributes of a property is essential to identify the market participants likely to purchase or rent the property and those likely to sell or lease it. Potential buyers or tenants and sellers or landlords represent the forces of demand and supply that create the dynamics of the subject market.

Adherents of this second school of thought argue that a property productivity analysis focusing on the characteristics and attributes of the subject property facilitates identification of competitive properties and, thus, definition of the subject market. After property productivity analysis is completed, these appraisers analyze demand and competitive supply in the delineated market area. Market-specific data are examined to arrive at estimates of current and future demand and an inventory of available and projected supply. The extent of market equilibrium or disequilibrium is determined, and future market conditions are forecast. To develop a complete understanding of the market for which a forecast is being made, the analyst studies critical variables such as the rate of employment growth, changes in population and household size, income levels, and retail sales.

Next these analysts consider the most probable alternative uses of the property in terms of present and prospective market support. This analysis will indicate which of the most probable alternative uses is most productive and thereby qualifies as the highest and best use of the property.

Whichever approach the appraiser chooses to follow, the purpose of the market analysis should guide the appraiser's efforts at all times. The purpose of market analysis is generally to establish whether appropriate market support exists for a property under a specified use or if there is evidence of market support for a proposed use at some time in the foreseeable future. Market analysis focuses on understanding how the local economy affects market conditions, specifically the conditions that characterize the market in which the subject property competes.

---

3. These practitioners subscribe to the writings of Richard U. Ratcliffe and James A. Graaskamp.

Fundamental Concepts

Market Definition

At the outset of the market analysis process, the appraiser must clearly identify the real estate product and the real estate market in which the subject competes. These two tasks may be considered complementary. Analyzing the characteristics and attributes of the real estate product helps the appraiser identify competitive properties. Defining the real estate market for the subject property clearly enhances the appraiser's understanding of how externalities affect the subject. Market analysis breaks down a specific real estate market into consumer submarkets or market segments. It also disaggregates the real estate product from other types of properties.

To understand market analysis, it is useful to reexamine the definition of a real estate market. *A real estate market is a group of individuals or firms that are in contact with one another for the purpose of conducting real estate transactions.* Market participants may be buyers, sellers, renters, lessors, lessees, mortgagors, mortgagees, developers, builders, managers, owners, investors, or brokers. Each market participant does not have to be in contact with every other participant; a person or firm is part of the market if that person or firm is in contact with another subset of market participants.

The actions of market participants are prompted by their expectations about the use or uses of a property and the benefits it will afford its users. Market segmentation, therefore, differentiates the most probable users of a property from the general population by their consumer characteristics. A real estate market is made up of market participants engaged in real estate transactions. The activity of these individuals focuses on a real estate product and the service it provides. Product disaggregation, therefore, differentiates the subject property and competitive properties from other types of properties on the basis of their attributes or characteristics.

To identify a specific real estate market, an appraiser investigates the following factors:

1. *Property type* (e.g., single-family residence, retail shopping center, office building)
2. *Property features* such as occupancy, customer base, quality of construction, and design and amenities
   a. *Occupancy*—single-tenant or multitenant (residential, apartment, office, retail)
   b. *Customer base*—the most probable users (Data on population, employment, income, and activity patterns are analyzed. For residential markets, data are broken down according to the profile of the likely property owner or tenant; for commercial markets, data are segmented according to the likely users of the space. For retail markets, the clientele that the prospective tenants will draw represents the customer base; for office markets the customer base reflects the space needs of prospective companies leasing office units.)
   c. *Quality of construction* (class of building)
   d. *Design and amenity* features
3. *Market area*—defined geographically or locationally (A market area may be local, regional, national, or international in scope. It may be urban or suburban; it may

correspond to a district or neighborhood of a city. Retail and residential market areas are often delineated by specific time-distance relationships.)

4. Available *substitute properties*—i.e., equally desirable properties competing with the subject in its market area, which may be local, regional, national, or international

5. *Complementary properties*—i.e., some other property or property type that is complementary to the subject (The users of the subject property need to have access to complementary properties, which are also referred to as *support facilities*.)

A market segment is delineated by identifying the market participants likely to be involved in transactions focused on the subject real estate and the type of real estate product and service it provides. The product disaggregation includes both the subject property and competitive and complementary properties. Thus, market analysis combines market segmentation and product disaggregation.

Market analysts often make use of survey data to delineate market areas. Surveys are especially useful in identifying consumer preferences, purchasing behavior, and lifestyles, which are significant factors in retail and residential market definition.

Demand

Demand reflects the needs, material desires, purchasing power, and preferences of consumers. Demand analysis focuses on identifying the potential users of a subject property—the buyers, renters, or clientele it will attract. For each particular type of property, demand analysis focuses on the end product or service that the real estate provides. Thus, a demand analysis for retail space would attempt to determine the demand for retail services generated by potential customers in the market area. A demand analysis for office space would attempt to identify businesses in the area that occupy office space and their space or staffing needs.

Demand analyses for residential and retail markets specifically investigate the households in the subject's market area. (A *household* is defined as a number of related or unrelated people who live in one housing unit; thus a single individual may constitute a household.) In addition to the number of households in the market area, these analyses focus on the disposable income or effective purchasing power of these households and the ages, gender, preferences, and behavioral patterns of household members. The following factors are important in demand analysis for a residential market:

- Population of the market area—size and number of households, rate of increase or decrease in household formation, composition, and age distribution
- Income (household and per capita)
- Employment types and unemployment rate
- Percentage of owners and renters
- Financial considerations such as savings levels and lending requirements (e.g., interest rates on mortgages, points charged, loan-to-value ratios)
- Land use patterns and directions of city growth and development

- Factors affecting the physical appeal of the neighborhood, e.g., geography and geology (climate, topography, drainage, bedrock, and natural or man-made barriers)
- Local tax structure and administration
- Availability of support facilities and community services (cultural institutions, educational facilities, health and medical facilities, fire and police protection)

The following factors are significant in demand analysis for a retail market.

- Population of trade area(s)—size and number of households, rate of increase or decrease in household formation, composition and age distribution of households
- Per capita and household income (mean and median)
- Percentage of household income spent on retail purchases and percentage of disposable income (effective purchasing power) spent on various retail categories
- Rate of sales retention in the trade area
- Required volume of sales for a retail facility to operate profitably and existing sales volume per square foot
- Retail vacancy rate in the market
- Percentage of retail purchases captured from outside the trade area
- Land use patterns and directions of city growth and development
- Accessibility (transportation facilities and highway systems) and cost of transportation
- Factors that affect the appeal of the retail center (image, quality of goods, and tenant reputation)

The following factors are considered in demand analysis for an office market:

- Area employers who use office space; current and estimated future staffing needs
- Average square foot areas of office space required by an office worker (Requirements vary according to the category of work, the rank of the office worker, and the location of the office in the suburbs or the central business district.)
- Vacancy rate for the specific class of office building
- Move-up demand for Class A and Class B buildings or fall-out demand for Class B and Class C buildings
- Land use patterns and directions of city growth and development
- Accessibility (transportation facilities and highway systems) and cost of transportation
- Factors that affect the appeal of the office building (quality of construction, management, and tenancy) and the availability of support facilities (shops, restaurants, recreational centers)

Demand in industrial and agricultural property markets is generally more limited than the demand in residential or commercial markets. As with all property types, market delineation is essential to identify demand for the property. The fundamentals of industrial and agricultural property markets are discussed at the end of this chapter.

The demand for housing and most retail space is projected on the basis of growth rates in population, income, and employment levels.[4] The key points discussed below can be especially useful in understanding demand projections.[5]

First, the rate of household formation varies significantly with income and age (cohort) groups in the existing population; this rate is even more sensitive to migration. Estimating the number of households in an area by dividing the total population by the average household size may result in considerable error. The rate of household formation is much higher for people between the ages of 25 and 34 and those between 35 and 54 than for people between the ages of 15 and 24. However, precise data may be difficult to obtain.

Second, household size is not a constant. Over the past decade, average household size has declined significantly. Between 1985 and 1993, household size in the United States fell from 2.69 to 2.63.[6]

Third, while average or median income is generally projected in current (inflationary) dollars, real income in the United States calculated in constant dollars did not grow between 1973 and 1984, increased very modestly between 1985 and 1989, and has again declined since 1990.[7] Income projections based on current dollars will thus reflect future, inflated dollars.

Finally, population projections for small areas are published by public agencies and market research firms, but such projections can be misleading. Therefore, the appraiser should also consult projections for the overall metropolitan area. The availability of land and the adequacy of the infrastructure in the subject area will help determine how much of the overall growth projected will go to that area.

Competitive Supply

Supply refers to the production and availability of the real estate product. To analyze supply the appraiser must compile an inventory of properties competitive with the subject. Competitive properties include the stock of existing units, units under construction that will enter the market, and projects in planning. Care must be exercised in developing and analyzing data on proposed or announced projects because some may not ultimately be constructed. The appraiser must also determine the number of units lost to demolition and the number added or removed through conversion. Data may be gathered from field inspection; by reviewing building permits (issued and acted upon), plat maps, and surveys of competitive sites; and through interviews with developers and city planners.

4. See Chapter 8 for a discussion of the data used to estimate the demand for and competitive supply of a specific property type or use.
5. Dowell Myers, "Housing Market Research: A Time for a Change," *Urban Land* (October 1988), 16-19.
6. U.S. Department of Commerce, Bureau of the Census, *Current Population Reports, Series P-20, No. 478,* March 1993.
7. U.S. Department of Commerce, Bureau of the Census, *The Statistical Abstract of the United States: 1990,* 10th ed (Washington, D.C.: U.S. Government Printing Office), 444, Table 716; and U.S. Department of Commerce, Bureau of the Census, *Current Population Reports, Consumer Income Series P-60, No. 184,* March, 1993.

Table 4.1 | **Projections of the Number of Households in the United States: 1995 to 2010**

	1995	Percent	2000	Percent	2005	Percent	2010	Percent
Total households	97,722,883	100	103,245,963	100	108,818,659	100	114,825,428	100
Under 35	23,609,506	24	22,011,573	21	21,945,230	20	23,149,719	20
35-54	40,479,445	41	45,123,324	44	46,483,668	43	45,863,333	40
55 and older	33,633,932	34	36,111,066	35	34,410,161	32	45,812,376	40
Family households	68,382,680	100	71,668,930	100	74,732,880	100	77,894,830	100
Under 35	15,707,012	23	14,274,241	20	13,884,370	19	14,395,388	18
35-54	31,977,088	47	35,174,523	49	35,772,737	48	34,843,630	45
55 and older	20,698,580	30	22,220,166	31	25,075,773	33	28,655,812	37
Nonfamily households	29,340,203	100	31,577,033	100	34,085,779	100	36,930,598	100
Under 35	7,902,494	27	7,737,332	24	8,060,860	24	8,754,331	24
35-54	8,502,357	29	9,948,801	32	10,710,931	31	11,019,703	30
55 and older	12,935,352	44	13,890,900	44	15,313,988	45	17,156,564	46

Demand for residential and commercial property is projected on the basis of household formation rates. The above projections are based on the following assumptions: The ages of couples at first marriage will continue to rise, but at a slower pace than previously, and the increase in the percentage of those never married will continue to decelerate. The leveling off of the divorce rate, which has shown a decline since 1979, is expected to continue as population cohorts in their 20s and 30s age.

Based on data in the *1990 U.S. Census* and population projections published in *Current Population Surveys* (CPS) by the U.S. Census Bureau.

To analyze the supply of competing properties, the following factors must be studied:

- Quantity and quality of available competition (standing stock)
- Volume of new construction (competitive and complementary)—projects in planning and under construction
- Availability and price of vacant land
- Costs of construction and development
- Currently offered properties (existing and newly built)
- Owner occupancy versus tenant occupancy
- Causes and number of vacancies
- Conversions to alternative uses
- Special economic conditions and circumstances
- Availability of construction loans and financing
- Impact of building codes, zoning ordinances, and other regulations on construction volume and cost

Market Equilibrium

Over the short term, the supply of real estate is relatively fixed and prices are responsive to demand. If demand is unusually high, prices and rents will start to rise before new construction can begin. The completion of a building may lag considerably behind the shift in demand. Thus, disequilibrium generally characterizes markets over the short term.

Theoretically, the supply of and demand for real estate move toward equilibrium over the long term. However, this point is seldom achieved. In some markets, such as those characterized by a very specialized economy, supply responds slowly to changing demand conditions. Even when an excess in the quantity of goods offered for sale becomes apparent, projects currently under construction generally have to be completed. More stock will continue to be added to the existing surplus causing greater disequilibrium. A decline in demand may also occur while new real estate units are being constructed, further exacerbating the oversupply.

Analysts and market participants describe the activity of real estate markets in a variety of ways. An *active market* is a market characterized by growing demand, a corresponding lag in supply, and an increase in prices. An active market is also referred to as a *seller's market* because the sellers of available properties can obtain higher prices. A *depressed market* is a market in which a drop in demand is accompanied by a relative oversupply and a decline in prices. A depressed market is also referred to as a *buyer's market* because buyers have the advantage.

Other terms applied to markets are subject to interpretation. For example, markets are sometimes characterized as "strong" or "weak." Strong markets may reflect either high demand and increasing price levels or a large volume of transactions. Weak, or soft, markets may be identified by low demand and declining price levels. Other loosely defined terms include "broad" and "narrow" markets, "loose" and "tight" markets, and "balanced" and "unbalanced" markets.[8]

All markets cannot be described with simple characterizations. Sometimes supply and demand do not act as expected. Supply may fail to respond to increasing demand because the rate of demolition exceeds the rate of new construction. In this case, prices will continue to rise. Or supply may outpace rising demand because of a glut of existing properties on the market, and prices will decline.

The activity of the real estate market is cyclical. Like the business cycle, the real estate cycle is characterized by successive periods of expansion, peak, contraction, and trough. The real estate cycle is not, however, synchronized with the business cycle. Real estate activity responds to two sets of stimuli, one of which operates over the long term and the other over the short term.

The long-term, or *secular*, cycle is a function of changes in the characteristics of existing employment, population, and income. If the local economy is able to provide stable employment and generate new jobs, the present population will remain in the area and others will migrate there seeking employment. The specific types of employment offered by the local economy determine the levels of disposable income in the community.

Shifts in consumer preferences may also occur over the long term, e.g., the growing interest in "signature" buildings and "big box" stores, restrictions on development caused by opposition from the conservation movement.

The short-term cycle is largely a function of the availability of credit. Interest rates serve as indicators of short-term cycles. Real estate activity, measured in the number of housing starts and home sales, is extremely sensitive to fluctuations in the interest rate. Therefore, the real estate industry generally takes the lead, anticipating upturns and downturns in the business cycle. Vacancy and absorption rates may be considered indicators of short-term cycles, although in especially depressed markets low rates may persist for many years. Industrial relocation and mass labor migration may also create short-term cycles.

Short-term indicators typically reflect only the immediate future. Interest rates are very volatile, and vacancy and absorption rates can rarely be forecast with any accuracy beyond two or three years. To develop a market forecast, an appraiser should identify long-term trends. Indicators of long-term trends include the economic base and planned infrastructure of the community. These factors, among others, determine the future growth potential of the area.

Sample Procedures for Conducting Market Analysis

A market analysis is performed to estimate the demand for a specific category of real estate (e.g., residential units, retail space, office space, industrial plant, agricultural operation) and the extent of market support for the subject property. Market analysis may be undertaken to examine an existing property under a specified use or the proposed use of a property that presently is vacant or put to another use. In either case, the objective of the market analysis is to demonstrate whether adequate market support

---

8. Carn et al, 76-77 and 81-82.

exists for a given property use.[9] The market analysis procedure is the same for existing properties and proposed properties.

For many existing properties, demand must be forecast. In some cases, the analyst can study the sales or income history of the property and infer its future performance and market capture. To perform market analysis for a proposed property, which is frequently required to evaluate project feasibility, the analyst has to determine whether the project will achieve a competitive level of performance. In addition to demand forecasting, the capture potential of a proposed property requires extensive analysis.

The procedures presented below reflect a conventional approach to market analysis, beginning with an economic overview and market identification rather than property productivity analysis.

Housing Demand

To forecast the demand for proposed units in a single-family subdivision over a given period (typically five years), an appraiser may follow the steps described below.[10]

1. *Preliminary economic overview.* Analyze the community's economic base by surveying the industries and businesses that generate employment and income as well as the rate of population growth, rate of household formation, and levels of income, which are generally functions of employment. Study economic activity and investigate the local real estate market by surveying the number of residential sales, the level of residential construction, and mortgage interest and absorption rates.

2. *Market and property identification.* Analyze the characteristics of likely buyers to whom the specified housing units would appeal. Develop a consumer profile describing income (i.e., ability to afford the housing), household size, age, and preferences. The market area of potential buyers may be defined in terms of time-distance relationships (the commuting time to employment centers), social or political boundaries (school districts, voting precincts), man-made or natural boundaries (major thoroughfares, physical barriers) and the location of competitive housing. Perform a preliminary analysis of the legal, physical, and locational attributes of the subject units and units in competitive subdivisions.

3. *Demand analysis.* Determine the size of the current and projected population within the defined market area. Determine the current and projected number of households, keeping in mind that household size varies with the age of the head of the household. Segment the number of current and projected households into those headed by owners and those headed by renters. There may be an overlapping category of renters who can afford to buy. Break down the number of owner-

---

9. Market analysis also provides an estimate of demand (e.g., a specific number of units) and helps determine the nature of the property to be developed (e.g., owner-occupied condominium units or renter-occupied apartment units).

10. Procedures for estimating housing, retail space, and office space demand are discussed in J.R. Kimball and Barbara S. Bloomberg, "The Demographics of Subdivision Analysis," *The Appraisal Journal* (October 1986) and J.R. Kimball, "Office Space Demand Analysis," *The Appraisal Journal* (October1987). The focus of the market analysis will determine the sequence of steps in the study. For example, a client may not specify the housing unit, retail facility, or office building to be developed, but may instead want to know the best type of unit, facility, or building to develop. In this case, the analyst must investigate supply and demand before the property can be identified.

headed households according to their income levels to determine the percentage of households that are or will be able to meet the mortgage payments required by local lending practices and interest rates and other housing costs such as expenses for maintenance, insurance, and taxes. Adjust the number of owner-headed households that are or will be able to afford the housing by the vacancy rate in the market to determine the existing and anticipated demand for the subject property.

4. *Competitive supply analysis.* Inventory existing competitive properties, proper-ties under construction, planned properties for which building permits have been obtained, and proposed properties within the subject's identified market area. Refine the inventory by checking the total number of building permits issued against those actually put to use in recent years. Tally the inventory of existing and anticipated competitive supply for the projection period. Rate the subject and its competition for specific amenities and attributes that give housing units a competi-tive advantage or disadvantage.

5. *Equilibrium or residual analysis.* Compare existing and potential demand with current and anticipated competitive supply to determine whether demand for additional units or square footage of housing (marginal demand) exists or when it may develop. Analyze the competitive rating to forecast the likely capture rate for the subject.

Retail Space Demand

To forecast the demand for an existing or proposed community shopping center at a specific site over a given period (i.e., five or 10 years), an appraiser might follow these steps:

1. *Preliminary economic overview.* Analyze the community's economic base by surveying the industries and businesses that generate employment and income as well as the rate of population growth and levels of income, both of which are functions of employment. Study economic activity as reflected in retail sales and the local real estate market by surveying the number of retail sales, the level of construction activity, and absorption rates.

2. *Market and property identification.* Define the trade area for the facility using techniques such as gravitational models and customer spotting, or by adjusting preliminary trade area boundaries for the specific geographic, demographic, and economic characteristics of the community. Perform a preliminary analysis of the legal, physical, and locational attributes of the subject retail center and competitive centers in or near its trade area.

3. *Demand analysis.* Identify the amount of supportable leasable retail space in the trade area using projected demographic and income data. An estimate of support-able leasable retail space may be obtained by multiplying the number of households in the trade area by the mean or median household income. To this figure apply the following percentages: the percentage of household income spent on retail purchases, the percentage of retail purchases made at a facility such as the subject, and the percentage of sales retention in the trade area. Then divide this estimate of total potential retail sales by an estimate of the sales per square foot required for

the facility to operate profitably. Adjust the resulting figure for the normal vacancy rate in the market to obtain an estimate of the supportable leasable retail space in the trade area. This estimate may be further adjusted to account for retail income from outside the trade area and leakage of retail income to other areas.

4. *Competitive supply analysis.* Determine the amount of existing retail space currently leased or vacant and the amount of space under construction or in planning in or near the defined trade area. Refine the inventory by checking the total number of building permits issued against those actually put to use in recent years. Rate the subject and its competition for specific amenities and attributes that give a retail center a competitive advantage or disadvantage.

5. *Equilibrium or residual analysis.* Compare the estimate of supportable leasable space with the amount of existing and anticipated retail space. The difference between the two will be the estimate of additional space needed. Sales per square foot in individual retail stores may also indicate the performance level of an existing shopping center, the center's share of the market, and whether there is opportunity for expansion. These data may be used to check the reasonableness of the estimate of additional space demanded. If there is a current surplus of retail space, the forecast of market conditions may identify when in the future the available retail space will have been absorbed and demand for additional retail space will begin to come on line. Analyze the competitive rating to obtain the likely market capture rate for the subject. A cost of occupancy analysis can establish whether a tenant's cost of occupancy is proportional or disproportional to the tenant's sales. (If the cost of occupancy is too high, the tenant will either not re-lease the space or only do so at a lower rent.) For example, if a comparison of occupancy costs (total rent plus taxes, insurance, and common area maintenance, which may or may not include utilities) and sales volume indicates a ratio of 1:10 or less, the anticipated rent levels may be met.

Office Space Demand

To forecast the demand for existing or additional office space in a particular node or district over a given period, an appraiser analyzes the relationship between supply and demand in the overall market area and the district's actual and potential share of the existing and projected demand. The time when a proposed building will reach stabilized occupancy can be forecast in this way. Demand for office space in the overall market area is estimated with the following steps:

1. *Preliminary economic overview.* Analyze the community's economic base by surveying the industries and businesses that generate total employment. Investigate the percentage of total employment that utilizes office space.

2. *Market and property identification.* Segment the market of property users according to the type of tenants leasing office units currently or in the future, their space or staffing needs, and the clientele they draw. For example, law firms may seek space in prestigious, centrally located buildings, while businesses providing other types of services may prefer suburban offices with ample parking facilities and reasonable rents. The market area for an office building is generally diffused

over a broad metropolitan area. Competitive office space is disaggregated on the basis of the class of building, tenancy, and location. A preliminary analysis of the subject and competitive buildings includes comparison of the nodes or clusters of office buildings within the metropolitan area as well as competitive buildings within the subject node. Determining the share of overall demand that a district will capture is discussed below.

3. *Demand analysis.* Project employment for the overall market area. Based on job projections provided by forecasting agencies such as municipal departments and econometric services, develop estimates of the number of office workers projected in each economic and occupational sector. Consider historical employment growth rates to check the reasonableness of these projections.[11] Convert the number of office occupants into the annual demand for office space. The average space required for an office worker ranges from 125 to 150 square feet.[12] In soft markets with high vacancy rates, businesses often lease extra space and employees may occupy more area. The total number of office workers estimated for a specific period is multiplied by the average space required per worker. Projections may be made in annual, biannual, or multiyear increments. If a 10-year forecast is being developed and steady growth is anticipated, the demand for the first period is subtracted from the demand for the last period and the difference is divided by the number of periods in the forecast to yield an annual demand estimate.

4. *Competitive supply analysis.* Inventory currently leased and vacant competitive space as well as competitive space under construction or in planning. The competitive supply inventory may also be affected by demolitions, renovations, and the adaptation of space now under other uses. Refine the inventory by checking the total number of building permits issued against those actually put to use in recent years. Rate the subject and the competition within the subject's node for specific amenities and attributes that give the office space a competitive advantage or disadvantage.

5. *Equilibrium or residual analysis.* Compare the existing and projected demand for office space with the total supply of current and anticipated competitive office space. If the projected demand for space exceeds the total quantity of space offered for lease, subtract the one from the other to arrive at the unsatisfied demand for office space. Refine the forecast by checking the accuracy of the projection of office space in demand against the historic pattern of demand. For Class A and Class B buildings, potential *move-up or fall-out demand* should be

---

11. Another way to calculate the number of office space occupants in economic and occupational sectors in past years involves establishing the ratio between the number of office workers and the number of total workers in each sector. In a sector such as finance, insurance, and real estate (FIRE), a high percentage (more than two-thirds) of all office workers occupy space in freestanding office buildings—i.e., buildings entirely occupied by office workers. The number of FIRE office workers in freestanding buildings may be estimated by multiplying the total number of workers by this percentage. In sectors such as manufacturing, however, a very low percentage of office workers occupy space in freestanding office buildings. Using these ratios, the number of office workers in each sector can be determined and the aggregate of office workers in all sectors can be calculated. See Ian Alexander, *Office Location and Public Policy* (New York: Chancer Press, 1979).

12. Very general estimates of average area requirements are published by the Building Owners and Managers Association (BOMA). Because the square foot area required per employee varies widely with community size and the type of employment in the community, market analysts should compare BOMA estimates with area-per-worker data developed as part of the competitive supply analysis. Estimates obtained from other national and local sources may also vary.

considered, i.e., some tenants move up from Class B to Class A space in a down market with declining rents, while others fall out from Class A to Class B space in an active market where rents are increasing.

In an in-depth analysis, also consider space subject to pre-leasing and space that will become vacant when current tenant leases expire. If demand for space is anticipated to grow at a steady rate, the total supply that is available for occupancy may be divided by projected annual demand to determine the absorption period. At the end of the absorption period, additional space will be required. This point in time represents a "window" for development.

Rank the subject against competitive office buildings based on location and amenity characteristics. Analyze the competitive rating to forecast the subject's likely *absorption* (short-term capture) and *share of the market* (long-term capture).[13]

To determine a particular node or district's share of the overall market projection, development patterns in the district must be analyzed. Central business districts are characterized by the greatest density of development, while suburban office complexes attract tenants with lower rents and easier access, both for employees and customers. Not all suburbs share equally in the market for office space. Development patterns in areas (analogs) that closely resemble the subject district should be compared. Key demographic features such as total population and educational and income levels are believed to be closely correlated with the ability of a suburban area to support an office building.

The appraiser can develop a ratio by dividing the amount of existing office space in the district by the amount of office space in the overall market area. Such a ratio only reflects the district's "fair share" of the market, however, and may not provide an accurate forecast. Market preferences must also be considered in determining the ratio. The projected demand for office space in the overall market area may be multiplied by this ratio.

The projected quantity of space in demand is compared with estimates of the current and anticipated amount of space offered for lease, and the accuracy of the projections are checked against historic patterns. These same procedures are used to analyze absorption in the overall market area.

To forecast when a *proposed building* will reach stabilized occupancy, the appraiser can estimate the construction period and an absorption rate based on pre-leasing and the historic performance of competitive buildings. Historic performance is interpreted and used to forecast expectations, but it must be considered in its proper context. Performance may have been especially high during periods of rapid growth and unusually low during periods of stagnation. Detailed data on occupancy may describe not only nodal and district patterns, but also absorption rates for different building types (e.g., low-, mid-, and high-rise) or different building classes (e.g., Class A, Class B, Class C) and different occupants (e.g., anchor tenants or nonanchor tenants, corporate management, research and development departments, professional services).

---

13. This usage is from John M. Clapp, *Handbook for Real Estate Market Analysis* (Englewood Cliffs, N.J.: Prentice-Hall, Inc., 1987), 5.

Industrial and Agricultural Properties

Market analysis for industrial and agricultural properties is complicated by three factors: the market areas for these properties are more widely scattered, demand is more limited, and supply is highly differentiated according to the operation of the enterprise.

The market for industrial real estate reflects the unique characteristics of the property type. High-priced industrial machinery is generally custom-built and, except for the flex space in multitenanted research and development (R & D) facilities, industrial plants are typically custom-designed to the needs of the particular production line. The owners and users of industrial real estate have necessarily made a long-term commitment. Apart from warehousing and distribution centers, most industrial firms are precluded from ever moving due to the difficulty and expense of relocation. The turnover rates for industrial plants, therefore, are relatively low.

Plants are often built with custom-financing, which is the result of lengthy negotiation. Transactions may vary considerably even for highly similar properties, and most transactions are confidential so market data are not readily available.

To conduct market analysis for agricultural properties, appraisers must examine factors as diverse as national and regional economic trends, ecological and environmental considerations, and the character of the subject agricultural district. Land prices are affected by both short-term commodity prices and long-term federal policy involving farm subsidies and the leasing of adjacent public lands for grazing range or timber stands. The condition of the regional economy generally exerts an influence on land prices also. For example, a boom or slump in an energy or extractive industry that represents a region's economic base (e.g., Texas or Colorado) may generally enhance or depress property values.

Rural appraisers must consult statistical data on soil productivity and crop yields as well as analyses of the effects of erosion on future soil productivity and forecasts of artesian (aquifer) reserves and waters available for irrigation. The appraiser should be aware of current and future environmental legislation and any momentum toward land or wildlife conservation.

Finally, the appraiser must be familiar with the characteristics of the immediate agricultural district and the specific types of agriculture and complementary land uses found in the area (e.g., fodder production for a livestock ranch or dairy farm). Other essential information includes local assessment rates, the principal type of ownership (e.g., family farm or agribusiness), and the level of recent sales activity or foreclosures.

Key Concepts

- Real estate markets do not have the characteristics of efficient markets.
- Five different real estate markets can be identified for five types of property: residential, commercial, industrial, agricultural, and special purpose.
- Real estate market definition, segmentation, and disaggregation are preliminary to market analysis.
- Market analysis investigates the relationship between the demand for and competitive supply of real estate in a defined market.

- Appraisers can approach market analysis in one of two ways: proceeding from an economic overview to the specific property or beginning with the property and then considering the economy.
- Specific real estate markets can be identified by property type, property features, market area, substitute properties, and complementary properties.
- The activity of real estate markets is subject to the effects of long-term (secular) and short-term cycles.
- The factors considered and the procedures followed in market analysis may vary depending on the property type and the purpose of the analysis.

Terms

absorption	market definition
active (seller's) market	market disequilibrium
capture	market equilibrium
competitive supply	market segmentation
demand	move-up demand
depressed (buyer's) market	real estate cycle
disaggregation	share of the market
economic base analysis	short-term cycle
fall-out demand	strong market
household	submarket
long-term (secular) cycle	supply and demand
market analysis	weak market

CHAPTER FIVE

The Valuation Process

T he concepts that are fundamental to appraisal thought form the basis for all the actions appraisers perform in addressing their clients' needs. These actions constitute *the valuation process, a systematic procedure employed to provide the answer to a client's question about real property value*. The valuation process is both a model and a mirror of appraisal activity and, as such, it reflects many attitudes, beliefs, techniques, and methods that relate to questions of value.

The theory of valuation, as distinct from the theory of value, began to take form in the late nineteenth century. Alfred Marshall (1842-1924), the British economist who formulated the neoclassical theory of value as a synthesis of earlier theories, anticipated and developed many of the concepts employed in contemporary appraisal practice. These concepts include the determination of site value through capitalization of income, the impact of depreciation on buildings and land, and the influence of different building types and land uses on site value.

Marshall is also credited with identifying the three traditional approaches to value: market (sales) comparison, replacement cost, and capitalization of income. Irving Fisher (1867-1947), an influential American economist associated with the neoclassical school, fully developed the income theory of value, which is the basis for the income capitalization approach used by modern appraisers.[1]

Modern Appraisal Theory

The writings of Marshall, Fisher, and other economists of the late nineteenth and early twentieth centuries were read by scholars and business professionals interested in economic thought. At the same time, the field of real estate appraisal was emerging and a few practitioners were gaining experience estimating market value and other kinds of value for properties of various types. In the 1920s and 1930s, several events helped to establish appraisal as a young, but viable, real estate function.

One motivating force was the introduction of land economics as an academic discipline. Land economics developed from the interrelationship of several disciplines and attracted scholars and students who contributed significantly to real estate and appraisal literature over the next 40 years.[2]

---

1. Paul F. Wendt, *Real Estate Appraisal: Review and Outlook* (Athens: University of Georgia Press, 1974), 18-19.
2. This influential group included Richard T. Ely (1854-1943), the founder of land economics as an academic subject, Frederick Morrison Babcock (1898-1983), Ernest McKinley Fisher (1893-1981), and Arthur J. Mertzke (1890-1970). Ely, Babcock, and Fisher contributed to the Land Economics series published by the National Association of Real Estate Board (now the National Association of Realtors®), which was the first major publication effort designed to provide real estate professionals with current technical information. The first texts in this series were Fisher's *Principles of Real Estate* (1923), Ely and Moorehouse's *Elements of Land Economics* (1924), and Babcock's *The Appraisal of Real Estate* (1924).

A significant event in appraisal history was the publication of *Real Estate Apprais-ing* by Arthur J. Mertzke in 1927, which adapted Alfred Marshall's ideas to develop a tangible link between value theory and valuation theory. Mertzke translated economic theory into a working appraisal theory, helped establish a clear emphasis on the three approaches to value, and explained the use of capitalization rates as indexes of security. The preeminence of the three approaches to value in the appraisal process was under-scored in publications by K. Lee Hyder, Harry Grant Atkinson, and George L. Schmutz.[3] Their works set forth systematic procedures for applying the sales comparison, cost, and income capitalization approaches. Schmutz presented a model in which appraisal activity leads to a conclusion of value, which was later incorporated into *The Appraisal of Real Estate*, first published by the American Institute of Real Estate Appraisers in 1951.

Appraisal theory has continued to evolve. Today's education requirements are stringent and appraisers make use of many analytical methods and techniques. Applying these methods and techniques to an expanding database presents new challenges and raises questions as to how applicable the valuation model is to actual appraisal assign-ments, how well it analyzes the forces that affect value, and how accurately it interprets the actions and motivations of market participants.

The Valuation Process

The valuation process begins when an appraiser identifies the appraisal problem and ends when he or she reports a conclusion to the client. Each real property is unique and many different types of value can be estimated for a single property. The most common appraisal assignment is performed to estimate market value; the valuation process contains all the steps appropriate to this type of assignment. The model also provides the framework for estimating any other defined value. Consulting assignments often call for value estimates which are derived through modification of the valuation process.

The valuation process is accomplished thorough specific steps; the number of steps followed depends on the nature of the appraisal assignment and the data available. The model indicates a pattern that can be used in any appraisal assignment to perform market research and data analysis, to apply appraisal techniques, and to integrate the results of these activities into an estimate of defined value.

Research begins after the appraisal problem has been defined. The analysis of data relevant to the problem starts with an investigation of trends observed at all market levels—international, national, regional, community, and neighborhood. This examination helps the appraiser understand the interrelationships among the principles, forces, and factors that affect real property value in the specific area. It also provides raw data from which to extract quantitative information and other evidence of market trends such as positive or negative percentage changes in property value over a number of years, the population movement into an area, and the number of employment opportunities available and their effect on the purchasing power of potential property users. These data can be analyzed and employed to estimate a defined value.

---

3. K. Lee Hyder, "The Appraisal Process," *The Appraisal Journal* (January 1936); Harry Grant Atkinson, "The Process of Appraising Single-Family Homes" *The Appraisal Journal* (April 1936); and George L. Schmutz, *The Appraisal Process* (North Hollywood, Calif.: the author, 1941).

Traditionally, appraisal techniques are the specific procedures within the three approaches that are applied to derive indications of real property value. Other procedures such as the use of inferential statistics and economic models also contribute to appraisals. One or more approaches to value may be used depending on their applicability to the particular appraisal assignment.

In assignments to estimate market value, the ultimate goal of the valuation process is a well-supported value conclusion that reflects all the factors that influence the market value of the property being appraised. To achieve this goal, an appraiser studies a property from three different viewpoints, which correspond to the three traditional approaches to value:

1. The value indicated by recent sales of comparable properties in the market—the sales comparison approach

2. The current cost of reproducing or replacing the improvements, minus the loss in value from depreciation, plus site value—the cost approach

3. The value of a property's earning power based on the capitalization of its income—the income capitalization approach

The three approaches are interrelated; each requires the gathering and analysis of sales, cost, and income data that pertain to the property being appraised. Each approach is outlined briefly in this chapter and discussed in detail in subsequent chapters.

From the approaches applied, the appraiser derives separate indications of value for the property being appraised. One or more of the approaches may not be applicable to a specific assignment or may be less reliable due to the nature of the property, the needs of the client, or the data available.

To complete the valuation process, the appraiser integrates the information drawn from market research and data analysis and from the application of approaches to form a value conclusion. This conclusion may be presented as a single point estimate of value or as a range within which the value may fall. An effective integration of all the elements in the process depends on the appraiser's skill, experience, and judgment.

The valuation process is depicted in Figure 5.1.

Definition of the Appraisal Problem

The first step in the valuation process is the development of a clear statement of the appraisal problem. This sets the limits of the appraisal and eliminates any ambiguity about the nature of the assignment. The statement of the problem should include:

- Identification of the real estate
- Identification of the property rights to be valued
- Use of the appraisal
- Definition of value
- Date of the value estimate
- Description of the scope of the appraisal
- Other limiting conditions

Figure 5.1 | **The Valuation Process**

Definition of the Problem

| Identification of real estate | Identification of property rights to be valued | Use of appraisal | Definition of value | Date of value estimate | Description of scope of appraisal | Other limiting conditions |

Preliminary Analysis and Data Selection and Collection

General	**Specific**	**Competitive Supply and Demand**
(Region, city and neighborhood)	(Subject and comparables)	(The subject market)
Social	Site and improvements	Inventory of competitive
Economic	Cost and depreciation	properties
Government	Income/expense and	Sales and listings
Environmental	capitalization rate	Vacancies and offerings
	History of ownership	Absorption rates
	and use of property	Demand studies

Highest and Best Use Analysis

Land as though vacant
Property as improved

Specified in terms of
use, time, and market participants

Land Value Estimate

Application of the Three Approaches

| Cost | Sales comparison | Income capitalization |

Reconciliation of Value Indications and Final Value Estimate

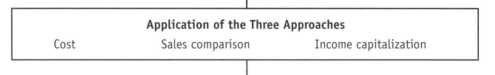

Report of Defined Value

Identification of the Real Estate

A property is first identified by a street address, a location, or some other descriptive data that enable it to be located. A complete legal description specifying the exact location and boundaries of the property is provided later. Examples of property identification follow.

Reference:	The Kennedy Building, commercial offices
Street address:	2600 South Zephyr Denver, Colorado
Legal description:	Lots 7-l0, inclusive, Block 3 of Sterns Addition, Fifth Filing, City and County of Denver, Colorado

If the property is identified with a legal description, the description should be accurate. The best source for the legal description is the owner's deed[4] or mortgage. Legal descriptions of real estate are usually derived from land surveys and preserved in public records in accordance with local or state law. Appraisers should be familiar with the specific system or systems used to describe land in various areas and be sure that the legal description is reasonable. Systems of land description include the metes and bounds system, the rectangular or government survey system, and the lot and block (or plat map) system. (Land description is discussed in Chapter 10.)

Identification of the Property Rights To Be Valued

The valuation of real property includes both the physical real estate and the rights that one or more individuals or legal entities may hold or contemplate holding in the ownership or use of the land and improvements. An appraiser may estimate the value of a fee simple estate or of partial interests created by the severance or division of ownership rights. Special attention must be given to limitations on ownership rights, which include easements, encroachments, liens, leases, and the disposition of air or subsurface rights. Financing must also be considered because both fee simple estates and partial interests can be mortgaged. The specific rights to be valued and the probable or actual financing involved must be ascertained at the start of the assignment because the complexity of these rights and terms will determine the procedures, skills, and time required to complete the assignment.

The fee simple estate in property is often valued before partial interests are considered. However, the dollar value of the fee simple estate is not necessarily equal to the sum of the values of all partial interests; the value of a partial interest may differ from the value of its contribution to the whole. For example, a 50% interest in a property in which the owner does not have majority control may have significantly less value than

---

4. A deed is the best source for the legal description, but there are many different types of deeds that an appraiser may consult, e.g., warranty deed, administrator's deed, bargain and sale deed, executor's deed, grant deed, quitclaim deed, and trust deed.

50% of the fee simple value; this lower value could be a direct result of dividing the fee simple estate. To estimate the market value of a partial interest in real property, direct market evidence of market attitudes toward the particular aspects of that partial interest is usually sought.

Use of the Appraisal

The use or function of an appraisal is the manner in which a client employs the information contained in an appraisal report. The client may specify the use of the appraisal when requesting it; if not, the appraiser may have to solicit this information, guiding the client to ensure a clear understanding of the question. Because an appraisal provides the basis for a decision regarding real property, the nature of the decision affects the character of the assignment and the appraisal report. A value estimate may be needed to determine the:

- Price at which to buy or sell
- Amount of a loan
- Basis for taxation
- Terms of a lease
- Value of real property assets in financial statements
- Basis for just compensation in eminent domain proceedings

To avoid wasted effort, the appraiser and the client must reach a mutual understanding concerning the use and ownership of the appraisal report and its conclusions.

Definition of Value

The purpose of the valuation process is to estimate the value of a real property interest, so the specific type of value and the interests involved must be clearly identified. The statement of purpose in the final report of defined value specifies the stated scope of the valuation assignment, i.e., to estimate a defined value of a real property interest. Types of appraised value include market value, use value, going-concern value, investment value, assessed value, and insurable value.

A written statement of the defined value to be estimated must be included in every appraisal report. This statement establishes the precise question to be answered for the client, the appraiser, and all readers of the report. It explains the data selected for consideration and the methods employed to analyze the data, thus supporting the logic and validity of the final value estimate. The statement also specifies whether the value estimate is reported in terms of cash, terms equivalent to cash, or other precisely revealed terms.

Date of the Value Estimate

The date of the value estimate must be specified because the forces that influence real property value are constantly changing. Although conditions observed at the time of the appraisal may persist for a considerable time after that date, an estimate of value is considered valid only for the exact date specified. Market value is generally seen as a reflection of market participants' perceptions of future economic conditions, and these perceptions are based on market evidence at a specific point in time. Value influences reflect economic conditions at a particular time, and sudden changes in business and real estate markets can dramatically influence value. The date of the value estimate is not to be confused with the date on the letter of transmittal, which is usually a different date.

Most appraisals call for current value estimates but, in some cases, a valuation as of a date in the past is required. Retrospective appraisals may be required for inheritance tax (date of death), insurance claims (date of casualty), income tax (date of acquisition),[5] lawsuits (date of loss), and other purposes. In condemnation proceedings appraisers may estimate property value as of the date of filing the declaration or petition to condemn, the date of trial, or another date stipulated by the parties involved or by the court. Historical market data are often available, so market value can be estimated in retrospect.

Appraisals as of a future date, or prospective appraisals, may be required to estimate the value of property interests in proposed developments or the value at the end of a cash flow projection. The anticipation of future benefits is involved whenever an appraiser estimates the present value of a projected income stream or reversion. Prospective value estimates for proposed developments are frequently required as of the time the development is to be completed and when the development is projected to achieve stabilized occupancy. Appraisers may be employed to derive opinions of prospective values that will be used by owners, buyers, investors, or lenders to make real estate-related decisions.[6]

Description of the Scope of the Appraisal

The scope of the appraisal refers to the extent of the process in which data are collected, confirmed, and reported. The scope is described to protect third parties whose reliance on an appraisal report may be affected by this information. An appraiser determines the extent of the work and of the report based on the significance of the appraisal problem and the agreement with the client. It is often important for the appraiser to indicate what was *not* done in the appraisal as well as what was done. The appraiser may want to indicate the time spent and the area searched to gather the data, especially if only limited data were available. The appraiser is responsible for describing the scope of the appraisal, but this may be accomplished in various sections of the report rather than in a separate section.[7] The description of the scope should also discuss any special assumptions or limiting conditions affecting the appraisal.

The Uniform Standards of Professional Appraisal Practice (USPAP) promulgated by The Appraisal Foundation distinguish between *complete appraisals* and *limited appraisals*. Limited appraisals are estimates of value performed under the Departure Provision of the Uniform Standards. In limited appraisals, the scope of the data collected and confirmed is typically narrower. Limited appraisals might include appraisals of real

---

5. It is sometimes necessary to estimate a property's value as of March 1, 1913, the date when the federal income tax system was established, to calculate the capital gain on a property owned since that date.

6. Retrospective and prospective value estimates are discussed in Statements in Appraisal Standards Nos. 3 and 4.

7. Kendall Thurston, "Complying with the Code and Standards (Part III)," *The Real Estate Appraiser* (April 1992), 49-51.

estate using only the sales comparison approach and property appraisals prepared to update value estimates done over the past year.

Other Limiting Conditions

Identification of the real estate and the property rights to be appraised, the date of the value estimate, the use of the appraisal, and the definition of value all qualify the appraisal. Typically, some limiting conditions are also applicable. Statements of limiting conditions are included in the report for the appraiser's protection and to inform and protect the client and other users of the report. For example, an appraisal report may state that the valuation of subsurface oil, gas, or mineral rights is not part of the appraisal. Another limiting condition might establish that the appraiser will not be expected to provide court or hearing testimony or to attend court proceedings unless arrangements are made a reasonable time in advance and compensation is agreed upon. (The courts may subpoena appraisers to testify despite a limiting condition to the contrary.) Other limiting conditions might specify that no engineering survey was made or that, except as specifically stated, property data were taken from sources considered to be reliable. (For further examples, see the discussion of assumptions and limiting conditions in Chapter 26.)

Preliminary Analysis and Data Selection and Collection

After defining the problem, the appraiser is ready to perform a preliminary analysis to determine the character and scope of the assignment and the amount of work that will be required to gather the necessary data. The preliminary analysis and work plan depend on the assignment and the type of property being valued. For example, much more information will be required in the valuation of a large apartment building than in the valuation of a single-family residence.

To complete an assignment quickly and efficiently, each step in the valuation process must be planned and scheduled. Time and personnel requirements will vary with the amount and complexity of the work. Some assignments may be completed in a few days; for more complex appraisal problems, weeks or months may be spent gathering, analyzing, and applying all pertinent data.

Some assignments can be performed by a single appraiser, while others require the assistance of other staff members or appraisal specialists. Sometimes the assistance of specialists in other fields is needed. For example, in valuing a rural property, the appraiser's findings may be augmented by the professional opinion of a soil engineer. Recognizing when work can or must be delegated improves efficiency and ensures accuracy.

A planned work schedule is helpful, particularly in performing large, complicated assignments. A clear and precise understanding of individual responsibilities can help expedite the work. Because the appraiser bears the ultimate responsibility, he or she must see the assignment as a whole as well as a collection of procedures and details. With a comprehensive view, the appraiser can recognize the type and volume of work to be done and schedule and delegate it properly.

The appraiser's work plan usually includes an outline of the proposed appraisal report. The major parts of the report are delineated and the data and procedures involved in each section are noted. Using this outline, data can be assembled intelligently and the appropriate amount of time can be allocated to each step in the valuation process.

Three types of data are gathered for appraisals: general data, specific data, and competitive supply and demand data. General data consist of information about trends in the social, economic, governmental, and environmental forces that affect property value. *A trend is a momentum or tendency in a general direction brought about by a series of interrelated changes*. Trends such as population shifts, declining office building occupancy rates, or increased housing starts in an area are identified by analyzing general data. General data can contribute significantly to an appraiser's understanding of the marketplace.

Specific data relate to the property being appraised and to comparable properties. These data include legal, physical, locational, cost, and income and expense information about the properties and the details of comparable sales. Financial arrangements that could affect selling prices are also considered. The history of ownership and use of the property should be researched to establish whether toxic wastes or hazardous materials may be present on the site.

Competitive supply and demand data relate to the competitive position of the property in its future market. Supply data include inventories of existing and proposed competitive properties, vacancy rates, and absorption rates. Demand data may consist of population, income, employment, and survey data pertaining to potential property users. From these data an estimate of future demand for the present or prospective use or uses of the property is developed.

The amount and type of data collected for an appraisal depend on the approaches used to estimate value. These approaches, in turn, relate directly to the appraisal problem. In a given valuation assignment, more than one approach to value is usually appropriate and necessary to arrive at a value indication. Depending on the problem or problems to be addressed, one approach may be given greater emphasis in deriving the final value estimate. In conducting a particular assignment, the appraiser's judgment and experience and the quantity and quality of data available for analysis may determine which approach or approaches are used.

The data collected should be meaningful and relevant. All value influences, pertinent facts, and conclusions about trends should be clearly indicated in the report and related specifically to the property being appraised. Because the data selected form the basis for the appraiser's judgments, a thorough explanation of the significance of the data reported ensures that the reader will understand these judgments.

Highest and Best Use Analysis

Analysis of the highest and best use of the land as though vacant and of the property as improved is essential in the valuation process. Through highest and best use analysis, the appraiser interprets the market forces that influence the subject property and identifies the use upon which the final value estimate is based. (Highest and best use analysis is discussed in detail in Chapter 13.)

Analyzing the highest and best use of the land as though vacant serves two functions. First, it helps the appraiser identify comparable properties. Whenever possible, the property being appraised should be compared with similar properties that have been sold recently in the market. In conformity with the principle of consistent use, the highest and best use of the land as though vacant for each comparable property should be the same as that of the subject property. Potentially comparable properties that do not have the same highest and best uses are usually eliminated from further analysis.

The second function of such an analysis relates to improved properties that produce income. Analysis of the property's highest and best use as though vacant identifies the use among alternative uses that would produce maximum income to the land after property income is allocated to the improvements. In the cost approach and some income capitalization techniques, a separate land value estimate is required. Estimating the land's highest and best use as though vacant is a necessary part of deriving a land value estimate.

There are also two reasons to analyze the highest and best use of the property as improved. The first is to help identify comparable properties. Each improved property should have the same or a similar highest and best use as the improved subject property.

The second reason to analyze the highest and best use of the property as improved is to decide whether the improvements should be cured of items of deferred maintenance and retained, modified (e.g., renovated, modernized, converted), or demolished. Improvements should be retained as long as the return from the property as improved exceeds the return that would be realized from a new use, after deducting the costs of demolishing the old improvement and constructing a new one. Identification of the existing property's most profitable use is crucial to this determination. In some situations, however, a property may be subject to restrictions (e.g., historic preservation) that prevent the improvement from being demolished and the property from being developed to its highest and best use.

The highest and best use conclusion should specify the optimal use, when the property will be put to this use or achieve stabilized occupancy, and the market participants who will support the use—e.g., an owner-user of the property, an equity or debt investor in the property.

Land Value Estimate

Land value is directly related to highest and best use. The relationship between highest and best use and land value may indicate whether an existing use is the highest and best use of the land.

Land value can be a major component of total property value. Appraisers often estimate land value separately, even when valuing properties with extensive building improvements. Land value and building value may change at different rates because improvements are almost always subject to depreciation. For many appraisals, a separate estimate of land value is required.

Although a total property value estimate may be derived in the sales comparison or income capitalization approaches without separating land and improvement values, it may be necessary to estimate land value separately to isolate the value the land contributes to the total property. In the cost approach the value of the land must be estimated and stated separately.

In the valuation model, land value estimate is a separate step. The most reliable way to estimate land value is by sales comparison. When few sales are available, however, or when the value indications produced through sales comparison need additional support, other procedures may be applied. The procedures used to obtain land value indications are: sales comparison, allocation, extraction, subdivision development, land residual, and ground rent capitalization. These techniques are described as follows:

1. *Sales comparison.* Sales of similar, vacant parcels are analyzed, compared, and adjusted to provide a value indication for the land being appraised.

2. *Allocation.* Either sales of improved properties are analyzed and the prices paid are allocated between the land and the improvements, or comparable sites under development are analyzed and the costs of the finished properties are allocated between the land and improvements. Allocation can be used in two ways: to establish a typical ratio of land value to total value, which may be applicable to the property being appraised, or to isolate the value contribution of either the land or the building from the sale for use in comparison analysis.

3. *Extraction.* Land value is estimated by subtracting the estimated value of the depreciated improvements from the known sale price of the property. This procedure is frequently used when the value of the improvements is relatively low or easily estimated.

4. *Subdivision development.* The total value of undeveloped land is estimated as if the land were subdivided, developed, and sold. Development costs, incentive costs, and carrying charges are subtracted from the estimated proceeds of sale, and the net income projection is discounted over the estimated period required for market absorption of the developed sites.

5. *Land residual technique.* The land is assumed to be improved to its highest and best use. The income attributable to the return *on* and *of* the capital invested in the improvement(s) is deducted from the net operating income. The result is the income attributable to the land. This income is capitalized to derive an estimate of land value.

6. *Ground rent capitalization.* This procedure is used when land rents and land capitalization rates are readily available, e.g., for appraisals in well-developed areas. Net ground rent, the net amount paid for the right to use and occupy the land, is estimated and divided by a land capitalization rate. Either actual or estimated rents can be capitalized using rates that can be supported in the market.

Application of the Three Approaches

The valuation process is applied to develop a well-supported estimate of a defined value based on an analysis of pertinent general and specific data. Appraisers estimate property value with specific appraisal procedures which reflect three distinct methods of data analysis—cost, sales comparison, and income capitalization. One or more of these approaches are used in all estimations of value; the approaches employed depend on the type of property, the use of the appraisal, and the quality and quantity of data available for analysis.

All three approaches are applicable to many appraisal problems, but one or more of the approaches may have greater significance in a given assignment. For example, the cost approach may be inappropriate in valuing properties with older improvements that suffer substantial depreciation, which may be difficult to estimate. The sales comparison approach cannot be applied to very specialized properties such as garbage disposal plants because comparable data may not be available. The income capitalization approach is rarely used to value owner-occupied residential interests, although it may be applied with market support. Income capitalization can be particularly unreliable in the market for commercial or industrial property where owner-occupants outbid investors. Wherever possible, appraisers should apply at least two approaches. The alternative value indications derived can serve as useful checks on one another.

Cost Approach

The cost approach is based on the understanding that market participants relate value to cost. In the cost approach, the value of a property is derived by adding the estimated value of the land to the current cost of constructing a reproduction or replacement for the improvements and then subtracting the amount of depreciation (i.e., deterioration and obsolescence) in the structures from all causes. Entrepreneurial profit may be included in the value indication. This approach is particularly useful in valuing new or nearly new improvements and properties that are not frequently exchanged in the market. Cost approach techniques can also be employed to derive information needed in the sales comparison and income capitalization approaches to value, such as the costs to cure items of deferred maintenance.

The current costs to construct the improvements can be obtained from cost estimators, cost manuals, builders, and contractors. Depreciation is measured through market research and the application of specific procedures. Land value is estimated separately in the cost approach.

Sales Comparison Approach

The sales comparison approach is most useful when a number of similar properties have recently been sold or are currently for sale in the subject property's market. Using this approach, an appraiser produces a value indication by comparing the subject property with similar properties, called *comparable sales*. The sale prices of the properties that are judged to be most comparable tend to indicate a range in which the value indication for the subject property will fall.

The appraiser estimates the degree of similarity or difference between the subject property and the comparable sales by considering various elements of comparison.

- Real property rights conveyed
- Financing terms
- Conditions of sale
- Expenditures made immediately after purchase
- Market conditions
- Location
- Physical characteristics
- Economic characteristics
- Use
- Nonrealty components of value

Dollar or percentage adjustments are then applied to the sale price of each comparable property (assuming the same real property interest is involved). Adjustments are made to the sale prices of the comparables because the prices of these properties are known, while the value of the subject property is not. Through this comparative procedure, the appraiser estimates the value defined in the problem identification as of a specific date.

Factors such as income multipliers and capitalization rates may also be extracted through sales comparison analysis. In the sales comparison approach, appraisers consider these data, but do not regard them as elements of comparison. These factors are usually applied in the income capitalization approach.

Income Capitalization Approach

In the income capitalization approach, the present value of the future benefits of property ownership is measured. A property's income streams and resale value upon reversion may be capitalized into a current, lump-sum value. There are two methods of income capitalization: direct capitalization and yield capitalization, or discounted cash flow analysis. In direct capitalization, two basic formulas are used.

$$\frac{\text{Income}}{\text{Rate}} = \text{Value}$$

$$\text{Income} \times \text{Multiplier*} = \text{Value}$$

where

$$\text{Multiplier} = \frac{1}{\text{Rate}}$$

* Traditionally, multipliers have been referred to as factors. Hence, the terms *factor* and *multiplier* are interchangeable.

Yield capitalization also employs two basic formulas. The future benefits of owning a property may be converted into an estimate of present value by discounting each future benefit at an appropriate yield rate.

$$PV = \frac{CF_1}{1 + Y} + \frac{CF_2}{(1 + Y)^2} + \frac{CF_3}{(1 + Y)^3} + \cdots + \frac{CF_n}{(1 + Y)^n}$$

where PV = present value; CF = cash flow for the period specified; Y = the appropriate periodic yield, or discount, rate; and n = the number of periods in the projection. In discounted cash flow analysis, periodic income and the reversion are converted into present value by applying a specified discount rate.

Using the other yield capitalization formula, an overall rate that explicitly reflects the investment's income pattern, value change, and yield rate is developed.

$$R_0 = Y_0 - \Delta_0 a$$

Where R_0 = the overall capitalization rate; Y_0 = the overall yield rate; and $\Delta_0 a$ = the product of the relative change in property value and an annual conversion factor.

Like the sales comparison and cost approaches, the income capitalization approach requires extensive market research. Data collection and analysis for this approach are conducted against a background of supply and demand relationships, which provide information about trends and market anticipation.

An investor in an apartment building, for example, anticipates an acceptable return *on* the investment as well as a return *of* the invested funds. The level of return needed to attract investment capital is a function of the risk inherent in the property. Moreover, the level of return required by investors fluctuates with changes in money markets and the returns offered by alternative investments. Appraisers must be alert to the changes in investor requirements indicated by the current market for comparable investment properties and by changes in the more volatile money markets, which may suggest future trends.

The specific data that an appraiser investigates in the income capitalization approach might include the property's gross income expectancy, the expected reduction in gross income caused by vacancy and collection loss, the anticipated annual operating expenses, the pattern and duration of the property's income stream, and the anticipated resale value or the value of other real property interest reversions. After income and expenses are estimated, the income stream or streams are capitalized by applying an appropriate rate or factor or converted into present value through discounting. In discounted cash flow analysis, the quantity, variability, timing, and duration of a set of periodic incomes and the quantity and timing of the reversion are specified and discounted to a present value at a specified yield rate. The rates used for capitalization or discounting are derived from acceptable rates of return for similar properties.

Final Reconciliation of Value Indications

The final analytical step in the valuation process is the reconciliation of the value indications derived into a single dollar figure or a range into which the value will most likely fall. The nature of reconciliation depends on the appraisal problem, the approaches that have been used, and the reliability of the value indications derived.

When all three approaches have been used, the appraiser examines the three, separate indications. The relative dependability and applicability of each approach are considered in reconciling the value indications into a final estimate of defined value. In the reconciliation section of the report, the appraiser can explain variations among the indications produced by the different approaches and account for any inconsistencies between the value conclusions and methods applied.

Report of Defined Value

The final estimate of defined value, which is the goal of the valuation process, may in some cases be reported as a range of value, but it is usually reported as a single figure. The assignment is not complete until the conclusion is stated in a report and presented to the client. A self-contained appraisal report includes all the data considered and analyzed, the methods applied, and the reasoning that led to the final value estimate. A concise valuation analysis allows the reader to understand the problem and the factual data presented and to follow the reasoning behind the appraiser's conclusion of value.

The value estimate is the appraiser's opinion and reflects the experience and judgment that he or she has applied to the study of the assembled data. The appraisal report is the tangible expression of the appraiser's work. In preparing a report, the appraiser should pay particular attention to writing style, organization, presentation, and overall appearance. The conclusions of an appraisal may be communicated to the client orally[8] or in writing. Written reports may be *self-contained reports*, *summary reports*, or *restricted reports*. A *form report* may be a summary or a restricted report. Chapter 26 describes the requirements for appraisal reports and the circumstances under which they are prepared and submitted. The appraisal report is the last step in the valuation process.

Key Concepts

- The valuation process is a systematic set of procedures employed to provide the answer to a client's question about real property value.
- Definition of the appraisal problem is the first step in the valuation process. The appraiser identifies the real estate, the property rights to be valued, the use of the appraisal, the date of the value estimate, the scope of the appraisal, and other limiting conditions.
- The appraiser selects and collects three types of data, i.e., general data on value influences and trends, specific data on the subject and comparable properties, and competitive supply and demand data for the specific market.
- Analysis of highest and best use includes consideration of both the land as though vacant and the property as improved. The conclusion is specified in terms of use, timing, and market participants.
- Of the six techniques that can be applied to estimate land value, sales comparison is the most reliable.

---

8. Oral reports are usually summary or restricted reports. According to Standards Rule 2-4, oral reports must meet the requirements of Standards Rule 2-2(b).

- Each of the three approaches—cost, sales comparison, and income capitalization—is especially effective in given situations. An appraiser often employs more than one approach.

- Value indications from different approaches are reconciled into a final estimate of value.

- The report of defined value, which is the last step in the valuation process, summarizes the data analyzed, the methods applied, and the reasoning that led to the value conclusion.

Terms

allocation

capitalization rate

cash flow

comparable sales

competitive supply and
    demand data

cost approach

date of the value estimate

definition of the appraisal
    problem

definition of value

direct capitalization

discount rate

extraction

final value estimate

general data

ground rent capitalization

highest and best use of land
    as though vacant

highest and best use of
    property as improved

identification of property rights

income capitalization approach

income multiplier

limiting conditions

land residual technique

land value estimate

preliminary analysis

present value

range of value

reconciliation of value
    indications

report of defined value

restricted appraisal report

sales comparison approach

scope of the appraisal

selection and collection
    of data

self-contained appraisal report

specific data

subdivision analysis

summary appraisal report

trends

use or function of the
    appraisal

valuation process

yield capitalization

yield rate

CHAPTER SIX

Money Markets
and Capital Markets

Money is the medium of exchange commonly employed in selling and purchasing goods and services. The parties to a business transaction agree on the value of the good or service and this value is expressed in terms of money. Each nation has a monetary system with a combination of coins and paper currency. The relative values of national currencies are established through trading and international banking agreements. In recent years, free trade practices and instantaneous wire fund transfers have made the exchange of currencies a global market operation influencing worldwide monetary conditions. Real estate is priced in terms of money and real estate investments are money, so the cost and value of money, which fluctuate daily in financial markets, influence real estate prices. Therefore, it is imperative that appraisers understand domestic and global monetary values.

The term *money* is difficult to define and various definitions are used by economists. Some believe that money is "currency in the hands of the public plus demand deposits at commercial banks." *Demand deposits* are funds that can be withdrawn at any time such as money in checking accounts. Others say that money is "currency plus demand and time deposits at commercial banks." *Time deposits* are funds that can be withdrawn only after proper notification such as money in certificates of deposit. Money has also been defined as "currency plus demand and time deposits plus the liabilities of nonbank financial intermediaries."[1] Economists and Federal Reserve statisticians disaggregate the money supply further into five components.[2]

Most of the money in circulation is in checking accounts. Whether the money supply is defined in terms of currency, account balances, or both, its value is influenced by its availability. The value of money is a global, rather than simply domestic, consideration. Although important relationships are well established, they are subject to variable exchange ratios for national currencies and the rapid movement of free-flowing funds.

---

1. Howard R. Vane and John L. Thompson, *Monetarism—Theory, Evidency and Policy* (New York: Halsted Press, 1979), 49.
2. *Transaction money* (M$_1$) consists of money used to buy and sell things. It includes money in circulation—i.e., coins and paper currency (*fiat money*), demand deposits, and interest-paying checking accounts. *Broad money* (M$_2$), which is also called *asset money* or *near-money*, includes M$_1$ plus savings accounts, small deposits of less than $100,000 (e.g., money market accounts), and overnight repurchase agreements and Eurodollars. *Additional near-monies* (M$_3$) consist of M$_2$ plus savings accounts or institutional time deposits of more than $100,000 (money market funds), term repurchase agreements, and term Eurodollars.
    Two *money-type assets* which may be added to M$_3$ are *liquid assets* (L), which include M$_3$ plus short-term U.S. Treasury securities, savings bonds, bankers' acceptances, and commercial paper and *total credit* (D), which includes L plus all debt of the domestic, nonfinancial sectors (e.g., mortgages, bonds, and similar instruments). See Paul A. Samuelson and William D. Nordhaus, *Economics*, 13th ed. (New York: McGraw-Hill, 1989), 227-230 and U.S. Department of Commerce, Bureau of the Census, *Statistical Abstract of the United States, 1990* (Washington, D.C.: U.S. Government Printing Office, 1990), Table No. 832, "Money Stock and Liquid Assets."

Money Supply and Demand

Supply and demand relationships set the cost, or price, of money. When money becomes plentiful, the price declines; as it becomes scarce, the price rises. The price of money is expressed as an interest rate—i.e., the cost to borrow funds. Interest rates are particularly important in the real estate industry because most investments are created by combining debt and equity funds. When the demand for money is high and its supply is low, capital costs, or interest rates, increase. These higher interest rates, which are components of the capitalization and discount rates developed for valuation, affect real property values.

There is a difference between money and other commodities on the supply side of the pricing formula. The demand for money is a product of the operation of economic forces. The supply of money available for lending is a function of the level of savings, which reflect personal, corporate, and governmental accumulation, both domestic and foreign.

Economics determines the amount of savings, but the quantity of U.S. currency is subject to regulation by the Federal Reserve (the Fed). The Fed has the power to regulate general interest rate levels, which strongly influence the discount rates and overall capitalization rates used in real estate valuation. In foreign countries, various central banks perform the same functions as the Fed, and they generally have the same powers. Because monetary operations are global, the availability of funds must be considered on a worldwide basis. This has become especially evident in recent years as the United States has become a net importer of capital, which has to be sought on terms and conditions established not by the Fed, but by international trading and exchange rates. The bills and coins that comprise money are interchangeable (fungible) and can be used in all economic activities. The holder of capital will invest in whatever he or she believes will produce the optimum yield, considering the risk and maturity involved. Competition for capital involves all economic sectors.

Trading Money Instruments

A money market represents the interaction of buyers and sellers who trade short-term money instruments. Short-term money instruments with maturities of less than one year include federal funds, Treasury bills, Treasury notes, and other government securities; repurchase agreements and reverse repurchase agreements; certificates of deposit; commercial paper; bankers' acceptances; municipal notes; and Eurodollars. Although it is called a "market," the money market is not formally organized like the New York Stock Exchange. Rather, it is an over-the-counter operation which employs sophisticated communications and computer systems to provide traders with accurate, readily available information on national and international transactions. Because the Federal Reserve regulates the money supply, it influences daily trading activity in the money market and the cost (i.e., interest rates) of money market funds. The money market, in turn, greatly affects the real estate industry because its short-term financing vehicles are needed to fund real estate construction and development. This is one of many ways in which the availability and cost of money regulates the volume and pace of activity in the real estate industry.

A capital market reflects the interaction of buyers and sellers trading long- or intermediate-term money instruments. Long- and intermediate-term instruments usually mature in more than one year and include bonds or debentures, stocks, mortgages, and deeds of trust. Although stocks are capital market items, they are equity investments with no fixed maturities. The distinction between money markets and capital markets is not sharply defined because both involve trading in funds for varying terms and both are sources of capital for all economic activities, including real estate.

In money markets and capital markets, there are observable relationships between various instruments that stem from differing interest rates, maturities, and investment risks. Normally an individual who invests in a long-term instrument is believed to assume greater risk than one who invests in a short-term instrument. Therefore, long-term instruments usually offer higher yields. This situation is graphically portrayed in what has come to be known as the *normal yield curve.* (See Figure 6.1.)

The relationship is sometimes reversed. In periods of high inflation, investors are reluctant to take long-term positions. They fear that escalating interest rates will erode their capital, so they try to keep their money in short-term instruments. The Federal Reserve, however, wants to combat inflation, so it causes interest rates to rise. This action is intended to be temporary, lasting just long enough to dampen investors' inflationary expectations. Consequently, in inflationary times short-term yields may be greater than long-term yields, and the yield curve is said to be inverse. (See Figure 6.2.)

Figure 6.1 | **Normal Yield Curve: Low Inflation Period—Certificates of Deposit**

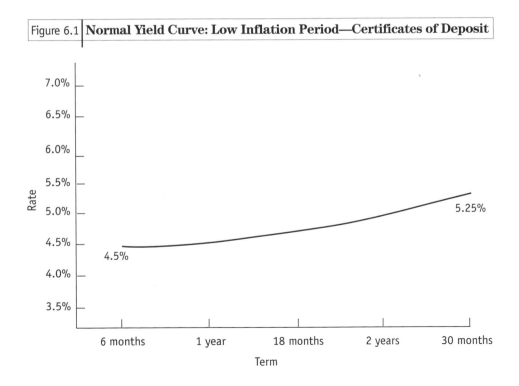

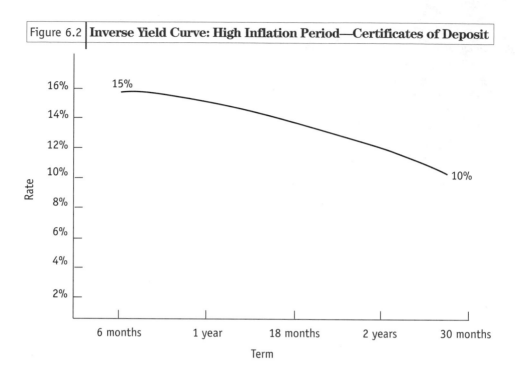

Figure 6.2 | **Inverse Yield Curve: High Inflation Period—Certificates of Deposit**

Fractional Reserve Banking

When a commercial bank makes a loan to a business or an individual, it credits the checking account of that business or person with the amount loaned. In a sense, banks manufacture money through this loan process because they create money by monetizing debt. Commercial banks effectively fund a large volume of loans by entering the money market. They raise the required cash by selling their paper—e.g., certificates of deposit— to a broad group of investors. Of course, the money-creating activities of banks are restricted because the Federal Reserve requires that they maintain reserves equal to specified percentages of their deposits. If a bank has a 20% reserve requirement, each dollar of its reserves could support four dollars of deposits, which can be created by extending four dollars in loans and crediting them to the borrowers' accounts. This arrangement is called *fractional reserve banking* and it is used by central banking systems throughout the world.

Federal Reserve System

In 1913 the U.S. Congress passed the Federal Reserve Act which created the Federal Reserve System, a central bank to manage money and credit, promote orderly growth of the economy, and serve as a lender of last resort. The framers of the act studied central banking in other countries and attempted to create a balanced banking system that was neither politically nor privately controlled. The Federal Reserve System is independent of Congress and the president; this independence distinguishes it from central banks in most other countries, which are government entities. Although the Fed is independent, it functions within the general structure of the U.S. government. Thus, the system operates in accordance with national economic policies, but has the power to exercise independent judgment.

The Fed is composed of 12 regional banks, which serve the 12 Federal Reserve regional districts, and a number of member banks, which include all nationally chartered commercial banks and many state-chartered banks. (See Figure 6.3.) The Fed is directed by a board of seven governors, who are appointed by the president and confirmed by the U.S. Senate for 14-year terms.

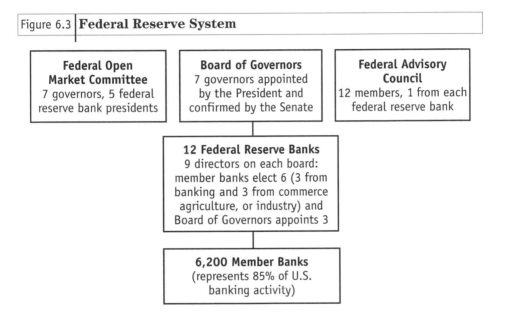

Figure 6.3 | **Federal Reserve System**

Federal Open Market Committee 7 governors, 5 federal reserve bank presidents	**Board of Governors** 7 governors appointed by the President and confirmed by the Senate	**Federal Advisory Council** 12 members, 1 from each federal reserve bank

12 Federal Reserve Banks
9 directors on each board:
member banks elect 6 (3 from
banking and 3 from commerce
agriculture, or industry) and
Board of Governors appoints 3

6,200 Member Banks
(represents 85% of U.S.
banking activity)

Members of the Federal Reserve Board cannot be dismissed during their term of service. The geographic distribution and occupations of board members are considered in their selection. Only one member from each region can serve at a time, so the regions have equal representation on the board. To avoid conflicts of interest, bank officers, directors, and stockholders cannot serve on the Federal Reserve Board.

Credit Regulation

Reserve requirements, the discount rate, and the Federal Open Market Committee are the three principal credit-regulation devices that the Fed uses to accomplish the duties assigned to it by Congress. In periods of economic crisis, the Fed supplies financial markets with necessary liquidity. For example, when the stock market crashed in October of 1987, the central bank immediately announced that, as a lender of last resort, it would supply necessary liquidity. The Federal Reserve regulates money and credit, which are the lifeblood of the real estate industry. Therefore, appraisers should be familiar with the Fed's day-to-day activities as they affect the supply of money and the level of interest rates. Because of the global nature of financial markets, the prevalence of instantaneous communications, and the securitization of realty interests, the monetary activities of the central bank can have an immediate impact on real estate markets.

Reserve Requirements

Within statutory limits, the Federal Reserve Board can fix the amount of reserves that member banks must maintain. One requirement of membership in the system is that member banks cannot make all their deposit liabilities available for business loans; they must agree to keep part frozen, and earning no interest in reserve accounts at Federal Reserve banks. The Federal Reserve changes the amount of its reserve requirements from time to time and these changes expand or contract the volume of money and credit available for business lending within the banking system. If the Fed wants to restrict the money supply, it increases deposit reserve obligations; if it wants to increase the supply, it lowers the obligations. In the mid-1990s, demand deposits (checking accounts) were subject to a reserve requirement between 3% and 10% (a 3% requirement on demand deposits in excess of $49,800,000; a 10% requirement on demand deposits in excess of $54,000,000), but time funds (savings accounts) were exempt from reserve requirements.

Federal Discount Rate

The federal discount rate is another major, credit-regulation tool. Banks in the Federal Reserve System can borrow from the Fed and obtain funds for their customers even in periods of great demand. To get these loans, member banks agree to pay the Federal Reserve interest at its established discount rate. The borrowing privilege of member banks is not unrestricted, however. The Fed denies loan requests when it believes that borrowing is not in the best interests of the national or regional economy. When credit is refused, it is said that "the discount window is closed."

The borrowing privilege is a vehicle for expanding the monetary supply; its curtailment limits or contracts credit. When the discount rate is low, banks are encouraged to borrow and the amount of money available to the economy expands. When the discount rate is high, member banks are reluctant to borrow and credit is generally restricted. Thus, the federal discount rate helps determine *the prime rate, the interest rate that a commercial bank charges for short-term loans to borrowers with high credit ratings*. The federal discount rate is generally about two percentage points below the prime rate. In 1994, the difference was 3.75 points, an especially broad span.

Federal Open Market Committee

The Fed's third credit-regulation tool is the Federal Open Market Committee (FOMC). The FOMC is probably the most extensively used and most potent of the Federal Reserve's credit-regulating devices. The committee is composed of the Federal Reserve Board of Governors, the president of the New York Federal Reserve Bank, and four district reserve bank presidents who serve for one-year terms on a rotating basis. The FOMC buys and sells U.S. government securities in the open market, thereby exerting a powerful influence on the supply of money and the interest rate. In fact, through its daily operations, the FOMC maintains short-term money rates at selected target levels. When the committee buys securities, money is infused into the banking system in an amount that can equal five to eight times the purchase amount.

The FOMC buys securities from bond dealers with Federal Reserve checks, which the dealers deposit in their accounts in the commercial banking system. These payments increase balances in member banks' reserve accounts, often creating free reserves which permit greater loan activity at these banks. In turn, the money supply is increased through such lending, which expands checking account balances. Fractional reserve requirements determine the monetary leverage obtained by banks when the Federal Open Market Committee buys securities. If, for example, banks have a reserve requirement of 12% on demand deposits, the amount of money infused into the economy when the FOMC purchases securities may be 8.33 times (100/12) the amount to be kept on deposit. Thus, by purchasing securities the FOMC stimulates economic growth and expansion. When the FOMC sells securities, it causes funds to be removed from member banks' reserve accounts, which reduces the supply of money and credit. Thus, economic growth is discouraged.

A notable example of such activity by the Fed occurred in the late 1980s and early 1990s. For five years (1989-1994), the Federal Reserve Bank had maintained downward pressure on interest rates. From near double-digit short-term rates, the Fed engineered a succession of 0.25% decreases in the federal funds rate. By the beginning of 1994, the rate bottomed out at 3.0%. During this period, all other short- and longer-term rates experienced significant declines. Then on February 7, 1994, the Fed changed direction by raising the federal funds rate target to 3.25%. The financial markets went into shock. The long series of rate decreases had been orchestrated to spur a lagging economy. In fact, in 1990 and 1991 there was an economic recession. As the recovery gained force in late 1993 and early 1994, the Fed stepped in to stop the expansion by means of a small rate increase. The Fed's rationale was to head off future inflation.

Usually, the FOMC meets once a month to set monetary policy strategies. The minutes of these meetings are kept secret for 30 days and then published. Before the minutes become public, money dealers watch the actions of the committee to infer its current policy. The Fed departed from this custom in February 1994 by publicly announcing the magnitude of the increase in the federal funds rate. Several, similar announcements were made later that year.

Financial market participants may be guided by the opinions of experts, called *Fed watchers*, who often correctly interpret and predict Fed policy by analyzing the committee's activities. Real estate investors and appraisers, whose success may depend on interpreting and forecasting financial markets, may profit from the extensive information provided by Fed watchers.

Fiscal Policy

While the Fed determines monetary policy, the Department of the Treasury manages the government's financial activities. The U.S. Congress and the president shape fiscal policy through their decisions regarding the federal budget, expenditures, and revenues. The Treasury Department implements these policy directives. Essentially, the U.S. Treasury raises funds and pays bills. It is authorized to generate currency, collect taxes, and borrow money. Expenditures for national projects and activities are made pursuant to congressional appropriations.

When income matches or exceeds spending, the federal budget is balanced. When the outflow of funds exceeds collections, a federal deficit results. Spending that is not covered by tax funds produces deficits, which are financed by the sale of public debt instruments such as government bonds, bills, and notes issued by the Treasury. When deficits are monetized by selling large amounts of debt, the Fed is tacitly expected, though not mandated, to cooperate by supplying the banking system with sufficient reserves to accommodate the debt sales program and still leave enough credit for the private sector.

In theory expenditures should expand the economy, increasing government tax collections and eventually producing an operating surplus that will reduce government debt. In practice, however, spending has grown much faster than revenues. In the late 1970s and early 1980s, government deficits materially contributed to severe inflation. Throughout this time, the Fed supplied whatever money was needed to fund the federal deficit. Financial institutions became concerned that excessive borrowing by the Treasury might use up credit supplies, short-changing private sector needs and crowding out smaller borrowers. The real estate industry was threatened by the loss of long-term mortgage capital due to the volatility of money markets and capital markets.

Inflation slowed and the economy recovered in the mid-1980s, which helped to stabilize the real estate industry, but the federal deficit continued to grow. Large amounts of this debt have been monetized by foreign investment. In 1989 and 1990, a long-running conflict between the fiscal policy of the Treasury Department and the monetary policy of the Fed came to a head. Controversy arose over the exchange value of the U.S. dollar with respect to foreign currencies, particularly the Japanese yen and German deutsche mark. In the years following 1985, the United States consistently ran trade deficits, importing more goods and services from foreign countries than it exported. At the same time, the size of the budget deficit was growing astronomically, and the United States found it necessary to borrow foreign funds, becoming a net importer of capital. The trade deficit worsened the existing strain on U.S. finances.

The Treasury Department concluded that a cheaper dollar would be a remedy for the trade deficit, making U.S. goods and services cheaper and more competitive in world markets. To lower the value of the dollar, the Treasury Department conducted a two-pronged campaign: "jawboning," or talking down the dollar's value, and encouraging the Fed to conduct large-scale sales of dollars in world money markets. This strategy met with appreciable success. However, the Fed voiced opposition to the policy, contending that it was inflationary. Cheaper dollars did not discourage imports, but made them more expensive, triggering price escalations. The tug-of-war between the two positions has continued. Much of the debate has taken place behind the scenes and off the record, but each side has defended its policy position with unusual candor.

This uneasy situation was exacerbated in 1994. With budget and trade deficits still at high levels, the value of the dollar declined sharply vis-a-vis the yen and deutsche mark, reaching its lowest postwar level. As confidence in the dollar eroded, global currency dealers exploited the situation. On at least two occasions, the Fed intervened to support the dollar by selling yen and deutsche mark on a vast scale in the currency markets, but to little avail. The decline of the dollar was so rapid that some observers characterized it as a "free fall." The devaluation of the dollar prompted calls for further action by the Fed, which was urged to support the dollar as an anti-inflationary measure. Such assistance seemed necessary to maintain the global marketability of dollar-denominated securities, particularly U.S. Treasury issues that play an important role in financing the deficit.

Money Market Instruments

The prices of financial instruments, which are established in a free and active money market, determine their investment yields. These yields consist of the instruments' face, or stated, interest rates plus any price discounts earned, or minus any price premiums paid. The price or cost of money is properly called an *interest rate* because when a borrowing instrument is created, it carries that day's market interest level for the risk rating and maturity involved.

If a six-month-term instrument is sold when it is three months old, and interest rates are higher than they were when the instrument was created, the buyer will not be satisfied with the face, or coupon, rate. To make a deal, the seller will have to discount the paper; the investment yield to the buyer will then be the face rate plus amortization of the discount. If lower interest rates prevail at the time of sale, the buyer cannot purchase at the coupon rate, because the seller will demand a premium. The yield to the buyer will then be the face rate minus amortization of the premium paid. These conditions are reflected in the real estate market, where buyers price property to provide good prospects for what they believe will be competitively attractive yields on the equity invested.

Money markets, which deal in instruments with maturities of one year or less, are especially important to real estate development activities. Construction loans are short-term mortgages with variable interest rates that are tied to market indexes. For example, borrowing costs in the market might be two to four percentage points above the floating *prime rate*, which is the short-term loan rate that commercial banks offer to favored customers. It is not unusual for building loan rates to be adjusted monthly with a floor, or minimum, rate, but no cap, or upper limit. When the demand for short-term money is intense and the supply is limited, market interest rates escalate and construction funds become extremely expensive. The high real estate project costs that result can destroy economic feasibility and cause project failures and bankruptcies.

The anticipated cost and availability of short-term funds are key considerations for developers, and their perceptions cause real estate activity to expand or contract. Appraisers must factor projected construction loan costs, which constitute a large portion of so-called *soft costs*, into their cost approach valuations. This is particularly important when appraising projects that will require more than one year to complete.

In money markets, various instruments and arrangements are offered and sold by the federal government, banks, corporations, and local governments. Important instruments include federal funds, Treasury bills, Treasury notes, other government securities, repurchase and reverse repurchase agreements, certificates of deposit, commercial paper, bankers' acceptances, municipal notes, and Eurodollars.

Federal Funds

When member banks experience intense loan demand, their reserve account balances may fall below the Federal Reserve System's requirements. To increase their reserves, these banks can borrow at the Fed's discount window or from other banks that have experienced slack demand and have excess reserves to loan for a short term. The funds borrowed or loaned from bank to bank are called *federal funds* because they are used to meet Federal Reserve requirements. To obtain federal funds, banks may deal directly with one another or they may employ brokers to arrange the transactions.

The federal funds rate is influenced by any or all of the Federal Reserve's credit-regulation devices and by the relationship between the supply of and demand for reserve funds held by banks. It is a key rate and its movements generate sympathetic trends in other money market and capital market costs. The rates for various instruments in these markets differ largely because of differences in their investment qualities and maturities. The federal funds rate is of particular interest to Fed watchers because it is the only money cost that is directly manipulated by the Federal Reserve System. It is clear that money and capital markets follow and react to variations in the federal funds rate.

Treasury Bills

A Treasury bill is a short-term, direct debt obligation of the U.S. government, usually with a maturity of three months, six months, or one year. Treasury bills are issued in denominations of $10,000, $15,000, $100,000, $500,000, and $1 million. These instruments do not bear a coupon interest rate; they are sold at a discount, which provides investor earnings. The yield on a Treasury bill is calculated for a 360-day year, but maturities are based on a 52-week year.

Treasury bills are backed by the full faith and credit of the U.S. government and are sold at frequent auctions. In preparing bids, purchasers study recent levels of and movements in the federal funds rate to determine the direction of monetary policy. This plainly demonstrates the close relationship between these money rates.

Treasury bills greatly influence real estate activity. Treasury bill rates remain the principal guide for short-maturity loan costs, particularly in the construction and development sectors of the real estate industry.

Other Government Securities

U.S. Treasury notes, which have longer maturities than most money market instruments, are traded in money and capital markets. They are backed by the full faith and credit of the U.S. government and are issued at auctions in maturities of one to 10 years. Many notes are issued for two to five years. Treasury notes are issued in denominations of $1,000, $5,000, $10,000, $100,000, and $1 million. They bear interest and carry a face rate.

After Treasury notes are issued, they are traded freely and priced to reflect current market yields. In these transactions, the remaining maturities are frequently short and the rates indicated fit typical patterns for similar money market investments. The earnings rates on Treasury notes also exert a strong influence on mortgage rates. To remain competitive in financial markets, lenders sometimes introduce new financing arrangements. One arrangement popular during the 1980s was the use of balloon mortgages. These short-term loans were made at fixed interest rates with the balance coming due at the end of the term and generally carried points to enhance the lender's yield.

Other important securities are created and sold by government-sponsored agencies such as the Federal National Mortgage Corporation, the Federal Farm Credit System, the Federal Home Loan Bank, the World Bank, and the Federal Land Bank. These instruments are supported by borrowing lines from the U.S. Treasury. They are freely and actively traded over the counter and offer yields slightly higher than those offered by direct Treasury obligations.

Repurchase Agreements and Reverse Repurchase Agreements

Repurchase agreements and reverse repurchase agreements are short-term financing arrangements made by securities dealers, banks, and the Federal Reserve System in which a person who needs funds for a short period uses his or her portfolio of money market investments as collateral and sells an interest in the portfolio with the obligation to repurchase it, with interest, at a specified future time. These agreements provide borrowers with needed liquidity and lenders with securities as collateral. Individuals and businesses with excess short-term cash invest in repurchase agreements. The time of repurchase may be one day or up to several months in the future.

The Fed has used these agreements to fine-tune money markets to achieve selected interest rate levels and smooth out seasonal distortions in the supply of and demand for money. By arranging a purchase from a securities dealer who is obligated to repurchase in a few days, the Fed temporarily creates additional bank reserves because the dealer deposits the transaction proceeds in a commercial bank. A reverse repurchase agreement is created when the Fed sells securities to dealers who must sell them back with interest. In this way the Fed temporarily withdraws reserves from the banking system because the dealer will pay with a check drawn on a commercial bank account.

Repurchase agreements enable corporations to lend excess cash for short periods. This is especially important because these businesses cannot engage in Federal Reserve funds trading, which is usually reserved for banking organizations. The interest rates applied in repurchase agreements are determined by prevailing supply and demand conditions in short-term money markets. They are also influenced by the quality of the collateral, which is usually excellent.

Certificates of Deposit

Certificates of deposit (CDs) are financial instruments that represent time deposits with banking organizations. Certificates of deposit may be issued for terms of one month, three months, six months, one year, or up to seven years. A CD is a contract between a bank or savings and loan institution and a depositor in which the institution agrees to pay negotiated rates of interest and the depositor agrees to maintain the deposit for a fixed period of time. A CD is backed only by the credit of the issuing bank, which is usually supported by FDIC insurance. Many CDs are negotiable and can be traded.[3]

Commercial Paper

Commercial paper is a corporation's promissory notes to borrow short-term funds for current operations. By trading commercial paper, organizations with excess cash can lend to those in need of money. This money market sector is well organized, and transaction data on prices and interest rates are widely and quickly disseminated by computer. Dealers specializing in commercial paper "make markets" and are able to consummate deals quickly and efficiently. Because commercial paper is backed solely by the credit of the corporations issuing it, only the largest, soundest companies can use it effectively. Due to the vagaries of money supply and demand conditions, commercial paper rates are frequently lower than bank loan costs; hence, large corporations benefit from the ability to use commercial paper.

In the real estate industry, commercial paper is used to raise short-term construction funds. For example, a real estate investment trust (REIT) might issue commercial paper to raise the money to fund construction loans. For the REIT, the key consideration is that interest rates on the commercial paper be sufficiently below construction mortgage rates to give the trust enough earnings to handle expenses and provide a satisfactory profit. Commercial paper is exempt from federal securities registration regulations provided 1) it is for a short term, 2) the funds are for current operations, and 3) there is an unequivocal takeout commitment for the loan. When these requirements are met, the Securities and Exchange Commission will issue "no action" letters.

Bankers' Acceptances

A bankers' acceptance is a bank's obligation or promise to pay. The main difference between commercial paper and bankers' acceptances is that commercial paper is backed by the corporation's credit only, while the corporation and the bank both stand behind bankers' acceptances. Thus, the latter carries less risk, which often causes yields on bankers' acceptances to be less than yields on commercial paper.

Bankers' acceptances are short-term, noninterest-bearing notes that are sold at a discount and redeemed at par, or the face amount, like Treasury bills. Most bankers' acceptances are created in the course of foreign trade, so large banks with foreign departments participate in this market. These instruments are not directly related to real estate operations, but they reflect trends in short-term interest rates for investments of varying quality.

---

3. For many years, the Federal Reserve imposed constraints on CD rates through its Regulation Q. Deregulation legislated in the early 1980s, however, relaxed or removed these limitations, and Congress established the Depository Institutions Deregulation Committee to ensure equality among all financial institutions.

Municipal Notes

Municipal notes are short-term obligations of local governments such as villages, cities, and counties that are used to finance current operations until satisfactory long-term funds are obtained. Because municipal notes are exempt from federal and state taxation, they are favored by many investors. This tax advantage has caused the interest rates on these notes to be relatively low. The earning rates on municipal notes may be some indication of a real estate investor's requirements for after-tax yields. Although real estate investments are generally for longer terms, studying the rates on municipal notes does provide some insight into investment strategies.

Eurodollars

Eurodollars are dollars deposited outside the United States. The growth of Eurodollars is aided by the fact that U.S. trading deficits are paid in dollars, world oil bills are settled in dollars, and an increasing number of multinational business operations are using and requiring dollars. Banks and businesses that require short- and intermediate-term financing have profited from borrowing this type of capital.

While the real estate investment trust (REIT) industry expanded, many trusts secured Eurodollar loans to fund mortgage lending operations. (REITs are discussed later in this chapter and in Chapters 20 and 28.) Eurobond and debenture issues with five- to seven-year maturities have been employed, but maturities of one to six months are more common. When supply and demand conditions generate favorable interest levels, Eurodollar loans can provide bridge financing for real estate ventures.

Yield Levels

Appraisers consult daily financial market reports to study money market activity for indications of changing monetary costs and values. These published reports provide information on various debt and equity instruments and their yield rates. Since this information represents the market's discounting of economic futures, it reflects the state of the economy and can be expected to affect real estate industry operations. Figure 6.4 is a sample report from the *New York Times* daily financial section. It shows the yield levels evidenced in the day's debenture trading. Other publications also provide this type of financial information.

Capital Market Instruments

Traditional capital market operations are described in this section, but readers must keep in mind that the conditions influencing the use of long-term, fixed- or variable-rate instruments may change over time. Appraisers and market analysts must keep abreast of shifts in monetary policy that invariably effect market changes and interpret how they may influence the financing arrangements discussed below.

Bonds

A bond is a capital market instrument with a fixed interest rate issued for a term of one year or more. The U.S. government, business corporations, states, and municipalities, among others, issue bonds to raise long-term capital for operations and development. Earnings from government-issued bonds are not free from federal taxation, but they are often exempt from local taxes. Generally, the short-term funding discussed earlier is used for project development, and long-term arrangements are made when the real estate project is completed.

Bonds are usually sold with a par value of $1,000; thus, if the issue carries an interest rate of 12%, each bond will earn $120 per year. The buyer will receive this earnings rate and, at maturity in 20 or 30 years, will be repaid the $1,000 principal.

The bond market is closely related to real estate investment activities. Real estate is normally bought with a combination of equity capital and medium- to long-term debt funds, called *mortgage money*. Most real estate deals are structured with a substantial amount of mortgage money and a smaller amount of equity, or venture, funds. Institutions with long-term capital to invest usually survey bond markets, then examine mortgage opportunities, and finally make investment decisions to secure the best earnings for the risk involved.

Figure 6.4

Key Rates

In percent	Yesterday	Previous Day	Year Ago
PRIME RATE	8.25	8.25	8.75
DISCOUNT RATE	5.00	5.00	5.25
FEDERAL FUNDS*	5.25	5.28	5.78
3-MO. TREAS. BILLS	5.21	5.14	5.40
6-MO. TREAS. BILLS	5.41	5.35	5.30
10-YR. TREAS. NOTES	7.04	7.04	6.03
30-YR. TREAS. BONDS	7.18	7.18	6.52
TELEPHONE BONDS	8.27	8.27	7.45
MUNICIPAL BONDS**	6.20	6.17	6.07

*Estimated daily average, source Telerate
**Municipal Bond Index, The Bond Buyer
Salomon Brothers and Telerate for Treasury's bell-wether bonds, notes and bills

Key Rates, July 9, 1996. These data are updated daily on the Web pages of the *New York Times* (WWW.nytimes.com) and *Wall Street Journal* (www.wsj.com).

Correlating bond market yields and mortgage capital costs can be intriguing. Until the 1970s and early 1980s when high inflation caused money market volatility, there was a close correlation between good-quality mortgages and AA-rated utilities bonds. The unstable financial conditions of this period reduced the availability of long-term, fixed-interest capital and created a need for new method of real estate investment analysis. During the 1980s, the widespread use of balloon mortgages and the charging of points (i.e., a percentage of the total loan amount paid to the lenders to enhance their yield) allowed lenders to remain competitive in capital markets. Today, mortgage-equity combinations may involve debt funds with variable interest rates, and property feasibility studies must account for expected rate changes. Appraisers must be aware of expert opinion about interest rate forecasts for the projected investment term and apply this knowledge in making their judgments.

Over the last 25 years, a huge, efficient secondary mortgage market has emerged. Much of this activity is generated by U.S. government agencies such as Fannie Mae (the Federal National Mortgage Association), Freddie Mac (the Federal Home Loan Mortgage Corporation), and Ginnie Mae (the Government National Mortgage Association). These organizations provide liquidity to banking institutions to facilitate their residential mortgage lending. Needed funds are raised through the sale of bonds and debentures and the sale of mortgage-backed certificates on a vast scale. The latter are debt instruments, paying interest and principal to holders. The cash flow for these distributions are generated by the pools of mortgages backing the issues. To secure investor funding, these securities compete with other securities in financial markets. They must offer yields that are competitive in terms of the risk ratings and maturities involved.

Daily, large-scale, open market trading sets yield levels. Certificates backed by Fannie Mae, Freddie Mac, and Ginnie Mae, which represent pools of residential mortgages, are now used as collateral security for issues of bond-type securities called collateralized mortgage obligations (CMOs). CMOs are traded daily in financial markets in amounts of hundreds of billions of dollars. Pricing reflects yields at various basis point spreads above the rates available on U.S. Treasury bonds and other comparable securities. Through this mechanism, the residential mortgage interest rate is inextricably linked to yield rate levels in the securities markets and fluctuates with their daily activities. The *securitization* of real estate interests has exploded and is becoming a force in commercial real estate as well. This suggests that other real estate rates may soon be similarly tied to the activity of financial markets. (Securitization is discussed in detail in Chapter 28.)

The municipal bond yields observed in daily trading reflect investors' after-tax earnings requirements for a wide range of risk ratings. A popular proxy for these bonds is the Bond Buyers Index, which is published in the financial press. Figure 6.5 shows "Active Bond Issues," a regular feature in the *New York Times*, which contains information on maturities, risk ratings, and daily price changes. The quoted yields are calculated from indicated prices and interest rates, assuming full payment at maturity. Some bonds are traded on organized exchanges such as the New York Stock Exchange, but many others are traded over the counter.

Figure 6.5	

ACTIVE BOND ISSUES

Issues	Moody's/S&P Rating	Bid	Asked	Yld. to Mat.	Chg.
Utility Bonds					
Southern Cal Ed 6.375's 06	A3/A	90.88	91.19	7.70	...
Alabama Power Co 7.0's 03	A1/A+	97.19	97.68	7.46	+ 0.03
Con Edison 6.625's 02	A1/A+	96.68	96.91	7.31	...
Corporate Bonds					
Browning-Ferris 7.875's 05	A2/A	102.06	102.38	7.49	+ 0.02
General Motors 7.1's 06	A3/A−	95.84	96.04	7.69	+ 0.03
Wal-mart 5.875's 05	Aa1/AA	89.09	89.40	7.48	+ 0.01
Intermediate Bonds					
Ford Motor Co 7.5's 99	A1/A+	101.03	101.33	7.04	− 0.01
Rockwell Intl 6.625's 05	Aa3/AA−	94.44	94.56	7.47	+ 0.02
Coca-Cola 7.875's 02	A3/AA−	102.34	102.80	7.25	...
High Yield Bonds					
USX Corp 7.2's 04	Baa3/BB+	96.16	96.21	7.87	− 0.02
Viacom 7.75's 05	Ba2/BB+	95.28	95.34	8.51	+ 0.07
Black & Decker 7.0's 06	Ba1/BBB−	94.75	95.07	7.74	+ 0.02

Source: Bloomberg Financial Markets

Active Bond Issues, July 9, 1996. These data are updated daily on the Web pages of the *New York Times* (www.nytimes.com) and *Wall Street Journal* (www.wsj.com).

Stocks

A stock is an ownership share in a company or corporation. A stock corporation is a common legal entity in which investors provide organizational capital by subscribing to shares that represent ownership and a right to all proprietary benefits. These shares are subject to the prior claims of operating expenses and debt service on the capital raised by selling bonds, debentures, and other money market instruments. Shareholder benefits consist of any cash or stock dividends declared, augmented by share price appreciation or diminished by price depreciation.

Marketing mechanisms in the form of stock exchanges—e.g., the New York Stock Exchange (NYSE) and the National Association of Securities Dealers (NASD)—were established to give business ventures ready access to capital sources and to provide a flexible, convenient means for trading shares. Through continuous refinement of exchange operations, orderly market conditions have been established and share values, declared dividends, and other important financial data are regularly published.

Mortgages

A mortgage is a legal instrument for pledging a described property interest as collateral or security for the repayment of a loan under certain terms and conditions. A mortgage constitutes a lien on the interest pledged. Mortgage loans supply most of the capital employed in real estate investments. A borrower gives a lender a lien on real estate as assurance that the loan will be repaid. If the borrower fails to make the payments, the lender can foreclose the lien and acquire the real estate, thereby offsetting the loss.

Traditional mortgage loans are made for long terms of 20 to 30 years and carry fixed interest rates. A level-payment mortgage, which requires the same dollar amount of payment each period for the entire loan term, is a popular contract. The payments are calculated to pay interest at a certain rate and to amortize the loan fully over its term so that less of each successive payment is required for interest and more is available for debt reduction. Other payment arrangements and schedules are also used, the most notable examples being variable-rate and balloon mortgages. The parties to a mortgage are usually free to contract in any fashion they desire, subject only to limitations of usury and public policy.

A borrower may pledge a real property interest to more than one lender, thereby creating several liens; in such cases, the time sequence or order of the liens is important. The first loan contract executed and recorded is the first mortgage, which has priority over all subsequent transactions. Second and third mortgages are sometimes referred to as *junior liens*. Because they involve more lending risk than first mortgages, higher rates of interest are charged for second and third mortgages, which typically have shorter terms.

Home equity loans are another common type of junior lien. Home equity loans generally run for terms of about five years, shorter than second or third mortgages, and the payments made generally cover only the interest on the loan. The principal is repaid in a lump sum at the end of the loan term. Many banks and thrift institutions deal in home equity loans on an enormous scale. Homeowners use this type of financing for non-real estate purchases such as cars or appliances, which were formerly made by install-ment contracts. Home equity loans are popular because the interest paid on such loans is deductible. Home equity loans are also used to establish credit lines. In this arrangement, the borrower only pays interest on the amount borrowed.

Another type of mortgage, the *reverse annuity mortgage* (RAM), is increasingly attractive to older home owners and business owners. A RAM is a negative amortization mortgage which allows owners to use some or all of the equity they have accumulated in their property as retirement and still retain ownership of the property. Typically, the loan increases as more money is borrowed and unpaid interest on the outstanding balance accumulates up to an agreed-upon amount, which is generally scheduled to coincide with the sale of the property.

Mortgages can be categorized based on how they are protected against the risk of default; the three major categories are guaranteed, insured, and conventional. Veterans Administration (VA) home mortgages are the most notable example of guaranteed mortgages; other state and national government agencies also provide guarantees. Federal Housing Administration (FHA) mortgages are the most common type of insured mortgages, but other government bodies and private insurance companies offer loan insurance as well. Conventional mortgages are neither insured nor guaranteed. Although regulations vary from state to state, in most states institutional lenders are limited to a 75% to 80% conventional loan-to-value ratio. Private mortgage insurance (PMI) is used to facilitate conventional loans with higher loan-to-value ratios. Although mortgage terms and interest rates are set by contractual agreement between the lender and the borrower, they are usually subject to usury limitations set by the states and other public policy restrictions.

The effects of competition for capital are clearly evident in mortgage markets. In a volatile economic climate, investors resist long-term positions and fixed-rate instruments because they provide little protection against inflation. In response to erratic conditions during the late 1970s and early 1980s, balloon mortgages and contracts such as variable-rate mortgages, adjustable-rate mortgages, renegotiable rate mortgages, and rollover mortgages were created. These mortgage instruments provide for periodic adjustment of interest rates to keep yields competitive with those available in capital markets. Although these contracts may cover long periods, the payment requirements change at frequent intervals so real estate owners cannot budget for fixed debt service. An owner managing a property subject to a variable-rate mortgage may feel impelled to arrange leasing programs that permit rapid rental adjustments to offset increases in mortgage payments caused by money market fluctuations.

Deeds of Trust

A mortgage is a contract between a borrower and a lender, but a deed of trust involves a third party as well. *A deed of trust is defined as a legal instrument similar to a mortgage that, when executed and delivered, conveys or transfers property title to a trustee.* In such an arrangement, a borrower conveys or transfers property to a trustee for the benefit of a lender. A deed of trust states the trustee's name and the lender's name. The borrower conveys title to the trustee, but retains the right to use and occupy the property. In many states where deeds of trust are used, they are recorded in the county and given to the lender or trustee for safekeeping until the loan is paid off.

Deeds of trust are used to eliminate the need for foreclosure proceedings against a defaulting debtor. A *trust agreement* accompanies the deed and sets forth the terms of the security and instructions to the trustee. If the buyer defaults, a public sale by the trustee in accordance with state law provides funds to compensate the trustee and repay the debt with interest. In some states, deeds of trust are used in place of mortgage contracts.

Nonmoney Credit Instruments

Land contracts, frequently called *installment sale contracts* or *contracts for deed*, are instruments that provide for the future delivery of a property deed to a buyer after certain conditions are met. A seller finances the sale of a property by permitting the buyer to pay for it over a period of time, but the title is delivered only after all payments are made. In the event of default, the buyer normally forfeits all payments made and the seller may also elect to hold the buyer to his or her contract. Because such contracts are sometimes not recorded, a buyer usually ensures that the agreement contains provisions to protect against any liens or encumbrances that may be filed against the property before title passes.

The purchase-money mortgage (PMM) is a common real estate financing device that often resembles a junior lien. A buyer may finance all or much of a property's purchase price by arranging for the seller to accept a purchase-money mortgage. A purchase-money mortgage is typically used to cover the difference between the buyer's down payment and a new first mortgage or an assumed mortgage. The contract specifies the required interest rate, the amortization payments, and a date for final and full repayment. To facilitate a transaction, a seller may take a purchase-money mortgage so that the buyer does not have to obtain funds from other sources. The buyer takes title immediately and becomes the property owner.

A purchase-money mortgage may or may not be subordinate to the new first mortgage or assumed mortgage, depending on how the financing was structured. If it is not and the buyer defaults on a payment or some other requirement, the seller may foreclose. Sometimes, however, the buyer takes back a purchase-money mortgage to complete the sale and it is the only mortgage on the property. When used for land acquisition, a purchase-money mortgage should contain release clauses that specify the principal payments that must be made to release parts of the property from the lien of the mortgage. Other procedural matters such as the order in which lots may be released are normally set forth as well.

Rate Relationships

Observing daily trading activity over a period of time may reveal relationships among the earning rates of various instruments traded in money and capital markets. For example, there may be a relatively constant spread of 50 basis points between the yields on three-month and six-month Treasury bills. However, market volatility can cause the spread between these yields to increase or decrease at times. Similarly, the spread between three-month and six-month commercial paper may widen to 70 basis points and remain steady at that level for several months. These observations are significant because they reveal how the length of an instrument's maturity influences its yield.

The federal funds rate is a foundational rate. In money and capital markets, fluctuations in this rate are closely followed and produce sympathetic reactions in prices and yields. Another key investment yield is reflected in the weekly auction of Treasury bills. Because these instruments represent top credit quality and short maturity, their yields establish a base from which market participants measure all short-term money costs, including real estate construction loan rates. Money market and capital market rate relationships are created by prime investment considerations, which include borrowers' credit, loan maturity, monetary supply and demand conditions, and existing and anticipated inflation rates. All of these factors are important in rating the risk of various investments.

With an understanding of rate relationships, appraisers can correlate real estate investment risk with the risks associated with actively traded capital market instruments, and thereby select market-driven and market-supported discount and capitalization rates. The financial press contains a plethora of pricing and yield information to facilitate this process. Capitalization rates obtained from any other source should be validated by comparing them with rate levels in the financial markets.

| Figure 6.6 | **Key Rate Trends** |

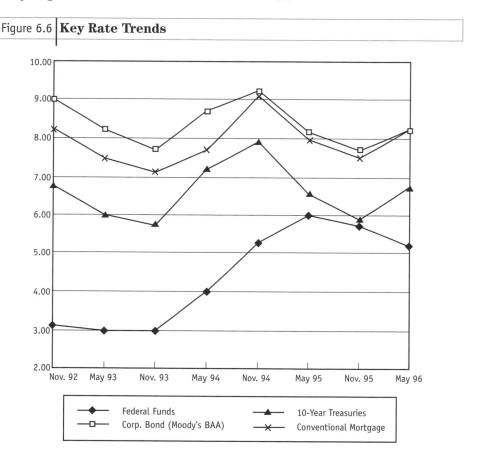

	Nov 92	May 93	Nov 93	May 94	Nov 94	May 95	Nov 95	May 96
Federal Funds	3.09	3.00	3.02	4.01	5.29	6.01	5.80	5.24
Corp. Bond (Moody's BAA)	8.96	8.21	7.66	8.62	9.32	8.20	7.68	8.30
10-Year Treasuries	6.87	6.04	5.72	7.18	7.96	6.63	5.93	6.74
Conventional Mortgage	8.31	7.47	7.16	7.68	9.17	7.96	7.38	8.30

Source. Federal Reserve Statistical Release

Cycles, Trends, and Inflation

Money and capital market conditions are cyclical. As the economy expands, competition for capital intensifies, the costs of goods and services increase, and inflation escalates. The Fed then seeks to combat inflation by tightening money and credit until the economy slows down. The demand for funds subsides, interest rates decline, and economic conditions become stable enough for businesses to expand. When the frequency of the economic cycle accelerates and its range increases, business and money conditions change drastically and rapidly. This creates an unattractive economic environment for long-term investments.

Inflation is often described as price escalations throughout the economy; when goods and services become increasingly expensive, inflation is at work. Inflation occurs when the general level of prices rises.[4] The *inflation rate* is the rate of change in the price level as reflected in the Consumer Price Index, or CPI. Inflation can be measured with the following formula:[5]

$$\frac{\text{Rate of inflation}}{(\text{year t})} = \frac{\text{price level} \quad \text{price level}}{(\text{year t}) - (\text{year t} - 1)} \times 100$$
$$\frac{}{\text{price level (year t} - 1)}$$

To apply this formula, consider the median price of a single-family home, which rose from $106,800 in 1993 to $109,900 in 1994 (year t).

$$\frac{\$109,900 - \$106,800}{\$106,800} \times 100 = 2.9\%$$

The rate of inflation during 1993 was 2.9%.

Inflation is also described as a proliferation of monetary units—i.e., a currency expansion. When monetary units proliferate with no apparent growth in underlying wealth, the value of each unit declines; more units are required in exchange for goods and services, and price levels rise.

The effect of inflation on real estate can be seen in the single-family residential market. Between 1970 and 1980, the supply of money (L) in the United States almost tripled; simultaneously, the median prices of new and used dwelling units escalated drastically, and these prices were accepted and supported by healthy demand. (Although the rate of growth in the money supply declined during the 1980s, the money supply continued to increase and doubled by 1990. In the early 1990s, the rate of growth in the money supply has been far more modest.)

The economic importance of inflation can be seen in the concept of "real" interest rates. Nominal interest rates which are reported daily in the financial press, are said to be composites of the "real" cost of funds, or the real interest rate, and the premiums that investors demand to protect their currency value from being eroded by inflation. Thus, the nominal rate equals the real interest rate plus an inflation premium. Economists

---

4. For a discussion of the differences between inflation and appreciation, which reflects an actual increase in value, see the discussion of expected and unexpected inflation in Chapter 20.
5. Paul A. Samuelson and William D. Nordhaus, *Economics*, 13th ed. (New York: McGraw-Hill, 1989), 306.

suggest that the real interest rate has remained steady at 3% to 4%. Therefore, if the capital market were to show a nominal rate of 11% for 10-year U.S. Treasury notes, the real interest rate concept would indicate an inflation premium of 7%.

11% (nominal rate) = 4% (real interest rate) + 7% (inflation premium)

This example demonstrates how investors' perceptions of inflation can affect prices in market trading and change the interest rates on instruments of different maturities.

Traditional real estate investment practices involve the use of two types of capital—debt and equity—and a typical venture is structured with a substantial mortgage amount and a smaller equity contribution. Before 1970 the largest suppliers of mortgage funds were thrift institutions such as savings banks, savings and loan associations, and life insurance companies. However, the high interest rates of the 1970s and early 1980s had a negative effect on these organizations' mortgage positions. Their portfolio yields became inadequate, their liquidity declined, and their mortgages were being repaid with funds that were cheaper than those originally loaned. High interest rates increased yields on competing investments, leading depositors to withdraw their funds to take advantage of alternative opportunities. Thus, traditional mortgage lenders were unable to offer as many loans. The term *disintermediation* was coined to describe these inflation-generated conditions.

Similarly, in the early 1990s, a financial crisis in the savings and loan institutions and a general economic recession provoked widespread concern over the soundness of real estate investments. Overwhelmed with foreclosures, lenders sought to avoid mortgage activity. Into the breach came Wall Street, with its massive and innovative capital-raising abilities. Through the underwriting of REIT issues and other real estate securitizations, Wall Street became a major source of real estate investment capital.

Business and Real Estate Cycles

Obviously money market and capital market activities and trends affect the real estate industry. In the years following World War II (1946-1966), distinct patterns emerged in real estate and general business cycles. As business prospered, the demand for capital intensified, inflation accelerated, and an oversupply of goods and services was produced. Then Federal Reserve monetary policy and other economic controls would be used to slow the pace of the economy and a recession would ensue.

When Congress wanted to revive the economy, the industry invariably selected to provide economic stimulation was real estate, particularly home building. Programs were developed to provide abundant, moderately priced mortgage money. These programs usually involved loan insurance or guarantees to induce capital managers to participate. Because there was a substantial demand for housing, the programs were well received and residential development expanded, increasing employment in all economic sectors. Manufacturers of hardware, supplies (e.g., heating, plumbing, and electrical), paints, furniture, equipment, and other goods saw business improve. The economy finally revived, then inflation started to accelerate, and the cycle was repeated. When loan insurance and guarantee programs supplied inexpensive long-term capital, real estate prospered and the general economy expanded.

Sources of Capital for Real Estate

The different aspirations of equity and debt investors are revealed in their market actions. The debt investor participates in bonds or mortgages, usually pursuing conservative paths in search of certain income and the repayment of principal. This type of investor expects a priority claim on investment earnings and often looks for security in the form of a lien on the assets involved. While a debt investor is relatively passive, an equity investor is active. An equity investor is more willing to assume risk, so the funds used for equity investment are known as *venture capital*.

Inflation tends to change traditional investor attitudes. Institutions that normally restrict their real estate positions to debt in the form of mortgages become dismayed when they realize that the rates of return they bargained for, and once deemed adequate, are too low. They also know that the expensive money they loaned will be repaid with cheap, inflated dollars. In the early 1980s, these conditions impelled institutional investors to alter their investment policies and seek real estate equity positions, which they believed to be reasonable hedges against inflation. The economic and monetary changes of the late 1980s, however, brought distress to the real estate investment industry, suggesting a return to more traditional investor attitudes and policies.

The ongoing securitization of real estate investment has been accompanied by the evolution of a four-quadrant capital market represented by public equity, public debt, private equity, and private debt investment. This development has brought about a structural change in capital market financing for real estate. The pricing of publicly traded asset shares reflects continuous transactions in the securities market. The pricing of asset shares in the private market quadrants is readily linked to activity in the public markets.

There are both advantages and disadvantages associated with investor-driven pricing. Returns on real estate investment are becoming even more closely related to the returns on non-real estate investment alternatives. Real estate is an economic sector, however, not just another asset class. The value of real estate depends on performance, not simply investor behavior. (Chapter 28 contains further discussion of the securitization of real estate investment capital and the pricing of securitized real estate investment in capital markets.)

Equity

Equity investors realize that their earnings are subordinate to a project's operating expenses and debt service requirements. Equity income earnings are called *dividends*; one-year's worth of income to an equity investment is an *equity dividend*. But equity dividends are only one part of the total return that the investor anticipates. Investors also expect that the value of their original investment will increase, although there is a risk that it will remain stable or decline. The total return the investor anticipates is called the *equity yield*. An *equity dividend* represents the cash flow component of the equity yield.

Trusts

Trust entities are used extensively to amass equity funds for real estate investment. *A trust is a temporary, conditional, or permanent fiduciary relationship in which the legal title to, and control of, property are placed in the hands of a trustee for the benefit of another person.*

One frequently employed trust is the Massachusetts business trust, in which holders of shares of beneficial interest have no personal liability for the trust's actions. Usually, this protection is achieved by using a corporate business structure. This type of trust also allows shareholders to avoid the double income taxation incurred by corporations. A corporate entity is taxed on its earnings, and from its after-tax net income it distributes dividends to shareholders, who are then personally taxed on that income. The earnings on a Massachusetts business trust, however, are passed through to beneficial shareholders; no income tax is paid by the trust and only a single tax is paid by the shareholders. Investors have found these income and tax pass-through arrangements very attractive.

Real estate investment trusts (REITs), which are usually organized as Massachusetts business trusts, have been successful in pooling the funds of small investors to acquire real estate investment positions that could not be handled by these people individually. REITS offer shareholders freedom from personal liability, the benefit of expert management, and readily transferred shares. To qualify for a tax pass-through, a REIT must pay dividends of at least 90% of its net income. With complicated income-measuring practices, these trusts attempt to pay out almost all their net income and, therefore, are substantially restricted in establishing reserves for possible losses.

Following the 1990-1991 recession, Wall Street managed to market a large group of new REITs. This vehicle became popular for two reasons. At a time when bank saving accounts were paying less than 3% interest, REITs were offering 6% cash dividends. In addition, the liquidity of these securities, which are traded on the major stock exchanges, is an attractive feature. REITs have raised billions of dollars of capital for real estate investment.

Partnerships

A partnership is a common vehicle for pooling real estate equity funds. *A partnership is a business arrangement in which two or more persons jointly own a business and share in its profits and losses.* There are two kinds of partnerships—general and limited.

A general partnership is an ownership arrangement in which all partners share in investment gains and losses and each is fully responsible for all liabilities. A general partner has complete liability for the acts of the other partners and is responsible for debts incurred by them. This is one major disadvantage of this type of business arrangement. General partners may legally participate in the active management of the business. The most attractive feature of a general partnership in a real estate investment is the ability to pass the tax-shelter benefits of depreciation, interest, and real estate taxes through to partners. In recent years new tax legislation has substantially changed the scope of these benefits.

A limited partnership is an ownership arrangement consisting of general and limited partners; general partners manage the business and assume full liability for partnership debt, while limited partners are passive and liable only to the extent of their own capital contributions. Limited partnerships are popular because they permit an uneven distribution of tax-shelter benefits. Although limited partners' financial liability is restricted to their capital contributions, they may receive tax benefits in excess of that amount.

Syndications

Another arrangement for raising real estate equity capital is a syndication. *A syndication is a private or public partnership that pools funds for the acquisition and development of real estate projects or other business ventures.* Private syndications are limited to small groups of investors and are relatively free from government regulation. Public syndications involve large groups of investors and generally operate in more than one state, so they are subject to Security Exchange Commission (SEC) registration regulations.

A syndication is often organized or promoted by a general partner, who has full financial liability for the partnership's activities. The other syndicate investors are limited partners. To attract investors, syndication agreements may provide for an unequal distribution of investment benefits, allocating the major share of tax-shelter benefits to purchasers of syndicate shares, not the general partner. With the help of very favorable tax laws, syndications became extremely popular in the late 1970s. Vast amounts of capital were poured into these investments, which offered returns primarily in the form of income tax benefits. Changes in the tax laws in the mid-1980s took away most of these benefits, resulting in the failure of many of these investments.

Joint Ventures

A joint venture is a combination of two or more entities that join to undertake a specific project. Although a joint venture often takes the form of a general or limited partnership, it differs from a partnership in that it is intended to be temporary and project-specific. The parties may later embark on other ventures, but each venture is the subject of a separate contractual agreement. General and limited partnership arrangements are popular in real estate joint ventures because they permit uneven distribution of tax-shelter benefits. Tenancy in common is a form of joint ownership that is usually employed in small property holdings.

A joint venture arrangement is frequently used in large real estate projects. One party, usually a financial institution, supplies most of the required capital and the other party provides construction or management expertise. Life insurance companies and pension trusts have joined with entrepreneurial building organizations in joint ventures to develop large offices, shopping malls, and other major real estate projects. If the financial partner wants the restricted liability of a limited partner, it must be willing to forego active project management.

Pension Funds

Private and government-operated pension funds are a huge and rapidly growing source of investment capital. Usually the pension contributions of employers and employees are placed with a trustee, who is obliged to invest and reinvest the money prudently, accumulate funds, and pay designated plan benefits to retirees. The trustee may be a government body, a trust company, an insurance company, or an individual. In performing these duties, an individual trustee may employ the trust departments of commercial banks, insurance companies, and other financial institutions.[6]

U.S. pension funds totaled approximately $4.78 trillion in 1993 and they are expected to increase steadily through the decade. A capital source of such huge proportions must have a major impact on the general economy and the real estate industry. Pension trusts are the only group that can feasibly consider some long-term investments because their funds are collected and their pension benefits are paid out over an extended period of time.

Traditionally, pension funds have been involved primarily in securities investments such as stocks and bonds. The development of pass-through securities by Ginnie Mae, however, has made it easier for pension funds to invest in mortgages, and they have made sizable investments. Pension trusts have also shown a willingness to invest in real estate equities by purchasing or participating in the real estate investments created by life insurance companies and commercial banks. Banks and life insurance companies acquire high-quality real estate equities, pool the investments in separate accounts, and supply the necessary portfolio management for a fee. Pension trusts commit funds to these accounts and share in all earnings, which consist of both income returns and sales profits.

Life Insurance Companies

Through normal insurance sales and operations, life insurance companies accumulate large amounts of funds which they place in diverse investments. Insurance companies are substantial mortgage lenders, and they make many real estate equity investments for their own accounts and as managers of separate accounts. Their investment officers regard equities as attractive earning situations that offer growth potential and reasonable protection against the capital erosion caused by inflation.

International Equity Capital

The investment activities of foreign individuals, countries, financial institutions, and pension funds also provide equity capital for the real estate industry. These off-shore capital sources have become increasingly important to U.S. real estate. Foreign investors often take a long-term investment view, bidding up prices, accepting relatively low initial cash flow returns, and looking to future income and value growth to supply a major part

---

6. To protect American workers covered by pension and other benefit plans, Congress adopted the Employee Retirement Income Security Act (ERISA) in 1974. ERISA and its subsequent amendments establish a comprehensive legislative framework governing the investment, management, and administration of employee pension plans, profit-sharing plans, and welfare plans. ERISA also empowers government agencies to conduct audit programs in performing their duties. After more than two decades, the administrative structure and doctrine of ERISA continue to evolve as the courts and regulatory agencies make judgments concerning compliance by plan administrators and the claims due beneficiaries. See *Fiduciary Responsibilities for Plan Investments, Plan Administration, and Plan Audits*, Federal Publications, Inc. (Washington, D.C., 1994), a-b, 1-17, 45-53, 57-76, 103-118.

of their anticipated total equity return. Often foreign investors do not hesitate to make 100% equity acquisitions when the properties involved are attractive and have exciting growth potential. Many of these investors will undoubtedly mortgage their properties later, when monetary conditions improve and lower interest rates permit positive leveraging.

International capital comes from a variety of sources, including individual and institutional investors abroad. Traditionally, the Western Europeans and Canadians have represented the principal foreign investors in U.S. real estate. Between the late 1970s and early 1980s, however, Middle Eastern and Japanese investors began entering the U.S. market. Middle Eastern investment has fallen off with the decline in world oil prices since the mid-1980s. Because the financing available from Japanese banks in the 1980s was superior to that being offered by U.S. banks, the Japanese were able to buy up many premier properties in the United States, especially in Hawaii and on the West Coast. In the early 1990s, a domestic recession (plus the costs of reconstruction after the 1995 Kobe earthquake) caused the Japanese to withdraw from the U.S. real estate market. Many of the properties they invested in have also experienced difficulties, which has dampened Japanese enthusiasm for U.S. real estate. It is too early to forecast what role, if any, the North American Free Trade Agreement (NAFTA) will have on stimulating investment from Canada and Mexico.[7] However, given the Canadian budget deficit and the Mexican trade deficit and devalued peso, it is unlikely that much capital will be available for export.

Although foreign investors supply needed equity capital to realty ventures in this country, they represent only a very small fraction of total U.S. real estate investment.

Debt

Because mortgage money is so important in real estate, investors, appraisers, and counselors must be familiar with the sources and costs of debt capital. Increased regulation in the wake of the savings and loan crisis has prompted many traditional providers of debt capital to restrict their lending activity in commercial real estate. The focus of these institutions has been redirected to residential lending. Although commercial banks and life insurance companies are not precluded from originating loans for commercial real estate, increased reserve requirements have made real estate a less attractive investment option. (Chapter 28 contains further discussion of these developments.)

Savings and Loan Associations

Savings and loan associations (S&Ls), like mutual savings banks, life insurance companies, credit unions, and others, are financial intermediaries. They receive savings

---

7. A foreign investor interested in buying U.S. property usually hires an American appraiser to value the property. A U.S. lender who is considering underwriting part of a real estate project in a foreign country also needs a meaningful appraisal report, and often retains an American appraiser to work on the assignment with a local appraisal firm. It is essential that the American appraiser understand the motivations of the foreign client or the behavior of foreign investors in general. For example, a favorable exchange rate or a special tax advantage may make investment in U.S. properties especially attractive. The investment horizon of foreign clients may be considerably longer than that of American investors. The appraiser should not ascribe the motives of typical U.S. buyers to foreign buyers whose perceptions may differ widely. For further discussion of international valuation, see Chapter 27.

deposits, lend them at interest, and distribute dividends to depositors after paying operating expenses and establishing appropriate reserves. When short-term interest rates are high, savers tend to withdraw funds and reinvest them in higher-yielding, short-term money market instruments and funds. Because savings and loan associations are financial intermediaries, high interest rates reduce the availability of mortgage funds and increase their cost.

Savings and loan associations promote thrift, pool savings, and invest funds in home mortgages. Such thrift institutions may be state or federally chartered. Until 1989 federal savings and loan associations were supervised by the Federal Home Loan Bank Board (FHLBB), which was created in 1932 to provide credit to thrift and home financing institutions and to alleviate liquidity problems in the savings and loan industry by assuring a constant flow of funds. In the late 1980s, S&L institutions suffered enormous financial losses. Hundreds of S&Ls failed and had to be taken over by the government. The assets of these thrift institutions ran into hundreds of billions of dollars.

The Financial Institutions Reform, Recovery and Enforcement Act of 1989 (FIRREA), the savings and loan bailout legislation, created the Office of Thrift Supervision (OTS) under the direction of the Treasury Department. In addition to taking over the functions of the damaged FHLBB, the OTS had been authorized to examine and supervise all federal and state savings and loans (and all savings and loans holding companies) and to establish strict uniform accounting standards for thrift institutions similar to those established for commercial banks. FIRREA also set up the Resolution Trust Corporation (RTC), which was charged with disposing of the assets of insolvent thrift institutions. This task involved handling hundreds of billions of dollars in deposits, performing and nonperforming mortgages, and real estate owned. As a result, the RTC quickly became the largest player in real estate markets. By 1994, the RTC had accomplished much of its mission and its position in the market was becoming less prominent. The assets of the now defunct Federal Savings and Loan Insurance Corporation (FSLIC) have been assumed by the Federal Deposit Insurance Corporation (FDIC). (See Appendix A for a summary of federal legislation affecting appraisers.)

The origins of the savings and loan crisis can be traced back to the escalating inflation of the late 1970s and early 1980s, which underscored the mismatch between the assets and the liabilities of the savings and loan industry. The assets of savings and loan institutions were overwhelmingly fixed-rate, long-term mortgages, while their liabilities consisted of demand deposits and other accounts with short-term maturities. During the years of high inflation, savings and loan institutions were seriously affected by disintermediation, as depositors withdrew funds to invest in higher-earning competitive investments.

The deregulatory legislation passed in the early 1980s to make savings and loan institutions more competitive phased out controls on interest rates, allowing thrift institutions to pay more competitive rates. However, the savings and loans ultimately had to pay more for the money deposited with them than their earnings rate allowed. Earnings were held down by their portfolios of fixed-rate, long-term mortgages. To liquidate such assets, the institutions resorted to selling at substantial price discounts.

They then gained legislative approval to get into new, purportedly high-earning lines of business such as equities, development loans, and so-called "junk bonds."

The collapse of real estate markets, starting in the Southwest, and the junk bond debacle wiped out the net worth of many thrift institutions. Legislation to remedy the situation took an inordinately long time to set up and, with the inexorable laws of compound interest, the problem grew exponentially. The cost of closing insolvent savings and loans exceeded $191 billion, and the long-term cost of the bailout is expected to run $400 billion.

These events have had a profound effect on real estate appraisers. Today federal agencies are required to retain state licensed or certified appraisers to perform appraisals of properties for *federally related transactions* with values above a specified threshold or *de minimis*, which in April 1994 was fixed at $250,000. Business loans of $1 million or less are exempt where the sale of, or income derived from, real estate is not the primary source of repayment. Many lending institutions are regulated by the FDIC. Other federal agencies either insure mortgages (i.e., FHA, HUD), or guarantee mortgages (i.e., the VA). Mortgage loans which originate with federally regulated lenders or which are insured or guaranteed by federal agencies qualify as *federally related transactions*. The *de minimis* requirement, therefore, has had widespread ramifications upon appraisers.

Commercial Banks

Commercial banks are privately owned institutions that offer a variety of financial services to businesses and individuals. They may be state or federally chartered. Commercial banks are managed by boards of directors, who are selected by stockholders but are subject to regulation by state agencies and the Federal Deposit Insurance Corporation (FDIC). (The FDIC is an independent agency that insures individual deposits in all state and federally chartered banks in the Federal Reserve System.) So-called *national banks* are also subject to regulation by the Office of the Comptroller of the Currency (OCC), which may call on them to submit reports of their operations for audit.

In keeping with their role as short-term lenders, commercial banks have traditionally supplied construction and development loans. For short-term, interim financing, developers are usually required to obtain commitments from long-term, permanent lenders, whereby the lenders agree to "take out" the "end loan" with the developer once the project has been completed. Large commercial banks have also become a principal source of takeout financing, i.e. long-term permanent mortgage loans and end loans, usually for commercial and industrial properties. In small communities, commercial banks are also expected to supply their customers with home loans.

One important real estate credit function of commercial banks is warehousing mortgages for mortgage bankers and other financial institutions. The banks provide mortgage bankers with short-term loans secured by their mortgage inventories. This arrangement gives mortgage bankers the liquidity to continue their lending operations while they try to sell the accumulated mortgages to a permanent lender.

Life Insurance Companies

Life insurance companies, which supply a large amount of real estate mortgage credit, are of two principal types—mutual and stock. Mutual life insurance companies are owned by policyholders, who share in net earnings by receiving dividends that can be used to reduce their premium expenses. The profits of stock life insurance companies belong to shareholders, who may or may not be policyholders.

Life insurance companies have always invested heavily in real estate. Their activities include both mortgage lending and property ownership. Life insurance companies usually acquire real estate positions that are long term and relate well to their regular business, in which policy premiums are collected over extended periods. The recent development and popularity of "universal" life insurance has deprived companies of much long-term investment capital. In this insurance arrangement, the policyholder, not the company, directs the investment of policy reserves.

The mortgage investments of life insurance companies cover the full range of realty types—e.g., residences, apartments, offices, shopping malls, hotels, and industrial properties. Because many companies have great financial resources, they have been important in mortgaging large, income-producing properties. Large companies prefer loans on offices and shopping malls.

Life insurance companies may acquire full ownership of real estate for their own investment accounts or for the separate investment accounts that they manage for pension trusts. Although real estate ownership may amount to only 3% to 5% of a company's assets, a large dollar investment is involved because major life companies may have billions of dollars in assets.

Mutual Savings Banks and Stockholder Owned Banks

Mutual savings banks are located in many states and are regulated by the FDIC and various state banking departments. They are very similar to mutual savings and loan associations, promoting thrift and investing substantial amounts of savings in real estate mortgages. Generally they have broader investment powers than savings and loan associations. Since deregulation in the early 1980s, mutual savings banks have expanded the scope of their activities, which now almost match those of commercial banks. Mutual savings banks have grown substantially and continue to change rapidly; they now control assets of more than $350 billion.

Savings banks are important mortgage lenders on local and national levels. When the FHA became dominant in home mortgage lending, savings banks participated extensively in FHA programs. Like savings and loan associations, mutual savings banks have supplied large amounts of mortgage funds for the one- to four-family residential real estate market. Savings banks have reasonably broad investment powers, but they usually concentrate on mortgages, which may account for 65% to 75% of a bank's assets. They also invest in government bonds, corporate bonds, and, to a lesser degree, real estate and stock equity investments.

As mentioned earlier, thrift institutions have been in the unfortunate position of borrowing short and lending long—i.e., their deposits are of the demand type, but they are invested in long-term mortgages. Disintermediation eroded many institutions' net worth and limited their lending. For the real estate industry, this has meant less available mortgage money and greater money costs. When interest rates escalate, fewer aspiring home purchasers qualify as acceptable credit risks because debt service would consume too much of their disposable income. These conditions depress home building and sales.

In the late 1980s and early 1990s, hundreds of mutual savings banks and savings and loan associations went public by converting to stock ownership. In the process, they raised vast amounts of new capital. As the net worth of these banks was augmented, their stock issues became very attractive to investors. Stronger financial positions have prompted many of these institutions to consider a return to lending activities.

Junior Mortgage Originators

Real estate investments are structured not only with first mortgages, but also with second, third, and fourth mortgages. Junior mortgages can be used to raise substantial amounts of mortgage funds and to achieve various investment goals, such as creating additional leverage and facilitating sales of properties with first mortgages that cannot be refinanced. In most jurisdictions, loans must be legally recorded to establish their priority. The first lien recorded takes priority over any that are subsequently filed. When a mortgagor defaults, junior lien holders must keep the senior positions financially current or they run the risk of being cut off by foreclosure of the prior liens. Obviously, junior mortgages involve greater risk than senior liens and therefore command higher interest rates.

Legal regulations usually preclude banks, savings and loan associations, and life insurance companies from making large junior mortgage loans. However, various regulatory "leeway" or "basket" clauses allow institutions to make junior mortgage loans in amounts that do not exceed 3% or 4% of institutional assets. Other private lenders such as REITs, financing companies, and factoring organizations provide secondary financing as a regular line of business. They offer expensive secondary financing in the form of junior mortgages or subordinated land sale-leasebacks, but they are not supervised to the same extent as banks and life insurance companies.

Secondary Mortgage Market

Government and monetary authorities often see housing activity as the most effective way to deal with a general economic slump. Government and private organizations stimulate home building through the secondary mortgage market. In this market, mortgagees sell packages of mortgages at prices consistent with existing money market rates. Selling mortgages frees up capital, creates liquidity, and permits mortgagees to lend when they might otherwise lack funds. The agencies discussed below are the principal operators in the secondary mortgage market.

Fannie Mae (Federal National Mortgage Association). Fannie Mae exerts a major influence on the secondary mortgage market. Its principal purpose is to help the housing industry by purchasing mortgages from primary mortgage markets, thus increasing the liquidity of primary lenders. The agency issues long-term debentures and short-term discount notes to raise most of its funds. Two important Fannie Mae programs are the over-the-counter program, in which the association posts the prices it will pay for the immediate delivery of mortgages, and the free market system commitment auction, in which separate, but simultaneous, auctions are held for FHA, VA, and conventional mortgages. Fannie Mae is a federal agency, but it is a privately owned corporation. Its stock is traded on the New York Stock Exchange. As a federal agency, Fannie Mae has extensive borrowing lines with the U.S. Treasury.

Freddie Mac (Federal Home Loan Mortgage Corporation). Freddie Mac was created in 1970 to increase the availability of mortgage funds and to provide greater flexibility for mortgage investors. Until 1989, the organization was directed by the Federal Home Loan Bank Board. Since then, the regulatory functions of the damaged FHLBB have been assumed by the Office of Thrift Supervision (OTS). Freddie Mac facilitates the expansion and distribution of capital for mortgage purposes by conducting both purchase and sales programs.

In its purchase programs, Freddie Mac buys single-family and condominium mortgages from approved financial institutions. This allows the banking or mortgage banking organization that sells the mortgages to remain liquid in times of credit stringency and continue making mortgage funds available for housing. Although Fannie Mae programs include insured and guaranteed mortgages, Freddie Mac's main interest is in conventional mortgage fields. Both whole mortgages and participations are purchased by Freddie Mac.

In its sales programs, Freddie Mac sells its mortgage inventories, acquiring funds from organizations that have excess capital. Through its purchases, the agency supplies these funds to other organizations that have shortages. Because its operations are conducted nationally, Freddie Mac generates mortgage capital availability throughout the United States.

Ginnie Mae (Government National Mortgage Association). Ginnie Mae is another agency that influences the secondary mortgage market. Its operations have made much mortgage capital available to housing markets. Fannie Mae is a private corporation, but Ginnie Mae is a government organization that gets financial support from the U.S. Treasury. Ginnie Mae provides special assistance in mortgage programs for loans that could not be handled without extraordinary support. It also manages and liquidates certain mortgages acquired by the government. Its most important role in the secondary market, however, is in the mortgage-backed security (MBS) program.

Ginnie Mae is authorized to guarantee the timely payment of principal and interest on long-term securities that are backed by pools of insured or guaranteed mortgages. The most popular security is a pass-through arrangement in which mortgage payments are passed on to the holder of the security. In this program mortgage originators pool their loans in groups of $1 million or more, issue covering securities, and obtain a Ginnie Mae guarantee. Through the program investors who do not have the capacity to originate mortgages can become involved in home finance markets. Because they are backed by the U.S. government, Ginnie Mae securities are traded extensively. Money and capital market investors regard the investment yields indicated by the agency as the current return on top-quality, long-term instruments.

The recent emergence of collateralized mortgage obligations (CMOs) as a major investment banking instrument was prompted by Ginnie Mae guarantee arrangements. CMOs are bonds issued and sold in the capital markets. They are attractive to investors because the debt involved is usually collateralized by Ginnie Mae certificates covering pools of residential mortgages. Because of Ginnie Mae's participation, these bonds receive an AAA, highest-quality risk rating and can be sold at attractively low interest rates. As CMOs have proliferated, they have involved collateral other than Ginnie Mae certificates, including Fannie Mae, Freddie Mac, and even conventional institutional mortgages. This vehicle has been a huge source of liquidity for the mortgage industry and has monetized the mortgage element in real estate investment.

A variation in the CMO field is the real estate mortgage investment conduit (REMIC) option, which transforms the CMO from a pure debt (bond) vehicle into an equity-type investment. In a REMIC arrangement, the certificate represents a proportionate share of ownership in a pool of mortgages. The issuing organization, often an investment bank, avoids adding debt to its balance sheet by using the REMIC. The investor in a REMIC enjoys the benefit of a tax pass-through similar to that of a REIT, and thereby avoids the double taxation incurred by investors in corporations. The issuing entity is not taxed. The holders bear the sole burden of taxes on earnings.

CMOs of all types have brought enormous amounts of capital into the mortgage field. Another variation, "stripped" CMOs, consists of securities which represent principal-only and interest-only components of the investment.[8] Through this type of securitization, pension trusts and other conservatively managed investment funds have assumed large positions in the real estate field, assured by the AA or AAA risk ratings granted CMOs by a major rating organization.

Securitization is rapidly spreading to real estate equity investments. The RTC initiated the large-scale securitization of both mortgage and equity interests in the S&L cleanup. Wall Street has taken securitization much further, successfully handling large portfolios for commercial banks and insurance companies. Many observers believe that in real estate finance, Wall Street has taken the place of traditional lenders.

The mechanism that the RTC used to liquidate the assets of insolvent S&Ls paved the way for large-scale securitization. This process involved the sale of pools of commercial mortgages, known as *commercial mortgage backed securities* (*CMBSs*), through investment bankers to nontraditional mortgage investors. The RTC initially set up a guarantee fund to secure CMBSs, thereby facilitating the risk rating of these debt instruments. More recently, collateralization of CMBSs has taken other forms. (Chapter 28 contains further discussion of the securitization of real estate investment capital.)

Farmer Mac (Federal Agricultural Mortgage Corporation). Established by the Farm Credit Act of 1987, the Federal Agricultural Mortgage Corporation serves the same function for rural properties as Fannie Mae does for urban and suburban properties. Like Fannie Mae, Farmer Mac is a federally chartered, but privately owned corporation. Farmer Mac is subject to the regulatory powers of the Farmers Credit Administration, which also oversees the system of cooperative banks that constitutes the Farm Credit System. Farmer Mac creates a secondary market for loans originated by private banks as well as federally guaranteed loans on agricultural real estate and rural housing.

Private sector transactions. Although most secondary mortgage market activity is generated by Fannie Mae, Freddie Mac, and Ginnie Mae, the private sector has also played a role. Banks and insurance companies with mortgage-originating capability often

---

8. STRIP is an acronym for Separate Trading of Registered Interest and Principal of Securities.

sell loan portfolios, or mortgage participations, to private or institutional investors. Some REITs have purchased mortgages from institutions, thereby supplying the sellers with the liquidity needed to continue their lending programs.

The development and growth of private mortgage insurance programs have facilitated private secondary mortgage activity. In the residential market, private programs have successfully insured mortgage loan increments that exceed legal ratios. This has encouraged private secondary market operations that could not have occurred otherwise.

Debt and Equity Relationships

In money markets and capital markets, when the risks associated with different investments are comparable, funds flow to the investment that offers the best prospective yield. Risks are related to rewards; if capital is to be attracted, competitive yields must be offered. Debt and equity investments have different characteristics and appeal to different investors. A survey of these investment attributes is presented here to clarify the distinction between a real estate venture's mortgage and equity components.

Equity yield is cash flow or dividend income that is augmented by growth or diminished by depreciation. This is true whether the investment is an equity interest in real estate or a common stock. From 1955 to 1975, most real estate appraisers and analysts based their opinions about competitively attractive equity yields on real estate market data. Throughout this period, capital was generally available at modest, stable costs.

After 1975 an inflation-induced recession slowed real estate investment activity, reducing the availability of market data that could be analyzed for appraisal purposes. The information that was gathered was difficult to interpret because rapid, intense monetary changes quickly impaired its market relevance. If, for example, interest rates change 10 times in one year, it is difficult to attach much importance to a capitalization rate that has been extracted from a sale transaction completed just six months ago. The adjustments required are too large to be reliable.

In an unstable economic climate, appraisers are well advised to search money markets and capital markets for data to support the conclusions they have developed from real estate data. There are hundreds of thousands of transactions each day in financial markets and billions of dollars are involved. These transactions reflect the discounting of economic futures by well-informed investors and provide useful insights for investment analysts.

The general, but unsteady, decline in interest rates after 1983 restored some reliability to real estate market data in equity yield analysis, but financial market data are of paramount significance. Every real estate investment depends on one commodity— money. The most persuasive indicators of competitive yield levels are found in money markets where billions of dollars of capital are traded daily, traders are sophisticated and well informed, and investments are often professionally rated for risk.

The largest equity market is the trading of common stocks. Transactions are reported daily, and share prices and current dividend rates are revealed. Most major newspapers carry full details on stock market operations, and financial publications offer abundant information about corporate earnings and general conditions in commercial and industrial enterprises. These data provide the basis for risk rating the securities issued by businesses. In the field of debt investments (bonds and debentures), the rating task is often performed by professionals such as Standard & Poor's and Moody's; their opinions are widely published and respected by the financial community.[9] Other information is furnished by the securities analysts of major banking institutions, brokerage companies, and the investment banking industry. Their opinions are readily available to investors. Financial analysts generally follow groups of companies, examining their business affairs in detail and forecasting their prospects for earnings and growth.

Analysts' reports and financial publications do not reveal prospective stock yields, but they do provide information from which investment indexes can be drawn. Because value is the present worth of future income and reversion combined, a key element of value is anticipated appreciation or depreciation. In the stock market, securities analysts are the best sources of the in-depth information on which the investment community bases its growth or depreciation forecasts. In this regard a securities analyst functions like a real estate appraiser, who arrives at an estimate of value by discounting market-supported income and reversion forecasts. With the ever-accelerating securitization of real estate interests, capitalization rates and discount rates are becoming inextricably linked to the levels and activities of the capital markets.

The second, larger component in real estate investment is the debt capital segment, or mortgage funds. Again, capital markets offer abundant information on investor yield requirements for a great variety of debt instruments with different maturities and risk ratings. In the bond and debenture markets, there are hundreds of thousands of daily transactions involving billions of dollars. Each transaction represents one investor's discounting of perceived future economic conditions. The entire volume of transactions presents an excellent picture of well-informed expectations of debt capital performance.

There are differences in the investment yields produced by debt and equity instruments. With a debt instrument, the original lender is entitled to interest at a specified rate, either fixed or variable, and full payment of the loan amount at maturity. The arrangement may call for periodic payments of interest only and full repayment of the principal at maturity, as in the case of bonds, or it may require periodic payments that combine interest and debt reduction, as in most mortgage loans.

If the original lender sells the investment during its contractual term, a different yield will be realized. If financial market conditions are tight and interest rates are higher than when the loan was originated, the lender must sell the position at a discount. If money is freer and rates are lower, the lender may be able to sell at a premium. The purchaser collects the amount of interest specified in the original contract, but the instrument's yield rate relates to a new investment basis. When the loan is repaid at maturity, the purchaser receives the full face amount, including any discount involved in the acquisition, minus any premium paid. The instrument's investment yield comprises the interest collected, plus any gain or minus any loss realized at loan maturity, and repayment.

9. Standard and Poor's Corporation and Moody's Investor Services, Inc. publish a variety of data on the performance of stocks and bonds. For a listing of these publications, see the bibliography.

It can be seen that the investment yield on a debt instrument is largely a contractual matter. Income earnings are defined in the instrument as a fixed or variable percentage of the debt's face amount paid at specified times over the term of the loan. The reversion is limited to the original face amount of debt, which may be more or less than the amount paid by the final holder of the instrument.

An equity investment has none of the contractual certainty or specificity of a debt position. The income or dividend earnings are simply the amount of a venture's income, if any, after operating expenses and debt service are paid. This cash flow can be positive or negative, depending on whether there is an excess or deficiency of income after all expenses. The reversion is simply the venture's market value at the end of the investment holding period—i.e., a future value. When entering into an investment, an investor considers the forecast dividend earnings and reversion in relation to the acquisition price; this relationship reflects the prospective equity yield. Upon termination of the investment, the dividends and reversion realized are related to the original amount of the investment to reflect the historic equity yield.

Key Concepts

- The price of real estate is expressed in money. The value of money is determined by supply and demand relationships.
- The two sources of capital for real estate are the money market, trading in short-term money instruments, and the capital market, trading in long-term money instruments.
- In the United States, the money supply is regulated by the credit policies of the Federal Reserve System and the fiscal policies of the Treasury Department.
- Short-term money market instruments include federal funds, Treasury bills and notes, repurchase and reverse repurchase agreements, certificates of deposit, commercial paper, bankers' acceptances, municipal notes, and Eurodollars.
- Long- and intermediate-term capital market instruments include bonds, stocks, mortgages (including junior liens, home equity loans, and reverse annuity mortgages), deeds of trust, installment sale contracts, and purchase-money mortgages.
- The securitization of real estate interests through the trading of secondary mortgage market issues, CMOs, REITs, and CMBSs links real estate capitalization and discount rates to financial market activity.
- Capital and money markets are affected by business cycles, monetary conditions, and governmental policies and agencies.
- The capitalization of real estate is divided into debt investment and equity investment, or venture capital.
- REITs, partnerships, syndications, joint ventures, insurance companies, and international equity capital are sources of equity investment.
- S&Ls, commercial banks, insurance companies, mutual savings and stockholder owned banks, junior mortgage originators, and the secondary mortgage market (CMOs, CMBSs) are sources of debt investment.

Terms

bankers' acceptances

basis point

bond

business cycle

capital market

certificates of deposit (CDs)

collateralized mortgage
  obligations (CMOs)

commercial bank

commercial mortgage backed
  securities (CMBSs)

commercial paper

debt

deed of trust

demand deposits

disintermediation

dividends

equity

Eurodollars

Fannie Mae

Farmer Mac

Federal Deposit Insurance
  Corporation (FDIC)

federal discount rate

federal funds

Federal Open Market Committee
  (FOMC)

Federal Reserve System

Financial Institutions Reform,
  Recovery and Enforcement
  Act (FIRREA)

fractional reserve banking

Freddie Mac

general partnership

Ginnie Mae

home equity loan

inflation

installment sale contract

insurance company

interest rate

interim financing

international equity capital

joint venture

junior lien

junior mortgage originators

key economic indicators

land contract

limited partnership

money

money market

mortgage

municipal notes

mutual savings bank

pension fund

purchase-money mortgage (PMM)

prime rate

real estate investment trusts
  (REITs)

real estate mortgage investment
  conduits (REMICs)

repurchase (and reverse
  repurchase) agreements

reserve requirement

reverse annuity mortgage

risk rating

savings and loan association

secondary mortgage market

securitization of real estate interests

stock

stock corporation

syndication

takeout financing

time deposits

Treasury bill or note

trust

venture capital

CHAPTER SEVEN

Fee Simple and Partial Interests

A ccording to the bundle of rights theory, complete real property ownership, or title in fee, consists of a bundle of distinct rights. Generally, each of these rights can be separated from the bundle and conveyed by the fee simple owner to other parties for an unspecified duration or for a limited time period. When a right is separated from the bundle and transferred, a partial, or fractional, property interest is created.[1]

Identifying Partial and Fractional Interests

Appraisers must understand partial and fractional interests to define appraisal problems. At the start of any appraisal assignment, the property rights to be valued must be clearly identified. Valuations of partial and fractional interests are often required because many forms of real property ownership and lease agreements involve less than the complete bundle of rights. Evaluations of fractional interests are also needed in real estate decision making.

Property interests may be examined from many perspectives because the ownership, legal, economic, and financial aspects of real estate overlap.

Ownership by an Individual or Entity

The ownership of property interests can be divided in various ways. For example, in business and marital partnerships two or more parties may have undivided partial and fractional ownership rights in a specific property through joint tenancies, tenancies in common, or tenancies by the entirety. A land trust or a real estate trust is a vehicle for partial property interests in which a group of property owners may continue to operate and manage a property, but the legal title is conveyed to a trustee. A corporation is an association of shareholders created under law. Corporations are title-holding entities in which the shareholders have an ownership interest. Other legal arrangements under which a legal entity holds title to property include partnerships, cooperative corporations, and condominium associations.

Legal Estates and Economic Interests

Separate legal and economic interests derived from the bundle of rights are involved in many kinds of income-producing properties, and each of these interests is distinct in its form and content. Leased fee, leasehold, and subleasehold estates are created through leases in accordance with established legal procedures.

---

1. For an historical view of how real property interests relate to U.S. law, see C. Reinold Noyes, *The Institution of Property* (London: Longmans, Green and Company, 1936).

The leasing of real estate is one practical and familiar application of the bundle of rights theory. The owner of a complete bundle of rights (the lessor) may convey to a tenant (the lessee) a smaller bundle of rights, including the rights to use and occupy a property for a fixed period of time. In return, the tenant agrees to pay periodic rent and to vacate the premises at the end of the lease.

The U.S. Constitution establishes the right of freedom of contract, which allows for flexibility in lease arrangements.[2] A variety of lease contract clauses and provisions have been developed and used, and many have been tested and interpreted by the courts. The flexibility of leasing arrangements has resulted in leasing practices that are responsive to changing economic and financial conditions.

In valuing the economic and legal interests created by leases, appraisers must consider the following factors, among others:

1. The relationship between contract rent and market rent
2. The length of the lease
3. The credit (risk) rating of the tenant
4. The division of expenses between the landlord and tenant

These factors may strongly influence the selection of discount rates. If, for example, the tenant has a low credit rating, an appraiser may not give much consideration to the lease arrangement. If the same lease is assumed by a tenant that is a major business entity with an AAA credit rating, the appraiser would give significant weight to the lease terms. The outlook for future income is much clearer in this case, and the value of the leased fee may exceed the market value of the property unencumbered by the lease, creating a positive leased fee estate (often called a *positive leasehold estate*). Interrelationships may create a variety of complex situations. For example, a below-market contract rent to be paid by a tenant with a poor credit rating may be more certain than an above-market contract rent to be paid by a tenant with a good credit rating.

Financial Interests

The financial aspects of property interests have a major impact on real estate investment practices. The analysis of mortgage and equity components is of particular importance. Mortgage funds are secured debt positions, while equity investments are venture capital. Fee simple, leased fee, and leasehold interests can all be mortgaged, thereby subdividing these interests into mortgage and equity components. Other possible financial arrangements include senior and subordinated debt, sale-leaseback financing, and equity syndications.

The ownership, legal, economic, and financial interests by which various rights can be identified illustrate the complexity and usefulness of the bundle of rights theory. A thorough understanding of the property rights to be valued in an appraisal assignment is needed not only to define the problem, but also to produce an appropriate solution.

---

2. Article I, Section 10 [1] of the U.S. Constitution states that "no state shall ... pass any ... law impairing the obligation of contracts..."

Types of Property Interests

Fee Simple Estates

Ownership of a title in fee establishes the interest in property known as the fee simple estate—i.e., *absolute ownership unencumbered by any other interest or estate, subject only to the limitations imposed by the governmental powers of taxation, eminent domain, police power, and escheat.*

Owners in fee simple may choose to improve or not to improve their property. They may also retain ownership or transfer property title by selling the property or giving it away. When a fee owner dies, the property passes to his or her legal heirs or to others named in the will. This transfers *an estate, a right or interest in property*. Inherited property interests are frequently the subject of valuation assignments.

Life Estates

A life estate is defined as the total rights of use, occupancy, and control, limited to the lifetime of a designated party. The designated party is generally known as the *life tenant* and is obligated to maintain the property in good condition and pay all applicable taxes during his or her lifetime. The second interest in a life estate which may require valuation is that of the *remainderman*, who acquires the possessory interest in the property upon the death of the life tenant. Life estates can be created by operations of law, by wills, or by deeds of conveyance. For example, a fee owner may leave a will that gives land to his widow for her remaining lifetime and, at her death, the land is passed on to their children. Thus, the widow acquires a life estate and functions as a life tenant with the children becoming the remaindermen. A living fee owner may deed his property to a family member as remainderman and, by the terms of the conveyance, retain a life estate for himself. This practice eliminates the expense of probating the will after the owner dies, but may also result in the assessment of a gift tax.

If the life estate generates an income, the appraiser may estimate its probable duration from life expectancy statistics compiled in actuarial studies. Once the net operating income from the estate and its duration are established, an appropriate discount rate can be selected and applied. If the life estate does not generate income, the appraiser may project its future value and then discount this value back to the current date. Since death is certain but its timing is indeterminable, discounting is generally accomplished by applying a safe rate. The discount rate selected also depends on the age and life expectancy of the person who holds the life estate.

A variation on this form of ownership is called a *determinable fee* or *defeasible estate*. This ownership interest continues until a specified condition or event occurs and the interest is automatically terminated. For example, the owner of a parcel of land may convey the parcel to the town for use as a park so long as the town remains a town. If the town is eventually incorporated as a city, the land parcel will revert to the former owner or the owner's heirs.

Lease Interests

Lease interests result when the bundle of rights is divided by a lease. The lessor and the lessee each obtain interests, which are stipulated in contract form and are subject to contract law. The divided interests resulting from a lease represent two distinct, but related, estates of property—the leased fee estate and the leasehold estate. The lease-holder, or tenant, receives specified rights in the real estate, such as the right of use and occupancy, for specific purposes over a defined period of time.

The leased fee estate is the lessor's, or landlord's, estate. *A leased fee estate is an ownership interest held by a landlord with specified rights that include the right of use and occupancy conveyed by lease to others; the rights of lessor (the leased fee owner) and lessee (leaseholder) are specified by contract terms contained within the lease.* Although the specific details of leases vary, a leased fee generally provides the lessor with rent to be paid by the lessee under stipulated terms; the right of repossession at the termination of the lease; default provisions; and the right of disposition, including the rights to sell, mortgage, or bequeath the property, subject to the lessee's rights, during the lease period. When a lease is legally delivered, the lessor must surrender possession of the property to the tenant for the lease period and abide by the lease provisions.

The leasehold estate is the lessee's, or tenant's, estate. *A leasehold estate is the interest held by the lessee (tenant or renter) through a lease transferring specified rights, including the right of use and occupancy, for a stated term under certain conditions.* When a lease is transmitted, the tenant usually acquires the rights to possess the property for the lease period, to sublease the property (if this is allowed by the lease and desired by the tenant), and perhaps to improve the property under the restrictions specified in the lease. In return, the tenant is obligated to pay rent, surrender possession of the property at the termination of the lease, remove any improvements the lessee has modified or constructed (if specified), and abide by the lease provisions.

Leases

When a property is encumbered by a lease, the legal interest typically appraised is the leased fee. The property is considered to be a leased fee regardless of the duration of the lease, the specified rent, or any other terms restricting the lessor and lessee (e.g., subleasing, buildout, tenant insurance). A property under a lease that specifies rent at market levels is thus appraised as a leased fee, not as a fee simple interest. The leased fee interest in a property under a lease that does not represent an arm's-length transaction must be given special consideration. Specific concerns in the valuation of leased fee interests are discussed in detail in Chapters 21 and 24.

Lease Terms

A lease is both an instrument and a contract. It is an instrument by which the landlord gives the tenant the right to occupy the property for the term specified in the lease. It imposes a contractual obligation on the tenant to pay rent to the landlord, and it may contain other promises and agreements between the landlord and the tenant. The legal interest held by the tenant is the leasehold estate. Leases may stipulate the terms of use and occupancy of structures or parts of structures. Ground leases specifically grant the right to use and occupy land.

Leases that cover a period of one year or more must generally be set down in writing. In some states leases for shorter periods may be verbal. A lease should clearly describe the rented property, specifying the geographic location, street address, and condition of the premises; it should also clearly delineate the lessor's and lessee's rights and obligations. The signatures of the lessor and the lessee effectively establish the legal power of a lease. The tenant's possession generally provides notice that the rights of the leasehold estate are being exercised. Long-term leases or lease memoranda are usually recorded.

Most leases contain clauses pertaining to the duration of tenancy, rent, security deposit, insurance, payment of public utilities, right of entry, assignment and subleasing, maintenance and repair, fixtures, taxes, eminent domain, default, and renewal options. Other contractual clauses may address purchase options, rent escalations or reductions, alterations, and use restrictions. Many types of leases (e.g., ground leases) contain provisions for leasehold mortgaging provided the arrangement is economically sound, the term of the lease is not too short, and leasehold mortgaging is not forbidden by the lease.

Lease clauses can influence property value. Therefore, it is imperative that appraisers read and understand all leases that affect the property interests being appraised. In some instances it may be necessary or advisable for an appraiser to consult an attorney for assistance in interpreting lease provisions. By leasing real estate a lessor receives some advantages, including the receipt of a certain income or annuity, favorable income tax considerations, and the benefit of tenant-built improvements, unless these are reserved as the personal property of the tenant. These advantages can, and frequently do, enhance property value and can provide the owner with a hedge against inflation. The potential advantages for a lessee include a minimum equity investment in property, an alternative to costly financing, favorable tax considerations, and reduced management responsibility.

Tenancy

When the bundle of rights is owned as separate property interests, tenancy is created. In real estate *tenancy* has two meanings: *1) the holding of property by any form of title, and 2) the right to use and occupy property as conveyed in a lease.* The first definition usually refers to co-ownership of real estate; the second definition concerns the nature of the relationship between a landlord and a tenant.

Co-ownership includes joint tenancy, tenancy by the entirety, and tenancy in common. *Joint tenancy is joint ownership by two or more persons with the right of survivorship.* Under this arrangement each party has an identical interest and right of possession. *Tenancy by the entirety is an estate held by a husband and wife in which neither has a disposable interest in the property during the lifetime of the other, except through joint action.* It has the same survivorship provision as a joint tenancy, but tenancy by the entirety applies only to spouses. *Tenancy in common is an estate held by two or more persons, each of whom has an undivided interest.* In this estate the undivided interest may or may not be equally shared by the holders and there is no right of survivorship.

The valuation of undivided partial interests poses a problem for appraisers. Because no party can exercise complete control, the interest of each party is usually not worth as much as the corresponding fraction of the property's market value. Minority interests have limited market appeal, so the appraiser must decide how to derive an appropriate value. Because either party can bring legal action to divide the property, which is known as *partition*, the cost of this proceeding is one measure of value diminution. However, a sale in partition is a forced sale, which does not reflect free market action, and the price paid may or may not reflect market value. Valuations of co-ownerships are not easy and may be disputed.[3]

The length of the relationship between a landlord and a tenant varies. *Tenancy from period to period* (periodic tenancy) and *tenancy for years* are two legally recognized ways to describe this relationship. In tenancy from period to period (e.g., month to month, quarter to quarter, year to year), the owner of the leasehold interest pays rent periodically and each payment renews the interest for an additional period. The ultimate length of the leasehold interest is not stated. In a tenancy for years, the beginning and end of the estate are clearly specified. If the tenant does not default, the estate continues until it expires on the specified termination date. A tenant who continues to pay rent after expiration of the lease is in a *holdover tenancy*. With the approval of the landlord, this estate is known as *tenancy at will*; without the approval of the landlord, it is known as *tenancy at sufferance*. Most situations involving the latter ultimately result in eviction proceedings.

Rental Payments

The three basic kinds of leases can be distinguished by identifying who is financially responsible for property expenses. Gross leases and net leases assign these responsibilities differently. *A gross lease is a lease in which the landlord receives stipulated rent and is obligated to pay all or most of the operating expenses and real estate taxes. A modified gross lease is a lease in which the landlord and tenant share the expenses according to the proportions specified by the lease. A net lease is a lease in which the tenant pays all or most of the property charges in addition to the stipulated rent.* Typical property charges include real estate taxes, insurance premiums, utilities, and the costs of maintenance and structural repairs. In net lease arrangements, the tenant assumes the risk that taxes may increase or the building may be destroyed. If the building is destroyed, the tenant may be obligated to rebuild the building and continue paying rent during its construction. The exact definitions of these lease types vary. Lawyers and brokers sometimes use terms such as *net net lease* and *triple net lease* to emphasize that it is the tenant who must meet most or all of the property charges. The appraiser must understand the precise terms of the lease under consideration.

---

3. The value of an undivided partial interest in a property can be estimated by first valuing the fee simple interest in the property using traditional valuation techniques. Then that value is divided by the proportion of the property that the partial interest represents and discounted. The appraiser's most difficult task is to find the percentage by which the undivided partial interest must be discounted. For further discussion and examples, see Chapter 21 of Frank E. Harrison, *Appraising the Tough Ones* (Chicago: Appraisal Institute, 1996).

The level and schedule of rental payments can also vary. *A flat rental, or level payment, lease has a specified level of rent that continues throughout the lease term.* In contrast, the payments required by a step-up or step-down lease change at specific points in time. *A step-up or step-down lease provides for a certain rent for an initial period, followed by an increase or decrease in rent over stated periods.* Other types of leases may stipulate that adjustments be made, although not necessarily at specified intervals. *An index lease provides for periodic rent adjustments based on the change in an economic index.* The Consumer Price Index (CPI) is frequently used to set rent levels in long-term leases. *A revaluation lease provides for rent adjustments at periodic intervals based on a revaluation of the real estate.* Rent payments can be annual, semiannual, quarterly, monthly, weekly, or even daily. They may be required at the beginning of the specified rental period or at the end. *An escalator lease may require the lessor to pay expenses for the first year of the lease and the lessee to pay any increase in expenses as additional rent over the subsequent years of the lease.* Leases may also contain an *expense stop or clause* which limits the lessor's expense obligation, with the lessee assuming any expenses above an established level. An expense stop safeguards the lessor from unexpected increases in expenses due to inflation.

Lease terms shape the quantity and quality of the future benefits likely to flow to the interests created by the contract. The lease agreement provides that the lessor will receive specified rent or services during the term of the lease and a reversion of the tenant's rights of use and occupancy when the lease expires. The contract generally gives the tenant exclusive rights of use and occupancy during the lease term, subject to rent or service obligations. Other divisions of rights are common. For example, an original tenant may sublet a property and both the leased fee and leasehold positions may be mortgaged. (Analysis of income and expenses and the procedures for valuing leased fee and leasehold estates are discussed in Chapters 20, 21, and 24.)

A lease sets rental terms and, presumably, indicates the gross income to the leased fee. As mentioned previously, appraisers estimating the market value of leased fee interests must always consider the relationship between contract rent and market rent, the length of the lease, the credit rating of the tenant, and the division of expenses between the landlord and the tenant.

Specialized Lease Interests

Leasehold Position

The leasehold is the interest held by a tenant or renter through a lease transferring the rights to use and occupy the leased premises under certain conditions. The most important obligation associated with these rights is the payment of rent. The relationship of contract rent to market rent greatly affects the value of a leasehold. *Contract rent is the actual rental income specified in a lease.* Rent is commonly paid by the tenant or tenants to the lessor according to a specified schedule. A leasehold interest usually has value when contract rent is less than market rent. If the lessee has a rent advantage, the leasehold interest has positive value. This, in turn, may affect the value of the leased fee.

A leased fee encumbered with a fixed rent that is below market rates may be worth less than the unencumbered fee estate.

Market rent is the rental income that a property would most probably command in the open market. Only in an ideally negotiated lease would contract rent equal market rent. When contract rent exceeds market levels, the leasehold may have negative value. Sometimes, market changes may also create a positive leasehold interest, and it is even possible for the leasehold interest to undergo several changes over the life of the lease. The date of the value estimate is critical because it identifies the point in time at which the appraiser has compared contract rent to market rent within the context of prevailing market conditions.

Subleasehold Position

Normally a tenant is free to sublease all or part of a property, but many leases require that the lessor's consent be obtained. *A sublease is an agreement in which the lessee in a prior lease conveys to a third party the same interest that the lessee enjoys (the right of use and occupancy of the property), but for a shorter term than that of the lessee. An assignment is a written transfer by the lessee of the entirety of interests the lessee enjoys in the property (the rights of use and occupancy of the property), to be held by another legal entity or to be used for the benefit of creditors.* Leases usually provide that the lessor's consent "will not unreasonably be withheld." Over the years, court decisions have established that subleasing should not be subject to undue constraint. To deny permission, lessors usually must show that the security of their position would be impaired.

In a sublease, the original lessee is "sandwiched" between a lessor and a sublessee. The original lessee's interest has value if the contract rent is less than the rent collected from the sublessee. Subleasing does not release the lessee from the obligations to the lessor defined in the lease agreement.

The discount rates used in valuing different lease interests will vary because the rates selected must reflect the risks involved. Generally, the lessor's interest, the leased fee, entails less risk than the lessee's interest, the leasehold, since the owner of the leased fee is usually entitled to a reversion whereas the owner of the leasehold is not. In turn, the lessee assumes less risk than the sublessee, whose position is exposed to greater risk. The subleasehold position is more risky because the subleasehold will only have value if it is rented to a sub-subtenant for an amount that is more than the sublessee pays the owner, but less than or equal to market rent.

A lease contract may contain a provision that explicitly forbids subletting. Without either the right to sublet or a term that is long enough to be marketable, a leasehold position cannot be transferred and, therefore, has no market value. Furthermore, the value of the leased fee would likely be diminished in this case since a lessee who no longer has need of the leased premises and is not allowed to sublease the space is likely to default on the lease. Of course, the leasehold position may have use value to the lessee. Valuations of leaseholds under contractual provisions that prohibit subletting are required for a variety of reasons (e.g., to establish estate taxes, to allocate a condemnation award between a lessor and lessee).

Mortgaged Lease Interests

Leasehold mortgaging is a type of mortgage-equity financing in which a lessee, or tenant, agrees to subordinate the leasehold interest to a mortgage covering the leasehold. Such a mortgage is often obtained by a lessee-developer who holds a ground lease to a land parcel and, with the lessor's consent, wants to build improvements. If the tenant defaults on the terms of lease, however, he or she is subject to eviction. It is important to remember that, in this situation, it is the lessee, not the lessor, who is subordinating the leasehold to a mortgage. The rights of the leasehold mortgagee would be forfeit if the tenant were evicted. The leasehold mortgagee may be protected by a "nondisturbance" clause in the lease or by a subordination of the lease to the leasehold mortgage. A "nondisturbance" clause gives the mortgagee the right to cure any default(s) by the lessee upon appropriate notice. In a lease subordination arrangement, the leasehold mortgagee can foreclose on the leasehold interest subject to the lease.

A leasehold mortgagee who finances building improvements should be certain that the rent required in the ground lease is not higher than a competitively attractive yield on the land value. The mortgagee should make sure that the lease terms include the right to cure any lessee default. If compelled to foreclose, the leasehold mortgagee can take possession of the leasehold interest and the improvements, subject to the terms of the lease, and is only obliged to pay the rent required in the lease.

In current investment practice, investors seek maximum financing for favorable leveraging and the best tax shelter. Leases, the mortgaging of lease interests, and subordinations provide the necessary tools. For major investment projects, a more complex set of arrangements may be worked out. For example, a property may be divided into a leased fee and a leasehold interest. The mortgage on the leased fee is arranged and a leasehold mortgage is set up to construct improvements. By using different legal entities, one party can hold both the fee position and the leasehold position. In such a situation, expert legal advice is needed to ensure that the documentation supports the separation of the interests and does not effect a merger.

In appraising a leasehold estate subject to a mortgage, the appraiser should investigate whether 1) the rent provisions of the ground lease are tied to the CPI, 2) the debt service on the fee mortgage is variable, and 3) the debt service on the leasehold mortgage includes an equity kicker or participation benefits. The appraiser must be aware of these provisions to appraise the property appropriately.

Other Partial and Fractional Interests

The bundle of rights includes interests other than those created by leases for the use and occupancy of the physical real estate. Property ownership may also be divided into planes of space. Vertical interests and other estates or interests, such as transferable development rights (TDRs), can be transferred and must be considered separately by the appraiser in sales, leases, mortgages, and other realty transactions.

Vertical Interests

One important dimension of real property ownership concerns the distinction between subsurface and air rights.[4] *A subsurface right is the right to the use and profits of the underground portion of a designated property.* The term usually refers to the right to extract minerals from below the earth's surface and to construct tunnels for railroads, motor vehicles, and public utilities. *Air rights are the property rights associated with the use, control, and regulation of air space over a parcel of real estate.* Both of these fractional interests represent portions of a fee simple estate, and each embodies the idea of land as a three-dimensional entity.

The vertical division of real property is based on the legal concept of land as a volume of space with boundless height and depth.[5] This concept is significant because technological developments continue to expand our ability to use the earth's subsurface and atmosphere. In urban areas in particular, engineering advances have dramatically affected land use and, therefore, highest and best use considerations. The development of steel-framed building construction, the passenger elevator, deep tunnel excavation techniques, and communications technology have all helped to shape our urban landscape.

Changes in land use also reflect the forces and factors affecting value. As the density of building in urban areas increases, fewer sites are available for new construction and land values escalate. This trend has produced a growing interest in developing air rights. As early as 1902, the air rights associated with highly valued land along the New York Central Railroad in New York City were beginning to be developed. Park Avenue is one outstanding example of real estate development built on the acquisition of air rights. Real estate development established on air rights can be found in urban areas around the world.

When a large building is to be constructed in a space to which air rights apply, the base of the site is visualized as a platform constructed at some level (e.g., 30 or 40 feet) above the present surface. In the case of Park Avenue development, however, the platform is actually located below grade, just above the railroad tunnel. The platform must be supported by columns, which normally rest on a caisson foundation built underground. In this manner, a number of discrete, interrelated "lots" are created; the air, column, and caisson lots associated with different portions of the three-dimensional space comprise the land or site in question. Figure 7.1 illustrates a division of vertical space.

Air rights can be sold in fee, with the seller retaining one or more easements for a specialized use such as the operation of a railroad. Air rights may also be subdivided; in this case the owner of the fee sells or leases only the land and air that are to be occupied by a particular improvement.

Air rights were subdivided to construct The Merchandise Mart in Chicago, which is shown in Figure 7.2. The structure was built between 1928 and 1931 in air space above

---

4. Rights to surface areas may be divided into smaller parcels by horizontal subdivision, but this does not create partial interests. Usually a large tract held in fee simple is divided into a number of smaller units, which are also held in fee simple. Rights-of-way over surface areas may be conveyed by easements, which are discussed later in this chapter.
5. B. Harrison Frankel, "Three-Dimensional Real Property Law: The Truth About 'Air Rights,'" *Real Estate Law Journal* (Spring 1984).

| Figure 7.1 | **Three-Dimensional Division of Space for Air or Tunnel Rights** |

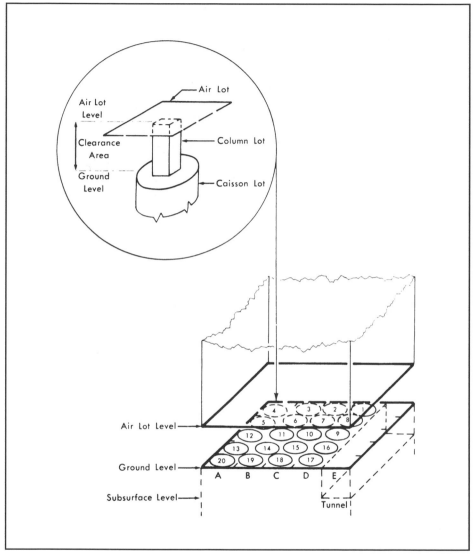

As an example, these divisions may be identified as air rights above air lot level; column lots between air lot level and ground (1-20); caisson lots below ground level (1-20); tunnel rights between ground level and subsurface (E)

The Chicago and Northwestern Railroad. The owners of the Mart, which is one of the world's largest mercantile buildings, actually possess 458 caisson lots extending 100 feet below ground, 458 column lots, a small surface parcel that houses building equipment, and the air lot 23 feet above Chicago's city datum level, where the building is constructed. The Merchandise Mart typifies the traditional development of air rights over existing railroad track; other developments may be more creatively designed.

| Figure 7.2 | **The Merchandise Mart in Chicago** |

(H. Armstrong Roberts, Inc.)

Easements

Easements represent another division of property ownership. *An easement is usually the right to perform a specific action on a particular parcel of property, or portion thereof, by the grantees who do not hold the underlying fee.* Easements frequently permit a specific portion of a property to be used for access to an adjoining property or as a public right-of-way. Although surface easements are the most common, subterranean and overhead easements are used for public utilities, subways, and bridges. Other easements prohibit the owner of the underlying fee from certain uses of the property without giving the owner of the easement any possessory interest in the real estate, e.g., scenic easements, facade easements.

Clearly, a property that enjoys the benefit of an easement gains additional rights; a property that is subject to an easement is burdened. The easement attaches to the property benefitted and is referred to as an *easement appurtenant*. The property whose owner acquires an easement is known as the *dominant estate or tenement*; the property that is subject to the easement is called the *servient estate or tenement*. Easement rights can be conveyed in perpetuity or for a limited time period.

An easement can be created by a contract between private parties or by adverse possession in accordance with state law. It can also be acquired by governmental entities or public utilities through the exercise of eminent domain. In these cases, a valuation is needed to estimate the price the easement owner should pay to the burdened party. In the valuation of easements for public acquisition, the measure of value is *always* the loss in the value of the burdened property—*not* the value of the easement to the taker.

An easement that affords ingress and egress to an otherwise landlocked parcel increases its value. Easement rights to a development's recreational facilities normally enhance the value of plots that have this advantage. The value of an easement appurtenant is usually estimated as some part of the amount of value it adds to the property it benefits; the burdened property's loss in value can also be used to indicate the value of an easement. This latter measure is used when an easement is acquired by a governmental entity or public utility. The value of an easement reflects the basic economic concept of contribution. No one should pay more for an easement appurtenant than the amount of value gained by the property it benefits. The holder of an easement realizes a gain by paying less than the added value.

When an easement is acquired by a public utility company, e.g., for overhead power lines, valuation becomes more complicated. In all cases, however, an easement is a partial interest that is held by another party and burdens the real property. It has measurable value.

Some easements, known as *easements in gross*, do not benefit other land, but rather have utility as an independent property interest. For example, an electrical transmission line easement has utility for the transmission of electrical power without being appurtenant to the property. *Conservation easements* restrict the future use of property and have independent utility for the purpose of conserving wildlife or habitat. Such easements are usually owned by a governmental entity or conservation group.[6] Open space easements set land aside for nonbuilding uses and may encumber land in three ownership categories: private open space adjacent to dwellings owned by individual residents, public open space owned by the government, and common open space owned by a community association and set aside for the use of residents.

Preservation easements are used to protect certain historic properties by prohibiting physical changes to the property and, in many cases, limiting the uses to which the property can be put.[7] Usually the owner must maintain the condition of the property at the time the easement is donated or immediately after a proposed restoration. Under federal law, a preservation easement can, in certain circumstances, be deeded to a qualified nonprofit organization or government agency. In such instances, the property owner donates the easement and receives an income tax reduction that can be equal to, but not more than, the market value of the real property rights donated.

The economic theory that underlies federal valuations of donated preservation easements is generally the same as that applied in federal eminent domain appraising, although the acquirer of a preservation easement receives rather than takes rights. The value of a preservation easement is based on the difference between the value of the entire property before the creation of the easement and the value of the remainder

---

6. Appraisers are increasingly called upon to value land subject to conservation easements. The deduction allowed by the IRS for the value of donated conservation easements is one of the few tax benefits left to investors, and the consequences are enormous. According to one valuation method employed by the IRS, the value of a conservation easement is estimated as the difference between the values of the land before and after the creation of the easement. IRS Regulation §1.170.A-14 (h)(3) deals specifically with the valuation of conservation easements donated for charitable deductions. When preparing appraisals for federal tax purposes, appraisers are advised to consult a tax attorney or tax expert.

7. Preservation easements often prevent a property from being developed to its highest and best use. The highest and best use of an older property which happens to have some local historical significance may be to raze the building and redevelop the site. A preservation easement may make this alternative impossible.

property after the easement is created. Often an increase in property value resulting from the easement may offset acquisition costs for the government.[8]

Each easement document contains specific controls and restrictions which must be carefully analyzed to determine their effect on the encumbered property. The effect of existing land use regulations, including any historic district controls or individual landmark designations, should be related to the subject property and the provisions of the easement.

Transferable Development Rights

Transferable development rights (TDRs) emerged in the real estate industry during the 1970s. *A transferable development right is a development right that is separated from a landowner's bundle of rights and transferred, generally by sale, to another landowner in the same or a different area.* Some TDRs are used to preserve property uses for agricultural production, open space, or historic buildings. In this arrangement, a preservation district and a development district are identified. Landowners in the preservation district are assigned development rights, which they cannot use to develop their own land, but can sell to landowners in the development district. These landowners can use these tranferred rights to build at higher densities than zoning laws in the development district would normally permit.

Another situation in which development rights are transferred results from the constrained capacity of an existing utility. For example, consider a community that decides to impose a construction moratorium pending the expansion of its present sewage plant or the building of a new plant. Before the moratorium, a landowner was granted the right to hook up 100 projected single-family residences to the existing plant. A second landowner, however, did not obtain the right to link up his 50 proposed single-family residences to the sewage treatment plant, and will have to wait for expansion of the plant's capacity. The second landowner risks financial loss if he cannot develop the land immediately, so he purchases the right to link up his 50 residential units to the plant from the first landowner.

Appraisers can value TDRs with ordinary sales comparison techniques if there are sufficient transactions to constitute a market. When market sales are lacking, the income capitalization approach may be applied. In such cases, the economic concept of contribution provides a foundation, and the value added to the property due to the acquisition of the TDR is adjusted for the administrative, legal, and other costs incurred. Some, though not all, of the property's net value increase can be attributed to the TDR; no one is likely to undertake such a complicated procedure without the prospect of a reasonable profit.

Air rights can be transferred in various ways. Often the air rights to one property are shifted to another within the same building zone under legal planning regulations. The transfer of air rights allows developers to adjust the density of land use without putting adverse pressure on owners, neighborhoods, or districts. This practice underscores the importance of local zoning authorities, which regulate building heights, building functions, setbacks, and other variables involved in the development of air rights.

---

8. *Uniform Appraisal Standards for Federal Land Acquisitions* (Washington, D.C.: U.S. Government Printing Office, 1992).

Special Forms of Ownership

Condominium Ownership

A condominium is a form of fee ownership of separate units or portions of multi-unit buildings that provides for formal filing and recording of a divided interest in real property. While residential and retail properties were once the main types of property held in condominium ownership, many other property types have begun to be "condominiumized," e.g., office condos, "dockominiums," and "landominiums."

A condominium unit is a separate ownership, and title is held by an individual owner. The unit may be separately leased, sold, or mortgaged. In a traditional condominium, the condominium owner also holds title to an undivided partial interest in the common areas of the total condominium project—e.g., the land, the public portions of the building, the foundation, the outer walls, and the spaces provided for parking and recreation. Thus, the owner possesses a three-dimensional space within the outer walls, roof or ceiling, and floors and, along with other owners, has an undivided interest in common areas. Recently, the concept of *limited common elements* has been applied to condominiums. In this arrangement, certain common elements, e.g., parking stalls, storage units, or plots of surrounding land, are reserved for the use of some, but not all, of the condominium owners.

The owners of units in a condominium project usually form an association to manage commonly held real estate in accordance with adopted bylaws. The expenses of management and maintenance are divided pro rata among the owners, who pay a monthly fee.

To value individual condominium units, appraisers generally use the sales comparison approach. Recent sales of units of comparable size, location, and quality are the best indicators of value. To value entire condominium projects, whether they are newly constructed buildings or conversions, appraisers usually apply the income capitalization approach (discounted cash flow analysis) in conjunction with the sales comparison approach (to establish unit prices). The amount and timing of all capital outlays, expected monetary receipts, and returns are estimated, and these amounts are discounted at a rate consistent with competitive investment yields. The estimates of future sellout prices and the timing of sales are key elements in the valuation.

Cooperative Ownership

In certain areas cooperative ownership of apartments is popular. *Cooperative ownership is a form of ownership in which each owner of stock in a cooperative apartment building or housing corporation receives a proprietary lease on a specific apartment and is obligated to make a monthly payment which represents the proportionate share of operating expenses and debt service on the underlying mortgage, which is paid by the corporation.*

A co-op is established when a stock corporation is organized to issue an authorized number of shares at a specified par value. The corporation takes title to an apartment building and prices the various apartments. The price per unit determines the number of shares that an apartment occupant must purchase to acquire a proprietary lease. The lease obligates the occupant to pay a monthly maintenance fee, which may be adjusted at times by the corporation's board of directors. The fee covers the expenses of management, operations, and maintenance of public areas. Because the shareholders can vote their shares in electing directors, they have some control over property conditions.

Recently, a new method for financing cooperatives has emerged in some areas. In the past cooperative corporations arranged mortgages on entire apartment properties. Cooperative shareholders had to fund their purchases with 100% equity or borrow the money from commercial banks using short-term, personal notes. Now, however, a cooperative corporation can arrange a mortgage on the total property, and individual apartment shareholders can mortgage their stock for up to 75% of its value. These new mortgage arrangements have made cooperative apartment properties much more marketable.

If the market for cooperative apartments is active, appraisers can value individual units with the sales comparison approach. However, appraisers must remember that prices are influenced by the amount and terms of the mortgage financing that the corporation has placed on the building. In recent years co-op mortgages have ranged from 25% to 50% of total value, with the balance financed by individual apartment shareholders as pure equity or with cooperative apartment mortgages. Often corporate bylaws impose limitations on the property's marketability, which can affect the validity of comparable sales data.

Timesharing

Fractional interests created by timesharing have been marketed extensively in recent years. *Timesharing involves the sale of either limited ownership interests in, or rights to use and occupy, residential apartments or hotel rooms.*

There are two forms of timesharing and it is imperative that the appraiser distinguish between them when appraising timeshare projects or analyzing timeshare comparables. The first form is known as *fee timesharing*. The purchaser of a fee timeshare receives a deed that conveys title to a unit for a specific part of a year, thereby limiting the ownership interest. The purchaser has the right to sell, lease, or bequeath this real property interest. The interest can be mortgaged and title can be recorded. The second form of timesharing is called *nonfee timesharing*, which does not convey a legal title in the property. Typically a purchaser receives only the right to use a timeshare unit and related premises.

There are subcategories for both types of timesharing. The two types of fee timesharing are timeshare ownership and interval ownership. In timeshare ownership, purchasers receive a deed to an undivided interest in a particular unit as tenants in common. Each purchaser agrees to use the unit only during the time period stipulated in his or her deed. In interval ownership, the owner receives a terminable fee in the form of a tenancy for years (the specified time period), which may last for the duration of the project. At the end of the tenancy for years, the fee interest is conveyed or reverts to the interval owners as tenants in common. They then have the option of selling the property and dividing the proceeds, or continuing as tenants in common and renewing the interval estate.

Timeshare owners and interval owners pay operating expenses, including a proportionate share of taxes, insurance, and other costs, and a fee for common area maintenance (CAM) and management. In many projects, 50 one-week intervals are created; the remaining two weeks of each year are reserved for maintenance and major repairs.

The three types of nonfee timesharing are known as leasehold interest, vacation license, and club membership.[9] The leasehold interest type of timesharing is essentially a prepaid lease arrangement. A vacation license involves the transfer of a license from the developer to the purchaser, giving the latter the right to use a given type of unit for specified time periods over the life of the vacation license contract. In the club membership form of ownership, timeshare patrons purchase membership for a specified number of years in a club which owns, leases, or operates the timeshare property. The purchaser receives the right to use a particular type of unit for a specified period during each year of membership.

The partial interests created by timesharing are valued through sales comparison. The appraiser begins by identifying the rights to be valued. The portion of the property allocated for use by the shareholder must be established as well as any personal property included. In appraising existing timeshare properties, resales of comparables generally provide reliable indications of value. To value new timeshare projects, appraisers must consider 1) the time required for sellout, 2) seasonal variations that affect sales, 3) all direct and indirect costs required to create a facility that will command the prices anticipated, and, most important, 4) competition in the market.

Ownership of Real Property by Legal Entities

Stock Corporations

The Corporate Ownership Entity and the Shareholder's Financial Interest

A stock corporation may be organized to hold title to a single asset, such as a parcel of real estate, or multiple assets, such as a portfolio of property investments. Ownership of the corporate entity is divided into partial interests by selling shares to an investment group. Any specific stock holding represents a percentage of total corporate ownership, which is derived from the ratio between the number of shares owned by a particular investor and the total number of shares issued by the corporation. The percentage is an ownership share in the corporation, and its book value is usually found by multiplying the corporate net worth by the ownership percentage.

Market Value and Book Value of the Shareholder's Interest

The market value of a share of stock in a corporation that has a parcel of real estate as its sole asset may be higher or lower than its book value. *Book value is defined as the capital amount at which property is shown on the account books.* Book value usually equals the original cost of the asset after subtracting accrued depreciation and adding the value of any additions or improvements. Book value and market value are usually not the same, so the values of the pro rata shares of ownership associated with each differ.

---

9. Under the laws of some states, vacation licenses and club memberships are not considered interests in real estate, but personal property.

Discounted Pro Rata Value of Shares: Minority Interests or Closely Held Corporations

Fractional corporate interests—i.e., shares of stock—typically sell for less than their pro rata value because a minority interest does not have the ability to control the investment. In a *closely held corporation* formed for a real estate venture, additional discounts may be required to reflect illiquidity because the market for shares is often limited.

Because stock market values often represent a discount from actual corporate net worth, the accounting profession and the Securities and Exchange Commission allow publicly owned real estate corporations to show both the book values and the current market values of assets on their annual financial statements. This practice, which is sometimes referred to as *current value accounting*, frequently reveals that present market values greatly exceed book values (i.e., cost less accumulated depreciation). Therefore, a corporation may have greater net worth than is indicated by book values. Publicly owned real estate corporations employ professional appraisers to estimate the current market values used in these reports.[10]

Land Trusts

The Land Trust Ownership Entity

Trusts are sometimes used as legal vehicles to create partial ownership interests or financial (mortgage) interests in real property. *A land trust is often a legal vehicle for partial ownership interests in real property in which independently owned properties are conveyed to a trustee. Land trusts may be used to effect a profitable assemblage or, in some cases, to facilitate the assigning of property as collateral for a loan.* The trustee holds legal title to the property for a specified time and performs only the functions outlined in the trust agreement. The trustee may or may not actively manage the property or collect rent; when not performed by the trustee, these duties remain the responsibility of the beneficiaries, who are the original owners. One important legal aspect of a trust arrangement is that a judgment against a beneficiary is not a lien against the real estate.

Valuation of the Beneficiary's Interest

To value a beneficiary's partial interest, the appraiser must first estimate the market value of the total property. The appraiser then adjusts the estimate to account for any effect on value that may result from the trust indenture provisions, which identify the rights and obligations of beneficiaries. The beneficiary's position will often call for significant downward adjustment.

General and Limited Partnerships

Partnerships are used extensively in real estate acquisition because they pool funds for property ownership and operation.

---

10. The International Valuation Standards Committee (IVSC) was formed in 1980 to establish worldwide standards for the valuation of fixed assets in financial statements. Under international accounting standards, fixed assets are divided into tangible assets, intangible assets, and financial assets. Many in the accounting and financial communities believe that evaluations of the current and historical performance of businesses should be made with reference to the current value of their assets. In the United States, historical costs are commonly used to report the value of fixed assets.

The General Partnership Entity and Valuation of the Partner's Interest

In a general partnership, all partners share in business gains and each is personally responsible for all liabilities of the partnership. To value a partner's partial interest, the appraiser estimates the market value of the partnership's total real property assets and adjusts the estimate to reflect the partner's percentage of ownership. Other adjustments are made in light of the terms of the partnership agreement, which define the partners' rights and liabilities in sales and liquidations. The partners' ability or inability to control business operations (i.e., to decide when to sell, to select property managers, and to approve or disapprove prospective leases) has a major effect on the value of a general partnership. Another important aspect of a partnership is that it automatically terminates when a general partner dies. Because the provisions of partnership contracts shape and limit ownership benefits, they also influence the value of the partial interests involved.

The Limited Partnership Entity and Valuation of the Partner's Interest

Limited partnerships have both general partners and limited partners. The general partners manage the business and assume full liability for partnership obligations. In contrast, the liability of each limited partner is restricted to his or her capital contributions.

The investment value of limited partnership interests or syndicate shares often includes income tax shelter benefits. At one time, such investments offered small income returns, at least during the early years, when the value of the investment was perceived to lie largely in its income tax benefits (tax deductions and tax deferrals). The Tax Reform Act of 1986 significantly reduced the income-sheltering of real estate investments.[11]

Limited Liability Companies

A limited liability company (LLC) incorporates features of a corporation and a partnership. The owners of a limited liability company are members rather than shareholders or partners. Unless otherwise specified, management is generally vested in the members in proportion to their contribution of capital to the limited liability company. Members may separate their right to a share of the company profits from the right to participate in management or to vote on matters affecting the company. These separated rights can then be assigned to a transferee. To value a member's interest in a limited liability company, the appraiser must determine whether the member holds a complete interest in the company or a transferee interest in the profits. Over the past two decades, many states have adopted legislation authorizing the establishment of LLCs, in large part as a means of attracting foreign investment. Outside the United States, LLCs are a common form of business organization.

Real Estate Equity Syndications

Equity syndication represents a means for selling interests or rights in real property. *A syndication creates a private or public partnership or other entity for the purpose*

---

11. Guide Note 1 to the Appraisal Institute's Standards of Professional Appraisal Practice addresses the valuation of real estate limited partnership interests.

of pooling funds toward the acquisition, development, holding, management, and/ or disposition of real estate. Syndications, which may be referred to as partnerships, are established when an individual or group purchases interests in real property for the purpose of transferring them to a limited partnership. The limited partnership interests are then sold to investors.

Such arrangements appear simple, but they may be very complex because syndications frequently purchase more than real estate, and the value of the interests in real estate and the aggregate value of the limited partnership interests differ in quality as well as quantity. Syndications convey property interests, which are grouped as securities. Their value depends not only on the property rights in the underlying real estate, but also on the additional, or more limited, rights created by contracts and other nonrealty considerations. Accordingly, any valuation of syndicated property other than a market value estimate of the fee simple rights involves valuing more than the rights or interests in the real property.

Real property interests and the interests of the limited partnership differ in value because many non-real estate items or conditions are involved in the latter. In addition to the real property interests conveyed, most sales of limited partnership interests by a syndicator include items such as 1) management services, 2) the ability to invest in a major property that an investor might not be able to invest in alone, and 3) the potential for improved liquidity. Potential capital appreciation and eligibility for tax benefits also influence investors and may affect market value. These factors and conditions are difficult to isolate, so analyses of comparable sales may be difficult.

Decreased inflation, the prosecution of individuals who abuse tax shelters, and the failure of financial institutions have brought some mortgage and syndication practices into question. Appraisers must exercise great care in determining the exact nature of the rights or interests to be valued in any assignment involving partnerships. The market values of syndicated partnership interests should not be presented as though they represent the assembled ownership of real property assets.

Key Concepts

- Property rights may be identified in terms of ownership, legal estates, economic benefits, and financial interests.
- Ownership may be held in fee simple or leased fee.
- Leases specify the rights of the lessor (e.g., to collect rent, to repossess the property upon lease expiration, to dispose of the property through sale or transfer) and the rights of the lessee (e.g., to use, occupy, improve, and sublease the property).
- Various tenancy arrangements apply to property ownership by two or more persons.
- Leases are classified as gross, modified gross, and net depending on whether the landlord or tenant pays the operating expenses and taxes.

- The market value of a leased fee interest depends on how contract rent compares to market rent. A leasehold interest may acquire value if the lease allows for subletting and the term is of a marketable duration.

- Partial or fractional interests also include vertical interests (e.g., subsurface or air rights), easements (e.g., conservation or preservation easements), transferable development rights (TDRs), and interests resulting from specialized forms of ownership (condominiums, cooperatives, timesharing).

- Partial interests in legal entities that own real property are created through stock corporations, land trusts, general and limited partnerships, limited liability companies, and equity syndications.

Terms

air rights
book value
condominium
conservation easement
contract rent
cooperative
easements
easements in gross
equity
equity syndication
fee simple
fractional interest
general partnership
gross lease
joint tenancy
land trust
leased fee
leasehold
leasehold mortgaging
lessee
lessor

life estate
limited liability company
limited partnership
market rent
modified gross lease
mortgage
net lease
partial interest
partnership
preservation easement
sandwich lease
stock corporation
sublease
subsurface rights
tenancy
tenancy by entirety
tenancy in common
timesharing
transferable development rights
(TDRs)
trust

CHAPTER EIGHT

Data Collection and Analysis

T he identification of property interests and other investigations that help define the appraisal problem provide direction for the collection of useful data. Appraisers need patience, judgment, and research skills to direct the preliminary steps of data collection and analysis and to gather and manage information. In real estate appraisal the quality and quantity of information available for analysis are as important as the methods and techniques used to process the data and complete the assignment. Therefore, the ability to distinguish between different kinds of data, to research reliable data sources, and to manage information efficiently is essential to appraisal practice.

General Data

General data consist of information on the social, economic, governmental, and environmental forces that affect property value. This information is part of the accumulated knowledge that appraisers bring to their assignments. All general data are ultimately understood in terms of how they affect the economic climate in which real property transactions occur. In analyzing general data, appraisers observe the operation of appraisal principles by studying the interaction of the four forces that affect property values in an area. Although the four forces provide convenient categories for examining general data, it is their interaction that creates trends and ultimately influences property value.

Economic Trends

The related series of events that comprise a trend are studied and used as historical evidence to support forecasts. Forecasting is an art that employs scientific processes to identify or quantify future events or conditions. Forecasts are developed by analyzing statistical data, examining the perceptions and behavior of market participants, and scrutinizing all assumptions upon which the forecast rests. The application of critical judgment is fundamental to forecasting. In making forecasts appraisers try to discern and consider all pertinent factors affecting future conditions. Appraisers cannot predict the future, but they are able to develop probable forecasts by observing past and current market trends and examining the perceptions of market participants. To forecast market conditions, appraisers scrutinize the likelihood that current trends will continue and that the events anticipated by market players will occur.

Appraisers must recognize and understand the economic trends that affect the value of real property. It is not enough to know that economic changes have occurred; the probable direction, extent, and impact of these changes must also be studied to identify and forecast trends.

The particular trends considered by an appraiser vary with the appraisal problem and the type of real estate being appraised. To estimate the market value of a shopping center with the income capitalization approach to value, for example, the base rent and overage rent under a percentage lease must be forecast.[1] The shopping center's total potential gross income depends on trends in the number of households in the trade area, the income of these households, and their typical expenditures on the goods and services supplied by the center; the availability of alternative shopping facilities also must be considered.

International Economic Trends

In the world economy, the economic well-being of one nation may directly and indirectly affect many other nations. There is much foreign investment in U.S. real estate, partly because land prices are relatively low and the stability of the U.S. government gives foreign investors some measure of protection. Thus, inflation and political instability in other countries influence the demand for, and value of, real estate in the United States.

The greater the intensity and duration of an economic trend, the wider its influence. Changes in basic national and international economic indicators, such as the balance of foreign trade, rates of foreign exchange, commodity price levels, wage levels, interest rates, industrial production levels, and the volume of retail sales, all merit consideration.

National and Regional Economic Trends

The state of the national economy is basic to any real estate appraisal. National economic conditions are indicated by the gross national product, gross domestic product, national income, the balance of payments to other nations, price level indexes, interest rates, aggregate employment and unemployment statistics, the number of housing starts and building permits issued, the dollar volume of construction, and other general data. A time series of economic indicators, which describes and measures changes or movements over a period of time, may reveal fluctuations in long-term trends and help put current statistics in perspective. Financial institutions must compete for funds to lend not only with one another, but also with money market mutual funds. Lending rates reflect this ongoing competition, and demand in the market adjusts itself accordingly.

Federal programs and tax policies can affect the value of real estate. One example is the investment tax credits available for the rehabilitation of older, nonresidential real estate and for historic preservation projects. These credits enhance the profitability of these properties and, ultimately, affect their value. Another example of how federal tax policy affects property value is the 1981 Economic Recovery Tax Act, which permitted use of an accelerated cost recovery system (ACRS) for buildings held to produce income or used in one's trade or business. Under ACRS, the cost of depreciable assets was recovered at prescribed rates over a predetermined recovery period, which was usually shorter than the asset's useful life. The Tax Reform Act of 1986 introduced a modified accelerated cost recovery system (MACRS) for properties placed in service after 1986. Under MACRS, the cost of depreciable assets is recovered over a predetermined recovery

---

1. See Chapter 21 for the definitions of *percentage lease, base rent* and *overage rent*.

period (generally longer than that specified under ACRS) using the depreciation method prescribed for the class of property.[2]

The national economy also reflects the economic condition of the various geographic regions of the United States. A region's economic health depends on the status of its economic activity, which in turn encompasses the economic activities in individual areas and communities within the region's geographical boundaries. Minor disruptions in the economic growth of one community may not appreciably affect the entire region if the regional and national economies are strong.

The extent to which an appraiser is concerned with the national or regional economy and the economy of the city or neighborhood depends on the size and type of property being appraised. For example, a large regional shopping center that serves a trade area of 500,000 people and an automobile assembly plant that employs 5,000 workers are more sensitive to the general state of the economy than are medical-dental office buildings or retail service operations in suburban residential areas.

Local Economic Trends

Analysis of a local economy often focuses on trends in population, employment, and income. Population change, net household formation, the diversity of the economic base of the community, the level and stability of employment, wage rates, and household or family income all indicate the economic strength of a community.

The conditions and potential of the local economy are relevant to most appraisal assignments. The value of real estate in a community is influenced by the demand for its use. The demand for various types of real estate, including vacant land, depends on the population of the market that the real estate serves, the effective purchasing power of this population, and their desire to own real estate. Demand may change for various types of real estate and between real estate and nonrealty investment sources.

Employment and economic base analysis. The population and income in a region or a community depend on the employment that constitutes the economic base of the area. *The economic base is the economic activity of a community that enables it to attract income from outside its borders.* The ability to attract income gives a community an advantage over other communities and makes it relatively more successful in providing products or services.[3] The advantage enjoyed by a community may be due to its proximity to commodity markets, the presence of natural resources, the availability of a trained work force, the climate, or a government decree that establishes the community as a county seat or state capital. As a result of this advantage, most of the community's work force may be engaged in specialized activities such as the production of durable goods or assembly and distribution.

---

2. The depreciation of residential rental property is determined by applying the straight-line method over 27.5 years; for nonresidential real property, the straight-line method is applied over 31.5 years. For properties placed in service after 1981 but prior to 1987, depreciation is determined using the accelerated cost recovery system; for properties placed in service before 1981, the Tax Reform Act prescribes the same method used in the past.

3. For further discussion of economic base analysis and the significance of demographic change, see Anthony Downs, "Characteristics of Various Economic Studies," and Jerome Dasso, "Economic Base Analysis for the Appraiser," in *Readings in Market Research for Real Estate* (Chicago: American Institute of Real Estate Appraisers, 1985). See also Stephen F. Fanning, MAI, Terry V. Grissom, MAI, PhD, and Thomas D. Pearson, MAI, PhD, *Market Analysis for Valuation Appraisals* (Chicago: Appraisal Institute, 1994), Chapter 6, and Morton J. Schussheim, "The Impact of Demographic Change on Housing and Community Development," *The Appraisal Journal* (July 1984).

The nature of employment in a community or region can affect population growth, the level and stability of income, the willingness of the population to spend disposable income, and the risk associated with investments in the area. These characteristics affect the demand for, and value of, all types of real estate. A community that has a diversified economic base with various types of employment is more attractive to investors than a single-industry town. The stability offered by a diversified local economy can reduce the risk of real estate investment and increase property values.

City origins and growth patterns. Appraisers of urban and suburban property recognize that growth and change in a community can affect neighborhoods, districts, and other areas differently. An appraiser must understand the factors that contribute to urban and suburban growth patterns to analyze the neighborhood or district where the subject property is located and to determine how the area affects the quantity, quality, and duration of the property's future income stream or the amenities that create value.

The structure of land uses in an urban community usually reflects the origin of the settlement to some extent; this is known as the *siting factor*. Some U.S. cities were established at transportation centers such as seaports, river crossings, or the intersection of trade routes. Other cities were founded near power sources useful to manufacturing, and still others were located for defensive, commercial, or political reasons. As the national standard of living improved, climate and other natural advantages became siting factors responsible for the development of retirement areas, recreational resorts, and other specialized communities. From its initial site, a community grows outward in a pattern dictated by the nature and availability of developable land, the evolution of technology, and the government's ability and willingness to provide essential public services.[4]

Communities such as New York and San Francisco, where land is scarce, experience an increase in the density of land use. Development corridors channel new construction to usable land. New technology, building materials, and construction methods make it possible to construct high-rise buildings in cities without bedrock and those subject to earth tremors.

Transportation improvements and the proliferation of automobiles have also shaped modern cities. Improved transportation allows urban settlements to grow in size and serve larger markets. The pattern of city growth is influenced by the local transportation network. Growth usually radiates from the central business district along major transportation routes; great dispersion is created by major freeway systems.

Trends Affecting Rural Land

Appraisers of rural land should understand the links between the local rural economy, the regional economic base (agricultural, extractive, or recreational), and the national economy. The appraiser should identify trends within the specific sector of economic activity, e.g., the size and complexity of business operations in farming, ranching, timber-

---

4. Various conceptual models of urban growth are used to describe land use patterns. These "social ecology" models include the concentric zone theory, the sector (wedge) theory, the multiple nuclei theory, and the radial (axial) corridor theory. For a more complete discussion of urban growth patterns, see W. B. Martin, "How to Predict Urban Growth Patterns," *The Appraisal Journal* (April 1984). See also Stephen F. Fanning, MAI, Terry V. Grissom, MAI, PhD, and Thomas D. Pearson, MAI, PhD, *Market Analysis for Valuation Appraisals* (Chicago: Appraisal Institute, 1994), Chapter 5.

harvesting, drilling, or mining; the level of mechanization and/or labor-intensiveness; the degree of dependence on government subsidies and/or government-leased lands; and prospective competition from imports. The subject property should be analyzed in relation to comparable properties in the immediate agricultural, mining/drilling, or recreational district.

Local Market Considerations

To understand how national and even international economic trends influence property value, an appraiser studies how the region and community where the subject property is located may respond to these trends. The appraiser should examine the economic structure of the region and the community, the comparative advantages that each possesses, and the attitudes of local government and residents toward growth and change. For example, the increasing number of elderly households in the nation is less significant to property values in Minnesota than to values in Sunbelt states, which attract more retirees. A community with a no-growth policy may have substantially different local demographics and economic potential than one that does not discourage growth.

Regional economics have an influence on local market conditions, but local markets do not necessarily parallel regional markets. Macroeconomic studies, which are concerned with broad areas such as cities and regions, are important to an understanding of real estate and real estate trends. These studies should not be confused with microeconomic studies, which appraisers perform to evaluate the factors influencing the market value of a particular real estate parcel. For example, regional trends may suggest an expected increase in population, but the local data available to the appraiser indicate that the particular area will not benefit from this trend. While both studies are important, local trends are more likely to influence property values directly.

Demographics

The population and its geographic distribution are basic determinants of the need for real estate. Households must have shelter, and the production and distribution of goods and services require plants, stores, hotels, hospitals, warehouses, and offices. An appraiser should be aware of the potential for change in the aggregate population and in the demographic attributes of the population that constitutes the market for the subject property. Population growth is affected by birth rates, death rates, and migration. In turn, these determinants of aggregate population reflect the rate of household formation, the age distribution of households, the state of medical technology, the standard of living, social mores, and the regulations imposed on immigration.

Aggregate population growth is distributed among regions in response to changing economic opportunities. In the past people migrated from the South to the North and Northeast, from rural areas to urban areas. During the 1970s an economic boom in the Sunbelt reversed this movement and people migrated from North to South. Recent economic recovery in the North has slowed the southward migration. The migration from urban to suburban areas has also slowed due to transportation costs and the expense of providing municipal services and utilities to outlying areas. As a result, the demand for housing in older urban neighborhoods is increasing in some cities.

Real estate improvements are provided in response to the demand generated by a population with effective purchasing power. *A household—i.e., persons who occupy a group of rooms or a single room that constitutes one housing unit*—imposes a basic demand for housing units. With sufficient income and a desire for property ownership, households transform their needs into effective demand. In analyzing a local housing market, a knowledge of trends in the formation of households and household characteristics is crucial. The age, size, income, and other characteristics of households must be considered to determine the demand for housing.

The demand for commercial and industrial real estate is created by a population's demand for the goods and services to be produced or distributed at these sites. Appraisers must be aware of changes in the characteristics and distribution of the population that consumes goods and services as well as changes in the work force that produces them. A changing population coupled with technological advances can rapidly alter the demand for the services provided by property, which can affect property value.

Government Regulations and Social Attitudes

General data include information about social attitudes and the government regulations and activities that reflect these attitudes. In response to social attitudes, the government establishes land use regulations and provides public services such as transportation systems and municipal utilities. Appraisers accumulate information on zoning, master plans, environmental impacts, transportation systems, local annexation policies, and other regulations that reveal governmental and social attitudes toward real estate.

Local zoning ordinances regulate land use and the density of development. In some areas retroactive zoning is employed to remove nonconforming uses gradually, giving owners time to alter property use. Zoning also can be used to preserve the architectural character of an area. With varying degrees of success, communities regulate zoning to halt or slow growth. To encourage new development, they may expand capital improvement programs and construct sewage treatment facilities, fire stations, streets, and public recreational facilities.

Zoning may also be used to enforce a community's land use plan or comprehensive plan, which is usually based on economic growth projections and may be modified for political reasons. The appraiser should be aware of the assumptions on which the land use plan is based and of the potential for revision. The appraiser must consider the date that the plan was adopted and its projection term. Land use plans are typically projected 5 to 10 years into the future. The more recently the land use plan was adopted, the more meaningful it will be.

Environmental concerns have prompted increased regulation of land development at state and local levels. Zoning ordinances and building codes have long imposed additional costs on developers. To preserve the quality of the environment, developers are required to consider the impact of large developments on the ecology of a particular area and on the larger environmental system. They may be required to improve public roads, construct sewage treatment facilities, preserve natural terrain, or take other actions to conform to the recommendations of local, regional, or state planning agencies. These regulations can add significantly to the time required to complete a development and increase its final cost. The value of subdivision land is obviously influenced by environmental regulations, which can affect the amount of time required to develop and sell the sites.

The creation or modification of a transportation system is a government action based on an analysis of the direct and indirect impact of the system on users and nonusers. An improvement in the transportation system can affect the accessibility of a site and, thus, its value. Improved transportation routes often cause new areas to be developed, which affects the value of other sites that must compete with the increased supply. To a great extent, the suburbanization of an urban population results from improvements in highways, commuter railroads, and bus routes.

The movement of commercial and retail enterprises between downtown areas and the suburbs has changed real estate markets and placed new emphasis on zoning systems, the administration of local government, and public expenditures. The highway system has opened certain regions to development and has increased their comparative advantage by decreasing the cost of transporting products to markets.

A municipality's willingness to annex and provide public services to outlying areas can affect the direction and amount of development. Conversely, sewer moratoriums have been used effectively to control local growth. This type of restriction can increase the value of developments that are already in place if demand is pressing on a limited supply.

In short, to estimate value properly, the appraiser should understand the government regulations and actions that affect the subject property. The comparable properties selected for analysis should be similar to the subject property in terms of zoning, accessibility, and other characteristics.

Purchasing Power

Households obtain personal income from wages and salaries, yields on savings and other investments, profits from businesses, private and government pensions, and government transfer payments such as social security, unemployment compensation, and farm subsidies. *Disposable income, the personal income that remains after deducting income taxes and all other payments to the government*, is either spent or saved. The amount of disposable income spent on goods and services indirectly determines the demand for properties such as shopping centers, industrial plants, office buildings, and warehouses.

Price Levels

Price level changes influence the quantity of goods and services that can be purchased. Nominal prices that have been adjusted for changes in the price level are called "real" prices. The sale prices, rents, operating expenses, construction costs, and interest rates used to estimate market value are typically expressed in nominal dollars, unadjusted for price level changes; the appraiser's final value estimate is also reported in nominal dollars.

Investments vary in their ability to retain real or constant value in inflationary periods. Owners of income-producing real estate often attempt to keep the real value of their property constant by including escalator clauses in leases. These clauses allow rents to be adjusted in accordance with an inflation index so that the tenant pays for increases in operating expenses.

Many lenders are unwilling to accept the risk of changing price levels and look for protection against that portion of inflation that may not be fully reflected in the mortgage interest rate. Many institutions making loans on income-producing property continue to ask for equity participation in the property's income and for a mortgage interest rate that includes a premium for anticipated inflation. Other lenders may use a floating rate tied to the prime rate or some other economic indicator. These loan provisions affect the net operating income and before-tax cash flows of properties and, therefore, the value indications derived using the income capitalization approach.

Building Fluctuations

Housing starts and the construction of commercial and industrial properties fluctuate in response to business cycles, political events, and the cost and availability of financing. These fluctuations follow the long-term trend of new construction, which has been moving upward. Short-term fluctuations result in temporary misallocations of supply, which can depress rents and prices.

The standing stock of housing units at any point in time consists of all units occupied by households as well as those that are vacant. The stock is continually altered by the construction or conversion of units in response to developers' perceptions of the demand for new housing and by the need to replace existing units.

Six months to two years may pass between the time a developer decides to supply units and the time they enter the market. During this period, changing conditions may reduce demand, and the units coming on the market may remain unrented and unsold, thus increasing vacancy rates. Developers may continue to produce additional units for some time, even in the face of rising vacancies. Once these excess units are produced, they remain on the market and can depress rents or prices until demand increases to remove the surplus. When the market tightens, the supply of units lags behind the increase in demand, resulting in abnormally low vacancy rates and upward pressure on rents and prices. Ultimately, supply materializes as developers respond to increased demand.

Fluctuations in the local supply of and demand for real estate are influenced by regional and national conditions. Therefore, an appraiser looks for regional and national trends that may indicate a positive or negative change in property values at the local level. Although all regions may not experience the same slump in construction, tight monetary policy affects the cost and availability of mortgage credit and exerts a moderating influence on supply, even in a rapidly growing region.

Commercial real estate is affected by business conditions and the cost and availability of financing. Because business firms pass their high financing costs on to consumers, residential construction may be restricted. If the demand for the goods and services produced or supplied by a business remains strong, the firm can raise prices and continue to expand even when credit is tight and interest rates are high.

The appraiser must recognize that a property's value as of a specific date may rise or fall due to fluctuations in building activity. Because market value is influenced by the balance of supply and demand at the time of the appraisal, the appraiser should make certain that the client understands the economic conditions that affect the subject property's value at a specific time.

Building Costs

The cost of replacing a building tends to follow the general price levels established over a long period, but these price levels vary from time to time and from place to place. Building costs generally decline or stabilize in periods of deflation and increase in periods of inflation. These costs are affected by material and labor costs, construction technology, architect and legal fees, financing costs, building codes, and public regulations such as zoning ordinances, environmental requirements, and subdivision regulations.

The cost of construction can alter the quantity and character of demand and, therefore, the relative prices of property in real estate submarkets. The high cost of new buildings increases the demand for, and prices of, existing structures. When the cost of new structures increases, rehabilitation of existing buildings may become economically feasible. High building costs increase prices in single-family residential submarkets, which can increase the demand for rental units and their prices. The size and quality of the dwelling units demanded decrease when building costs increase more rapidly than purchasing power.

Taxes

Real estate taxes are levied by both municipalities (cities, townships, or counties) and school districts. The taxing body reviews the annual budget to determine the amount that needs to be raised. The balance remaining after revenues from other sources (e.g., sales or income taxes, state or federal revenue sharing, interest on investments) are deducted must come from property taxes. Assessing officers generally estimate the value of each parcel of real estate in the jurisdiction periodically. Real estate taxes are based on the assessed value of real property, hence the term *ad valorem* (according to value) taxes. The assessed value of property is normally based on, but not necessarily equivalent to, its market value.

If, for example, the tax rate is $60 per $1,000 of assessed value and the assessed value is 50% of market value, then the annual real estate tax equals 3% of market value.

$$\frac{\$60}{\$1,000} \text{ x } 50\% = 3\%$$

If assessed value is not consistent with market value, the formula is modified to reflect the inconsistency. The ratio of assessed value to market value is called the *common level ratio or assessment ratio*.

Often, both a general tax and a school tax are levied on property. For example, a jurisdiction which assesses property at 40% of its market value may have a general tax rate of $50 per $1,000 of assessed value and a school tax rate of $62.50 per $1,000 of assessed value. If the market value of a property is $120,000, its assessed value would be $48,000 ($120,000 x 0.40), the general taxes to be paid on the property would be $2,400 (48 x $50.00), and the school taxes to be paid would be $3,000 (48 x $62.50).

A tax rate can also be expressed as a mill rate. A mill is $0.001, or one-tenth of one cent. A 5% rate is equivalent to $50.00 per $1,000 of assessed value, $5.00 per $100, or 50 mills. For example, consider a municipality which assesses at 75% of market value, has a general tax rate of 21 mills, and a school tax rate of 19 mills. If the market value of a property is $450,000, its assessed value is $337,500 ($450,000 x 0.75), the general taxes to be paid on the property are $7,087.50 ($337,500 x 0.021), and the school taxes to be paid are $6,412.50 ($337,500 x 0.019).   An effective tax rate is calculated by dividing the total amount of taxes by the market value of the property. Thus, the effective tax rate for the property in the first example with a market value of $120,000 and taxes of $5,400 ($2,400+$3,000) is 4.5% ($5,400/$120,000). The effective tax rate for the $450,000 property with taxes of $13,500 ($7,087.50+6,412.50) is 3% ($13,500/$450,000). Effective tax rates can be used to compare the tax burden on properties.

In jurisdictions where ad valorem real estate tax assessments have an established or implied relationship to market value, appraisal services may be required to resolve tax appeals. In some communities, the trend in real estate taxes is an important consideration. In cities where public expenditures for schools and municipal services have increased, the heavy burden of taxes can affect real estate values adversely. Under these circumstances, new construction may be discouraged. There may be several tax districts in a metropolitan area, each with a different policy. Understanding the system of ad valorem taxation in an area facilitates the appraiser's analysis of how taxes affect value.

Although income taxes are not usually treated as an expense in appraisal calculations, they can influence property value. Currently homeowners can deduct mortgage interest and property taxes when they itemize deductions on their income tax return. This tax benefit influences the overall price level of single-family residences and condominiums.

Different levels of sales taxes and taxes on earnings can also affect the relative desirability of properties. Although these taxes may be uniform within a state, properties in different states often compete with one another. To attract new residents and industries, a state may impose taxes that are lower than those of surrounding states. This may increase demand and enhance property values in the state relative to values in bordering states.

Financing

Because the cost and availability of financing help to determine the demand for, and supply of, real estate, financing affects real estate values. The cost of financing includes the rate of interest on the mortgage instrument, deed of trust, or installment contract as well as any points, discounts, equity participations, or other charges that the lender requires to increase the effective yield on the loan. Financing depends on the borrower's ability to qualify for a loan, which may be determined based on the loan-to-value ratio, the housing expense-to-income ratio required for loans on single-family homes, and the debt coverage and breakeven ratios required for loans on income-producing properties. (These ratios are discussed in Chapter 22.) The cost and availability of financing typically have an inverse relationship; high interest rates and other costs usually are accompanied by a decrease in the availability of credit.

The cost and availability of credit for real estate financing influence both the quantity and quality of the real estate demanded and supplied. When interest rates are high and mortgage funds are limited, households that would have been in the home ownership market find that their incomes cannot support the required expenses. Purchases are delayed and smaller homes with fewer amenities are bought. The cost of land development financing and construction financing is reflected in the higher prices asked for new single-family homes, which result in a further reduction in the quantity demanded.

The rental market is affected by the demand pressure of households that continue to rent and by the high cost of supplying new units, which results in part from financing costs. Occupancy rates and rents rise. Businesses try to pass on their higher occupancy costs to customers by increasing the prices of their products or services. If they cannot fully recover the increased occupancy cost, the quantity of commercial and individual space demanded is reduced.

Sources of General Data

The general data needed to appraise real property are available from a wide variety of sources. A substantial amount of information is compiled and disseminated by federal, state, and local agencies; trade associations and private business enterprises may also provide data.

The largest body of national, regional, and city data comes from the federal government. The *Economic Report of the President*, published by the Council of Economic Advisors, includes data and analysis of housing starts and financing. *Economic Indicators* is a monthly publication prepared by the Council of Economic Advisors for the Joint Economic Committee. The *Federal Reserve Bulletin* and *Historical Chart Book*, which are published by the Federal Reserve Board, contain information on the gross national product, the gross domestic product, national income, mortgage markets, interest rates, and other financial statistics; installment credit; sources of funds; business activity; the labor force, employment, and industrial production; housing and construction; and international finance. The National Office of Vital Statistics compiles and disseminates statistics on birth and death rates.

The U.S. Department of Commerce, Bureau of the Census, publishes the *Census of Population,* the *Census of Housing*, the *Census of Manufacturers*, the *Census of Agriculture*, the *Annual Housing Survey*, and the *Statistical Abstract of the United States*, as well as various series on current population, population estimates, and population projections; consumer income; and housing completions, housing permits, and other housing statistics. These publications provide detailed information on population and housing characteristics for the nation, states, counties, metropolitan statistical areas (MSAs), municipalities, census tracts, and blocks in metropolitan areas. Interim reports on selected population, income, and housing data are also published by the Bureau of the Census. (See Chapter 9, footnote 1, for source references pertaining to the use of census data and other information in neighborhood and district analysis.)

The U.S. Department of Commerce, Bureau of Economic Analysis, publishes the *Survey of Current Business*. This is a source for data on the Consumer Price Index, the wholesale price index, mortgage debt, and the value of new construction. The U.S. Department of Housing and Urban Development issues reports on FHA building starts, financing, and housing programs administered by the department. It also disseminates FHA vacancy surveys for selected metropolitan areas. The U.S. Department of Labor, Bureau of Labor Statistics, publishes the *Monthly Labor Review,* which contains the Consumer Price Index, wholesale prices, and monthly and annual employment and earnings figures.

At state and local levels, departments of development, local and regional planning agencies, and regional or metropolitan transportation authorities can provide appraisers with data on population, households, employment, master plans, present and future utility, and transportation systems. Often such agencies publish directories of manufacturers that list, by county, the names of firms, their products, and their employment figures.

A state bureau of employment service can provide county data on employment, unemployment, and wage rates. Chambers of commerce offer a variety of information on local population, households, employment, and industry, which they often obtain from other secondary sources such as the census.

Trade associations can also be very useful sources. The National Association of Realtors[R] compiles information on existing home sales for the nation as a whole and for individual regions. The national association and its affiliates put out many publications with data useful to appraisers. The National Association of Homebuilders disseminates information on new housing starts as well as prices, construction costs, and financing. *Sales and Marketing Management Magazine, Survey of Buying Power* contains information on households, income distribution, and retail sales by county and for selected cities.

Other meaningful data can be gathered from private sources such as banks, utility companies, university research centers, private advisory firms, multiple listing services, and cost services such as E. H. Boeckh and Marshall Valuation Service. These sources offer a variety of information on bank debt, department store sales, employment indicators, land prices, corporate business indicators, mortgage money costs, wage rates, construction costs, deeds, mortgage recordings, and the installation of utility meters.

In recent years many databases have been developed for on-line access to information. Large databases are also accessible to small computers through CD-ROM technology. Such databases cover a broad range of topics and offer many options to appraisers performing general or specialized research. The information available is virtually unlimited and includes topics such as current and historical news; industry analyses and reports; corporate earnings and analyses; local, regional, and national Yellow Page listings; and publication indexes and articles.

General data are an integral part of an appraiser's office files. Data obtained from various sources can be catalogued and cross-indexed. General data such as multiple listing information and census data can be stored and accessed by computer. Many local and regional planning and development agencies computerize information on housing inventory and vacancies, demolitions and conversions, commercial construction, household incomes, new land use by zoning classification, population and demographics, and housing forecasts by geographic area.

Recent developments in computer software and hardware have resulted in low-cost, high-performance databasing combinations for appraisers. Hundreds of individual programs are now used with desktop systems in appraisal offices. Some databases are contained in a single computer, while others are shared by several computers or terminals through local or telecommunication networks. Improvements in telecommunication programs and facilities, word processing, and electronic spreadsheets have facilitated appraisal analysis and report writing, as well as the use of database information.[5]

Specific Data

Specific data include details about the property being appraised, comparable sales and rental properties, and relevant local market characteristics. In appraisals these data are used to determine highest and best use and to make the specific comparisons and analyses required to estimate market value. The specific data about a subject property provided in land and building descriptions help the appraiser select comparable specific data pertaining to sales, rentals, construction costs, and local market characteristics.

In analyzing general data, national, regional, and local trends in value are emphasized; in an analysis of specific data, the characteristics of the subject property and comparable properties are studied. From relevant comparable sales, an appraiser extracts specific sale prices, rental terms, income and expense figures, rates of return on investment, construction costs, the expected economic life of improvements, and rates of depreciation. These figures are used in calculations that lead to an indication of value for the subject property.

An appraiser needs specific data to apply each of the three approaches to value. The appraiser uses the data to derive adjustments for value-influencing property characteristics, to isolate meaningful units of comparison, to develop capitalization rates, and to measure accrued depreciation. By extracting relevant data from the large quantity of data available, an appraiser develops a sense of the market. This perception is an essential component of appraisal judgment, which is applied in the valuation process and in the final reconciliation of value indications. The validity of a final estimate of market value depends to a great extent on how well it can be supported by market data.

Specific data are analyzed through comparison. In each approach to value, certain items of information must be extracted from market data to make comparisons. Specific data are studied to determine if these information items are present and if they can be used to make reliable comparisons with the subject property. If, for example, the subject property is an apartment building of three-bedroom units, the appraiser may be able to use data from sales of similar apartment buildings to make adjustments for the time of sale, the location, and physical property characteristics. The appraiser may also need to analyze data on competitive properties that have not been sold recently to obtain information on the rental rates and expenses for apartment buildings in the area.

---

5. For further information on databases and electronic commerce, see William B. Rayburn and Dennis S. Tosh, "Artificial Intelligence, the Future of Appraising," *The Appraisal Journal* (October 1995), 429-435; Paul Gilon and C.A. Cardenas, "Appraisers and Cyberspace: the Internet," *The Appraisal Journal* (October 1995), 469-481; and Jay T. Fitts, "Technology: Friend Not Foe," 1995 Appraisal Institute Symposium, "Retooling of a Profession."

The appraiser's analysis of the highest and best use of the land as though vacant and the property as improved determines what comparable specific data are collected and analyzed. The nature and amount of research needed for a specific assignment depend on the property type and the purpose of the appraisal. The appraiser should gather all available data that may be pertinent to the assignment, organize the data, and perform a preliminary analysis before applying any analytical techniques.

Investigation of Market Transactions

A detailed description and classification of the characteristics and components of a property are assembled in land and building analyses. From these analyses the appraiser selects and analyzes data in the sales comparison, cost, and income capitalization approaches. The data used for comparison in the three approaches should be derived from properties that are similar to the property being appraised. To use sales as a valid basis for further analysis, the appraiser inventories the relevant characteristics and components of the properties selected as comparables.

To select comparable sale properties, the appraiser examines public records, published sources, office files, and information from buyers, sellers, and other knowledgeable persons. Interviews with property owners may reveal relevant sales that have not been recorded. Realtors®, salespeople, developers, and other appraisers are also good sources of sales and rental data. The selection of comparables is directed to some extent by the availability and scope of the data. Investigation of an active market usually reveals an adequate and representative number of transactions within a restricted area and time period.

The geographic area from which comparable sales can be selected depends on the property type. In valuing certain types of retail property, only properties with main street frontage may be pertinent. For many large industrial properties and most investment properties, the entire community should be studied; for larger properties, the national market may be relevant. For a residential appraisal, adequate data can sometimes be found within a block of the subject property. Even in these cases, however, the appraiser should consider the broader market to place the subject property and the comparables in a general market context.

In selecting market data for analysis, an appraiser focuses on transactions pertinent to the subject property's specific market. In general, comparable properties fall into two categories. The first and preferred category includes those that are comparable to and competitive with the property being appraised or have a demonstrable effect on prices or other relevant components of the market in question. The second category includes those that are comparable to, but not competitive with, the subject. With computer analysis, a large number of properties can be studied in the course of a single assignment, which may generate a deeper understanding of each property's contribution to, and influence on, a given market.

Appraisers seek data that will facilitate accurate comparisons, but because every real estate parcel is unique, absolute comparability is impossible. The comparability of properties varies, and the appraiser may find it necessary to place less confidence on a given comparable. Nevertheless, the appraiser may still want to consider this comparable for its evidence of, and effect on, the marketplace.

Appraisers have a special responsibility to scrutinize the comparability of all data used in a valuation assignment. They must fully understand the concept of comparability and should avoid comparing properties with different highest and best uses, limiting their search for comparables, or selecting inappropriate factors for comparison.

The first determinant of useful data is their degree of comparability. A second determinant is the quantity of information available, and a third, but equally important, factor is the authenticity and reliability of the data. An appraiser must not assume that all data pertinent to an assignment are completely reliable. Sales figures, costs, and other information subject to misrepresentation should be scrutinized for authenticity.

When comparable sales data are scarce in the subject property's immediate area, the appraiser may need to extend the data search to adjacent neighborhoods and similar communities. When the selection of data is limited to an unacceptably narrow sample of current market activity, the appraiser may decide to use sales that are less current or to interview brokers, buyers, sellers, owners, and tenants of similar properties in the area to obtain evidence of potential market activity such as listing prices or offers to purchase. Listings, which represent the owner's perception of the value of the property, usually reflect the upper limit of value; offers, which represent the buyer's perception, commonly set the lower limit of value. Listings and offers may be analyzed for comparability, but are not generally adjusted.

An appraiser gathers broad information about a market from its pattern of sales. Important market characteristics can be revealed by significant factors such as the:

- Number of sales
- Period of time covered by the sales
- Availability of property for sale
- Rate of absorption
- Rate of turnover (i.e., volume of sales and level of activity)
- Characteristics and motivations of buyers and sellers
- Terms and conditions of sale
- Use of property before and after its sale

While analyzing data to select comparable sales, an appraiser begins to form certain conclusions about the general market, the subject property, and the possible relationships between the data and the subject property. The appraiser ascertains market strengths and weaknesses; the probable supply of, demand for, and marketability of properties similar to the property being appraised; and the variations and characteristics that are likely to have the greatest impact on the value of properties in the market. Thus, an appraiser analyzes data against a background of information about the particular area and the specific type of property.

The information needed to apply the cost and income capitalization approaches must often be obtained from market sources other than sales. This information may also be used to refine adjustments made in the sales comparison approach. In the investigation of general and neighborhood data, an appraiser learns about trends in construction costs, lease terms, typical expenses, and vacancy rates. Examining trends in the market where the subject property is located provides additional specific data that can be used to derive value indications and successfully complete evaluation assignments.

Sources of Specific Data

Like sources of general data, sources of specific data are diverse. In addition to the data obtained from public records and published sources, personal contact with developers, builders, Realtors®, financial and legal specialists, property managers, local planners, and other real estate professionals can provide useful information. Thus, practicing appraisers need communication skills as well as analytical techniques to research sales, improvement costs, and income and expense data thoroughly and complete appraisal assignments.

Sources of sales data include public records; published news; Realtors®, appraisers, managers, and bankers; multiple listing books; listings and offers; and other local sources.

Public records. The appraiser searches public records for a copy of the property deed. The deed provides important information about the property and the sales transaction, including the full names of the parties involved and the transaction date. A legal description of the property, the property rights included in the transaction, and any outstanding liens on the title are indicated.

Occasionally the names of the parties may suggest that unusual motivations were involved in the sale. For example, a sale from John Smith to Mary Smith Jones may be a transfer from a father to a daughter; a sale from John Smith, William Jones, and Harold Long to the SJL Corporation may be a change of ownership in name only, not an arm's-length transaction arrived at by unrelated parties under no duress.

In some states the law requires that the consideration paid upon transfer of title be shown on the deed. However, this consideration does not always reflect the actual sale price. To reduce transfer taxes, some purchasers (e.g., buyers of motels or apartments) deduct the estimated value of personal property from the true consideration paid. Because these personal property values are sometimes inflated, the recorded consideration for the real property may be less than the true consideration. In one case, the consideration indicated on the deed may be overstated to obtain a higher loan than is warranted; in another, the consideration may be understated to justify a low property tax assessment. Although some states require that the true and actual consideration be listed on the deed, other states allow the consideration to be reported as "$10 and other valuable consideration."

The local tax assessor's records may include property cards for the subject property and comparables properties, with land and building sketches, area measurements, sale prices, and other information. In some locations, legal or private publishing services issue information about revenue stamps and other facts pertaining to current property transfers.

Published news. Most city newspapers feature real estate news. Although some of the news may be incomplete or inaccurate, an appraiser can use it to confirm details because the names of the negotiating brokers and the parties to a transaction are usually published.

Realtors®, appraisers, managers, and bankers. Other real estate professionals can often provide information about transactions and suggest valuable leads. Individual sources may be definitive, but if the information obtained from real estate professionals is third-party data, the appraiser should look for separate verification.

Multiple listing services. In many communities multiple listing services (MLS) publish books and maintain electronic databases. These sources primarily contain data on residential properties listed for sale during the calendar year or fiscal quarter and cite their listing prices. They contain fairly complete information about these properties, including descriptions and brokers' names. However, details about a property's square footage, basement area, or exact age may be inaccurate or excluded. In certain areas, multiple listing books or access to electronic databases can be purchased. Multiple listing services sometimes publish the sale prices of properties that have been sold. Only a small percentage of commercial, industrial, or special-purpose properties are included in MLS books.

Listings and offers. Whenever possible, an appraiser should gather information on listings of properties offered for sale. An appraiser can request that his or her name be added to the mailing lists of banks, brokers, and others who offer properties for sale. Classified ads of properties offered for sale suggest the strength or weakness of the local market for a particular type of property and the sales activity in a particular area. Information on offers to purchase may also be obtained from brokers or managers. Listings are generally higher than actual transaction prices; offers are generally somewhat lower.

Electronic data interchange (EDI). Electronic data interchange (EDI) is the electronic exchange of information between entities using standard, machine-processable, structured data formats. Efforts by various mortgage originators, insurers, and secondary mortgage market agencies to set up a computer-to-computer information exchange led to the creation of EDI in 1994.[6] Translation software for EDI enables individual computer users to electronically access a standardized database on residential properties created from EDI-formatted appraisals prepared on the Uniform Residential Appraisal Report (URAR). EDI was created to streamline the work of mortgage underwriters, reduce mortgage origination costs, and improve service to consumers.

As EDI technology reengineers the mortgage loan process, the lending industry has actively pursued the establishment of data standards for all mortgage market functions involving interaction among sellers, servicers, and investors in mortgages. Federal and secondary mortgage market agencies also have mandates to implement and standardize electronic information procurement.[7]

---

6. Among the 27 firms and organizations that participated in the National Property Data Service Work Group and helped coordinate EDI were the Mortgage Bankers Association, Fannie Mae, Freddie Mac, and the Appraisal Institute. The Data Interchange Standards Association (DISA) is responsible for ensuring that EDI meets acceptable standards for electronic data transmission. The Accredited Standards Committee X12 of the American National Standards Association has approved the transaction sets used to format appraisal reports for EDI.
7. W. Lee Minnerly, *Electronic Data Interchange (EDI) and the Appraisal Office* (Appraisal Institute: Chicago, 1995), 1-12.

The potential for misuse of such pooled data is a concern. Any attempt to reduce the appraisal process to the perfunctory application of statistical and regression analyses is a disservice to both consumers and lenders.

Improvement Cost Data

Useful construction cost data may be obtained from many sources. Contractors and suppliers of construction materials can provide cost information about recently constructed buildings that are similar to the subject property. Cost estimators may also be consulted for information on the costs involved in constructing building improvements. Appraisers should be aware that published cost estimates may or may not include indirect costs such as loan interest during construction. In an active market, cost information can also be obtained by interviewing local property owners who have recently added building or land improvements similar to those found on the subject property. If work contracts and accounting records of recently improved properties are available, they can provide significant details.

Cost estimates are made by assembling, cataloging, and analyzing data on actual building costs. Detailed costs should be divided into general categories such as residential construction or commercial building costs; separate figures should be provided for special finishes or equipment. Costs for individual structural components should also be researched and kept on file.

Several cost-estimating services publish manuals or maintain electronic databases that break down costs into square foot increments. Unit costs for building types usually start with a building of a certain size (i.e., a base area), which serves as a benchmark. Then additions or deductions are made to account for the actual number of square feet in the subject property. Data provided by cost estimating services can be used to confirm estimates developed from local cost data.

Cost manuals and electronic databases are updated periodically by including cost index tables that reflect changes in the cost of construction over a period of years. Cost indexes convert a known cost as of a past date into a current cost estimate. However, there are practical limitations in applying this procedure because, as the time span increases, the reliability of the current cost indication tends to decrease. Sometimes cost index tables can be used to adjust costs for different geographic areas.

The use of cost index tables can pose further problems because it may be difficult to ascertain which components are included in the original cost reported. Capital expenditures for improvements added after the original construction must be considered, and added improvements may affect the estimates of cost and accrued depreciation.

Some appraisers rely almost entirely on cost-estimating services; others maintain files of specific cost comparables similar to their files of sale comparables. These files may be based on information furnished by contract-reporting services. Contract-reporting services may indicate building areas or a general building description, the low bids, and the contract award. The appraiser can then obtain any missing information, such as the breakdown of office and warehouse space, and classify the building type for filing purposes. When cost comparable files are carefully developed and managed, they can supply authentic square-foot costs on buildings of all types for use in appraisal assignments.

Income and Expense Data

To derive pertinent income and expense data, an appraiser investigates comparable sales and rentals of competitive income-producing properties in the same market. For investment properties, current and recent incomes are reviewed and vacancy and collection losses and typical operating expenses are studied. Finally, data on the mortgage terms, or debt service, should be examined and refined by the appraiser to make forecasts of future incomes and expenses.

Published and electronic information on property values for several consecutive years can suggest the rate of appreciation or depreciation applicable to various property types. Interviews with owners and tenants in the area can provide lease and expense data. Lenders may be contacted for information on available terms of financing.

Appraisers try to obtain all income and expense data from the income properties used as comparables. These data are tabulated in a reconstructed operating statement and filed by property type. (See Chapter 21 for a suggested format for reconstructed operating statements.)

Like expense data, rental information is difficult to obtain. Therefore, appraisers should take every opportunity to add rents to their rental databases. Long-term leases are usually on public record. A separate county index that cites the parties to recorded leases and the volume and page where leases are recorded may also be available. Sometimes this information is listed with deeds and mortgages, but it is usually coded for easy identification. In certain cities, abstracts of recorded leases are printed by private publishing services. Classified ads may also provide rental information. Many appraisers periodically check advertised rentals and recorded rental information by property type or area. It is convenient to file rental data under the same classifications used for sales data.

Income and expense comparables should be filed chronologically and by property type so they can be retrieved easily and used to estimate the expenses for a similar type of property. Income and expense figures should be converted into units of comparison for analysis. For example, income may be reported in terms of rent per apartment unit, per room, per hospital bed, or per square foot. Income is usually stated in terms of dollars per unit or units over a specified time period. Expenses for insurance, taxes, painting, decorating, and other required maintenance can be expressed in the same units of comparison used for income, or they can be expressed as a percentage of the effective gross rent. The unit of comparison selected must be used consistently throughout the analysis.

Rental property data may show vacancy rates and operating expenses as a percentage of the effective gross income. These data are essential in valuing income-producing property. The age and type of construction and any utilities provided by the owner should be specified.

Capitalization Rates

Capitalization rates are another essential type of market data. They are rates or multipliers (e.g., a gross rent multiplier for a single-family property) that are extracted from market data. When net operating income and sale price information are available, an overall rate (R_o) can be calculated; if mortgage information is also available, the equity capitalization rate (R_E) can be calculated. Whenever possible, an appraiser should calculate these rates from available data and consider their meaning in the analysis. In making comparisons, capitalization rates are analyzed in light of the similarity between the comparable sale's characteristics and the characteristics of the subject property. (The derivation of capitalization rates is discussed in detail in Chapters 22 and 23.)

The overall and equity capitalization rates derived from sales can also be used as bases for deriving other capitalization rates. When possible, overall property rates and equity yield rates should be extracted from market evidence.

Competitive Supply and Demand Data

The valuation process requires that a property be appraised within the context of its market. Of particular significance to the analysis are the supply of competitive properties, the future demand for the property being appraised, and its highest and best use. After inspecting the subject property and gathering property-specific data, the appraiser inventories the supply of properties that constitute the major competition for the property in its defined market.

Required Analysis

Competitive Supply Inventory

The supply inventory includes all competitive properties: rental units, properties that have been sold, properties being offered for sale, and properties that will come on the market at some future time. The appraiser must recognize that the subject property will always compete in a future market. Thus the appraiser's investigation must cover not only existing competition, but also prospective projects that will compete with the subject.

Demand Study

Along with the supply inventory of major competitive properties, the appraiser analyzes the prospective demand for the subject property. The appraiser cannot assume the current use is necessarily the use for which the most demand will exist in the future. Even in the most stable markets, subtle shifts in the market appeal or utility of a category of properties can put some properties at a competitive disadvantage and benefit others. Even in volatile markets characterized by rapid change due to factors such as accelerating growth, precipitous decline, or an upturn in proposed construction, appraisers need to quantify demand in some manner.

The specific techniques applied to study market demand can be highly sophisticated and may fall outside the scope of normal appraisal practice. In these cases the appraiser might use data compiled by special market research firms (proprietary data) to supplement the appraisal. All appraisers should, however, develop an understanding of market research techniques and acquire the skills needed to conduct basic demand studies.

Vacancy Rates and Offerings

One approach to understanding local demand is to study the vacancy rates and offerings of competitive properties. A large number of vacancies may indicate an oversupply in relation to current demand, or it may suggest that the rents asked for this type of space are too high. Very few vacancies and offering prices that are higher than recent sale prices or rental rates may indicate an increase in unsatisfied demand or an underpricing of space. Vacancies and offerings are studied to support the appraiser's absorption projection and the forecast of prospective demand for the appraised property.

The inventory of competitive properties extends beyond the analysis of comparable sales and rentals. The use and occupancy of competitive properties that have not recently been sold or are subject to long-term leases can indicate the overall health of the local market. It is also important that the appraiser recognize potential demographic and economic shifts that may affect future competition for the appraised property.

The appraiser should research and report listings and offerings of competitive properties. Appraisers are justifiably reluctant to base an appraised value on listings. Listings do not meet the normal appraisal criteria for comparable sales data, which specify completed, arm's-length transactions. Nevertheless, listings may be seen as collateral evidence of market activity.

Listings and offerings can be useful indicators of the values anticipated by sellers and buyers and reflect the likely turnover of competitive properties. Listings are usually set at a level that will excite market interest and therefore may be employed to test market activity. They are relevant market phenomena which the appraiser should consider in analyzing competitive supply and demand. The appraiser may find that tabulating information about competitive properties in a market data grid facilitates comparing the market position of the subject property to that of the competition.

Sources of Competitive Supply and Demand Data

A competitive supply inventory is compiled in several steps. The appraiser first conducts a field inspection to inventory competitive properties in the subject neighborhood and competitive neighborhoods. The appraiser then can interview owners, managers, and brokers of competitive properties in the area as well as developers and city planners. Field inspection and interviews are especially important because investors rely heavily on local competitive supply and demand analyses. An examination of building permits (both issued and acted upon), plat maps, and surveys of competitive sites provides insight into prospective supply. Data on available space as well as vacancy, absorption, and turnover rates in specific property markets can be obtained from electronic databases and reports prepared by real estate research firms.

Demand can be estimated using demographic data (population and vital statistics) and economic data (employment and income statistics) for the market area. The Census Bureau (Department of Commerce) and Bureau of Labor Statistics compile statistical data which are available in published form and on computer tape. Other private and public sources provide historic data and projections based on small area populations. Appraisers who rely on projections prepared by market research firms should have a clear understanding of the methodology used to make the projection; otherwise the data may represent little more than a blind data set. To test the reasonableness of small area projections, comparisons should be made between the demographic data and the supply data collected in the specified market. Supply data may include building permits and market sales or absorption rates kept by public agencies such as building inspection, city planning, and public works departments.

Personal observation is also useful in estimating local demand. For example, the planned closing of an army base should be considered in analyzing the future demand for adjacent commercial properties such as dry cleaners, motels, bars, and restaurants. An appraiser who had observed development near highway interchanges will be able to anticipate that a proposed freeway interchange will generate future demand for shops, service stations, and motels catering to the needs of motorists and tourists.

The Topographically Integrated Geographic Encoding and Reforming (TIGER) file established by the 1990 census is of special relevance to appraisals of sites being considered for development. The TIGER file is a Geographic Information System (GIS) for assembling data about microlevel locations. These data include information on traffic analysis zones (TAZs), acreage available for development, and zone densities. The spatial analysis format integrates a spreadsheet model with geographic information. The software for this system is competitively priced and readily available for use with microcomputers.[8]

Other GIS databases contain information on local taxes (e.g., property assessments, school levies) and infrastructure (e.g., gas lines).

Organization and Array of Data

Understanding the content and sources of general and specific appraisal data facilitates their analysis in valuation and consulting assignments. Before undertaking any analysis, however, an appraiser must organize all the specific data accumulated in the investigation. *Market data grids* are carefully constructed spreadsheets that provide a tabular representation of market data organized into useful, measurable categories. If the information to be analyzed is very complex, the appraiser may need to design several market data grids to isolate and study specific data.

The first type of market data grid is called a *data array grid*. The appraiser lists significant characteristics of the subject and comparable properties that has been isolated. This type of grid summarizes the data presented and allows the appraiser to identify those factors that may account for differences in value and those that probably do not. The data array grid only presents data; it is not used for comparing the properties. In a second type of grid, an *adjustment grid*, the sale properties are compared to the subject and specific adjustments are made to their prices.

The data array grid should include the total sale price of each comparable property and the date of each sale, which can be expressed in relation to the subject property's date of valuation (e.g., one month ago, 16 months ago). The grid also includes informa-

8. See Lynn Bodin Wombold, "Tracking Population Change" and Michael L. Robbins," Forecasting Retail Sales with Geographic Information Systems: A Preliminary Methodology" in *Forecasting: Market Determinants Affecting Cash Flows and Reversions*, Research Report 4 (Chicago: American Institute of Real Estate Appraisers, 1989). See also, Bruce R. Weber, "Application of Geographic Information Systems to Real Estate Market Analysis and Appraisal," *The Appraisal Journal* (January 1990).

tion about the property rights conveyed, the financial arrangements of the sale, and any unusual motivations of the buyer or seller that may have resulted in a negotiating advantage, such as a desire to liquidate a property for inheritance tax or to acquire a particular property for expansion. Because financial arrangements and unusual motivations can significantly influence a property's sale price, they must be carefully examined.

The data array grid can include characteristics of the subject and comparable properties, information on sales transactions, and pertinent market data from other sources. An appraiser may choose to use two or more data array grids, i.e., one grid for comparable sales data and other grids for information derived from other sources. Isolating specific data may indicate the type of information the appraiser will be able to derive from the collected data and identify variations among properties that may be significant to their value.

In examining the data array grid, the appraiser may find that certain data are not pertinent and will not be useful in applying the approaches to value. For example, if an appraiser who is valuing an industrial property finds that the subject and the comparables all occupy one-acre sites, site size will probably not account for differences in the properties' sale or unit price. If the percentages of office space in the properties vary, however, this factor probably does have an effect on value.

Analysis of the data array grid may indicate that additional data are required and that the appraiser needs to create other grids to include more information or to isolate the data required for specific approaches. Appraisers should see data analysis as a developing process and the data array grid as a tool that facilitates this process and the derivation of valid indications of property value.

Figures 8.1 and 8.2 show sample grids for the organization and array of market data. Figure 8.1 is a data array grid of comparable sales to be analyzed in the sales comparison approach to value. (Further discussion and examples of the use of adjustment grids for data analysis are provided in Chapters 18 and 19.) Figure 8.2 shows how a basic data array grid can be used to organize data on rental properties, which may be used to derive market rent estimates for application in the income capitalization approach to value.

Units of Comparison

Units of comparison, which are almost always size-related, are used in analyzing data in all three approaches to value. In the sales comparison approach, the sale price may be divided by the unit of comparison. By reducing the sale price to a size-related unit price, the appraiser usually eliminates the need to make any subsequent size adjustments. (For a discussion of adjusting for differences in economies of scale, see Chapter 18.) In the cost approach, the total cost of construction and total accrued depreciation may be divided by the unit of comparison. In the income capitalization approach, the income and expense items and the net operating income may be divided by the unit of comparison selected. Several, different units of comparison may be used in each approach, depending on the information needed and the focus of the analysis. However, the unit of comparison selected must be consistently applied to the subject property and all comparable sales properties in each analysis.

| Figure 8.1 | **Data Array Grid** |

Element	Subject	Sale 1	Sale 2	Sale 3	Sale 4	Sale 5
Sale price	?	————	————	————	————	————
Property rights conveyed	————	————	————	————	————	————
Financing	————	————	————	————	————	————
Conditions of sale (motivation)	————	————	————	————	————	————
Date of sale (market conditions)	————	————	————	————	————	————
Location	————	————	————	————	————	————
Gross building area (GBA)	————	————	————	————	————	————
Rentable area	————	————	————	————	————	————
Land area	————	————	————	————	————	————
Lease expiration dates	————	————	————	————	————	————
Rent concessions	————	————	————	————	————	————
Escalation	————	————	————	————	————	————
Market rent	————	————	————	————	————	————
Potential gross income (PGI)	————	————	————	————	————	————
Effective gross income (EGI)	————	————	————	————	————	————
Net operating income (NOI)	————	————	————	————	————	————
Income multiplier	————	————	————	————	————	————
Overall cap rate (R_o)	————	————	————	————	————	————
Equity cap rate (R_E)	————	————	————	————	————	————
Property yield rate (Y_o)	————	————	————	————	————	————
Equity yield rate (Y_E)	————	————	————	————	————	————

Figure 8.2 | Organization and Array of Market Data for Rental Properties

Element	Subject	Sale 1	Sale 2	Sale 3	Sale 4	Sale 5
Sale price	?	$600,000	$920,000	$850,000	$990,000	$920,000
Property rights conveyed	Leased fee	Leased fee	Leased fee	Leased fee	Leased fee	Leased fee
Amount seller received	?	$600,000	see[a]	$850,000	see[b]	$920,000
Cash equivalent price	?	$600,000	$800,000	$850,000	$900,000	$920,000
Unit of comparison (number of sq. ft.)	400,000	200,000	320,000	430,000	380,000	480,000
Dollars per sq. ft. of GBA	?	$3.00	$2.50	$1.98	$2.37	$1.92
Conditions of sale (motivation)[c]	?	Arm's-length	Arm's-length	+10%	Arm's-length	Arm's-length
Date (market conditions)[d]	?	Current	+6%	Current	+2%	Current
Location[e]	Corner lot	Similar	+5%	Similar	+5%	Similar
Size[f]	Small lot	-5%	-2%	Similar	Similar	+2%
Other physical characteristics[g]	High ground	Similar	Similar	Similar	+5%	Similar
Zoning[h]	C-3	Similar	Similar	-10%	Similar	+15%
Contract rent[i]	Same as market rent	Similar	Similar	+30%	Similar	Similar
Dollars per sq. ft. of GBA after addition of percentage adjustments	?	$2.85	$2.72	$2.57	$2.65	$2.25
Rent per sq. ft. of GBA	?	$0.30	N/A	$0.18	$0.24	N/A
Gross income multiplier (GIM)	?	10.0	N/A	11.0	9.9	N/A
Percentage of NOI to GI	?	81%	N/A	89.5%	80.4%	N/A
Overall capitalization rate (R_O)	?	8.10%	N/A	8.14%	8.12%	N/A
Mortgage capitalization rate (R_M)	?	9.2%	9.4%	10.5%	10.1%	9.6%
Equity capitalization rate (R_E)	?	7.4%	7.3%	7.6%	7.5%	7.4%

a. In Sale 2 the seller received $120,000 in cash and a note for $800,000 (including any interest) payable in 18 months; the cash equivalent value of the note is $680,000.

b. In Sale 4 the seller received $200,000 in cash and a note for $790,000, with a 20-year amortization schedule, quarterly payments including 8.5% interest, a seven-year call provision, and a balloon arrangement.

c. In Sale 3 the seller had to dispose of the property to settle an estate.

d. Considering the rate of inflation and the popularity of the neighborhood, a 2% increase is indicated for a one-year-old sale and a 6% increase is indicated for a two-year-old sale.

e. Sales 2 and 4 are not corner lots; the subject and the other sales are.

f. Within this range of sizes, small plots are worth more per square foot than large plots due to greater demand.

g. Sale 4 includes one-half acre of floodplain land.

h. Sale 3 includes two acres of land with R-5 zoning; the subject and the other sales are all zoned C-3. Sale 5 includes a nonexclusive vehicle right-of-way for the use of the subject property.

i. Sale 3 is leased at a rent that is 8.5% below market rent and there are three years remaining in the lease term.

Typically, different units of comparison are used with different property types. Comparisons can be made based on the price, cost, income, or expenses per unit, depending on the approach applied. The following list shows common property types and the typical units of comparison used in their appraisal.

Single-family residences

- Entire property
- Gross living area

Vacant land

- Entire property
- Acreage and price per acre
- Square footage
- Front footage
- Potential subdivided lot
- Building units per acre

Agricultural properties

- Acreage and price per acre
- Animal unit (AU)—for pastureland
- Thousand board feet (MBF)—for timberland

Apartments

- Square footage of livable area
- Number of apartments
- Number of rooms

Warehouses

- Square footage of gross building area
- Cubic footage
- Loading docks and doors—for truck terminals

Factories

- Square footage of gross building area
- Machine unit

Offices

- Square footage of net leasable area
- Square footage of gross building area—especially for office condominiums and single-tenant or owner-occupied buildings

Hospitals

- Square footage
- Number of beds

Theaters

- Square footage
- Number of seats

The fundamental features of data analysis in the sales comparison, cost, and income capitalization approaches are described in the following section.

Data Analysis

Cost Approach

In the cost approach, appraisers often use sales data and cost and depreciation information derived from the market. Both types of information may contribute significantly to the cost approach, and each may serve as a check on the other. An analysis of sales data can supplement cost and depreciation data obtained from other sources. Sales analysis can provide direct indications of accrued depreciation, entrepreneurial profit, and the value contribution of buildings or land improvements. The cost of an improvement recently added to a sale property may indicate current construction costs.

To develop cost estimates from data obtained through observation and interviews, the appraiser must ascertain precisely what the reported expenditure represents in relation to the total actual cost of property improvements. If entrepreneurial profit is evident, it should be included in the appraisal estimate. Quoted costs for improvements may not reflect the owner's related risk, labor and equipment costs, financial charges, the costs of land preparation, engineering costs, or other indirect expenses. The appraiser must also recognize that cost estimates for the reproduction or replacement of improvements as of the appraisal date, which are developed in data analysis, may not reflect any profit that the current owner realized due to the change in the property. Of course, final cost estimates should include this profit if it is evident in the market.

Sales Comparison Approach

In the sales comparison approach to value, an appraiser analyzes data gathered primarily from comparable sales. The purpose of this analysis is to identify differences that affect the value of the subject property and the comparable sale properties so the value of these differences can be measured. The analysis of sales data reveals which features the market perceives to be valuable. Mathematical computations can then be applied to the known values of the comparables to arrive at indications of the total or per-unit value of the subject property.

The first step in data analysis is the selection of one or more appropriate units of comparison. In appraising single-family residential property, adjustments are typically made to the total property sale price; therefore, the basic unit of comparison is the total property. The total property unit is seldom used in appraising nonresidential properties because their sizes vary significantly.

After the appropriate unit of comparison is chosen, the appraiser reviews the data to determine which characteristics of the properties and which sales transactions should be used in the sales comparison approach. The dates of the sales indicate which properties will provide the best initial indication of change in value over time. Ideally, this indication is derived from a recorded sale and a subsequent resale of a property that was not substantially changed between the sales.

Further data analysis will suggest where the appraiser should begin to solve for the values contributed by individual property characteristics. Because properties usually have many components, the appraiser starts by finding a single component for which a value can be derived. For example, a data array grid shows that two properties vary only in that one is fully landscaped and the other is not. The appraiser can estimate the contributory value of the landscaping by comparing the two sales and make the appropriate adjustment on the adjustment grid. Another market variable can then be isolated from other sales, and a second adjustment can be estimated. (Further discussion of paired data analysis can be found in Chapter 18.)

The analysis of sales is progressive. An appraiser isolates and solves for one variable at a time, comparing known indications against unknown characteristics. This analytical process gives the appraiser an indication of the data that will be most useful in applying the sales comparison approach and suggests the pattern of calculations that will be needed to derive a value indication. Moreover, a careful review of market data may reveal that additional data are needed to substantiate the value indication reached through the sales comparison approach, or that more weight should be attributed to the value indications derived through the cost and income capitalization approaches.

Income Capitalization Approach

Comparable sales data, comparable rental data, and income and expense statements provide a variety of information for use in the income capitalization approach. Much of the data needed for this approach is derived from interviews with individuals who are familiar with the subject property or comparable sale and rental properties. An appraiser may also interview owners and managers of similar properties for information on typical rents, lease terms, vacancy rates, management fees, and other operating expenses.

If an appraiser is valuing an apartment building in an area where there is a relative scarcity of apartment sales or other property data, the appraiser may study apartment complexes located elsewhere to suggest income and expense trends and indicate the various relationships between income and value. If sufficient comparability exists, these data can provide support for the analysis.

When the data available provide adequate information on the income, expenses, and mortgage terms associated with each sale, the appraiser can derive an estimate of the net operating income (*NOI*) and pre-tax cash flow, or equity dividend, of each sale property. The overall capitalization rate and equity capitalization rate reflected in each sale can then be calculated.

This calculation is meaningful only if the appraiser uses the same income and expense categories to derive net operating incomes from comparable sales and to project the net operating income of the subject property. If, for example, an allowance for replacements is made in the expense statement for one comparable property and not in the others, the overall capitalization rate derived for that property will not be comparable to the rates derived for other properties.

By analyzing the market-derived overall capitalization rate and equity capitalization rate indicated by each comparable sale, the appraiser can develop an appropriate rate or rates, which can be used to derive a value indication for the subject property with direct capitalization techniques. When adequate comparable sale and rental data are available, it is often possible to calculate both an overall capitalization rate and an equity capitalization rate for the subject property. Although yield capitalization may produce a more detailed analysis, market-derived rates should be analyzed and explained in market value appraisals. If the results obtained with direct and yield capitalization methods differ, the appraiser must find market support for his or her conclusions and explain them in light of the market. (Yield capitalization techniques are discussed in Chapter 23.)

Key Concepts

- Data collection and analysis are essential to appraisal.
- The economic base of a community attracts income from outside the area, which affects population growth and the disposable income of the community.
- General data include information on social, economic, governmental, and environmental forces. Sources of general data include federal government publications, state/local government offices, trade associations, and private research firms.
- Specific data comprise information on the subject property, comparable properties, and market transactions. Sources of specific data are public records (e.g., deeds, recorded leases), newspapers (e.g., advertised sale prices and rentals), multiple listing services, cost-estimating manuals, brokers, lenders, contractors, owners, and tenants.
- Market data on competitive supply and demand allow the appraiser to estimate current and future demand for the property. Some sources of market data are field inspections, interviews with market participants, building permits and plat maps, proprietary data, and demographic and economic data compiled by the Census and Labor bureaus.
- Technological advances such as Geographic Information System (GIS) and the Electronic Data Interchange (EDI) are important sources of spatial data and specific data.
- Market data are analyzed by appraisers using data array grids and adjustment grids.

Terms

absorption rate	balance of trade
accelerated cost recovery system (ACRS)	building permit
	building start
adjustment grid	business cycle
ad valorem tax	capitalization rate
arm's-length transaction	competitive supply

consideration
construction cost
Consumer Price Index (CPI)
cost-estimating manual
data array grid
debt service
demand
depreciation
disposable income
economic base
economic base analysis
economic indicator
economic life
Electronic Data Interchange
    (EDI)
field inspection
forecasting
general data
Geographic Information
    System (GIS)
gross domestic product
gross national product
household
household formation
improvement cost data
income and expense data
listing

macroeconomic factor
market data grid
microeconomic factor
modified accelerated cost recovery
    system (MACRS)
nominal price
offering
operating expense
plat map
price level
prime interest rate
proprietary data
purchasing power
real price
school tax
siting factor
specific data
Topographically Integrated
    Geographic Encoding and
    Referencing (TIGER) datafiles
transactional data
unemployment rate
units of comparison
vacancy and collection loss
volume of retail sales
wage level

CHAPTER NINE

Neighborhoods and Districts

S ocial, economic, governmental, and environmental forces influence property values in the vicinity of a subject property, which affect the value of the subject property itself. Therefore, the boundaries of the area of influence must be delineated to conduct a thorough analysis. The area of influence is the area within which the forces affect surrounding properties in the same way they affect the property being appraised. Although physical boundaries may be drawn, the significant boundaries are those that fix the limits of influences on property values. By coincidence, these limits may be observable.

The area of influence is commonly called a *neighborhood. A neighborhood is a group of complementary land uses.* A residential neighborhood, for example, may contain single-family homes and commercial properties that provide services for local residents. A clear distinction can be drawn between a neighborhood and a district. *A district is a type of neighborhood that is characterized by homogeneous land use.* Districts are commonly composed of apartments or commercial, industrial, or agricultural properties.

To identify neighborhood or district boundaries, an appraiser examines the subject property's surroundings. The investigation begins with the subject property and proceeds outward, identifying all relevant actual and potential influences on the property's value that can be attributed to its location. The appraiser extends the geographic search far enough to encompass all influences that the market perceives as affecting the value of the subject property. At the physical point where no factors influencing the value of the subject and surrounding properties are found, the boundaries for analysis are set. The appraiser's conclusions regarding the impact of the neighborhood or district on the subject property's value are significant only if area boundaries have been properly delineated.

Neighborhood or district analysis provides a framework, or context, in which property value is estimated. It identifies the area of analysis and establishes the potential limits within which the appraiser searches for data to be used in applying the three approaches to value. Realistic boundaries allow the appraiser to identify comparable properties in the same neighborhood or district; the sale prices of these properties usually require little or no adjustment for location.

Neighborhood or district analysis helps the appraiser determine the stability of an area and may indicate future land uses and value trends.

Characteristics of Neighborhoods and Districts

A neighborhood exhibits a greater degree of uniformity than the larger surrounding area. Obviously, no group of inhabitants, buildings, or business enterprises can possess identical features or attributes, but a neighborhood is perceived to be relatively uniform. Many shared features may be evident in a neighborhood, including similar building types and styles, population characteristics, economic profiles of occupants, and zoning regulations that affect land use. The variables that suggest similarity are not limited to physical characteristics. The social, economic, and governmental forces operating within a neighborhood contribute as much to its definition as the physical environment. The varied nature of different neighborhoods reflects this fact. Similarity may also be indicated by the dominant land use, rent and occupancy levels, the credit strength of occupants, and the ages of buildings.

Neighborhood and District Boundaries

Neighborhood and district boundaries identify the physical area that influences the value of a subject property. These boundaries may coincide with observable changes in prevailing land use or occupant characteristics. Physical features such as the type of structures, street patterns, terrain, vegetation, and lot sizes tend to identify land use districts. Transportation arteries (highways, major streets, and railroads), bodies of water (rivers, lakes, and streams), and changing elevation (hills, mountains, cliffs, and valleys) can also be significant boundaries.

   The neighborhood of a house in a single-family subdivision usually ends where land uses change to commercial, apartment, or industrial use. However, another house in the same subdivision that is nearer to these different land uses may be influenced by them; the neighborhood of this house may not end at the same point.

   In defining a district, variations in the relevant characteristics of properties may indicate that more limited boundaries should be established. For example, consider an urban area where many high-rise apartment buildings are constructed along a natural lakeshore and separated from other land uses by major transportation arteries. In this type of district, there may be great variation in apartments, prices, sizes, views, parking availability, proximity to public transportation, and building ages. These variations suggest limited district boundaries which must be identified to reveal market and submarket characteristics.

   The properties closest to a subject property tend to exert the greatest influence on its value. Any property, even a commercial one, that is on the fringe of a residential area and near attractive, well-maintained, desirable properties tends to have a higher value than it would if it were located near less attractive, poorly maintained, undesirable properties.

   Legal, political, and economic organizations collect data for standardized or statistically defined areas, so information about income and educational levels may be available for cities, counties, tax districts, census tracts, or special enumeration districts. Although these data may be relevant, they rarely conform to the area boundaries identified for property valuation. If secondary data are used to help identify neighborhood boundaries, the appraiser should verify and supplement the data with primary research.

To identify neighborhood and district boundaries, an appraiser follows several steps.

Step 1. Examine the area's physical characteristics. The appraiser should drive or walk around the area to develop a sense of place, noting the degree of similarity in land uses, types of structures, architectural styles, and maintenance and upkeep. Using a map of the area, the appraiser can identify points where these characteristics change and note any physical barriers—e.g., major streets, hills, rivers, railroad tracks—that coincide with these points.

Step 2. Draw preliminary boundaries on a map. The appraiser draws lines on a map of the area to connect the points where physical characteristics change. The physical barriers that coincide with or are near these points are identified.

Step 3. Test preliminary boundaries against demographic data. The appraiser then obtains accurate data on the ages, occupations, incomes, and educational levels of neighborhood residents.[1] The information generally available for census tracts, zip code regions, and counties must be segmented to represent pertinent subareas and neighborhoods. Reliable data may also be available from local chambers of commerce, universities, and research organizations.

In unusual cases an appraiser might consider sampling area residents to identify relevant characteristics. Appraisers may also interview neighborhood occupants, businesspeople, brokers, and community representatives for their perceptions of how far the neighborhood extends. Through experience, an appraiser learns to observe changes and understand how neighborhoods are perceived.

Change

In neighborhood and district analysis, an appraiser recognizes the propensity for change and tries to determine how a particular neighborhood may be changing. Appraisers usually consider trends in historic growth and neighborhood composition when analyzing patterns of change. When values in a neighborhood are increasing, the appraiser must determine whether the subject property's value can be expected to exceed, equal, or lag behind the neighborhood trend. Similarly, if neighborhood values are stable or declining, the appraiser analyzes the value of the subject property relative to these trends.

Evidence of Change

Neighborhood change is often indicated by variations within the neighborhood. New uses may indicate potential increases or decreases in a neighborhood's property values. For example, a neighborhood in which some homes are well maintained and others are not may be undergoing either decline or revitalization. The introduction of different uses, such as rooming houses or offices, into a single-family residential neighborhood also indicates potential change.

---

1. Every 10 years the Bureau of the Census, U.S. Department of Commerce, collects data on population and housing characteristics, employment, and earnings. For information on applying census and other data to neighborhood and district analysis, see Stephen F. Fanning, MAI, Terry V. Grissom, MAI, PhD, and Thomas D. Pearson, MAI, PhD, *Market Analysis for Valuation Appraisals* (Chicago: Appraisal Institute, 1994), Chapters 7 and 8.

Changes in one neighborhood are usually influenced by changes in other neighborhoods and in the larger area of influence. In any relatively stable city, the rapid growth of one neighborhood or district may adversely affect a competing neighborhood or district. A city may grow until its center is not accessible from its more remote districts. In such instances new, competing business centers may be established to serve the needs of outlying areas.

Suburban business centers may have an adverse effect on a city's central business district. Newer residential areas may affect older areas. The added supply of new homes may induce residents to shift from old homes to new ones and place older homes on the market. This increase in supply may affect the market values of all homes in the area. If the location of a neighborhood makes it attractive for conversion to a more intensive use, the existing improvements may be extensively remodeled or torn down to make way for redevelopment.

Growth causes changes in the utility of both vacant and improved parcels of real estate. Utility may increase or decrease, and changes in value may result. No neighborhood or district is static; although it usually proceeds slowly, change is constant and inevitable.

Neighborhood or District Life Cycle

Because neighborhoods and districts are perceived, organized, constructed, and used by people, each has a dynamic quality of its own. Appraisers describe this quality as the *life cycle* of a neighborhood or district. The complementary land uses that comprise neighborhoods and the homogeneous land uses that comprise districts typically evolve through four stages.

1. Growth—a period during which the neighborhood gains public favor and acceptance
2. Stability—a period of equilibrium without marked gains or losses
3. Decline—a period of diminishing demand
4. Revitalization—a period of renewal, modernization, and increasing demand

Although these stages describe the life cycle of neighborhoods or districts in a general way, they should not be used as specific guides to market trends. No set number of years is assigned to any stage in the cycle. Many neighborhoods and districts remain stable for a very long time; decline is not necessarily imminent in all older areas. Unless decline is caused by a specific external influence—e.g., the construction of a new highway that changes traffic patterns—it may proceed at a barely perceptible rate and can be interrupted by a change in use or a revival of demand. There is no set life expectancy for a neighborhood or district, and the life cycle is not an inexorable process. At any point in the cycle, a major change can interrupt the order of the stages. For example, a strong negative influence can cause a neighborhood that is in a stage of growth to decline precipitously rather than stabilize.

After a period of decline, a neighborhood may undergo a transition to other land uses or its life cycle may begin again due to revitalization. Neighborhood revitalization often results from organized rebuilding or restoration undertaken to preserve the architecture of significant structures. It may also be caused by a natural rekindling of demand. The rebirth of an older, inner-city neighborhood, for example, may simply be due to changing preferences and lifestyles, with no planned renewal program.

Gentrification and Displacement

One relatively recent neighborhood phenomenon is *gentrification, whereby middle- and upper-income people purchase neighborhood properties to renovate or reha- bilitate them.* The residents displaced by this process are often lower-income individuals, who moved into these older, urban neighborhoods when middle- and upper-income groups left or began to find the neighborhoods unappealing and unattractive. Often two or more low-income households would occupy what was formerly a single-family resi- dence. Such neighborhoods often became blighted.

Gentrification, which reverses the process of decline, appears to be the result of a preponderance of small families and single people who choose to live in urban areas.

Neighborhood renovation

Analysis of Value Influences in Neighborhoods

The forces that influence value, which are evident in the similar characteristics of properties in a neighborhood, are important in neighborhood analysis. Similar character- istics point to influences that have affected value trends in the past and may affect values in the future. The forces that influence value in districts are important in district analysis. The discussion that follows focuses on neighborhoods, but generally applies to districts as well.

Social Considerations

A neighborhood's character may be revealed by examining why occupants live or work in the area. Occupants are attracted to a location for its status, physical environment, services, affordability, and convenience.

In performing a neighborhood analysis, an appraiser identifies relevant social characteristics and influences. To identify and describe these characteristics, the appraiser must be aware that the characteristics that have the greatest influence on property values in a neighborhood tend to overlap. The overall desirability of the subject neighborhood in relation to other, competing neighborhoods is, of course, reflected in their respective price levels.

In neighborhood analysis, relevant social characteristics include

- Population density, which is particularly important in central business districts and high-rise residential neighborhoods
- Occupant skill levels or employment categories, which are particularly important in industrial or high-technology districts
- Occupant age levels, which are particularly important in residential neighborhoods
- Occupant employment status, including types of unemployment (temporary, seasonal, or chronic)
- Extent or absence of crime
- Extent or absence of litter
- Quality and availability of educational, medical, social, recreational, cultural, and commercial services
- Presence or absence of community or neighborhood organizations such as improvement associations, block clubs, and crime watch groups.

It is difficult, if not impossible, to identify the social preferences of the many individuals who comprise a given market and to measure how these preferences affect property value. Therefore, an appraiser should not place too much reliance on social influences in arriving at a value conclusion. From an appraiser's viewpoint, the social characteristics of a residential neighborhood are significant only when they are considered by the buying public and can be objectively and accurately analyzed. Although race, religion, and national origin are social characteristics, they have no direct relationship to real estate values. Professional appraisers know that they must perform unbiased neighborhood analyses.

Economic Considerations

Economic considerations relate to the financial capacity of neighborhood occupants and their ability to rent or own property, to maintain it in an attractive and desirable condition, and to renovate or rehabilitate it when needed. The physical characteristics of the area and of individual properties may indicate the relative financial strength of area occupants and how this strength is reflected in neighborhood development and upkeep. Ownership and rental data can also provide clues to residents' financial capability. The income levels revealed by recent census information, newspaper surveys, and private studies may indicate the prices at which occupants can afford to rent or purchase property. Using vacancy statistics compiled by newspapers, the U.S. Postal Service, and other fact-finding agencies along with information on the number of properties for rent or sale found in classified newspaper ads, an appraiser can estimate the strength of demand

and the extent of supply.

The presence of vacant lots or acreage suitable for development in an area may suggest future construction activity or indicate a lack of demand. Current construction creates trends that affect the value of existing improvements. A careful study of these trends can help an appraiser predict the future desirability of an area. Block-by-block information helps identify the direction of growth. A neighborhood may be developing, static, declining, or in a period of revitalization. A trend may be a local phenomenon or it may affect the entire community. A change in the economic base on which a community depends (e.g., the addition or loss of a major employer) is frequently reflected in the rate of population growth or decline. Ownership demand tends to remain strong and rental occupancy levels are high when the population is growing; demand weakens and occupancy levels decrease when the population is declining.

To analyze a neighborhood's economic characteristics, an appraiser expands the analysis to include economic trends over a three- to five-year period. Then the appraiser decides which economic variables significantly contribute to value differences among neighborhoods and compares the current economic characteristics of competing neighborhoods.

The economic characteristics that an appraiser may consider include

- Occupant income levels
- Extent of owner occupancy
- Property rent levels
- Property value levels
- Vacancy rates for various types of property
- Amount of development and construction
- Effective ages of properties
- Changes in property use

Governmental Considerations

Governmental considerations relate to the laws, regulations, and taxes that affect neighborhood properties and the administration and enforcement of these constraints. Some buyers are interested in neighborhoods that are subject to effective zoning laws, building codes, and housing and sanitary codes. The property tax burden associated with the benefits provided and the taxes charged for similar benefits in other neighborhoods are considered. The enforcement of applicable codes, regulations, and restrictions should be equitable and effective. An appraiser gathers data on the governmental characteristics of the neighborhood and compares them with the characteristics of other, competing neighborhoods.

Tax burdens in different neighborhoods can vary significantly and variations in taxes are a significant basis for comparison. Sometimes the level of special assessments in a location can become so heavy that the marketability of property is seriously affected. The benefits resulting from these assessments may not enhance the sale prices that can be obtained for properties in proportion to their cost; nevertheless, the cost must be offset. As a rule, properties that are subject to special assessments can be expected to bring lower sale prices than comparable properties that are not subject to these taxes. For example, consider two identical properties located in the same block on different streets that are each worth $75,000 free of encumbrances. If one is subject to a special assessment lien of $3,000, its market value subject to the lien may be calculated by deducting the present value of the future payments on the $3,000 lien from $75,000. (The balance on a special assessment declines each time a share is paid off.)

Divergent tax rates may also affect market value. Local taxes may favor or penalize certain property types. Therefore, an appraiser should examine the local structure of assessed values and tax rates to compare the tax burdens created by various forms of taxes and ascertain their apparent effect on the values of different types of real estate.

Counties or cities may have the authority to impose optional taxes such as sales and earnings taxes on residents. When the sales and local earnings taxes applicable to competing communities vary, the relative desirability of the communities may be affected. Variations in optional taxes often have a more pronounced influence on the marketability and value of commercial and industrial property than real estate taxes do.

Most communities have detailed zoning ordinances, which are designed to implement a comprehensive plan. Zoning laws typically identify zones or districts where certain land uses are permitted and others are prohibited. The broadest zoning categories are residential (often indicated by R), commercial (indicated by either C or B for business) and industrial (indicated by either I or M for manufacturing). These categories are divided into subcategories, such as R1a for detached, single-family residences constructed on lots of a specified minimum size, shape, and frontage. Smaller lots may be allowed in areas zoned R1b; R2 zoning may allow duplexes and R3 zoning might permit low-density apartments. The zoning code for a moderate-sized city may consist of several hundred pages which identify and explain the various zones. An appraiser should examine the zoning requirements for the neighborhood in question and attempt to assess their adequacy and enforcement provisions.

Private restrictions on land use may be established by private owners through provisions in deeds or plat recordings. These restrictions may specify lot and building sizes in a subdivision, permitted architectural styles, and property uses. Condominium bylaws also restrict property use. The appraiser should make certain that private restrictions do not limit property uses inordinately. In the absence of zoning, the appraiser should determine if the private restrictions in force are adequate to protect long-term property values.

The governmental characteristics to be considered in neighborhood analysis include

- Tax burden relative to services provided, compared with other neighborhoods in the community
- Special assessments
- Zoning, building, and housing codes
- Quality of fire and police protection, schools, and other governmental services

Environmental Considerations

Environmental considerations consist of any natural or man-made features that are contained in or affect the neighborhood and its geographic location. Important environmental considerations include building size, type, density, and maintenance; topographical features; open space; nuisances and hazards emanating from nearby facilities such as shopping centers, factories, and schools; the adequacy of public utilities such as streetlights, sewers, and electricity; the existence and upkeep of vacant lots; general maintenance; street patterns, width, and maintenance; and the attractiveness and safety of routes into and out of the neighborhood.

Certain buildings may be overimprovements or underimprovements due to their excessive or deficient cost, quality, or size relative to their sites and surrounding properties. For example, a six-bedroom, four-bathroom house in an area of three-bedroom, one-bath houses might be an overimprovement, or it may signal a trend toward larger homes in the area. Overimprovements may be worth less than their cost new, particularly in middle- and lower-income neighborhoods.

Topographical features can have positive or negative effects on neighborhood property values. The presence of a lake, river, bay, or hill in or near a neighborhood may give the area a scenic advantage. Conversely, the presence of a wetland may preclude development unless costly mitigation procedures are feasible. A hill may mean little in a mountainous area, but in a predominantly flat area, an elevated or wooded section can enhance property value. A river subject to severe flooding may cause the value of homes along its banks to decline due to the risk of such a hazard. Sometimes a river, lake, or park serves as a buffer between a residential district and commercial or industrial enterprises. Land features may give a neighborhood protection against wind, fog, or flood, or they may expose it to damage.

The presence of asbestos or PCBs in buildings and any environmental liabilities incurred due to past contamination may reduce property values. In certain areas, radon, a colorless, odorless gas linked to lung cancer, is released by the radioactive decay of radium atoms in the soil. The U.S. Environmental Protection Agency (EPA) has published interim guidelines for the design of buildings in radon-affected areas. Excessive traffic, odors, smoke, dust, or noise from commercial or manufacturing enterprises can also limit the desirability of a residential neighborhood.

Gas, electricity, water, telephone service, cable television, and storm and sanitary sewers are essential to meet the accepted standard of living in most municipal areas. A deficiency in any of these services tends to decrease property values in a neighborhood. The availability of utilities also affects the direction and timing of neighborhood growth or development.

A neighborhood's environmental characteristics cannot be judged on an absolute scale; rather, they must be compared with the characteristics of other, competing neighborhoods. An appraiser asks: Do the terrain, vegetation, street patterns, structural density, property maintenance, public utilities, and other attributes of this neighborhood make it more or less desirable than other neighborhoods? In other words, what is the relative desirability of the neighborhood's location?

Location

Location has micro and macro dimensions. *Location* may refer to the siting of a property and the effect of siting on accessibility (e.g., corner vs. interior lot) or to the time-distance relationships, or linkages, between a property or neighborhood and all other possible origins and destinations of people going to or coming from the property or neighborhood. Time and distance are measures of relative access. Usually all the properties in a neighborhood have the same or very similar locational relationships with common origins and destinations.

To analyze the impact of neighborhood location, an appraiser must identify important linkages and measure their time-distances by the most commonly used types of transportation. The type of transportation usually depends on the preferences and needs of neighborhood occupants. It is not enough to note that transportation exists; the type of service provided and how it addresses the needs of neighborhood occupants must be considered.

Linkages should be judged in terms of how well they serve the typical users of real estate in the neighborhood. For example, in analyzing a single-family residential neighborhood, an appraiser considers where typical occupants need to go. If adequate facilities are not available for necessary linkages, the neighborhood will not be regarded as favorably as competing neighborhoods that have better linkages. For single-family residential neighborhoods, linkages with schools, grocery stores, and employment centers are usually the most important; linkages with recreational facilities, houses of worship, restaurants, and retail stores are less important. When current zoning does not restrict changes from the present land use, or when a change in the predominant land use is evident, the appraiser may need to examine linkages in terms of both the current land use and the anticipated predominant land use in the neighborhood.

Public transportation is important because some people do not own automobiles and others prefer not to use them often. Thus, residential properties in remote areas with unreliable or infrequent public transportation may command lower rentals and prices than properties that are more conveniently located or have better service. The distance to public transportation is considered in relation to the people who will use it.

A study of neighborhood transportation facilities must consider the territory through which users must pass. Most people would rather avoid poorly lighted streets and rundown areas. Generally, the closer a property is to good public transportation, the wider its market.

The market's perception of the desirability of different neighborhoods can be studied by analyzing comparable sales. The dollar and percentage differences among the sale prices of similar properties in different locations can provide the basis for this analysis.

Some important environmental characteristics to be considered in neighborhood analysis are

- Land use patterns
- Lot size and shape
- Terrain and vegetation

- Environmental liabilities
- Street patterns and width
- Density of structures and amount of open space
- Property maintenance and upkeep
- Availability and quality of utilities
- Nuisances and hazards (e.g., odors, noises, litter, vibrations, fog, smoke, and smog)
- Access to public transportation and type of system (e.g., bus, rail)
- Access to schools and quality of schools
- Access to stores and service establishments
- Access to parks and recreational facilities
- Access to houses of worship
- Access to workplaces

Environmental Liabilities

In recent years the federal government has issued more than 70,000 pages of environmental laws and regulations; state and local governments have added thousands more. This vast network of regulations defines the natural and man-made conditions that constitute environmental liabilities affecting property values. Natural areas to be protected include wetlands, aquifer replenishment areas, and habitats for endangered or threatened species. Man-made liabilities may be indicated by the presence of underground storage tanks, asbestos, PCBs, or other hazardous materials. The existence of one or more environmental conditions can reduce the value of a property to a fraction of its potential value.

The typical appraiser may not have the knowledge or experience needed to detect the presence of hazardous substances or to measure their quantities. Like buyers and sellers in the open market, the appraiser must often rely on the advice of others. Appraisers are not expected or required to be experts in the detection or measurement of hazardous substances.

The role and responsibility of the appraiser in detecting, measuring, and considering environmental substances affecting a property are addressed in Advisory Opinion 9 and Guide Note 8 of the Standards of Professional Appraisal Practice. Advisory Opinion 9, which was adopted December 8, 1992, addresses the following areas of concern:

- An appraiser who is requested to complete a checklist as part of a process to detect contamination should only respond to those questions that can be answered competently by the appraiser within the limits of his or her particular expertise.
- An appraiser may reasonably rely on the findings and opinions of qualified specialists in environmental remediation and compliance cost estimation.
- An appraiser may appraise an interest in real estate that is or is believed to be contaminated based on the hypothesis that the real estate is free of contamination when 1) the resulting appraisal is not misleading, 2) the client has been advised of the limitation, and 3) the Ethics Provision of USPAP is satisfied.

- The value of an interest in impacted or contaminated real estate may not be measurable by simply deducting the remediation or compliance cost estimate from the estimated value as if unaffected.

Guide Note 8 was adopted January 1, 1991, and amended January 25, 1994. This guide note takes its direction from the Competency Provision of USPAP, which requires the appraiser to have the knowledge and experience necessary to complete a specific appraisal assignment competently, or alternatively to disclose his or her lack of knowledge or experience to the client, take all steps necessary or appropriate to complete the assignment competently, and describe in the report his or her lack of knowledge or experience and the steps taken to competently complete the assignment.

The Property Observation Checklist, developed and adopted by the Appraisal Institute in 1995, is consistent with Advisory Opinion 9 and Guide Note 8. The checklist provides appraisers conducting property inspections with a uniform, easy-to-use, and (to the extent possible) liability-limiting guideline for recording observations about the physical presence of possible environmental factors. Use of the checklist is voluntary. It was not developed for single-family residential or agricultural properties. The Property Observation Checklist appears at the end of Appendix A.

Even if there is no reason to believe that the property being appraised is affected by hazardous substances, appraisers are advised to include a standard disclaimer or statement of limiting conditions concerning hazardous substances in their appraisal reports. Such a statement clarifies the normal limits of the appraisal, discloses the appraiser's lack of expertise with regard to hazardous substances, and disclaims responsibility for matters beyond the appraiser's experience. (An example of such a disclaimer is provided in Chapter 26.) The determination of due diligence remains at issue, even when a disclaimer is used. This matter is discussed below.

Comprehensive Environmental Response, Compensation, and Liability Act of 1980 (CERCLA)

The most far-reaching of all federal environmental laws is the Comprehensive Environmental Response, Compensation, and Liability Act of 1980 (CERCLA), commonly known as Superfund. The act was created by Congress to serve as a mechanism for cleaning up contaminated sites without long and costly legal entanglements. The assignation of liability under CERCLA has been criticized by property owners and lenders as both inequitable and unpredictable. In June of 1994, Congress approved a reform proposal put forth by the Environmental Protection Agency (EPA) calling for changes in the way CERCLA works.

Under CERCLA, the adjudication of liability has been strict, joint, several, and retroactive. *Strict liability* refers to the assigning of liability without regard to intentional fault or proof of negligence. *Joint and several liability* means that if several persons or entities have contributed hazardous waste to a site, each (several) and any (joint) is liable for the cost of assessing the damage, cleaning it up, and restoring the environment to an uncontaminated condition. Since many of the contamination issues that CERCLA addresses occurred in the past, the legislation is, by definition, *retroactive*.

The parties held liable include the generators, transporters, and disposers of hazardous waste materials. Through the legislation's retroactive provisions, the previous owner or operator of a property may be subject to CERCLA liability. The legal language is intentionally broad enough to apply to temporary owners, lessees, lessors, trustees, and even stockholders. The law empowers the EPA to find ways to pay for waste cleanup by holding the perpetrators liable for the "deep pocket" costs. If no demonstrably liable party can be found, the federal government will use Superfund monies to clean up severely contaminated sites.

Congress attempted to remedy certain inequities in the CERCLA legislation by passing the Superfund Amendments and Reauthorization Act (SARA) in 1986. SARA addressed the matter of the so-called "innocent" purchaser. One of the few exemptions from charges of liability under CERCLA was the action or omission of a third party who could demonstrate no contractual relationship to the defendant. (Contractual relationships may include land contracts, deeds, or instruments transferring title or possession.) SARA extended this exemption to cover third parties who acquired real property after the disposal or placement of hazardous substances provided that these parties, at the time of the acquisition, "did not know and had no reason to know that any hazardous substance was disposed of on, in, or at the facility." SARA further specified that "all appropriate inquiry into the previous ownership and uses of the property" must have been undertaken to establish that the defendant had no reason to know of the presence of hazardous substances. SARA also recognized the exemption of defendants who acquire property by inheritance and government entities that acquire property through involuntary transfer or the exercise of eminent domain. (See Appendix A for a summary of federal legislation affecting appraisers.)

Reform provisions in recent EPA policy statements more clearly delineate the circumstances under which owners and lenders may be liable for environmental cleanup costs, specify the steps owners and buyers must take to fulfill CERCLA's due diligence requirements, and extend current tax laws involving the cost recovery of environmental cleanup expenses to cover cleanup costs as deductible repairs.

Environmental Site Assessments and Environmental Property Assessments

Because the potential liability for a contaminated site is so far-reaching, some buyers, sellers, and lending institutions have routinely begun to commission *environmental site assessments* (ESAs) or *environmental property assessments* (EPRAs) before executing a sale or a loan agreement. Most environmental assessments required for real estate transactions are conducted by environmental consultants who are trained to investigate a broad range of environmental issues. Specialized investigations are performed in phases. Phase I is focused on evidence of potential contamination; in Phase II, tests are conducted to determine whether the suspected contaminants are present. A Phase III assessment describes the extent of the contamination. The enviromental consultant may also recommend a course of action to accomplish the cleanup and estimate the cost of remediation.

A Phase I environmental assessment is most commonly associated with real estate transactions. Typically it includes a site visit; examination of aerial photographs; study of the records kept by local, state, and federal environmental agencies; and a review of pertinent regulatory legislation. During the site visit, the investigator interviews occupants of the subject and neighboring properties and looks for signs of contamination, such as a stained ground, defoliation, noxious odors, areas of inconsistent surface height or depth, uneven pavement, and the presence of drums or other debris.

If a Phase I environmental assessment uncovers evidence of possible contamination or past or present violations of environmental regulations, a Phase II environmental assessment should be undertaken. Phase II normally includes invasive sampling of the soil. A Phase III environmental assessment calls for further invasive sampling to establish the horizontal and vertical extent of soil and groundwater contamination.[2] In a Phase III assessment the investigator usually draws up a plan for remediation or mitigation, including a timetable and the estimated costs associated with the environmental cleanup.

An environmental assessment cannot guarantee that a property is totally free of hazardous substances. An investigation does provide limited legal protection for the innocent purchaser, however, and a reasonable margin of assurance that contamination from asbestos, PCBs, or other hazardous substances is unlikely. To guarantee that a property is completely free of contaminants, every building component would have to be examined for asbestos and every cubic foot of soil and groundwater to the earth's core would have to be tested. The question "How clean is clean?" continues to be debated in the courts.

Although an appraiser may state in the assumptions and limiting conditions section of an appraisal report that he or she is not knowledgeable in environmental matters and has had to rely on the expertise of another party, i.e., an environmental engineer, a question remains. In accepting the work of the environmental engineer, has the appraiser exercised due diligence, i.e., has the appraiser determined whether the specific testing requirements for Phase II and III assessments have been followed?

The role of intermediaries. The action of intermediaries, i.e., the various people involved in transactions other than buyers and sellers, is becoming a significant factor in the disclosure of environmental problems. As states enact regulations that require the disclosure of environmental problems in real estate transactions, intermediaries play a larger role in focusing attention on environmental concerns. Even if the buyer and seller are willing to complete a sale, the transaction may not be consummated or the terms and conditions of the transaction may have to be altered because of the involvment of real estate brokers, lenders, appraisers, and title insurance companies.

To date, the disclosure of contamination has been relatively good in transactions involving commercial real estate. This is attributable to the sophistication of the parties involved and their awareness of liability issues. This has not been the case in residential transactions. The disclosure requirements mandated by various states have a substantial

---

2. See Robert V. Colangelo and Ronald D. Miller, *Environmental Site Assessments and Their Impact on Property Value: The Appraiser's Role* (Chicago: Appraisal Institute, 1995), 218-219 and the workbook for the seminar, titled *Environmental Risk and the Real Estate Appraisal Process* (Chicago: Appraisal Institute, 1994), 78-80. This seminar was developed by Richard J. Roddewig with the research assistance of Gary Papke.

effect on the residential market. The residential appraisal report form includes a section that requires discussion of environmental problems. Many states require that the listing agent interview the seller to elicit information on environmental matters pertaining to the property; this information is included as part of an environmental checklist.

Impact on use of property as collateral. Despite the Superfund legislation and the EPA's pronouncements that innocent owners of contaminated properties may not be held liable for cleanup costs, environmental problems can have a substantial impact on the use of property as collateral. A property owned free and clear of any encumbrances can be used as collateral to obtain loans, e.g., home equity loans, but lenders may be unwilling to accept a property as collateral if there is an environmental problem. Lenders express concern about both the diminution in the value of a property as collateral and also the possibility of repossessing a property subject to the costs of an environmental cleanup. With the loss in the value of the property as collateral, the marketability of the property is also jeopardized.

Concealed Environmental Hazards

Although the environmental liabilities associated with industrial plants are well known, many of the same liabilities may be present in residential and agricultural properties. One cannot assume that green rural properties that appear clean are actually free of environmental liabilities.

In the 1940s and 1950s farmers commonly used cattle vats, trenches filled with fuel oil through which cattle were led to rid them of mites and small insects. The fuel oil was often treated with DDT and other pesticides. When this practice fell into disuse, the trenches were simply filled in. Farms often have aging underground storage tanks that held gasoline used to fuel farm vehicles. Farmland may also be contaminated by the accumulation of fertilizers and pesticides. Old railroad beds can also constitute an environmental hazard because railroad ties were commonly soaked in creosote-filled trenches dug on site when tracks were laid. Timberlands are not free of contaminants either. Old turpentine stills are often found in areas where forests were once harvested.

Environmentally Stigmatized Properties

A stigma is an externality that negatively impacts the value of properties in proximity to it. Two sets of risks are associated with stigmatized properties.[3] The first set of risks are real or scientifically quantifiable risks, such as the cost to cure or manage the problem. The second set consists of perceived risks, which vary with the characteristics of the contamination (i.e., whether it can be concealed, how much it disrupts everyday activities, and what degree of peril is associated with it), the extent of media exposure, and the nature of the liability (to an individual or entity).

Because an environmental stigma is likely to evoke a reaction from both buyers and lenders, it often results in the effective cessation of mortgage lending for an entire area. Different types of hazardous and toxic materials have different stigmatic effects. Few problems are associated with contained asbestos insulation in buildings, but suspected

---

3. Bill Mundy, "Stigma and Value," *The Appraisal Journal* (January 1992).

leakage of a contaminant (plume) into the groundwater can stigmatize property greatly even if the contaminant is absent from the ground under the property being appraised.

Objectivity in Neighborhood Analysis

All amenities and detrimental conditions revealed in neighborhood or district analysis should be described specifically and impartially in the appraisal report. A general reference to "pride of ownership" in a report is too vague and subjective to indicate any actual effect on property value. Such references ascribe motives and attitudes to people, which should be avoided. Rather than generalities, the appraiser should record specific, impartial observations made during a personal inspection of the neighborhood. Descriptive phrases such as "many broken windows," "tall weeds present," "no litter present," and "well-kept lawns" reflect directly observable, value-influencing factors.

Appraisers' conclusions regarding neighborhood conditions and their effects on property values are considered by buyers, sellers, brokers, lenders, courts, arbiters, public officials, and other decision makers and advisers. Appraisers are often asked to provide specific evidence of neighborhood conditions and trends and to explain their findings in written reports.

Districts

The unique characteristics of districts require that special factors be considered in their analysis. The specific value influences affecting apartment districts, commercial districts, industrial districts, agricultural districts, and other types of districts are frequently not the same as the influences affecting single-family residential neighborhoods. One important factor that affects land value in all districts is the availability of public utilities, including sanitary sewers and municipal or well water. Prevailing levels of real estate and personal property taxes also influence the desirability of districts and may be reflected in real estate values. Of course, the four forces that influence all real estate value affect districts.

Apartment and Multifamily Districts

In large cities apartment and multifamily districts usually cover an extensive area; in smaller cities such districts may be dispersed or limited in size. Apartment design may be multistory, garden, row, or townhouse; units may be rented or privately owned as cooperatives and condominiums.

Although apartment and multifamily districts differ from single-family residential areas, they are subject to many similar influences. Therefore, an appraiser can identify the characteristics and amenities that affect an apartment district in a manner similar to that applied to a single-family residential neighborhood, but with a change of emphasis. In apartment and multifamily districts, desirability and value may be influenced by

- Access to workplaces
- Transportation service
- Access to shopping centers and cultural facilities
- Neighborhood reputation

- Residential atmosphere, neighborhood appearance, and protection against unwanted commercial and industrial intrusion (Proximity to employment, however, may be highly desirable for multifamily districts, which often act as buffers for commercial and industrial districts.)

- Proximity to parks, lakes, rivers, or other natural features

- Supply of vacant apartment sites that are likely to be developed and could make present accommodations more or less desirable

- Parking for tenants and guests

- Vacancy and tenant turnover rate

High-rise apartment district
(H. Armstrong Roberts, Inc.)

These characteristics and other pertinent data form the basis for an appraiser's study of rental housing. In some cities, statistics on the supply of apartments, vacancy rates, and rent levels are available. When statistics are not available, the appraiser must gather data through research.

Commercial Districts

A commercial district is a group of offices or stores that influences the use and value of the commercial property being appraised. Included in this category are highway commercial districts (i.e., the enterprises along a local business street or freeway service road and developments adjacent to a traffic intersection), regional or neighborhood shopping centers, and downtown central business districts (CBDs).

To analyze a commercial district, an appraiser identifies its trade area—the area the businesses serve. A commercial district and its property values are affected by factors that influence the values of surrounding properties. Therefore, the type and character of nearby land uses affect commercial districts.

In the 1950s and 1960s, trends in population growth, suburbanization, and the availability of automobiles powered by inexpensive energy encouraged outward urban expansion. This period saw the widespread development of shopping centers outside of CBDs. By the mid-1970s, large regional shopping centers and smaller community centers were beginning to supplant older central business districts. Commercial businesses located in shopping centers often benefitted from their association with complementary establishments. Businesses in downtown areas and strip developments did not fare as well, and commercial activity in many downtown areas declined. To forestall the prospect of further decline, some CBDs made efforts at revitalization, which met with varying degrees of success.

The mid-1980s to late 1980s witnessed an unprecedented building boom. The construction of many new regional and community malls glutted an already abundant inventory of retail space. The sluggish economy of the early 1990s resulted in a rather depressed selling environment. Consequently, by the mid-1990s, the retail market was evidencing a dramatic decline in shopping center construction, with retailers pulling out of many centers and the closure of more than 10% of all regional malls.

To analyze a commercial district's trade area, an appraiser focuses on the quantity and quality of the purchasing power of the population likely to patronize the shopping area. The appraiser also considers other factors, including

- Significant locational considerations such as the time-distance from potential customers, access, highway medians, and traffic signals
- Economic trends in the buying power of the residential neighborhood served
- Physical characteristics such as the visibility, attractiveness, quality of construction, and condition of properties
- Direction of observable growth
- Character and location of existing or anticipated competition
- Retailers' inventory, investments, leasehold improvements, and enterprise
- Availability of land for expansion and customer parking
- Pedestrian or vehicular traffic count
- 100% location or anchors and core groupings

When analyzing a group of local retail enterprises that are not located in a shopping center, an appraiser also examines the zoning policies that govern the supply of competing sites, the reasons for vacancies and business failure, and the level of rents compared with current rent levels in new buildings.

Central Business Districts

A central business district (CBD) is the core, or downtown area, of a city where the major retail, financial, governmental, professional, recreational, and service activities of the community are concentrated. Over the past quarter of a century, CBDs have not experienced the same pattern of growth and development as other commercial districts. The development of surburban commercial centers and the countervailing decline of inner urban areas have undercut the former predominance of CBDs.

Appraisers should be aware of the general trend for CBDs, but should also recognize that some CBDs have brighter outlooks than others. The CBDs of Boston, San Francisco, New York, Chicago, and Washington, D.C. are cases in point. Transportation facilities in most cities are oriented to the CBD. Through downtown development associations, many merchants have attempted to revitalize CBDs with improved public transportation, larger parking areas, better access, and coordinated sales promotion programs.

The diverse enterprises located in CBDs usually reflect several types of land use, e.g., retail stores, offices, financial institutions, and entertainment facilities. Retail clothing stores may primarily serve office employees and other retail establishments tend to locate where large numbers of people work, shop, and live. Financial institutions are often found in areas with other financial institutions. Major entertainment and cultural facilities usually operate in or near CBDs to serve the greatest number of residents and out-of-town visitors. Different parts of the CBD attract different uses, and the enterprises within a single general use category may be diverse. For example, office buildings in different parts of a CBD may house a wide variety of business and professional firms.

Appraisers should recognize that shifting functions within CBDs can lead to changes in land use and potential increases in real estate values. For example, a shift from commercial use to office and entertainment uses may attract more restaurants, art galleries, and specialty shops to a downtown area. Over the past decade, many CBDs have come to represent destinations, with prominent stores that enjoy name recognition and are near to complementary entertainment or recreational facilities. Quite often, destination shopping is a dual-purpose outing which allows the entire family to participate in both shopping and recreational activities.

To assess the viability of a CBD, an appraiser must consider the sales potential of various commercial products and services and determine whether establishments in the CBD can attract a share of the market. To evaluate the utility of a particular location within a CBD, the appraiser considers which use or mix of uses—e.g., office, hotel, retail, or entertainment—is most appropriate.

Regional Shopping Centers

A regional shopping center provides a variety of general merchandise, apparel, furniture, home furnishings, service, and recreational facilities built around one or more full department stores of at least 100,000 square feet each. Regional shopping centers contain the same type of stores found in neighborhood centers, but in greater variety and number. A regional center may also have banks, service establishments, medical and business offices, and theaters.

A regional shopping center's trade area may include several neighborhood centers. Although neighborhood centers may compete with a regional center for certain segments of economic support, neighborhood centers serve their immediate areas and may be seen as supplementing, rather than competing with, the major shopping services provided by a regional center.

The largest shopping centers are the superregional centers, which generally serve large metropolitan areas. *A superregional shopping center provides an extensive variety of general merchandise, apparel, furniture, home furnishings, service, and recreational facilities built around at least three major department stores of at least 100,000 square feet each.* The gross leasable area of a superregional center may exceed 1,000,000 square feet.

In addition to the major department stores and other businesses found in regional centers, superregional centers contain specialty shops, arcades, and restaurants. Because a superregional center offers an exceptionally wide variety of retail goods and services, its trade area is extensive. Trade areas are also extended by major transportation arteries and linkages, so the trade areas for some superregional centers transcend state boundaries.

The siting of a superregional shopping center is a complex task, which includes consideration of existing regional shopping centers, demographic trends, and transportation corridors. The land costs for superregional centers are high, and a center can significantly affect the value of surrounding properties by creating a demand for uses that complement the uses found within the center.

Like superregional shopping centers, regional centers generate substantial value for the land they occupy and significantly influence the values of surrounding sites and tracts. Generally, regional centers increase the value of adjacent or nearby land because they create a demand for satellite stores, office buildings, and other commercial uses. These centers may also stimulate demand for new single-family or multifamily residential development.

Community Shopping Centers

A community shopping center is a center of between 100,000 and 300,000 square feet that usually contains one junior department store, a variety store or discount department store, a supermarket, and specialty shops. Community shopping centers may also offer professional and financial services and recreational facilities. A community shopping center is part of the community or area it serves.

A community center's customers usually come from areas that are 10 to 20 minutes away by car. The viability of such a center depends on the sales potential for the various products and services it offers. The market allocates this potential among the various competing establishments in the service area. Sales potential may be estimated from surveys of consumer buying patterns, which are conducted by the U.S. Department of Commerce, and from information gathered by universities, private companies, and trade organizations. Historical patterns and changes in the number and types of competing establishments may also be studied to determine the market share of a particular center.

Neighborhood Shopping Centers and Strip Shopping Centers

A neighborhood shopping center is the smallest type of shopping center, with a gross leasable area of between 30,000 and 100,000 square feet. Neighborhood shopping centers provide for the sale of convenience goods (e.g., food, drugs, and sundries) and personal services (e.g., laundry, dry cleaning, shoe repair, and hair styling) to satisfy the daily needs of those residing in the immediate neighborhood. Neighborhood shopping centers must offer easy access and adequate parking and they must be situated in good locations, on or near public transportation routes. Since so many neighborhood shopping centers are located along well-trafficked roads, they are often referred to as *strip shopping centers*.

Specialty Centers

In addition to regional, community, and neighborhood shopping centers, there are many retail centers that may be classified as types of *specialty centers*. Specialty shopping centers are characterized by an absence of a traditional anchor tenant, whose role may be taken over by another type of tenant or by a grouping of tenants which collectively function as an anchor.[4] Specialty shopping centers include:

---

4. James D. Vernor and Joseph Rabianski, *Shopping Center Appraisal and Analysis* (Chicago: Appraisal Institute, 1993), 11-16.

- *Festival center.* A group of shops catering to impulse buying and characterized by a mix of restaurants and food vendors
- *Fashion center.* A concentration of boutiques and sometimes one or more high-quality apparel stores
- *Outlet mall.* A mall containing several factory outlet stores
- *Discount or wholesale center.* Similar to a community shopping center but with a discount department store as the anchor
- *Power center.* Generally a center with four or more anchor tenants
- *"Big box" general merchandise store.* Value retailers
- *Hypermart.* Similar to a community shopping center in terms of the selection of retail goods, but more akin to a regional shopping center in market dominance
- *Warehouse club.* Similar to a discount center but only open to dues-paying members

Office Districts

Office districts consist of groups of office buildings, which can range in size from small structures to large, multistory buildings. They may contain offices primarily for members of one profession, such as doctors or lawyers, or offices that serve a variety of tenants. The offices may be executive suites of multinational corporations or back offices for small service companies.

Office districts include planned office parks and strip developments on or near major traffic arteries. Office parks, which are also known as *business parks*, often have industrial users among their tenants because the parks offer good locations, easy access, attractive surroundings, and utility without the congestion and high rents of the CBD. Office parks are increasingly providing facilities for service industries as well.

Office park
(H. Armstrong Roberts, Inc.)

Industrial Districts

Land and building values in an industrial district are influenced by the nature of the district, the labor supply, transportation facilities, the economics of bringing in raw material and distributing finished products, the political climate, the availability of utilities and energy, and the effect of environmental controls. To arrive at an informed conclusion about the value of an industrial property, the appraiser must obtain pertinent data on these influences.

Industrial districts range from those that contain heavy industry, such as steel plants, foundries, and chemical companies, to those that house assembly and other "clean" operations. In most urban areas, heavy industry and light industry districts are established by zoning ordinances, which may limit uses and place controls on air pollution, noise levels, and outdoor operations. In older manufacturing or warehouse districts, obsolete, multistory, elevator buildings are typical and parking and expansion areas are limited. Newer manufacturing districts and industrial parks usually consist of one-story buildings. Each industrial district has a value pattern which reflects the market's reaction to its location and the characteristics of its sites and improvements.

Availability of labor. A district is desirable to industry only if it has an adequate and suitable work force, so an appraiser must ascertain whether there is an acceptable labor supply. The characteristics and pay levels of the labor force are important, as is the recent history of local labor-management relations.

Industrial park
(H. Armstrong Roberts, Inc.)

Because industry depends on a labor supply, many industrial districts are located near residential communities. Workers may be attracted to a particular plant by special inducements such as a company cafeteria, other employee facilities, or social activities; a plant's parklike appearance may be an advantage.

Availability of materials. Manufacturing operations need a convenient, economical source of raw or semifinished materials and facilities to distribute manufactured products conveniently and inexpensively. The desirability of a district or site depends greatly on its access to raw materials.

Distribution facilities. The size, weight, and nature of commodities and the distance to their destination determine how they are shipped—by air, rail, truck, or water. Access to major highways, adequate ingress and egress, and on-site parking and maneuvering areas are crucial considerations for most manufacturing and warehouse operations.

The environmental liabilities incurred by industrial properties are considerably more complex than those that affect other property types. Industrial properties may contain underground storage tanks for a broad range of chemicals. The presence of asbestos and PCBs may be more widespread. Long-term contamination tends to be more severe and cleanup costs can be very high.

Farm district
(H. Armstrong Roberts, Inc.)

Agricultural Districts

Agricultural districts vary in size from a portion of a township to several counties. Most important value influences relate to individual properties rather than an entire agricultural district because farms may be far apart. Nevertheless, the physical features of an agricultural district are usually representative of the individual farms and contribute to their desirability. To define an agricultural district, an appraiser considers soil types, the crops grown, the animals raised, typical land use, the average size of the farming operations in the district, and whether the operations are run by owners or tenants.

Grain farm districts are usually characterized by soil types and topography that are conducive to growing and harvesting crops such as corn and wheat. Orchards and groves make up another type of district in which the soil type and climate combine to create a distinct economy. Areas that cannot produce cash crops may be adapted to growing certain grasses. Generally, grasslands are used for livestock production and their boundaries are determined by altitude and climate.

Dairies are found where the soil is suited for growing pasture grasses and hay. These areas are served by highways that lead to marketing centers where farm products are sold. Like an urban neighborhood, the farm community depends on government services such as roads and schools and on the availability of electricity.

Environmental liabilities for agricultural properties may include cattle vats, turpentine stills, fertilizers, pesticides, and underground storage tanks.

Specialty Neighborhoods and Districts

Some areas that contain specialized activities qualify as neighborhoods or districts. An area can be regarded as a district or a neighborhood if it has common functions or land uses. Although similar procedures are used to analyze all neighborhoods and districts, the specific characteristics that contribute to the desirability and value of an area vary according to its function.

Medical Districts

A district may be composed entirely of hospitals, health care facilities, and physicians' offices. A medical district may include one or more hospitals with related facilities such as parking lots and patient services buildings, a number of physicians' offices, and several pharmacies. Medical districts can be found in densely populated urban areas and in spacious, parklike settings.

The desirability and value of a property such as a doctors' office building depend on its age and proximity to hospitals and other medical offices. The quality of professional personnel and the availability of modern equipment are also important considerations.

The disposal of medical waste and potentially infectious materials has become highly controversial. Many hospitals incinerate their waste, while others have it shipped offshore.

Research and Development Parks

Research and development parks may contain the research and development departments of large drug, chemical, or computer companies, or they may cater to firms that specialize in research activities. Research firms are usually small and specialize in identifying and developing new products, which are sold to other firms. Occasionally a small research firm will create, develop, and market a new product with considerable success, but then the nature of the firm must shift from research to marketing. Research and development parks are often sponsored and promoted by universities. Proximity to a university can provide a research operation with a convenient source of technical expertise and qualified employees. Universities may sponsor a park to sell excess land, provide employment for students and faculty, and raise an area's level of economic activity.

High Technology Parks

Firms engaged in high-tech activities often locate near one another or in parks where technical expertise may be available from a nearby university or research park. Electronics and computer firms have dominated high technology parks, but firms involved with space equipment, drugs, cosmetics, and aviation may also have offices in these areas.

Education Districts

Local schools, colleges, and universities may constitute a district if they have several buildings or facilities and are considered an integral part of the surrounding residential neighborhood. Education districts may contribute economically as well as socially and culturally to the surrounding community. Colleges and universities often attract students from far away who bring income to the community and thus contribute to its economic base. In some towns and smaller cities, universities and colleges may provide most of the economic base. An education district should be readily accessible to the surrounding residential neighborhood.

Historic Districts

Since 1931 when the first historic district zoning ordinance was passed in the United States, interest in preserving historically and architecturally significant properties has grown and given rise to a unique type of district.[5] The establishment of historic districts is one of the most widely applied and rapidly developing techniques for preserving cultural heritage.

Historic districts may be informally perceived by observers, or they may be formally designated by local, state, or federal agencies. Historic districts are federally certified only after stringent requirements have been met, including substantial compliance with the criteria of the National Register of Historic Places.[6] Once districts are federally certified, developers, investors, and renovation specialists can qualify for tax incentives such as the liberal tax credits allowed under the Economic Recovery Tax Act of 1981 (which were subsequently reduced by the Tax Reform Act of 1986). Historic preservation has also been aided in many cities by using federal Urban Development Action Grants (UDAGs) to fund preservation projects in blighted neighborhoods.

Historic districts may include residential property, commercial property, industrial property, or other types of property alone or in combination with one another. Appraisers must become thoroughly familiar with the criteria applicable to each district's designation status and how these criteria are, or may be, applied to properties within district boundaries.

---

5. Russell V. Keune, ed., *The Historic Preservation Yearbook* (Bethesda, Md.: Adler & Adler, 1984), 461. See also William E. Lockard, Jr. and Dudley S. Hinds, "Historic Zoning Considerations in Neighborhood and District Analysis," *The Appraisal Journal* (October 1983); Virginia O. Benson and Richard Klein, "The Impact of Historic Districting on Property Values," *The Appraisal Journal* (April 1988); and Paul K. Asabere and Forrest E. Huffman, "Historic Designation and Residential Market Value," *The Appraisal Journal* (July 1994).
6. Keune, 328.

Neighborhood and District Analysis in Form Reports

Some organizations, businesses, and federal agencies have developed forms to standard-ize the reporting of appraisal data. The most widely used form is the Uniform Residential Appraisal Report (URAR) form. Appraisal forms such as the URAR include spaces for recording information on the many variables important to neighborhood analysis. (See Figure 9.1.)

A form report is not simply an exercise in checking boxes. The form must usually be supplemented by comments and addenda that communicate the additional informa-tion required to complete the appraisal. In some cases self-contained reports, which provide a broader scope and accommodate more detail, may better serve the needs of the appraisal client.

Standard 2 of the Uniform Standards of Professional Appraisal Practice requires that any report communicating the results of an appraisal comply with specific reporting guidelines.

> In reporting the results of a real property appraisal an appraiser must com-municate each analysis, opinion, and conclusion in a manner that is not misleading.

> *Standards Rule 2-1.* Each written or oral real property appraisal report must: (a) clearly and accurately set forth the appraisal in a manner that will not be misleading; (b) contain sufficient information to enable the person(s) who are expected to receive or rely on the report to understand it properly; (c) clearly and accurately disclose any extraordinary assump-tion or limiting condition that directly affects the appraisal and indicate its impact on value.

Key Concepts

- In neighborhood and district analysis, an appraiser studies how value influences affect property.
- Neighborhoods are defined by a combination of factors, e.g., physical features, the demographic and socioeconomic characteristics of the residents or tenants, the condition of the improvements (age, upkeep, ownership and vacancy rates), and land use trends.
- Neighborhoods often pass through a four-stage life cycle of growth, stability, decline, and revitalization. Some neighborhoods may bypass stages in this cycle.
- Neighborhood analysis focuses on the four forces—social, economic, governmental, and environmental—that influence value. Analysis of the four forces is performed by investigating specific factors pertaining to each.
- Extensive environmental legislation has passed since 1980 (e.g., CERCLA, SARA, reform provisions in EPA policy statements) to remediate environmental contami-nation and delineate the liability of property owners.

Figure 9.1 | Neighborhood Analysis Section of the URAR

NEIGHBORHOOD

Location	☐ Urban	☐ Suburban	☐ Rural
Built up	☐ Over 75%	☐ 25-75%	☐ Under 25%
Growth rate	☐ Rapid	☐ Stable	☐ Slow
Property values	☐ Increasing	☐ Stable	☐ Declining
Demand/supply	☐ Shortage	☐ In balance	☐ Over supply
Marketing time	☐ Under 3 mos.	☐ 3-6 mos.	☐ Over 6 mos.

Predominant occupancy
☐ Owner
☐ Tenant
☐ Vacant (0-5%)
☐ Vacant (over 5%)

Single family housing

PRICE $(000)	AGE (yrs)
Low	
High	
Predominant	Predominant

Present land use %
One family _____
2-4 family _____
Multi-family _____
Commercial _____
(_____) _____

Land use change
☐ Not likely ☐ Likely
☐ In process
To: _____

Note: Race and the racial composition of the neighborhood are not appraisal factors.

Neighborhood boundaries and characteristics: _____

Factors that affect the marketability of the properties in the neighborhood (proximity to employment and amenities, employment stability, appeal to market, etc.): _____

Market conditions in the subject neighborhood (including support for the above conclusions related to the trend of property values, demand/supply, and marketing time...such as data on competitive properties for sale in the neighborhood, description of the prevalence of sales and financing concessions, etc.): _____

- Advisory Opinion 9 and Guide Note 8 of the Standards of Professional Appraisal Practice address the responsibility of appraisers in detecting environmental problems. The Property Observation Checklist of the Appraisal Institute may be used to inspect a property and to record observations about possible environmental factors.
- Environmental site assessments (ESAs) and environmental property assessments (EPRAs) are often required for approval of a sale or loan. The extent of an environmental assessment may correspond to one of three phases.
- Broad diversity exists within the basic categories of neighborhoods and districts, e.g., residential, commercial, business, industrial, medical, education, agricultural, and historic.

Terms

agricultural district

apartment and multifamily
  district

business district

central business district (CBD)

commercial district

community shopping center

Comprehensive Environmental
  Response, Compensation, and
  Liability Act of 1980 (CERCLA)

decline

destination shopping

displacement

district

education district

environmental hazards/liabilities

environmental property
  assessment (EPRA)

Environmental Protection Agency
  (EPA)

environmental remediation/cleanup

environmental site assessment
  (ESA)

gentrification

growth

high technology parks

historic district

industrial district

innocent purchaser

joint and several liability

linkages

location

medical district

neighborhood

neighborhood or district boundaries

neighborhood or district life cycle

neighborhood and strip shopping
  center

nuisance

office district

Property Observation Checklist

regional shopping center

research and development park

residential district

revitalization

single-family residential
  neighborhood

siting

specialty center

stability

stigmatized property

strict liability

Superfund Amendments and
  Reauthorization Act of 1986
  (SARA)

superregional shopping center

time-distance linkage

trade area

CHAPTER TEN

Land or Site Description

A ppraisal assignments may be undertaken to estimate the value of land only or the value of both land and improvements. In either case the appraiser must make a detailed description and analysis of the land. Land can be raw or improved; raw land can be undeveloped or in agricultural use. Land may be located in rural, suburban, or urban areas and may have the potential to be developed for residential, commercial, industrial, agricultural, or special-purpose use.

A site is land that is improved so that it is ready to be used for a specific purpose. A site can have both on-site and off-site improvements which make it suitable for its intended use or development. Off-site improvements may include water, drainage, and sewer systems; utility lines; and access to roads. On-site improvements may include landscaping, accessory buildings, and support facilities.

In appraising any type of property, an appraiser must describe and analyze the land or site. *A land or site description is a detailed listing of factual data, including a legal description, other title and record data, and information on pertinent physical characteristics.* A land or site analysis goes further. *A land or site analysis is a careful study of factual data in relation to the neighborhood characteristics that create, enhance, or detract from the utility and marketability of the land or site as compared with competing land or sites.*

Improved real estate consists of two distinct entities—the land and the improvements. Although the two are joined physically, it is often desirable and sometimes necessary to value them separately. Separate valuations may be required for specific purposes such as

- Local tax assessment
- Estimating building depreciation
- Application of specific appraisal techniques
- Establishing ground rent
- Estimating casualty loss
- Valuation of agricultural land

One primary objective of land or site analysis is to gather data that will indicate the highest and best use of the land or site as though vacant so that land value can be estimated in terms of that use. (See Chapter 13 for a full discussion of highest and best use.) Whether a site or raw land is being valued, the appraiser must determine and evaluate its highest and best use. When the highest and best use of land is for agriculture, an appraiser usually analyzes and values the land by applying the sales comparison and income capitalization approaches. If the land will be developed for urban residential or commercial use, the appraiser may use subdivision development analysis, a special application of the income capitalization approach.

Land or site description and analysis are conducted to provide

- A description of the property being appraised
- A basis for selecting comparable sales
- A basis for allocating values to the land and the improvements
- An understanding of the property being appraised and its present use
- A foundation for determining the property's highest and best use

This chapter focuses on the description and analysis of the land component of real property. Because appraisers typically deal with land that has been improved to some degree, the term *site* is used except when raw land is specified. The information needed to complete a full site description and analysis is noted and explained, and sources for obtaining this information are presented. Although this discussion relates primarily to the property being appraised, the same type of data are collected and examined in analyzing the comparable properties used in the appraisal.

Legal Descriptions of Land

Land boundaries differentiate separate ownerships and the land within one set of boundaries may be referred to as a *parcel*, *lot*, *plot*, or *tract*. These terms may be applied to all types of improved and unimproved land.

A parcel of land generally refers to a piece of land that may be identified by a common description and is held in one ownership. Every parcel of real estate is unique. To identify individual parcels, appraisers use legal descriptions. A legal description identifies a property in such a way that it cannot be confused with any other property. Because it specifically identifies and locates a parcel of real property, a legal description is often included in an appraisal report. The legal description of a property is usually entered on a deed, which may be obtained from the owner of the property or from county records.

In the United States three methods are commonly used to describe real property legally—the metes and bounds system, the rectangular survey system, and the lot and block system. An appraiser should be familiar with these forms of legal description and know which form or forms are accepted in the area where the appraisal is being conducted.

Metes and Bounds

The oldest known method of surveying land is the metes and bounds system, in which land is measured and identified by describing its boundaries. The system is centuries old, dating back to a time when property boundaries were set by a buyer and a seller walking the perimeter of a property and establishing landmarks along the way. Surveying tracts by metes and bounds was common in Western Europe and, when North America was colonized, the system was employed extensively in transferring property from crown governments to colonists and in transfers between colonists. Because this system was used when the colonies were settled, it is the primary method for describing real property in the original 13 states. Eight other states have adopted the method as well. Metes and bounds descriptions are used extensively throughout the United States, often in conjunction with the government survey system. An example of a metes and bounds description is shown in Figure 10.1.

A metes and bounds description of a parcel of real property describes the property's boundaries in terms of reference points. To follow a metes and bounds description, one starts at the point of beginning (POB), a primary survey reference point that is tied to adjoining surveys, and moves through several intermediate reference points before finally returning to the POB. The return is called *closing* and is necessary to ensure the survey's accuracy.

| Figure 10.1 | **Metes and Bounds System** |

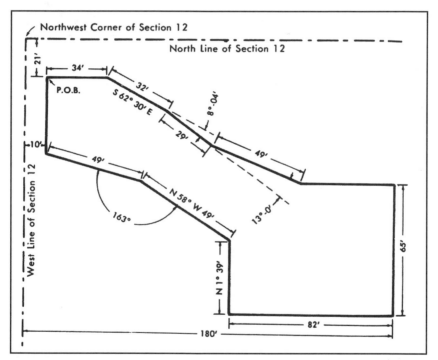

Description of Tract: Commencing at the Northwest corner of Section 12 thence South along the section line 21 feet; thence East 10 feet for a place of beginning; thence continuing East 34 feet; thence South 62 degrees, 30 minutes East 32 feet; thence Southeasterly along a line forming an angle of 8 degrees, 04 minutes to the right with a prolongation of the last described course 29 feet; thence South 13 degrees, 0 minutes to the left with a prolongation of the last described line a distance of 49 feet; thence East to a line parallel with the West line of said Section and 180 feet distant therefrom; thence South on the last described line a distance of 65 feet; thence due West a distance of 82 feet; thence North 1 degree West 39 feet; thence North 58 degrees West a distance of 49 feet; thence Northwesterly along a line forming an angle of 163 degrees as measured from right to left with the last described line a distance of 49 feet; thence North to the place of beginning.

Bounds refer to the POB, which is also the point of return, and all intermediate points. Points, which are sometimes called *monuments,* may refer to marked stones, trees, a creek, or the corner of another property, or they may be simply survey reference points. *Metes* describe the direction one moves from one reference point to another and the distances between points. One moves from point to point by knowing the courses of each point, which are identified in degrees, minutes, and seconds of an angle from the north or south. Thus, in moving from one point to another, one is moving from the vertex of one angle to the vertex of another.

Distances between angles are measured linearly in feet. Sometimes, however, this measurement between angles is found to be inaccurate. When this happens, the actual distance between points or monuments is measured; actual distance takes precedence over angle measurement, especially in boundary disputes. Permanent benchmarks, which are survey markers set in heavy concrete monuments, are used to eliminate possible confusion regarding points of beginning.

Today surveyors in the field increasingly rely on "total stations" to collect data in digital form. These data are then "dumped" into the surveyor's office computer. Computer software allows for more accurate determinations of directions, distances, and areas.

The metes and bounds system is the primary method of describing real property in 21 states, and it is often used in other states as a corollary to the rectangular survey system, especially in describing unusual or odd-shaped parcels of land.

Rectangular Survey System

As the United States began to expand to the south and west, a more convenient system of land description was needed to facilitate the sale of large tracts of land that the federal government had acquired through purchases, treaties, and war. Because the government needed to generate revenue by selling the land quickly in a simple and orderly fashion, the U.S. Rectangular Survey System was created.

The rectangular survey system, which is also known as the *government survey system*, was established by a land ordinance passed on May 20, 1785. In 1786 the first public land surveys in the United States were made in Ohio.[1] The rectangular survey system became the principal method of land description for most land west of the Ohio and Mississippi rivers. Florida, Alabama, and Mississippi were also included in the system, but land that was settled or colonized prior to the ordinance was not. Public lands in 30 states were surveyed in accordance with this system.

The initial reference points for government surveys were established under the direction of the Geographer of the United States. From each point specified, true east-west and north-south lines were drawn. The east-west lines are called *base lines* and the north-south lines are called *principal meridians*. Each principal meridian has a unique name and is crossed by its own base line. Using these base lines and principal meridians, land can be located accurately.

---

1. The government survey system evolved over half a century. Initially, exterior township lines with sectional corners at one-mile intervals were established (1785). Then the sections were numbered (1796) and subdivided into half sections (1800). The practice of allowing for excesses or deficiencies in measurement in the most westerly and northerly half mile of each township also dates back to 1800. The sections were further subdivided into quarter sections (1805) and quarter quarter sections (1832); the lines of division for half quarter sections run on an east-west axis.

The land surveyed under the rectangular survey system is divided by north-south lines six miles apart called *range lines*, and by east-west lines six miles apart called *township lines*. The rectangles created where these lines intersect are called *townships*. The standard township is six miles square and contains 36 square miles. When applied to surveying, the term *township* has two meanings: a location on a line north or south of a base line and a square of land that measures six miles by six miles. (In some states, *township* also refers to a political subdivision similar to a county.)

The intersection of a base line and a principal meridian is the starting point from which the range lines and township lines are counted to locate a specific township in a legal description. Ranges are numbered east and west from the principal meridian; townships are numbered north and south from the base line.

In Figure 10.2, the shaded township is four township rows north of the base line

---

Figure 10.2 | **Government Survey System**

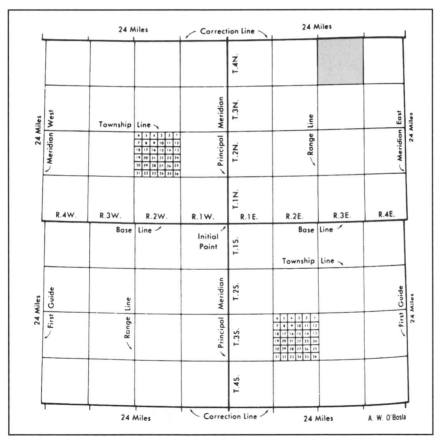

Description of the shaded township: Township 4 North, Range 3 East (T.4N., R.3E.). The township is four township rows north of the base line and three range lines east of the principal meridian. (The township is located in northern California, so the base line and principal meridian may be further identified as Mt. Diablo Base and Meridian.)

Source: John S. Hoag, *Fundamentals of Land Measurement* (Chicago: Chicago Title Insurance Company, 1976), p. 8. Reprinted through courtesy of Chicago Title Insurance Company.

and three range lines east of the principal meridian. If this property were located in northern California, it would be called Township 4 North, Range 3 East, Mt. Diablo Base and Meridian, which would be abbreviated T.4N, R.3E., M.D.B.& M.

Townships are divided into 36 sections, each of which is one mile square and contains 640 acres. For a more specific description of a parcel, a section may be divided into quarter sections and fractions of quarter sections (see Figure 10.3). To accommodate the spherical shape of the earth, additional lines called *guide meridians* are drawn every 24 miles east and west of the principal meridian. Other lines, called *standard parallels*, are drawn every 24 miles north and south of the base line. These correction lines are used to adjust the rectangular townships to fit the curvature of the earth.

Sectioned land descriptions are commonly used and easily understood. A properly

Figure 10.3 | Division of a Section of Land

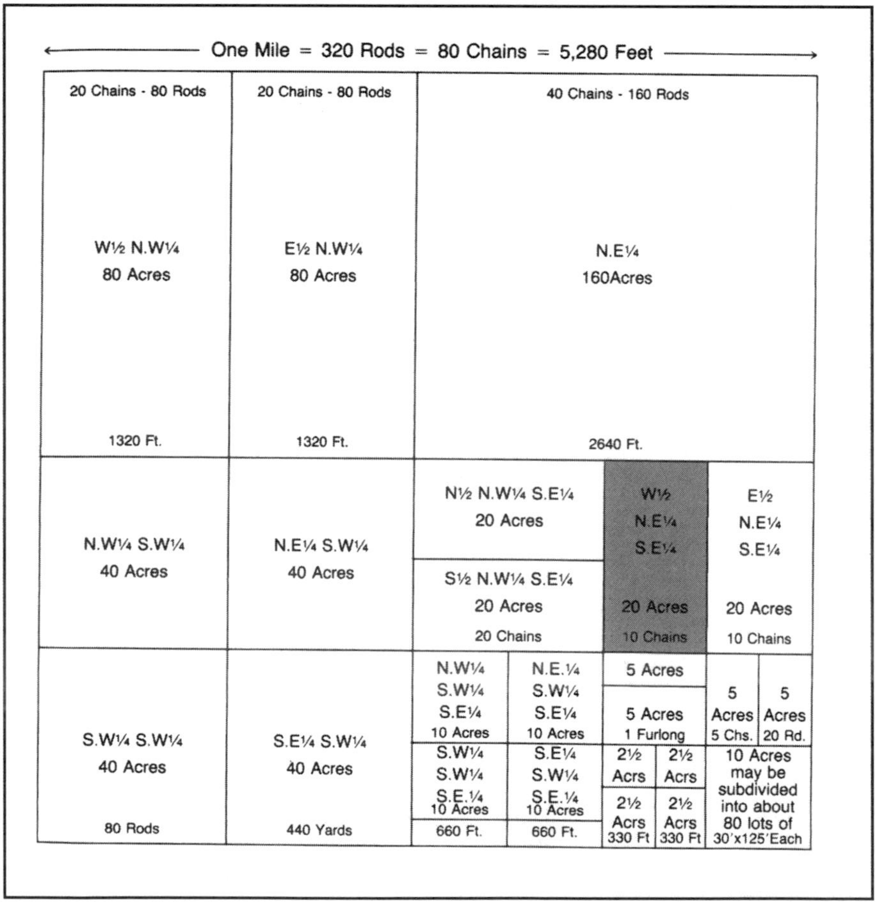

Description of the shaded 20-acre parcel located in the southwestern part of the section: The west half of the northeast quarter of the southeast quarter of Section 10, Township 4 North, Range 3 East (Mt. Diablo Base and Meridian).

written legal description goes from the immediate location to the sectional boundaries—i.e., it begins with the particular site and ends with the base and meridian. The township illustrated in Figure 10.2 is called Township 4 North, Range 3 East. Similarly, Figure 10.3 shows a shaded, 20-acre parcel located in the southeast part of the section, which is properly described as follows: The west half of the northeast quarter of the southeast quarter of Section 10, Township 4 North, Range 3 East, Mt. Diablo Base and Meridian.

Townships are adjusted for the curvature of the earth. As a result, some sections do not contain precisely 640 acres, so this parcel may not contain exactly 20 acres. Furthermore, the township's northern boundary is not exactly six miles long, due to the curvature of the earth and to the convergence of the meridians. This discrepancy and any others caused by errors in measurement are allowed for in the most westerly and northerly half-mile of the township. Irregular townships may also exist due to preexisting land grants and the boundaries of navigable waters.

Shortages and overages in the acreages of sections are usually found in the north and west corners of townships. Fractional sections and government lots may be found where adjustments were necessary.

Lot and Block System

The lot and block system was developed as an outgrowth of the rectangular survey system and can be used to simplify the locational descriptions of small parcels. The system was established when land developers subdivided land in the rectangular survey system and assigned lot numbers to individual sites within blocks. (The numbering of lots and blocks is illustrated in Figure 10.4.) The maps of these subdivisions were then filed with the local government to establish a public record of their locations. Each block was identified precisely using a ground survey or established monuments.

| Figure 10.4 | **Lot and Block System** |

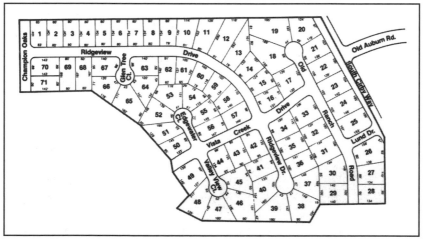

Description of a lot in the rectangular survey area: Lot 10 of Woodridge Creek Unit (Block) 1, a Subdivision of the Southeast quarter of Section 18, Township 10 North, Range 7 East (Mt. Diablo Base and Meridian). (Owner: Sunrise Properties, Sacramento, Calif.; Engineer: Morton and Pitalo, Sacramento, Calif.)

Applying the lot and block system to old, unsurveyed communities helped to identify each owner's site or parcel of land. Typically a surveyor located the boundaries of streets on the ground and drew maps outlining the blocks. Then lot lines were established by agreement among property owners. A precise, measured description was established for each lot and each was given a number or letter that could be referred to in routine transactions. For example, a lot in a rectangular survey area might be described as follows: Lot 5 of Block 18 of Adam's Orangegrove Colony, a Subdivision of the southwest quarter of Section 10, Township 3 North, Range 3 East, Mt. Diablo Base and Meridian.

Title and Record Data

Before making an on-site inspection, an appraiser should obtain necessary property data from published sources and public documents. Most jurisdictions have a public office or depository for deeds where transactions are documented and made public. The accessibility of public records, which is legally known as *constructive notice*, ensures that interested individuals are able to research and, if necessary, contest deed transfers. Most county recorders' offices keep index books for land deeds and land mortgages, from which the book and page number of a recorded deed may be found. An appraiser might also find pertinent information in the property's *abstract of title*, which includes a summary of conveyances, transfers, and other facts used as evidence of title as well as any other public documents that may impair title. In addition, official county plat books may be examined in the county auditor's office.

Sometimes public records do not contain all relevant information about a particular property. Although official documents are the most dependable sources of information, they may be incomplete or not suited to the appraiser's purposes. Useful support data can be found in land registration systems, land data banks, and assessors' maps.

Ownership Information

A property's legal owner and type of ownership can be ascertained from the public records maintained by the county clerk and recorder. Local title or abstract companies may also provide useful information.

The most common form of property ownership is ownership in fee simple. If a property is not to be appraised in fee simple, the elements of title that are to be excluded should be indicated and carefully analyzed. If, for example, an appraiser is asked to estimate the value of a fractional ownership interest, he or she must understand the exact type of legal ownership to define the property rights to be appraised.

An appraiser must also find out if the property being appraised has any outstanding rights that may affect its value. The Uniform Standards of Professional Appraisal Practice require that appraisers investigate any previous property ownership occurring within a specified number of years.[2] The appraiser should also investigate the ownership of surface and subsurface rights. He or she may have access to a title report, an abstract of title, or other documentary evidence of the property rights to be appraised. Title data indicate easements and restrictions, which may limit the use of the property, as well as

---

2. See Standards Rule 1-5 of the Uniform Standards of Professional Appraisal Practice.

special rights and obligations such as air rights, water rights, mineral rights, obligations for lateral support, and easements for common walls.

Easements, rights-of-way, and private and public restrictions affect property value. Easements may provide for electrical transmission lines, underground sewers or tunnels, flowage, aviation routes, roads, walkways, and open space. Some easements or rights-of-way acquired by utility companies or public agencies may not be used for many years and the appraiser's physical inspection of the property may not disclose any evidence of such use. Nevertheless, the appraiser should search diligently for information pertaining to any limitations on ownership rights.

Restrictions cited in the deed may limit the type of building or business that may be conducted on the property. A typical example is a restriction that prohibits the sale of liquor or gasoline in a certain place. Often a title report will not specify the details of private restrictions; a copy of the deed or other conveyance must be obtained to identify the limitations imposed on the property.

Zoning and Land Use Information

Land use and development may be regulated by city or county government, but they are often subject to regional, state, and federal controls as well. In analyzing zoning and building codes, an appraiser considers all current regulations and the likelihood of a change in the code. Usually a zone calls for a general use, such as residential, commercial, or industrial, and then specifies a type or density of use. Zoning regulations often control the height and size of buildings, lot coverage, the number of units allowed, parking requirements, sign requirements, building setbacks, plan lines for future street widenings, and other factors of importance to the highest and best use of the site.

Most zoning ordinances identify and define the uses to which a property may be put without reservation or recourse to legal intervention. They also describe the process for obtaining nonconforming use permits, variances, and zoning changes, if permitted. Although zoning ordinances and maps are public records that are available at zoning offices, an appraiser may need help from planning and zoning staff to understand the impact of zoning regulations. Often an appraiser must contact several agencies. Many zoning and land use restrictions are not listed in the recorded title to a property, so confirmation from controlling agencies may be necessary.

In areas subject to floods, earthquakes, and other natural hazards, special zoning and building regulations may impose restrictions on construction. In coastal and historic districts, zoning restrictions may govern building location and design.

Public land use and government programs in an area can also affect land uses and values. The construction of public parking garages in an area, for example, may enhance or detract from property values. Requirements for the provision of mixed low- and high-cost housing can directly affect land use.

Probable changes in government regulations must also be considered. If, for example, a building moratorium or cessation of land use applications is in effect for a stated period, a property's prospective highest and best use may have to be delayed.

The reasonable probability of a zoning change must be considered. Highest and best use recommendations may rely on the probability of a zoning change. One of the criteria for the highest and best use conclusion is that the use must be legally permissible. If the highest and best use of a site is predicated on a zoning change, the appraiser must investigate the probability that such a change will occur. The appraiser may interview planning and zoning staff and study patterns of zoning change to assess the likelihood of a change. The appraiser can generally eliminate those uses that are clearly not compatible with existing uses in the area as well as uses that have previously been denied. The appraiser may also prepare a forecast of land development for the area. If the zoning of the subject site is not compatible with the probable forecast uses, the likelihood of a change in the zoning is especially high. The appraiser should recognize, however, that a zoning change is *never* 100% certain.

Assessment and Tax Information

Real property taxes in all jurisdictions are based on ad valorem assessments. The records of the county assessor or tax collector can provide details concerning a property's assessed value and annual tax burden. Often, an appraiser obtains the property inventory on which the property assessment is based before conducting his or her own physical inspection and inventory of the property.

Taxation levels are significant in considering a property's potential uses. From the present assessment, the current tax rate, and a review of previous tax rates, the appraiser can form a conclusion about future trends in property taxation. Assessed values may not be good indicators of the market value of individual properties because mass appraisals based on statistical methodology tend to equalize the application of taxes to achieve parity among district assessment levels. Nevertheless, in some areas and for some property types, assessed value may approximate market value. The reliability of local assessments as indicators of market value varies from district to district.

Tax Parcels

Some government authorities lay out tax parcels using a variation of the lot and block system. Typically tax parcels are established by numerical reference to the coded map books maintained by the assessing authority. Tax parcels are identified with numbers that refer to the map book, the page, the block, and the parcel number.

Physical Characteristics of Land

In site description and analysis, an appraiser describes and interprets how the physical characteristics of the site influence value and how the physical improvements relate to the land and to neighboring properties. Important physical characteristics include site size and shape, corner influence, plottage, excess land, surplus land, topography, utilities, site improvements, accessibility, and environment. The physical characteristics that are important in analyzing agricultural land are soil, drainage, and irrigation.

Size and Shape

A size and shape description states a site's dimensions, street frontage, width, and depth, and sets forth any advantages or disadvantages caused by these physical characteristics.

The appraiser describes the site and analyzes how its size and shape affect property value. Special attention is given to any characteristics that are unusual for the neighborhood. The effects of the size and shape of a property vary with its probable use. For example, an odd-shaped parcel may be appropriate for a dwelling, but unacceptable for certain types of commercial or industrial use.

Land size is measured and expressed in different units depending on local custom and land use. Land suitable for agriculture and large industrial tracts are described in acres. The size of residential and commercial sites is usually expressed in square feet, although acreage may also be used. Dimensions are expressed in feet and tenths of feet for easy calculation.

Frontage is the measured footage of a site that abuts a street, stream, railroad, or other feature recognized by the market. The frontage may or may not be the same as the width of the property because a property may be irregularly shaped or have frontage on more than one side.

Often a site that is larger or smaller than normal will not have the same square foot or acreage value as neighboring sites. Size differences can affect value and are considered in site analysis. Reducing sale prices to unit prices facilitates the analysis of comparable sites. Generally, as size increases, unit prices decrease; conversely, as size decreases, unit prices increase. The functional utility of a site often results from an ideal, or optimum, size and frontage-to-depth ratio. An appraiser should recognize this fact when appraising sites of unusual size or shape. Value tendencies can be observed by studying market sales or leases of lots of various sizes.

Corner Influence

Properties with frontage on two or more streets may have a higher or lower unit value than neighboring properties with frontage on only one street. The advantage of easier access to corner sites may be diminished by a loss of privacy or a loss of utility due to setback requirements. An appraiser must determine whether the local market considers a corner location to be favorable or unfavorable.

In the layout of building improvements and the subdivision of large plots, corner sites allow more flexibility than interior properties. A residence situated on a corner may have a garage or carport at either the side or the rear of the property. Most interior lots have only one possible position for garages or carports. A corner location usually reduces the number of abutting owners from three to two. For commercial properties, a corner location may enhance value by providing added exposure and a convenient rear service entrance. A corner site provides advantageous ingress and egress for a drive-in business.

Corner sites can also have disadvantages. The original cost of constructing off-site improvements for corner sites is higher. Although some or all street costs are apportioned to all the lots in a development, a developer frequently demands and receives higher prices for corner sites. Residences on corner sites are exposed to more traffic noise and danger and provide less security. Owners of corner sites may pay higher costs for front-footage sidewalks and assessments, and the side street setback may affect the permitted size of the building.

For mass appraisal work such as ad valorem taxation, assessors and others compile data and derive mathematical formulas to compute how the site affects a property's value. They use corner influence tables and size adjustments based on mathematical curves. If an appraiser uses the values derived with these formulas, however, unsound value estimates can result. More accurate adjustments for site depth, corner influence, and size can be made by carefully analyzing zoning restrictions, sales data, market attitudes, and preferences.

Plottage or Assemblage

Plottage or assemblage is an increment of value that results when two or more sites are combined to produce greater utility. Sometimes highest and best use results from assembling two or more parcels of land under one ownership. If the combined parcels have a greater unit value than they did separately, plottage value is created. For example, there may be great demand for one-acre lots in an industrial park where most of the platted lots are of one-half acre. By itself, a half-acre lot has a value of $1.00 per square foot. If it were combined with an adjacent half-acre lot, however, the value would increase to $1.50 per square foot. Plottage value may also apply to an existing site of a special size or shape which has greater utility than more conventional, smaller lots. Neighboring land uses and values are analyzed to determine whether an appraised property has plottage value.

Plottage is significant in appraising agricultural land. Properties of less-than-optimum size have lower unit values because they cannot support the modern equipment needed to produce maximum profits. In an urban area, plottage of commercial office and retail sites and of residential apartment sites may increase the unit values of the lots assembled.

Excess Land and Surplus Land

The portion of a property's land area that represents an optimal site for the existing improvements will reflect a typical land-to-building ratio. Land that supports the existing improvement is generally called *utilized land. Excess land, in regard to an improved site, is the land not needed to serve or support the existing improvement.* In regard to a vacant site or a site considered as though vacant, excess land is the land not needed to accommodate the site's primary highest and best use. Such land may have its own highest and best use or may allow for future expansion of the existing or anticipated improvement. If the excess land is marketable or has value for a future use, its market value as vacant land is added to the estimated value of the economic entity.

Surplus land is land that does not serve or support the existing improvement, but cannot be separated from the property and sold off. Surplus land does not have an independent highest and best use.

Topography

Topographical studies provide information about land's contour, grading, natural drainage, soil conditions, view, and general physical usefulness. Sites may differ in value due to these physical characteristics. Steep slopes often impede building construction. Natural

Figure 10.5 | **Topographic Map**

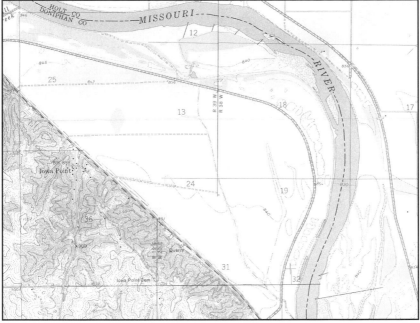

U.S. Geological Survey

drainage can be advantageous, or it can be disadvantageous if a site is downstream from other properties that have the right to direct excess flowage onto it. Adequate storm drainage systems can offset the topographic and drainage problems that would otherwise inhibit the development of such a site.

In describing topography, an appraiser must employ the terminology used in the area. What is described as a steep hill in one part of the country may be considered a moderate slope in another. In some instances, descriptions of a property's topography may be taken from published sources such as contour maps.

Geodetic Survey Program

As part of the rectangular survey system, the U.S. government maintains an active geodetic survey program. Geodetic surveys are performed to map large land areas, taking into account the curvature of the earth's surface. These technically sophisticated surveys are performed for a number of purposes, including the compilation of land elevation data to create topographic maps. The nation's geodetic survey effort is conducted by both the U.S. Coast and Geodetic Survey and the U.S. Geological Survey.

The topographic maps prepared under the direction of the U.S. Geological Survey, which are referred to as *quadrangles*, provide much information that is useful in land descriptions. (See Figure 10.6.) Base lines, principal meridians, and township lines are shown along with topographic and man-made features. The topographic features commonly depicted on these maps include land elevations, which are represented by

Figure 10.6 | **U.S. Department of the Interior Geological Survey**

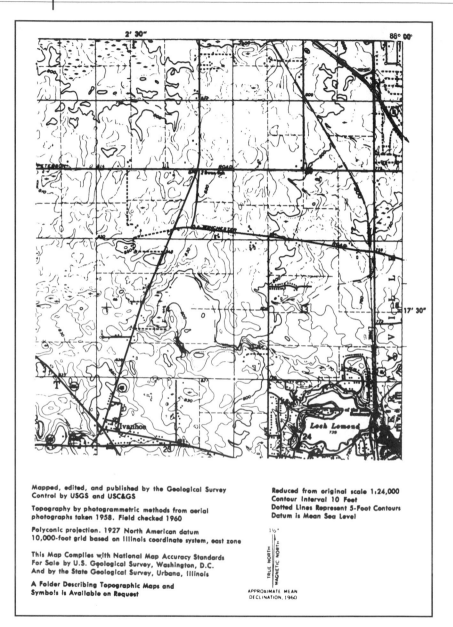

Mapped, edited, and published by the Geological Survey
Control by USGS and USC&GS

Topography by photogrammetric methods from aerial
photographs taken 1958. Field checked 1960

Polyconic projection. 1927 North American datum
10,000-foot grid based on Illinois coordinate system, east zone

This Map Complies with National Map Accuracy Standards
For Sale by U.S. Geological Survey, Washington, D.C.
And by the State Geological Survey, Urbana, Illinois

A Folder Describing Topographic Maps and
Symbols is Available on Request

Reduced from original scale 1:24,000
Contour interval 10 Feet
Dotted Lines Represent 5-Foot Contours
Datum is Mean Sea Level

APPROXIMATE MEAN
DECLINATION, 1960

contour lines at specified intervals, rivers, lakes, intermittent streams and other bodies of water, poorly drained areas, and forest. The man-made features identified include improved and unimproved roads, highways, bridges, power transmission lines, levees, railroads, airports, churches, schools, and other buildings.

Topographic maps are published in series, which refer to the number of minutes of longitude and latitude representing the boundary of a quadrangle. The two most popular series are 7.5 minute and 15 minute, representing scales of 1:24,000 (one inch = 2,000 ft.) and 1:62,500 (one inch = approx. 1 mile), respectively. Quadrangles published in the 7.5 minute series provide greater topographic and cultural detail, but their applicability to land description depends on the nature of the appraisal assignment.[3]

Soil Analysis

Surface soil and subsoil conditions are important for both improved properties and agricultural land. The soil's suitability for building is important for all types of improved property, and it is a major consideration when the construction of large, heavy buildings is being contemplated. The need for special pilings or floating foundations has a major impact on the adaptability of a site for a particular use and, therefore, on its value.

Agronomists and soil scientists measure the agricultural qualities of soil; engineers trained in soil mechanics test for soil consistency. Subsoil conditions are frequently known to local builders, developers, and others, but if there is any doubt about the soil's bearing capacity, the client should be informed of the need for soil studies. All doubts must be resolved before the land's highest and best use can be successfully analyzed.

Floodplain and Wetlands Analysis

The appraiser should check floodplain maps prepared by local governments to determine whether the site is in or near a flood zone of a 100-year floodplain. Such maps are also published by the Federal Emergency Management Agency (FEMA). On these maps, each panel is identified by a FEMA number. Wetlands, as defined by Section 404 of the Clean Water Act, are those areas that are inundated or saturated by surface or groundwater at a frequency and duration sufficient to support, and under normal circumstances do support, a prevalence of vegetation typically adapted for life in saturated soil conditions. Swamps, bogs, fens, marshes, and estuaries are subject to federal environmental law.

Utilities

An appraiser investigates all the utilities and services available to a site. Off-site utilities may be publicly or privately operated, or there may be a need for on-site utility systems such as septic tanks and private water wells. The major utilities to be considered are sanitary sewers; domestic water; types of raw water for commercial, industrial, and agricultural uses; natural gas; electricity; storm drainage; telephone service; and cable television.

Although neighborhood analysis describes in general the utility systems that are available in an area, a site analysis should provide a detailed description of the utilities

---

3. Indexes of U.S. Geological Survey quadrangles for states east of the Mississippi River are available from the Eastern Distribution Branch, U.S. Geological Survey, 1200 S. Eads Street, Arlington, VA 22202. To obtain quadrangles for states west of the Mississippi, contact the Western Distribution Branch, U.S. Geological Survey, Box 25286, Federal Center, Denver, CO 80225.

Figure 10.7 | **Floodplain Map**

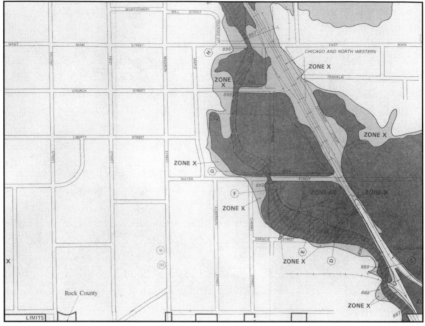

Federal Emergency Management Agency (FEMA)

Figure 10.8 | **Wetlands Map**

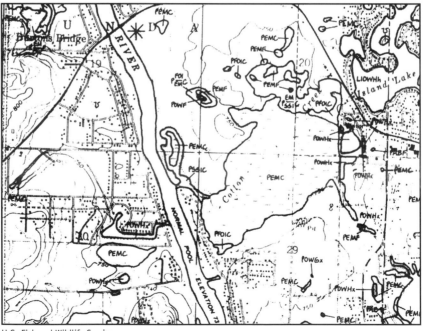

U.S. Fish and Wildlife Service

that are available to the appraised site. The exact size, location, and capacity of the utilities should be determined. It is not sufficient simply to establish which utilities are available. Any limitations resulting from a lack of utilities are important in highest and best use analysis, and all possible, alternative sources of utility service must be investigated.

The rates for utility service and the burden of any bonded indebtedness or other special utility costs should also be considered. Of particular concern to commercial and industrial users are the quality and quantity of water and its cost; the costs and dependability of energy sources; the adequacy of sewer facilities; and any special utility costs or surcharges that might apply to certain businesses.

Accurate information on public utilities can be obtained from local utility companies or agencies, local public works departments, and providers of on-site water and sewage disposal systems.

Site Improvements

In a site description an appraiser describes off-site, as well as on-site, improvements that make the site ready for its intended use or development. Then the appraiser analyzes how the site improvements affect value. The quality, condition, and adequacy of sewer and drainage lines, utility hookups, access roads, and other off-site improvements influence a site's use and value. The appraiser also describes and analyzes on-site improvements such as grading, landscaping, fences, curbs, paving, and walks. The value of off-site site improvements is typically considered with site value.

The location of existing buildings on a site must also be described and analyzed. Many appraisers make plot plans, which show all major buildings in relation to lot lines. Land-to-building ratios are usually quite significant. In a residential area where a typical building covers one-half of the lot, a four-to-one building-to-land ratio may diminish a property's value. The space allotted for parking influences a site's value for business and commercial use, so the parking space-to-building ratio in a commercial property must be analyzed.

The appraiser also notes on-site improvements that add to or detract from a property's probable optimum use. For example, a lot zoned for residential apartments may be improved with an 18-unit apartment building that is too valuable to demolish. If the lot could accommodate a 24-unit building, but the present structure blocks access to the potential location of additional units, the appraiser may conclude that the site is underimproved and not being put to its highest and best use.

Accessibility

Site analysis focuses on the time-distance relationships between the site and common origins and destinations. An appraiser describes and analyzes all forms of access to and from the property and the neighborhood. In most cases, adequate parking area and the location and condition of streets, alleys, connector roads, freeways, and highways are important to land use. Industrial properties are influenced by rail and freeway access and the proximity of docking facilities. Industrial, commercial, and residential areas are all affected by the location of airports, freeways, public transportation, and railroad service.

After noting the facilities available to the site and their conditions, the appraiser analyzes how these facilities affect the site and the uses to which it can be put. Residential sites, for example, are influenced by their access to workplaces, schools, shopping areas, recreational facilities, and places of worship. The appraiser also analyzes how well the transportation facilities serve the needs of property owners in the area.

Traffic volume may be either advantageous or disadvantageous to a site, depending on other conditions that affect its highest and best use. High-volume local traffic in commercial areas is usually an asset; heavy through traffic is deleterious to most retail stores, except those that serve travelers. The volume of traffic passing a property is determined by a traffic count, which can usually be obtained from local or state road departments. Traffic counts indicate average daily traffic, peak hours, and directional flow. Observing the speed and turning movements of actual vehicles helps an appraiser judge how traffic affects a property's highest and best use.

The noise, dust, and fumes that emanate from a heavily traveled artery or freeway are detrimental to most low-density, residential lots. On the other hand, the advertising value of locations on major arteries can benefit offices and shopping centers, unless congestion restricts the free flow of traffic. The visibility of a commercial property from the street is an advertising asset; this asset is most valuable when the driving customer can easily exit the flow of traffic and enter the property.

Median strips, left-turn restrictions, one-way streets, and access restrictions can all limit the potential uses of a parcel. In site analysis the appraiser should test any probable uses of the site in relation to the flow of traffic. Any planned changes in access should be verified with the appropriate authority and considered in the appraisal.

Environment

Appraisers also analyze land use in light of environmental conditions. Environmental considerations include factors such as the local climate, availability of groundwater, pattern of drainage, quality of air, presence of wildlife habitats, location of earthquake faults, and proximity to streams, rivers, lakes, or oceans. Air and water pollution are by-products of increased population and urbanization. Public concern over pollution has prompted political action and legislation to protect the environment. In areas subject to extreme air pollution, regulations may exclude certain industries and limit the volume of traffic; such restrictions impact land use in these jurisdictions. Pollution rights have also become a salable commodity.[4] In locations near natural water sources, industrial uses may be prohibited while recreational uses are promoted. Environmental and climatic advantages and constraints must be thoroughly analyzed to determine the proper land use for a site. Future land uses must be compatible with the local environment.

A site in a specific location may be influenced by its exposure to the sun, the wind, or other environmental factors. A very windy location can be disastrous to a resort, but beneficial to a fossil-fuel power plant. The sunny side of the street is not always the most

---

4. The Clean Air Act of 1990 regulated the tonnage of acid-rain emissions that smokestack industries may release in proportion to plant size. Industries that do not use their full legal allowance can transfer or sell their pollution rights to other industries. Since 1993 pollution rights have been sold on both the Chicago Board of Trade and in the off-exchange pollution-rights market. By 1995, however, the price of pollution rights had nearly collapsed.

desirable for retail shops. In hot climates, the shady side of the street ordinarily gets more pedestrian traffic and greater sales, thus producing higher rents and higher land values.

Analysis of a site's environment focuses on the interrelationships between the appraised site and neighboring properties. The effects of any hazards or nuisances caused by neighboring properties must be considered. Of particular importance are safety concerns—e.g., the safety of employees and customers, of occupants and visitors, of children going to and from school.

A site's value is also influenced by nearby amenities and developments on adjoining sites such as parks, fine buildings, and compatible commercial buildings. The types of structures surrounding the property being appraised and the activities of those who use them can greatly influence site value.

Special Characteristics of Agricultural Resource Land

The following characteristics of agricultural resource lands should be investigated.[5]

- *Soil.* Precise soil surveys that indicate the soils found on properties, appropriate crops, and expected production are often available. These surveys are useful in comparing agricultural properties.

| Figure 10.9 | **Soil Map** |

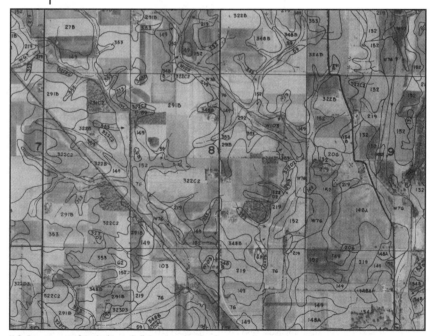

U.S. Department of Agriculture, Soil Conservation Service

---

5. For a thorough discussion of the methods used to describe and analyze the significant characteristics of land used for agricultural production, see *The Appraisal of Rural Property* (Chicago: American Institute of Real Estate Appraisers, 1983), and *Rural Appraisal Manual* (Denver: American Society of Farm Managers and Rural Appraisers, 1991).

- *Drainage and irrigation.* The long-term dependability and cost of adequate drainage and water supplies should be analyzed. (Evaluating on-site drainage and irrigation may require special expertise.)
- *Climate.* General climatic conditions and growing seasons can affect crop production and, therefore, land value.
- *Potential crops.* The crops grown on a property are related not only to climate, soil, and irrigation, but also to the availability of labor, transportation, and access to the markets that make, transport, and sell the products produced from crops.
- *Environmental controls.* Cropping patterns are influenced by regulations on herbicides, insecticides, fertilizers, air and water pollution, and wildlife protection. Underground storage tanks, asbestos in farm buildings, and cattle vats are common environmental liabilities.
- *Other considerations.* The locations of minerals, wildlife habitats, and streams and lakes; the distances from populated areas; and the potential for recreational land uses are among the many other considerations to be analyzed in appraising agricultural land. Special tax provisions, such as reduced taxes on agricultural or resource properties, should also be studied.

Key Concepts

- A land or site description is a detailed listing of data, including a legal description, other title and record data, and information on the physical characteristics of the land.
- In the United States, the three principal methods used to describe real property are the metes and bounds system, the rectangular survey system, and the lot and block system.
- Title information may be gleaned from public records which include indexes of land titles and mortgages, abstracts of title, and plat books.
- To prepare a land description, the appraiser investigates zoning regulations, probable zoning changes, building codes, public land use plans, and the physical constraints of the site. Assessment information may be useful in suggesting potential uses for the site.
- The physical characteristics of a site relate to size, shape, plottage potential, corner influence, the presence of excess or surplus land, topography, available utilities, on-site and off-site improvements, location, and environment.
- Topographical characteristics, surface soil and subsoil quality, grade, drainage, and the bearing capacity of the soil determine the suitability of a land parcel for an agricultural use or a proposed improvement. The cost of installing utilities is considered in the highest and best use conclusion.
- Location refers to time-distance linkages and the accessibility of the site.

Terms

abstract of title

assessed value

base line

constructive notice

corner influence

economic unit

excess land

Federal Emergency Management
    Agency (FEMA)

floodplain

frontage

geodetic survey program

government survey system

land or site analysis

land-to-building ratio

legal description

lot and block system

metes and bounds system

off-site improvement

on-site improvement

point of beginning (POB)

plat book

plottage

plottage value

principal meridian

quadrangle

range line

raw land

rectangular (government) survey
    system

site

subdivision development analysis

surplus land

tax parcel

total station

township

township line

wetlands

CHAPTER ELEVEN

Building Description

A n important part of every appraisal is the description of the building or buildings on the site. An appraiser describes each building's design, layout, and construction details, which include structural components, materials, and mechanical systems. The appraiser also determines building size and the condition of each element described. The building description provides the basis for comparing the subject property's improvements with improvements that are considered typically in the subject property's market.

Accurate building descriptions are essential to all valuation assignments. The appraiser needs a thorough understanding of the physical characteristics of the subject property to identify and select suitable comparables. Building descriptions also enable the appraiser to identify the extent and quality of building improvements, calculate their reproduction or replacement costs, and determine most forms of depreciation. Therefore, the quality of building descriptions directly affects the value estimate produced by applying the three approaches to value.

Elements of a Building Description

An appraiser prepares a building description by considering a variety of specific information in sequence. Primary concerns are the type of use represented by the existing building, the codes and regulations affecting this use, and the building size, plan, and construction. Also important are the structural details of the exterior and interior of the building and its equipment and mechanical systems—those included in the original construction and subsequent improvements. An appraiser must view a building objectively and analytically, paying careful attention to all components that ultimately contribute to the determination of the building's highest and best use as improved and any alternative highest and best uses to be considered in the assignment.

Use Classification

Real estate is usually divided into five major use groups: residential, commercial, industrial, agricultural, and special purpose. The planning, construction, and use of buildings are restricted by various laws, codes, and regulations, which are enacted at all levels of government to protect the health, safety, and welfare of the public.

Zoning regulations establish the permitted uses of property. Existing and potential property uses must be checked against zoning regulations to determine if they are conforming or nonconforming uses. When the present use does not conform to current zoning regulations, the appraiser should consider how this fact might affect property value.

Building design and construction are controlled by building, plumbing, electrical, and mechanical codes. When violations exist, the appraiser estimates the cost to correct the problem and judges the effect on value.

Building Codes

Building codes are enacted at local, state, and federal levels. Many states have codes that control the kinds of buildings that are constructed within their borders. Federal regulations are established to ensure occupational health and safety, environmental protection, pollution control, and consumer protection. Building codes establish requirements for the construction and occupancy of buildings and contain specifications for building materials, methods of construction, and mechanical systems. These codes also establish standards of performance and address considerations such as structural strength, fire resistance, and adequate light and ventilation.

To describe a building completely, an appraiser should be familiar with the codes in the area and determine whether the building complies with all applicable codes. A building that is not in compliance probably has less value than a similar building that is. If compliance is an absolute requirement, bringing a building up to code may produce additional expenses for its owners. On the other hand, the ultimate impact on expenses may be favorable if bringing the building up to code is expected to increase the net income the building is able to generate. Moreover, noncompliance may impact the highest and best use and marketability of the property.

Because building codes are not uniformly established and enforced, industrial and professional groups have developed model codes, which are gradually being accepted throughout the country, especially in large communities.

Size

To prepare a building description, an appraiser must determine the building's size. This may be a formidable task because the methods and techniques used to calculate building size vary regionally, differ among property types, and may reflect biases that significantly affect value estimates. The appraiser must know the measurement techniques used in the area where the building is located as well as those used to describe properties elsewhere. Appraisers should apply measurement techniques and report building dimensions consistently within each assignment because failure to do so can impair the quality of the appraisal report.

An appraiser uses the system of measurement commonly employed in the area and includes a description of the system in the appraisal report. One of the most common measurements, gross building area, must always be calculated, but other building measurements can sometimes be ascertained from plans, if they are available. Measurements taken from plans should be checked against actual building measurements because alterations and additions are often made after plans are prepared. The areas of attached porches, freestanding garages, and other minor buildings are always calculated separately.

Standards for measuring residential property have been developed by several federal agencies, including the FHA, the VA, Fannie Mae, and Freddie Mac. Because there is a close relationship between these agencies and the mortgage market industry, these standards have been used in millions of appraisals. The agencies use gross living area (*GLA*) to measure single-family residences and gross building area (*GBA*) to measure multifamily buildings. *Gross living area is defined as the total area of finished, above-grade residential space.* It is calculated by measuring the outside perimeter of the structure and includes only finished, habitable, above-grade living space. Finished basements and attic areas are not generally included in total gross living area. Local practices, however, may differ. *Gross building area is the total floor area of a building, excluding unenclosed areas, measured from the exterior of the walls.* It includes both the superstructure floor area and the substructure or basement area. Gross building area is also the standard of measurement for industrial buildings.

Gross leasable area (*GLA*)[1] is commonly used to measure shopping centers. *Gross leasable area is defined as the total floor area designed for the occupancy and exclusive use of tenants, including basements and mezzanines.* It is measured from the center of joint partitioning to the outside wall surfaces.

Office buildings present special problems for appraisers because they are measured differently in different areas.[2] Office building descriptions should include measurements of gross, finished, and leasable building areas. Once most office buildings were measured in terms of net usable area, which is the area actually occupied by a tenant. Now, however, the total floor space is measured, excluding vertical openings such as elevator shafts, stairwells, and air ducts. Some methods of office measurement allocate a pro rata portion of the restrooms, elevator lobbies, and corridors to each tenant; one method also includes a pro rata portion of the ground floor main lobby in each tenant's leased area. Office building management may measure single-tenant and multitenant floors in the same building differently. Because these measurements vary with occupancies, the appraiser must apply a consistent method in calculating the floor-by-floor rentable area of a building.

The appraiser should not accept a statement about the size of a subject or comparable property without knowing the basis for the calculation. If unverified size information is used in an appraisal, the resulting value estimate could be erroneous or misleading. Building measurement is further complicated by different practices of description in local and regional markets.

Accurate measurement of building size is essential in the sales comparison approach, especially when the subject and comparable properties vary in size. The subject and the comparables should be measured consistently. Units of comparison are selected based on market analysis, experience, and judgment. The subject property's size measurement can be adjusted to reflect the system of measurement used in the marketplace, or all the properties analyzed can be reduced to a representative unit such as price per square foot of gross living area or gross building area. Since most units of comparison

1. Note that the acronym *GLA* can stand for two different area measurements. Residential appraisers use *GLA* for gross living area; nonresidential appraisers use it to refer to gross leasable area.
2. The Building Owners and Managers Association International (BOMA) in Washington, D.C., has established a methodology for measuring office building floor area. This widely used method is described in BOMA's "Standard Method for Measuring Floor Area in Office Buildings," which is updated periodically.

are related to size, reducing sale prices to unit prices usually eliminates the need to make size adjustments.

Building size is also important in estimating effective rent in the income capitalization approach to value. Comparable rentals rarely reflect buildings of exactly the same size. Reducing rental data to unit rent often facilitates comparison. Size differences can be further considered in reconciliation. Often comparable rental information is converted into rent per square foot. The rent for the subject property is estimated by multiplying the adjusted rent derived from the comparable data by the number of square feet of leasable area. Expense figures obtained from market data are also converted into square foot units, which may be used for income analysis as well.

The calculations used in the cost approach to value require measurements of the entire building and of certain building components. Two similar buildings with the same square footage will have different costs if their exterior or interior walls are of different lengths. All significant differences must be considered when the cost of a comparable building is used to estimate the cost of the building being appraised.

Building Description Format

A complete building description includes information about the details and condition of a building's exterior, interior, and mechanical systems. Although there is no prescribed method for describing all buildings, the following outline may be used to establish a format for building descriptions.

A. Exterior description
1. Substructure
   a. Footings
   b. Slabs
   c. Piles
   d. Columns
   e. Piers
   f. Beams
   g. Foundation walls
2. Superstructure
   a. Framing
   b. Insulation
   c. Ventilation
   d. Exterior walls
   e. Exterior doors
   f. Windows, storm windows, and screens
   g. Facade
   h. Roof and drain system
   i. Chimneys, stacks, and vents
   j. Special features
B. Interior description
1. Interior walls, partitions, and doors
2. Division of space

      a. Storage areas

      b. Stairs, ramps, elevators, escalators, and hoists

  3. Interior supports

      a. Beams, columns, and trusses

      b. Flooring system (subflooring)

      c. Ceilings

  4. Painting, decorating, and finishing

      a. Basements

      b. Floor coverings

      c. Walls, partitions, and ceilings

      d. Molding and baseboards

      e. Fireplaces

  5. Protection against decay and insect damage

  6. Miscellaneous and special features

C. Equipment and mechanical systems

  1. Plumbing system

      a. Piping

      b. Fixtures

  2. Systems that use energy

      a. Hot water system

      b. Heating systems

         (1) Warm or hot air

         (2) Hot water

         (3) Steam

         (4) Electric

      c. Heating fuels

         (1) Fuel oil

         (2) Natural gas

         (3) Electricity

         (4) Coal

      d. Air-conditioning and ventilation systems

      e. Electrical systems

  3. Miscellaneous equipment

      a. Fire protection

      b. Elevators, escalators, and speed ramps

      c. Signals, alarms, and call systems

      d. Loading facilities

      e. Attached equipment—process related

Exterior Description

In describing a building's exterior, an appraiser provides information about the details of the building's substructure and superstructure. When a group or complex of buildings is being described, the appraiser may also need to include information about the infrastructure. *The infrastructure is the core of development in a group of buildings or in a complex that serves as the common source of utilities or support services.* For example, the infrastructure of a building complex may include a boiler and an electrical system that serve several structures.

Substructure

Substructure usually refers to a building's entire foundational structure, which is below grade, or ground, and includes such foundation supports as footings, slabs, piles, columns, piers, and beams. Piers do extend above ground but, in general, the substructure provides a support base on which the superstructure rests.

Footings

Footings are support parts that prevent excessive settlement or movement. The most common type of footing is a perimetric base of concrete that rests on undisturbed earth below the frost line. This base distributes the load of the walls over the subgrade. Other types of footings include plain footings, which are unreinforced and designed to carry light loads, and reinforced footings, which contain steel to increase their strength. Columns are long, relatively slender pillars. Spread footings are frequently used where the soil has poor load-bearing capacity.

Because footings are visible only when a building is under construction, an appraiser must obtain information about them from plans or by consulting architects, contractors, or builders. Footings that are improperly designed and constructed often cause settling and wall cracks. An appraiser must observe any structural problems in the building and evaluate their effect on the property's value. If the problems can be corrected, the cost of correction is estimated. Some defects are ignored by the market and have little effect on a property's value, while others result in substantial value decreases.

A building's foundation is made of natural or prepared material. Today most foundations are made of poured concrete walls or of concrete or cinder block walls that rest on concrete footings. The foundations of many older buildings are made of cut stone or stone and brick. Mat and raft foundations, known as *floating foundations*, are used over soils that have poor load-bearing capacity. They are made of concrete slabs that are heavily reinforced with steel so that the entire foundation functions as a unit. Pile foundations are made of columnar units of concrete, metal, or wood that transmit loads through soil with poor load-bearing capacity to lower levels where the soil's load-bearing capacity is adequate. The columnar units serve as substitutes for footings. Columns, piers, and grade beams are other types of foundation supports that can be used separately or in combination.

Superstructure

Superstructure usually refers to the portion of the building above grade. In multipurpose buildings, however, components such as parking garages that are above grade but not used for habitable space are often considered part of the substructure.

Framing

The structural frame is the load-bearing skeleton of a building to which the exterior and interior walls are attached. The structural frames of most houses in the United States are

Figure 11.1 | **Basic Systems and Components of a Building**

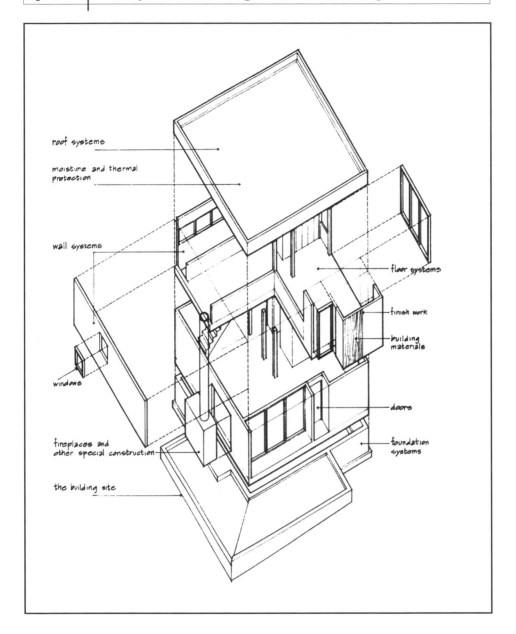

roof systems

moisture and thermal protection

wall systems

floor systems

finish work

building materials

windows

doors

fireplaces and other special construction

foundation systems

the building site

Reprinted with permission from Frank Cheng and Cassandra Adams, *Building Construction Illustrated* (New York: Van Nostrand Reinhold, 1991).

made of wood. The two most common types of wood frame construction are platform and post and beam; platform framing is more prevalent.

In *platform construction* one story of a building is constructed at a time and each story serves as a platform for the next. *Studs*, which are the vertical framing members, are cut at the ceiling height of the first story, then horizontal plates are laid on top, and more studs are cut for the second story.

Post and beam framing is composed of beams that are spaced up to eight feet apart and are supported on posts and exterior walls. The framing members used for this type of construction are much larger and heavier than those used in the other framing systems. Exposed wood construction may enhance a building's architectural design. The post and beam system was used in colonial houses and barns and it began to regain popularity in the mid-1970s.

One relatively new method of framing employs panels of framing members and siding or subflooring that are prefabricated at a mill or built at the site. Construction begins on the ground and materials are subsequently lifted as a unit and installed in place. Some buildings are constructed with solid masonry exterior walls, which function as part of the framing system. Often interior framing is made of steel beams or reinforced concrete; older masonry buildings have interior framing of wood beams and posts.

The form of industrial buildings has changed a great deal in the past century. At the turn of the century, the most popular type of industrial building was the multistory mill building, which had exterior masonry walls and heavy post and beam framing systems that were often supported by solid interior masonry walls and columns. After 1900 steel began to replace timber framing, and by 1910 many multistory industrial buildings were built of reinforced concrete with rectangular columns and beams and heavy slab floors. By 1920 round, mushroom-capped columns were generally used under rectangular areas of heavier slab floors. Later several other types of integral beam and slab construction became common (e.g., the T-beam floor design with hollow tile between the T-beams, the use of pans to form beams or waffle patterns), especially in buildings that required lower live-load capacities.

Today large residential, commercial, and industrial buildings often have framing systems of steel beams or reinforced or precast concrete. Precast units with prestressed, reinforced steel are widely employed. Tilt-up construction uses precast concrete slabs, which can be lifted into a vertical position to become exterior bearing walls or curtain walls. The interior frame may consist of precast and prestressed concrete beams and columns with lighter precast slabs used for the structural roof.

There has been a trend toward constructing more functional, single-story, horizontal buildings for industrial plants. The framing for these buildings is usually made of steel. Bays, which are the areas between columns, have become increasingly large. Bays of 30 to 50 feet are quite common, and some aircraft plants have been built with more than 100 feet between columns. When the frame must support heavy cranes, the structural steel members used are heavier and larger.

A wood framing system that is defective can cause walls to crack, exterior walls to bulge, windows to stick, and doors to open or close improperly. In addition, the space between wall siding and a masonry chimney may be too wide. Steel framing is usually less expensive than precast or reinforced concrete, and it is easier and faster to erect. Steel framing does have one major disadvantage, however. Unless it is encased in heat-resistant, fireproof material such as plaster or concrete, the steel will buckle and bend in a fire, pulling adjacent members out of position and greatly increasing fire damage to the building. Reinforced and precast concrete framing is the most expensive and difficult to construct, but it is highly resistant to damage by fire.

Insulation

Insulation provides a number of benefits. It not only helps economize on fuel and ensure the comfort of occupants in both warm and cold climates, but it also reduces noise transmission and impedes the spread of fire. The adequacy of building insulation and other energy conservation features should be noted by the appraiser in a building description.

Before World War II, most buildings were constructed without added insulation; the heavy building materials used at the time provided some insulation. Newer buildings are more energy efficient. Many older buildings are being renovated to increase their energy efficiency by adding insulation. Insulation is classified by its form, which may be loose-fill, flexible, rigid, reflective, or foamed-in-place.

Loose-fill insulations, which are poured or blown by a machine into a building's structural cavities, are manufactured from mineral wool (e.g., rock, slag, or glass wool) or cellulosic fiber (e.g., recycled newsprint, wood chips, or other organic fibers). Before the 1970s, loose-fill insulations were often manufactured from asbestos-containing materials (ACMs).

Flexible insulations are manufactured in batt and blanket form from mineral wool or cellulosic fibers and are available in three forms. The insulation may be wrapped with kraft paper on the edges and a vapor barrier on one or both sides, faced with a vapor barrier on one side only, or friction-fit without any covering because the interlaced fibers are resilient enough to remain upright in the cavity. Flexible insulations are generally used where it is not practical to install loose-fill insulation or where the foil or kraft paper facing is needed as a vapor barrier.

Asbestos is a nonflammable, natural mineral material that separates into fibers. Asbestos-containing materials (ACMs) were widely used in structures built between 1945 and 1970 as thermal and acoustical insulation or for fireproofing and soundproofing. Other ACMs were used in siding and roofing shingles. Airborne asbestos fibers pose a threat to human health when they are distributed in the air. The potential of any ACM to release fibers depends on its degree of friability—i.e., how easily it is crumbled or pulverized. Dry, sprayed-on thermal insulation over structural steel is highly friable. Densely packed, nonfibrous ACMs such as vinyl asbestos floor covering and pipe insulation are not considered friable under normal conditions. Nevertheless, these materials will become friable if they are broken, sawed, or drilled.

Encapsulation or enclosure of asbestos is effective as a short-term solution. The Environmental Protection Agency (EPA) has guidelines for the removal of asbestos when a building is being demolished or renovated, but these regulations have been difficult to enforce.

The EPA regulates asbestos under the authority provided by the Clean Air Act and the Toxic Substances Control Act. The National Emissions Standards for Hazardous Air

Pollutants (NESHAP), which were drawn up as part of the Clean Air Act, apply to asbestos emissions in manufacturing, waste disposal, building demolition, and renovation. The Asbestos Hazard Emergency Response Act (AHERA), which was amended to the Toxic Substances Control Act in 1986, empowered the EPA to regulate asbestos in public schools when it poses a hazard and to promulgate regulations for asbestos removal.

Opinions differ on the effect of asbestos on the value of income-producing properties. There is little evidence, however, that investors are willing to sell properties at sharp discounts because of the problem.

Rigid insulations that can be used in many parts of a building have become popular. They are available in four forms: structural wall insulation, fiberboard, structural deck insulation, and rigid board insulation. Reflective insulation made of foil reflects heat that is transferred by radiation. This type of insulation should be installed facing an air space of at least three-quarters of an inch and should remain free of dust and other materials that could reduce its reflective qualities.

There are two basic types of foamed-in-place insulation: urethane foam insulation and urea-formaldehyde foam insulation (UFFI). Both types rely on a chemical reaction that causes the mixture to expand to approximately 30 times its original size and solidify in approximately 24 hours.

In April of 1982 the Consumer Product Safety Commission banned urea-formalde-hyde foam insulation in residences and schools. The ban resulted from the commission's investigation of the effects of formaldehyde gas, which can be released from the insulation at very high levels, especially immediately after installation. The ban took effect in August of 1982 and was lifted in April of 1983 by a federal court of appeals which held that the risks had not been proven. The ban was not retroactive, so it did not affect the approximately 500,000 homes in the United States that have urea-formaldehyde foam insulation. However, the chemical breakdown of the toxic gas released by urea-formalde-hyde foam insulation over a certain period of time renders UFFI harmless.

The ability of an insulation material to resist the flow of heat is measured in R values. R value is derived by measuring the British thermal units (Btus) that are transmitted in one hour through one thickness of the insulation.[3] The higher the R value, the better the insulation. There is no universal standard for the amount of insulation required in a structure because the amount varies with the climate and the type of building. For example, overceiling or underroof insulation with an R value of 13 might be satisfactory in a mild climate if there is gas or oil heat and no air-conditioning. In cold or hot climates and in structures with electric heat or air-conditioning, insulation with an R value of 24 might be necessary. There has been a growing trend to superinsulate structures using insulation with much higher R values.

Ventilation

In many buildings ventilation is needed to reduce heat in closed-off areas such as attics and spaces behind walls. Ventilation also prevents the condensation of water, which collects in unventilated spaces and causes building materials to rot and decay. When

---

3. A Btu is the quantity of heat required to raise the temperature of one pound of water at or near 39.2 degrees Fahrenheit by one degree.

condensation seeps into insulation, it reduces its R rating. Ventilation can be accomplished with holes that range in size from one inch to several feet in diameter; these holes should be covered with screening to keep out vermin. Ventilation can also be increased by using fans.

Exterior Walls

The two basic types of exterior walls are load-bearing and nonload-bearing walls. Load-bearing walls are often made of solid masonry, such as cement block, brick, or a combination of these materials. Load-bearing walls can also be made of poured concrete, pre-stressed concrete, steel beams covered with siding material, or wood framing heavy enough to support the weight of the roof and the upper stories. Load-bearing walls can be strengthened with masonry pilasters that are attached to the exterior of the wall.

Nonload-bearing walls, which are commonly used in larger buildings, are attached to the framing system. They can be made of porcelain enamel, steel, aluminum, precast aggregate concrete slabs, or glass. For industrial buildings, less attractive, but serviceable, materials such as corrugated iron, tilt-up precast concrete slabs, asbestos board, fiberglass, and metal sandwich panels are used. When the quality of the exterior walls is below the standard for buildings in the same market, the property may suffer a loss in value.

Exterior Doors

Exterior doors are usually made of solid wood, metal, or glass. Hollow exterior doors are a sign of poor-quality construction. Commercial and industrial buildings often have large steel truck doors. A variety of special-purpose doors are available and many have automatic door openers. Special automatic doors must be described in a building description. The presence or absence of energy-conserving material such as weatherstripping around doors should also be noted. To prevent air leakage through cracks at the bottom of a door, door shoes, weatherproof thresholds, and sweeps can be attached.

Windows, Storm Windows, and Screens

Wood was the material first used for framing windows and it is still commonly used in houses. It has good insulating properties, is readily available, can take either a natural or painted finish, and is easy to install and repair. Aluminum and steel are also used for window framing in residential, commercial, and industrial buildings. In describing a building, the appraiser notes the type of window and its material or manufacture. Window types include single- and double-hung windows, casement windows, and horizontal sliding windows as well as clerestory, fixed, awning, hopper, center pivot, and jalousie windows.

Because windows are a major source of heat and cooling loss, their design and installation is important. There is a trend toward reducing the size of windows and placing them higher to conserve energy and increase security. Windows should be tightly sealed, with caulking at the joints and between the wall and the window. The use of insulated glass, multiple glazing, and storm sashes helps keep cold air out and heat in. The appraiser should describe these energy-saving features in a building description.

In residential construction, storm doors and windows are used to provide insulation. They can save typical home owners 10% to 20% of their fuel costs. In commercial and industrial buildings, windows of double or triple glazing are generally installed and, occasionally, casement windows may be used.

Modern storm doors and windows are often made of aluminum and permanently installed with screens. Wooden storm doors and windows that must be removed and stored during the summer are becoming obsolete. Appraisers may find it difficult to judge how much storm windows and doors add to the value of a building, but analyzing what is typical in the market can be helpful.

In most parts of the country, screens are needed for all windows that open. Most screens have aluminum frames and, in residences, screens are often combined with storm windows. An appraiser should inventory all removable window and door screens and note if any are missing.

Facade

Many houses, stores, office buildings, and industrial buildings have a facade, or front, that differs from the design and construction of the rest of the building. Frame houses may have extra masonry veneer on the facade or contrasting siding. Retail stores often have elaborate fronts of glass and other decorative materials; even some industrial buildings have facades that are more elaborate than their exteriors. The appraiser describes a special facade and considers its cost and effect on the property's value.

In modern industry and commerce, public image is important. An attractive store, warehouse, industrial plant, or office building has both advertising and public relations value to the occupant. Ornamentation, identifying signs, lighting, and landscaping all contribute to a building's attractiveness.

Roof and Drain System

A roof is designed and constructed to support its own weight and the pressure of snow, ice, wind, and rain. There are many types of roofs. Flat roofs are used extensively in industrial and commercial buildings, but are less common in residences. Lean-to roofs, often called shed roofs, are used on saltbox houses, and gambrel roofs are popular for barns and Cape Ann and Dutch Colonial houses. Other types of roofs include gable, hip, and mansard roofs. In industrial construction, monitor and sawtooth roofs are sometimes used.

The most prevalent systems of roof construction for houses are trusses, joists or horizontal beams, joists and rafters, and posts and beams. In commercial and industrial construction, the roof structure may be of steel or wood trusses, glued wood beams, or a steel or concrete frame with wood joists or purlins or with steel bar joists. These systems support the roof sheathing, which may be plywood, steel roof deck, lightweight precast concrete slabs, reinforced concrete slabs, or insulated sheathing in large sheets.

The roof covering prevents moisture from entering the structure. In most regions, residential roofs are covered with asphalt shingles, which are available in various weights and styles, including lock-tab and seal-tab varieties. Other common residential roof coverings are shingles and shakes made of wood (usually cedar), asbestos, and cement.

Fiberglass shingles have recently been introduced and metal, clay tile, slate, and built-up or membrane roofs are also found on houses.

Many of these residential roof coverings are also used for commercial and industrial buildings. The flat roofs of these buildings are made of built-up layers of felt or composition material that are nailed to the sheathing and covered with tar. Gravel or another surfacing material helps keep the roof from drying out and cracking. Membrane roof assemblies are becoming popular for commercial and industrial buildings.

Joints in roofs are created where two different roof slopes meet or where the roof meets adjoining walls or projections such as chimneys, pipes, and ventilation ducts. All joints must be flashed. Flashing is usually accomplished by nailing strips of galvanized metal, aluminum, or tin across or under the point, applying a waterproofing compound or cement, and securing the roofing material over the edges to hold it permanently in place.

An appraiser investigates the condition of a roof to determine its remaining useful life. Most roofs need to be replaced several times during a building's life, so a roof's condition and age are considered in the valuation process.

The water that falls on a roof must be directed to the ground or into a drain system. Gutters and downspouts channel water from roofs to prevent damage and protect the appearance of walls when roof overhangs are not provided. Gutters or eave troughs catch rainwater at the edge of the roof and carry it to downspouts or leaders, the vertical pipes that carry the water to the ground or into sewers, dry wells, drain tiles, or splash pans. In large buildings, storm water collects in roof drains, which are connected to storm drains by pipes in the building. Even so-called "flat" roofs may be slightly pitched to direct water to drains and gutters. Gutters and downspouts must be made of galvanized steel, aluminum, or copper.

Chimneys, Stacks, and Vents

Chimneys, stacks, and vents should be structurally safe, durable, and smoketight; they should also be able to withstand the action of flue gases. The efficiency of any fuel-burning heating system depends on its chimney, stack, or vent. Chimneys and stacks with cracked bricks, loose mortar joints, or other leaks may be serious fire and health hazards. Exhaust systems range from simple metal vents and flues to complex masonry fireplaces, industrial chimneys, and ventilation systems. A building's chimneys, stacks, and vents and their apparent condition are described in an appraisal report.

Special Features

Some buildings have special features that must be carefully described and considered in the valuation process. Special features might include artwork, ornamentation, exterior elevators, solar and wind equipment, unique window installation, special masonry work and exterior materials, and items required for the commercial or industrial use of buildings. Unique building features can present a valuation problem. The appraiser must decide if the item or items add to the property's market value or are of value only to the current user. In the latter case, the item or items may add use value, but little or no market value. If such items are costly to remove, they can have a negative effect on value because they may not appeal to a future owner.

Interior Description

The interior description of a building includes information about the interior walls and the areas between them, including how the space is divided and finished.

Interior Walls, Partitions, and Doors

In residences most interior walls are made of wood studs covered with drywall materials such as gypsum board, wood panels, ceramic tile, plywood, or hardboard. Plaster walls were once popular, but they are used less frequently now. Masonry houses often have masonry interior walls. The interior walls of commercial and industrial buildings may range from simple wire partitions to solid masonry walls that provide fire protection. Glass, wood, plywood, hardboard, metals, tiles, concrete, brick, and a number of other materials are used in wall construction. Interior walls can be painted, wallpapered, or decorated in other ways. Partitioning is also used to divide space. Partitions are generally nonload-bearing and movable.

Types of interior doors include simple hollow-core doors, which are used in most residential construction; solid-core doors, which are found in older buildings and office buildings; complex, self-closing, fire-resistant doors, which are found in commercial and industrial buildings; specialty, self-opening and closing doors, which are used in offices and commercial buildings; and special-purpose doors such as those used in bank vaults. Because hanging a door is complicated, it is often done improperly. Most poorly hung doors close improperly or fail to make contact with an edge of the frame when closed.

Division of Space

A building description provides a complete list of the number of rooms in the structure and their uses; room sizes may also be stated. The number of bedrooms and bathrooms in a residential property usually influences the market for the property and its value. The number of units in an apartment building, and the types and sizes of the rooms within the units, significantly influence the property's income-producing potential. Similarly, the amount of office space in an industrial property and the partitioning of office suites may affect property value.

In certain parts of the United States, many types of buildings have basements. In these areas buildings without basements may have substantially less value than similar buildings with basements. If basements are not common in the area, a basement may add little or no value to a building.

Storage Areas

An appraiser must describe and consider the adequacy of a building's storage areas. Home owners often complain about a lack of adequate storage space, especially in kitchens. Ample cabinets, closets, and other storage areas are important, particularly in homes without basements. Storage is particularly important in multifamily residential buildings. The value of apartment and condominium projects is often enhanced by the availability of storage space. Frequently, mini-storage facilities are located near apartment complexes because apartment units often have inadequate storage space. Storage problems can also exist in commercial and industrial buildings.

Stairs, Ramps, Elevators, Escalators, and Hoists

Designing and constructing even the simplest staircase is a complicated task. In public buildings codes often regulate where stairs are located, how they are designed and constructed, and how they are enclosed for fire protection. Public buildings may also have to be barrier-free to provide access for handicapped people. The Americans with Disabilities Act (ADA) of 1990 established accessibility guidelines and a 1997 deadline for their implementation. In a residence, a well-planned stairway provides for safe ascent and descent, with adequate headroom and space for moving furniture and equipment. Railings should be installed on the sides of all interior stairways, including stairways in attics and basements, where they are often omitted.

Appraisers must evaluate how efficiently the elevators and escalators in a building move people and freight. The elevators and escalators in many multistory buildings are inadequate and do not meet current market standards. Curing these deficiencies is often extremely expensive or impossible.

Recent legislation dictates that handicapped persons be provided with access to public buildings, which may require that ramps be installed both inside and outside the structure. An appraiser cannot assume that a building complies with these requirements. The enforcement of such requirements can be triggered by a change in use or a title transfer.

Special elevators and hoists are often considered part of a building, although they may be studied under the category of equipment. These building components must be carefully described, and their contribution to the value of the building must be estimated.

Interior Supports

A building description includes consideration of the building's internal supports, which include beams and columns, the flooring system, and ceilings.

Beams, Columns, and Trusses

Many residential, commercial, and industrial buildings have basements or crawl spaces that are too large for the first-floor joists or subfloor systems and cannot be supported by the foundation walls alone. Therefore, foundation walls are an important part of the main framing system in large buildings, and they are designed to support heavy loads. Bearing beams that rest on columns of wood, masonry, or steel provide additional support. Cracked or sagging beams may be an early indication of more serious problems in the future. If an appraiser observes these signs, he or she should consider and report them. As interior support systems, traditional joist construction is being replaced by trusses— both roof and floor trusses.

Flooring System

Subflooring provides safe support for floor loads without excessive deflection and an adequate base for the support and attachment of finish floor material. Bridging stiffens the joists and prevents them from deflecting.

Ceilings

In residences with gypsum walls, ceilings are often made of the same material; in other buildings, tiles may be used. In some structures, the underside of the upper story is an adequate ceiling. Ceiling height must be measured and considered by the appraiser. Ceilings that are too low or high for the property's current highest and best use as improved may be considered an item of functional obsolescence and decrease the property's value.

Painting, Decorating, and Finishing

The primary purpose of interior painting and decorating is to give the building an attractive appearance. Most buildings are decorated many times during their useful lives. An appraiser reports the condition of the painting and decorating in a structure and notes when they will need to be redone.

The attractiveness of painting and decorating is subjective. Many new owners and tenants will redecorate to suit their personal tastes. Unusual decorations and colors may have limited appeal and, therefore, may detract from a building's value. The quality of decoration is sometimes an important consideration in valuing a restaurant, store, or other commercial building.

Basements

In residences and some commercial buildings, basements may be finished and used for purposes other than storage. If these uses are accepted and typical in the area, they can add significantly to the property's value.

Dampness, which is often a problem in basements, may be caused by poor foundation wall construction, excess groundwater that is not properly drained by ground tiles, poorly fitted windows or hatches, poor venting of equipment, or poorly constructed or operating roof drains that allow water to enter. Signs that may indicate a wet basement include a powdery white mineral deposit a few inches off the floor, stains near the bottom of walls and columns or equipment that rests close to the floor, and the smell of mildew.

Flooring and Floor Coverings

A wide variety of flooring is available, and some flooring materials are selected primarily for their low cost and durability. Sand, compressed dirt, bituminous paving, brick, stone, gravel, concrete, and similar products are suitable for many industrial buildings, warehouses, garages, and basements. In many commercial and industrial buildings, floors must be especially thick or reinforced to support heavy equipment. Terrazzo flooring, which is made of colored marble chips that are mixed into cement and ground smooth, is used for high traffic areas such as the lobbies of public buildings.

Wood in various forms continues to be a popular material for floors. Planks and blocks are used for industrial floors, and many commercial buildings use wood floors to conform with the design and overall decoration. Wood planks and hardwood strips are found in many residences, although other types of flooring have become more popular. Resilient, ceramic, and quarry tiles are used in all types of buildings. Resilient flooring, which is usually a combination of vinyl and asphalt, is also produced as sheet goods.

Carpeting was once considered a luxury in residences, offices, stores, and commercial buildings, but today it is widely used in all types of buildings. An appraiser should consider whether floor coverings can endure wear and tear and how they conform to a building's design and decoration.

Walls, Partitions, and Ceilings

The types and finishes of various components should be differentiated. For example, partitioning can be wood or metal. Ceilings can be drywall, plaster, or suspended panel (drop ceilings). Walls and partitions may be painted, papered, or paneled. Supplemental finishings include ceramic tile and wainscot paneling.

Molding and Baseboards

In the past architects often designed unique moldings for buildings, but now moldings are of a standard size and shape and their use is decreasing. Nevertheless, beautiful, restored molding can add value to older houses. Simple baseboards are used in many types of buildings to protect the walls from damage caused by furniture or cleaning equipment.

Fireplaces

Fireplaces are popular in homes and commercial buildings such as restaurants, inns, and specialty stores. Most fireplaces do not provide a building's primary source of heat; in fact, because of their design, many have little heating power.

A typical fireplace has a single opening with a damper and a hearth. More complex designs feature two or more openings. Because fireplaces are difficult to construct, many are badly made and function poorly. One common problem is downdraft, whereby smoke is blown into the building by the wind outside. This can happen if the chimney does not extend at least two feet above any part of the roof within 10 feet of the chimney.

Many prefabricated fireplaces and flues are sold and installed in buildings that did not originally have fireplaces. Unless they are approved by Underwriters Laboratories and installed according to the manufacturer's instructions, these fireplaces can be potential fire hazards. To be safe, a fireplace should be supported with noncombustible material and have a noncombustible hearth that extends at least 16 inches in front of the opening and at least eight inches on each side. A carpet or rug that comes within a few inches of the front of a fireplace is a definite fire hazard.

Protection Against Decay and Insect Damage

All wood is susceptible to decay and insect damage. When wood is consistently exposed to moisture and water, destructive organisms propagate on or beneath its surface. The most prevalent of these organisms are aerobic fungi, which thrive where a proper combination of moisture, temperature, oxygen, and food exist. Sapwood of all species is subject to decay; heartwood varies in susceptibility from low to very high resistance, depending on the species.

Insects damage wood more rapidly and obviously than decay. Although several species of insects destroy wood, subterranean, dampwood, and drywood termites are by far the most destructive. Subterranean termites are very adaptable and are found across the United States. They colonize in moist soil and infest both damp and dry wood.

Dampwood and drywood termites are more limited in their geographic distribution. Drywood termites colonize in wood and create infestations that are extremely difficult to eradicate.

To protect against decay and insect damage, builders may slope the ground away from foundations for good drainage and put vapor barriers on the interior sides of exposed walls. They may also use polyethylene as a soil cover in crawl spaces; flashing gutters, downspouts, and splash blocks to carry water away from foundation walls; poured concrete foundation walls; concrete caps over unit masonry foundations; wood treatments; soil treatments; and metal termite shields. Building with dry, naturally durable woods and conducting regular maintenance inspections can also help prevent insect infestation and damage.

Miscellaneous and Special Features

Many industrial and commercial buildings are designed for special purposes. Steel mills, oil refineries, chemical plants, concrete factories, and mines are constructed for highly specialized functions. Commercial establishments often have unique design features (e.g., drive-in restaurants), or special facilities (e.g., the cooling room in a furrier's shop). Other properties with special-purpose improvements include amusement parks, sports complexes, wharfs and docks, transportation terminals, and TV and radio transmission towers, studios, and theaters.

In valuing industrial and commercial properties, an appraiser may find it helpful to distinguish between two categories of equipment. The first category comprises equipment and mechanical systems that provide for human comfort. Plumbing, heating, air-conditioning, and lighting are human comfort items that will be discussed later in this chapter. The second category includes fixed building equipment that is process-related. Air hoses, process piping, craneways, bus ducts, heavy electrical lines, and freezer equipment are process-related items found in special-purpose industrial buildings. An appraiser must decide what contribution these special-purpose items make in terms of their use value, keeping in mind that their contribution may be different when measuring other types of value such as market or insurable value.

Equipment and Mechanical Systems

Most buildings cannot perform the functions for which they were designed and constructed unless their equipment and mechanical systems are in good working order. Each item of equipment and each mechanical system should be inspected and described by the appraiser.

Major equipment and mechanical systems can be divided into those that do not consume a significant amount of energy and those that do. A plumbing system is not basically an energy consumer, although it may have pumps that use some electricity. The systems that consume energy are the hot water system (which is distinct from the plumbing system), the heating system, the air-conditioning and ventilation system, and the electrical system. Some buildings have other mechanical systems and equipment as well. Most of these systems use some electricity, but are not major energy consumers.

Figure 11.2 | **Mechanical Systems**

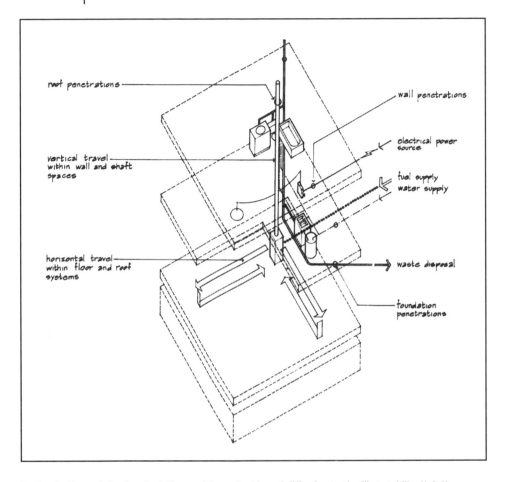

roof penetrations

wall penetrations

electrical power source

vertical travel within wall and shaft spaces

fuel supply
water supply

horizontal travel within floor and roof systems

waste disposal

foundation penetrations

Reprinted with permission from Frank Cheng and Cassandra Adams, *Building Construction Illustrated* (New York: Van Nostrand Reinhold, 1991).

Plumbing System

Plumbing is an integral part of most buildings. It consists of piping, which is usually covered or hidden except in industrial buildings, and fixtures, which are visible. Laundries, laundromats, and certain industrial buildings have elaborate plumbing systems.

Piping

Much of the cost of a plumbing system may be due to piping, which consists of supply pipes that carry water (and occasionally other fluids) under pressure, waste pipes that depend on the flow of gravity, and vent pipes that are used in concrete construction to permit air in the structure to escape. The quality of the materials used, the way the pipes were installed, and how easily they can be serviced are significant considerations in estimating how long the pipes will last and how much they will cost to maintain. Worn galvanized steel, lead, or brass water pipes may need to be replaced. Copper is an excellent pipe material with a long life. Virtually all piping that supplies drinking water is copper. Cast iron is good for below-grade waste lines. In many areas and many types of buildings, a high-quality piping system will last as long as the building. However, many buildings have pipes that do not last. An appraiser describes the conditions of the pipes and notes when they will probably need to be replaced.

Plastic pipes are widely used for waste and vent lines. The durability and serviceability of plastic pipes should be checked. Water pipes must be strong enough to withstand the pressure needed to move water through them. Because there is no pressure in a waste drain line, these pipes must be slanted so that waste will flow from each fixture through the main line into the sewer or sewage disposal system. Building sewers should be installed to guard against sewer backup in heavy rains.

Fixtures

The plumbing fixtures used in bathrooms include lavatories, or washbasins; bathtubs; showers; toilets, which are known as water closets in the building trades; bidets; and urinals. High-quality fixtures are made of cast iron covered with acid-resistant vitreous enamel; fiberglass and other materials are also used.

The design of bathroom fixtures has changed substantially, and old fixtures may become obsolete during a building's economic life. An appraiser should report the need for modernization, but old fixtures of good quality, such as porcelain pedestal basins and footed tubs, are often rehabilitated.

Kitchen plumbing fixtures include single or double sinks, which should be installed in countertops and made of Monel metal, stainless steel, enameled steel, or cast iron covered with acid-resistant enamel. Other kitchen fixtures include garbage disposals, dishwashers, and instant hot water units. Some homes may have specialized plumbing fixtures such as laundry tubs, wet bars, swimming pools, or saunas.

Fittings, which are important parts of plumbing fixtures, include faucets, spigots, drains, shower heads, and spray tubes. The water in many areas is hard—i.e., it contains minerals such as calcium, magnesium, sulfates, bicarbonates, iron, and sulfur, which react unfavorably with soap and make it difficult to rinse from clothing, hair, and skin. Often hard water cannot be used until it is treated, either with simple equipment or with automatic, complex, multistage systems.

Commercial and industrial buildings have many of the same fixtures found in homes, and they also may have drinking fountains, janitor sinks, handwashing and eyewashing fountains, floor drains, and other special-purpose fixtures. An appraiser must decide which building fixtures are part of the real estate and which are personal property.

Systems That Use Energy

As mentioned earlier, the systems that consume energy are the hot water system, the heating system, the air-conditioning and ventilation system, and the electrical system.[4] An appraiser must describe all these systems and indicate the type of fuel used in the heating system.

---

4. Heating, ventilation, and air-conditioning systems are commonly referred to as HVAC systems.

Hot Water System

All homes and many commercial and industrial buildings need an adequate supply of hot water. A typical residential hot water system gets its heat from a self-standing water heater, which is powered by electricity, gas, or oil. Houses with inadequate hot water systems suffer from functional obsolescence. The size of the hot water tank needed in a residence is determined by the number of inhabitants and their water-using habits and by the recovery rate of the tank. Commercial and industrial buildings often require much more hot water than homes, so they often have large cast iron or steel boilers and storage tanks.

Heating Systems

Most heating systems use warm or hot air, hot water, steam, or electricity. The amount of heat a system can produce is rated in Btus. The heating capacity required relates to the cubic content, exposure, design, and insulation level of the structure to be heated. An appraiser describes the heating system and analyzes whether it is appropriate in the local market area.

Warm or hot air heating systems. Heating systems based on warm or hot air depend on the natural force of gravity or use a pressure blower to push heated air through the ducts. The air is heated in a furnace that is fired by gas, oil, electricity, or coal and is distributed through one or more registers directly from the furnace or through ducts connected to registers throughout the building. Air circulation is maintained with a fan and a return duct system. Thermostats, filters, humidifiers, air cleaners, and air purification devices may be included in the heating system.

In some buildings the central air-conditioning equipment uses the same ducts as the heating system. This is not always possible, however, because the air-conditioning may require ducts of a different size. Furthermore, heating registers should be placed low on the walls, while air-conditioning registers should be higher up or in the ceiling.

Some older heating systems relied on gravity and the use of larger ducts, with simple distribution patterns for circulation. Warm air systems are used in new apartment construction, especially for garden apartments and townhouse developments. When gas is used, the warm air system may function through unit heaters, radiant gas heaters, wall or floor furnaces, or individual gas furnaces. Gas-fired heating units need adequate ventilation. Indeed, all open-flame heating sources must have a sufficient air supply to support complete combustion.

Hot water heating systems. Heating systems based on hot water are called *hydronic systems*. In a hydronic system, water is heated in a cast-iron or steel boiler and moved by gravity (in older systems) or pumped by a circulator (in modern systems) through a one-pipe system to radiators where the heat is transferred by convection and radiation to the areas being heated. The colder water then returns to the boiler where it is reheated and the process is repeated.

Radiant heating is a type of hot water heating system in which hot water is circulated by a pump, called a *circulator*, through narrow pipes that are embedded in floors, walls, and ceilings. This system depends primarily on heat being transferred by radiation, rather than by convection, which characterizes a conventional system. In a conventional hot water heating system, air is warmed as it passes over the heated metal of a radiator and is then circulated in an area of colder air. Radiant heat can also be produced by electric heating elements embedded in floors, walls, and ceilings.

Steam heating systems. In some structures, steam is produced in a boiler fueled by gas, oil, coal, or electricity and distributed through a piping system. In a simple, one-pipe gravity system (identical to that used in hot-water systems), which may be used in small buildings, radiators are served by a single riser from the main pipe. The condensate returns to the boiler through the same riser and is used again. More complex and expensive two-pipe systems are found in larger, high-quality structures.

At one time vertical section, cast-iron boilers were used in large installations. These units were fairly efficient when covered with insulated metal casings or jackets. Steel boilers were usually of a low-pressure, fire-tube type, in which combustion gases passed through tubes inserted into a cylindrical drum that contained water. Several types of two-pass or three-pass boilers were designed for better efficiency. Recently, small, efficient "package boilers" have become popular for heating and generating process steam.

Steam systems also use radiators to transfer heat by radiation and convection. Common cast-iron radiators successfully transfer heat, but improvements are still being developed to operate steam heating more efficiently. Zone control is now widely used to stabilize the effects of different heating needs in different parts of a building. The amount of heat available for distribution can be controlled by separate temperature controls.

In many states licenses are required for certain classes of steam boilers. Appraisers must be familiar with local boiler license laws and ascertain whether boilers have current, valid licenses.

Electrical heating systems. The equipment used in electrical heating systems includes heat pumps, wall heaters, baseboard units, duct heating units, and heating units installed in air-conditioning ducts. Such equipment gives an electrical heating system both heating and cooling capacity. Radiant floors, walls, and ceilings that have panels or cables under the surface; infrared units; and electric furnaces that use forced warm air or hot water can also be used in electrical heating systems. An electrical resistance system produces heat in the immediate area or room that is to be heated. It is the least expensive system to install because it requires no furnace, furnace room, ducts, flue, or plumbing. However, it does require substantial electrical service and a great deal of wiring to each unit in the building.

Heat pumps that combine heating and cooling functions are increasingly popular. A heat pump is actually a reverse refrigeration unit. In the winter, the pump takes heat from the outside air, the ground, or well water and distributes it inside the house. When the weather is very cold, the efficiency of the unit decreases and must be supplemented with resistance heating. In the summer, the pump cools by extracting heat from inside the house like a typical air-conditioning unit.

Convectors are finned heating elements that are installed in baseboards or concealed in walls or cabinets. A convector combined with a fan becomes a unit or room heater. Unit heaters are found in commercial and industrial buildings such as stores, warehouses, and garages, where large spaces must be heated. The units are usually placed near the ceiling in the space to be heated.

The automatic regulation of a heating system helps it operate efficiently. A multiple-zone system with separate thermostats is more efficient than a single zone system with one thermostat. Complex systems provide an individual temperature control for each room. The efficiency of certain systems can be increased by putting a thermostat on the outside of the building. This helps building operators anticipate how much heat the system will need to produce.

Heating Fuels

The type of fuel used in a building's heating system should be explained in the building description. Depending on the area and the type of building, one type of fuel may be more desirable than another. Nevertheless, many building heating systems do not use the most economical fuel. For any specific use, different fuels have different advantages and disadvantages, which are subject to change.

Fuel oil. In spite of its high cost, fuel oil is a popular energy source which is easy to transport and store. On-site, 275-gallon tanks are used in millions of houses and tanks that hold thousands of gallons of fuel oil are buried on industrial and commercial sites.

Natural gas. Natural gas is a convenient type of fuel because it is continuously delivered by pipelines; no storage tank is needed. In many parts of the United States, natural gas is the most economical fuel. Liquid petroleum gas, such as butane and propane, is used in many rural areas. It requires on-site storage tanks and is usually more expensive, but in other respects it is similar to natural gas.

Electricity. Like oil, gas, or coal, electricity can be used to produce heat in a furnace or to heat water in a boiler. In most areas electrical heating costs are high, but good insulation and control can eliminate waste.

Coal. In the past coal was the most popular fuel for heating; it is still used in electrical generating plants and to generate power for some industrial and commercial uses. Coal is also used in residences for stoves and fireplaces, but the burning of certain types of coal creates environmental pollution.

An appraiser cannot assume that a building's existing heating system contributes maximum value to the property. The heating system that was installed when the building was constructed may not be acceptable to potential buyers today.

New technology has continued to reduce energy consumption for large heating systems. Many industrial users who once depended on gas alone now install more efficient, oil or electric systems to provide heat when the gas supply is curtailed. Electric heat has become so costly in some areas that buildings using it sell for substantially less than similar properties that use other types of fuel. *Cogeneration*, the simultaneous production of electrical energy and low-grade heat from the same fuel, is also being used in some parts of the country.

Buyers are sensitive to energy costs. Apartments in which the owner supplies heat and hot water usually sell for less than similar properties in which tenants pay for utilities. Buildings that have high ceilings, many openings, and poor insulation may be at a disadvantage in the market.

Solar heating and domestic hot water systems have attracted much interest, and many such systems are on the market. Appraisers should keep up-to-date on the development of solar energy and its use in particular areas. A solar heating system should be carefully described and its contribution to the property's value should be estimated. When residential appraisals are reported on Freddie Mac and Fannie Mae forms, solar heating and other special energy systems must be described and valued separately.

Air-Conditioning and Ventilation Systems

Before World War II ducts, fans, and open windows were used to reduce heat and provide fresh air in most buildings. In many buildings ducts and fans are still used to cool and provide fresh air. In certain parts of the western United States, where the humidity is low even when it is very hot, buildings can be cooled with *swamp coolers*, simple systems that blow air across wet excelsior or another water-absorbing material. Package units that employ this method are still manufactured for home and commercial use. Because these units use less power, they are less expensive to operate than conventional air-conditioning systems.

The most common type of air-conditioning system consists of an electrically powered compressor that compresses Freon from gas into liquid outside the area being cooled. The heat released in this process is either blown away or carried away by water. The compressed Freon is then directed into thin tubes in the area being cooled, where it expands and absorbs heat from the air that is directed over the tubes by one or more fans. Another type of air-conditioning system is powered by gas, rather than electricity, and uses ammonia, not Freon, as the refrigerant. Air-conditioners range from small, portable units to units that provide many tons of cooling capacity. The capacity of an air-conditioning unit is rated in tons of refrigeration, which is equal to the amount of heat needed to melt a ton of ice in 24 hours, or 12,000 Btus per hour.

Commercial and industrial air-conditioning and ventilation systems are more complex. Some simply bring in fresh air from the outside and distribute it throughout the building; others merely remove foul air. Still others combine these two functions, but do not have any cooling or heating capacity. More complex systems wash, filter, and add or remove humidity from the air. The most complex systems perform all of these functions and also heat and cool air through a complex system of ducts and fans. In larger systems that use less electricity, water cools the pipes in which the gas has been compressed. The water is then conserved in towers that cool it for reuse.

An appraiser describes the air-conditioning and ventilation system in a building and decides whether it is appropriate to the geographic area. To do this the appraiser may have to investigate whether the building's system meets current standards. If the appraiser concludes that the building has too much or too little air-conditioning, the appraisal report should include the data on which this conclusion is based.

Electrical Systems

A well-designed electrical system will provide sufficient power for all the electrical uses in the building. Sometimes, one electrical service may supply power to more than one building.

In an electrical system, power is distributed from the electrical service station through branch circuits, which are wires located throughout the building, to electrical outlets. Each branch circuit starts at a distribution box, where it is separated from the main service by a protection device such as a fuse or circuit breaker. When a short circuit or overload occurs on the branch circuit, the fuse or circuit breaker disconnects the circuit from the power supply to prevent a fire.

The wiring between the distribution boxes and the outlets may be a rigid or flexible conduit. This type of wiring is common in commercial and industrial buildings. In most houses BX or armored cable is used. Plastic-coated wire is used in certain areas, and the old knob-and-tube wiring is still used in rural areas and older buildings, although it is considered obsolete.

Most electrical wire is copper. After World War II aluminum wire became popular as the price of copper escalated, but its resistance to fire has been seriously questioned. In some sections of the country, aluminum wiring is prohibited by electrical or building codes.

A typical residential electrical system is a single-phase, three-wire system that provides a minimum of 100 amperes of electricity. The old 30-ampere systems are certainly obsolete and residences that have 60 amperes of service normally sell for less than those with larger services. Ampere services of 150, 200, 300, and 400 are needed when electric heating and air-conditioning are used. Most of these services can provide up to 220 volts by connecting three wires to the outlet.

Power wiring is used in commercial and industrial buildings to operate utility systems, appliances, and machinery. The electrical power is generally carried at higher voltages (e.g., 240, 480, 600 volts or more) and is usually three-phase or three-phase-four-wire, which allows both lighting and three-phase power loads to be delivered by the same supply.

Power wiring is carried in conduit or by means of plug-in bus ducts. Overhead bus ducts are frequently found in manufacturing plants where flexible service is needed. Large-capacity power wiring may contribute to the value of an industrial improvement. However, if the wiring is an uncommon type and adds to a building's operating costs or will be expensive to remove, it may result in functional obsolescence. Similarly, any building with insufficient electrical service or wiring suffers from functional obsolescence.

Switches and lighting fixtures are also part of the electrical system. Because lighting fixtures are stylized and styles change, they are often obsolete before they wear out. Fluorescent lighting, which may be suspended, surface-mounted, or recessed, is used extensively in commercial and industrial buildings. Often continuous rows are used in large spaces. Incandescent fixtures may be used for smaller rooms, accents, or special purposes.

In newer lighting design, the intensity and quality of light over work areas and display surfaces are important considerations. The degree of intensity will vary with the type of use. Sodium, mercury vapor, halogen and halide lights are often installed in industrial buildings. Some installations are designed so that air moves past the lighting fixtures to augment the heating system.

Floor outlets or floor duct systems are extensively used in commercial and office buildings. These systems provide convenient electrical outlets for office machines and telephone outlets at desks using a minimum number of cords. Some houses and commercial buildings have low-voltage switching systems, in which many outlets and lights can be controlled from one place.

Miscellaneous Equipment

In preparing building descriptions, appraisers must also consider miscellaneous equipment, some of which is discussed below.

Fire Protection

Fire protection equipment includes fire escapes, standpipes and hose cabinets, alarm services, and automatic sprinklers. A wet sprinkler system must have adequate water pressure to ensure that the pipes are always filled. A dry system has pressurized air in the pipes. When a sprinkler head opens, the pressure is relieved and water enters. Dry systems are used on loading docks and in unheated buildings where there is a danger of water freezing.

Elevators, Escalators, and Speed Ramps

Elevators are usually classified as passenger or freight and may be either electric or hydraulic. The type, speed, and capacity of an elevator and the number of floors it serves are related to the type of property and its utility. Hydraulic elevators are suitable for low-speed, low-rise operations. Passenger elevators that need full-time operators are costly and now practically obsolete. Most modern elevators are high-speed and completely automatic. Control systems collect signals and distribute service among all the elevators in the system. Some elevators have auxiliary controls so that they can be manually operated if necessary.

The movement of large numbers of people up and down or along horizontal or gradual slopes can be accomplished with escalators and speed ramps. This equipment must be adequate to accommodate those who use the building.

Signals, Alarms, and Call Systems

Signals, alarms, call systems, and similar devices should not be overlooked by appraisers. Smoke detectors are increasingly common in residential and multifamily structures and are required by law in many areas. Security alarm systems, which warn occupants of forced entry, fire, or both, are available for residential, commercial, and industrial use. Because fire and safety regulations change, systems that were adequate when they were installed may later be considered substandard.

Other items to be noted by an appraiser include clocks, pneumatic tube systems, mail chutes, incinerators, and telephone wiring. In small buildings the telephone company supplies the wiring and equipment; larger buildings may have extensive systems of built-in cabinets, conduits, and floor ducts for telephone service. The telephone service in a building may be suitable for the current occupant, but unsuitable for a potential buyer.

Loading Facilities

Facilities for loading and unloading trucks and freight cars may be important in commercial and industrial buildings. Off-street loading docks are usually required by zoning ordinances. Many older buildings have loading doors only or substandard loading facilities. Loading docks may be open or covered. The floor of an efficient, one-story industrial building may be built above grade at freight car or truck-bed level. In some buildings docks are enclosed for trucks and freight cars, and leveling devices are provided to assist in loading or unloading. A properly designed industrial building has space in front of truck docks so that vehicles can maneuver.

Attached Equipment

Process-related fixed building equipment includes air hoses, process piping, industrial wiring for heavy electrical capacity, bus ducts, and freezer equipment. Although this equipment may be a part of another utility systems (e.g., plumbing or electrical), its contributory role in a specific industrial process warrants attention. The appraiser should consider attached equipment in terms of its use value.

Quality and Condition Survey

A building description includes a quality and condition survey in which the appraiser analyzes and explains the quality and condition of the items described. The character, quality, and appearance of building construction are reflected in each of the three approaches to value. The quality and condition of building components have a major influence on the cost estimate, the accrued depreciation estimate, the ability of the property to produce rental income, and the property's comparability with other properties. Analysis of the quality of construction and the methods and materials used complements the appraiser's analysis of the building's structural design and architecture.

A structure can have a good, functional layout and an attractive design but be built with inferior materials and poor workmanship. These deficiencies increase maintenance and utility costs and adversely affect the property's marketability. Conversely, a building can be built too well or at a cost that cannot be justified by its utility. Most purchasers will not pay for these excess costs and only part of the original investment can be recaptured by the original owner through reduced maintenance expenses.

Practical or reasonable economy of construction results in an improvement that will produce rental income or value commensurate with its cost. Maintenance and operating expenses for an economically constructed building may be slightly higher than minimum expenses, but this is usually preferable to a building of superior construction which will have higher taxes. To achieve the desired level of construction quality and cost, building materials and construction methods must be chosen and used properly. Appraisers should recognize that an appropriate combination of elements results in a building that is adequate for its intended purpose.

The maintenance and age of a building affect its condition. In a quality and condition survey, the appraiser generally distinguishes among items in need of immediate repair on the date of the appraisal (deferred maintenance items), items that may be repaired or replaced at a later time, and items that are expected to last the full economic life of the building.

Items in Need of Immediate Repair

Although a building may be in excellent condition, the appraiser usually finds some items in need of repair on the date of the appraisal. Repairing these items will normally add as much or more value to the property than the cost of their repair. When the cost approach to value is applied, these are considered items of curable physical deterioration.

The appraiser's repair list should include items that constitute a fire or safety hazard. Many clients request that these items be listed separately in the report. Sometimes the appraiser is asked to estimate the cost of each repair, which is called *cost to cure*. The following list indicates some repairs that are commonly needed.

- Touch-up exterior paint on buildings and the removal of graffiti
- Minor carpentry repairs on stairs, molding, trim, floors, and porches
- Redecorating interior rooms
- Fixing leaky or noisy plumbing
- Loosening stuck doors and windows
- Repairing torn screens and broken windows
- Rehanging loose or damaged gutters and leaders
- Replacing missing shingles, tiles, and slates and repairing leaky roofs
- Fixing cracked sidewalks, driveways, and parking areas
- Doing minor electrical repairs
- Replacing rotten floor boards
- Exterminating vermin
- Fixing cracked or loose tiles in bathrooms and kitchens
- Repairing septic systems
- Eliminating safety hazards such as windows that have been nailed shut
- Eliminating fire hazards such as paint-soaked rags in a storage area

Short-lived Items

During the building inspection, an appraiser usually encounters other items that show signs of wear and tear, but would not be economical to repair or replace on the date of the appraisal. The economic life of a building is the period over which the improvements contribute to property value. Many building components have to be repaired at some time during the economic life of the building. If the remaining life of the component is shorter than the remaining economic life of the structure as a whole, the component is identified as a *short-lived item*.

The appraiser must decide if an item needs immediate repair or replacement or whether this work can be done later. (The consideration of deteriorated items is discussed in Chapter 17.) If the repair or replacement will add less to the value of the property than it will cost, the maintenance should usually be delayed. For example, a building with a sound, 10-year-old roof may hold up well for at least another five years. Although the roof has suffered some deterioration, replacing it probably would not add more value to the property than the cost of a new roof. Short-lived items that will eventually require repair or replacement include:

- Interior paint and wallpaper
- Exterior paint
- Floor finishes
- Shades, screens, and blinds (often considered personal property)
- Waterproofing and weatherstripping
- Gutters and leaders
- Roof covering and flashing
- Water heater
- Furnace
- Air-conditioning equipment
- Carpeting
- Kitchen appliances (considered short-lived items only if built-in)
- Sump pump
- Water softener system (often rented, not owned)
- Washers and dryers (often considered personal property)
- Ventilating fans

The appraiser should consider whether repairing an item is necessary to preserve other components. For example, sometimes the roof cover must be replaced or the economic life of the other components will be reduced. The appraiser should note whether the condition of the short-lived item is better or worse than the overall condition of the building.

Long-lived Items

The final step in a quality and condition survey is to describe the condition of those items that are not expected to require repair or replacement during the economic life of the building, assuming they are not subject to abnormal wear and tear or accidentally damaged. A building component with an expected economic life that is the same as the remaining economic life of the structure is called a *long-lived item*. Repair may not be required because the component has been built to last and has been well maintained. All the long-lived components of a building are rarely in the same condition; the appraiser identifies those items that are not in the same condition as the rest of the building.

Some defective long-lived items are not considered in need of repair because the cost of their replacement or repair is greater than the amount these items contribute to the value of the property. A serious crack in a foundation wall, for example, would probably be considered incurable physical deterioration. Incurable depreciation that results from problems in the original design of a structure is considered incurable functional obsolescence.

Some long-lived items are listed below.

- Hot and cold water pipes
- Plumbing fixtures (may also be considered functional components)
- Electric service connection (may also be considered functional components)
- Electric wiring
- Electric fixtures
- Ducts and radiators

Key Concepts

- A building description includes specific information on the size, design or layout, structural components, construction materials, equipment, and mechanical systems of a building.
- A building description addresses the current use, the zoning codes that govern that use, the plan and construction of the structure, relevant building codes, and the size of the building.
- Systems for measuring residential and commercial properties vary. Gross building area *(GBA)* is measured for all property types. Gross living area *(GLA)* and gross leasable area *(GLA)* are other common measurements.
- A building description includes a description of the exterior, the interior, and the equipment and mechanical systems.
- An exterior description provides information on the substructure (foundation), superstructure (framing, insulation, ventilation, exterior walls and doors, roof and drains, and chimneys), and infrastructure (utilities and support services) of a building.
- An interior description provides information about the interior walls and doors, flooring, space divisions, stairways, internal supports, painting, decorating, finishing, and protection against decay and pests.
- Equipment and mechanical systems provide for human comfort; industrial buildings also contain process-related equipment.
- Heating, plumbing, ventilation, electrical, and lighting systems are differentiated by component materials, principles of operation, and sources of power.
- In a quality and condition survey, the appraiser distinguishes among items in need of immediate repair (deferred maintenance items), short-lived items that can be replaced at a later date, and long-lived items expected to last for the remaining economic life of the building.

Terms

Americans with Disabilities Act
(ADA) of 1990
asbestos-containing materials
(ACMs)
bays
building code
building description
cogeneration
deferred maintenance items
economic life
equipment and mechanical
systems
exterior description
facade
floating foundation
footings
framing
gross building area (*GBA*)
gross leasable area (*GLA*)
gross living area (*GLA*)
heating, ventilation, and
air-conditioning (HVAC)
system
immediate repair items

infrastructure
insulation
interior description
internal supports
joists
long-lived items
obsolescence
platform construction
post and beam framing
process-related equipment
purlins
quality and condition survey
R-value
remaining economic life
short-lived items
solar heating
strut
studs
substructure
superstructure
use classification
ventilation
zone control

CHAPTER TWELVE

Building Style and Function

A rchitectural style and functional utility are interrelated, and their combined effect on property value must be analyzed by appraisers. *Architectural style is the character of a building's form and ornamentation. Functional utility is the ability of a property or building to be useful and to perform the function for which it is intended, according to current market tastes and standards.* Functional utility also relates to the efficiency of a building's use in terms of architectural style, design and layout, traffic patterns, and the size and type of rooms. Both architectural style and functional utility influence human lives by providing or withholding beauty, comfort, security, convenience, light, and air. They may also ensure reasonable maintenance expenditures, preserve valuable traditions, and indicate the need for change.

A building may have functional utility but lack architectural style, or it may have admirable style but little utility. Form and function work together to create successful architecture. Functional utility is not necessarily exemplified by minimal space or form; people's need for comfort and pleasure must also be considered in the design of offices, stores, hospitals, and houses. An appraiser must recognize and rank market preferences regarding style and functional utility and then relate these preferences to market value.

Considerations of style and functional utility are integral to an appraisal. They are noted along with other physical characteristics during property inspection. Using comparable data an appraiser can analyze how style and function influence a property's market value. Style and functional utility are examined in terms of the use for which a particular property was designed, its actual or contemplated use, and its most economic use. These three uses may or may not be the same.

Architectural Style and Utility

Architecture is the art or science of building design and construction. It is the formal organization of three-dimensional elements on a large scale to serve various human needs. Because architecture interprets human needs, it is a fundamental reflection of culture. Architectural style affects the market value of property, so an understanding of its nature is important to appraisers. Two basic types of styles are distinguished in American architecture: formal architecture and vernacular architecture.

Formal architecture refers to the art and science of designing and building structures that meet the aesthetic and functional criteria of those trained in architectural history. Formal architectural styles are identified by common attributes of expression and are frequently named in reference to a geographic region, cultural group, or time period. Italianate, Second Empire, and Prairie School are examples of formal architectural styles.[1]

Vernacular architecture identifies structures designed and built without reference to the aesthetic and functional criteria of architectural history. Vernacular architecture reflects custom and responds to the environment and contemporary lifestyles. Vernacular styles share common attributes and may be technologically simple or sophisticated. These styles are usually unnamed because they are not formally studied by architectural historians. The sod houses built on the prairies of the American West and the mass-produced homes constructed in modern subdivisions are examples of vernacular styles. The traditional barn is another successful type of vernacular building.

Architectural style is influenced by market standards and tastes. Market standards are accepted norms, which reflect a culture's shared attitudes and beliefs. They are established forms and methods of construction which have not yet been surpassed by advances in technology or been perceived as aesthetically undesirable.

Market tastes are preferences, which may be shared by groups or expressed individually. Commonly shared tastes characterize most of the market for real estate. In a free economy, tastes shift either in reaction to, or in accordance with, market standards. Market tastes and standards are influenced both by the desire to preserve tradition and by the desire for change, variety, and efficiency. Architectural trends respond to the market's desire to preserve tradition by including elements of past architectural styles; the market's desire for change provides the impetus for developing new elements of architectural design.

Changes in architectural trends are precipitated by the market's reaction to current styles. When a style becomes too extreme, a shift to elements of past styles frequently occurs. Thus, extreme ornateness may be replaced by forms that are spare. A reactive shift, then, provides contrast to the preceding, dominant architectural style. Such changes also produce avant-garde or experimental building styles, which are ultimately tested in the market. An experimental style is eventually discarded or it becomes an accepted standard. However, design elements that are discarded in a reactive swing are not lost; old forms may disappear for a time and then reappear in a modified form.

Changes in architecture can also be generated by external forces. For example, rising energy costs have prompted new developments in the heating, ventilation, and air-conditioning systems used in office buildings. These developments include the installation of solar energy panels, the trend toward stand-alone HVAC systems, and the use of new exterior materials that conserve energy.

Architectural styles are modified over periods that are loosely related to the economic life cycles of buildings. Newly constructed buildings usually contrast in style with buildings of the previous period. Newly constructed buildings of all architectural styles enjoy broad market appeal, whether they are professionally designed or not. When a building is no longer new, however, it is compared with other buildings in terms of the quality and usefulness of its architectural style. Form and structure, the most basic

---

1. Literature on American architectural history is abundant. For a description of architectural styles in a real estate appraisal context, see Judith Reynolds, MAI, *Historic Properties: Preservation and the Valuation Process*, 2d ed. (Chicago: Appraisal Institute, 1996). Other sources are cited in the bibliography of this text.

components of architectural style, limit and define a building's potential uses (and changes in use); these factors become more influential as time passes.

Architectural styles reflect the complex relationship between cultural premises and human activity. Thus, descriptions of architectural styles provide appraisers with a record of architectural history and a catalog of social expression. Figures 12.1 and 12.2 illustrate formal and vernacular architectural styles in America.

Style Adaptations

Architectural style is reflected in a number of building components. A building's materials, structure, equipment, and siting all shape and change its style. The availability of natural materials such as wood, stone, and clay and lime for making brick was primarily responsible for the different architectural styles that have emerged and prevailed in various areas of the United States. When post-and-beam construction was developed, greater spaces could be spanned. This type of construction made it possible to build the large fabricating mills of the Industrial Revolution. The evolution of lightweight balloon framing and machines to mass-produce nails changed the form of buildings in the nineteenth century. Balloon framing allowed buildings to be constructed much more rapidly because precut components were used.

Technology and Design

The development of the Franklin stove and central heating systems changed the shape and number of rooms in all structures because fireplaces were no longer needed to provide heat. The mass production of domestic commodities and equipment in the early twentieth century eliminated the need for root cellars, pantries, and large laundry rooms, which decreased the size of dwellings and changed room arrangements.

In the mid-twentieth century, central air-conditioning and heating became common in residential, commercial, and industrial buildings. This resulted in a standardization of architectural styles, particularly housing styles, throughout the country and nearly obliterated the regional building styles developed in response to variations in climate.

For example, the thick, mud masonry walls and small windows of houses in the Southwest were well-suited to the hot, dry weather of the region. Houses in the rainy Northwest had overhanging roofs so that windows could be opened for ventilation without admitting the rain. The saltbox houses of New England were protected against the harsh northern wind because the windowless, steeped-roof side of the house faced north. Although regional building styles temporarily lost favor, structural defenses against climate were reincorporated into construction in the mid-1970s. Because the market has become energy-conscious, climate-compatible design has returned. Such design considerations are important in estimating market value because consumers increasingly desire energy-saving features.

Advances in computers and semiconductors, wiring networks and switching devices, and satellite communications have affected building design. In modern business facilities, much attention is devoted to the installation, routing, and expansion capabilities of communications systems. The networking of information services and telecommunications facilities (telephones, fax lines, modems) has significantly impacted building construction and design. Design considerations for contemporary office buildings include

Figure 12.1 | **Formal Architecture**

Jeffersonian

Art Deco

Georgian

Gothic Revival

Second Empire

Queen Anne

Courtesy of the United States Committee of the International Council on Monuments and Sites, the National Park Service, the National Trust for Historic Preservation, the Smithsonian Institution Traveling Exhibition Service, the Historic American Buildings Survey, the Preservation Press, and the Brown Foundation.

Figure 12.2 | **Vernacular Architecture**

(Both photos from
H. Armstrong Roberts, Inc.)

the capacities of feed conduit and electrical service to accommodate a wide variety of transmission linkages, the presence or absence of roof reinforcement to support satellite and microwave antennae, and the ability of HVAC systems to handle the increased heat output of office computers. These factors affect the size of conduit and risers, the amount and quality of electricity required, ceiling height, and other structural considerations.

Construction Materials

The use of steel for framing and the invention of the elevator made the construction of taller buildings possible. Steel studs have become prevalent in all types of construction, even residential. Steel does not warp, is cheaper and more available than wood, and can be installed under most conditions. Curtain walls of glass and metal are well-suited to the box-like forms of modern buildings built in the International style. Curtain-wall construction separated the functions of support and enclosure, which were inseparable in multistory buildings of heavy masonry. Curtain walls can be made of metal, masonry, precast concrete, or glass.

Steel bar joists have twice the load-bearing capacity of solid joists, so greater spaces can be spanned and pipes, ducts, and conduit can be threaded through open webbing. Trusses (especially roof and floor trusses) have replaced more traditional joist systems and are used in framing for all types of new construction. Lightweight structural support systems and the use of lamination and plastic glues developed in the aircraft industry have facilitated the creation of new building components such as butterfly and arcaded roofs.

Construction techniques developed since the 1940s have allowed buildings to take new shapes because concrete can now be used in large slabs, building blocks, or beams.

Elevator buildings constructed of reinforced concrete are an alternative to steel framing construction and are less vulnerable to fire. Building a structure with poured concrete is slow and must stop in cold weather, but precast concrete assembly can proceed nearly as quickly as steel construction. For additional strength, posttensioning can be used to tighten reinforcing rods while the concrete hardens. Concrete column reinforcement allows concrete buildings to be built as high as steel-framed towers. Lightweight aggregate can also be used in cement to reduce the load.

Styrofoam forming is a relatively new system of construction that is replacing traditional concrete construction. Two sheets of rigid styrofoam held together by steel rods are used as forms into which concrete is poured. The steel rods prevent the styrofoam from spreading. When the concrete hardens, the styrofoam is left in place, providing rigid insulation for both sides of the concrete wall. This system of construction is now used in all types of construction.

As materials, structural components, and equipment become more refined, architectural styles change. Technological advances are integrated into evolving architectural styles and may modify architectural trends.

Siting

Architectural design is also influenced by the placement of a building on its site. Every building has a physical setting that includes the space around it. In cities where buildings abut one another directly, there is little choice about placement. In some locations there is more flexibility, however, and a building's design, placement, and landscaping can provide a defense against the climate. Appropriate placement on a site can also reduce energy costs and enhance a building's architectural design.

Architectural design can be adjusted to suit the climate and the individual site. Trees can provide shade, act as windbreaks and sound barriers, and filter and add moisture to the air. Deciduous trees should be placed on the west side of a property, where they can provide shade from the afternoon sun in summer and allow the sun to shine through in winter. Conifers planted on the north side of a property act as windbreaks. The effects of shade and sunlight can also be moderated by the angle and direction of overhanging roofs. These roofs deflect the high-angle rays of the summer sun, but allow the low-angle rays of the winter sun to be admitted through the building's windows.

Because increasing fuel costs have created the need for alternative energy sources, active and passive solar features have been introduced into some building designs. Active solar heating systems make use of glass roof panels or glass attached to one side of the building. Warm air is stored in a medium such as water or pumped directly into the structure. Passive solar heating techniques include strategically placed windows or glass walls, insulation, heat-retaining walls and floors, and careful siting. Rooms, roofs, and windows can be situated to allow warm air to flow freely through the structure or to provide maximum ventilation and air cooling.

Earth-sheltered construction, solar heating techniques, climate-specific siting, and other energy-related building adaptations should be considered in terms of their acceptance in the market and their influence on sale prices, rents, and other market value indicators.

Functional Utility

To be functional an item must work and be useful. The definition of functional utility, however, is subject to changing expectations and standards. Optimal functional utility implies that the design and engineering of a building are considered to best meet perceived needs at a given time.

Functional inutility is an impairment of the functional capacity of a property or building according to market tastes and standards. It becomes equivalent to functional obsolescence when ongoing change, caused by technological advances and economic and aesthetic trends, renders building layouts and features obsolete. Functional inutility must be judged in light of market standards of acceptability, specifically the standards of buyers who make up the market for a particular type of building within a particular period of time.

As objectives of building design, functional utility and aesthetics are sometimes in conflict; market standards generally reflect a compromise between the two. Extremely utilitarian housing designs that omitted basements, entrance halls, and dining rooms were eventually rejected by much of the market and replaced with more flexible designs. Similarly, the trend toward ultimate efficiency in office building interiors produced standard space with low ceilings, plain walls, and vinyl asbestos floors. This type of interior finish was soon considered substandard.

Functional utility represents more than practical utilitarianism. Superadequacies—i.e., superadequate structural components or space—are also items of functional obsolescence because their costs exceed their value. When an expensively finished retail space with high ceilings is included in an office building located where there is no market for retailing, the building incorporates functional obsolescence in the form of superadequacy.

Standards of functional utility vary with the type and use of property. Specific considerations for different types of property are discussed in the remainder of this chapter. Some general standards of functional utility to be considered by appraisers include

- Suitability or appropriateness
- Comfort
- Efficiency
- Safety
- Security
- Accessibility
- Ease and cost of maintenance
- Market standards
- Attractiveness
- Profitability

One additional standard must be given special consideration. In determining the functional utility and appropriateness of an architectural style, an appraiser must consider compatibility.

Compatibility

Compatibility means that a building is in harmony with its use or uses and its environment. Compatibility should extend to a building's form, materials, and scale. Styles of different periods frequently clash; a cubistic dwelling would not be in harmony with eighteenth-century colonial buildings. Similarly, a monumental or ostentatious building is often out of place in a modest setting. Two-story structures tend to be overwhelmed in a row of skyscrapers, so their market value may be diminished by incompatibility of design. There are other types of incompatibility as well. A structure can be incompatible with its function, its various elements can be incompatible with one another, or the structure can be incompatible with its site or location in the neighborhood.

Compatibility is influenced by zoning, historical districts, construction and maintenance costs, land value, physical features, architectural trends, and technology. Sometimes these factors impose conformity, which is important in the analysis of highest and best use. Usually the predominant uses and building styles in an area are readily observable. A trend in development may be more difficult to discern; an architectural style that appears atypical may actually conform to an emerging trend.

A building design that is typical in an area has less influence on value than a design that is atypical, so the impact of nonconformity must be considered carefully. Many property owners strive to achieve a degree of individuality, e.g., in the color of exterior paint or the use of landscaping and fencing. In most markets, a modicum of individuality is acceptable as long as it does not violate conformity. When a homeowner takes the expression of individuality to an extreme, however, conformity is lost and property value is generally penalized.

For example, a slightly unusual design that is attractive and generally in harmony with other, nearby buildings could command a higher price than its more typical neighbors. A building with an incongruous design, however, will probably be sold at a price below the general market level; if this is not the case, there may be offsetting qualities.

Occasionally, assessing the value influence of a nonconforming design may require unsupported, but reasoned, appraisal judgment. In many cases, however, the effect on value can be determined from market data. For example, international style office buildings in a particular location may regularly be sold at lower prices per square foot than buildings of a different style.

Sometimes there may be sufficient demand for a nonconforming design, such as a detached dwelling in a neighborhood of row houses or an art nouveau movie theater in a retail shopping district dominated by nineteenth-century buildings. If demand exists, it may support a market value equal to or greater than that of more typical structures. Functional utility and location may override design as a primary market requirement. There may be no design penalty if the general proportions and scale of an atypical building are in harmony with the surroundings, the demands of functional utility are met, and the location is appropriate.

Building materials should be in harmony with one another and with a building's architectural style. A building that is designed to be constructed of one material will not necessarily be effective when constructed of another. Building materials should not be excessively varied nor should an architectural design have too many distracting features. The design and building materials used should be well-integrated and in harmony with the site. A frame building in a wooded, hilly area will probably be in better harmony with its setting than a brick building, assuming wood is appropriate for the structure's function. A frame building in an urban area dominated by masonry usually suffers a market value penalty; similarly, an office building with a metal facade may be penalized if stone facades are typical in the area.

Design and Functional Utility by Building Type

Marketability is the ultimate test of functional utility. Generally, a building is functional if it successfully serves the purpose for which it was designed or adapted. Specific design considerations that affect the functional utility of residential, commercial, industrial, agricultural, and special-purpose buildings are discussed below.

Residential Properties

Trends in single-family and apartment design change and building components such as porches, balconies, fireplaces, dining rooms, large kitchens, entry halls, and family rooms may be included or excluded. Housing standards vary widely for different income levels and in different regions. Historic houses are often less functional, but they may be in great demand due to their preservationist appeal. To evaluate the functional utility of residential buildings, appraisers should analyze standard market expectations. Nevertheless, the functional utility of a single-family or multifamily dwelling results primarily from its layout, accommodation of specific activities, adequacy, and ease and cost of maintenance.

Layout

The layout of an apartment or house relates to traffic patterns—i.e., where kitchens and bathrooms should be located for convenience and how private and public areas should be separated. A layout has functional inutility if it causes awkward traffic patterns. For example, inutility may result if people have to cross the living room to get to a bedroom, if the dining area is not adjacent to the kitchen, or if groceries have to be brought through the living room to the kitchen.

Full bathrooms, which include facilities for bathing, are most convenient, accessible, and private when they are near the bedrooms; they should be accessed directly or through a hall, not through a second bedroom. Powder rooms should be located off a hall and near, but not too near, the living room or dining room. Poor floor plans are easily recognized by those who make up the market for apartments and houses, but standards often vary with current trends in a region and neighborhood.

The location of various rooms in relation to the site can increase or diminish a dwelling's privacy, comfort, and serenity. In urban areas, the bedrooms and living rooms are increasingly found in the rear of residences, often accessible to the garden or backyard. This trend is relatively new. Formerly it was considered desirable for the living room and largest bedroom to be at the front of the house, oriented to the street. Kitchens, which were once relegated to the rear, are now just as likely to be on one side of a hall in the middle or at the front of a residence.

The popularity of condominium ownership has encouraged versatility in apartment design. Clustered, duplex, and townhouse units are constructed in interesting configurations that maximize their market appeal. Structures designed for other uses are now being converted to apartments. Silos, breweries, warehouses, and schools have been successfully converted into multiunit projects. Two-story duplexes with vertical access from within the unit, rather than from public space, have strong market appeal. Multiunit housing is also built in stacked configurations with access on more than one level to minimize stair climbing. Low-rise, multifamily housing projects can be designed in a great many ways. Elevator apartment buildings tend to have more standardized, predictable floor plans to make the best use of space within a simple rectangular configuration.

Accommodation of Specific Activities

In residential building design, the specific activities of occupants are accommodated by providing separate areas for food preparation, eating, conversation, sleeping, hygiene, hobbies, and relaxation. Throughout much of this century, the trend in American housing has been toward combining the functions of many rooms into fewer rooms. The "great room" concept reflected in a combined living room, dining room, and family room exemplifies this trend.

Adequacy

Adequacy is a primary consideration in evaluating functional utility. The adequacy of building size, windows, doors, rooms, ceiling height, closets, security, privacy, and comfort are all considered in planning dwellings and in estimating their value.

Standards of adequacy vary. The one-bathroom apartment or house has, for the most part, become an anachronism. New kitchens and baths are larger, better equipped, and more expensively finished than the small, utilitarian kitchens and baths of the recent past. Dishwashers, garbage disposals, and wall ovens are usually standard in new construction and their absence may create a value penalty. Ceramic tile in baths and more elegant fixtures are becoming commonplace. The master bedroom frequently has its own compartmentalized bath with a spa tub and a separate dressing area. Closets are abundant in new apartments and houses and ceiling heights have increased, especially in living rooms, despite high energy costs.

In general more people have better housing today. Many amenities are now considered necessities and their inclusion is taken for granted. Even in periods of high construction and financing costs when average houses are smaller, the tendency is to retain extra bathrooms, labor-saving devices, and fireplaces.

Although an apartment is a dwelling unit within a larger structure, it must be seen as an integral part of the whole. Security, convenience, and ease of maintenance are primary considerations for apartments, whether they are rented or owned as cooperatives or condominiums. Amenities tend to be more important than space; apartment buyers and sellers often prefer a fireplace or an extra bathroom to an additional 200 square feet of area. Because most apartments do not have gardens or yards, they should provide light, air, and an interesting view. Amenities such as convenient parking, swimming pools, tennis courts, and exercise facilities are important to apartment projects when these features are not available nearby.

Smaller kitchens and bathrooms tend to be more acceptable to the market for apartments than the market for houses. A dining area that is a part of the living room or kitchen is generally acceptable. Family rooms and living rooms may be spacious to offset the smallness of other rooms and closet space must be plentiful.

Kitchen and bath finishes and equipment that are unusual or faddish can make an apartment less desirable to the market. Pastel ceramic tile in bathrooms and dark-colored kitchen equipment may be undesirable where all-white or neutral color schemes are the norm. Dishwashers, garbage disposals, and central air-conditioning have become standard for apartments, and laundry equipment is becoming common in more expensive units.

The mix of units in an apartment project should meet market demands; an improper unit mix may indicate functional inutility.

Ease and Cost of Maintenance

The ease and cost of maintaining a single-family dwelling or condominium unit are increasingly important to its marketability. More family members have become wage earners and less time is available for home maintenance. Interior and exterior finishes that require extensive maintenance can make a structure less competitive.

The efficient use of energy is a primary consideration in the residential market because heating, cooling, lighting, and cooking fuels are expensive. As alternatives to electricity, natural gas, and oil, buyers have turned to insulation, fireplaces, wood stoves, ventilating fans, and passive solar techniques. In most markets a house that wastes fuel and electricity suffers major functional obsolescence.

Energy-conserving features are particularly important in multifamily dwellings and often make the difference between a profitable operation and an unprofitable one. A large portion of the energy used in buildings is needed to offset heat lost through cracks, window openings, and the building envelope. Insulation, properly installed windows with double or triple glazing, caulking, and weatherstripping help reduce heat loss in the winter; shade trees, blinds, and solar screens can help keep units cooler in the summer. Energy-efficient equipment and controls also help meet new standards of functional utility in multifamily buildings.

Commercial Properties

Commercial buildings are used for offices, stores, banks, restaurants, and service outlets. Hotels constitute an important subcategory of commercial property. Frequently, two or more commercial uses are combined in a single building.

The structural and design features of commercial buildings are constantly changing. Developers want the most competitive building possible, within the cost constraints imposed by economic pressures, so they incorporate technological changes to meet the demand for innovation whenever possible.

The efficiency of commercial construction today is much greater than it was in the past. Greater utility can be observed both in the portion of the total area enclosed by the structure, which produces direct income in the form of rent, and in the structural facilitation that has evolved out of new materials and construction methods. No single method of commercial building construction predominates; methods vie with one another, and one may surpass others in a given area at a particular time. Steel and reinforced concrete are the most commonly used structural materials.

Appraisers examine a number of specific elements of functional utility in commercial buildings.

- Column spacing
- Bay depth
- Live-load floor capacity
- Ceiling height
- Module width
- Elevator facilities
- The work letter
- HVAC adequacy
- Energy efficiency
- Public amenities
- Parking ratios

Important safety and security concerns may be affected by the treatment of these specific elements.

Column Spacing

Column placement relates to a building's total height; greater spans are more expensive to construct. Closely spaced columns limit the possibilities for interior partitioning. In some areas columns are typically placed at 20 to 22 feet on center, but this placement is far more limiting than column placement at 28 to 30 feet on center. Tenants usually prefer the wider spacing, but the costs of construction may prove prohibitive. The widespread use of trusses in commercial construction has reduced the importance traditionally placed on column spacing and bay depth.

Bay Depth

Bay depth is the distance from the tenant side of the corridor wall to the exterior wall. Bay depth controls the layout of interior space and is dictated by the depth and width of the site, which prescribes the building's configuration. The box-like configuration of contemporary office buildings is cost efficient because the ratio of perimeter wall to enclosed area is optimized. A long, thin building is more expensive to construct than a square one with the same area. The shallower bays of older buildings are more adaptable to the needs of smaller tenancies, but greater bay depths are more profitable to build if they do not exceed market demand. Tenants are often more concerned with the configuration of the space and its ability to house staff and equipment than with the amount of square foot area.

Live-Load Floor Capacity

Floor load capacity is measured in live-load pounds per square foot. Inadequate floor load capacity is a type of functional obsolescence that often decreases a building's marketability and is expensive to cure. Live load includes everything that can be moved, excluding parts of the structure. A floor load capacity of 100 pounds per square foot, up from 70 pounds a generation ago, is generally considered adequate for commercial buildings. Microfilm and microfiche record storage and the use of small-frame computer equipment have begun to reverse the trend toward ever-increasing, live-load floor capacity.

Ceiling Height

New commercial buildings usually have finished ceilings. Finished ceiling heights depend on the building heights permitted by zoning, on market standards and preferences, and on the cost to heat and cool the enclosed space. Higher ceiling heights within a normal range are generally preferred for office space.

Module Width

Building modules are based on the distance between window mullions, which determines the size of partitioned offices in a building. Ceiling tiles and other finish components also determine the dimensions of contemporary office space modules.

When older commercial buildings have architectural charm or other desirable structural qualities, it may be cost-effective to retrofit them with modern lighting, ventilation, and elevators, even if their design does not conform to contemporary standards. Structures with high ceilings, narrow bay depths, wide public corridors, tall doors, and elaborate woodwork may be successfully preserved and adapted to meet the demand of markets that do not require streamlined space.

Elevators

The elevators in multilevel office buildings should be adequate in terms of speed, load capacity, safety, and number, and they should be able to meet peak period demands. Appraisers judge the adequacy of elevators using established standards. A building should have one elevator for every 25,000 to 40,000 square feet of leasable area. The elevators should be able to transport from 10% to 30% of the building's occupants within five minutes at speeds of 300 to 350 feet per minute.

The standards for elevators vary with a building's tenants. For example, a building that houses a single organization may require more elevator service due to heavy interfloor traffic. The Americans with Disabilities Act of 1990 guarantees reasonable access to public and commercial facilities. The control panels within elevator cars should be accessible and interior corridors and doors should be wide enough for wheelchairs.

Elevator capacity is expressed in weight and number of occupants. Electric elevators are faster than hydraulic ones and serve multistory buildings better; hydraulic elevators are sometimes used to connect two or more floors.

In assessing the functional utility of elevator service, an appraiser should consider the number of tenants, the number of floors, and the total building area served by the elevators, as well as the quality of elevator service in competing buildings.

Work Letter

A work letter is an agreement, usually part of a lease, that specifies the level of build-out, i.e., the interior finish and equipment that the landlord is to provide to the tenant, including lighting, partitioning, door allowance, and electrical capacity. The quality and dollar value of these standard installations vary. A typical work letter may include the following specifications:

- One linear foot of partitioning for every 12 to 15 square feet of office space
- One suite entrance door for every 5,000 square feet of office space and one interior door for every 200 to 300 square feet of space
- One 2 ft.-by-4 ft. lighting fixture for every 80 square feet of office space
- One light switch for each room
- One duplex receptacle for every 125 square feet of space
- One telephone outlet for every 150 square feet of space
- One linear foot of closet door for every 800 square feet of space and one bifold closet door for every 5,000 square feet of space

Inadequacies or superadequacies in the level of finish specified in a work letter can result in market value penalties; variations may result in a tenant payment or credit, or in a rental addition or concession.

HVAC Adequacy

Another aspect of a building's functional utility is the adequacy of the heating, ventilation, and air-conditioning (HVAC) systems. It is particularly important that a building's principal use matches its mechanical equipment. For example, medical office buildings usually have substantially more plumbing lines and connections, ventilating diffusers, electrical wiring, and partitioning than typical office structures. To remain in use, a medical office building cannot be subject to any form of functional obsolescence. A medical office building that exhibits significant functional obsolescence caused by superadequacy will probably have to be adapted to an alternative office use.

Energy Efficiency

Energy consumption is increasingly significant for commercial buildings. To remain competitive, office buildings must incorporate technological advances such as computer-programmed controls, zoned heating and cooling, and highly efficient mechanical equipment. Public pressure to economize on energy consumption has increased due to rising energy costs, peak load pricing policies, and the threat of energy allocation.

In inefficient commercial buildings energy expenditures range from 125,000 to 150,000 Btus per square foot per year. In buildings that house computers, energy costs are significantly higher. With improved building design, energy consumption can be reduced to 60,000 to 80,000 Btus per square foot per year; experimental buildings can operate on less than 50,000 Btus per square foot per year.

Most newer commercial buildings in urban areas have been constructed with fixed-sash fenestration, but some are now being built with windows that open to admit fresh air and regulate temperatures. If energy allocation occurs and certain fuels become scarce or unavailable at times, fixed-sash windows could become functionally obsolete.

Public Amenities in Retail Space

Amenities can contribute to a building's functional utility. Building amenities may include attractive public areas, well-kept grounds, and adequate, well-located restroom facilities. The type and use of a property may dictate building amenities. For example, a retail center must have good delivery access, suitable traffic patterns for shoppers, strong lighting, adequate column spacing, and a sufficient number of escalators. Surface and finish elements should be durable and easily maintained. A retail center must also have areas for shoppers and workers to rest, ample restroom facilities, and attractive, coordinated signs.

The specialty shopping center is the newest type of retail grouping. It houses a number of retailers, most of which offer nonessential goods and services. A specialty shopping center usually has no anchor tenants, so it must project its image with a central feature, integrated design elements, or attractive landscaping. Restaurants and entertainment facilities such as movie theaters are also included in specialty shopping centers.

The quality and distribution of public amenities in shopping centers are important appraisal concerns. The need for adequately distributed amenities influences the design of shopping centers, which are as competitive in the market as office buildings. The configuration of the typical shopping center has changed even more drastically than the design of the typical office building.

Trends in shopping centers change so rapidly that many structures become functionally obsolete before they deteriorate physically. Because retail space is relatively easy to renovate, many centers are streamlined and modernized when they lose their market appeal. Shopping centers have evolved from the small strip centers developed after World War II into huge regional and superregional centers, which may occupy up to 100 acres of land and include more than one million square feet of building area. Despite the trend toward greater size, however, most existing and newly built shopping centers have less than 200,000 square feet of space; more than half have less than 100,000 square feet of area.

Supermarkets and drugstores were once the anchor tenants of large suburban shopping centers. They now tend to be free-standing structures located near, but not within, shopping centers. This change is the result of increased merchandising competition among supermarkets, department stores, drugstores, and smaller stores. Large suburban shopping centers are frequently town centers, where people go to shop, socialize, be entertained, and attend civic meetings.

Parking Ratios

Parking ratios are crucial to the success of all retail centers, except those located in dense urban areas. The emergence of multiuse shopping centers and the trend toward smaller cars between the mid-1970s and mid-1980s have increased the ratio between gross leasable store area and parking spaces. One parking space for every 180 square feet of gross leasable store area is usually adequate. Orientation to a means of access is crucial for all commercial buildings.

Users of commercial space tend to occupy separate structures in areas of low-density development. These buildings are usually accessed by automobile, so sufficient, adjacent parking is essential. Pedestrian traffic from buildings to parking areas should also be accommodated. Access to both public transportation and parking is important for commercial buildings located in densely developed urban areas.

Security and convenience govern the placement of parking facilities; the route between a commercial facility and its parking area must be direct and visible. The amount of parking provided is determined by the proximity and availability of alternative sources of access, such as public transportation, and the amount of parking provided by similar buildings. Some commercial buildings in urban areas do not include on-site parking because other forms of transportation are convenient or adequate parking facilities are located nearby.

In an efficiently designed parking garage, columns are placed every 28 feet, which permits three cars to be parked between columns. With the advent of smaller cars, the capacity of outdoor parking lots increased; more cars could be accommodated by restriping spaces. Parking garage design has not changed fundamentally because columns are still needed but, when possible, drive aisles have been reduced from 26 to 25 feet in width.

The standard parking space has been reduced from an area of 9 feet by 18 feet to 8 3/4 feet by 17 1/2 feet. A compact car needs a space approximately 8 1/4 feet by 16 1/2 feet. Most self-park garages average 300 to 350 gross rentable square feet per car, which includes aisles and ramps; garages with attendant parking allow substantially less than 300 square feet per car. The most efficient configuration for a garage is 90-degree-angle parking. A typical parking ratio in an area without good public transit is one parking space for every 200 square feet of leasable area.

Hotels

Hotels range from tiny inns with fewer than a dozen rooms to huge convention hotels with more than a thousand rooms.[2] All hotels and motels were once measured against standard, current designs. This tendency continues for medium-priced hotels, but in appraising older facilities and luxury hotels, variation in architectural styles and interior finish must be considered.

Many older hotels and apartment buildings that have been rehabilitated as hotels have unique architectural styles and an atmosphere of luxury that is difficult to replicate in newer structures. The desire to rehabilitate older buildings is widespread, affecting large, historic structures in urban centers as well as small inns in picturesque country settings.

All lodging facilities benefit from suitable fireproofing, soundproofing, and security systems. Beyond these basic considerations, the physical configuration of a hotel or motel is determined by the type of patrons it serves. A motor hotel, or motel, must be oriented to the needs of drivers who wish to spend a minimum amount of time on the premises; a

---

2. For a thorough discussion of hotels, see Stephen Rushmore, MAI, *Hotels and Motels: A Guide to Market Analysis, Investment Analysis, and Valuations* (Chicago: Appraisal Institute, 1992) and *The Computerized Income Approach to Hotel-Motel Market Studies and Valuations* (Chicago: Appraisal Institute, 1990).

resort hotel, on the other hand, must provide a variety of entertainment facilities for its guests. Although automobile parking is still needed at resorts, it is usually out of sight.

Functional inutility in hotel structures, like other types of buildings, can be categorized in terms of superadequacies, deficiencies, poor layout, inappropriate structural quality or finishes, and inefficient equipment.

The amount of hotel space devoted to guest rooms varies. A hotel that is a major meeting and entertainment center has a much lower proportion of guest rooms to public areas than an apartment hotel. Many apartment hotels are successful transient operations which consist entirely of suites with small equipped kitchens, living rooms, and separate bedrooms. These hotels usually have small lobbies and restaurants.

The layout of guest rooms also varies with the clientele. Large rooms, separate dressing areas, and large closets are needed when most guests stay for several nights. Room size is usually geared to the necessary amount of furniture; the room should be large enough to provide ample space around and between the pieces of furniture. Business travelers need desks, while vacationers usually do not. The trend toward larger beds requires larger rooms, but rooms that are too large do not use space efficiently.

Support space for guest rooms includes hotel office and operations areas, restaurants, lounges, public meeting rooms, and often athletic facilities.

Industrial Properties

Like all properties, an industrial property must have a site, buildings, and equipment that function as an operating unit. Inutility is measured against the standard of optimal efficiency for similar properties in the market.

Some industrial properties are designed and equipped to meet the needs of a specific occupant and have limited appeal to others. Buildings used for industries that involve bulky or volatile materials and products have specialized equipment and building designs, so they have few potential users. Buildings used for research and development or for light manufacturing and processing are less limited in their appeal.

All industrial buildings are measured in terms of gross building area (GBA). To make comparisons and measure buildings in terms of market standards, the GBA can be divided into finished and unfinished space. The most flexible design for industrial buildings, and the one with the greatest appeal on the open market, is a one-story, square or nearly square structure that complies with all local building codes.

Industrial buildings can be constructed of many types of material, but concrete and steel are used most often. The building method commonly applied is tilt-up construction, which incorporates concrete walls that are cast horizontally and put in place vertically. The walls are often designed to be load-bearing. Flat roofs supported by steel bar joists are also common. Prefabricated steel buildings are less expensive to build, and their appearance is now considered more acceptable than it was in the past. Plastic skylights can be installed for natural light instead of expensive monitor and sawtooth roofs.

Industrial properties must have land-to-building ratios that allow plenty of space for parking, truck maneuvering, yard storage, and expansion. Other locational considerations include reasonable real estate taxes, an available supply of labor, adequate utility service, beneficial zoning, proximity to supply sources and customers, and ease of transportation, which is vital to the receipt of raw materials and the distribution of finished products.

The popularity of business parks combining industrial and commercial uses in recent years has been detrimental to traditional industrial parks, which are characterized by groups of industrial buildings with similar uses. In addition to industrial uses, business parks often have research and development buildings and office and commercial space occupied by banking facilities, restaurants and taverns, and day-care centers. With good landscaping, ample setbacks, building and lot size minimums, and professional architecture, engineering, and management, business parks provide an environment that is acceptable to occupants and to government land-planning groups.

The combination of old and new industrial space may create substantial functional obsolescence if the new construction contributes less than its cost to the value of the whole. The layout of industrial space should allow operations to be carried out with maximum efficiency. Typically, receiving functions are performed on one side of the building, shipping functions on the other, and processing or storage functions in the middle. Some industrial buildings include special features such as sprinkler systems, scales, loading dock levelers, cranes, and craneways, refrigeration areas, conveyor systems, process piping (for compressed air, water, and gas), power wiring, and employee lockers and lunchrooms.

Storage Buildings

Storage structures range from simple cubicles, known as *miniwarehouses*, to huge regional warehouses with one million square feet of area. Functional utility and location have a major impact on the market value of storage buildings; obsolescence usually occurs before the structures deteriorate physically. The functions of warehouses are

- To store materials in a protected environment
- To organize materials so that they can be easily inventoried and removed
- To provide facilities for efficient delivery
- To provide facilities for efficient access and shipping

For optimal functional utility, warehouses should have adequate access, open areas, ceiling height, floor load capacity (often 300 pounds or more for heavy-duty industrial storage buildings), humidity and temperature controls, shipping and receiving facilities, fire protection, and protection from the elements.

The primary consideration in warehouse location is good access. Trucking is the most common means of transporting goods, but certain warehouse operations also need access to rail, water, and air transportation. Operations that depend on trucks to transport goods should be near an arterial highway. The highway's access street or frontage road and the truck maneuvering area at the warehouse loading dock must allow for efficient use of loading facilities at all times. If a warehouse site slopes downward from a frontage road, the loading dock can be constructed at truck-bed level. For rail access, one portion of the site must be long and level.

Forklifts, conveyor belts, and automatically guided vehicle conveyor systems are used to move materials inside warehouses. Truck docks must be wide enough to accommodate truck widths and the interior servomechanism used to move goods and materials. If electric trucks are used, a battery-charging area should be included. Most storage operations are palletized—i.e., pallets, or portable platforms, are used for moving and storing materials. Therefore, ceiling heights in warehouses should accommodate the stacking of an ideal number of pallets. Because wide spans provide maximum flexibility, a square structure generally is the most cost-effective.

Office space in warehouses may constitute as little as 1% of the total area, but generally approximately 5% of the total gross building area is used for offices. In distribution facilities, office space may comprise up to 35% of the total gross building area. Office space in warehouses should be adequately heated, cooled, and lighted, but its finish is generally utilitarian.

Sprinkler systems are needed in warehouses where flammable goods are stored. The nature of the stored material determines whether the system should be wet or dry, using water or chemicals.

Miniwarehouses are usually one-story rectangular structures located near those who will use them. These properties should be visible, accessible, and include sufficient land for parking and maneuvering. The individual units within miniwarehouses vary; they usually include small storage units, which have passage doors, and larger units, which have roll-up truck doors.

Buildings on Agricultural Properties

In most of the United States, there is a trend toward fewer, larger farms. Therefore, the contribution of farm buildings to the total value of farm real estate has been steadily decreasing. Statistics from the U.S. Department of Agriculture indicate that farm buildings represent less than 20% of the total value of farm property. The number of farm buildings per acre of farmland has also decreased.

Farms are operated by families and by large, specialized business concerns. The equipment and management needed to run agricultural operations have become increasingly specialized.

Farming operations are conducted in fewer types of farm buildings because each operation is responsible for fewer functions. Farm buildings must accommodate the type of machinery and equipment currently used in farming. More large machine sheds are needed to house tractors, combines, discs, plows, harrows, cultivators, pickers, trucks, and other equipment. Pipeline milking machines and overhead feed bins dictate the requirements for milking parlors and loafing sheds where livestock are sheltered. Changes in the care and feeding of poultry have substantially modified the design of poultry farm buildings. Facilities for the storage of grain and produce such as silos, corn cribs, storage barns, and refrigerated units for fruit and vegetables are also important to a farm operation.

The history of the United States is reflected in certain types of buildings. Barns have successfully combined functional utility with picturesque design and become emblems of American culture. Form, function, and materials come together in a unique way to make barns the most successful type of vernacular buildings. Some barns have traditionally been multifunctional, providing animal shelter, grain storage, and a threshing floor; other structures, such as tobacco barns and modern farm buildings, serve a single, specialized function.

The traditional American barn is 60 feet long and 30 feet wide, with two gable ends, a loft, and double doors. Most barns are built of wood, but some are made of stone, logs, or brick. Old barns are suitable for modern, general-purpose farming if they are sufficiently adaptable. The use of baled, rather than loose, hay and the increased use of ensilage have lessened the need for barn storage. Silos, however, have become more prevalent and larger. Virtually all newer barns have pre-engineered pole construction, which is less expensive and can accommodate more farming activities than older, multistory barns. Two major developments in agriculture have made many older barns outmoded. First, milking parlors with central milking stations have replaced dairy barns with traditional stanchions. Second, hay is no longer baled and stored in barns, but rolled and stored in fields under inexpensive tarp coverings.

Animal shelters should be dry and clean, provide protection from the wind and sun, and be adaptable to equipment storage. To be useful each farm building must contribute to the operating efficiency of the entire farm. Each building's usefulness relates to the type and size of the farm. Functional inutility can result from having too many farm buildings when fewer would be more efficient.

Special-Purpose Buildings

The architecture of some buildings tends to limit them to a single use. Although most buildings can be converted to other uses, the conversion of special-purpose buildings generally involves extra expense and design expertise. Special-purpose structures include churches, synagogues, theaters, sports arenas, and other types of auditoriums.

The functional utility of a special-purpose building depends on whether there is continued demand for the use for which the building was designed. When there is demand, functional utility depends on whether the building conforms to competitive standards. For example, there is a continued demand for movie theaters, but their design has changed due to high maintenance and utility costs. Ornate movie theaters have been replaced with simple, unembellished structures. Older movie theaters are increasingly converted into concert halls and legitimate theaters.

The design and materials used in synagogues and churches are simpler today to keep maintenance and utility costs down. The functional utility of these structures, like sports and concert arenas, is primarily related to seating capacity. The structure's support facilities, general attractiveness, and appeal must also be considered.

The adaptive-use movement has generated public interest in the conversion of special-purpose buildings. Buildings usually outlive their function, and energy shortages, the decline of modernism, and disproportionate construction costs have contributed to the preservation movement. Railroad stations, schools, firehouses, and grist mills are popular structures for conversion. The functional utility of these buildings relates to how much they deviate from building codes and how the cost of rehabilitation compares with the potential economic return. A typical item of functional inutility in adaptive-use projects is an insufficient number of staircases to meet building codes. By contrast, a high ceiling in a specialty property does not indicate functional inutility if it is considered a desirable architectural feature that contributes to net income.

Mixed-Use Buildings

Many buildings successfully combine two or more uses. The construction of mixed-use buildings, which began in the late 1950s and 1960s, reflects postwar developments such as suburban shopping centers and the planned business and residential communities of urban America. One prevalent example is the mixed-use development (MUD), which comprises at least three revenue-producing uses such as retail, office, and residential or hotel/motel facilities.

Mixed-use developments are characterized by the physical and functional integration of their components. They are megastructures built around centrally located shopping galleries or hotel courtyards. Walkways, plazas, escalators, and elevators provide an interconnecting pedestrian thoroughfare with easy access to parking facilities located underground, at street level, or aboveground. Because mixed-use developments bring together diverse participants, they require extensive, extraordinarily coherent planning.[3]

In mixed-use buildings each type of use reflects a number of design criteria, which must be analyzed separately. The structure must also be considered as a whole to determine how successfully it combines uses. The uses combined should be compatible, but minor incompatibilities can be alleviated with separate entrances, elevators, and equipment. In a mixed-use building without separate entrances and elevators, the residential units on upper floors and the office units below would both suffer. Only in a rather large building can the extra expense of separate features be justified. A hotel located in an office building should have its own entrance and elevators. Security and privacy should characterize a building's residential area, while a professional, prestigious image is desirable for the office portion of the structure.

Mixed-use buildings are an architectural challenge. Traditional residential and commercial buildings look different and are easily distinguished from one another. These differences have been diminished, however, by the eclecticism of postmodern architecture.

Key Concepts

- In architecture, style and functional utility are necessarily interrelated because form and function work with design and construction to create a successful product.
- American architecture is characterized by both formal and vernacular styles.
- Market preferences are influenced both by the desire to maintain tradition and by an expectancy of innovation.
- Architectural style depends on the availability of building materials, the state of technology, and the potential of the specific site.

---

3. For a comprehensive analysis of mixed-use developments, see Robert E. Witherspoon, Jon P. Abbett, and Robert M. Gladstone, *Mixed-Use Developments: New Ways of Land Use* (Washington, D.C.: Urban Land Institute, 1976).

- Building design and construction have been influenced by changes in framing, HVAC systems, and telecommunications technology.
- Functional utility depends on several interactive factors, i.e., design or layout, ease and cost of maintenance, amenity or comfort level, safety and security, market standards for the property, the compatibility of the building and its use and environment, and property marketability.
- Functional inutility is judged in relation to the market standard.
- Standards for functional utility vary according to property type, i.e., residential (single-family, multifamily), commercial (retail and hotel), industrial (manufacturing, research and development, warehouse), farm, special-purpose, and mixed-use.

Terms

adequacy	hotel design
agricultural building design	industrial building design
Americans with Disabilities Act	live load/load-bearing capacity
architectural style	market standard
architecture	mixed-use development (MUD)
bay depth	pre-engineered construction
ceiling height	parking ratio
column spacing	public amenities
commercial building design	regional building styles
compatibility	reinforced concrete
conversion	siting
elevator capacity	special-purpose design
energy conservation	storage building design
energy efficiency	styrofoam forming
floor load	temperature control system
formal architecture	truss system
functional inutility	vernacular architecture
functional utility	work letter
gross building area (*GBA*)	
heating, ventilation,	
air conditioning (HVAC)	
systems	

CHAPTER THIRTEEN

Highest and Best Use Analysis

T he economic principles of supply and demand, substitution, balance, and conformity are basic tools for analyzing market behavior and the value of property. The
interdependent factors that influence value—i.e., utility, scarcity, desire, and
effective purchasing power—are economic in origin. Modern value and appraisal theory
has evolved from neoclassical economic thought.

The relationship between economic behavior and appraisal is evident in real estate
markets. In these markets, where buyers and sellers of property rights interact, market
value has great significance to debt and equity capital investors and to professional
appraisers. In all types of property transactions, market value estimates based on careful
analyses of economic behavior are needed to shape financial decisions that affect
individuals, neighborhoods, businesses, and governments.

An understanding of market behavior is essential to the concept of highest and best
use. Market forces create market value, so the interaction between market forces and
highest and best use is of crucial importance. When the purpose of an appraisal is to
estimate market value, highest and best use analysis identifies the most profitable,
competitive use to which the property can be put. Therefore, highest and best use is a
market-driven concept.

Analyzing the highest and best use of a property may require detailed study.
Elaborate studies of highest and best use are typically performed for consulting assignments. In many appraisals, however, the nature of the assignment sets limits on the
extent of highest and best use analysis to be undertaken, and the characteristics of the
property limit the number of alternative uses to be considered.

In the valuation process, highest and best use analysis has traditionally been placed
before the application of the three approaches to value. In many appraisal assignments,
however, the final tests of financial feasibility and maximum productivity can only be
completed with information obtained from the application and development of the
approaches. The conclusion of highest and best use, therefore, may be finalized after the
approaches are applied.

Definition

Highest and best use may be defined as

> the reasonably probable and legal use of vacant land or an improved prop-
> erty, which is physically possible, appropriately supported, financially fea-
> sible, and that results in the highest value.

To clarify the distinction between the highest and best use of 1) land or a site as though vacant, and 2) property as improved, consider a single-family residential property. If the property is located in an area zoned for commercial use, the maximum productivity of the land as though vacant will most likely be based on commercial use. If, however, the competitive level of demand is greater for a residential use, then the highest and best use of the property as improved will likely be for residential use.

Appraisal theory holds that as long as the value of a property as improved is greater than the value of the site as unimproved, the highest and best use is use of the property as improved. Once the value of the vacant land exceeds the value of the improved property, the highest and best use becomes use of the land as though vacant. In practice, however, a property owner who is redeveloping a site may often raze and remove an improvement even when the value of the property as improved exceeds the value of the vacant site. Many investors will not pay large sums for the underlying land simply to hold onto the property until the value of the remaining improvement has abated. The costs of demolition and any remaining improvement value are worked into the redevelopment of the site.

The highest and best use of a specific parcel of land is not determined through subjective analysis by the property owner, the developer, or the appraiser; rather, highest and best use is shaped by the competitive forces within the market where the property is located. Therefore, the analysis and interpretation of highest and best use is an economic study of market forces focused on the subject property.[1]

Market forces also shape market value, so the general data that are collected and analyzed to estimate property value are also used to formulate an opinion of the property's highest and best use as of the appraisal date. In all valuation assignments, value estimates are based on use. The highest and best use of a property to be appraised provides the foundation for a thorough investigation of the competitive positions of market participants. Consequently, highest and best use can be described as the foundation on which market value rests.

When potential buyers contemplate purchasing real estate for personal use or occupancy, their principal motivations are the perceived benefits of their enhanced enjoyment, prestige, and privacy. Purchasers of investment property are frequently motivated by the promise of net income or capital accumulation and certain tax advantages. Investors are directly concerned with *feasibility, an indication that a project has a reasonable likelihood of satisfying the explicit objectives they have set for financial success*. These objectives may include assured occupancy, low management costs, and potential value enhancement.

Like highest and best use and market value, highest and best use and feasibility are interrelated. However, feasibility analyses may involve data and considerations that are not directly related to highest and best use determinations. Such analyses may be more detailed than highest and best use analyses, have a different focus, and/or require additional research. Generally, the feasibility of developing real estate under a variety of

---

1. The benefit a real estate development produces for a community or the amenity contribution provided by a planned project (i.e., the public space in a park-like area) is not considered in the appraiser's analysis of highest and best use. Highest and best use is driven by economic considerations and market forces, not by public interest. See Chapter 2 for a discussion of "public interest value."

alternative uses is studied. (See Figure 13.1.) The use that maximizes value represents the highest and best use. Traditionally highest and best use analysis has been associated with land residual analysis, which is derived from classical economics. In a classic land residual analysis, value is attributed to the income that remains after improvement costs are compensated. Highest and best use of the land as though vacant indicates only how the land should be used if it were vacant. Although it is primarily a tool for land valuation, it is also used by appraisers to measure a building's value contribution on the assumption that property value minus land value under highest and best use equals improvement value.

Figure 13.1	**Comparison of Real Estate Analyses**

Market Analysis	**Feasibility Analysis**	**Highest and Best Use Analysis**
To identify demand for alternative uses	To determine respective values based on criterion variables (e.g., residual land value, rate of return, capitalized value of overall property)	To determine the use resulting in the maximum value
Supply and demand analysis to forecast absorption rate and probable rents for:	Calculation of *NOI*/cash flows and selection of appropriate cap rate/ discount rate to determine property value based on criterion variables for:	Specification in terms of use, timing, and market participants
use no. 1, use no. 2, use no. 3, use no. 4	use no. 1, use no. 2, use no. 3, use no. 4	(i.e., user of the property, equity investor, debt investor)

While buildings can be changed, the essential characteristics of sites cannot. The income to any particular site depends on the use decision. When an individual site can be substituted for another site in a particular market, the difference in value between the two sites is attributable to the superior features of one of the parcels of land. From this vantage point, therefore, land value is the driving force and property values in a specific market are a function of the income to the land.

With respect to the highest and best use of the land as though vacant, the first question to be asked is: Should the site be developed or left vacant? If the answer to this question is that the site should be developed, a second question is: What kind of improvement should be built? The third question to be asked relates to the highest and best use of the property as improved.

The highest and best use of property as improved is a distinct concept developed by valuation theorists and practitioners to answer an important question that the original concept does not address. This question is: Should the existing improvements on the property be maintained in their current state, or should they be altered in some manner to make them more valuable?

In answering these two sets of questions, an appraiser considers options ranging from the demolition and removal of the existing improvements, to the curing of items of deferred maintenance, to the rehabilitation, renovation, or modernization of the improved property.

Highest and Best Use of Land as Though Vacant

Analysis of the highest and best use of land or a site as though vacant assumes that a parcel of land is vacant or can be made vacant by demolishing any improvements. With this assumption, uses that create value can be identified and the appraiser can begin to select comparable properties and estimate land value. Land as though vacant is a fundamental concept of valuation theory and a basic component of the cost approach. Because many appraisals include an allocation of property value between land and building(s), a highest and best use analysis of the land as though vacant is performed. When a site is improved with a building that contributes to property value, the determination of the site's highest and best use as vacant often becomes a theoretical exercise.

The questions to be answered in this analysis are: 1) If the land is, or were, vacant, what use should be made of it? and 2) What type of building or other improvement, if any, should be constructed on the land and when?

When a reasonable forecast of a property's highest and best use indicates a change in the near future, the present highest and best use is considered an interim use. For example, the highest and best use of a farm in the path of urban growth would be for interim use as a farm, with a potential future highest and best use as a residential subdivision. If the farm is ready for development at the time of the appraisal, there is no interim use. If the farm has no subdivision potential, its highest and best use is as a farm with no interim use.

In some cases an appraiser may conclude that the highest and best use of a parcel of land is to be held for speculation—i.e., to remain vacant until development is justified by market demand. This occurs frequently when real estate markets are oversupplied. For many parcels of land, however, achieving the highest and best use requires some change or improvement. The highest and best use of land as though vacant may call for its subdivision into smaller parcels of land or its assemblage with other land.

If an improvement is needed to realize the highest and best use of the land, the appraiser must determine the type and characteristics of the *ideal improvement* to be constructed. The ideal improvement is one that would take maximum advantage of the site's potential, conform to current market standards, and contain the most suitably priced components. For example, should the parcel of land be improved with an office building, a retail building, or a hotel? If an office building would be the highest and best use, how many stories should it have? How many offices should it contain? What size should the offices be? Which features should be included? What rental should be charged and what level of operating expenses would be incurred? How much would such a building cost? In short, the conclusion of highest and best use for a parcel of land should be as specific as the marketplace suggests. General categories such as "an office building," "a commercial building," or "a single-family residence" may be adequate in some situations, but in others the particular use demanded by market participants must be specified.

Even when a site is not vacant, appraisal theory enjoins the practitioner to analyze the site as though it were. Such analysis seeks to determine how desirable the current use is and whether it should be continued or superseded. The appraiser considers the site as if it were vacant to determine whether a building with the same use, size, quality, and function as the existing building should be constructed on it. If this new improvement were to be the highest and best use of the land as though vacant, it presumably would have no physical deterioration or functional obsolescence. Thus, any difference in value between the existing improvement and the new improvement would be attributable to these forms of depreciation. The appraiser also must consider external obsolescence, which would affect the existing improvement and the new improvement equally.

The present use of a site may not be its highest and best use. The land may be suitable for a much higher, or more intense, use. For instance, the highest and best use of a parcel of land as though vacant may be for a 10-story office building, while the office building that currently occupies the site has only three stories.

Highest and Best Use of Property as Improved

Highest and best use of a property as improved pertains to the use that should be made of an improved property in light of its improvements. The existing improvement is compared with the ideal improvement. For example, an appraiser may ask, Should a 30-year-old hotel building be maintained as it is or should it be renovated, expanded, or partly demolished? Would these changes contribute more to the value of the property than they would cost? Alternatively, should the hotel building be replaced with a different type or intensity of use?

The use that maximizes an investment property's value, consistent with the rate of return and associated risk, is its highest and best use as improved. If the potential uses considered require no capital expenditures for remodeling, their estimated returns can be compared directly. If capital expenditures would be required to convert the structure from its existing use to other potential uses, rates of return must be calculated for these property uses, considering the total investment in the property and all capital expenditures. These rates of return can then be compared with rates of return for uses that do not require capital expenditures.

In analyzing the highest and best use of owner-occupied properties, appraisers must consider any rehabilitation or modernization that is consistent with market preferences. For example, the highest and best use of a luxury residence should reflect all rehabilitation that would be required for maximum enjoyment of the property. The program of rehabilitation should ensure the maximum profit upon future resale of the property. For a tenanted property, rehabilitation should focus on maximizing profit (rental income) to the owner-landlord.

Purpose of Highest and Best Use Analysis

An appraiser should distinguish between highest and best use as though vacant and highest and best use as improved in the appraisal analysis. The appraisal report should clearly identify, explain, and justify the purpose and conclusion for each type of use.

Highest and Best Use of Land as though Vacant

The value of land is generally estimated as though vacant.[2] When land is already vacant, the reasoning is obvious; an appraiser values the land as it exists. When land is not vacant, however, its value depends on how it can be utilized. Therefore, the highest and best use of land as though vacant must be considered in relation to its existing use and all potential uses.

Land value can be based on potential, rather than actual, use. (This is the basis for the cost approach.) For example, consider a valuable commercial site in an excellent location that is currently improved with a service station that is free of any negative environmental features.[3] A purchaser who wants to build a high-rise office building on the site may pay a price for the property that includes no value, or even negative value, for the existing improvements. The potential use, not the existing use, usually governs the price that will be paid.

Any building can be demolished; the fact that most buildings are not does not negate the possibility. The possibility of removing existing improvements is the premise for the concept of highest and best use of land as though vacant. Land values are not penalized so long as the existing buildings have economic value. If the buildings no longer have value, demolition is appropriate. As mentioned earlier, buildings can be changed, but the basic physical characteristics of sites cannot.

Historic district zoning controls have made demolition permits difficult, if not impossible, to obtain in some areas. Furthermore, special tax incentives for older buildings can substantially enhance their value and alter the highest and best use of the property in many cases.

Several appraisal techniques require a separate estimate of land value. The highest and best use of land must be identified to estimate land value under its optimal use. The highest and best use of any comparable properties analyzed should be the same or similar to that of the subject property since land use influences value. In short, there are three reasons to identify the highest and best use of land as though vacant in an appraisal: to estimate a separate land value, to identify comparable sales of vacant land, and to identify external obsolescence.

---

2. Standards Rule 1-3(a) directs an appraiser to "consider the effect on use and value of the following factors: existing land use regulations, reasonably probable modifications of such land use regulations, economic demand, the physical adaptability of the real estate, neighborhood trends, and the highest and best use of the real estate." Standards Rule 1-3(b) recognizes "that land is appraised as though vacant and available for development to its highest and best use and that the appraisal of improvements is based on their actual contribution to the site." The comment to this rule explains, "This guideline may be modified to reflect the fact that, in various legal and practical situations, a site may have a contributory value that differs from the value as if vacant."

3. When the highest and best use of the land as though vacant is different from that of the property as currently improved, demolition may be considered as one alternative. At this time the costs of demolition are addressed as well as the costs of curing any environmental problems—e.g., the removal of underground storage tanks, the abatement of asbestos, the replacement of transformers containing PCBs.

Highest and Best Use of Property as Improved

The highest and best use of property as improved is analyzed for two reasons. The first is to identify the property use that can be expected to produce the highest overall return for each dollar of capital invested. This information is important to informed buyers who are economically motivated. If, for example, a property is currently being used as rental apartments, a sophisticated buyer will want to know if this use will continue to provide maximum benefits. If not, would the rate of return be increased by converting the property to an apartment hotel? The value of the property will differ under these two use assumptions, and the use that provides the highest present value is the highest and best use.

The second reason to estimate the highest and best use of property as improved is to help identify comparable properties. Both the highest and best use of land as though vacant and property as improved should be the same or similar for each comparable property as for the subject property. For example, it may be inappropriate to use a comparable property that has a highest and best use as an office building in appraising a subject property that has a highest and best use as a hotel.

Criteria in Highest and Best Use Analysis

The highest and best use of both land as though vacant and property as improved must meet four criteria. The highest and best use must be legally permissible, physically possible, financially feasible, and maximally productive. These criteria are often considered sequentially.[4] The tests of legal permissibility and physical possibility *must* be applied before the remaining tests of financial feasibility and maximal productivity. A use may be financially feasible, but this is irrelevant if it is legally prohibited or physically impossible. Only when there is a reasonable possibility that one of the prior, unacceptable conditions can be changed is it appropriate to proceed with the analysis. If, for example, current zoning does not permit a potential highest and best use, but there is a reasonable probability that the zoning could be changed, the proposed use could be considered on that basis. Physical limitations that prevent a site from achieving its optimal use can often be overcome by applying additional capital.

Legally Permissible

In all cases the appraiser must determine which uses are legally permissible. Private restrictions, zoning, building codes, historic district controls, and environmental regulations must be investigated because they may preclude many potential uses. Nonconforming uses are discussed later in this chapter.

A long-term lease can also affect a property's highest and best use because, over the remaining term of the lease, property use may be limited by lease provisions. If a property is subject to a land lease that has 12 more years to run, for example, it may not be economically possible to construct a new building with a 40-year remaining economic

---

4. Although the criteria are considered sequentially, it does not matter whether legal permissibility or physical possibility is addressed first, provided both are considered prior to the test of financial feasibility. Many appraisers view the analysis of highest and best use as a process of elimination. The test of legal permissibility is often applied first because it eliminates most alternative uses and does not require a costly engineering study. It should be noted that the four criteria are interactive and may be considered in concert. Matrix analysis can be used to plot their interaction.

life.[5] In such a case the appraisal report should state that the highest and best use determination is influenced by the lease's impact on future utility. A distinction, however, must be made between the highest and best use of property and a legal requirement to use property for a particular purpose beyond its economic life.

Private restrictions and deed restrictions relate to the covenants under which some properties are acquired. These restrictions may prohibit certain uses or specify building setbacks, heights, and types of materials. If deed restrictions conflict with zoning laws or building codes, the more restrictive guidelines usually prevail.

If there are no private restrictions, the property uses allowed by the zoning laws prevail, but the possibility of a change in zoning should also be considered. If a particular use of the site or property is not allowed under current zoning, but there is a reasonable probability that a change in zoning could be obtained, this eventuality should be considered in determining highest and best use. Uses that are not compatible with existing uses and uses that have been previously denied can be eliminated. The appraiser may prepare a land development forecast for the area. If the social and economic characteristics of neighborhoods nearby have been changing, the likelihood of a change in zoning may be especially high. The appraiser must fully disclose all pertinent factors relating to a possible zoning change, including the time and expense involved and the risk that the change will not be granted. The probability of a zoning change is never 100% certain.

Building codes can prevent land from being developed to its highest and best use by imposing burdensome restrictions that increase the cost of construction. This is particularly common in metropolitan areas that include municipalities or jurisdictions with restrictive building codes. Residential development in metropolitan areas has been greatly influenced by various building code requirements, especially requirements for off-site improvements. Less restrictive codes typically result in lower development costs, which attract developers; more restrictive codes tend to discourage development. In some areas building codes are used to slow new construction and limit growth.

Concern over the effects of land use has resulted in increased environmental regulation. Appraisers must be familiar with environmental regulations pertaining to clear air, clean water, and wetlands and should be sensitive to the public's reaction to proposed development projects. Resistance from local residents and the general public has stopped many real estate developments.

Physically Possible

The size, shape, area, terrain, and accessibility of a parcel of land and the risk of natural disasters such as floods or earthquakes affect the uses for which it can be developed. The utility of a parcel may also depend on its frontage and depth. Irregularly shaped parcels can cost more to develop and, after development, may have less utility than regularly shaped parcels of the same size. Ease of access enhances the utility of a site.

Certain parcels can achieve their highest and best use only as part of an assemblage. In such a case, the appraiser must either determine the feasibility and probability of assembly or make the highest and best use determination and other appraisal deci-

---

5. If a lease buyout were possible, the present value of the buyout plus the cost of demolition or conversion would have to be considered.

sions conditioned on such an assembly. For example, a large petrochemical plant may be constructed on a site that has been created by assembling smaller tracts. The individual tracts may not have had the potential for industrial use separately and, therefore, may have had much lower unit values.

The capacity and availability of public utilities are important considerations. If a sewer main located in front of a property cannot be tapped because of a lack of capacity at the sewerage disposal plant, the property's use is limited.

When the topography or subsoil conditions of a site make development difficult or costly, its utility is adversely affected. All sites available for a particular use compete with one another. If the cost of grading or constructing a foundation on the subject site is higher than is typical in the area, the site may be economically unusable for the highest and best use that would otherwise be indicated.

The highest and best use of a property as improved also depends on physical considerations such as size, design, and condition. The condition of the property and its ability to continue in its current use may be relevant. If the property should be converted to another use, the cost of conversion must be analyzed in light of the returns to be generated by the new use. Obviously, the costs of conversion depend on the property's existing physical condition and location.

Financially Feasible

In determining which uses are legally permissible and physically possible, an appraiser eliminates some uses from consideration. Then the uses that meet the first two criteria are analyzed further. If the uses are income-producing, the analysis will study which are likely to produce an income, or return, equal to or greater than the amount needed to satisfy operating expenses, financial obligations, and capital amortization. All uses that are expected to produce a positive return are regarded as financially feasible. If the uses are not income-producing, the analysis will determine which are likely to create a value or result in a profit equal to or greater than the amount needed to develop and market the property under those uses. Analyses of supply and demand and of location are needed to identify those uses that are financially feasible and, ultimately, the use that is maximally productive.

To determine the financial feasibility of potential income-producing uses, the appraiser estimates the future gross income that can be expected from each. Vacancy and collection losses and operating expenses are then subtracted from each gross income to obtain the likely net operating income (*NOI*) from each use. A rate of return on the invested capital can then be calculated for each use. If the net revenue capable of being generated from a use is sufficient to satisfy the required rate of return on the investment and provide the requisite return on the land, the use is financially feasible.

To determine the financial feasibility of a non-income-producing use, the appraiser compares the value benefits that accrue or the profit that results from the use against the expenses involved. If the value benefits or the expected profits exceed the costs, the use is considered feasible. If the value benefits or expected profits fall below the costs or exceed costs by only a marginal amount, the use may not be financially feasible.

Maximally Productive

Of the financially feasible uses, the use that produces the highest residual land value consistent with the rate of return warranted by the market for that use is the highest and best use. To determine the highest and best use of land as though vacant, appropriate rates of return that reflect the associated risk are often used to capitalize income streams from different uses into their respective values. This procedure is suitable if all competing uses have similar risk characteristics. The use that produces the highest residual land value is the highest and best use.

The residual land value can be found by estimating the value of the proposed use (land and improvements) and subtracting the cost of the labor, capital, and entrepreneurship expended to create the improvements. Alternatively, the land value can be estimated by capitalizing the residual income to the land.

The land income that is capitalized into value is the residual income remaining after operating expenses and the return attributable to the improvements have been deducted from the income to the total property. Using a land residual technique, the value of the improvements is multiplied by a building capitalization rate determined in the market. (Building capitalization rates are discussed in Chapter 20.) The income attributable to the improvements is then subtracted from the net operating income for the total property, and the remaining income is allocated to the land. This procedure is illustrated in the next section.

The potential highest and best uses of land are usually long-term land uses, which are expected to remain on the site for the normal life of the improvements. Normal life expectancy depends on building type, quality of construction, and other factors. The stream of benefits, or income, produced by the buildings reflects a carefully considered, and usually very specific, land use program.

Testing Highest and Best Use

To test the highest and best use of land as though vacant or a property as improved, an appraiser analyzes all feasible alternatives. The market usually limits the number of property uses to a few logical choices. Each alternative use must first meet the tests of physical possibility and legal permissibility. The uses that meet the first two tests are then analyzed to ascertain how many financially feasible alternatives must be considered.

For example, market analysis may indicate the need for a large office building in a community. If the subject site is surrounded by modern, single-family residential developments, however, a large, multistory office building would probably not be logical, even if it were legally permitted. Similarly, a housing development for the elderly might be a permissible use for a site, but if most residents of the area are under 40 years old, this use may be illogical and would probably not meet the criterion of financial feasibility.

Appraisers must exercise caution in performing market analysis to support estimates of highest and best use. Although a given site may be particularly well-suited for a specific use, there may be a number of other sites that are equally or more appropriate. Therefore, the appraiser must test the highest and best use conclusion to ensure that existing and potential competition from other sites has been fully recognized.

An appraiser must also consider the competition among various uses for a specific site. For example, competition for available sites along a commercial strip development may be intense. Developers of community retail uses, garden office uses, and fast food franchises may bid against one another for these sites. The highest and best use and the value of the sites will reflect this competition. In turn, the competing commercial uses will price their goods and services to accommodate the competitive prices dictated by the market. Indeed, if only one use was appropriate for a particular site, the value of the site would probably suffer some diminution in value.

The same observation may be applied to CBDs. The market may define the highest and best use of land in the CBD simply as high-rise development, which often includes a mix of uses such as office, retail, hotel, and residential condominium. At times, the highest and best use conclusion for a CBD site does not indicate a specific highest and best use, but rather a class of uses that is supported by neighborhood trends and reflects a consistent density of development. Although the appraiser considers specific uses in determining highest and best use, the appraiser's analysis of these uses is often general, based on commonly accepted operating expense ratios and other data inputs. Often the appraiser stops short of detailed feasibility analysis, which may involve extensive consultation with planners, architects, engineers, and cost estimators.

The examples that follow are presented to illustrate the determination of the highest and best use of property as though vacant and as improved.

Highest and Best Use of Land as though Vacant

Example 1. Single-Family Residence

Consider a site in an area zoned for detached, single-family residences, some of which have already been built. The first highest and best use question is whether the site should be developed or left vacant. Since the residual value of the site as though residentially improved is positive, the highest and best use of the site as vacant is to develop it.

The second highest and best use question is what type of residence to construct on the site. The builder has narrowed down the logical development alternatives to two types of houses, both of which are compatible with other houses in the neighborhood. Use A calls for the construction of a large house with an estimated market value of $250,000, including the lot value. Use B calls for the construction of a more modest house which would be worth approximately $200,000 with the lot. Similar sites in the area have been selling to developers for approximately $32,000 to $33,000. The estimated costs of constructing the two houses and their respective value estimates can be used to identify the highest and best use of the appraised land. The calculations are shown below.

	Use A	Use B
Market value	$250,000	$200,000
Cost to construct new	- 187,000	- 150,000
Developer's fee	- 30,000	- 24,000
Land value	$ 33,000	$ 26,000

The answer to the second highest and best use question as to which residential improvement should be built is Use A, the larger house. It is the use that results in the higher residual land value. Similar sites can be expected to sell for about $32,000 to $33,000. Thus, if $33,000 was paid for the lot and the smaller house was built, the builder would incur a financial loss.

Example 2. Income-Producing Use

To select a single highest and best use among various income-producing uses, the available uses are generally analyzed in terms of their potential rates of return and perceived income stability. For example, consider a 150-ft.-by-150-ft. site on a commercial strip that has been valued at $160,000 using the sales comparison approach. Development trends in the area suggest that the site be developed as either a retail convenience store or a commercial office building. Under either commercial use the residual value of the site is positive, so the highest and best use of the site as vacant is to develop it. To determine which commercial use should be developed, the appraiser estimates the development costs, potential net operating incomes, and overall rates of return under the two possible uses. The data are shown below.

	Retail Use	Office Use
Potential *NOI*	$ 55,000	$ 60,000
Overall capitalization rate	11%	10%
Capitalized *NOI*	500,000	600,000
Development costs	- 300,000	- 450,000
Residual land value	$200,000	$150,000

Thus, the retail use should be developed because it requires a smaller investment and produces a greater residual land value.

Example 3. Income-Producing Use: Alternative Approach

In the previous example, land value was calculated by deducting development costs from the estimated property value. Land value was the residual amount. Another approach is to assume that the income available to the land is the residual. Consider a 100-ft.-by-200-ft. site that is zoned for apartment, office, or retail use. If the logical, alternative uses are an apartment building, an office building, and a retail building, the appraiser must assemble data on the construction costs, net operating income, and market rate of return that can be anticipated for each alternative use. Cost and income figures are shown below. The return on the improvements is expected to be 12% of their cost and the market capitalization rate for the land is 10%. (Market-derived land and building capitalization rates are discussed in depth in Chapters 20 and 22.) Under these uses, the improvement accounts for between 84% and 89% of *NOI*.

	Apartment Building	Office Building	Retail Building
Cost to construct	$1,200,000	$950,000	$800,000
NOI	162,000	135,000	110,000
Income to improvement (12%)	- 144,000	- 114,000	- 96,000
Income to land	$18,000	$21,000	$14,000
Residual land value (income to land capitalized at 10%)	$180,000	$210,000	$140,000

The site's highest and best use would be represented by the office building because this use produces the greatest residual value for the land. The land residual technique is useful in testing highest and best use alternatives, but it is rarely employed to measure land value.

As the examples indicate, highest and best use is not determined by a single item such as cost, size, total income, or rate of return. Highest and best use results when an optimal combination of factors creates a maximum residual land value.

Highest and Best Use of Property as Improved

An analysis of the highest and best use of a property as improved may indicate that little or no capital expenditure is required, or it may suggest that significant expenditures are required to convert the property to a different use or to rehabilitate or remodel the existing use.

Example 1. No Capital Expenditure

Consider a single-family residence that could be converted into a combination apartment-rooming house or could be used for single-family occupancy. The first use would require no capital expenditure. The first floor could be rented to a family, while the three upstairs bedrooms would be rented as is to college students. The downstairs would be rented for $500 per month and each of the three upstairs rooms would be rented for $100 per month. Property expenses for heat, electricity, repairs and maintenance, real estate taxes, insurance, and additional management cost would be approximately $2,000 per year. These expenses would be paid by the owner. Some vacancy or collection loss must be anticipated for both the downstairs and upstairs rentals.

As an alternative, the property could be rented as a single-family residence for $575 per month net—i.e., the renters would pay all property-related expenses, including property taxes and insurance. Some vacancy or collection loss must be anticipated for this use also.

Assuming that an overall capitalization rate of 10% would be appropriate for either use, the calculations comparing the uses are shown below.

	Combination Apartment-Rooming House Use	Single-Family Occupancy Use
Gross income	$9,600	$6,900
Vacancy or collection losses (10%)	-960	-690
Effective gross income	$8,640	$6,210
Expenses	-2,000	-0
NOI	$6,640	$6,210
Overall capitalization rate*	10%	10%
Value	$66,400	$62,100

* Overall capitalization rates are discussed in Chapter 22.

The figures suggest that the highest and best use of the property as improved would be a combination apartment-rooming house.

Example 2. Capital Expenditure Required

A warehouse property can be rented for $75,000 total net to the owners. However, the owners are considering converting some of the warehouse space into office space and increasing the rent. The conversion would cost approximately $125,000 and would probably add to the market value of the property, which is currently $600,000. An appraiser estimates that with the new office space the annual rent could be increased to $85,000, even though the amount of warehouse space would be reduced. The calculations used for the highest and best use analysis are shown below.

	Warehouse Use Only	Warehouse with Office Space
NOI	$75,000	$85,000
Overall capitalization rate	12.5%	12.5%
Capitalized NOI	$600,000	$680,000
Conversion cost	0	- 125,000
Property value	$600,000	$555,000

The warehouse without offices is the highest and best use of the property as improved.

Highest and Best Use Statements

All appraisal reports should contain statements that describe the appraiser's analyses and conclusions pertaining to the highest and best use of the land or site as though vacant or of the property as improved; both must be described in market value assignments where a separate site valuation is always included. As a general rule, the highest and best use statement should summarize the discussion that precedes it and follow the sequence of the four tests. A logically structured review of the four tests forms a foundation for the opinion of value.

When the highest and best use conclusion is the primary objective of a consulting assignment, the income and return calculations and the reasoning employed should be included. If an appraiser concludes that the highest and best use of an improved property is different from its existing use, justification for this conclusion should be included in the market value appraisal report. When the highest and best use conclusions are based on techniques applied to identify the highest and best use among two or more potential uses, the full analysis is usually included in the appraisal report.

When a separate estimate of land value is presented in an appraisal, it is appropriate for the report to discuss the highest and best use of the land as though vacant as well as the highest and best use of the property as improved.[6] If a separate estimate of land value is not presented and the appraisal is conditioned on continued use of the property as improved, the appraiser usually discusses only the highest and best use of the property as improved. In such cases the existing improvements may not represent the highest and best use of the site, but they are expected to continue in use and thus add value to the site.

Each parcel of real estate may have a highest and best use of the land or site as though vacant and a different highest and best use of the property as improved. If an appraiser comments on both the highest and best use of the land as though vacant and the property as improved, each highest and best use must be identified separately in the highest and best use section of the appraisal report. The highest and best use of the land or site is presented first, with a statement that the determination was made under the theoretical presumption that the land is vacant and available for development. Then the highest and best use of the property as improved is given with a statement that the determination was based on the future potential of the land and the existing improvements.

If the land is already improved to its highest and best use, the two statements may be combined. Nevertheless, the report should specifically state that the determination is the same for both the land as though vacant and the property as improved, or that the land is improved to its highest and best use.

An appraisal report should also identify the highest and best uses of the comparable sale properties, both as though vacant and as improved. If the improved comparable properties have different highest and best uses of the land as though vacant and of the property as improved, this must also be explained. The difference could affect value, especially in the sales comparison approach.

Special Situations in Highest and Best Use Analysis

The premises of highest and best use analysis are fundamental to all studies of the uses to which vacant land or improved properties can be put. In identifying and testing highest and best uses, however, special considerations are required to address single uses, interim uses, legally nonconforming uses, uses that are not highest and best, multiple uses, special-purpose uses, speculative uses, and excess land.

---

6. Standards Rules 1-3(b) and 1-4(a) of USPAP, which are specific guidelines rather than binding requirements, advise appraisers in developing a real property appraisal to "recognize that land is appraised as though vacant and available for development to its highest and best use and that the appraisal of improvements is based on their actual contribution to the site;" and to "value the site by an appropriate appraisal method or technique."

Single Uses

The highest and best uses of land or sites as though vacant and property as improved are generally consistent with, and similar to, surrounding uses. For example, a single-family residential use is usually not appropriate in an industrial neighborhood. However, a property's highest and best use may be unusual or even unique. For example, market demand may be adequate to support one large, multistory office building in a community, but it may not support more than one. A special-purpose property such as a museum may be unique and highly beneficial to the site, but it may not be supported by surrounding land uses or comparable properties. Land value should be based on the highest and best use of property, regardless of its most likely use as suggested by surrounding land uses and comparable properties.

Interim Uses

In many instances a property's highest and best use may change in the foreseeable future. A tract of land at the edge of a city might not be ready for immediate develop-ment, but current growth trends may suggest that the land should be developed in a few years. Similarly, there may not be enough demand for office space to justify the construc-tion of a multistory office building at the present time, but increased demand may be expected within five years. In such situations, the immediate development of the site or conversion of the improved property to its future highest and best use is usually not financially feasible.

The use to which a site or improved property is put until it is ready for its future highest and best use is called an *interim use*. Thus, interim uses are current highest and best uses that are likely to change in a relatively short time, i.e., five to seven years. Farms, parking lots, old buildings, and temporary buildings may be interim uses. Mining and quarry operations may be considered special cases of interim uses which usually continue until depletion of the resource.

The principle of *consistent use*, which holds that land cannot be valued based on one use while improvements are valued based on another, must be addressed when properties are devoted to temporary, interim uses. The value of a site under a temporary, interim use may differ substantially from the value of the same site as though vacant and available for development under its long-term highest and best use.

An interim use may or may not contribute to the value of the site or improved property. Farming vacant land does not contribute to the site's value unless the income produced exceeds a typical return for similar vacant land that is not used for agricultural purposes. (In interim use situations, favorable tax treatment may be a more important consideration than the return from the agricultural operation.) If old buildings or other uses cannot produce gross revenues that exceed reasonable operating expenses, they do not contribute to property value. If their net return is less than the amount that could be earned by the vacant land, the buildings do not have contributory value. Indeed, the value of such improved properties may be less than the value of their sites as though vacant when demolition costs are considered. The value of these sites is based entirely on their potential highest and best uses.

Many outmoded improvements clearly do not meet the tests of highest and best use, but they do create increments of value over the value of the vacant land. These improvements may appear to violate the consistent use theory but, in fact, the market simply acknowledges that, during transition to a new use, old improvements may make a property worth more than the vacant land.

Interim uses such as farming operations, parking lots, and golf courses may be contributory uses. In comparing a subject property with other properties, differences in their interim uses must be taken into account even though their future highest and best uses are identical. For example, consider two sites that are expected to be economically ready for high-rise office building construction in about five years. One property has a commercial interim use that produces $40,000 more net operating income per year than the other property, which has a parking lot as its interim use. The site with the commercial interim use might be worth $150,000 more than the other site ($40,000 for five years discounted at 10.5% with a factor of 3.743).

Parking lot as an interim use of property
(H. Armstrong Roberts, Inc.)

If the demolition costs for the two present uses are different, this must be considered and an adjustment must be made. If the present value of the future cost to demolish the commercial building is $50,000 and the parking lot will entail no demolition cost, the difference in values could be only $100,000 ($150,000 - $50,000). The appraiser must identify the interim uses of the property being appraised and all comparable properties. Differences in the prices paid may be due to different return requirements and different anticipated demolition costs. See the calculations that follow:

Site 1	Site 2
Under a 5-year commercial interim use	Under a 5-year interim use as a parking lot
$140,000 *NOI* Additional value of Site 1 based on *PV* of $40,000 for 5 years: $40,000 x 3.743 = $149,720 Rounded $150,000	$100,000 *NOI*
$50,000 = *PV* of future cost to demolish	0 = *PV* of future cost to demolish

Thus, Site 1 is worth $100,000 more under a 5-year interim commercial use than Site 2 under a 5-year interim use as a parking lot.

Legally Nonconforming Uses

A legally nonconforming use is a use that was lawfully established and maintained, but no longer conforms to the use regulations or the yard and bulk regulations of the zone in which it is located. This kind of use frequently results from new zoning laws or a change in the zoning ordinance. Zoning changes may create underimproved or overimproved properties.[7] A single-family residence located in an area that is subsequently zoned for commercial use is an underimproved property. In this case the residence will most likely be removed so that the site can be improved to its highest and best use, or the house will be considered an interim use until conversion to commercial use is financially feasible.

Nonconforming, overimproved properties result when zoning changes reduce the permitted intensity of property use. For example, an old country store may be located in a neighborhood that has been rezoned for low-density residential use. Nonconforming uses may also result from changes in the permitted density of development and changes in development standards that affect features such as landscaping, parking, setbacks, and access. Zoning ordinances vary with the jurisdiction; they usually permit a preexisting use to continue, but prohibit expansion or major alterations that support the nonconforming use. When the nonconforming use is discontinued or terminated, it usually cannot be reestablished.

When valuing land with a legally nonconforming use, an appraiser must recognize that the current use may be producing more income, and thus have more value, than the property could produce with a conforming use. It may also produce more income and have a higher value than comparable properties that conform to the zoning. Therefore, when the value of a legally nonconforming-use property is estimated by comparing it with similar, competitive properties in the sales comparison approach, the appraiser should

---

7. J. Mark Quinlivan and Vance R. Johnson, "Nonconforming-Use Properties: The Concept of Positive Economic Obsolescence," *The Appraisal Journal* (January 1981). Other sources of information on highest and best use analysis are *Readings in Highest and Best Use Analysis* (Chicago: American Institute of Real Estate Appraisers, 1981) and Lincoln W. North, *The Concept of Highest and Best Use* (Winnipeg: Appraisal Institute of Canada, 1981).

consider the higher intensity of use allowed for the subject property. The site should be considered as though vacant and available for development under a less intense use.

In most nonconforming use situations, the property value estimate reflects the nonconforming use. Land value, however, is based on the legally permissible use, assuming that the land is vacant. The difference between the property value and the land value reflects the contribution of the existing improvements and possibly a bonus for the nonconformance.[8] The appraiser should recognize the separate value of the nonconforming improvements and the bonus created by the nonconforming use.

Legally nonconforming uses that correspond to the highest and best use of the property as improved are often easy to recognize. Sometimes, however, it is not clear whether an existing nonconforming use is the site's highest and best use. The question can only be answered by carefully analyzing the income produced by the nonconforming use and the incomes that would be produced by alternative uses if the property were brought into conformity with existing regulations. Some jurisdictions specify a time period for phasing out legally nonconforming uses. In most jurisdictions, a nonconforming use must be eliminated if the property suffers major damage.

Uses That Are Not Highest and Best

Many existing buildings and other improvements do not represent the highest and best use of their sites as though vacant. Nevertheless, the highest and best use is generally in the same category as the existing use. For example, the highest and best use of a site improved with a 10-year-old apartment building may be for a new, more functional apartment building. Similarly, the highest and best use of a residential site improved with a 20-year-old house may be for a new, more modern, single-family residence. In such cases the improvement does not suffer from external obsolescence, so its value need not be discounted for inappropriate use of the site.

For certain sites the general category of highest and best use may have changed— e.g., from apartment to industrial use or from single-family residential to commercial use. If the improvements on these sites existed prior to the neighborhood change, they suffer from external obsolescence and are likely to have less value than similar improvements on more appropriate sites. It would be incorrect to value such an improvement as if it were located on an appropriate site. According to the concept of consistent use, an improvement must be valued based on a use that is consistent with the site's highest and best use.

To understand the importance of valuing a site and its improvements according to a consistent use, consider the following situation. An apartment building is located on a site that has an industrial use as its highest and best use. The land as though vacant is worth approximately $1 million, considerably more than the land value that would result if its highest and best use were for apartment use. The existing apartment building on the site is worth $1.5 million, which reflects a penalty on its value; its value would be $2 million if it were located on a site appropriate for apartment use. Because both the site and the

---

8. Alternatively, some practitioners believe that the value added in a downzoning should not be attributed solely to the improvement, but should be allocated between the improvement and the land. This is commonly accomplished by applying a ratio to the overall property value which reflects typical ratios of the contributions of land and improvements to value in similar market properties not affected by downzoning.

improvement must be valued according to the same highest and best use, the appraiser must consider the building's value to be $1.5 million. Consequently, the total value of the property would be $2.5 million—$1.5 million for the building and $1 million for the site. If the appraiser had used $2 million as the building value and a lower land value consistent with the apartment use, an erroneous total property value would have resulted.

Multiple Uses

Highest and best use often includes more than one use for a parcel of land or a building. A large tract of land might be suitable for a planned unit development with a shopping center in front, condominium units around a golf course, and single-family residential sites on the remainder of the land. Business parks often have sites for retail stores in front and warehouse or light manufacturing structures in the rear.

One parcel of land may serve many functions. Timberland or pastureland may also be used for hunting, recreation, and mineral exploration. Land that serves as a right of way for power lines can double as open space or a park. Public streets with railroad siding are also considered multiple-use land.

A building can have multiple uses too. A hotel may include a restaurant, a bar, and retail shops in addition to its guest rooms. A multistory building may contain offices, apartments, and retail stores. A single-family, owner-occupied home may have an apartment upstairs.

Appraisers can often estimate the contributory value of each use on a multiple-use site or in a multiple-use building. If, for example, the market value of a timber tract that can be leased for hunting is compared on a unit basis with the value of another timber tract that cannot, the difference should be the value of the hunting rights. In oil-producing areas, appraisers are often asked to segregate the value of mineral rights from the value of other land uses. Properties with mineral rights value can be compared with properties that do not have such value. In multiple-use assignments, the sum of the separate use values may be less than, equal to, or greater than the value of the total property.

Special-Purpose Uses

Because special-purpose properties are appropriate for only one use or for a very limited number of uses, appraisers may encounter practical problems in specifying their highest and best uses. The highest and best use of a special-purpose property as improved is probably the continuation of its current use, if that use remains viable. For example, the highest and best use of a plant now used for heavy manufacturing is probably continued use for heavy manufacturing, and the highest and best use of a grain elevator is probably continued use as a grain elevator. If the current use of a special-purpose property is physically or functionally obsolete and no alternative uses are feasible, the highest and best use of the property as improved may be realized by demolishing the structure and selling the remains for their scrap or salvage value.

Sometimes a special-purpose property must be analyzed and appraised on the basis of two highest and best uses—i.e., continuation of the existing, special-purpose use (value in use) and conversion to an alternative use (value for an alternative use). In such a situation, some appraisers contend that it is possible to estimate more then one market value depending on how the market is defined. For example, a church may first be analyzed based on its highest and best use as a church; in this analysis the contributory value of the improvements may be supported by cost or sales comparison data. If there is a congregation willing to buy a church, they may be willing to purchase the subject property at a value that reflects its present use as a church. If the demand for churches is low, however, the appraiser may also project a highest and best use as commercial office space. The estimated value of the improvements for conversion to this use would probably be derived from a detailed cost study or from sales data on churches converted to commercial uses. The value of the prop-

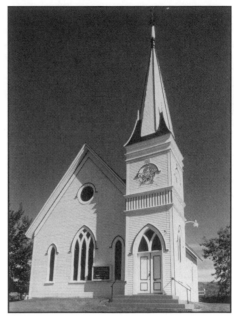

A church is a special-purpose property.

erty converted to a commercial use would probably differ from its value as a church.

Speculative Uses

Land that is held primarily for future sale may be regarded as a speculative investment. The purchaser or owner may believe that the value of the land will increase, but there may be risk that the expected appreciation will not occur while the speculator holds the land. Nevertheless, the current value of the land is a function of its future highest and best use, so the appraiser should discuss its potential highest and best use. The appraiser may not be able to predict the exact future highest and best use, but the general *type* of future use (e.g., as a shopping center or industrial park) is often known or indicated by the zoning, surrounding land-use patterns, or comprehensive city plan. Because there may be several types of potential highest and best use (e.g., single-family or multifamily residential developments), appraisers usually cannot identify a specific future highest and best use; they can, however, discuss logical alternative uses and anticipated income and expense levels.

Excess Land and Surplus Land

Some parcels of land are too large for their principal highest and best uses. Improved sites may have either *excess land* or *surplus land* that does not support the existing improvement. Vacant sites or sites considered as though vacant may have land that is not needed to accommodate the site's primary highest and best use. In some cases the highest and best use of *excess land* is for open space or nondevelopment. In other situations the highest and best use of *excess land* may be for future expansion of the existing or anticipated buildings or for future development as a separate entity. When the additional land does not support the existing improvement but may not be separated from the property and sold off, it has no independent highest and best use and represents *surplus land*.

Land that supports the property's primary use, such as a parking lot for an office building or a playground for a school, is not excess land. Only land beyond the normal needs of a particular use, as determined in the market, can be considered *excess* or *surplus land*. An appraiser should clearly identify any *excess* or *surplus land* and, if appropriate, indicate its unit value separately.

Some large sites are not considered to have excess land because the acreage that is not needed for the particular use cannot be used separately. As noted earlier, this acreage is *surplus land*. An overly large lot in an area that is 100% built up contains *surplus land* as does a site that cannot be divided because of the location of its buildings.

Key Concepts

- Highest and best use is the reasonably probable and legal use of vacant land or an improved property which is physically possible, legally permissible, appropriately supported, financially feasible, and that results in the highest land value.

- Highest and best use is a market-driven concept that is fundamental to both valuation and feasibility analyses.

- The highest and best use of a property is concluded after each potential use has been tested using the four criteria. The use that fulfills the four criteria and maximizes value is the highest and best use.

- A distinction is made between the highest and best use of the land or site as though vacant and the highest and best use of the property as improved.

- Highest and best use of the land or site as though vacant may be the existing use, a projected development, a subdivision, an assemblage, or speculative holding.

- The highest and best use of a property as improved may be continued maintenance, renovation, rehabilitation, expansion, adaptation or conversion to another use, partial or total demolition, or some combination of these alternatives.

- The statement of highest and best use should be as specific as the market suggests.

- To test financial feasibility and maximum productivity, the respective values under alternative uses are estimated by analyzing criterion variables such as land value, rate of return and risk associated with the use, and capitalized overall property value.

- Single uses, interim uses, legally nonconforming uses, uses that are not highest and best, multiple uses, special-purpose uses, speculative uses, and excess and surplus land require special consideration.

Terms

alternative use

appropriately supported

consistent use

criteria variable

excess land

existing use

feasibility

financially feasible

four criteria

highest and best use

highest and best use of land or
    site as though vacant

highest and best use of property
    as improved

ideal improvement

intensity of use

interim uses

land residual

legally nonconforming uses

legally permissible

maximally productive

multiple uses

physically possible

potential use

single uses

special-purpose uses

speculative uses

surplus land

use density

value in use

CHAPTER FOURTEEN

Land or Site Valuation

The supply of land is relatively stable. Although vast changes have occurred in the earth's surface over the ages, and slight modifications in the supply and quality of land may occur over a lifetime, these natural events rarely affect the land with which appraisers are concerned.

There are, however, a few notable exceptions to the permanence of land, such as the accretion or erosion of land along a shoreline, the pollution of land with harmful wastes, the exhaustion of agricultural land through improper farming methods, and the transformation of arable land into desert due to ecological imbalances. Earthquakes may change the surface of the earth and faults beneath the surface can create vast sinkholes. Fortunately, these occurrences are rare.

Land has value because it provides potential utility as the site of a structure, recreational facility, agricultural tract, or right-of-way for transportation routes. If land has utility for a specific use and there is demand for that use, the land has value to a particular category of users. Beyond the basic utility of land, however, there are many principles and factors that must be considered in land valuation. Although it is sometimes considered the simplest of appraisal tasks, the valuation of land requires careful analysis of a complex variety of factors.

Land Valuation Theory

Value Concepts and Principles

Anticipation, change, supply and demand, substitution, and balance are appraisal principles that influence land value. Anticipation means that value is created by the expectation of benefits to be derived in the future. If buyers anticipate that sites in a certain location will be in demand for office use within the next five years, they may be motivated to acquire land for development even though the development of office space is not presently tenable. The competition among buyers who make up the market for these sites creates a price level for the land that may have little to do with its current use. In such circumstances, the highest and best use of the sites could be speculative holding for eventual office development.

The supply of and demand for sites in a particular location tend toward equilibrium. If supply declines and demand remains stable or increases, prices rise. Conversely, if the supply of sites for a particular use increases and demand remains stable or declines, prices fall. Temporary imbalances between supply and demand are usually resolved over time and equilibrium is reestablished. The price of property reflects this relationship.

When prices drop sufficiently, supply will contract because existing uses will be retained. When prices rise, a new supply may be created through rezoning, annexation, or abandonment of existing uses.

Although the supply of and demand for sites tend toward ultimate equilibrium, this principle may not apply in the short run. If one type of site is very scarce in a particular location, the pressure of intense market competition may increase the value of such sites beyond the level indicated by their profitability. For example, the rents that can be obtained for office space in a particular location may not justify the high prices being paid for office sites. Similarly, the prices that can be obtained for improved residential properties may not justify the high prices paid for the last few lots in a popular location. Nevertheless, market value is generally the most probable price the market can sustain. Eventually, the equilibrium among prices and land values will be reestablished; if all other factors remain constant, values will rise or prices will fall.

Land value is substantially affected by the interplay of supply and demand, but it is the economic use of a site that determines its value in a particular market. For example, the price that a developer can afford to pay for a warehouse site is determined by the net income that the warehouse will earn and the cost of constructing it. Intense competition for choice sites or for the last remaining sites in a particular location can cause prospective owners or owner-occupants to pay more for a particular site than is indicated by the broad spectrum of market activity and the highest and best use of the site.

The principle of substitution, which holds that a buyer will not pay more for one site than for another that is similar or equal, applies to land values and indicates that the greatest demand will be generated for the lowest-priced sites. The principle of balance is also applicable to land values. When the various elements of a particular economic mix or a specific environment are in a state of equilibrium, value is sustained; when the balance is upset, values change. If, for example, a district has too much industrially zoned land, property values will probably fall. Because prices are usually quoted in inflated, not constant, dollars, prices may appear to be increasing when they are actually falling or remaining level.

Property Rights and Public Controls

The appraisal of land focuses on valuing the property rights attached to the land. These include the rights to develop the land within certain limits, to lease it to others, to farm it, to mine it, to alter its topography, to subdivide it, to assemble it, and to use it for waste disposal. Whenever possible, an appraiser should consult public records to identify easements, rights-of-way, and private or public restrictions that affect the subject property.

Because the supply of land cannot keep pace with the demand for it, governments regulate how land can be used and developed. Most municipalities and counties have some form of zoning that specifies how a parcel of land can be developed. In addition to zoning, many jurisdictions now have master plans that specify long-term development goals. Developers frequently must provide public amenities such as open space, streets, and adjacent or off-site public improvements to acquire development rights. Sometimes developers can proceed with development only after they submit approved site plans. In some areas citizen groups may protest a development they do not like, and their wishes frequently influence the type of development that is finally approved.

Through the power of eminent domain, the government can remove land from private use to augment the supply of public land or modify land use through urban renewal programs. In some rural jurisdictions land use is influenced by government-sponsored transferable development rights (TDRs), which compensate farmers for retaining land in agricultural use and shift the cost of development to developers. Lower ad valorem taxes on agricultural land also affect rural land use; this form of tax subsidy tends to extend the duration of agricultural uses.

A significant amount of land in the United States has been encumbered with open space or conservation easements in perpetuity. These permanent encumbrances limit or prohibit the subdivision of land to prevent further development. Land subject to perpetual open space or conservation easements is usually restricted to its existing use, as specified in the deed of easement. These deeds are vested in preservation or conservation trusts. Other encumbrances prohibit the demolition or alteration of historic structures.

Physical Characteristics and Site Improvements

The physical characteristics of land, the utilities available, and site improvements affect land use and value. The physical characteristics of a parcel of land that an appraiser must consider include size and shape, frontage, topography, location, view, and topographical characteristics such as contour, grade, and drainage.

The availability of utilities—i.e., water, sewers, electricity, natural gas, and telephone service—also influences the use and development potential of a parcel of land. Utilities may be provided by off-site facilities such as public water mains, sewers, and power lines or by on-site facilities such as spring basins, drilled domestic wells, and septic tanks.

A parcel of land becomes a *site* when it is improved and ready to be used for a specific purpose. A site may have both on-site and off-site improvements that make it suitable for its intended use or development. Necessary on-site improvements include grading, landscaping, paving, and utility hookups for water, gas, electricity, and telephone. Essential off-site improvements include streets, curbs, sidewalks, drains, and connecting utility lines. Off-site improvements are typically considered with site value; only rarely are they valued with other property improvements. Like buildings and other structures, on-site improvements are subject to physical deterioration and functional obsolescence.

Highest and Best Use

Land value must always be considered in terms of highest and best use. Even if the site has improvements, the value of the land is based on its highest and best use as though vacant and available for development to its most economic use. Consideration of the land as though vacant is a commonly accepted procedure which facilitates the orderly analysis and solution of appraisal problems that require land to be valued separately. Land has first claim to any income generated by the property and priority over any return on the improvements. Land value may be equal to, or even greater than, total property value, even when substantial improvements are located on the site.

Highest and best use is also affected by how much existing improvements contribute to property value. The contribution of the improvements is estimated by subtracting the value of the land from the value of the total property. Land is said to *have value*, while improvements *contribute to value*. When improvements do not contribute to property value, demolition is indicated. In this case the cost of converting the property into a vacant site is a penalty, or negative building contribution, to be deducted from the value of the land.

In some circumstances the appraisal of a property may require that the site be considered in terms other than its highest and best use. In an appraisal to estimate the use value or legal, nonconforming use value of an improved site, an appraiser may need to value the site according to its specified use or the existing improvements, not its highest and best use. In this case the appraiser should value the site both in terms of its highest and best use and its conditional use.

Land Valuation Techniques

The procedures used to value vacant land are:

1. Sales comparison
2. Allocation
3. Extraction
4. Income capitalization, divided into
   - Direct capitalization techniques
     Land residual
     Ground rent capitalization
   - Yield capitalization techniques
     Discounted cash flow analysis
     (subdivision development analysis)

All these procedures are derived from the three traditional approaches to value. Sales comparison and income capitalization are listed; the allocation and extraction procedures indicated reflect the influence of the sales comparison and cost approaches.

Sales Comparison

The sales comparison approach may be used to value land that is actually vacant or land that is being considered as though vacant for appraisal purposes. Sales comparison is the most common technique for valuing land and it is the preferred method when comparable sales are available. To apply this method, sales of similar parcels of land are analyzed, compared, and adjusted to provide a value indication for the land being appraised. In the comparison process, the similarity or dissimilarity of the parcels is considered.

The appraiser gathers data on actual sales as well as listings, offers, and options; identifies the similarities and differences in the data; adjusts the sale prices of the comparables to account for the dissimilar characteristics of the land being appraised; and forms a conclusion as to the market value of the subject land.

Elements of comparison include property rights, financing terms, conditions of sale (motivation), market conditions (sale date), location, physical characteristics, available utilities, and zoning. Physical characteristics of the site include its size and shape, frontage, topography, location, and view. (For a more complete discussion of elements of comparison, see Chapter 18.) Unit prices may be expressed as price per square foot, front foot, lot, dwelling unit, or other unit used in the market.

If sale prices have been changing rapidly over the past several years and an adequate amount of sales data is available, the sales selected for comparison should take place as close to the effective appraisal date as possible. When current data on local sales are not available, the appraiser may need to expand the search to another neighborhood, which usually necessitates an adjustment for location, or extend the search back in time in the same neighborhood, which usually necessitates an adjustment for market conditions. The decision to use sales from another neighborhood or older sales should be based on which adjustment has more support—the location adjustment or the market conditions adjustment.

Size is generally a less important element of comparison than date and location. Most types of development have an optimal site size; if the site is too large, the value of the excess land tends to decline at an accelerating rate. Because sales of different sizes may have different unit prices, appraisers ordinarily give more weight to comparables that are approximately the same size as the subject property. Reducing a sale price to a size-related unit price usually eliminates the need to make a size adjustment.

Zoning is often the most basic criterion in selecting comparables. Sites zoned the same as the subject property are the most appropriate comparables. If sufficient sales in the same zoning category are not available, data from similar categories can be used after adjustments are made. As a general rule, the greater the dissimilarity between the subject and the comparables, the more potential there is for distortion and error in sales comparison.

In addition to recorded sales and signed contracts, appraisers should consider offers to sell and offers to purchase. Offers provide less reliable data than signed contracts and recorded sales. Usually the final sale price is lower than the initial offer to sell, but higher than the initial offer to buy. Negotiations can take place in several stages.

Data on land sales are available from sources such as electronically transmitted and printed data services, newspapers, and deed and assessment records. Interviews with the parties involved in transactions—i.e., the buyers, sellers, lawyers, and brokers—can provide more direct information. After comparable data are collected and categorized and the comparable properties are examined and described, sales data can be assembled in an organized, logical manner. Sales are commonly arranged on a market data grid that has separate lines for important property characteristics. Adjustments for dissimilarities between the subject property and the comparable properties are made to the sale or unit prices of the comparables by means of a variety of techniques. (Paired data analysis and other techniques for sales comparison are discussed in Chapter 18.)

Generally, separate adjustments are made to the comparable sale prices for each element of comparison. The magnitude of each adjustment is indicated by the data. Land parcels of different sizes sell at different unit prices because the optimal size of a parcel depends on its use. Unit prices also vary with the date of sale and location. If the data selected are not sufficient to indicate the magnitude of the adjustments required, the appraiser can either gather and analyze additional comparable data or exercise appraisal judgment.

A sale price adjustment may be simply an acknowledgment of a property's superiority or inferiority; alternatively, it may be a precise dollar amount or percentage. Adjustments can also be totaled and factored into the comparable sale prices. Typically, adjustments are made in a particular order—i.e., adjustments for property rights, financing, and sale and market conditions are made before adjustments for location and physical characteristics. All adjustments should be presented in the appraisal report in a logical and understandable manner.

Allocation

Vacant sites in densely developed urban locations may be so rare that their values cannot be estimated by direct comparison. Similarly, sales of vacant sites in remote rural areas may occur so seldom that sufficient comparable data are not available. In such cases land value can be estimated by allocation or extraction.

The allocation method is based on the principle of balance and the related concept of contribution. Both affirm that there is a normal or typical ratio of land value to property value for specific categories of real estate in specific locations. Meaningful support for an allocation ratio may be derived from mass appraisals prepared by assessors or through consultation with developers who sell improved properties and can allocate sale prices between the land and the improvements based on their costs. The allocation method does not produce conclusive value indications, but it can be used to establish land value when the number of vacant land sales is inadequate.

For example, allocation could be used in an appraisal assignment to value the site under an older home in a fully developed residential neighborhood. Assume that no sales of vacant land have occurred recently, but the appraiser has ascertained that homes in the neighborhood that are similar to the subject have been sold for $140,000 to $150,000. A citywide study conducted by the local assessor's office indicates a land-to-property value ratio of approximately 10%. Accordingly, the value of the subject site estimated by allocation would be $14,000 to $15,000.

Because of the difficulty of supporting a land-to-property value ratio, allocation is a rarely used land valuation technique.

Extraction

Extraction is a method in which land value is extracted from the sale price of an improved property by deducting the value contribution of the improvements, estimated as their depreciated costs. The remaining value represents the value of the land. Improved sales in rural areas are frequently analyzed in this way because the building's contribution to total property value is generally small and relatively easy to identify.

For example, assume an appraiser is estimating the value of the site under an older, deteriorated, two-bay automobile service garage that was recently sold for $275,000. No vacant lots have been sold in the neighborhood recently. The appraiser estimates the replacement cost new of the improvement at $200,000 and total depreciation at 75%, indicating that the depreciated cost new of the improvement is $50,000. Deducting $50,000 from the $275,000 sale price, the appraiser obtains a residual land value of $225,000 by the extraction technique.

Income Capitalization Procedures

Direct Capitalization: Land Residual

The land residual technique may be used to estimate land value when sales data on similar parcels of vacant land are not available. The technique is applicable when 1) building value is known or can be accurately estimated, 2) net operating income to the property is known or can be estimated, and 3) both building and land capitalization rates can be extracted from the market.

To apply land residual, an appraiser first determines what actual or hypothetical improvements represent the highest and best use of the site. Then the net operating income to the property is estimated from market rents and operating expenses as of the date of the appraisal. Next, the appraiser calculates how much of the income is attributable to the building and subtracts this amount from the total net operating income. The remainder is the residual income to the land, which is capitalized at a market-derived capitalization rate to provide an estimate of land value. Chapter 20 discusses the extraction of land capitalization rates (R_L).

To illustrate the application of the land residual technique, assume that a developer engages an appraiser to estimate the value of a site that he plans to purchase. The developer intends to use the site to construct a professional office building, which is considered the highest and best use of the site. The appraiser's investigation of the local market indicates that the total property can be expected to produce a net operating income of $100,000 per year. The market indicates a building capitalization rate of 11% and a land capitalization rate of 6%. The value of a new building with no depreciation is estimated to be $800,000.

NOI	$100,000
Less income to the building	
$(I_B = V_B \times R_B)$ $800,000 \times 0.11 =$	88,000
Income attributable to the land	$12,000
Land value	
$(V_L = I_L/R_L)$ $12,000/0.06 \quad =$	$200,000

In this example the property is assumed to be free and clear of debt. If the purchase of the land or the construction of the improvement were to be financed, other items would have to be considered. With sufficient market data to indicate the value of the building, the property's anticipated net operating income, and the land and building capitalization rates, the value of the land can be calculated.

There are several variations of the land residual technique. In one variation, the property is valued as improved and the cost of the improvements and any profit are deducted. The sum remaining is the residual value of the land. The land residual technique can be used when comparable sales are lacking and as a check on the sales comparison approach. It is most useful in testing the feasibility of alternative uses of a particular site.

Direct Capitalization: Ground Rent Capitalization

Ground rents can be capitalized at an appropriate rate to indicate the market value of a site. *Ground rent is the amount paid for the right to use and occupy the land according to the terms of the ground lease.* It corresponds to the value of the landowner's interest in the land, the leased fee interest. Market-derived capitalization rates are used to convert ground rent into market value. This procedure is useful when an analysis of comparable sales of leased land indicates a range of rents and capitalization rates. If the current rent corresponds to market rent, the value indication obtained by applying a market capitalization rate will be equivalent to the market value of the fee simple interest in the land. If the ground rent paid under the terms of the existing contract does not correspond to market rent, the ground rent must be adjusted for the difference in property rights to obtain an indication of the market value of the fee simple interest.

Ground leases can have different terms and escalation clauses, so the appraiser should consider all benefits to the lessor during the term of the lease and the option periods and determine when the reversion of the property will take place. An alternative method of ground rent capitalization involves discounting the anticipated cash flows (rental income) over the holding period and the reversion, or lump-sum benefit, received upon termination of the investment.

Yield Capitalization: Discounted Cash Flow Analysis (Subdivision Development Analysis)

Discounted cash flow analysis (subdivision development analysis) is used to value vacant land that has the potential for development as a subdivision when that use represents the likely highest and best use of the land. The development of any project extends over two stages: the construction stage and the marketing stage.

To perform subdivision development analysis, data on development sales and costs for the developed lots must be available. Subdivision development analysis may involve residential, commercial, or industrial tracts of land that are large enough to be subdivided into smaller lots or parcels and sold to builders or end users. A planned subdivision can create a higher, better, and more intense use of the property when zoning, available utilities, access, and other influential elements are favorably combined.

An appraiser begins the analysis of a subdivision development by determining the number and size of the lots that can be created from the appraised land physically, legally, and economically. The proposed lots must conform to jurisdictional and zoning requirements with regard to size, frontage, topography, soil quality, and off-site improvements—e.g., water facilities, drainage, sewage, streets and curbs. The lots must also meet the demands of the market in which the property is located. Without surveys and engineering studies, an appraiser cannot know exactly how many lots can be created from a particular parcel of land. However, a reasonable estimate of the number of potential lots can be deduced from zoning and subdivision ordinances or, preferably, from the number of lots created in similar subdivisions. Allowances must also be made for the land needed for streets and green space.

The appraiser obtains a preliminary development plan for the hypothetical subdivision of the vacant land being appraised. The development plan specifies the number and size of the lots, the construction work to be accomplished, the hard and soft construction costs, the probable time required to subdivide the land and construct the on-site and off-site infrastructure, and the expenses to be incurred during the marketing period. The appraiser then undertakes a preliminary marketability analysis to assess the supply and demand situation and the probable absorption rate and marketing period for the lots. The appraiser estimates the projected retail prices of the lots by applying the sales comparison approach. The appraiser also estimates the amount of profit a typical developer would require to develop the land or, alternatively, to both develop and market the lots.

In the next phase of subdivision development analysis, the appraiser projects cash flows for income and expenses, noting the periods in which they will occur (i.e., either in semiannual or quarterly periods, depending on the market). The projection periods begin with the property as is and continue until sellout is completed or stabilized occupancy is achieved. The net cash flow for each period is discounted back to point zero to arrive at the present value of the net cash flows. (Discounting is discussed in Chapter 23). The discount rate applied, which is derived from and supported by the market, should reflect the risk involved.

The following example illustrates the application of discounted cash flow analysis to a tract of vacant land that is being considered for development as a residential subdivision. The 20-acre tract of vacant land is to be subdivided into 48 residential lots. The market supports an average retail sale price of $40,000 per lot. It will take six months to plat the subdivision and construct all the infrastructure. After construction is completed, the developer anticipates a two-year marketing period to be conducted in four, semiannual phases. Expenses are projected as follows.

- Marketing costs equal to 7% of the retail sale prices
- Legal and closing costs equal to 2% of the retail sale prices
- Real estate taxes of $1,300 during the first six-month construction phase for the land as undeveloped and $400 per year for each developed lot in inventory thereafter
- Average annual project overhead and maintenance of $200 per lot for the average number of lots in inventory during each period (calculated for 48 lots during the first period due to higher overhead costs during construction)
- An annual developer's fee of $40,000 for coordination and supervision

- Entrepreneurial or developer's profit (shown in the example as a "below-the-line" expense)[1] equal to 15% of the gross sale price
- Construction costs, including all soft costs, of $10,500 per lot, or a total cost of $504,000 (spread over Periods 1, 2, and 4).

The DCF analysis assumes that sale prices and all expenses will remain constant over the 30-month projection. The 12% discount rate to be applied is based on market conditions. The DCF analysis shown in Table 14.1 results in a value indication of $612,000 for the parcel of vacant land.

Table 14.1 DCF Analysis (Subdivision Development Analysis)

| | Semiannual Periods | | | | | |
	1	2	3	4	5	Total
Beginning inventory of lots	0	48	36	24	12	
Number of developed lots	48	0	0	0	0	
Number of lots sold	0	12	12	12	12	48
Ending inventory of lots	48	36	24	12	0	0
Cumulative no. of lots sold	0	12	24	36	48	48
Average price per lot	$40,000	$40,000	$40,000	$40,000	$40,000	
Gross lot sales income	0	$480,000	$480,000	$480,000	$480,000	$1,920,000
Expenses						
Marketing costs	0	$33,600	$33,600	$33,600	$33,600	$134,400
Legal/closing costs	0	9,600	9,600	9,600	9,600	38,400
Real estate taxes	1,300	8,400	6,000	3,600	1,200	20,500
Overhead/maintenance	4,800	4,200	3,000	1,800	600	14,400
Coordination/supervision	20,000	20,000	20,000	20,000	20,000	100,000
Total	$26,100	$75,800	$72,200	$68,600	$65,000	$307,700
Developer's profit	0	72,000	72,000	72,000	72,000	288,000
Development costs	384,000	95,000	0	25,000	0	504,000
Net cash flow	($410,100)	$237,200	$335,800	$314,400	$343,000	$820,300
Present value	($386,887)	$211,107	$281,944	$249,034	$256,310	$611,508

Indication of land value $611,508
$612,000 (rounded)

1. The timing of developer's profit is controversial. Some appraisers feel it is an expense that the developer has already incurred upon completion of the project and thus should be deducted as an "above-the-line" expense—i.e., before the calculation of annual net sales proceeds or cash flows. Other practitioners believe that the developer does not earn the profit by simply platting and constructing the infrastructure of a subdivision; the developer can expect compensation only after completing the development and selling or leasing the property as improved. These appraisers deduct developer's profit as a "below-the-line" expense. If the developer's profit is deducted as an "above-the-line" expense, the rate selected to discount the cash flows will be lower than the rate chosen if the developer's profit is deducted as a "below-the-line" expense. For further discussion, see Douglas D. Lovell and Robert S. Martin, *Subdivision Development* (Chicago: Appraisal Institute, 1993) and Chuck Munson, "Lender Residential Subdivision Evaluation Using Discounted Cash Flow Analysis," *The Appraisal Journal* (October 1994), 572-579.

The use of subdivision development analysis to value vacant land is most applicable in cases where sales data on vacant tracts of land are inadequate but market data are available on the probable sale prices of developed lots and the demand for such lots. This application of DCF analysis is also useful as a method of checking the reasonableness of value indications derived from other methods of estimating the value of vacant land with development potential. Comparing the value indication derived from DCF analysis with a value indication derived from sales comparison allows an appraiser to test the feasibility of a proposed project. If the value indication from the DCF analysis is less than the value indication from the sales comparison approach, the proposed project may be judged to be unfeasible.

Key Concepts

- An appraiser begins the valuation of a parcel of land by identifying the real estate and property rights to be valued, any encumbrances on those property rights (e.g., easements, rights-of-way, use restrictions in deeds or zoning ordinances), the site's physical characteristics, and the available utilities and site improvements. Comparable data on similar parcels are collected and the highest and best use of the subject site is analyzed.

- Sales comparison is the most commonly used and preferred method of valuing land. Data on sales of similar parcels of land are analyzed, compared, and adjusted for their dissimilarity to the subject property.

- The allocation method is based on typical ratios of land value to improvement value for specific categories of real estate in specific locations. Allocation is useful when transactional data on comparable sites are not available.

- To apply the extraction method, an estimate of the depreciated cost of the improvement(s) is deducted from the total sale price of the property to arrive at the land value. Extraction is used to estimate the land value of improved properties in rural areas and properties in which the improvements contribute little to total property value.

- Three income capitalization procedures are applicable to land valuation. Two of these—land residual and ground rent capitalization—are direct capitalization techniques. Subdivision development analysis is a yield capitalization technique.

- In the land residual method, the net operating income (*NOI*) attributable to the land (i.e., the amount that remains after the *NOI* attributable to the improvement is deducted from total *NOI*) is capitalized to produce an indication of land value. Several variants of the land residual method may be used. Land residual is applied when sales data on similar parcels are not available.

- Ground rent capitalization is used when ground rent corresponds to the owner's interest in the land, i.e., the leased fee interest. Market-derived capitalization rates are used to convert ground rent into an indication of land value.

- Subdivision development analysis is applied when subdivision and development represent the highest and best use of the land and sales data on finished lots are available. The number and size of the finished lots, their likely sale prices, the length of the development and marketing periods, and the absorption rate are estimated. Gross income and expenses are projected when they are expected to occur; the resulting net sales proceeds are then discounted back to arrive at an indication of land value. Several variants of subdivision development analysis may be used.

Terms

absorption rate	marketing period
adjustments	offers
allocation	off-site improvements
deed restriction	on-site improvements
depreciated cost	operating income
developer's profit	net operating income (*NOI*)
development period	net sales proceeds
direct capitalization	right-of-way
discounted cash flow analysis	sales comparison
easement	site
extraction	site improvements
gross income	subdivision development
ground rent	unit price
ground rent capitalization	yield capitalization
land	zoning
land residual	

CHAPTER FIFTEEN

The Cost Approach

L
ike the sales comparison and income capitalization approaches, the cost approach to value is based on comparison. In the cost approach, the appraiser estimates the value of a subject property in comparison to the cost to produce a new subject property or a substitute property, whichever the market suggests would be a more suitable comparison. The cost is compared with the value of the existing property and adjusted for differences in the age, condition, and utility of the subject property. The comparative framework used depends on the market standard for the subject property.

When applicable, the cost approach reflects market thinking because market participants relate value to cost. Buyers tend to judge the value of an existing structure not only by considering the prices and rents of similar buildings, but also by comparing the cost to create a new building in optimal physical condition with optimal functional utility. Moreover, buyers adjust the prices they are willing to pay by estimating the costs to bring an existing structure up to the physical condition and functional utility they desire.

In applying the cost approach, an appraiser attempts to estimate the difference in worth to a buyer between the property being appraised and a newly constructed building with optimal utility. The appraiser estimates the cost to construct the existing structure and site improvements (including direct costs, indirect costs, and an appropriate entrepreneurial profit) and then deducts all accrued depreciation in the property being appraised from the cost of the new structure as of the effective appraisal date. When the value of the site is added to this figure, the result is an indication of the value of the fee simple interest in the property.

The data used in the sales comparison approach reflect the market's reaction to items of depreciation. One way to estimate the total amount of depreciation in a comparable property is by allocating its sale price between the land and the improvements and then deducting the contribution of the improvements from their estimated cost. If the price allocated to the improvements is less than their current reproduction or replacement cost, there is depreciation. In applying the cost approach, an appraiser attempts to identify and quantify the causes of depreciation and relate them to the subject property. Appraisal methodology continues to evolve, and practitioners who apply the cost approach must adapt it to both the needs of the appraisal problem and the conventions of contemporary appraisal practice.

Relation to Appraisal Principles

Substitution

The principle of substitution is basic to the cost approach. This principle affirms that no prudent buyer would pay more for a property than the cost to acquire a similar site and construct improvements of equivalent desirability and utility without undue delay. Older properties can also be substituted for the property being appraised, and their value is measured relative to the value of a new, optimal property. In short, the reproduction cost of a property on the effective date of the appraisal plus its site value provides a measure against which prices for similar improved properties may be judged.

Supply and Demand

Shifts in supply and demand cause prices to increase or decrease. Thus, one property may have different values over time. If costs do not shift in proportion to price changes, the construction of buildings will be more or less profitable and the value of existing buildings will increase or decrease commensurately.

Balance

The principle of balance holds that the agents of production and the various property components must be in proper proportion if optimum value is to be achieved or sustained. An improper economic balance may result in an underimprovement or an overimprovement. An underimprovement is created by too little investment in the improvements relative to the value of the site; an overimprovement is created by too much investment.

Any excess or deficiency in the proportionate contributions of the site and the improvements may result in a loss in value relative to their cost. An imbalance in the various components of the improvements may also produce a loss in value. In the cost approach, the effect on value of an excess or deficiency is addressed in the estimation of depreciation.

Externalities

When supply and demand are in balance and credit is available, the cost of new improvements, plus an appropriate entrepreneurial incentive (profit), minus depreciation, plus the value of the site equals market value. The cost of production and market value may be affected differently by externalities. An externality such as inflation may sometimes increase material and labor costs while not affecting market values. On the other hand, completion of a sewer line may increase value but have no impact on cost. Gains or losses in value caused by externalities may accrue to both land and buildings. Rising construction costs often can significantly affect the market value of new construction and, in turn, the market value of older, substitute properties.

In the cost approach a loss in building value due to external causes is ascribed to external obsolescence, one of the three major types of depreciation. If, for example, an industrial plant that depends on trucks to transport its product is located a great distance from a recently completed highway, the property may suffer from external obsolescence.

External conditions can also cause a newly constructed building to be worth more or less than its cost. If properties of a certain type are scarce or it is difficult to construct new competitive properties, the value of a newly constructed building may be higher than its cost. On the other hand, an economic recession might create an oversupply of a particular type of property, which would cause the value of a new property to be less than its cost. In the late 1980s and early 1990s, external obsolescence has most often been attributed to declining market conditions. Externalities may have an especially strong effect on older properties.

Highest and Best Use

The concept of highest and best use is fundamental to real property value. In one application of the concept, a site is valued as though vacant and available to be developed to its highest and best use; in the other application, the highest and best use of the property as improved is concluded. Thus, a site may have one highest and best use as though vacant, and the existing combination of the site and improvements may have another highest and best use. Existing improvements have a value equal to the amount they contribute to the site or they may penalize value by an amount equal to the cost to remove them from the site.

If the existing improvements do not develop the site to its highest and best use, the improvements are worth less than their cost. A new building that is poorly designed is worth less than its cost due to the functional obsolescence in its design. Thus, the improvement that constitutes highest and best use is the one that adds the greatest value to the site.

Historical Background

The appraisal procedures that are now identified as the three approaches to value were developed after the stock market crash of 1929. The economic crisis that ensued had an immediate impact on the appraisal practices of the time. The collapse of the real estate market in the 1930s seemed to discredit the notion that market price is central to value. A dearth of construction activity made it difficult to derive accurate cost estimates for many types of property. Investors were wary of risking their money in new developments. The primary consideration was economic feasibility—i.e., whether effective demand could transform cost into value.

The depression era was characterized by a public backlash against the speculative excesses of the 1920s, which went unchecked in a business environment devoid of government regulation. During the depression the federal government entered the picture. The Federal Housing Administration (FHA) was established by the National Housing Act of 1934. By insuring mortgages, the FHA created a more stable mortgage market. It also promoted better-quality single-family housing by requiring builders to comply with government housing standards. As a precaution, the FHA required property appraisals before purchase so that it would not be left holding unsalable properties if the mortgagors defaulted.

Federal policy guidelines for appraisals specifically endorsed use of the replacement cost approach. By this means the FHA intended to stimulate construction because the cost of building new dwellings was clearly greater than the value of the dwellings in the market at the time. The emphasis on quality construction during this period was reinforced by the background of many appraisers, whose appraisal skill was based on a direct knowledge of building costs and quality.

In the building boom that followed World War II, some appraisers criticized the impracticality of estimating the costs of existing structures and the difficulty of tracking increasingly complex construction costs. The building costs services established before World War II helped maintain the validity of the cost approach throughout the 1940s, 1950s, and 1960s.

As investment analysis techniques became more sophisticated and the real estate industry grew more income-oriented, the position of the cost approach was further jeopardized. By the 1980s appraisal clients were mainly interested in the investment potential and market characteristics of properties. The cost approach was not of direct relevance to many real estate investors. Proponents of the cost approach rightly contend that the approach imparts a unique understanding of the economics of real estate. On the other hand, the usefulness of the cost approach in valuing existing improvements has been criticized on the grounds that information on direct costs and materials is better computed by building professionals than by appraisers. Yet the cost approach continues to show vitality. In the oversupplied markets of the late 1980s and early 1990s, some speculative investors purchased buildings because they recognized that their prices were a fraction of replacement cost.

Applicability and Limitations

Because cost and market value are usually most closely related when properties are new, the cost approach is important in estimating the market value of new or relatively new construction. The approach is especially persuasive when the site value is well supported and the improvements are new or suffer only minor accrued depreciation and, therefore, approximate the highest and best use of the site as though vacant. The cost approach can also be applied to older properties when adequate data are available to measure depreciation.

The cost approach is used to estimate the market value of proposed construction, special-purpose or specialty properties, and other properties that are not frequently exchanged in the market. Buyers of these properties often measure the price they will pay for an existing building against the cost to build a replacement, minus depreciation, or the cost to purchase an existing structure and make any necessary modifications. If comparable sales are not available, they cannot be analyzed to estimate the market value of such properties. Therefore, current market indications of depreciated cost or the costs to acquire and refurbish an existing building are the best reflections of market thinking and, thus, of market value.

In any market, the value of a building can be related to its cost. The cost approach is particularly important when a lack of market activity limits the usefulness of the sales comparison approach and when the properties to be appraised—e.g., single-family residences—are not amenable to valuation by the income capitalization approach. To estimate market value in these situations, an appraiser can calculate the cost of the building and then make a deduction for the amount of depreciation present in the existing improvement.

When the physical characteristics of comparable properties differ significantly, the relative values of these characteristics can sometimes be identified more precisely with the cost approach than with sales comparison. Because the cost approach starts with the cost to construct a substitute property with optimal physical and functional utility, it can help an appraiser determine accurate adjustments for physical differences in comparable sale properties. If, for example, an appraiser must make an adjustment for inadequate elevators in a comparable property, the cost to cure the deficiency can be used as a basis for this adjustment. The cost approach provides the appraiser with data to use both in estimating depreciation and in deriving an adjustment to apply in the sales comparison approach.

Because the cost approach requires that land and improvements be valued separately, it is also useful in appraisals for insurance purposes, when noninsurable items must be segregated from insurable items. In appraisals for accounting purposes, the cost approach is applied to estimate depreciation for income taxes.

The cost approach is especially useful when building additions or renovations are being considered. The approach can be used to determine whether the cost of an improvement, including profit, will be recovered through an increased income stream or anticipated sale price; its use can prevent the construction of overimprovements.

Finally, an estimate of probable building and development costs is an essential component of feasibility studies, which test the investment assumptions on which land use plans are based. Financial feasibility is indicated when a property's market value exceeds its total building and development costs plus a reasonable, market-supported entrepreneurial profit.

When improvements are older or do not represent the highest and best use of the land as though vacant, the physical deterioration, functional obsolescence, and external obsolescence of the structure are more difficult to estimate. Furthermore, relevant comparable data may be lacking or the data available may be too diverse to indicate an appropriate estimate of entrepreneurial profit.

In valuing investment properties, the persuasiveness of the cost approach is seriously diminished by the premise that improvements be constructed without undue delay. The development and construction of investment properties may take several months to several years; in the eyes of some investors, this constitutes an unacceptable delay.

When value estimates derived with the cost approach are not supported by market data, they must be regarded with caution. Because the estimation of depreciation and entrepreneurial incentive (profit) is difficult, the cost approach may be of limited usefulness in valuing older improved properties. Moreover, the cost approach results in an indication of the value of the fee simple interest in a property. To value real estate held in leased fee or property subject to other partial interests, appraisers must make adjustments to reflect the specific real property rights being appraised. Finally, appraisers must make adjustments in the cost approach to reflect expenses incurred during lease-up of the proposed improvement(s).

Procedure

After inspecting the neighborhood, the site, and the improvements and gathering all relevant data, an appraiser follows a series of steps to derive a value indication by the cost approach. The appraiser will

1. Estimate the value of the site as though vacant and available to be developed to its highest and best use.

2. Estimate the direct (hard) and indirect (soft) costs of the improvements as of the effective appraisal date.

3. Estimate an appropriate entrepreneurial incentive (profit) from analysis of the market.

4. Add estimated direct costs, indirect costs, and the entrepreneurial incentive (profit) to arrive at the total cost of the improvements.

5. Estimate the amount of accrued depreciation in the structure and, if necessary, allocate it among the three major categories: physical deterioration, functional obsolescence, and external obsolescence.

6. Deduct the estimated depreciation from the total cost of the improvements to derive an estimate of their depreciated cost.

7. Estimate the contributory value of any site improvements that have not already been considered (Site improvements are often appraised at their contributory value, i.e., directly on a depreciated-cost basis.)

8. Add the site value to the total depreciated cost of all the improvements to arrive at the indicated value of the property.

9. Adjust the indicated value of the property for any personal property (e.g., fixtures, furniture, and equipment) that may be included in the cost estimate and, if necessary, adjust this value, which reflects the value of the fee simple interest, for the property interest being appraised to arrive at the indicated value of the specified interest in the property.

Site Value

In the cost approach, the estimated market value of the site is added to the depreciated cost of the improvements. The value of the site depends on its potential highest and best use. Site value can be estimated using various techniques, which are discussed in Chapter 14. Appraisers must remember that the site value estimates produced with these techniques reflect the value of the fee simple interests in the site. If another interest, e.g., land lease, is being appraised, the site value indication may have to be adjusted.

Reproduction or Replacement Cost of the Improvements

The cost to construct an improvement on the effective appraisal date may be developed as the estimated reproduction or replacement cost of the improvement. The theoretical base for the cost approach is reproduction cost, but replacement cost is commonly used since it is easier to obtain. An important distinction must be made between the terms.

Reproduction cost is often difficult to estimate because the improvements may include materials that are now unavailable and construction standards may have changed. Nevertheless, reproduction cost usually provides a basis for measuring depreciation from all causes when such measurement is necessary. In estimating reproduction cost, appraisers must ensure that their data sources are thorough and reliable. This function may sometimes be delegated to an engineer or builder.

The use of replacement cost, rather than reproduction cost, eliminates the need to estimate *some* forms of functional obsolescence, but other forms of functional obsolescence, physical deterioration, and external obsolescence must still be measured. The decision to use replacement cost or reproduction cost is often related to the purpose of the appraisal.

Cost Estimates

To develop complete building cost estimates, appraisers must consider direct (hard) and indirect (soft) costs. Both types of cost are essential to a reliable cost estimate. Direct construction costs include the costs of material and labor as well as the contractor's profit required to construct the improvement on the effective appraisal date. Indirect costs are other costs not included in the direct construction of improvements—e.g., professional fees, financing costs, taxes during construction, and carrying charges such as leasing commissions, sales commissions, and absorption expenses during the lease-up or sellout period. Cost estimating methods are discussed in Chapter 16.

An incentive sufficient to induce an entrepreneur to incur the risk associated with a building project must also be estimated. Interviews with developers about anticipated profit may help in estimating entrepreneurial incentive. The difference between the total cost of development and marketing and the market value of a property after completion and achievement of stabilized occupancy is the entrepreneurial profit (or loss) realized. Whether the entrepreneur actually realizes a profit depends on how well he or she has analyzed the market demand for the property, selected the site, and constructed the improvements. In the case of income-producing properties, the profit realized will also depend on the entrepreneur's ability to obtain the proper tenant mix and negotiate leases. An in-depth discussion of entrepreneurial profit is provided in Chapter 16.

Depreciation

Depreciation is the difference between the reproduction or replacement cost of the improvements on the effective date of the appraisal and the market value of the improvements on the same date. Depreciation is caused by deterioration or obsolescence in the property. Deterioration is evidenced by wear and tear on the structure. Functional obsolescence is caused by internal property characteristics such as a poor floor plan, inadequate mechanical equipment, or functional inadequacy or superadequacy due to size or other characteristics. External obsolescence is created by conditions outside the property such as a lack of demand, changing property uses in the area, or national economic conditions. Some types of depreciation interact with one another, and the analysis of depreciation from all causes is cumulative. The various methods used to estimate depreciation are discussed and illustrated in Chapter 17.

Final Value Indication

The appraiser should make sure that the value indicated by the cost approach is estimated as of the effective appraisal date and that it is consistent with value indications derived from the other approaches to value. For example, an appraiser may be asked to estimate the market value of the fee simple interest in an income-producing property both upon completion of the building improvements and when stabilized occupancy is achieved. The cost estimates used in the cost approach should reflect the construction time required to complete the improvements as well as all marketing, sales, or lease-up costs incurred to achieve stabilized occupancy or the required sales in a normal market. Thus, an adjustment for external obsolescence or a prolonged absorption period should be made to reflect current occupancy if the building has not achieved stabilized occupancy as of the effective appraisal date. *Stabilized occupancy is defined as occupancy at that point in time when abnormalities in supply and demand or any additional transitory conditions cease to exist and the existing conditions are those expected to continue over the economic life of the property.* The concept of value at stabilization is based on stabilized occupancy—i.e., occupancy without significant fluctuations.

In reconciling the value indications derived from the various approaches to value, care must be taken to ensure consistency in the effective appraisal date and the purpose of the appraisal. This is especially important when the appraiser is reconciling prospective value indications. Any unusual physical deterioration or functional or external obsolescence evidenced in the subject property, but not in the comparable sales, should be reflected in the adjustments made in the sales comparison approach. Such factors should also be considered in the income capitalization approach and accounted for by assuming a temporary or permanent rent loss or making an appropriate adjustment to the final value indication. Finally, an adjustment for property rights should be made to the indicated value, if appropriate, to reflect the property interest being appraised.

Key Concepts

- In the cost approach, the value of a property is based on a comparison with the cost to build a new or substitute property. The cost estimate is adjusted for the depreciation evident in the existing property.
- The cost approach is most applicable in valuing new or proposed construction when the improvements represent the highest and best use of the land and land value is well supported.
- The cost approach is also used to estimate the value of special-purpose properties and properties that are not frequently exchanged in the market. It is an essential component of feasibility studies.
- The difficulty of estimating depreciation in older properties diminishes the reliability of the cost approach.
- The appraiser begins the cost approach by estimating the value of the land as though vacant and available for development under its highest and best use.

- The appraiser's estimate of the replacement or reproduction cost of the improvement(s) as of the effective date of the appraisal includes direct costs, indirect costs, and an estimate of entrepreneurial incentive or profit.

- From the total estimated cost of the improvement(s), the appraiser deducts an estimate of depreciation, which includes physical deterioration, functional obsolescence, and external obsolescence.

- The estimated depreciated cost of the improvements plus land value represents the value of the fee simple estate. This estimate is adjusted, if necessary, to arrive at the value of the property interest being appraised. An adjustment for costs incurred during the lease-up period is required for proposed improvements.

- Cost may be estimated on two different bases—replacement cost or reproduction cost. Specific types of obsolescence would be precluded by a replacement cost estimate.

Terms

carrying charges	feasibility study
contractor's profit	functional obsolescence
cost approach	functional utility
cost estimate	incurable depreciation
curable depreciation	indirect costs (soft costs)
depreciated cost	physical deterioration
depreciation	replacement cost
direct costs (hard costs)	reproduction cost
entrepreneurial incentive (profit)	stabilized occupancy
external obsolescence	

CHAPTER SIXTEEN

Building Cost Estimates

T o apply the cost approach to value, an appraiser must prepare an estimate of the cost of the improvements as of the effective date of appraisal. Such an estimate can be prepared by an appraiser who understands construction plans, specifications, materials, and techniques and can access a variety of data sources or computer programs available for this purpose. Alternatively, the work can be done with the assistance of expert cost estimators. In either case, the appraiser is responsible for the result. Existing improvements should be carefully inspected and described by all individuals who are delegated to estimate costs. Proposed improvements may be valued based on plans and specifications provided the appraiser discloses that the improvements do not exist and that the appraisal is conditioned on their completion as specified.

This chapter explains the distinction between estimates of reproduction and replacement cost and identifies and discusses the components of cost: direct costs, indirect costs, and entrepreneurial incentive (profit). It also briefly describes sources of cost data and presents the three methods appraisers use to estimate cost: the comparative-unit method, the unit-in-place method, and the quantity survey method.

Reproduction and Replacement Cost Estimates

From a theoretical standpoint, the cost estimate used in the cost approach to value is the cost to create duplicate improvements as of the effective appraisal date. This is known as an estimate of *reproduction cost*. An existing building, however, may incorporate materials, construction techniques, or design elements that are now out-of-date and would not be reproduced. Or a structure may exhibit a combination of features that diverge from the current standards for building components, for which cost estimates are readily available. In these situations it is common appraisal practice to estimate the cost to create improvements that would provide comparable utility. This produces an estimate of *replacement cost*. Cost estimates can vary significantly depending on whether reproduction cost or replacement cost is used; the cost basis selected for a particular appraisal must be clearly explained in the report to avoid misunderstanding.

Reproduction cost is the estimated cost to construct, at current prices as of the effective appraisal date, an exact duplicate or replica of the building being appraised, using the same materials, construction standards, design, layout, and quality of workmanship, and embodying all the deficiencies, superadequacies, and obsolescence of the subject building.

Replacement cost is the estimated cost to construct, at current prices as of the effective appraisal date, a building with utility equivalent to the building being appraised, using modern materials and current standards, design, and layout.

Costs

Capital expenditures that are directly related to the construction of the physical improvements (e.g., contract costs) are called *direct* or *hard costs*. Capital costs that are indirectly related to the construction of the improvements (e.g., financing) are called *indirect* or *soft costs*. Because the entrepreneur provides the inspiration, drive, and coordination involved in the overall project, the difference between the cost of development and the value of a property after completion is the *entrepreneurial profit* realized. The true measure of entrepreneurial profit is determined by surveying profit expectations in the market. The estimate of reproduction cost new or replacement cost new is not complete until all costs, including entrepreneurial profit, have been considered.

Direct Costs

Direct costs are expenditures for the labor and materials used in the construction of improvements. The overhead and profit of the general contractor and various subcontractors are part of the usual construction contract and, therefore, represent direct costs that should always be included in the cost estimate. Direct costs also include the cost of:

- Building permits
- Materials, products, and equipment
- Labor used in construction
- Equipment used in construction
- Security during construction
- Contractor's shack and temporary fencing
- Material storage facilities
- Power line installation and utility costs
- Contractor's profit and overhead, including job supervision; worker's compensation; and fire, liability, and unemployment insurance
- Performance bonds

A building can cost substantially more than is typical if items such as walls and windows are insulated or thicker slabs are used to accommodate greater floor loads. Because the quality of materials and labor greatly influences costs, the appraiser should be familiar with the costs of the materials used in the subject property. The competitive situation in the local market can also affect cost estimates. Actual contractor bids based on the same set of specifications can vary substantially. A contractor who is working at capacity is inclined to make a high bid, while one who needs the work is likely to submit a lower figure.

Indirect Costs

Indirect costs are expenditures or allowances that are necessary for construction, but are not typically part of the construction contract. Indirect costs may include:

- Architectural and engineering fees for plans, plan checks, surveys to establish building lines and grades, and environmental studies
- Appraisal, consulting, accounting, and legal fees
- The cost of carrying the investment in land and contract payments during construction (If the property is financed, the points, fees or service charges, and interest on construction loans are indirect costs.)
- All-risk insurance expense and ad valorem taxes during construction
- The cost of carrying the investment in the property after construction is complete, but before stabilized occupancy is achieved
- Supplemental capital investment in tenant improvements or leasing commissions
- Marketing costs, sales commissions, and title transfers
- Administrative expenses of the developer
- The cost of title change

The items cited above reflect typical indirect costs incurred in a balanced market. In markets that are out of balance, higher costs may result from a prolonged absorption period—e.g., additional carrying costs, tenant improvements, leasing commissions, and marketing and administrative expenses. These costs should be considered as part of the estimate of external obsolescence.

Some indirect costs, such as architectural fees and property taxes, are generally related to the size and cost of the project; these are best estimated as a percentage of direct costs. Other costs, such as leasing and sales commissions, are related to the type of property or market practice. Still others, such as appraisal fees and environmental studies, are a function of the time required to accomplish the task. The indirect costs of carrying an investment during and after construction is a combination of all of the above. Although total indirect costs are sometimes estimated as a percentage of direct costs, more detailed studies of these costs are recommended. Such studies should become easier to compile as more computer applications are developed.

Entrepreneurial Incentive and Entrepreneurial Profit

Entrepreneurial incentive is a market-derived figure that represents the amount an entrepreneur expects to receive as repayment for his expenditure (direct and indirect costs) and as compensation for providing coordination and expertise and assuming the risks associated with the development of a project. Entrepreneurial profit is the difference between total cost of development and marketing and the market value of a property after completion and achievement of stabilized occupancy. Entrepreneurial incentive is what motivates an entrepreneur—the reward the entrepreneur anticipates receiving. The frame of reference for entrepreneurial incentive is forward-looking. The amount the entrepreneur actually achieves by the end of the development and marketing periods is entrepreneurial profit. The frame of reference for entrepreneurial profit is backward-looking.

If the cost of developing a property is used to provide an indication of value, the appraiser must recognize the contribution of the entrepreneur and consider the inclusion of entrepreneurial profit in addition to direct and indirect costs. An entrepreneur pays no more for land and improvements than is needed to provide an appropriate profit on the specific project. If realizing a profit does not appear feasible, the entrepreneur will not proceed with the project. This does not mean that the entrepreneur is guaranteed a reward for his or her efforts. Expenditures do not guarantee value. There is no certainty that any component of cost will create commensurate value, and the residual nature of an entrepreneurial reward makes it far from certain. Nevertheless, entrepreneurship represents a legitimate cost of development and should be included in the estimate of development costs.[1] Entrepreneurial profit can take the form of profit on a sale, additional return on an investment in an operating property, or use value to the entrepreneur.

The amount of profit is related to the stage of development. The developer starts earning a profit from the start of the project. This profit increases as the land is acquired, plans are drawn up, permits are approved, financing is secured, contracts are doled out, construction is completed, and the units are sold off. It is difficult to estimate exactly how much is earned at each phase of the project.

In the cost approach, entrepreneurial profit is added to the direct and indirect costs of developing the property. In the development method, which is a specific application of the income capitalization approach, entrepreneurial profit is included among the costs of development deducted from the anticipated gross sales price of the finished units to arrive at an estimate of land value.

Potential Problems in Estimating Entrepreneurial Profit

The estimation of entrepreneurial profit may present problems for an appraiser in four ways. First, some appraisers point out that the value associated with the amenities of a property may be such that its sales price far exceeds the sum of the development costs (land, building, and marketing). These practitioners contend that it would be a mistake to attribute the entire difference between the sale price and the total development costs to entrepreneurial profit. Thus, to ensure the reasonableness of the entrepreneurial profit estimate, an appraiser should carefully examine the source of additional property value over and above the cost of development.

Second, some practitioners observe that in owner-built, owner-occupied properties, entrepreneurial profit often represents an intangible. Entrepreneurial profit is realized

---

1. In analyzing the components of reward and compensation anticipated by an entrepreneur, the appraiser may choose to further distinguish between the concepts of entrepreneurial incentive and developer's fee. *Entrepreneurial incentive* reflects the projected return required to attract an entrepreneur to invest capital in a project, based on market expectations. Entrepreneurial incentive may be expressed as a rate or percentage of cost.

   In larger projects, a *developer's fee* is often considered; this fee is distinct from entrepreneurial incentive. The developer's fee represents compensation for the overall management of the project, i.e., the time, energy, and experience the developer invests in the project and the risks the developer takes. The developer's fee is equivalent to the salary the developer might otherwise obtain. The developer's fee may also be expressed as a rate. Care should be taken to distinguish the developer's fee from the fee paid to a project management firm for the supervision of on-site contractors or subcontractors in the event the developer delegates the construction management role. Finally, the developer's fee should not be confused with the contractor's profit and overhead, which are considered among the direct costs of construction.

   Some practitioners identify *project profit* as the difference between the total cost of the project and its sale price or market value. In a well-conceived enterprise, project profit may be expected to cover both entrepreneurial incentive and the developer's fee. In a poorly conceived project, there may be no project profit, and perhaps even a project loss. In such a scenario entrepreneurial incentive may not be realized.

   To avoid confusion, it is advisable to define *entrepreneurial profit* and *developer's fee* specifically in the appraisal report. The terms are sometimes used interchangeably, and both are subject to multiple interpretations. Some practitioners associate developer's fee primarily with subdivision development. Others use the term to refer to oversight of project development from inception to completion, and include it among the direct and indirect costs of development.

only when the property is first sold, even if the sale takes place years after the property was built. Over time, entrepreneurial profit becomes obscured by the appreciation in property value.

Third, the way in which comparable properties have been developed affects the availability of data. Appraisers are usually able to calculate entrepreneurial profit from actual cost comparables for speculatively built properties such as condominiums and multifamily developments. In the value estimate of a speculatively built property, entrepreneurial profit represents a return to the developer for the skills employed and the risks incurred, although this return may differ from the return that was anticipated. In large-scale developments, however, the issue is complicated because the developer's profit may not reflect the proportionate contributions of the improved site and the improvement to the overall property value. Developers of tract subdivisions, for example, often realize most of their profit on the value of the houses built on the finished lots, not the value of the lots.

Data on entrepreneurial profit for custom-built properties may not be available if the property owner who contracted the actual builders was acting as the developer. The prices of upscale, custom-built properties often reflect the attractiveness of these amenity-laden properties as well as the high costs of the materials used. Thus, the breakdown of costs for custom-built properties may not be comparable to the breakdown for speculatively built properties, which further complicates the task of estimating a rate of entrepreneurial profit. Theoretically, however, the value of custom-built properties should also reflect an entrepreneurial profit.

Fourth and finally, the appraiser must scrutinize the cost data on which the value estimate is based to determine whether or not an allowance for entrepreneurial profit has already been made. If this is not done, the developer's profit could be included twice. Data derived from sales of comparable sites often include a profit for the land developer. Cost estimating services quote direct costs (e.g., contractor's profit) and indirect costs (e.g., sales costs), but they do not usually provide estimates of developer's profit. Since different sources of data reflect costs in different ways, the appraiser should identify where the developer's profit is considered in the estimate, i.e., whether it is an item already included in cost plus land value or a stand-alone item added to cost plus land value.

Estimating Entrepreneurial Profit

Depending on market practice, entrepreneurial profit may be estimated as a percentage of direct costs, direct and indirect costs, direct and indirect costs plus site value, or the value of the completed project. In the following example, the dollar amounts and ratios, or relative percentages, of entrepreneurial profit are presented only for purposes of illustration. In this case, the developer's fee, as distinct from entrepreneurial profit, is included among indirect costs.

Base	% Applied		Entrepreneurial Profit
Direct cost	$ 545,000 x 22.0%	=	$120,000 (rounded)
Direct cost + indirect cost	$ 545,000 55,000 $ 600,000 x 20.0%	=	$120,000
Direct cost + indirect cost + land value	$ 545,000 55,000 200,000 $ 800,000 x 15.0%	=	$120,000
Direct cost + indirect cost + land value + entrep. profit	$ 545,000 55,000 200,000 120,000 $ 920,000 x 13.0%	=	$120,000 (rounded)

Presumably, the entrepreneurial profit would be the same amount regardless of how it is calculated—i.e., as 22%, 20%, 15%, or 13% of the base cost selected. The final calculation of entrepreneurial profit as a percentage of the value of the completed project would actually be expressed as follows:

$$(\$ 800,000 \times 0.13)/(1 - 0.13) = \$ 120,000 \text{ (rounded)}.$$

Potential entrepreneurial profit should be derived through market analysis and interviews with developers to determine the expectations of profit required as motivation or incentive to undertake a particular development. Less emphasis should be given to historical profit margins. Historical profits are records of results and often differ from the anticipated profit that originally motivated the entrepreneur to proceed with a project. Profit is not as important as incentive.

In depressed markets the appraiser should focus on whether diminished entrepreneurial profit or entrepreneurial loss represents a form of external obsolescence. Considering entrepreneurship as a component of cost in a depressed market helps establish a basis for estimating the level of rent required to induce new construction, which may in turn provide some insight into problems of absorption and stabilized occupancy.

Estimating an appropriate amount of entrepreneurial profit is a continued challenge for appraisers because expectations of profit vary with different market conditions and property types. Typical relationships between profit and other costs are difficult to establish.

Cost Data Sources

Construction contracts for buildings similar to the building being appraised are primary sources of comparable cost data, but in their absence local building contractors and professional cost estimators can be reliable data sources. Some appraisers maintain comprehensive files of current cost data that include current costs for completed houses, apartments, hotels, office buildings, retail buildings, and industrial buildings. These costs can provide a basis for calculating the cost to construct an existing or proposed building.

Many cost-estimating services publish data for estimating the current cost of improvements. A few of these services are Marshall and Swift Publication Company; Boeckh Publications, a division of Thompson Publishing Corporation; and the F. W. Dodge Corporation.

Published cost manuals usually include direct unit costs, but an appraiser must research the market to find which costs are most applicable to the appraisal assignment. Manuals almost always include such direct costs as contractor's overhead and profit and some indirect costs such as escrow fees, legal fees, interest on construction loans, financing fees, carrying charges, and property taxes, but they may not include permanent financing fees and lease-up, sales, marketing, or carrying costs on the investment after construction, but before stabilized occupancy is reached. National cost services list the costs of many site improvements separately, rather than as part of building costs. These data include the costs of demolition, roads, storm drains, rough grading, soil compaction, utilities, and jurisdictional utility hookup fees and assessments. Entrepreneurial profit is rarely, if ever, included in cost service data. The appraiser must estimate such costs separately and include them in the total reproduction or replacement cost estimate. Computer-assisted cost-estimating services may also provide useful data.

Cost-Index Trending

Cost services often provide cost indexes, which are used to convert a known historical cost into a current cost estimate. The manuals identify base year and regional multipliers for specific building components. Cost index trending is useful for estimating the current cost of one-of-a-kind items when standard costs are not available.

The following example illustrates the application of cost-index trending. Assume the contract cost for constructing a building in January of 1994 was $1,000,000. The index for January of 1994 is 285.1 and the current index is 327.3. To trend the historical cost into a current cost, the current cost index is divided by the historical cost index and the result is multiplied by the historical cost. In this case the current cost is calculated as follows:

$$327.3 \div 285.1 = 1.148$$

$$1.148 \times \$1,000,000 = \$1,148,000$$

Problems can arise when cost index data are used to estimate current cost. The accuracy of the figures cannot always be ascertained, especially when it is not clear which components are included in the data (i.e., only direct costs or direct costs and some indirect costs). Furthermore, historical costs may not be typical for the time period, and the construction methods used at the time of the historical cost may differ from those used on the effective appraisal date. Although cost-index trending may be helpful in confirming a cost estimate, it is not a reliable substitute for the cost-estimating methods described in the following section.

Cost-Estimating Methods

The three traditional cost-estimating methods are the comparative-unit method, the unit-in-place method, and the quantity survey method. The quantity survey method produces a cost estimate based on a detailed inventory of the labor, materials, and equipment used in the subject improvements. The comparative-unit and the unit-in-place methods provide less detail, but they are the bases for the cost estimates used in most appraisals.

Measurement

Although buildings can be measured in several ways, appraisers should measure buildings according to local custom. To use cost service data effectively, an appraiser must understand the measurement technique used by the service.

Area measurement is widely used for all types of structures. It is most appropriate for buildings constructed to meet basic standards of height. A building's outside measurements are used to compute gross area. Then the area of all projections or cantilevered space are added, and the areas of insets or recesses are subtracted. The gross building area is the sum of the areas of all floor levels in the structure. In certain locations dwellings are measured in terms of the area of ground floor coverage; in others the gross area of living space is calculated. For example, a two-story house that measures 24 feet by 24 feet with an unfinished basement and attic has an area of 1,152 square feet (24 x 24 x 2). Guidelines established by the Fannie Mae call for the measurement of gross living area, which is defined to include finished and habitable, above-grade living area only. On Fannie Mae residential appraisal forms, finished basement or attic areas must be calculated and shown separately in the cost estimate.

The three standard measures used by commercial and residential appraisers are net rentable area, gross leasable area (upon which shopping center rents are based), and gross living area for residential space. Net rentable area (*NRA*) is the floor area of a building occupied by tenants, excluding hallways, elevator shafts, stairways, toilets, and wall thicknesses. Gross leasable area (*GLA*) is the total floor area designed for occupancy and the exclusive use of tenants, including basements and mezzanines, and measured from the center of the interior partitioning to outside wall surfaces. Gross living area (*GLA*) is the total area of finished, above-grade residential space, excluding unheated areas such as porches and balconies.

Comparative-Unit Method

The comparative-unit method is used to derive a cost estimate in terms of dollars per unit of area. The method employs the known costs of similar structures adjusted for market conditions and physical differences. Indirect costs may be included in the unit cost or computed separately. If the comparable properties and the subject property are in different markets, the appraiser may need to make an adjustment for location.

Unit costs vary with size; all else being equal, unit costs decrease as buildings increase in area. This reflects the fact that plumbing, heating units, elevators, doors, windows, and similar building components do not usually cost proportionately more in a larger building than in a smaller one.

The comparative-unit method is relatively uncomplicated, practical, and widely used. Unit-cost figures are usually expressed in terms of gross building dimensions converted to square feet. Total cost is estimated by comparing the subject building with similar, recently constructed buildings for which contract prices are available. The trend in costs between the date of the contract (or construction) and the effective appraisal date must be factored into the comparison.

In the absence of contract prices, an indication of the total cost new of a building can be extracted from sales of similar, newly constructed buildings so long as these tests are met: 1) the improvements reflect the highest and best use of the site; 2) the property has reached stabilized occupancy; 3) supply and demand are in balance; and 4) site value can be reasonably ascertained. The value of the site is subtracted from the sale price of each comparable property and the residual indicates the cost new of the improvements.

Most appraisers using the comparative-unit method apply unit-cost figures developed using data from a recognized cost service. Unit costs for the benchmark buildings found in cost-estimating manuals usually start with a base building of a specified size to which additions or deductions are made. If the subject building is larger than the benchmark building, the unit cost is usually lower; if the subject building is smaller, its unit cost will probably be higher.

Because few buildings are identical in terms of size, design, and quality of construction, the benchmark building is often different from the subject building. Different roof designs and irregular perimeters and building shapes can affect comparative-unit costs substantially. The following example illustrates this situation:

	Building A	Building B
Building dimensions	100 x 100	50 x 200
Building area in square feet	10,000	10,000
Perimeter walls in linear feet	400	500
Ratio: area to perimeter	25:1	20:1
Cost of walls		
Per linear foot	$50	$50
Total cost	$20,000	$25,000
Per square foot of building	$2.00	$2.50

To develop a reliable estimate with the comparative-unit method, an appraiser should calculate the unit cost from similar improvements or adjust the unit-cost figure to reflect variations in size, shape, finish, and HVAC equipment. The unit cost applied should also reflect any changes in cost levels between the date of the benchmark unit cost and the effective appraisal date. The ratio between the costs of equipment and the basic building shell has increased consistently through the years. Equipment tends to increase unit building costs and depreciate more rapidly than other building components.

To use area cost estimates, an appraiser assembles, analyzes, and catalogs data on actual building costs. These costs should be divided into general construction categories, and separate figures should be used to account for special finishes or equipment. The overall area unit cost can then be broken down into its components, which may help the appraiser adjust a known cost for the presence or absence of items in later comparisons.

The apparent simplicity of the comparative-unit method can be misleading. To develop dependable unit-cost figures, an appraiser must exercise judgment and carefully compare the subject building with similar or standard structures for which actual costs are known. Errors can result if an appraiser selects a unit cost that is not comparable to the building being appraised. When it is correctly applied, however, the method produces reasonably accurate reproduction or replacement cost estimates.

The warehouse shown in Figure 16.1 will be used to illustrate the comparative-unit method (and later the unit-in-place, or segregated cost, method). A detailed description of the warehouse follows Figure 16.1.

| Figure 16.1 | **Plan of a Warehouse** |

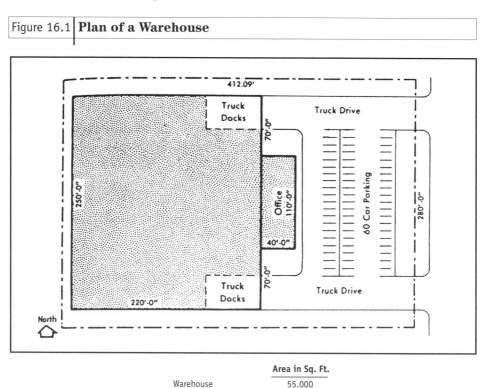

	Area in Sq. Ft.
Warehouse	55,000
Office	4,400
Total building	59,400

Basic Construction

Exterior walls, block and brick facade; structural steel columns, steel deck; rigid insulation; built-up tar and gravel roofing. Structure has full sprinkler system. Other details are typical.

Warehouse Area

Heating to 65°F at -10°F outside temperature; clear ceiling height, 18 feet; bays, 41½ x 36½ feet; structural steel framing; insulated roof deck and slab over steel bar joists; 6-in.

concrete floor slab at grade, waterproofed; electric service, 600 amperes, 120/240 volts. Four overhead wood truck doors; one washroom that contains three fixtures.

Office Area

Heated, with air-conditioning equipment rated at 15 tons; ceiling height, 9 feet; flooring, asphalt tile over concrete slab; illumination, 60 foot-candle intensity, fluorescent lighting; ceiling, acoustic tile; partitions, stud and drywall; two washrooms that contain six fixtures.

Table 16.1 shows how comparative-unit costs from a published cost manual can be applied to the warehouse building. Calculations such as those shown can be used to confirm a cost indication obtained from construction contracts for similar properties in the same market as the property being appraised on or about the effective appraisal date. Published data can be used independently when no local cost data are available.

In Table 16.1 an adjustment for the warehouse's sprinkler system was made using a square-foot unit cost. In other cases similar adjustments may be appropriate for observed physical differences in the amount of office area, construction features, or specific equipment.

Cost manuals rarely include all indirect costs or an allowance for entrepreneurial profit, so adjustments must often be made to obtain an indication of the total cost new. In Table 16.1 adjustments are made for: 1) indirect costs not included in the base price quoted in the cost manual; 2) indirect costs after construction but before stabilized occupancy is reached; and 3) entrepreneurial profit calculated as a percentage of total direct and indirect costs. The estimate of the value of the site and site improvements was derived through sales comparison.

Table 16.1 indicates the cost new of the warehouse building plus the site value, but the result shown is more likely to represent the value of a close substitute than a duplicate structure. Cost services use typical buildings for their base cost, so an appraiser can apply the comparative-unit method, develop reliable adjustment amounts and factors, and produce a reasonable property value estimate.

Construction contracts normally include other improvements to the land such as auxiliary buildings, driveways, pools, underground drainage facilities, rail sidings, fences, and landscaping. The possible combinations and varied value contributions of these improvements can cause a wide divergence in unit cost if the total contract is related to the size of the major improvement only. Therefore, when actual contract costs from the local market are used in the comparative-unit method, it is imperative that the costs of these other improvements be excluded from the base price.

Unit-in-Place Method

In the unit-in-place, or segregated cost, method unit costs for various building components as installed are applied to the number of components in the structure or to linear, area, volume, or other appropriate measures of these components. Using this method the appraiser computes a unit cost based on the actual quantity of materials used plus the labor of assembly required for each square foot of area. For example, the cost can be applied based on the square feet of floor area or linear feet of wall of a certain height. The same procedure is applied for other structural components.

Table 16.1	**Warehouse Property--Comparative-Unit Method**	
Base cost per sq. ft.		$ 27.22
Add for sprinkler system per sq. ft.		1.14
Subtotal		$ 28.36
Adjustment for ceiling height variations		x 1.086
Subtotal		$ 30.80
Adjustment for area/perimeter		x 0.895
Subtotal		$ 27.57
Current cost multiplier		x 1.120
Subtotal		$ 30.88
Local cost multiplier		x 0.980
Total cost per sq. ft. (from manual)		$ 30.26
Indirect costs not included in cost manual data*†		x 1.050
Subtotal		$ 31.77
Indirect costs from completion to stabilized occupancy*†		x 1.070
Subtotal		$ 33.99
Entrepreneurial profit at 10.0% of total direct & indirect costs		
$33.99 x 0.10		+ 3.39
Subtotal		$37.38
Total cost new for warehouse building:		
59,400 sq. ft. @ $37.38	=	$ 2,220,372
		$ 2,220,000 (rounded)
Site value & site improvements per sq. ft. of building		
59,400 sq. ft. @ 10.94	=	$ 650,000 (rounded)
Total value indicated by the cost approach	=	$ 2,870,000

Source: *Marshall Valuation Service* (Los Angeles: Marshall and Swift Publication Co.).

* Note. Contractor's overhead and profit and some other indirect costs are included in these base costs and adjustments. The source of published cost data should be studied for a complete understanding of what is included in quoted costs.

† For purposes of simplicity, a percentage was applied to account for indirect costs. A breakdown of the costs that comprise these estimates should be provided by the appraiser to support the percentages applied.

Unit-in-place cost estimates are made using standardized costs for structural components as installed. Excavating costs are typically expressed in dollars per cubic yard; foundation costs may be expressed in dollars per linear foot or cubic yard of concrete. Floor construction may be reduced to dollars per square foot and interior partitions may be expressed in dollars per linear foot. The basic unit for roofing is called a *square*, which represents 100 square feet. The unit-in-place measure on which the cost is based may be the measure employed in a particular trade, such as the cost per ton of air-conditioning; alternatively, any appropriate unit of measurement may be selected.

All constituent unit costs are totaled to provide the estimated direct cost of the entire improvement. Contractor's overhead and profit may be included in the unit cost figures provided by some cost services, or they may be computed separately. The appraiser must ascertain exactly what is included in any unit price quoted. Indirect costs are usually computed separately.

The following example shows how the cost of a brick veneer wall would be calculated on a unit-in-place basis. Costs such as these vary with market conditions and location; the figures shown are used only for purposes of illustration.

Cost	Unit	Description
$460.00	per 1,000	4-in. face brick, installed: common bond, ½-in. struck joints, mortar, scaffolding, and cleaning included
$360.00	per 1,000 bd. ft.	Dimension lumber, erected: 2-in.-x-4-in. wood stud framing, 16 inches on center
$0.42	per sq. ft.	Sheathing, installed: impregnated 4 ft. x 8 ft., ½-in.
$0.22	per sq. ft.	Insulation, installed: 2½-in. foil backing on one side
$0.30	per sq. ft.	Drywall: ½-in. with finished joints
$0.25	per sq. ft.	Paint: primer and one coat flat

From these data the cost per square foot of wall can be estimated as follows:

Cost	Unit	Description
$3.45	per 7½	Bricks
$0.24	per ⅔ bd. ft.	Wood stud framing
$0.42	per sq. ft.	Sheathing
$0.22	per sq. ft.	Insulation
$0.30	per sq. ft.	½-in. drywall
+ $0.25	per sq. ft.	Paint
$4.88	per sq. ft.	Total for finished wall

After calculating the unit cost of $4.88 per square foot, the appraiser can estimate the total cost of a veneer wall that meets these standards without detailing the quantities of material and labor. In practice, a cost analyst would refine the procedure by adjusting for waste and for extra framing for windows and doors, which require wall openings, lintels, and facing corners.

The unit costs for all components can be calculated in a similar fashion and, once these are established, the appraiser can estimate the cost of an entire building. However, specialized knowledge may be required to assemble the basic costs of equipment, material, and labor and to combine these costs into a final cost estimate. When fully developed, the unit-in-place method provides a substitute for a complete quantity survey and produces an accurate cost estimate with considerably less effort.

The unit-in-place concept is not limited to cubic, linear, or area units. It may also be applied to the cost of complete, installed components such as the cost of a roof truss that is fabricated off site, delivered, and erected. Unit-in-place cost estimates may be based on an appraiser's compiled data, but they are usually obtained from a cost-estimating service that provides updated monthly figures.

Table 16.2 illustrates how the unit-in-place method can be used to estimate the reproduction cost of the warehouse shown in Figure 16.1.

Table 16.2	Warehouse Property--Unit-in-Place Method			
Excavation	59,400 cu. ft.	@	$ 0.24	=	$ 14,256
Site	115,385 sq. ft.	@	$ 0.17	=	19,615
Foundation	59,400 sq. ft.	@	$ 1.79	=	106,326
Framing	59,400 sq. ft.	@	$ 4.82	=	286,308
Floor (concrete)	59,400 sq. ft.	@	$ 3.12	=	185,328
Floor (asphalt tile)	4,400 sq. ft.	@	$ 1.02	=	4,488
Ceiling (acoustical tile)	4,400 sq. ft.	@	$ 4.35	=	19,140
Plumbing (3 rooms)					
Fixtures	9 fixtures	@	$2,525	=	22,725
Drains	6 units	@	$ 380	=	2,280
Sprinkler system	59,400 sq. ft.	@	$ 1.48	=	87,912
HVAC	55,000 sq. ft.	@	$ 0.84	=	46,200
	4,400 sq. ft.	@	$ 4.20	=	18,480
Electrical & lighting	59,400 sq. ft.	@	$ 1.70	=	100,980
Exterior wall					
Concrete block	15,180 sq. ft.	@	$12.09	=	183,526
Brick facade	5,060 sq. ft.	@	$13.80	=	69,828
Partitions					
Walls	8,650 sq. ft.	@	$ 3.70	=	32,005
Doors	10 sq. ft.	@	$ 103	=	1,030
Overhead doors (10 ft.x 12 ft.x 4 ft.)	480 sq. ft.	@	$18.25	=	8,760
Roof joists & deck	59,400 sq. ft.	@	$ 6.86	=	407,484
Roof cover & insulation	59,400 sq. ft.	@	$ 2.18	=	129,492
Misc. specified items					30,000
Subtotal					$1,776,163
Current cost multiplier: (Different base from Table 16.1)					x 1.030
Subtotal					$1,829,448
Local cost multiplier					x 0.980
Total cost (from manual—$30.18 per sq. ft.)					$1,792,859

Table 16.2 continued	

Total cost	$1,792,859
Indirect costs not included in cost manual*†	x 1.100
Subtotal	$1,972,145
Indirect costs from completion to date of stabilized occupancy*†	x 1.050
Subtotal	$2,070,752
Entrepreneurial profit at 10.0% of total direct & indirect costs	
$2,070,752 x 0.10	= 207,075
Total cost new ($38.35 per sq. ft.)	$ 2,277,827
	(rounded) $ 2,278,000
Plus site value & site improvements	650,000
Total project value	$ 2,928,000

Source: *Marshall Valuation Service* (Los Angeles: Marshall and Swift Publication Co.).

* Note. Contractor's overhead and profit and some indirect costs are included in the base costs; architect's fees and other indirect costs are not. The source of published cost data should be studied for a complete understanding of what is included in the quoted costs.

† For purposes of simplicity, a percentage was applied to account for indirect costs. A breakdown of the costs that comprise these estimates should be provided by the appraiser to support the percentages applied.

In Table 16.2 adjustments are made for: 1) indirect costs not included in the cost manual's base price; 2) indirect costs after construction, but before stabilized occupancy is reached; and 3) entrepreneurial profit calculated as a percentage of total direct and indirect costs. The value of site improvements may be estimated separately on a depreciated cost basis and added to the depreciated cost of the improvements. More typically, the value of site improvements, estimated either on a depreciated cost basis or extracted from market data, may be added as a contributory amount to total property value.

Quantity Survey Method

The most comprehensive and accurate method of cost estimating is the quantity survey method. A quantity survey is a computation that reflects the quantity and quality of all materials used in the construction of an improvement and all categories of labor hours required. Unit costs are applied to these figures to arrive at a total cost estimate for materials and labor; then the contractor adds a margin for contingencies, overhead, and profit.

Depending on the size of the project and the resources of the contractor, the quantity survey and cost calculations may be prepared by a single cost estimator or by a number of subcontractors whose bids are compiled by a general contractor and submitted as the final cost estimate. In either case, the analysis details the quantity, quality, and cost of all materials furnished by the general contractor or subcontractor and the appropriate cost allowances.

A general contractor's cost breakdown for the warehouse shown in Figure 16.1 is summarized in Table 16.3. This is only a summary; the specific quantities and costs are not indicated.

Table 16.3	Warehouse Property—Contractor's Breakdown

General conditions of contract	$ 7,854
Excavating & grading	24,781
Concrete	182,053
Carpentry	25,473
Masonry	194,231
Structural steel	280,343
Joist, deck, & deck slab	329,827
Roofing	57,494
Insulation	32,378
Sash	5,256
Glazing	11,329
Painting	7,611
Acoustical material	5,803
Flooring	3,335
Electric	75,334
HVAC	67,560
Piping	6,458
Plumbing & sprinkler system	77,461
Subtotal	$1,394,581
Contingencies @ 5.0%	69,729
Contractor's overhead & profit @ 12.0%	167,350
Total proposed contract costs ($27.46 per sq. ft.)	$1,631,660
(rounded)	$1,631,700
Indirect costs before, during, and after construction*	x 1.27
Subtotal	$2,072,259
Entrepreneurial profit	
$2,072,259 x 0.10	+ 207,226
Total reproduction cost new	$2,279,485
Plus site value & site improvements	+ 650,000
Total project value	$2,929,485
(rounded)	$2,929,000

* For purposes of simplicity, a percentage was applied to account for indirect costs. A breakdown of the costs that comprise these estimates should be provided by the appraiser to support the percentages applied.

Contractor bids do not usually include indirect costs or entrepreneurial profit. The analysis illustrated in Table 16.3 reflects indirect costs and the calculation of entrepreneurial profit as a percentage of total direct and indirect costs. In the examples presented, indirect costs are considered in various stages of the cost estimating procedure.

Although site improvements such as parking facilities, landscaping, and signage are commonly included in a general contractor's bid, they are not detailed in Table 16.3. They should be included in a cost estimate of all improvements. In a cost estimate of an existing building, a separate itemization of site improvements facilitates the consideration of accrued depreciation. Because the quantity survey method produces a cost estimate of a duplicate building, Table 16.3 indicates the reproduction cost of the warehouse building as of the effective appraisal date.

In recent years the percentage of a general contract that is subcontracted out has increased. Subcontractors have become more efficient in their specializations. Subcontractor unit-in-place costs compare favorably with the cost of work done by employees of the general contractor, and the general contractor can operate with reduced overhead. To produce a quantity survey estimate, each contractor and subcontractor must provide a breakdown of materials, labor, overhead, and profit. The contractor's profit may depend on the volume of work that the contractor has lined up.

Although the quantity survey method produces a complete cost analysis of the improvements being appraised, it is time-consuming, costly, and frequently requires the services of an experienced cost estimator. For these reasons this method is seldom used in routine appraisal assignments.

Key Concepts

- Replacement cost refers to the cost to construct, at current prices, a substitute property that provides utility equivalent to that of the property being appraised, using modern materials and current standards, design, and layout. Replacement cost is used in most appraisals.

- Reproduction cost refers to the cost to construct, at current prices, a duplicate or replica of the property being appraised, using the same materials, construction standards, design, layout, and quality of workmanship, and embodying all the deficiencies, superadequacies, and obsolescence found in the subject property.

- Direct (hard) costs are capital expenditures directly related to the physical construction of the improvement, e.g., labor and materials.

- Indirect (soft) costs are capital expenditures that are not typically a part of construction, e.g., professional fees, financing, property taxes and all-risk insurance during construction, and marketing and lease-up costs.

- Entrepreneurial profit is that portion of cost that reflects the entrepreneur's contribution and reward for the risk and expertise associated with the development. The estimation of entrepreneurial profit is problematic, but the estimate is a necessary component of total cost. Several methods can be used to estimate entrepreneurial profit, but the estimate should reflect the market.

- Cost data may be obtained from construction contracts, building contractors, and published or computer-assisted cost-estimating services. Cost-index trending may be used to convert historical data into a current cost estimate.

- Building costs may be estimated using one of three methods: the comparative-unit method, the unit-in-place method, or the quantity survey method.

- In the comparative-unit method, costs are expressed in terms of dollars per unit of area or volume, based on known costs of similar structures that are adjusted for market conditions, location, and physical differences.

- The unit-in-place, or segregated cost, method estimates total building cost by adding together the unit costs of the various building components as installed.
- The quantity survey method is the most comprehensive means of estimating total cost. The quantity and quality of all materials used and all categories of labor required are estimated and unit cost figures are applied to arrive at a total cost estimate for labor and materials.

Terms

base cost	gross leasable area (*GLA*)
benchmark building	gross living area (*GLA*)
comparative-unit method	indirect costs
contractor's overhead and profit	net rentable area (*NRA*)
cost index	project profit
cost-index trending	quantity survey method
developer's fee	replacement cost
direct costs	reproduction cost
entrepreneurial incentive and profit	segregated cost method
gross building area (*GBA*)	unit-in-place method

CHAPTER SEVENTEEN

Depreciation Estimates

D epreciation is the difference between the market value of an improvement and its reproduction or replacement cost.[1] In the cost approach, an improvement's cost is considered to be an indicator of the value the improvement would have if it were new. By estimating the depreciation incurred by an improvement and deducting this estimate from the improvement's reproduction or replacement cost, an appraiser can conclude the depreciated cost of the improvement. This depreciated cost approximates the improvement's market value.

Depreciation in an improvement can result from three major causes operating individually or in combination. These causes are physical deterioration, functional obsolescence, and external obsolescence. The market recognizes the occurrence of depreciation; the appraiser merely interprets how the market perceives the effect of depreciation.

Physical deterioration refers to wear and tear from regular use and the impact of the elements. The common perception in the market is that a new structure is better than an old one. *Functional obsolescence* is caused by a flaw in the structure, materials, or design that diminishes the function, utility, and value of the improvement. The market perceives that a proper balance is better than too much or not enough. *External obsolescence* is an impairment of the utility or salability of an improvement or property due to negative influences outside the property. External obsolescence may result from adverse market conditions. Because of fixed location, real estate is subject to external influences that cannot be controlled by the property owner, landlord, or tenant.

Theoretically, depreciation can begin the moment construction is completed, even in a functional building that represents the highest and best use of a site. Improvements are rarely built under ideal circumstances and their construction takes considerable time. During the construction process, physical deterioration can be temporarily halted or even corrected, but physical deterioration tends to persist throughout the life of the improvements and usually accelerates as a building ages. Moreover, as time goes on and a building's features become dated in comparison to new buildings, functional obsolescence sets in. Consider, for example, an industrial building that was built in the early 1970s. The structure's 12-ft. ceilings, which were the market standard then, might be considered totally inadequate today when 18-ft. story heights are the norm. New buildings can also have functional obsolescence even before they are constructed, which is usually attribut-

---

1. Many of the terms appraisers use are also used by accountants, economists, and other real estate professionals. The term *accrued depreciation*, which appeared in previous editions of *The Appraisal of Real Estate,* was originally borrowed from accounting practice where it refers to the total depreciation taken on an asset from the time of purchase to the present, normally deducted from an asset's account value to derive net book value. While *accrued depreciation* has long been used in an appraisal context, the more concise term, *depreciation*, is equally suitable and has been used throughout this edition.

able to poor design. An appraiser may be able to spot the poor design of a prospective property by comparing the architect's plans with market standards, and perhaps the functional obsolescence can be eliminated before construction begins.

In the cost approach, the replacement or reproduction cost of the improvement(s) is estimated; the depreciation attributable to all causes is calculated and deducted from the cost new to arrive at the depreciated cost; and an estimate of the value of the land and site improvements is added to the depreciated cost to provide an indication of the market value of the property. Depreciation is a penalty only insofar as the market recognizes it as causing a loss in value. For some older buildings, the value loss due to depreciation may be offset by a temporary scarcity relative to demand or by an improvement's historical or architectural significance. In these situations, an appraiser should exercise caution. An imbalance in supply and demand is usually short-lived, and the scarcity's ability to offset any penalty for depreciation can quickly be eliminated. Similarly, when the historical or architectural significance of an improvement has offset the depreciation typically anticipated, the highest and best use of the property should be analyzed very carefully.

An appraiser's use of replacement cost rather than reproduction cost to derive a current cost estimate will affect the estimation of depreciation. Some forms of functional obsolescence are automatically eliminated when replacement cost is used, but other forms remain unaffected. Consider an industrial building with a poor layout and a 20-ft. story height in a market where 16-ft. story heights are the norm. A replacement cost estimate would be based on a building with a 16-ft. story height, while a reproduction cost estimate would be based on a 20-ft. story height. By using replacement cost instead of reproduction cost, the appraiser eliminates the superadequacy attributable to the story height, but not the poor layout. Moreover, any additional costs of ownership caused by the superadequacy would not be eliminated in the replacement cost estimate. If the appraiser uses replacement cost, he or she must consider any excess operating costs associated with the superadequate construction.

All three causes of depreciation--physical deterioration, functional obsolescence, and external obsolescence--reduce the value of an improvement based on its reproduction or replacement cost. Using one or more of the techniques described in this chapter, the appraiser can calculate the total amount of depreciation in a structure and, as appropriate to the assignment, allocate it among its various forms. Depreciation is then deducted from the replacement or reproduction cost of the improvement to estimate the contributory value of the improvement to the property.

Depreciation in Appraising and Accounting

The term *depreciation* is used in both accounting and appraisal so it is important to distinguish between the two usages. *Book depreciation* is an accounting term that refers to the amount of capital recapture written off for an asset on the owner's books. The term is typically used in income tax calculations to identify the amount allowed for the retirement or replacement of an asset under the tax laws. Book depreciation may also be estimated according to a depreciation schedule set by the Internal Revenue Service. Book depreciation is not market-derived, in contrast to depreciation estimates developed by appraisers which are. An appraiser's estimate of depreciation may help a client reach a conclusion about book depreciation, but the two concepts are distinct and should not be confused.

Age and Life Relationships

The appraisal concept of depreciation is based on age and life relationships, which relate to the entire improvement and also to its various components. Depreciation occurs over the life of an improvement or a component; theoretically an improvement or component will lose all of its value over its life. For example, assume that the typical life expectancy of a freestanding retail store in a market is 40 years. Theoretically, when the building is 40 years old, it will have reached the end of its life expectancy and will have lost all of its value to depreciation. The life expectancy of a water heater installed in the building will be much shorter than 40 years, and some components may have to be replaced several times over the building's 40-year life. In the development of depreciation estimates, age-life relationships are primarily used to estimate the total depreciation of the improvement and the physical deterioration of the improvement's components.

In estimating the total depreciation of an improvement, the age-life concepts most important to an appraiser are *economic life*, *effective age*, and *remaining economic life*. With respect to deterioration in the physical components, the most important age-life concepts are *useful life*, *actual age*, and *remaining useful life*.

Economic Life and Useful Life

Economic life is the period of time over which improvements contribute to property value. An improvement's economic life begins when it is built and ends when the building no longer contributes any value to the property. This period is usually shorter than the improvement's useful life, which is the total period the improvement can be expected to exist physically. If buildings are adequately maintained and worn items are periodically replaced, buildings may remain on the land long after they cease to contribute economically to property value. At the end of a building's economic life, there are several options available to the property owner: renovation, rehabilitation, remodeling or, in extreme cases, demolition and replacement with a suitable new structure.

To estimate an improvement's economic life, an appraiser studies the typical economic life expectancy of recently sold improvements similar to the subject in the market area. This technique is described in greater detail in the discussion of market extraction later in this chapter. All aspects of a property and its market, including the quality and condition of the construction, the functional utility of the improvements, and market and locational externalities must be considered in the estimation of a property's economic life. The condition and functional utility of an improvement as well as market and locational factors must also be taken into account in estimating an improvement's effective age. Although the economic life of an improvement is difficult to predict, it is shaped by a number of factors, including:

- Physical considerations--i.e., the rate at which the physical components of an improvement wear out, given the quality of construction, the use of the property, maintenance standards, and the region's climate.

- Functional considerations--i.e., the rate at which construction technology, tastes in architecture, energy efficiency, and building design change. These factors can render an improvement functionally obsolete, regardless of its age and/or condition.

- External considerations--i.e., short-term and long-term influences such as the stage of a neighborhood's life cycle, the availability and affordability of financing, and supply and demand factors.

Many physical, functional, and external considerations may not have any effect on the value of an improvement on the date of the value estimate, but they are certain to have a profound effect at some future time, say in 20, 50, or even 100 years. Although, it is difficult to forecast economic life expectancy, market study and analysis of historical trends may provide important information.

Useful life is a term that relates to the physical components of an improvement. It is the period of time over which the components of the improvement may reasonably be expected to perform the functions for which they were designed. Although the useful life of some physical components, such as concrete and steel, may be hundreds of years, it is unlikely that the improvements containing these components will have economic life expectancies that long. Accordingly, if a 40-year-old industrial building were being demolished so that its site could be redeveloped, it is probable that all components of the building would be demolished, regardless of their remaining useful life expectancies.

The components of an improvement are divided into two types. The first type, called *long-lived components*, include those elements which have a useful life at least as long as the improvement's economic life expectancy. These are usually the structural components of a building, including foundations, framing, and underground piping. The second type, called *short-lived components*, are elements which have a useful life that is shorter than the improvement's economic life expectancy. These elements usually include HVAC components, roof covering, interior decorating, and floor finishes. The importance of distinguishing between long-lived and short-lived components becomes apparent when breakdown techniques are applied. These techniques are discussed in a subsequent section.

Remaining Economic Life and Remaining Useful Life

Remaining economic life is the estimated period over which existing improvements are expected to continue to contribute to property value. Usually improvements can be regarded as investments designed to contribute to value over a long period of time. Some depreciation occurs between the date when the improvements begin to contribute to value (usually at the end of construction and/or after lease-up) and the date of the value estimate; the remaining economic life extends from the date of the value estimate to the end of the improvement's economic life. An improvement's remaining economic life is always less than or equal to its total economic life, but never more than its total economic life provided there is no change in the highest and best use of the property. *Remaining useful life* is the estimated period from the actual age of a component to the end of its total useful life expectancy. The remaining useful life of any long-lived component is equal to or, typically, greater than its remaining economic life.

Actual Age and Effective Age

Actual age, which is sometimes called *historical age* or *chronological age*, is the number of years that have elapsed since building construction was completed. Actual age serves two purposes in depreciation analysis. First, it is the initial element analyzed in the estimation of effective age. Second, it is fundamental to the age-life analysis needed to estimate physical deterioration in the long-lived and short-lived components of an improvement.

Effective age is the age indicated by the condition and utility of a structure. Similar buildings do not necessarily depreciate at the same rate. The maintenance standards of owners or occupants can influence the pace of building depreciation. If a building is better maintained than other buildings in its market area, the effective age of the building will be less than its actual age. If a building is poorly maintained, its effective age may be greater than its actual age. If a building has received typical maintenance, its effective age and actual age may be the same.

Effective age is related to remaining economic life in that the sum of the effective age and the remaining economic life is the total economic life. Conversely, the total economic life of similar structures, minus the effective age of the improvement, will approximate the remaining economic life of the subject.

Methods of Estimating Depreciation

Several methods may be used to estimate depreciation. Each is acceptable so long as the appraiser applies the method consistently, logically, and cautiously, and provided the method reflects the reaction of an informed and prudent buyer to the condition and quality of the property and the market in which the property is found. The primary goal of depreciation analysis is to identify all forms of depreciation recognized by the market, to treat all these forms of depreciation, and to charge only once for each form of depreciation. The various methods of estimating depreciation may be used in combination to solve specific problems or each may be applied individually to test the reasonableness of the estimates derived from other methods.

The three principal methods for estimating depreciation are the *market extraction method*, the *age-life method*, and the *breakdown method*. The market extraction and age-life methods are used primarily to estimate the total depreciation of a property; the breakdown method is used primarily to allocate a known amount of total depreciation among its components, i.e., physical deterioration, functional obsolescence, and external obsolescence.

Applying the market extraction method, an appraiser develops a depreciation estimate by studying sales of comparable properties that have depreciated to a similar degree as the subject improvement. The value of the land and site improvements at the time of sale is subtracted from the price of each comparable property to obtain the depreciated value of the improvement(s). The depreciated value of the improvement(s) is then subtracted from the reproduction or replacement cost of the comparable to arrive at a total dollar estimate that reflects all forms of depreciation. This dollar amount is converted into a percentage by dividing it by the reproduction or replacement cost. This percentage is then reconciled into a rate appropriate to the subject improvement(s) and used to develop a total depreciation estimate for the subject. If there are differences between the sales in age, location, or degree of maintenance, it may be appropriate to annualize the percentage by dividing it by the actual age or, if there is a significant difference between the actual age and the effective age, by the effective age estimate. By analyzing several comparables, a range of annual percentages of depreciation can be established. The appraiser reconciles the range and applies the concluded rate to the age of the subject improvement to develop a total depreciation estimate. The annual percentage can also be used to develop an estimate of the total economic life expectancy for the subject, which is then used in the age-life method.

When the age-life method is applied, the appraiser estimates the total economic life expectancy of the existing structure as well as its effective age, based on an analysis of sales of similar structures. The ratio of effective age to total economic life reflects the extent to which the improvement has depreciated. This ratio is directly applied to the reproduction or replacement cost of the structure to arrive at a lump-sum estimate of all forms of depreciation, which is then deducted from the cost figure.

The breakdown method is primarily used to allocate a known amount of total depreciation, estimated by either the market extraction method or the age-life method, into its components. When there are not enough comparable sales available to estimate total depreciation by market extraction or age-life methods, the breakdown method can be applied independently. Each form of physical deterioration, functional obsolescence, and external obsolescence must be estimated separately, using specific methods appropriate to that form of depreciation. The sum of the depreciation estimates for all items is then subtracted from the reproduction or replacement cost of the structure.

Regardless of the method applied, the appraiser must ensure that the final estimate of depreciation reflects the loss in value from all causes and that no form of depreciation has been considered more than once. Double charges for depreciation may produce inappropriately low value indications in the cost approach. The breakdown method can also be used to estimate the cost to cure curable items of depreciation, which should be recognized in the application of the other approaches. This is typically accomplished in the sales comparison and income capitalization approaches by deducting the cost to cure at the conclusion of the approach.

Reproduction and Replacement Cost Bases

An appraiser must estimate depreciation using the same basis from which costs were calculated--either reproduction or replacement cost. A reproduction is a virtual replica of the existing structure, employing the same design and similar building materials. A replacement is a structure of comparable utility employing the design and materials that are currently used in the building market. A reproduction may contain more items of functional obsolescence than a replacement structure. These items might include nonstandard story heights, insufficient electrical service, or the use of outdated and expensive building materials. The reproduction of obsolete items usually costs more in the current market, but does not produce a proportionate increase in utility or value. An amount must be deducted from reproduction cost to account for items of functional obsolescence.

The use of replacement cost usually eliminates the need to measure many, but not all, forms of functional obsolescence. Replacement structures usually cost less than reproduction structures because they are constructed with materials and techniques that are more readily available and less expensive in today's market. Thus a replacement cost figure is usually lower and may provide a better indication of the existing structure's contribution to value. A replacement structure typically does not suffer functional obsolescence resulting from superadequacies. However, if functional problems are found in the existing structure, an amount must be deducted from the replacement cost. Estimating replacement cost generally simplifies the procedure for measuring depreciation in components of superadequate construction. Common examples of functional obsolescence include structural defects and excessively thick foundations in an existing improvement. Such obsolescence would be corrected in a replacement building.

To avoid errors in measuring depreciation, an appraiser must be consistent and understand the purpose of this step in the cost approach. The estimate of depreciation is deducted from the cost to create a new reproduction or replacement improvement to arrive at the value contribution of the existing improvement. Even a newly constructed improvement may not have as much value as the cost to create it. Although it has no physical deterioration, a reproduction or replacement structure may suffer from functional obsolescence and/or external obsolescence. Any feature causing a loss in value measured against the cost standard must be accounted for as an item of depreciation.

Market Extraction Method

The market extraction method relies on the availability of comparable sales from which depreciation can be extracted. It is the most direct means of measuring depreciation because it is based on the transactions of market participants. It is primarily used to extract total depreciation, to establish total economic life expectancy, and to estimate external obsolescence. The market extraction method includes eight steps.

1. Find and verify sales of similarly improved properties that appear to have incurred a comparable amount of depreciation as the subject property. Although it is desirable, it is not essential that the comparables be current sales. Similarly, the comparables do not have to be from the subject's market; they can be from a comparable, but not necessarily competitive, market.

2. Make appropriate adjustments to the comparable sales for certain factors, including property rights conveyed, financing, and conditions of sale. If an appraiser can quantify curable depreciation for either items of deferred maintenance or functional obsolescence, this estimate should be applied to the sale price as an adjustment. (Depreciation extracted in this way will exclude curable items.) A market conditions adjustment is *not* made because the appraiser is estimating depreciation *at the time of the sale*. Adjustments for other physical, functional, or external impairments are not made either because these factors are the source of the depreciation in the comparable sale.

3. Subtract the value of the land at the time of sale from the sale price of each comparable property to obtain the depreciated cost of the improvements. (For residential properties in which the contributory value of the site improvements is low, their estimated value is included in the land value estimate. For more complex properties in which the contributory value of the site improvements is more substantial, the estimated cost of the site improvements is generally included with the cost of the main improvements.)

4. Estimate the cost of the improvements for each comparable at the time of sale. The type of cost (reproduction or replacement) should be the same as that used for the subject. Typically replacement cost is estimated. The cost estimate should include all improvements.

5. Subtract the depreciated cost of each improvement from the cost of the improvement to arrive at total depreciation in dollars. If no adjustments have been made to the sale prices for curable items, this extracted depreciation will include all forms of depreciation, both curable and incurable, from all three causes. If adjustments have been made to the sale prices for curable items, the extracted depreciation will not include curable items; it will represent a lump-sum depreciation estimate for all incurable items from all causes.

6. Convert the dollar estimates of depreciation into percentages by dividing each estimate of total depreciation by the cost new. If the ages of the sales are relatively similar to the age of the subject property, the percentages of total depreciation can be reconciled into a rate appropriate to the subject property. This rate is applied to the subject's cost estimate to derive an estimate of the subject's total depreciation.

7. If there are differences between the sales (e.g., in age, location, degree of maintenance), the appraiser annualizes the percentages of total depreciation by dividing each percentage by the actual age of the property or, if there is a significant difference between the actual age and the effective age, by the effective age estimate. Whether actual or effective age is used, the same age should be applied consistently to all sales. Because accurate estimates of effective age cannot always be derived for every comparable sale, the most consistent range of annual depreciation rates is developed using the actual ages of the comparables.

8. Reconcile the range of annual percentage rates into a rate appropriate to the subject improvement(s). This rate is then used to develop a total depreciation estimate for the subject property.

Examples

The market extraction method is demonstrated in the following example. Assume that all the sales are of a fee simple interest.

	Sale 1	Sale 2	Sale 3
Sale price	$215,000	$165,000	$365,000
Less value of site	- 60,000	- 40,000	-127,750
Depreciated cost of improvements	$155,000	$125,000	$237,250
Replacement cost of improvements	$230,000	$195,000	$375,000
Less depreciated cost of improvements	-155,000	- 125,000	-237,250
Lump-sum dollar depreciation	$ 75,000	$ 70,000	$137,750
Lump-sum percentage depreciation	32.61%	35.90%	36.73%

In this case the range of lump-sum percentage depreciation estimates is so narrow that it is not necessary to annualize them. Assuming that the replacement cost of the subject improvement(s) is $240,000 and the percentage of depreciation is estimated to be 33% of replacement cost, the total lump-sum dollar depreciation estimate comes to $80,000. Another aspect of the market extraction method is demonstrated in the following example. As in the preceding example, assume that all the sales are of a fee simple interest.

	Sale 1	Sale 2	Sale 3
Sale price	$998,000	$605,000	$791,000
Less value of site	-140,000	- 100,000	-125,000
Depreciated cost of improvements	$858,000	$505,000	$666,000
Replacement cost of improvements	$950,000	$627,000	$934,000
Less depreciated cost of improvements	-858,000	-505,000	-666,000
Lump-sum dollar depreciation	$ 92,000	$122,000	$268,000
Lump-sum percentage depreciation	9.68%	19.46%	28.69%
Age of sale	8	14	19
Average annual depreciation rate	1.21%	1.39%	1.51%

Here the range of lump-sum percentage depreciation estimates is so wide that they are difficult to reconcile and it becomes necessary to annualize the percentage estimates of depreciation. This narrows the range of annual depreciation rates to between 1.21% and 1.51% per year. It becomes apparent that as a building ages, the annual rate of deprecia-tion increases. Assuming that the subject improvements are 15 years old, reconciliation could result in an annual depreciation rate of 1.4% per year. The total depreciation for the subject improvements would be 21% (15 x 0.014) and this rate can be applied to the subject's replacement cost.

Applicability and Limitations

When sales data are plentiful, the market extraction method usually provides a reliable estimate of depreciation. However, the comparable properties should be similar to the subject and they should have incurred similar amounts and types of depreciation. When the comparable properties differ in design, quality, or construction, it is difficult to ascertain whether differences in value are attributable to these differences or to a difference in depreciation. The market extraction method is also difficult to apply when the type or extent of depreciation varies greatly among the comparable properties. If the sales analyzed were affected by special financing or unusual motivation, the problem is further complicated. The usefulness of the method depends heavily on the accuracy of the site value estimates and the cost new estimates for the comparable properties. If the sales are located in districts or neighborhoods that are not comparable to the subject's, the method may not be appropriate. Market extraction considers all types of depreciation in a lump sum and does not break down the estimate into the various components of depreciation. This method also assumes that depreciation occurs in a straight-line pattern. In spite of its limitations, the market extraction method often provides extremely reliable and convincing results.

Age-Life Method

Depreciation occurs over the economic life of an improvement, and at the end of its economic life a structure will be 100% depreciated. If a structure has not reached the end of its economic life, it cannot be 100% depreciated. The effective age and economic life expectancy of a structure are the primary concepts used by an appraiser in measuring depreciation by age-life relationships. In the age-life method, total depreciation is estimated by calculating the ratio of the effective age of the property to its economic life expectancy and applying this ratio to the property's reproduction or replacement cost. The formula is

Effective age/total economic life x reproduction/replacement cost = depreciation

Although it is not always as accurate as other techniques, the age-life method is the simplest way to estimate depreciation. The method is applied in three steps.

1. Conduct research to identify the anticipated total economic life of similar structures in the market area and estimate the effective age of the subject building. (The effective age may be the same as the actual age if the building's maintenance has been typical.)

2. Divide the effective age of the subject by the anticipated total economic life of similar structures. The resulting ratio is then applied to the subject's reproduction or replacement cost to estimate lump-sum depreciation.

3. Subtract the lump-sum estimate of depreciation from the replacement or reproduction cost of the subject improvement to arrive at the improvement's contribution to property value.

Example

The age-life method is illustrated in the following example. This information is given:

Replacement cost	$668,175
Site value	$180,000
Estimated effective age	18 years
Total economic life	50 years

The total percentage depreciation is determined by dividing the estimated effective age of 18 years by the total economic life expectancy of 50 years. Thus the age-life formula indicates total percentage depreciation of 36%. When this rate is applied to the replacement cost of $668,175, the total depreciation indicated is $240,543. The cost approach is applied as follows:

Replacement cost	$668,175
Less total depreciation	240,543
Depreciated replacement cost	$427,632
Plus value of site	180,000
Indicated value by the cost approach	$607,632

Age Factors

The age of a building is the period between the time it begins to contribute to value (usually at the end of construction and/or after lease-up) and the date of the value estimate. Actual age is a chronological figure. Effective age is based on an appraiser's judgment and interpretation of market perceptions. Depending on the circumstances, effective age can be greater than or less than a building's actual age. If a building has been exceptionally well-maintained or has been remodeled, renovated, rehabilitated, or modernized, its effective age will probably be less than its actual age. If a building has not been maintained or modernized or is in very poor condition, its effective age will probably be greater than its actual age. In the age-life method, the starting point for estimating a building's effective age is to establish its actual age.

Assume that the subject property is a 23-year-old strip retail center. It has been redecorated on the inside but has not been modernized. The original roof and HVAC components are still in place. It would probably have an effective age estimate of 23 years. The small amount of work done in redecorating is usually not sufficient to reduce the effective age. Now assume that, in addition to the redecorating, the roof and furnace have been replaced in the 23-year-old building. In this case the building would probably have an estimated effective age of less than 23 years. If the same 23-year-old building were in poor condition, had not been redecorated, had a defective HVAC system, and had below-average occupancy because of poor maintenance, it would probably have an estimated effective age greater than 23 years.

Economic Life Factors

The economic life of a building is the period of time over which it continues to contribute to value. An improvement's life expectancy can be affected by many different factors, including the quality of construction, the age and condition of the short-lived items, the overall condition and maintenance of the improvement, the functional utility of the improvement, and market and locational externalities.

The total economic life of a structure is determined within the context of its market. A building in one market may have a total economic life expectancy significantly different from that of an identical building in another market. The primary method for estimating total economic life involves adding a step to the market extraction method. Total economic life can also be estimated through judgments based on neighborhood analysis and investigation of demolition permits for properties undergoing a change in highest and best use (which usually occurs when a building has reached the end of its economic life expectancy).

Employing the additional step in the market extraction method, the appraiser calculates the reciprocal of the average annual depreciation rate, which indicates the total economic life expectancy of the sale as of the date of sale. For example, assume that a sale indicates an annual rate of depreciation of 2%. The reciprocal of this rate is calculated by dividing 100% by the rate. Thus, 100% divided by 2% results in a total economic life expectancy for the sale of 50 years as of the date of the value estimate. This does not mean that the total economic life expectancy of the sale has always been and will always be 50 years. It simply means that, at the time the property was sold, its average annual rate of depreciation indicated a total economic life expectancy of 50 years.

In the second example of market extraction, average annual rates of depreciation of 1.21%, 1.39%, and 1.51% were calculated for Sales 1, 2 and 3. The reciprocals of these three annual rates are 83 years, 72 years, and 66 years. A pattern can be observed here. As a building ages and the average annual depreciation rate increases, the total economic life expectancy decreases. Sale 1, an eight-year-old building, had an annual depreciation rate of 1.21% and a total economic life expectancy of 83 years. Its remaining economic life expectancy is therefore 75 years (83 - 8 = 75). In contrast, Sale 3, a 19-year-old building, had an annual depreciation rate of 1.51% and a total economic life expectancy of 66 years. Its remaining economic life expectancy is 47 years (66 - 19 = 47). Reconciliation should be based on the improvement that is most similar in age to the subject property. The subject property is 15 years old, so the improvement closest to it in age is Sale 2, which is 14 years old and has a total economic life expectancy of 72 years (100%/1.39%). In light of this similar sale and the pattern indicated by the market data, the appraiser could reasonably reconcile the total economic life expectancy for the subject property at 70 years. Applying the age-life formula, the total depreciation would equal 21.43% (15/70) of the property's replacement cost.

Applicability and Limitations

The age-life method is simple, easy to apply, and easy to understand. It allows an appraiser to determine total depreciation, which can subsequently be allocated among its various causes using breakdown procedures. Although this method is usually the simplest way to estimate depreciation, it does have certain limitations. First, because the percentage of depreciation is represented by the ratio of effective age to total economic life, this method assumes that every building depreciates on a straight-line basis over the course of its economic life. In other words, a 20-year-old industrial building is assumed to incur twice as much depreciation as a similar, 10-year-old industrial building; obviously, this is rarely true. The method is flawed because depreciation does not always occur on a straight-line basis. In some markets, buildings tend to depreciate more rapidly as they approach the end of their economic lives. In other markets a different pattern may be observed. The straight-line pattern of depreciation is only an approximation, although it is usually a sufficiently accurate one.

Second, the age-life method does not divide depreciation into its various components. Like the market extraction method, the age-life method does not distinguish between the different causes of value loss. In districts and neighborhoods where comparable properties incur different types and different amounts of depreciation than the subject property, the age-life method may be difficult to justify.

Third, the age-life method does not recognize the difference between short-lived and long-lived items of physical deterioration. Because a single figure is taken to reflect depreciation in the structure as a whole, varying amounts of deterioration in short-lived items are not directly indicated in the age-life method. For example, a structure as a whole may be estimated to be 20% depreciated except for the roof which, unlike other roofs in the neighborhood, is estimated to be 90% depreciated. In this situation, the breakdown method would allow an appraiser to make a more refined analysis.

Finally, one part of the denominator of the age-life ratio, i.e., the total economic life of similar structures, refers to a future period of time. Any forecast of future events calls for judgment, so total economic life may be difficult to establish.

Variation 1—Known Curable Items

In some situations, the cost to cure the curable items of depreciation (both physical and functional) is either known or can be easily and accurately estimated and the cost to cure these items is deducted from the replacement cost of the improvements *before* the age-life ratio is applied. This procedure mirrors what typical purchasers consider when deciding on whether to invest in a property. It is most meaningful when the subject property has curable depreciation not typically found in the market. When the curable items are dealt with first, the appraiser may have to consider using a shorter effective age and/or a longer economic life expectancy in calculating the age-life ratio.

Consider a 20-year-old property with a replacement cost of $892,000. The roof needs total replacement at a documented cost of $82,500. Sales of similar buildings which were sold *after* their roofs had been replaced were used to extract a total economic life expectancy of 100 years. In deriving a total economic life expectancy for each comparable building, the appraiser used an effective age that was 25% lower than the building's actual age. This simulated the thinking of investors in the market, who feel that the effective age of a building will be lower than its actual age once the roof has been replaced. After the roof is replaced, the subject's effective age is assumed to be 15 years, i.e., 25% lower than its actual age of 20 years. Dividing 15 years by the market-extracted total economic life expectancy of 100 years indicates total depreciation (exclusive of the roof) of 15%. This ratio is applied to the subject's replacement cost less the cost of roof replacement ($892,000 - $82,500, or $809,500) to derive a depreciation estimate of $121,425. Assuming a site value estimate of $100,000, the cost approach can be applied as follows:

Replacement cost	$892,000
Less cost to replace roof	82,500
Remaining cost	$809,500
Less depreciation	
(Remaining cost x age-life ratio:	
$809,500 x 15%)	121,425
Depreciated replacement cost	$688,075
Plus site value	100,000
Indicated value by cost approach	$788,075

Variation 2—Known External Obsolescence

In some situations where external obsolescence is present, another variation of the age-life method is applied. If external obsolescence is affecting the subject property and there are sales of properties in the subject market that have incurred the same external obsolescence, the appraiser should use the total economic life extracted from these sales in the age-life ratio. However, if external obsolescence is affecting the subject property and there are no sales in the subject market similarly affected, the appraiser should estimate depreciation *exclusive of external obsolescence* using a market-extracted economic life expectancy in the age-life ratio, and then estimate external obsolescence using techniques from the breakdown method. The estimated depreciation from the age-life method and the estimated external obsolescence from the breakdown method would be added together to arrive at an estimate of total depreciation.

Consider a subject property in a district where there is an oversupply of competitive properties. This has resulted in a 10% reduction in rents, which the appraiser equates with a 10% loss in building value. Land value is not affected. The replacement cost of the 10-year-old building improvement is $696,000. The market extraction method, applied to comparables in the subject's market a year ago when there was no oversupply, indicated a total economic life expectancy of 50 years. Using the age-life method, depreciation is thus estimated at 20% (10/50).

The depreciation estimated for the subject by the age-life method is $139,200 ($696,000 x 0.20) and the additional external obsolescence is estimated to be $69,600 ($696,000 x 0.10). Total depreciation, therefore, is $208,800, allocated as follows: $139,200 to all causes *except* external obsolescence and $69,600 to the external obsolescence. Note that the external obsolescence is caused by an oversupply in the market, and it is unlikely that such a situation will be permanent. As supply and demand again approach equilibrium, the oversupply will probably disappear.

Breakdown Method

The breakdown method is the most comprehensive and detailed way to measure depreciation. When used in conjunction with market extraction and age-life methods, the breakdown method disaggregates a total depreciation estimate into its component parts. The market extraction or age-life methods yield total depreciation as a lump-sum estimate. The breakdown method allows such lump-sum estimates to be allocated among their various components. The breakdown method is also used when the market extraction and age-life methods *cannot* be applied. In such situations, the breakdown method is used to estimate all items of depreciation individually and the estimates are added together to arrive at a total depreciation estimate.

Types of Depreciation

The three types of depreciation estimated by the breakdown method are physical deterioration, functional obsolescence, and external obsolescence. Physical deterioration is caused by wear and tear from regular use, the impact of the elements, and the effect of normal aging. Careful maintenance can slow the process of deterioration and neglect can accelerate it. Physical deterioration may be curable or incurable. The three main physical components of a building are items of deferred maintenance, short-lived components, and long-lived components. All physical components in a building fall into one of these three categories. In the breakdown method, all items of physical deterioration are estimated and the estimates are then totaled. Elements of total depreciation that are *not* physical deterioration *must be* some form of obsolescence. In addition to physical deterioration, a building may suffer damage or vandalism, which is treated separately.

Functional obsolescence is caused by a flaw in the structure, materials, or design of the improvement. It is attributable to defects *within* the property, as opposed to external obsolescence, which is caused by external factors. Functional obsolescence may be curable or incurable. Functional obsolescence can be caused by a deficiency, which means that the subject property is below standard in respect to market norms. It can also be caused by a superadequacy, which means that the subject property exceeds market norms. There are five types of functional obsolescence: curable functional obsolescence caused by a deficiency requiring an addition (installation) of a new item, curable functional obsolescence caused by a deficiency requiring the substitution (replacement) of an existing item ("curing a defect"), curable functional obsolescence caused by a superadequacy which it is economically feasible to cure, incurable functional obsolescence caused by a deficiency, and incurable functional obsolescence caused by a superadequacy. In the breakdown method, all items of functional obsolescence are estimated and the estimates are added up. Elements of total depreciation which represent *neither* physical deterioration *nor* functional obsolescence *must be* external obsolescence. The only ways that functional obsolescence can be offset are to cure it, when this is economically feasible, or for market norms to change.

External obsolescence is a loss in value caused by factors *outside of* the subject property. This can be an economic factor, such as an oversupplied market or very expensive financing, or a locational factor, such as poor siting or proximity to a negative environmental influence. External obsolescence is generally incurable on the date of the value estimate, but this does not mean that it is permanent. External influences can affect both the site and the improvements. When this is the case, the loss in value attributable to the externality may have to be allocated between the site and the improvements.

Calculating Depreciation in the Breakdown Method

There are five primary techniques used to calculate the different types of depreciation in the breakdown method. These include estimation of cost to cure, application of an age-life ratio, application of the functional obsolescence procedure, analysis of paired data, and capitalization of rent loss. Cost to cure is a measure of both curable physical deterioration and curable functional obsolescence. An age-life ratio is used to measure curable physical deterioration and incurable physical deterioration for both short-lived and long-lived components. The functional obsolescence procedure may be used to estimate all types of functional obsolescence. Analysis of paired data and capitalization of rent loss may be used to estimate incurable functional obsolescence caused by a deficiency as well as external obsolescence.

Applying the Breakdown Method

The breakdown method can be applied in two different ways: 1) by allocating a known total depreciation estimate developed from the market extraction or age-life methods among its various components or 2) by developing a total depreciation estimate.

When the breakdown method is used to allocate a lump-sum depreciation estimate, the first step is to calculate all items of physical deterioration, add them up, and subtract the total from the lump-sum depreciation estimate. The residual amount, if any, represents depreciation attributable to functional and external obsolescence. In the second step, all items of functional obsolescence are calculated, added up, and subtracted from the total amount of obsolescence. Any residual represents the depreciation attributable to external obsolescence. Damage or vandalism, if present, is calculated on a cost-to-cure basis and is added to the total depreciation amount.

When using this procedure, several cautions and considerations should be kept in mind. First, if the sum of all items of physical deterioration estimated using the breakdown method is equivalent to the total depreciation derived from market extraction or age-life methods, then probably little or no obsolescence has occurred. Second, if the sum of all items of physical deterioration and functional obsolescence estimated with breakdown techniques is equivalent to the total depreciation derived from market extraction or age-life methods, then it is likely that little or no external obsolescence is present. Finally, if the sum of the items of depreciation estimated by the breakdown method substantially exceeds the total depreciation derived from market extraction or age-life methods, all the methods applied should be reviewed. There are several reasons why there might be a difference in the results obtained from the breakdown method and the market extraction or age-life methods. The total depreciation derived from the market extraction or age-life methods may have been estimated incorrectly. The subject property may suffer from an element of depreciation that is indicated in the breakdown method, but not in the market extraction or age-life methods. One or more of the breakdown techniques may have been applied incorrectly. Or certain applications of the breakdown method may have resulted in a "double depreciation" charge.

When the breakdown method is applied to develop a total depreciation estimate, the first step is to calculate all items of physical deterioration, using the appropriate techniques, and then to add up all estimates to arrive at total physical deterioration. Next, all items of functional obsolescence are calculated, again using appropriate techniques, and these estimates are added together to arrive at total functional obsolescence. External obsolescence is calculated either through analysis of paired data or by capitalization of rent loss. The estimate of external obsolescence may have to be allocated between the site and the improvements, depending on how it is derived. Damage, if present, is calculated on a cost-to-cure basis. Finally, all physical deterioration, functional obsolescence, external obsolescence, and damage are added together to arrive at an estimate of total depreciation.

Calculating Curable Physical Deterioration

Curable physical deterioration, also known as *deferred maintenance*, applies to items in need of repair on the effective date of the appraisal. Some examples include broken windows, friable asbestos wrapping on boiler pipes, a hole in an interior partition, and a cracked lavatory. For most properties, deferred maintenance involves relatively minor items. Deferred maintenance items are 100% physically deteriorated (broken). The age of such an item is equal to or greater than its total useful life expectancy. The item must be fixed, replaced, or repaired for the building to continue to function as it should.

There are two major tests of curability. First, if spending the money to "cure" the item will result in a value increment equal to or greater than the expenditure, the item is normally considered curable. Second, if spending the money to cure the item will *not* result in a value increment equal to or greater than the expenditure, but will allow other existing items to maintain their value, the item is normally considered curable.

Deferred maintenance is measured as the cost to cure the item or to restore it to a new or reasonably new condition. The cost to cure may exceed cost new. Cost to cure is analogous to an age-life procedure since the age of a curable item equals (or exceeds) its total useful life expectancy, resulting in 100% deterioration. All deferred maintenance items are 100% physically deteriorated, and therefore they may all be treated together in the breakdown method.

Example—Items of Deferred Maintenance

During the inspection of an office, the appraiser notes that the exterior walls need to be scraped, primed, and painted. A painting contractor quotes a price of $5,000 to do the work; however, according to the appraiser's cost manual, the job should only cost $3,500. In this instance the correct measure is $5,000. If the painting were done during the original construction, the contractor would probably not have had to scrape the walls; he could have just primed and painted them. The extra cost is the difference between the cost to cure and the cost new. The higher amount should be used by the appraiser as the cost to cure.

Calculating Incurable Physical Deterioration—Short-Lived Items

Short-lived items are those that are not ready to be replaced on the date of the value estimate, but will probably have to be replaced in the foreseeable future. Examples include the roof covering, interior floor finish, furnaces, and water heaters. A short-lived item is not 100% physically deteriorated, so it does not yet need to be cured. However, like market participants, the appraiser recognizes that the items will be 100% deteriorated before the end of the building's total economic life expectancy and will have to be replaced; whenever that occurs, they will become curable items. Generally, the age of short-lived items is less than their total useful life expectancy. The same tests of curability that are applied to items of deferred maintenance are applied to short-lived items.

The deterioration in short-lived items is measured by estimating a separate age-life ratio and applying it to the cost to replace each item on the date of the value estimate. As with items of deferred maintenance, the cost to cure may exceed cost new. Since all short-lived items ultimately will become deferred maintenance items, and since deferred maintenance items are measured by the cost to cure, the proper place to begin analysis of the short-lived components is with the estimation of the cost to cure each item. Since each short-lived item usually has a different age and a different total useful life expectancy, a separate age-life ratio must be calculated for each item.

Example—Short-lived components. The boiler in an apartment building is 20 years old. According to a boiler contractor, the total useful life expectancy of a boiler such as this is 25 years. On the date of the value estimate, the boiler was operative and there was no need to replace it. However, a prudent purchaser or owner would recognize that the boiler *will* have to be replaced within a few years. If the boiler were replaced on the date of the value estimate, the cost would be $30,000. The age-life ratio is used to estimate a depreciation rate of 80% (20/25 = 0.80). When this ratio is applied to the cost to replace the boiler ($30,000), the deterioration indicated is $24,000 ($30,000 x 0.80). The boiler would *not* be considered a short-lived item if its remaining useful life were equal to or greater than the remaining economic life of the overall property.

Calculating Incurable Physical Deterioration—Long-Lived Items

Long-lived items include all items that were not treated as items of deferred maintenance or as short-lived items. Long-lived items all have the same age and life expectancy and, therefore, are all treated together. Examples of long-lived items include studs, underground piping, foundation walls, and insulation. A long-lived item is not 100% physically deteriorated; therefore, it does not need to be cured. In addition, such an item is not normally replaced except under extraordinary circumstances, e.g., a damaged foundation wall. The same tests of curability that are applied to the other physical components are applied to the long-lived items. The deterioration of long-lived items is measured by estimating an age-life ratio and applying it to all components of cost that have not already been treated for physical deterioration.

Example—Long-lived components. A small industrial building has a replacement cost of $700,000. It is 35 years old and has a total useful life expectancy of 100 years. The cost to cure the curable items is $10,000; the cost to replace the boiler is $40,000; the cost to replace the roof covering is $60,000; and the cost to replace the floor finish is $20,000. There are no other short-lived items. The age-life ratio is calculated to be 35% (35/100 = 0.35). The cost attributable to the long-lived items is $570,000. Physical deterioration in these long-lived items is estimated by deducting the cost to cure the curable items ($10,000) and the sum of the costs to replace the short-lived items ($120,000) from the replacement cost of the structure ($700,000). The age-life ratio (35%) is applied to the untreated costs ($570,000). The resulting amount of deterioration attributable to the long-lived items is $199,500 ($570,000 x 0.35).

Estimating Physical Deterioration Using the Age-Life Procedure

Figure 17.1 illustrates an age-life procedure that can be used to estimate all forms of physical deterioration, both curable and incurable. In addition to showing the correct methods to estimate all items of physical deterioration, the diagram was designed to ensure that no items of physical deterioration are treated more than once. This age-life procedure works whether the breakdown method is being used to allocate a known total depreciation amount among its components or to develop an estimate of total depreciation.

The procedure has four steps. First, the reproduction or replacement cost is allocated among the curable items, the incurable short-lived items, and the incurable long-lived items. Second, an age-life ratio is calculated for each allocated cost item. Third, the appropriate age-life ratio is applied to the estimated cost of each item. Finally, the individual items of physical deterioration are added together to develop an estimate of total physical deterioration.

The top row of the diagram, Line A, is where the appraiser enters the overall reproduction or replacement cost of the improvement. Note the arrows leading from Line A to Line B. The first column on the left is for the curable items. Since they are all 100% physically deteriorated, they are grouped together. The last column on the right is for the long-lived items. Since they all have incurred the same extent of physical deterioration, the long-lived items are all grouped together too. In the center of the diagram, there are separate columns for each short-lived item since each has a different age and a different total useful life. The number of interior columns depends on the number of short-lived items observed by the appraiser.

Line B is used to separate the various construction items into curables, short-lived components, and long-lived components. The column on the left labeled "Curables" groups all curable items together. Each of the interior columns represents a short-lived component, such as roof covering or exterior painting. The column on the right labeled "Long-lived Items" groups all long-lived items together.

Line C is used to allocate the improvement's overall reproduction or replacement cost on Line A among the curable items, the short-lived items, and the long-lived items. The sum of the cost to cure all curable items is entered in the left column. The cost to replace each of the short-lived items is entered in the appropriate column in the central portion of the diagram. The cost to cure the curable items and the individual costs to replace all short-lived items on Line C are added up and the total is deducted from the reproduction or replacement cost on Line A. The result is entered in the column on the right, which represents the remaining costs attributable to the long-lived items. All of the items on Line C, when added together, should equal the overall reproduction or replacement cost on Line A. By allocating costs before estimating the deterioration in any item, the appraiser is assured that all items will be treated for physical deterioration and none will be treated more than once.

Line D is where the age-life ratio of each item is entered. Since all curable items are 100% deteriorated, 100% should be entered in the left-hand column of Line D. A separate age-life ratio is calculated for each short-lived item, using the actual age and useful life

Figure 17.1 **Age-Life Procedure for Estimating All Items of Physical Deterioration**

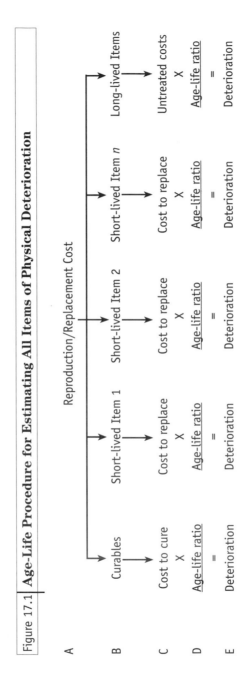

expectancy of the specific item.[2] Each age-life ratio is entered into the appropriate column on Line D. An age-life ratio is calculated based on the actual age of the long-lived items, usually equivalent to the chronological age of the building, and the total useful life expectancy of the long-lived items, usually extracted from the market.[3] This age-life ratio is entered in the appropriate column on Line D.

Physical deterioration estimates are calculated on Line E. The age-life ratio in each column on Line D is applied to the corresponding cost on Line C. The result is the physical deterioration for each item. The deterioration estimates on Line E should be less than the costs on Line C for all columns except the first, where the deterioration estimate on Line E should equal the cost on Line C. The total physical deterioration for the subject property is calculated by adding up all of the items on Line E.

Example—Age-life procedure for estimating all forms of physical deterioration. The subject is a 25-year-old industrial building in average condition. Its overall replacement cost is $800,000 (See Figure 17.2.). On the date of inspection, the appraiser found one overhead door damaged beyond repair, which will cost $5,000 to replace. The roof was replaced five years ago and has a 20-year guarantee; the cost to replace it is $60,000. The HVAC components are original and should last another five years; thus they are 83⅓% deteriorated (25/30). The cost to replace the HVAC components is $72,000. The offices were just completely redecorated at a cost of $10,000. The appraiser estimates that they will not have to be redecorated for another five years. Based on an analysis of demolition permits, the appraiser concludes that the total useful life expectancy of the long-lived items is 100 years.

In this example, the total physical deterioration is the sum of the individual deterioration calculations, $5,000 + $15,000 + $60,000 + $163,500, or $243,250.

Damage/Vandalism

Damage or vandalism can affect short-lived or long-lived items. The measure of damage is the cost to cure. Damage or vandalism must be treated separately in the breakdown method because it is not considered in the reproduction or replacement cost estimate. By

---

2. Total useful life for short-lived items may be obtained from the actual age of a component at the time of its replacement, analysis of manufacturer warranties, and information from contractors and suppliers, i.e., building equipment stores and lumber yards.

3. With respect to the total useful life expectancy of long-lived items, the appraiser must recognize that useful life tends to be longer than economic life. Moreover, regardless of how long physical components may last (e.g. concrete might last indefinitely), an economic factor must also be considered. Economic reasons will prevail when a building reaches the end of its economic life and is torn down.

  Total useful life for long-lived components can be estimated using neighborhood data, information from structural engineers, analysis of demolition permits, or market extraction. If a building is torn down and the site is redeveloped with a use similar to the use of the building that was torn down, the age of the building at the time it was torn down may be indicative of the building's useful life.

  Total useful life can also be extracted from a sale. Assume the subject is a 15-year-old structure with a replacement cost of $750,000 and no observed functional or external obsolescence. Using market extraction, a total economic life expectancy of 50 years is developed. At 30% of replacement cost, total depreciation comes to $225,000. There are $1,000 in curable physical items, and the costs to replace the roof ($40,000) and the HVAC components ($35,000) come to $75,000. Accordingly, the residual cost attributable to the long-lived items is $674,000. The total depreciation is $225,000. The total deterioration attributable to the curable and short-lived items, using age-life analysis, is $52,000. (The roof costs $40,000, is 15 years old, has a 20-year life, and thus is 75% deteriorated, indicating physical deterioration of $30,000. The HVAC costs $30,000, is 15 years old, has a 25-year life, and thus is 60% deteriorated, indicating physical deterioration is $21,000; curable physical items are estimated at $1,000.) Thus the residual deterioration attributable to the long-lived items is $173,000 ($225,000-$52,000), or 25.67% of the cost of the long-lived items. The average annual rate of physical deterioration in the long-lived items is 1.71% (25.67%/15). Calculating the reciprocal of this rate indicates a total useful life of the long-lived items of 58 years. Obviously, the total useful life (58 years) exceeds the total economic life (50 years).

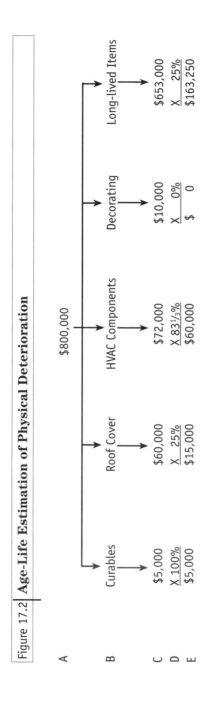

Figure 17.2 Age-Life Estimation of Physical Deterioration

curing damage or vandalism, the life of the damaged component is neither renewed nor prolonged; it simply is restored to its condition prior to the damage. For example, consider a brick wall that has been spray painted with graffiti. The cost of sandblasting the wall to remove the graffiti is $5,000. The item *must* be treated separately from the other items of physical deterioration because nowhere in the replacement cost is there a provision for the removal of graffiti. The measure of damage in this instance would be $5,000. Typically, the cost to cure damage is added to the curable physical deterioration and included among the items of physical deterioration in the breakdown method.

Calculating Functional Obsolescence

Functional obsolescence is a loss in value that may be caused by a deficiency or a superadequacy. Some forms of functional obsolescence are curable, while others are incurable. A *deficiency* may be a component or system that should be in the property but is not, or it may be a substandard or defective component or system in the property that does not work properly. A *superadequacy* is a component or system in the property that exceeds market requirements and does not contribute to value an amount equal to its cost.

There are two major tests of curability for a deficiency or superadequacy. First, if spending the money to cure the item will result in a value increment equal to or greater than the expenditure, the item is normally considered curable. Second, if spending the money to cure the item will *not* result in a value increment equal to or greater than the expenditure, but will allow existing items to maintain their value, the item is also normally considered curable. When it is possible and reasonable to cure an item but there is no economic advantage to curing it, the item will generally be considered incurable. For this reason, most superadequacies are incurable.

The Functional Obsolescence Procedure

Figure 17.3 diagrams a procedure that can be used to calculate all forms of functional obsolescence caused by a deficiency or a superadequacy, whether the obsolescence is curable or incurable. Use of this model ensures that all components of functional obsolescence will be treated in a consistent manner, that none of the items will be treated more than once, and that no double charges will be made for items that have already been depreciated, i.e., charged under physical deterioration, which is particularly important for superadequacies.

The procedure has five steps. First, the cost of the existing item is identified. This cost is derived from the replacement cost estimate. Of course, if the item is a form of curable functional obsolescence caused by a deficiency, there will be no cost for the item and zero will be entered on this line. In the second step, any depreciation that has already been charged for the item is deducted. In nearly all instances, this depreciation will be physical deterioration. As in the first step, if the item does not already exist in the building, no depreciation will have been charged and zero will be entered on this line.

If the functional obsolescence is curable, the next step is to add all costs associated with curing the item, which can include the cost of installing a new item, the cost of removing the old item, and net salvage value. Regardless of the type of functional obsolescence, the appraiser will have to calculate the cost to cure to determine whether the item is curable or not. If the functional obsolescence is incurable, the next step is to add the value of the loss attributable to the obsolescence. This value can be obtained by capitalizing a rent loss (using an income multiplier or a capitalization rate) or through paired data analysis. Again, the appraiser will have to calculate the value of the loss due to the functional obsolescence to determine whether the item is curable or not.

The fourth step is to enter a deduction for the cost of the item as though installed new on the date of the value estimate, if appropriate. As the final step, the appraiser adds up all of the entries to derive the total functional obsolescence attributable to each factor.

The model described works for all types of functional obsolescence. In Step 3, however, the appraiser needs to determine whether the functional obsolescence is curable or incurable. If it is curable, the entire cost to cure is used in the model. If it is in incurable, the value of the loss, which can be estimated by alternative techniques, is used in the model. The procedure is outlined in Figure 17.3. The applications that follow demonstrate how the procedure is used to estimate different types of functional obsolescence.

Figure 17.3	**Procedure for Estimating All Forms of Functional Obsolescence**
Step 1. Cost of existing item	$ xxx,xxx
Step 2. Less depreciation previously charged	- xxx,xxx
plus	
Step 3. Cost to cure (all costs)	+ xxx,xxx
or	*or*
Value of the loss	+ xxx,xxx
Step 4. Less cost if installed new	- xxx,xxx
Step 5. Equals depreciation for functional obsolescence	$ xxx,xxx

Curable functional obsolescence caused by a deficiency requiring an addition. A "deficiency requiring an addition" means that the subject suffers functional obsolescence because it lacks something that other properties in the market have. The functional obsolescence is curable when it is economically feasible to do so. Since the item is not present, the property cannot be penalized for any depreciation the item may have incurred. However, because it usually costs more to add an item to an existing property, the *excess cost to cure* is what the property is penalized for. For example, consider an office without air-conditioning. The additional rents that would be generated by installing air-conditioning would more than offset the cost and gross rent would increase by $2,000 per year. The current effective gross income multiplier (*EGIM*) is 7.0. Because of retrofit requirements, it is more costly to install the air-conditioning now than it would have been as a part of the original construction. The current cost of installing the air-conditioning is $12,000; if the work had been done as a part of new construction, the cost would have been only $10,000.

Cost of existing item	$ 0
Less depreciation previously charged	– 0
plus	
Cost to cure (all costs)	+ 12,000
or	
Value of loss	+ 0
Less cost if installed new	– 10,000
Equals depreciation for functional obsolescence	– $ 2,000

Note that since the lack of air-conditioning is a deficiency, no deterioration was charged. The functional obsolescence is curable because the value increase ($14,000) is greater than the cost to cure ($12,000). The cost to install the air-conditioning as a part of new construction on the date of the value estimate is $10,000, but the actual cost to retrofit and install the air-conditioning is $12,000. The curable functional obsolescence is the excess cost to cure, or $2,000.

Curable functional obsolescence caused by a deficiency requiring substitution or modernization. A curable deficiency requiring substitution or modernization is caused by something that is present in the subject property, but is either substandard compared to other properties on the market or is defective and thereby prevents some other component or system in the property from working properly. It is considered curable when it is economically feasible to do so. The measure is the cost to cure. (Theoretically, this is calculated as the cost of the modern component, plus installation, minus the physically depreciated value of the existing component, plus net salvage value. Because the salvage value of a component is offset by the costs to demolish, remove, and transport the item, it is often virtually nil. In such cases, it is not deducted from depreciated value. The appraiser must assess each situation accordingly.)

For example, consider a light industrial building with a 200-ampere electrical system which is substandard and must be updated. If the electric capacity were increased, the tenant would be willing to pay a higher rent, which would more than offset the cost of updating the electric service. The cost of the existing system is $5,000 as indicated by the replacement cost estimate. The electrical system is considered a long-lived component, and was physically depreciated by 50%. If the electric capacity is increased, the tenant will pay additional rent which will increase the net operating income by $1,000. The building capitalization rate for this type of property is 10%. The cost to remove the existing item and install a modern system is $8,000. If an ample capacity system had been installed at the date of construction, it would have cost $6,000.[4]

---

4. Note that this printing of *The Appraisal of Real Estate,* 11th ed., includes a deduction for this cost consideration in the three subsequent examples since many practitioners follow this procedure.

Cost of existing item	$ 5,000
Less depreciation previously charged	– 2,500
plus	
Cost to cure (all costs)	+ 8,000
or	
Value of loss	+ 0
Less cost if installed new	– 6,000
Equals depreciation for functional obsolescence	$ 4,500

Note that the substandard electrical service represents a defect and is considered curable because the value increment ($10,000) is greater than the cost to cure ($8.000). The $5,000 cost of the existing service, less the previous $2,500 charge for deterioration, plus the $8,000 cost to remove the inadequate system and install an adequate one, less the $6,000 cost if new, would be the measure of the curable functional obsolescence. In addition, any salvage value remaining in the outdated system (a benefit) would have to be considered in the depreciation estimate.

Curable functional obsolescence caused by a superadequacy. A superadequacy is a type of functional obsolescence caused by something in the subject property that exceeds market requirements, but does not contribute to value an amount equal to its cost. A superadequacy is only curable if it can be removed and value is added to the property (plus salvage value) because of its removal. If this is not the case, the superadequacy is incurable.

The subject property is a former duplex which has been converted into an office. The duplex had two furnace rooms, each of which contains a furnace capable of heating the entire building. The tenant who now uses the property as an office needs more room; he will gladly pay $200 more per month in rent if one furnace can be removed and the furnace room housing it is remodeled into office space. The additional rent will more than offset the costs of removing the second furnace and retrofitting the space. The effective gross income multiplier (*EGIM*) is 7.0. A contractor estimates it will cost $7,500 to remove the second furnace and remodel and retrofit the space. If the room had originally been finished as office space, it would have cost $4,400. In the replacement cost estimate, the second furnace had a replacement cost of $5,000, was considered a short-lived item, and was 80% physically deteriorated. The second furnace room was included as a long-lived item, had a replacement cost of $8,000, and was 25% physically deteriorated. This $6,000 has already been included in the cost estimate and should not be considered again.

Cost of existing item	$ 5,000
Less depreciation previously charged	– 4,000
plus	
Cost to cure (all costs)	+ 7,500
or	
Value of loss	+ 0
Less cost if installed new	– 4,400
Equals depreciation from functional obsolescence	$ 4,100

Note that the second furnace and furnace room are superadequacies. The situation is curable because the value increment ($16,800) is greater than the cost to cure ($7,500). The measure of this type of functional obsolescence is the $5,000 cost of the existing item, less the $4,000 charge for deterioration, plus the $7,500 cost to remove the furnace and remodel and retrofit the space, less the $4,000 that the finish would have cost.

Calculating Incurable Functional Obsolescence

Like curable functional obsolescence, incurable functional obsolescence may be caused by a deficiency or a superadequacy. A deficiency is a lack of something other properties in the market have. It is incurable when it is not economically feasible to cure it.

Incurable functional obsolescence caused by a deficiency. Consider a three-story office building without an elevator. If an elevator could be installed, the rents on the upper two floors would increase, and $10,000 more per year in effective gross income could be realized. Structurally, however, the building cannot support an elevator, even if there were space to install one (which there is not). Therefore, the annual rent loss will continue indefinitely. The *EGIM* for this type of property is 8.0. But if the building had been designed to accommodate an elevator, its installation with the original construction would have cost $30,000.

Cost of existing item	$ 0
Less depreciation previously charged	− 0
plus	
Cost to cure (all costs)	+ 0
or	
Value of loss	+ 80,000
Less cost if installed new	− 30,000
Equals depreciation from functional obsolescence	$ 50,000

Note that the lack of an elevator is an incurable deficiency because there is no way to install an elevator in the building. The value of the loss caused by this deficiency is estimated by applying an effective gross income multiplier of 8.0 to the income loss ($10,000), resulting in an estimate of $80,000. A similar estimate could be obtained by capitalizing the net rent loss by a building capitalization rate. The effect of this loss is partially offset by the $30,000 that would have been expended.

Incurable functional obsolescence caused by a superadequacy. An item of incurable functional obsolescence caused by a superadequacy is a property component that exceeds market requirements. It represents a cost without any corresponding increment in value, or a cost that the increment in value does not meet. This form of functional obsolescence is incurable because it is not economically feasible to cure it. In most applications of the cost approach, the need to estimate the functional obsolescence attributable to an incurable superadequacy is eliminated by using replacement cost instead of reproduction cost; superadequacies are not replicated in a replacement cost estimate. Nevertheless, whether replacement or reproduction cost is used, any extraordinary expense of ownership associated with the superadequacy must be quantified and deducted as a penalty from the value of the property.

For example, assume the subject is an industrial building with 24-ft. ceiling heights where the market norm is 16-ft. ceilings. The reproduction cost of a building with 24-ft. ceilings is $1,200,000 whereas the replacement cost of a building with 16-ft. ceilings is $1,000,000. The subject building costs $5,000 more per year to heat and air condition than comparable properties in the subject's market. Obviously, there is no way to cure this superadequacy. Because the ceiling height is an excess compared to the market norm, it is a superadequacy. In this market, the extra eight feet of ceiling height add no value to the property. Therefore, the amount entered as cost if intalled new is zero. The building capitalization rate in this market is 12.5%. The superadequate component is a long-lived item and has already been charged 10% for physical depreciation.

Cost of existing item	$200,000
Less depreciation previously charged	− 20,000
plus	
Cost to cure (all costs)	+ 0
or	
Value of the loss ($5,000/0.125)	+ 40,000
Less cost if installed new	− 0
Equals depreciation from functional obsolescence	$220,000

Note that if replacement cost is used, the $200,000 cost of the superadequacy will be eliminated and the measure of functional obsolescence would be only the capitalized additional costs of ownership. The extra ceiling height costs the subject $5,000 more per year than the costs incurred by competitive buildings, and the building capitalization rate is 12.5%. The incurable functional obsolescence in this instance is estimated to be $40,000 ($5,000/0.125).

If reproduction cost is used, the additional $200,000 cost of the superadequacy will *not* be eliminated. The incurable functional obsolescence would be measured as the cost of the superadequate item, less the physical deterioration already charged, plus the capitalized additional costs of ownership. Assuming that a 10% charge has already been levied for incurable physical deterioration due to the extra ceiling height, the incurable functional obsolescence would be the cost of the superadequate item ($200,000), less the physical deterioration already charged ($20,000), plus the added costs of ownership ($40,000). The resulting depreciation estimate is $220,000.

Calculating External Obsolescence

External obsolescence is a loss in value caused by factors outside a property. It is often incurable. External obsolescence can be either temporary, e.g., an oversupplied market, or permanent, e.g., proximity to an environmental disaster. External factors frequently affect both the land and building components of a property's value. External obsolescence is usually marketwide when its cause is economic, e.g., insufficient demand for a certain type of use or product the subject property was designed to provide, increased costs associated with governmental regulations (ADA requirements), changing technology, negative economic conditions such as high interest rates, unaffordable financing, or economic recessions. External obsolescence may affect only the subject property when its cause is location, e.g., negative environmental factors or the absence of zoning and land use controls.

When market data are studied to develop an estimate of external obsolescence, it is important to isolate the effect of the obsolescence on land value from the effect on the value of the improvements. In some situations, external obsolescence may be imputed entirely to the land; in other situations, it may be imputed entirely to the improvements. Often external obsolescence can be allocated between land and improvements. This is critical if external obsolescence is already reflected in the estimate of land value. A building-to-property-value ratio derived through district or neighborhood analysis may be used to determine the loss in value to be imputed to the building.

The two primary methods of measuring external obsolescence are paired data analysis and the capitalization of a rent loss. Paired data analysis is a useful technique when market evidence is available.

Example—External obsolescence estimated by paired data analysis.

The subject property is a 12-unit apartment building located downwind of a relatively new asphalt batching plant. Sale A is a vacant lot adjacent to the subject which is zoned for a 12-unit apartment building and was just sold for $36,000 ($3,000 per unit). Sale B is a vacant site on the other side of town which is also zoned for a 12-unit apartment building and was recently sold for $48,000 ($4,000 per unit). Sale C is a 9-unit apartment building in the subject's neighborhood which was recently sold for $459,000 ($51,000 per unit). Sale D is a 10-unit apartment building on the other side of town which was sold for $540,000 ($54,000 per unit). Using Sales C and D, the external obsolescence attributable to the property as a whole is estimated at $3,000 per unit. The subject property would thus incur $36,000 in external obsolescence (12 units x $3,000). Sales A and B indicate that $12,000 of this external obsolescence ($1,000 per unit) is attributable to the land; the remaining $24,000, therefore, is attributable to the building.

When a property produces income, the rent loss caused by the external obsolescence can be capitalized into an estimate of the loss in total property value. The portion attributable to the improvement can then be isolated from the portion attributable to the land. This procedure is applied in three steps. First, the market is analyzed to quantify the rent loss. Next, the rent loss is capitalized to obtain the value loss affecting the property as a whole. Third, the resulting total loss in value is allocated between the two property components as appropriate. If the rent loss is anticipated to be permanent, it can be capitalized by means of direct capitalization. This involves applying either a multiplier to a gross income loss or a capitalization rate to a net income loss. If the rent loss is not anticipated to be permanent, it can be capitalized using discounted cash flow analysis.

Example—External obsolescence estimated by capitalization of rent loss.

The subject property is 4,000-sq.-ft. retail establishment in an oversupplied market. In a normal market, net operating income would be $8.00 per square foot. However, since the oversupply began, net operating income has fallen to $6.25 per square foot. The oversupply, which is unique to the subject's market, was caused by overbuilding. It is anticipated to continue indefinitely. The overall capitalization rate indicated by the market is 10%. Since the oversupply is anticipated to continue indefinitely, the external obsolescence can be calculated by direct capitalization. The total rent loss of $7,000 ($8.00 - $6.25 = $1.75 x 4,000 square feet) is capitalized by the overall capitalization rate of 10%. The resulting external obsolescence of $70,000 would probably be attributed entirely to the improvements.

If the oversupply were anticipated to continue for a relatively short period of time, the external obsolescence could be calculated by discounted cash flow analysis. Assume that the $7,000 rent loss will only last three years and that the appropriate discount rate for this type of investment is 13%. The external obsolescence could be calculated as the present value of $7,000 per year for three years, discounted at 13% (*PV* of $1 per period at 13% for three years = 2.361153), or $16,528. As in the previous example in which direct capitalization was used, it is likely that the entire amount of external obsolescence would be attributable to the improvement.

Key Concepts

- Depreciation is the difference between the market value of an improvement and its reproduction or replacement cost. The depreciated cost of the improvement can be considered an indication of the market value of the improvement.

- Depreciation may be caused by physical deterioration, functional obsolescence, or external obsolescence.

- In the cost approach, the reproduction or replacement cost of the improvement(s) is estimated; the depreciation attributable to all causes is calculated and deducted from cost new to arrive at depreciated cost; and an estimate of the value of the land and site improvements is added to depreciated cost to provide an indication of the market value of the property.

- Age-life relationships used to develop an estimate of total depreciation include economic life, effective age, and remaining economic life; age-life relationships used to estimate deterioration in physical components include useful life, actual age, and remaining useful life.

- Physical components include items of deferred maintenance, short-lived items, and long-lived items.

- The three methods used to estimate depreciation are the market extraction, age-life, and breakdown methods.

- The market extraction and age-life methods are easy to apply. Both are limited in that they assume a straight-line pattern of depreciation, lump depreciation from all causes into an overall estimate, do not distinguish between short-lived and long-lived items, and rely on forecasts of remaining economic life.

- The breakdown method may be used in conjunction with market extraction or age-life methods to allocate an overall depreciation estimate among its components. The method can also be used to develop an overall estimate of depreciation independently.

- Deterioration in items of deferred maintenance is measured by the cost to cure or to restore to a (reasonably) new condition. Deteriorated short-lived items are considered curable if the cost to cure results in an increment in value equal to or greater than the cost or if curing the item is required to maintain the value of other building components. Deteriorated long-lived items rarely need to be cured. Any cost to cure damage or vandalism may also have to be estimated.

- Functional obsolescence may be caused by a deficiency or a superadequacy; some forms are curable and others are incurable.

- External obsolescence may be caused by economic or locational factors. It may be temporary or permanent, but is not considered curable on the part of the owner, landlord, or tenant.

- The age-life procedure is a useful model for ensuring that all forms of physical deterioration are correctly estimated and dealt with only once. The functional obsolescence procedure ensures that all items of functional obsolescence will be treated consistently, that none will be considered more than once, and that double depreciation charges will not be made.

- External obsolescence may be estimated by paired data analysis or by capitalization of rent loss.

Terms

actual age	functional obsolescence
age-life method	functional obsolescence procedure
age-life procedure for physical deterioration	incurable physical deterioration/ functional obsolescence
book depreciation	long-lived component
breakdown method	market extraction method
capitalization of rent loss	paired data analysis
cost to cure	physical deterioration
cost to replace	remaining economic life
curable physical deterioration/ functional obsolescence	remaining useful life
damage	replacement cost
deferred maintenance (items)	reproduction cost
deficiency	salvage value
depreciation	short-lived component
economic feasibility	superadequacy
economic life	total life expectancy
effective age	useful life
external obsolescence	vandalism

CHAPTER EIGHTEEN

The Sales Comparison Approach

T he sales comparison approach is the process in which a market value estimate is derived by analyzing the market for similar properties and comparing these properties to the subject property. The comparative techniques of analysis applied in the sales comparison approach are fundamental to the valuation process. Estimates of market rent, cost, depreciation, and other value parameters may be derived in the other approaches to value using similar comparative techniques. Often these elements are also analyzed in the sales comparison approach to estimate the adjustments to be made to the sale prices of comparable properties.

In the sales comparison approach, market value is estimated by comparing properties similar to the subject property that have recently been sold, are listed for sale, or are under contract (i.e., for which purchase offers and a deposit have been recently submitted). A major premise of the sales comparison approach is that the market value of a property is directly related to the prices of comparable, competitive properties.

Comparative analysis focuses on similarities and differences among properties and transactions that affect value. These may include differences in property rights appraised, the motivations of buyers and sellers, financing terms, market conditions at the time of sale (the comparative numbers of buyers, sellers, and lenders), size, location, physical features, and, if the properties produce income, economic characteristics. Elements of comparison are tested against market evidence to estimate which elements are sensitive to change and how they affect value.

Relationship to Appraisal Principles

The concepts of anticipation and change, which underlie the principles of supply and demand, substitution, balance, and externalities, are basic to the sales comparison approach. Guided by these principles, an appraiser attempts to consider all issues relevant to the valuation problem in a manner that is consistent and reflects local market conditions.

Supply and Demand

Property prices result from negotiations between buyers, sellers, and lenders. Buyers constitute market demand, and the properties offered for sale make up the supply. If the demand for a particular type of property is high, prices tend to increase; if demand is low, prices tend to decline. Shifts in the supply of improved properties frequently lag behind shifts in demand because supply is created by time-consuming construction and reduced by conversion to other uses, while satisfiable demand can change rapidly. The analysis of real estate markets at a specific time may seem to focus on demand, but the supply of properties must also be considered. Proposed construction, conversion, and demolition may change the supply-demand relationship and affect prices. To estimate demand, appraisers consider the number of potential users of a particular type of property, their purchasing power, and their tastes and preferences. To analyze supply appraisers focus on existing unsold or vacant properties as well as properties that are being constructed, converted, or planned. Shifts in any of these factors may cause the prices of the subject property and comparable properties to vary. Sales activity is also influenced by lenders, whose terms can cause the market to accelerate, decelerate, grind to a halt, or shift elsewhere.

Substitution

The principle of substitution holds that the value of a property tends to be set by the price that would be paid to acquire a substitute property of similar utility and desirability within a reasonable amount of time. This principle implies that the reliability of the sales comparison approach is diminished if substitute properties are not available in the market.

Balance

The forces of supply and demand tend toward equilibrium, or balance, in the market, but absolute equilibrium is almost never attained. The balance between supply and demand changes continually. Due to shifts in population, purchasing power, and consumer tastes and preferences, demand varies greatly over time. The construction of new buildings, conversion to other uses, and the demolition of old buildings cause supply to vary as well.

Another aspect of this principle holds that the relationship between land and improvements and the relationship between a property and its environment must both be in balance for a property to reflect its optimum market value. If, for example, a property has too much land in relation to its improvements or too many expensive amenities for its location, an imbalance is created. Appraisers must watch for imbalances in the market and within properties because they can cause the market to impute different prices to otherwise comparable properties.

Externalities

Positive and negative external forces affect all types of property. Periods of economic development and economic depression influence property values. An appraiser analyzes the neighborhood of the subject property to identify all significant external influences. To a great extent, these external forces are reflected in the adjustments made for property location. Two properties with identical physical characteristics may have quite different market values if one of the properties has less attractive surroundings. The condition and lighting of streets, the convenience of transportation facilities, the adequacy of police protection, the enforcement of municipal regulation, and the proximity to shopping and restaurant facilities vary with location. These factors must be considered by the appraiser to establish whether they have a positive or negative effect on the value of the property being appraised.

Applicability and Limitations

The sales comparison approach is applicable to all types of real property interests when there are sufficient recent, reliable transactions to indicate value patterns or trends in the market. For property types that are bought and sold regularly, the sales comparison approach often provides a supportable indication of market value. When data are available, this is the most direct and systematic approach to value estimation.

When the market is weak and the number of market transactions is insufficient, the applicability of the sales comparison approach may be limited. For example, the sales comparison approach is rarely applied to special-purpose properties because few similar properties may be sold in a given market, even one that is geographically broad. The income capitalization approach may be equally inapplicable. To value special-purpose properties, the cost approach may be more appropriate and reliable. Nevertheless, data on sales and offers for similar properties may establish broad limits for the value of the property being appraised, which may help support the findings of the other value approaches applied.

Generally, the sales comparison approach has broad applicability and is persuasive when sufficient data are available. It usually provides the primary indication of market value in appraisals of properties such as houses which are not usually purchased for their income-producing characteristics. Most single-family residential properties are amenable to direct sales comparison because many similar properties are commonly bought and sold in the same market, and many prospective buyers have chosen not to rent or build. Typically, the sales comparison approach also provides the best indication of value for small, owner-occupied commercial and industrial properties.

Buyers of income-producing properties usually concentrate on a property's economic characteristics, most often focusing on the rate of return for an investment made in anticipation of future cash flows. Thoroughly analyzing comparable sales of large, complex, income-producing properties is difficult because information on the economic factors influencing buyers' decisions is not readily available from public records or interviews with buyers and sellers. For example, an appraiser may not have sufficient knowledge of the terms of the existing leases applicable to a multitenanted, neighborhood shopping center that is comparable to the subject. Or the appraiser may not be fully informed of the investment parameters of the buyer. In some circumstances the real estate may represent only one component of value in an enterprise whose sale price reflects customer lists, accounts receivable, patents, goodwill, and an assembled work force. Sales data on comparable income-producing properties may be of limited use to the appraiser. Without complete information it will be difficult to arrive at a reliable indication of value for the subject property.

Rapidly changing economic conditions and legislation can also limit the reliability of the sales comparison approach. Perhaps the single greatest criticism of sales comparison is that the approach lags behind the market, resulting in appraisals that are based on dated information. The availability and cost of financing, changes in income tax laws and zoning regulations, or moratoriums on building and infrastructure development may result in a lack of recent comparable sales that reflect the impact of such changes over a given time period. An appraiser will have difficulty finding reliable market data on which to base an adjustment for the change. Rapid inflation or deflation can also jeopardize the reliability of an appraiser's adjustments.

Often little comparable data can be found to estimate the value of the first property to be renovated in an area of deteriorated buildings or the only property of a given type in a neighborhood. The appraiser may need to expand the search for sales data to other comparable neighborhoods.

To ensure the reliability of value conclusions derived by applying the sales comparison approach, the appraiser must verify the market data obtained and fully understand the behavioral characteristics of the buyers and sellers involved in property transactions. Caution should be exercised when sales data are provided by someone who is not a party to the transaction. Incorrect conclusions may result if the appraiser relies on such data without considering the motivation of the parties to the transactions. Similarly, errors can result if database characteristics, anticipated income and expense schedules, or potential changes in use are not considered.

It is imperative that the appraiser identify and analyze the strengths and weaknesses of the data compiled and the comparative analyses undertaken in the sales comparison approach. All relevant facts and opinions must be communicated in the appraisal report. Statements concerning the reliability of the data, the analyses performed, and the final conclusion of value should be presented in both the reconciliation section of the sales comparison approach and the final reconciliation of the value estimate.

The sales comparison approach is a significant and essential part of the valuation process, even when its reliability is limited. Although the dissimilarities in factors affecting property value cannot always be properly identified and quantified, the sales comparison approach may still provide a probable range of value in support of a value indication derived using one of the other approaches. Furthermore, data needed to apply the other approaches (e.g., overall capitalization rates for the income capitalization approach or depreciation estimates for the cost approach) are often obtained in the comparison process.

Required Data and Sources

To apply the sales comparison approach, an appraiser gathers data on sales, contracts, offers, refusals, options, and listings of properties considered competitive with, and comparable to, the subject property. Data from completed transactions are considered the most reliable value indicators. First, the appraiser thoroughly researches the prices, real property rights conveyed, financing terms, motivations of buyers and sellers, and dates of the property transactions. Then details on each property's location, physical and functional condition, and economic characteristics must be examined. Since conclusions must be market-derived, the appraiser will rely heavily on interviews, personal contacts, and proprietary research.

Most appraisers maintain data files on the details of market transactions and add information as new transactions occur. The potential sources of sales data are many and varied. Primary sources include courthouse records; government sales tax records; commercially available data from electronic reporting and multiple listing services; real estate periodicals; and interviews with the parties to transactions, their employees, attorneys, appraisers, counselors, brokers, property managers, and lenders. Assessment data should generally not be used to develop an estimate of market value.

Appraisers should verify information to ensure its accuracy and to understand the motivation behind each transaction. The buyer's perspective of what was being purchased at the time of sale is very important. Sales that are not arm's-length market transactions should be identified and used with caution. To verify sales data an appraiser confirms statements of fact with the principals to the transaction, if possible, or with the brokers, closing agents, or lenders involved. Owners and tenants of neighboring properties may also provide helpful information. Sometimes income and expense data for income-producing properties are unobtainable. If data on a particular sale are unavailable, imputing rents and expenses "based on market parameters" is improper.

The geographic limits of the appraiser's search for sales data depend on the nature and type of real estate being valued. Market boundaries define the area where potential buyers of comparable properties would look. If similar properties are commonly bought and sold in the same neighborhood as the subject property, the search will probably be relatively limited. At times, however, the appraiser must extend the area of the search to similar neighborhoods or market areas. Certain types of properties have regional, national, and even international markets. To estimate the values of regional shopping malls, office buildings, resort hotels, large multi-use complexes, and large industrial properties, appraisers may scrutinize data from a wide geographic area within which the competitive properties are located.

A sale price reflects many different factors that affect a property's value in varying degrees. Qualitative and quantitative techniques are employed to determine the relative significance of these factors. Appraisers employ mathematical applications to derive quantitative adjustments. When sufficient data to support a quantitative adjustment are not available, appraisers investigate qualitative relationships through direct comparison of market data and analysis of market trends.

After sales information has been collected and confirmed, it can be organized in a variety of ways. One convenient and commonly used method is to arrange the data on a market data grid. Each important difference between the comparable properties and the subject property that could affect property value is considered an element of comparison. Each element is assigned a row on the grid and total property prices or unit prices of the comparables are adjusted to reflect the value of these differences. The adjustments made reflect the thought processes and judgments of a typical buyer before an offer to buy or an actual purchase is made. A sample market data grid and the procedures used to make adjustments on such a grid are presented later in this chapter.

Procedure

To apply the sales comparison approach, an appraiser follows a systematic procedure. A general outline of the basic procedure follows.

1. Research the market for information on sales transactions, listings, and offers to purchase or sell involving properties that are similar to the subject property in

terms of characteristics such as property type, date of sale, size, physical condition, location, and zoning.

2. Verify the information by confirming that the data obtained are factually accurate and that the transactions reflect arm's-length, market considerations. Verification may elicit additional information about the market.

3. Select relevant units of comparison (e.g., price per acre, price per square foot, price per front foot) and develop a comparative analysis for each unit.

4. Compare comparable sale properties with the subject property using the elements of comparison and adjust the price of each comparable to the subject property *or* eliminate the sale property as a comparable.

5. Reconcile the various value indications produced from the analysis of comparables into a single value indication or a range of values. In an imprecise market subject to varying occupancies and economies, a range of values may be a better conclusion than a single value estimate.

Units of Comparison

After sales data have been gathered and verified, systematic analysis begins. Because like units must be compared, each sale price should be stated in terms of appropriate units of comparison. The units of comparison selected depend on the appraisal problem and nature of the property. Apartment properties are often analyzed on the basis of price per apartment unit. (Price per square foot of gross building area or gross leasable area is also widely used.) Warehouses and industrial properties may be compared based on price per square foot or cubic foot of gross building area. Hotels and motels are typically analyzed in terms of price per guest room; restaurants, theaters, and auditoriums in price per seat; golf courses in price per round (annual number of rounds played) or membership; and tennis and racquetball facilities in price per playing court. Mobile home parks are compared using price per parking pad; marinas, price per slip; automobile repair facilities, in price per bay; and vacant land, price per front foot, per square foot, or per acre. The typical units of comparison for single-family residential property are total property price and price per square foot of gross living area.

Units of comparison are used to facilitate comparison of the subject and comparable properties. When sale prices are reduced to size-related unit prices, the need to make adjustments for size differences is usually eliminated. Differences in size are considered in reconciliation, and the unit(s) of comparison selected can have a significant bearing on the reconciliation of value indications in this approach. It may sometimes be necessary to adjust for differences in *economies of scale*. For example, assume two industrial sites are studied as comparables. The first, a five-acre site, is almost identical to the subject in acreage. The second, a 15-acre site, is highly comparable to the subject, but it may sell for less on a per-acre basis, all other factors being equal.

Adjustments can be made either to total property prices or to appropriate units of comparison. Often adjustments for property rights conveyed, financing, conditions of sale (motivation), and date of sale (market conditions) are made to the total sale price. The adjusted price is then converted into a unit price (e.g., per square foot, per apartment unit, per acre) and adjusted for other elements of comparison such as location and physical characteristics.

Income multipliers and overall capitalization rates are not quantitatively adjusted in sales comparison analysis. Comparable prices are not adjusted on the basis of percentage differences in net operating income per unit because rents and sales prices tend to move in relative tandem. However, the appraiser should consider why the income from units varies among the sale properties. Sensitivity and trend analyses may be performed to gain an understanding of this variance.

For example, an appraiser may analyze sales of income-producing properties to derive potential and effective gross income multipliers, overall and equity capitalization rates, and even total property yield rates. These factors are not adjusted quantitatively. Instead, the appraiser considers their ranges and the similarities and differences between the subject and comparable sale properties that cause the multipliers and rates to vary. Qualitative adjustments based on sensitivity, trend, and grouped data analyses may be used to support quantitative adjustments that establish a bracket of rates for the subject. These techniques address the market sensitivities influencing the differences in rates. The appraiser then selects the rate from within the bracket that is most appropriate to the property being appraised for use in the income capitalization approach.

Income multipliers, capitalization rates, and yield rates are applied in the income capitalization approach to value, but it is appropriate to extract such rates and factors from comparable properties in sales comparison analysis.

Elements of Comparison

Elements of comparison are the characteristics of properties and transactions that cause the prices paid for real estate to vary. The appraiser considers and compares all discernible differences between the comparable properties and the subject property that could affect their values. Market evidence should be tested to identify the variables to which property values are especially sensitive. Statistical measures such as standard deviations and coefficients of variability[1] may be used in the judgment process.

Adjustments for differences are made to the price of each comparable property to make the comparable equal to the subject on the effective date of the value estimate. Adjustments for differences in elements of comparison may be made to the total property price, to a common unit price, or to a mix of both, but the unit prices used must be consistently applied to the comparable properties. The amount of adjustment made for each element of comparison depends on the extent to which each comparable property differs from the subject property. Appraisers must be sure to consider all appropriate elements of comparison and avoid adjusting for the same difference more than once.

There are ten basic elements of comparison that should be considered in sales comparison analysis.

---

1. If the volume of data permits, a basic statistical analysis using means, medians, standard deviations, and coefficients of variability may be developed. The coefficient of variability represents the standard deviation divided by the mean value. The unit(s) of comparison with the lowest coefficient of variability tend to reflect market thinking best and are generally consistent with buyer and seller expectations.

1. Real property rights conveyed
2. Financing terms
3. Conditions of sale
4. Expenditures made immediately after purchase
5. Market conditions
6. Location
7. Physical characteristics (size, construction quality, condition)
8. Economic characteristics (operating expenses, lease provisions, management, tenant mix)
9. Use (zoning)
10. Non-realty components of value

In most cases these elements of comparison cover all the significant factors to be considered, but on occasion additional elements may be relevant. Other possible elements of comparison include governmental restrictions such as conservation or preservation easements and water and riparian rights, access to the property, and off-site improvements required for the development of a vacant site. Often a basic element of comparison is broken down into subcategories that specifically address the property factor being analyzed. For example, physical characteristics may be broken down into subcategories for age, condition, size, etc.

If the appraiser's investigation uncovers only a few truly comparable properties or none at all, properties with more divergent characteristics may be included among the market evidence. If properly analyzed and adjusted, a broad sample of more diverse properties can offer a good perspective on the value of the subject property. A small number of comparable sales is often insufficient to support adjustments for differences in several elements of comparison; a range of value indications based on small samples of comparable data may distort the appraiser's conclusions and the final value estimate. The larger the database from which adjustments are extracted, the more reliable the conclusion. More extensive market evidence can provide an appraiser with greater insight into property value differences attributable to elements such as zoning, site size, and location (e.g., corner vs. interior lot).

Real Property Rights Conveyed

A preliminary step in the valuation process is to determine the real property interest to be appraised. Once this is established, the appraiser can relate the market data to the subject property. The appraiser must also precisely identify the real property rights conveyed in each comparable transaction selected for analysis. Thus, one of the first adjustments to be considered is the adjustment for differences in real property rights.

A transaction price is always predicated on the real property interest conveyed. Many types of real estate, particularly income-producing property, are sold subject to existing leases. The revenue-generating potential of a property is often fixed or limited by the terms of existing leases. In the valuation process, adjustments must be made to reflect the difference between properties leased at market rent and those leased either below or above market levels. The duration of existing leases affects these adjustments as do other lease terms that influence the income generated. To develop an adjustment for property rights, an appraiser must have specific information on the income structure and leasing conditions of the sale property. It is impossible to support a property rights adjustment without such information.

The transaction price of a property sold subject to existing leases reflects the contract rent that it will generate during the term of each lease and the market rent that will likely be achieved thereafter. In these situations the real property interest that is sold or being appraised is the leased fee estate. The value of a fee simple estate is based on market terms for rents.

For example, assume the fee simple interest in an office building is being appraised. A comparable building was fully leased at the time of sale, the leases were long-term, and the credit ratings of the tenants were good. To compare this leased fee estate to the subject fee simple estate, the appraiser must determine if the contract rent of the comparable was above, below, or equal to market rent. If the market rent for office space is $25 per square foot, and the average rent for the comparable sale property was $24 per square foot, the difference between market and contract rent is $1 per square foot.

The comparable sale property in question is a 100,000-sq.-ft. office building. The market indicates that 10% is an appropriate overall capitalization rate, the vacancy rate for the market in which the subject property is located is 5%, and 4% of effective gross income is a reasonable management expense.[2] The *effective* difference between the market rent of $25 per square foot and the contract rent of $24 per square foot is estimated by deducting the vacancy allowance (5%) and management expenses (4%) from the *actual* difference between these rents ($1). This amount is then multiplied by the total area of the sale property to derive the annual rent loss for the remaining term of the lease.

$1.00 - 0.05 (5% vacancy) = $0.95
$0.95 - 0.04 (4% management) = $0.91 (rounded)
$0.91 x 100,000 sq. ft. = $91,000

Other expenses are not considered because the leases are net leases and expenses do not constitute percentage charges against income.

The annual rent loss is then discounted over the remaining term of the lease. In the above example, the lease has 10 more years to run and market evidence supports a discount rate of 12%. Discounting the $91,000 annual loss in income over 10 years at 12% indicates an upward adjustment of $514,000. The present value of the $91,000 annual loss for 10 years at 12% is calculated below.

5.650223* x $91,000 = $514,170, or $514,000

* PV of $1 per period factor, 10 years @ 12%

The calculation is based on the assumption that the $1.00 difference between market rent and contract rent remains constant over the entire 10 years.

Calculating an adjustment for differences in real property rights is also necessary when just the leasehold interest is to be conveyed. For example, consider an office

2. The appraiser should make sure that the operating expenses of the properties are comparable. Generally the higher the rent the tenant pays, the more services the landlord provides.

building that is sold separately from its site, which is subject to a 99-year ground lease. The 100,000-sq.-ft. building, which is leased at market rent, sold for $7,500,000, or $75.00 per square foot. To determine the value of the fee simple estate in the total property, the value of the leased fee estate (the land) must be added to the value of the leasehold estate (the building).

One way to calculate the value of the leased fee estate is to capitalize the rent that accrues to the land. The annual ground rent is $200,000, which is consistent with current market rents, and market evidence supports a land capitalization rate of 8%. The calculation is

$$\text{Income to the land divided by } R_L = \$200,000/0.08$$

$$\text{Value of the leased fee} \qquad = \$2,500,000$$

Typically, the capitalization rate for the land will be lower than the rate for the building because the building incurs physical deterioration. In this case, an upward movement of $2,500,000 for property rights conveyed would be shown in the sales comparison grid.

In many situations, there may be an advantage associated with a leasehold interest in the land. For example, if the market value of the land in fee simple exceeds the market value of the land in leased fee, a leasehold owner who holds both an interest in the building and a favorable, long-term ground lease is at an advantage. In many U.S. cities (e.g., New York, Los Angeles, Houston), ground leases are typically long term. An adjustment for the advantage accruing from a long-term leasehold in the land can be derived by capitalizing the difference between contract rent and market rent.

If the real property rights conveyed for the comparable properties and the subject differ and no numerical adjustments are made for these differences in the sales comparison approach, the dissimilarities must be addressed elsewhere in the appraisal report— e.g., in the qualitative analysis and reconciliation of value indications from the sales comparison approach or in the reconciliation and final value estimate section. The appraiser should also consider any differences in the other approaches and estimate how they affect the value indication derived.

Financing Terms

The transaction price of one property may differ from that of an identical property due to different financing arrangements. For example, the purchaser of a comparable property may have assumed an existing mortgage at a favorable interest rate. In another case a developer or seller may have arranged a buydown, paying cash to the lender so that a mortgage with a below-market interest rate could be offered. In both cases the buyers probably paid higher prices for the properties to obtain below-market financing. Conversely, interest rates at above-market levels often result in lower sale prices.

Other nonmarket financing arrangements include installment sale contracts, in which the buyer pays periodic installments to the seller and obtains legal title only after the contract is fulfilled, and wraparound loans, which are superimposed on existing mortgages to preserve their lower interest rates. These loans offer below-market or blended interest rates to borrowers (buyers). Below-market rates are sometimes extended to individuals who have substantial bank accounts and are therefore especially creditworthy.

A financing adjustment may or may not include an adjustment for conditions of sale. A conditions of sale adjustment recognizes that some sales are transacted by parties under duress, who are at a disadvantage. A combined adjustment results when favorable financing is a function of the seller's need to sell the property quickly. Appraisers should recognize that, in some situations, these factors are interdependent.

In cash equivalency analysis an appraiser investigates the sale prices of comparable properties that appear to have been sold with nonmarket financing to determine whether adjustments to reflect typical market terms are warranted. First, sales with nonmarket financing are compared to other sales transacted with market financing to determine whether an adjustment for cash equivalency can be made. *Market evidence is always the best indicator of such an adjustment.* However, buyers rarely, if ever, rely on strict dollar for dollar cash equivalency adjustments.

Financing adjustments derived from precise, mathematical calculations for analyzing cash equivalency must be rigorously tested against market evidence. Realizing a profit provides the incentive for both the buyer and seller. Strict mathematical calculations may not, therefore, reflect market behavior. Market evidence must support whatever adjustment is made. If the cash discount indicated by the calculations is not recognized by buyers and sellers, the adjustment is not justified.

The definition of market value recognizes cash equivalent terms provided the calculation of these terms reflects the market. Conditions of sale may reveal other, noneconomic interests on the part of buyers or sellers. Confirmation of the intent of buyers and sellers is one way to verify a cash equivalency adjustment. Caution must continually be exercised in applying cash equivalency calculations. The final adjustment must always be derived from the market.

Cash equivalency calculations vary depending on the kind of financing arrangement that requires adjustment.[3] Two common situations involve points that the seller pays and loans that the seller finances. When the seller rather than the buyer pays points—i.e., the percentage that the lender charges for making the loan—the appraiser often deducts the full dollar amount from the sale price.

Appraisers may calculate adjustments for atypical financing by analyzing paired data sets or discounting the cash flows (e.g., payments and balloons) created by the mortgage contract at market interest rates. If discounting is used, the appraiser should not assume that the buyer will hold the property for the life of the mortgage. Market evidence often indicates otherwise. A mortgage is often discounted for a shorter term, but the balloon payment must still be included.

Buyers of real estate consciously commit to 1) the amount to be invested as equity and 2) the fixed periodic dollar payment to amortize the debt and pay the interest. Thus, debt components vary with the periodic loan payment and the constant debt cost. Differences in loan amounts and terms warrant the adjustment of sale prices. In cash equivalency analyses, direct market evidence is used to make the appropriate adjustments. The appraiser tries to locate sales with and without atypical financing, makes

---

3. For further discussion and examples of cash equivalency calculations, see David C. Lennhoff, "Defining the Problem," *The Appraisal Journal* (April 1986) and Halbert C. Smith and John B. Corgel, "Adjusting for Nonmarket Financing: A Quick and Easy Method," *The Appraisal Journal* (January 1984).

adjustments for other differences, and attributes the remaining price differential to the financing terms. This method can be used as a guide even if substantial data on transactions with special financing are not available.

When paired data analysis is used to derive a cash equivalency adjustment, the calculations for discounting and adjusting for atypical conditions of sale are often combined. In other words, the adjustments for financing and conditions of sale can be represented by a single figure.

For example, consider a house that sells for $125,000 with a down payment of $25,000 and a seller-financed $100,000 mortgage at 8% interest. The mortgage is amortized over 25 years with a balloon payment due in 8 years. To determine the appropriate discount rate, the appraiser checks the market for sales financed by similar mortgage arrangements and finds that an $80,000, 8% note has been sold for $65,000. The discount rate for this note is calculated as follows:

$$($80,000 - $65,000)/$80,000 = 0.1875 \text{ or } 18.75\%$$

This discount rate may be applied to the $100,000 loan to arrive at the cash equivalent value of the mortgage.

$100,000 - ($100,000 x 0.1875)	$81,250
Plus down payment	$25,000
Sale price adjusted for financing	$106,250

Calculating a cash equivalency adjustment by discounting cash flows can be accomplished in different ways. When a seller finances a mortgage at a below-market interest rate, the appraiser can estimate the present value of the mortgage by applying a present value factor to the monthly mortgage payment at the market interest rate for the stated term of the mortgage. For example, an appraiser might find a comparable sale of a single-family residence that was sold for $110,000 with a down payment of $25,000 and a seller-financed mortgage of $85,000 for a 20-year term at 10% interest. Homes in the market area are typically held for the full, 20-year term and the market-derived rate is 13%. The sale can be adjusted to cash equivalency as follows:

Mortgage: $85,000, 20 years, 10%
Monthly payment: $820.27
Present value of $820.27 per month for 20 years @ market rate of 13%

85.355132* x $820.27 = $70,014	
PV of mortgage, rounded	$70,000
Plus down payment	$25,000
Sale price adjusted for financing	$95,000

---

* PV of $1 per period factor, 20 years @ 13%, compounded monthly

Another way to calculate the present value of the mortgage is to divide the monthly payment factor (monthly constant) at the contract interest rate by the monthly payment factor at the market interest rate and multiply the mortgage by the result. In this case,

0.00965/0.011715 = 0.82373, x $85,000 = $70,017. (Implicit in this method is the assumption that the difference between the market interest rate and the contract interest rate will remain constant for the entire 20 years.)

Discounting cash flows to calculate a cash equivalency adjustment may also take into account the expectation of a balloon payment. The following example incorporates the same mortgage terms set forth in the previous example, except that the mortgagor (borrower) holds the mortgage for only seven years. (The average mortgage life for loans on different types of properties can be ascertained from sales data on loans that were paid off or refinanced rather than assumed by a buyer.) In the following example, the present value of the mortgage is computed as the sum of two components: the present value of the mortgage payments at the market interest rate for the expected life of a mortgage and the present value of the future mortgage balance at the market interest rate. One way to obtain the latter is first to calculate the value in seven years of the remaining 13 years of monthly payments at the contract rate and then to calculate the present value of that lump sum.

Monthly payment: $820.27
Present value of $820.27 per month for 7 years @ 13%
  54.969328* x $820.27 = $45,090, rounded $ 45,000
Value of remaining mortgage payments in 7 years
  PV of $820.27 per month for 13 years @ 10%
  87.119542† x $820.27 = $71,462
PV of mortgage balance
  0.425061‡ x $71,462 = $30,376 (rounded)   30,000
PV of mortgage $ 75,000

Plus down payment   25,000
Sale price adjusted for financing $100,000

---

* PV of $1 per period factor, 84 months @ 13% (monthly frequency)
† PV of $1 per period factor, 156 months @ 10% (monthly frequency)
‡ PV of $1 factor, 7 years @ 13% (annual frequency)
Note. The quantitative difference resulting from the choice of a discount factor at an annual frequency rather than a discount rate at a monthly frequency is insignificant. If the monthly frequency of the PV of $1 factor for 7 years @ 13% (0.404499) had been used in the above example, the adjusted sale price would have come to $99,000 (rounded). Errors in discounting are generally attributable to the choice of the discount rate, not the frequency of that rate.

Alternatively, the outstanding mortgage balance at the end of seven years can be calculated. Although these methods require more calculation, they are preferable because they reflect the typical holding period more accurately.

Transactions involving mortgage assumptions can be adjusted to cash equivalency with the same method applied to seller-financed transactions. However, the appraiser should be certain that the existing loan was assumed, not paid off. Other atypical mortgage terms include payments of interest only, followed by payments that include the repayment of the principal. This type of mortgage can also be adjusted to its cash equivalent value using the adjustment procedure described here. The present values of the payments (monthly, quarterly, semi-annual, or annual) at the market rate, year by year, are derived using present value factors. If balloon payments are involved, present value factors may be applied to isolate the contributory market value of the unpaid balance of the mortgage.

The cash equivalency of any set of financing terms can be computed, but adjustments are needed to reflect the market conditions and financing terms under which the property is expected to be sold. These adjustments may indicate that the effect of the financing terms suggests a value that differs from the cash equivalency calculation. For example, beneficial financing may be offered to expedite the marketing time on a parcel of distressed real estate. In such a situation, the purchaser would refuse to pay a premium for beneficial financing. It is also likely that the seller would be offering the property at a discount.

Appraisers must make sure that cash equivalency adjustments reflect market perceptions. In selecting an appropriate adjustment for use in cash equivalency analysis, the appraiser should give greater emphasis to the market-derived adjustment than to one derived by calculation.

Conditions of Sale

Adjustments for conditions of sale usually reflect the motivations of the buyer and the seller. In many situations the conditions of sale significantly affect transaction prices. For example, a developer may pay more than market value for lots needed in a site assemblage because of the anticipated plottage value resulting from the greater utility of a larger site. A sale may be transacted at a below-market price if the seller needs cash in a hurry. A financial, business, or family relationship between the parties to a sale may also affect the price of property. Interlocking corporate entities may record a sale at a nonmarket price to serve their business interests. One member of a family may sell a property to another at a reduced price, or a buyer may pay a higher price for a property because it was built by his ancestors.

When nonmarket conditions of sale are detected in a transaction, the sale can be used as a comparable but only with great care. The circumstances of the sale must be thoroughly researched before an adjustment is made, and the conditions must be adequately disclosed in the appraisal.

Although conditions of sale are often perceived as applying only to sales that are not arm's-length transactions, some arm's-length sales may reflect atypical motivations or sale conditions due to unusual tax considerations, lack of exposure on the open market, or the complexity of eminent domain proceedings. If the sales used in the sales comparison approach reflect unusual situations, an appropriate adjustment must be made for motivation or conditions of sale. Again, the circumstances of the sale must be explained in the appraisal report.

Expenditures Made Immediately After Purchase

A knowledgeable buyer considers expenditures that will have to be made upon purchase of a property because these costs affect the price the buyer agrees to pay. Such expenditures may include the costs to demolish and remove any buildings, costs to petition for a zoning change, or costs to remediate environmental contamination.

Market Conditions

Comparable sales that occurred under different market conditions than those applicable to the subject on the effective date of the value estimate require adjustment for any differences that affect their values. An adjustment for market conditions is made if, since the time the comparable sales were transacted, general property values have appreciated or depreciated due to inflation or deflation or investors' perceptions of the market have changed.

Changes in market conditions may also result from changes in income tax laws, building moratoriums, and fluctuations in supply and demand. Sometimes several economic factors work in concert to cause a change in market conditions. A recession tends to deflate all real estate prices, but specific property types will be affected differently. A decline in demand may affect only one category of real estate. If the demand for a specific type of property falls during a period of inflation, sales transacted during that period may not provide a reliable indication of the value of a similar property in a different period unless appropriate adjustments are made. Sales of other types of real estate transacted during the same period may better reflect the market conditions for the specific property being appraised. In a depressed economy, recent sales are often difficult to find. Older sales may be discounted over a reasonable holding period, which corresponds to the estimated time required for the market segment to recover. The decline in office rents over a specified period may also be analyzed when there are few, recent sales data.

Although the adjustment for market conditions is often referred to as a "time" adjustment, time is not the cause of the adjustment. Market conditions which shift over time create the need for an adjustment, not time itself. If market conditions have not changed, no adjustment is required even though considerable time may have elapsed.

Appraisers must also recognize that the sale of a property may be negotiated months or even years before its final disposition. The buyer and the seller agree as of the contract date, but the agreement does not become effective until the closing date (and there are often changes in the agreement during the interim). An adjustment for changes in market conditions between the date the contract is signed and the effective date of value may be appropriate. Appraisers may also be called on to estimate retrospective and prospective value, which necessarily entails consideration of changes in market conditions. (For guidance on the estimation of these values, see Statements Nos. 3 and 4 of the Uniform Standards of Professional Appraisal Practice).

Changes in market conditions are usually measured as a percentage of previous prices. While change is continuous, it typically occurs in discrete intervals. If the physical and economic characteristics of a property remain unchanged, analyzing two or more sales of the same property over a period of time will indicate the percentage of price change. An appraiser should always attempt to examine several sets of sales to arrive at an appropriate adjustment; an adjustment supported by just one set of sales may be unreliable.

Sales and resales of the same properties often provide the best indication of the change in market conditions over time. If data on resales are unavailable, however, sales of similar properties in the same market can be used. In either case, the sale transactions must be examined very carefully. Analysis of sale and resale data from the same property may indicate that nonmarket conditions were involved in one or both transactions.

Simple linear regression analysis and scatter diagrams may also be used to extract an annual rate of change in market conditions. The reliability of this analysis is affected by the number of market transactions studied. Unit prices can be graphed over time to indicate the trend in the market. Similarly, rents can be plotted on scatter diagrams to show differences over time.

Location

An adjustment for location may be required when the locational characteristics of a comparable property are different from those of the subject property. Excessive locational differences may disqualify property from use as a comparable. Locational differences are often handled with quantitative adjustments.

Most comparable properties in the same neighborhood have similar locational characteristics, but variations may exist within a neighborhood. Consider, for example, the difference between a property with a pleasant view of a park and one located two blocks away with an unattractive view. Adjustments for location may also be needed to reflect the difference in demand for various office suites within a single building, the retail advantage of a corner location, the privacy of the end unit in a residential condominium project, or the value contribution of an ocean view.

A property's location is analyzed in relation to the location of other properties. Although no location is inherently desirable or undesirable, an appraiser can conclude that the market recognizes that one location is better than, equal to, or worse than another. To evaluate the desirability of one location relative to other locations, appraisers must analyze sales of physically similar properties situated in different locations. Although the sale prices of properties in two different areas may be similar, properties in one area may be sold more rapidly than properties in the other.

For example, the subject of the appraisal is an interior vacant lot. The appraiser considers two sales of vacant lots similar to the subject in most respects except for location. Comparable A, a corner lot with frontage on two streets, was sold for $12.00 per square foot. Comparable B, an interior lot with frontage on only one street, was sold for $9.00 per square foot. The adjustment for location can be extracted by comparing the prices of the comparable on the corner lot with the comparable on the interior lot.

$$\$9.00/\$12.00 = 0.75$$

It can therefore be concluded that an interior lot is worth only 75% of the value of a corner lot. To bring the value of Comparable A, the corner lot, in line with the value of the interior subject lot, a percentage adjustment of 75% is applied to the unit price of Comparable A.

$$\text{Value of the subject} = \$12.00 \text{ per sq. ft. x } 0.75$$
$$= \$9.00 \text{ per sq. ft.}$$

The sale price of Comparable A, adjusted downward for its corner location, indicates a value of $9.00 per square foot for the subject interior lot. This relationship could also be expressed in terms of the complement of the value of Comparable A, i.e., the value of the subject equals the value of Comparable A less 25% of that value.

$$\text{Value of the subject} = \$12.00 - (0.25 \times \$12.00) = \$9.00$$

Physical Characteristics

If the physical characteristics of a comparable property and the subject property differ in many ways, each of these differences may require comparison and adjustment. Physical differences include differences in building size, quality of construction, architectural style, building materials, age, condition, functional utility, site size, attractiveness, and amenities. On-site environmental conditions may also be considered.

The value added or lost by the presence or absence of an item in a comparable property may not equal the cost of installing or removing the item. Buyers may be unwilling to pay a higher sale price that includes the extra cost of adding an amenity. Conversely, the addition of an amenity sometimes adds more value to a property than its cost.

Economic Characteristics

Economic characteristics include all the attributes of a property that affect its income. This element of comparison is usually applied to income-producing properties. Characteristics that affect a property's income include operating expenses, quality of management, tenant mix, rent concessions, lease terms, lease expiration dates, renewal options, and lease provisions such as expense recovery clauses. Investigation of these characteristics is critical to proper analysis of the comparables and development of a final value estimate.

Appraisers must take care not to attribute differences in real property rights conveyed or changes in market conditions to different economic characteristics. Caution must also be exercised in regard to units of comparison such as net operating income per unit. *NOI*s per unit reflect a mix of interactive economic attributes, many of which should only be analyzed in the income capitalization approach. Sales comparison analysis must not be presented simply as a variation of the income capitalization approach, applying the same techniques to reach an identical value indication.

Use/Zoning

Any difference in the current use or the highest and best use of a potential comparable and the subject property must be addressed. The appraiser must recognize the difference and determine if the sale is an appropriate comparable and, if so, whether an adjustment is required. In most cases the buyer or buyer's agent must confirm the ultimate use for which the comparable was purchased.

For example, an apartment complex purchased for conversion to condominiums may reflect a sale price above the market level for apartment properties. This property would not be an appropriate comparable for the "as is" valuation of an apartment complex for which no change in use is intended or one for which the highest and best use remains an apartment use.

In the valuation of vacant land, zoning is one of the primary determinants of the highest and best use of the property because it serves as the test of legal permissibility. Thus, zoning or the reasonable probability of a zoning change is typically a primary criterion in the selection of market data. When comparable properties with the same zoning as the subject are lacking or scarce, parcels with slightly different zoning that have a similar highest and best use to that of the subject may be used as comparables. These comparables may have to be adjusted for differences in utility if the market indicates that this is appropriate.

A difference in the uses permitted under the two zoning classifications does not necessarily require an adjustment if the parcels have the same use. When sale prices are reduced to compatible units (e.g., price of land per square foot of permissible building area), however, there may still be dissimilarities due to the different zoning classification requirements. For example, because of differences in parking requirements or landscaping requirements, site development costs for two parcels under different zoning classifications may differ even if the parcels have the same highest and best use. These dissimilarities must be considered.

Non-Realty Components of Value

Non-realty components of value include personalty, business concerns, or other items that do not constitute real property but are included in either the sale price of the comparable or the ownership interest in the subject property. These components should be analyzed separately from the realty. In most cases the economic lives, associated investment risks, rate of return criteria, and collateral security for such non-realty components differ from those of the realty.

Furniture, fixtures, and equipment in a hotel or restaurant are typical examples of personalty. In appraisals of properties in which the business operation is essential to the use of the realty, the value of the non-realty component must be recognized, estimated, and reported. Properties such as hotels and timeshare condominiums, which have high expense ratios attributable to the business operation, typically include a significant business value component.

Identification and Measurement of Adjustments

Various analytical techniques may be used to identify and measure adjustments. Comparative analysis includes the consideration of both quantitative and qualitative factors. Quantitative adjustments are developed as either dollar or percentage amounts. Factors that cannot be quantified are dealt with in qualitative analysis. Various techniques used in quantitative and qualitative analyses are listed below.

Quantitative
Paired data analysis (sales and resales of the same or similar properties)
Grouped data analysis
Statistical analysis
Graphic analysis
Sensitivity analysis
Trend analysis

Cost analysis (cost-to-cure, depreciated cost)
Secondary data analysis
Direct comparisons
Capitalization of rent differences

Qualitative
Relative comparison analysis
Ranking analysis
Personal interviews

The first step in any comparative analysis is to identify which elements of comparison affect property values in the subject market. Each of the basic elements of comparison must be tested using one or more of the techniques listed above to determine whether an adjustment is required. For example, in appraising a vacant, 50-acre parcel of land, an appraiser may find sales data on comparables that range in size from 35 acres to 65 acres, but show no significant difference in their prices per acre. The appraiser must not assume that an element of comparison affects value unless its influence is indicated by the market data.

Quantitative Analysis

When quantitative analytical techniques are applied, mathematical processes are used to identify which elements of comparison require adjustment and to measure the amount of these adjustments. When market evidence indicates that one or more elements affect value, those elements can be isolated by means of paired data analysis. Using this technique an appraiser can measure the difference between a comparable that does not contain the distinguishing element and a comparable that does. When more than one element of comparison is involved, additional pairs can be studied to isolate and abstract the differing elements.[4] Paired data analysis is a process of mathematical deduction. Appraisers shall recognize that this type of analysis has limited applicability, because identical paired data sets are rare and there is the potential for misuse. Special caution must be taken when analyzing pairs of adjusted values since the difference measured may not represent the actual difference attributable to the distinguishing characteristic. Pure pairings, i.e., pairs of sales that are identical except for the single element being measured, should be analyzed first. For example, data on a sale and resale of the same property may be compared to derive a time adjustment. Pairings of adjusted sales should only be used as a secondary analytical tool and should be identified as such.

When market evidence clearly supports differences between sales attributable to specific elements of comparison, paired data analysis can be a very effective technique. Ideally the sales being compared will be identical or very similar in all respects except for the single element being measured. However, this is rarely the case. In the absence of pure paired data, the appraiser's judgment becomes critical. Frequently an appraiser

---

4. Comparable properties that contain different unit or inventory mixes should be adjusted for this difference before pairing analysis is conducted. Examples of properties with different unit or inventory mixes include apartment buildings with one-, two-, and three-bedroom units and agricultural lands differentiated by Class I or Class II soils. A unit or inventory mix adjustment is required to ensure that comparables and subject are commensurate. The appraiser may be able to extract this adjustment by investigating the value relationships among the different classes of properties within the same property type.

must undertake a series of paired data analyses to isolate the effect of a single characteristic. A detailed example of paired data set analysis is presented in the next chapter.

Although paired data analysis is a theoretically sound method, it is sometimes impractical because only a narrow sampling of sufficiently similar properties may be available and it is difficult to quantify the adjustments attributable to all the variables present. An adjustment derived from a single pair of sales is not necessarily indicative, just as a single sale does not necessarily reflect market value. Even when limited data are available, however, the appraiser should not discard the technique. Rather, he or she should estimate the amount of adjustment indicated by the data and use other analytical procedures or judgment to test the reasonableness of the adjustment derived. It is imperative that the appraiser use all analytical tools appropriate to the appraisal problem.

A related technique, grouped data analysis, involves grouping data by independent variables such as date of sale and calculating equivalent typical values. The groups are studied in pairs to identify the dependent variable (e.g., the property's price per acre, front-foot-per-acre ratio, or topographic quality). Paired data and grouped data analysis are variants of sensitivity analysis.

Sensitivity analysis is a method used to isolate the effect of individual variables on value. Often associated with risk analysis, sensitivity analysis studies the impact of varied assumptions on different measures of return.

The statistical analysis of market data is becoming increasingly common in appraisal literature and appraisal practice. Appropriate statistical methods include statistical inference and regression analysis. Linear and multiple regression can be excellent tools of analysis in certain market situations if an appropriate database can be compiled. The effectiveness of regression analysis is limited by the number of elements or factors influencing a sale price; the more factors a sale reflects, the larger the database must be to identify relationships. Regressions for specific elements, however, may be used in conjunction with other techniques. Full discussion of the statistical methods applicable to the sales comparison approach is beyond the scope of this text. Appendix B provides a review of basic statistical techniques.[5]

Graphic analysis is a variant of statistical analysis in which the appraiser arrives at a conclusion by visually interpreting a graphic display of data and applying statistical curve fit analysis. A simple graphic display of grouped data may illustrate how the market reacts to variations in the elements of comparison. In curve fit analysis, different formulas may be employed to determine the best fit for the market data being analyzed. The most reliable equation for the best fit curve can be plotted, or the most appropriate equation of those commonly used to solve for an adjustment can be identified.

Trend analysis is applicable when large amounts of market data are available. It is especially useful when there is a limited number of closely comparable sales data, but a broad database on properties with less similar characteristics. The various elements influencing a sale price can be tested to determine their market sensitivity. Once the

---

5. Two texts with information on applying statistical analysis to appraisals are Freeman F. Elzey, *A First Reader in Statistics*, 2d ed. (Belmont, Calif: Brooks/Cole Publishing Company, a division of Wadsworth Publishing Company, Inc., 1974) and Norman R. Benedict, MAI, and Ted H. Szatrowski *Statistical Primer for Real Estate Problem Solving* (Chicago: American Society of Real Estate Counselors, 1989). *The Appraisal Journal* has published numerous articles on advanced statistical applications.

appraiser has determined which elements show market sensitivity, patterns for their adjustment can be analyzed.

In cost analysis cost indicators such as depreciated building cost, cost to cure, or permit fees are used as a basis for adjustments. The appraiser should make certain that the adjustments derived are reasonable and approximate market expectations.

Secondary data analysis is a method for determining adjustments that make use of data that do not directly pertain to the subject or comparable properties. These secondary data describe the general real estate market and are usually collected by a research firm or government agency.

Direct comparisons can be made between comparables that are similar in all but one characteristic, e.g., a residential property with a garage that is not up to market standards or an industrial property on a site that contains excess land.

Capitalization of rent differences can be used to derive an adjustment when the rent loss incurred by a comparable reflects a specific deficiency in the comparable, e.g., lack of an elevator in a low-rise office building or inadequate parking facilities for a convenience store.

Qualitative Analysis

Relative comparison analysis is the study of the relationships indicated by market data without recourse to quantification. Many appraisers use this technique because it reflects the imperfect nature of real estate markets. To apply the technique the appraiser analyzes comparable sales to determine whether the comparables' characteristics are inferior, superior, or equal to those of the subject property. Unlike quantitative analysis, the adjustments considered in relative comparison analysis are not expressed as dollar or percentage amounts. A detailed example of relative comparison analysis is presented in the next chapter.

Ranking analysis is a variant of relative comparison analysis. In ranking analysis the comparable sales are ranked in an descending or ascending order. Then the appraiser analyzes each sale to determine the relative position of the subject in the array. An example of such an array is provided in the next chapter. Ranking analysis may also be used to array or sort the comparable data for differences specific elements of comparison, e.g., size, siting (corner or interior lot), frontage. Specific value trends can thereby be established.

Personal interviews can reveal the opinions of knowledgeable individuals participating in the subject's market. This information must be regarded as secondary data and should not be used as the sole criterion for estimating adjustments or reconciling value ranges.

Comparative Analysis

Comparative analysis is the general term used to identify the process in which quantitative and/or qualitative techniques are applied to derive a value indication in the sales comparison approach. The two types of techniques may be used separately or in combination.

The adjustments derived in comparative analysis and applied to the sale prices of the comparables may be expressed as percentages, as dollar amounts, or in descriptive terms that clearly convey the magnitude of the difference in the element of comparison between the comparable and the subject. Five general steps are involved in the analytic process.

1. Identify the elements of comparison that affect the value of the type of property being appraised.

2. Compare the attributes of each comparable with those of the subject property and measure the difference in each element of comparison between the comparable and the subject. Each quantitative adjustment must be adequately explained to ensure that a third party would understand the reasoning behind the adjustment.

3. Derive a net adjustment for each comparable and apply it to the sale or unit price of the comparable to arrive at a range of adjusted sale or unit prices for the subject property. (A net adjustment is calculated as the difference between total positive and negative adjustments.)

4. Compare all the adjusted comparables and array them according to those that are superior to the subject, those that are similar, and those that are inferior to the subject. This process will result in a bracket of values identifying those comparables that are superior to the subject and those that are inferior to the subject.

5. Perform qualitative analysis to reconcile the range of values to the subject property.

When quantitative adjustments are being applied, the appraiser considers the array of value indications obtained in the third step to be the range of probable value indications for the subject property. The appraiser then determines the most probable position of the subject within this range of indications and reaches a final value conclusion. In this way the comparables most similar to the subject are given the greatest weight.

Applying qualitative analysis, the appraiser will normally divide the adjusted comparables into two groups: those that are qualitatively superior to the subject and those that are qualitatively inferior. The adjusted prices of these two groups will bracket the value of the subject by indicating a probable range of values. By considering those comparables most similar to the subject, some higher and some lower in value, the appraiser can conclude a single value indication for the subject property. If all the comparables are rated either superior or inferior to the subject, it may not be possible to determine a reliable range of value and reach a single value indication using qualitative analysis.

An appraiser may use both quantitative adjustments and qualitative analysis in comparative analysis, but not concurrently. Generally, quantitative adjustments are made before qualitative analysis is performed. Care must be exercised to ensure that the reader of the appraisal report will not be confused. Appraisal reports that include qualitative analysis often require more extensive discussion of the reasoning that the appraiser applied.

Types of Adjustments

The adjustments derived with quantitative techniques can be applied to a comparable property as either percentage or dollar amounts. The manner in which the adjustment is derived from the market determines how it is expressed. Percentages are usually converted into dollar amounts that may be added to or subtracted from the price of the comparable on the market data grid.

Adjustments can be applied in several ways depending on how the relationship between the properties (i.e., subject and comparable, comparable and subject, or comparable and comparable) is expressed or perceived by the market. This relationship is expressed as an equation which is solved to determine the amount of adjustment to be made for the differences between the properties.

An appraiser uses logical calculations to make adjustments, but the mathematics should not control the appraiser's judgment. Using computer and software technology, an appraiser can effectively apply mathematical techniques that were once prohibitively time-consuming. These techniques can be used to narrow the range of value, but a market value estimate is not determined by calculations. Appraisal has a creative aspect in that appraisers use their judgment to analyze and interpret quantitative data. Quantification helps the appraiser analyze market evidence and identify how various factors affect property value; qualitative analysis can be used to identify a bracket in which the final value estimate should fall and weight the value indicators based on market evidence. Preparing an organized grid that includes both quantitative and qualitative elements can help ensure that all elements of comparison are considered. If market evidence is inconclusive, the grid should clearly indicate this.

Percentage Adjustments

Adjustments for differences between a comparable property and a subject property are frequently expressed in percentages. Percentage adjustments are often used to reflect differences in market conditions and location.

For example, the data may indicate that market conditions have resulted in a 5% increase in overall property prices during the past year or that prices for a particular category of property have recently increased 0.5% per month. Similarly, an appraiser may analyze market data and conclude that properties in one location are sold for prices approximately 10% higher than the prices of similar properties in another location. These percentages may be converted into dollar amounts, which are then added to or subtracted from the price of the comparable. The percentages may also be directly applied to the sale price or unit price of the comparable. Of course, if the comparable is equal to the subject for all practical purposes, no adjustment is necessary.

The relationship between the subject property and the comparable property should be stated in a manner that corresponds to the way it is perceived by market participants.

Dollar Adjustments

Adjustments can also be computed in dollars. For example, an appraiser may conclude that the favorable financing terms involved in the sale of a comparable property resulted in the buyer paying a $100,000 premium. In analyzing major investment properties, an appraiser can frequently use discounting to derive a dollar adjustment for financing terms. Adjustments for many physical characteristics may also be estimated in dollar amounts, which are added to or subtracted from the sale price of the comparable.

Sequence of Adjustments

The sequence in which adjustments are applied to the comparables is determined by the market data and the appraiser's analysis of those data. The sequence presented in Table 18.1 is provided for purposes of illustration. This sequence is often applicable when percentage adjustments are calculated and added, either in conjunction with other percentage adjustments or in combination with dollar adjustments. However, this is not the only order in which quantitative adjustments may be made. Adjustments may be applied in other sequences if the market and the appraiser's analysis of the data so indicate. Using the adjustment sequence, the appraiser applies successive adjustments to the prices of comparable properties. In Table 18.1, the percentage adjustments are applied to the price of a comparable property to reflect the comparable's superiority or inferiority with regard to real property rights conveyed, financing, conditions of sale, market conditions, location, physical characteristics, economic characteristics, use, and non-realty components. Table 18.1 relates to a hypothetical subject property and a comparable property and the relationship between the properties is presented strictly for purposes of illustration.

Adjustments for property rights conveyed, financing terms, conditions of sale, and market conditions are often expressed in percentages. However, once the percentages are extracted from market data, a dollar adjustment for each element of comparison is typically calculated and applied to the sale price of the comparable in the market data grid. For example, if the change in market conditions from the date of the comparable sale to the date of value is estimated at 5% per year, a lump-sum dollar adjustment based on that 5% is applied to the price of the comparable. Once adjustments for these four elements of comparison have been made, the adjusted sales price is typically converted into a relevant unit price for further comparative analysis. Most property types, except single-family residences, are adjusted on a unit price basis. Subsequent adjustments for location, physical characteristics, economic characteristics, use, and non-realty components are typically applied to a unit price.

The first adjustment applied to the transaction price is for the property rights conveyed. This adjustment accounts for differences in the legal estates of the subject property and the comparable property. The second adjustment converts the price of the comparable into its cash equivalent price or modifies it to match the financing terms of the subject property. The third adjustment is made for conditions of sale and reflects the difference between the actual sale price of the comparable and its probable sale price if it had been sold in an arm's-length transaction. If the financing terms or conditions of sale of the comparable had been the same as those typical in the market for the subject

Table 18.1	Sequence of Adjustments

Element of Comparison	Market-Derived Adjustment	Adjustment Applied to Price
Sale price		$100,000
Adjustment for property rights conveyed	+5%	+5,000
Adjusted price		$105,000
Adjustment for financing terms	−2%	−2,100
Adjusted price		$102,900
Adjustment for conditions of sale*	+5%	+5,145
Adjusted price		$108,045
Adjustment for expenditures immediately after purchase	+0%	+0
Adjustment for market conditions	+5%	+5,402
Adjusted price		$113,447
Adjustment for		
Location	+3%	+3,403
Physical characteristics	−5%	−5,672
Economic characteristics	−5%	−5,672
Use	+2%	+2,269
Non-realty components	+3%	+3,403
Indication of value of the subject		$111,178

* The conditions of sale adjustment may be combined with another adjustment depending on how it is extracted from the market.

property, adjustments of zero would have been shown in the chart. At this stage in the sequence, the adjusted price figure is $108,045, which represents the amount for which the comparable property would have been sold under normal financing and sale conditions. This figure is approximately 108% of the actual transaction price. If any expenditures are to be made immediately after purchase, these are then deducted. In this example, none were required.

The next adjustment is for market conditions. It reflects the change in the prices paid for real estate due to changes in market conditions and the purchasing power of money over time. This adjustment is applied after the adjustments for property rights conveyed, financing, and conditions of sale. The adjustment would be distorted if it were applied directly to the actual transaction price, which was influenced by nonmarket considerations in the form of atypical financing. After the adjustment for market conditions, the adjusted price is $113,447, which represents the amount for which the comparable property would be sold as of the date of appraisal on the open market, provided the characteristics of the sale were the same as those of the property being appraised. The adjusted price is approximately 113.4% of the transaction price.

Adjustments for location, physical characteristics, economic characteristics, use, and non-realty components are made as needed to account for differences between the comparable property and the subject property. In this particular example, no other adjustments are required. After all adjustments have been made to the price of the comparable, the resulting value indication for the subject property is $111,178.

Sample Market Data Grid

The sample market data grid shown in Table 18.2 reflects the first four elements of comparison in a typical sequence; blank lines are provided for other elements of comparison. If the comparable sales are similar to the subject in regard to an element of comparison, no adjustment is required for that element. The sample grid includes separate lines for each comparison and adjustment to ensure that adjustments are made in a consistent manner.

The section labeled "For reconciliation purposes" is provided to help the appraiser analyze the degree of comparability of each sale, which indicates the relative reliability of the separate value indications derived. Each final adjusted sale price is a possible value indication for the subject property; together these prices may constitute a range of value within which the value of the subject property will likely be found. Each adjusted sale price can be analyzed to show the total, or absolute, adjustment made to the sale price of the comparable and the percentage of the sale price that is reflected by this total adjustment. With these value estimates, the appraiser can rank the comparability of the sales to the subject and select an appropriate estimate of value, assuming the value conclusion is to be reported as a point estimate. The sale that requires the least significant or lowest total adjustment (i.e., the absolute adjustment based on the sum of the adjustments regardless of sign) is often the most comparable and generally should be given the most weight in reconciling the value indications from the sales comparison approach. The weighting of value indicators is illustrated in the next chapter. In reconciling the value indications derived in the sales comparison approach, the appraiser must also consider the reliability of the data used to make adjustments.

Key Concepts

- In the sales comparison approach, an appraiser estimates market value by analyzing market activity involving similar properties (e.g., sales, listings), comparing these properties to the subject property, and adjusting the prices of the comparables for differences.

- The sales comparison approach is applicable when sufficient data on recent market transactions are available. It is commonly used to value single-family residential properties. Essential information on income-producing properties derived through sales comparison is used in the income capitalization and cost approaches.

- To apply the sales comparison approach, the appraiser gathers data from sales,

Table 18.2 | **Sample Market Data Grid: Comparison and Adjustment of Market Data**

Element	Subject	Sale 1	Sale 2	Sale 3	Sale 4
Sale price	unknown	_____	_____	_____	_____
Real property rights conveyed adjustment	_____	_____	_____	_____	_____
Adjusted price*					
Financing adjustment	_____	_____	_____	_____	_____
Conditions of sale adjustment	_____	_____	_____	_____	_____
Adjusted price†	_____	_____	_____	_____	_____
Market conditions adjustment	_____	_____	_____	_____	_____
Adjusted price‡	_____	_____	_____	_____	_____
_____	_____	_____	_____	_____	_____
_____	_____	_____	_____	_____	_____
_____	_____	_____	_____	_____	_____
Final adjusted sale price	_____	_____	_____	_____	_____
For reconciliation purposes:					
Total adjustment	_____	_____	_____	_____	_____
Total adjustment as % of sale price	_____	_____	_____	_____	_____

* Sale price adjusted for property rights conveyed
† Sale price further adjusted for financing and conditions of sale
‡ Sale price further adjusted for market conditions

contracts, offers, refusals, and listings of competitive properties. Sources of this information include public records, multiple listing services, real estate brokers, real estate periodicals, and interviews with the parties involved in market transactions.

- A systematic, five-step procedure for applying the approach includes 1) researching transactional data, 2) verifying the data as accurate and representative of arm's-length transactions, 3) selecting relevant units of comparison, 4) comparing the comparables with the subject and adjusting their prices for differences in various elements of comparison, and 5) reconciling multiple value indications into a single value or range of value.

- Elements of comparison identify the characteristics of properties and transactions that cause the prices paid for real estate to vary. The most common elements of comparison are real property rights conveyed, financing terms, conditions of sale, market conditions, any expenditures immediately after purchase, location, physical characteristics, economic characteristics, use, and non-realty components of value.

- Both quantitative and qualitative techniques are employed in comparative analysis. Quantitative adjustment techniques include paired data analysis, grouped data analysis, statistical analysis, graphic analysis, sensitivity analysis, trend analysis, cost analysis, secondary data analysis, direct comparisons, and capitalization of income differences. Qualitative analysis includes relative comparison analysis, ranking analysis, and personal interviews.

- Quantitative adjustments may be applied to comparable sales prices as percentage or dollar amounts.

- In qualitative analysis comparables are identified as either superior or inferior overall to the subject to bracket the probable value range of the subject property.

- Quantitative and qualitative methodologies are often combined in practice. Quantitative adjustments are applied before qualitative analysis is undertaken.

- To assist in the analysis of comparable sales, appraisers make use of data array and adjustment grids.

- As a part of reconciliation, the appraiser checks to ensure that value indications are expressed in the same units of comparison and reflect estimates as of the same date.

Terms

absolute adjustment	paired data analysis
adjusted sale price	percentage adjustments
adjustment grid	physical characteristic
arm's-length transaction	property rights conveyed
bracketing	qualitative analysis
cash equivalency	quantitative adjustments
comparative analysis	ranking analysis
conditions of sale	reconciliation
data array grid	relative comparison analysis
dollar adjustments	sales comparison approach
economic characteristic	secondary data analysis
elements of comparison	sensitivity analysis
expenditures made after purchase	sequence of adjustments
financing terms	statistical analysis
graphic analysis	transactional data
grouped data analysis	trend analysis
location	units of comparison
market conditions	use
non-realty components of value	zoning

CHAPTER NINETEEN

Applications of the Sales Comparison Approach

T he basic theory and procedures of the sales comparison approach were described in Chapter 18 and a number of specific techniques were introduced. Many of these techniques are illustrated in the pages that follow. Quantitative and qualitative techniques may both be employed in the application of the sales comparison approach. Adjustments derived by quantitative techniques are applied prior to qualitative analysis. Differences in specific elements of comparison which elude precise mathematical adjustment are subsequently considered in qualitative analysis. The two methodologies are complementary and are often used in combination.

In the following examples, quantitative adjustments are applied to the appraisal of a single-family residence and qualitative analysis is used to value an office building and an apartment complex. Paired data analysis is illustrated in the single-family residence example; relative comparison analysis is demonstrated in the office and apartment building examples. A combined application of paired data and relative comparison analyses is demonstrated in a fourth example, which concerns a warehouse.

Other techniques can also be used to identify and estimate adjustments. The appraiser should consider all applicable techniques to determine which ones are most appropriate to the appraisal. Generally, the more complex the property being appraised, the greater the number of techniques that may be applied to its valuation.

Quantitative Adjustments

Paired Data Analysis of a Single-Family Residence

The property being appraised is a single-family residence with 1,200 square feet of gross living area and a finished basement. It has six rooms, three bedrooms, one and one-half baths, and no garage. The area of the site is 10,000 square feet. The site improvements are average for the neighborhood; all building and site improvements are in average condition. The five comparables used in this analysis are all located in the same neighborhood as the subject. These properties are described below. Total sale price is the unit of comparison typically used to analyze single-family residential properties.

Comparable A is a 1,200-sq.-ft., frame ranch house situated on a 10,000-sq.-ft. lot with an unfinished basement and an attached, two-car garage. It has six rooms, three bedrooms, and one and one-half baths. It was sold three weeks before the date of the appraisal for $67,000 with financing at a below-market interest rate, which resulted in a price that was $5,000 higher than it would have been otherwise.

Comparable B is a 1,450-sq.-ft., frame ranch house situated on a 12,000-sq.-ft. lot with an unfinished basement and an attached, two-car garage. It has seven rooms, three bedrooms, and one and one-half baths. It was sold one month before the date of the appraisal for $75,000 with financing at a below-market interest rate, which resulted in a price that was $5,000 higher than it would have been otherwise.

Comparable C is a 1,200-sq.-ft., frame ranch house situated on a 10,000-sq.-ft. lot with an unfinished basement and an attached, two-car garage. It has six rooms, three bedrooms, and one and one-half baths. It was sold one year before the date of the appraisal for $56,500 with market financing.

Comparable D is a 1,450-sq.-ft., frame ranch house situated on a 12,000-sq.-ft. lot with a finished basement and an attached, two-car garage. It has seven rooms, three bedrooms, and one and one-half baths. It was sold one year before the date of the appraisal for $70,000 with market financing.

Comparable E is a 1,200-sq.-ft., frame ranch house situated on a 10,000-sq.-ft. lot with an unfinished basement and no garage. It has six rooms, three bedrooms, and one and one-half baths. It was sold one year before the date of the appraisal for $53,200 with market financing.

The summary grid shown in Table 19.1 indicates that the comparable properties differ from the subject property in terms of financing, market conditions at time of sale, size (i.e., living area, number of rooms), lot size, and the presence or absence of a garage and a finished basement. Paired data analysis can be used to derive adjustments for differences in these elements of comparison.

No adjustment for property rights is needed because all the properties are held in fee simple. The adjustment for financing terms can sometimes be derived by comparing the sale prices of the comparables with favorable financing to the sale prices of other comparables with market financing. The appraiser interviewed the buyers and sellers of the comparable properties and calculated the effect of the favorable financing terms on each sale price by discounting the buyer's advantage to present value. The adjustment for financing terms was based on the actual price that would be required for the seller to recapture the buydown the seller paid the lender. (The paired data from which the adjustment was derived are not shown in the table.) The appraiser concluded that the adjustment for the favorable financing terms of Comparables A and B is $5,000.

Comparables A and C differ only in their financing terms and market conditions at the time of sale. After the adjustment is made to Comparable A for financing terms, the adjustment for market conditions (date of sale) can be calculated as follows:

$$(\$62,000 - \$56,500)/\$56,500 = 0.097345, \text{ or } 9.7\%.$$

This 9.7% adjustment is rounded to 10% and the corresponding dollar amount is applied as an adjustment to Comparable C. The 10% adjustment for market conditions is also applied to Comparables D and E.

The difference in size between Comparables A and B can be attributed to the additional building area of Comparable B. (The lot on which Comparable B is located is also 20% larger than Comparable A's lot.) The size adjustment is made after both prices have been adjusted $5,000 downward for financing terms. The adjustment for size is calculated as $70,000 - $62,000 = $8,000.

Comparables C and E are identical except for the garage in Comparable C. Thus the garage adjustment can be calculated as the difference between their sale prices prior

Table 19.1 **Market Data Grid: Single-Family Residence Appraisal**

	Subject	A	B	Comparable C	D	E
Sale price	—	$67,000	$75,000	$56,500	$70,000	$53,200
Real property rights conveyed		Fee simple	Fee simple	Fee simple	Fee simple	Fee simple
Adjusted price	—	$67,000	$75,000	$56,000	$70,000	$53,200
Financing terms	—	Nonmarket	Nonmarket	Market	Market	Market
Adjustment for financing	—	-$5,000	-$5,000	0	0	0
Conditions of sale	—	Arm's length	Arm's length	Arm's length	Arm's length	Arm's length
Adjustment for conditions of sale	—	0	0	0	0	0
Adjusted price	—	$62,000	$70,000	$56,500	$70,000	$53,200
Market conditions	—	-3 weeks	-1 month	-1 year	-1 year	-1 year
Adjustment for market conditions	—	0	0	+$5,650	+$7,000	+$5,320
Adjusted price	—	$62,000	$70,000	$62,150	$77,000	$58,520
Location	—	Similar	Similar	Similar	Similar	Similar
Adjustment for location	—	0	0	0	0	0
Size in sq. ft.	1,200	1,200	1,450	1,200	1,450	1,200
Adjustment for size	—	0	-$8,000	0	-$8,000	0
Garage	None	2-car	2-car	2-car	2-car	None
Adjustment for garage	—	-$3,300	-$3,300	-$3,300	-$3,300	0
Finished basement	Yes	No	No	No	Yes	No
Adjustment for finished basement	—	+$7,000	+$7,000	+$7,000	0	+$7,000
Adjusted price	—	$65,700	$65,700	$65,850	$65,700	$65,520
For reconciliation purposes:						
Total net adjustment		$1,300	$9,300	$9,350	$4,300	$12,320
Total net adjustment as % of sale price		1.9%	12.4%	16.5%	6.1%	23.2%
Total gross adjustment		$15,300	$23,300	$15,950	$18,300	$12,320
Total gross adjustment as % of sale price		22.8%	31%	28.2%	26.1%	23.2%

to any other adjustment, i.e., $56,000 - $53,200 = $3,300. The adjustment for the absence of a garage is applied to Comparable C and to Comparables A, B, and D as well.

The adjustment for the finished basement in Comparable D is calculated by comparing Comparables B and D after Comparable D has been adjusted $7,000 upward for market conditions and Comparable B has been adjusted $5,000 downward for financing terms. The adjustment is calculated as $77,000 - $70,000 = $7,000.

Now the value indications derived for the comparables must be reconciled into a single value indication. Appraisers sometimes find it preferable to derive a range of values and then conclude a single value indication. The appraiser considers the range of value indications, the number of adjustments applied to each comparable, the total percentage adjustment to each comparable calculated as an absolute value (i.e., the gross adjustment), the total percentage adjustment to each comparable calculated as the difference between positive and negative adjustments (i.e., the net adjustment), any particularly large adjustments applied, and other factors indicating that a particular comparable should be given greater weight.

In this case the appraiser considers the range of value indications ($65,520 to $65,850) and gives the greatest weight to the comparable that required the least amount of adjustment. The fewest adjustments (only two) were applied to Comparable E, which also required the smallest gross adjustment ($12,320). Thus, if Comparable E is given the most emphasis and the adjusted sale price of Comparable E indicates the subject's value to be $65,520, the value of the subject is estimated to be approximately $65,500.

Reconciliation can also be approached statistically. In the weighting technique illustrated below, the most comparable property is weighted 5, while the least comparable is weighted 1.

	Sale A	Sale B	Sale C	Sale D	Sale E
Adjusted price	$65,700	$65,700	$65,850	$65,700	$65,520
Sales weighting	x 5	x 1	x 2	x 3	x 4
Product	328,500	65,700	131,700	197,100	262,080

Sum of the products = 985,080
Sum of the weights = 15
Value of the subject = 985,080/15 = $65,672, or $65,670

In this example, the percentage of total gross adjustment was used to weight the reliability of the comparable sales' value indications—i.e., the higher the percentage, the lower the weighting.

Adjustments can also be derived using grouped data analysis. The following example shows how a market conditions adjustment can be calculated from grouped data on sales in an industrial park over the past few years.

Sale	Sale Date	Group Average	Price/Acre	Group Average	Change
1	16 Jan 90		24,500		
2	01 May 90		29,200		
3	26 Jul 90		30,800		
4	08 Nov 90	13 Jun 90	17,600	25,525	
5	06 Mar 91		21,800		
6	27 May 91		28,800		
7	12 Jun 91		27,600		
8	17 Aug 91	31 May 91	29,100	26,825	5.1%
9	03 Feb 92		27,200		
10	03 Jun 92		27,900		
11	13 Oct 92	06 Jun 92	29,300	28,133	4.9%
12	10 Jan 93		29,900		
13	12 Apr 93		28,300		
14	05 Aug 93		30,800		
15	14 Dec 93	18 Jun 93	29,400	29,600	5.2%

The individual sale dates within each year of data groupings are spaced sufficiently far apart so that more detailed interpretation is not required. Sale prices are increasing at an average rate of 5% annually. If market conditions do not change substantially, the typical increase in mean value in 1994 will be about $1,375 per acre, calculated as follows:

$$\$25,525 + \$26,825 + \$28,133 + 29,600 = \$110,083$$
$$\$110,083/4 = \$27,521$$
$$\$27,521 \times 0.05 = \$1,376$$

The 1994 value of $30,975 per acre is calculated by adding $1,375 to the 1993 mean value of $29,600 per acre.

Qualitative Analysis

After quantitative adjustments are applied, qualitative analysis can be undertaken. Qualitative differences may be analyzed by ranking comparables according to their degree of similarity to the subject property. The magnitude of the differences may be used to decide which comparables are the more reliable indicators of the value of the subject and should provide the basis for reconciliation. Qualitative analysis acknowledges the inefficiencies of real estate markets and the difficulty of precisely measuring of the differences between the sale properties and the subject.

Relative Comparison Analysis of an Office Building

The property being appraised is a five-year old, multitenanted office building with 36,000 square feet of gross building area and 31,800 square feet of rentable area (88% of *GBA*). Its occupancy rate is 90%, which is considered stable in the subject market. The amount of space occupied by individual tenants ranges from 2,500 square feet to 7,000 square feet. The building is of average construction (Class B) and is in average condition. The ratio of rentable area to gross building area is low in comparison to the average for the subject market area, which is approximately 93%. The site is appropriately landscaped. The open-space parking provided is both adequate and in compliance with the zoning code. The location, which may also be considered average, is an interior site accessed from a major arterial highway.

Current base rents range from $12 per square foot to $13 per square foot of rentable area. Rent for the overall building averages $12.60 per square foot and the quality of the tenants is good. With the exception of telephone service, the landlord pays all expenses including janitorial and electrical. Operating expenses are typical for the market. The leases have three- and four-year terms; they contain an option to renew for three more years at the then-current market rent. All leases are less than 18 months old, and the rents and terms they specify are standard for the current market. Leasehold positions in the subject property do not accrue any particular advantage. The leased fee interest in the property is the interest to be appraised.

Five comparable sales are used in the analysis. All the comparables are mid-rise, multitenanted office properties located in the subject's market area and all were financed at market rates with conventional loan-to-value ratios. All the comparables were sold in leased fee. The unit of comparison employed in this analysis is price per square foot of rentable area. The five comparables are described below and shown in Table 19.2.

Comparable A was sold five months ago for $2,930,000. It is six years old and in average condition. The building contains 40,000 square feet of gross building area and 37,600 square feet of rentable area (94% of GBA). The indicated price per square foot of rentable area is $77.93. Average rent is $12.80 per square foot of rentable area. The landlord pays all expenses and occupancy is 87%. The rents, lease terms, and expenses of the property are at market levels. The site is located at the intersection of a major arterial highway and a collector road. Parking is adequate. The ratio of parking spaces to rentable area in Comparable A is approximately the same as that of the subject.

Comparable B was sold four months ago for $2,120,000. The building is four years old and contains 32,000 square feet of gross building area and 29,700 square feet of rentable area (93% of GBA). Its unit price is calculated to be $71.38 per square foot of rentable area. Site improvements are average, and the ratio of parking area to rentable area is similar to that of the subject property. The property is in average condition. The leases provide tenants with full services. Occupancy is 85% and the average base rent is $11.80 per square foot of rentable area, which is slightly below market levels. The lengths of the leases and property expenses are considered to be at market levels. The property is located on an interior site accessed from a major collector street. Parking is adequate.

Comparable C was sold nine months ago for $2,450,000. The building contains 35,000 square feet of gross building area and 32,200 square feet of rentable area (92% of GBA). Its unit price is $76.09 per square foot of rentable area. The improvements were constructed five years ago and are in average condition. Rent averages $12.60 per square foot of rentable area. All tenant services are provided by the landlord. The building has an occupancy rate of 90%, and all rents and lease terms are at market levels. The total expenses for the building are slightly higher than is typical for the market because two tenants who occupy 15% of the total space use excessive electricity; they do not pay additional rent to compensate for the extra expense. The property's location is an interior site accessed from a major arterial highway. The property has a parking ratio similar to that of the subject.

Comparable D was sold two months ago for $2,160,000. The building is six years old and in average condition. It contains 30,000 square feet of gross building area and 26,700 square feet of rentable area (89% of *GBA*). The unit price is $80.90 per square foot of rentable area. The rent averages $13.00 per square foot of rentable area, and the lease terms and building expenses are at market levels. The occupancy rate is 95%. The site is located at the intersection of two major arterial highways in a district zoned for higher-density development than is permitted in the subject district. Thus, the ratio of parking area to rentable area is lower than that of the subject property.

Comparable E was sold six months ago for $2,470,000. The building was constructed four years ago and is in average condition. It contains 38,000 square feet of gross building area and 33,800 square feet of rentable area (89% of *GBA*). Its unit price is $73.08 per square foot of rentable area. The location is an interior site accessed by a major collector street. The occupancy rate for the building is 90%. Rents average $12.30 per square foot of rentable area. Full tenant services are provided by the landlord. Rents, lease terms, and property expenses are at market levels. The property has adequate parking, and the parking ratio is similar to that of the subject property.

Qualitative analysis recognizes the inefficiencies of real estate markets and the difficulty in expressing adjustments with mathematical precision. It is essential, therefore, that the appraiser explain the logic applied in arriving at the adjustments so that readers of the appraisal report will understand how they were derived.

The appraiser first analyzes the market data and determines that all the office building sales involved the transfer of a leased fee interest. Thus, no adjustment for differences in property rights conveyed is necessary. (The below-market rent of Comparable B will be considered subsequently.) All sales were transacted with market financing, so no adjustment for this element of comparison is required either. Because all of the transactions were conducted at arm's length, there is no adjustment for conditions of sale. The comparables used were recent transactions, all occurring within nine months of the date of valuation. There have been no significant changes in rent levels and occupancy, so no adjustments are warranted for market conditions. The relative comparison analysis of dissimilar elements is described below.

Comparable A has an indicated unit price of $77.93 per square foot of rentable area. Its location at the intersection of a major arterial highway and a collector road is superior to the location of the subject property. The building has an average rentable area ratio, but it is a more efficient building than the subject. The building occupancy rate for Comparable A is slightly lower than the subject's and lower than the rate considered typical for stabilized occupancy in the market. In short, Comparable A has more superior than inferior attributes and these attributes are considered more significant. This indicates a unit value for the subject property of less than $77.93 per square foot of rentable area.

Comparable B has an indicated unit price of $71.38 per square foot of rentable area. Effective contract rent is lower than market rent. The location of this property on a major collector street is inferior to the subject property's location on a major arterial

Table 19.2 | **Market Data Grid for Relative Comparison Analysis**

Element of Comparison	Subject	Comparable A	Comparable B	Comparable C	Comparable D	Comparable E
Sale price	–	$2,930,000	$2,120,000	$2,450,000	$2,160,000	$2,470,000
Price/sq.ft. of rentable area	–	$77.93	$71.38	$76.09	$80.90	$73.08
Property interest	Leased fee	Leased fee	Leased fee	Leased fee	Leased fee	Leased fee
Age	5 years	6 years	4 years	5 years	6 years	4 years
Sq. ft. of *GBA*	36,000	40,000	32,000	35,000	30,000	38,000
Sq. ft. of rentable area	31,800	37,600	29,700	32,200	26,700	33,800
Rental area ratio	88%	94%	93%	92%	89%	89%
Occupancy rate	90%	87%	85%	90%	95%	90%
Construction quality and condition	Average	Average	Average	Average	Average	Average
Ratio of parking spaces to rental area	Good	Similar	Similar	Similar	Inferior	Similar
Average rent per sq. ft. of rentable area	$12.60	$12.80	$11.80	$12.60	$13.00	$12.30
Location	Average	Superior	Inferior	Similar	Superior	Inferior
Expense ratio	Market norm	Similar	Similar	Higher	Similar	Similar
Overall comparability	–	Superior	Inferior	Superior	Superior	Inferior

highway. Comparable B has a superior rentable area ratio, indicating that the property will yield a higher net income. The occupancy rate for the comparable is below the market rate for stabilized occupancy. In all, more of the attributes of Comparable B are inferior than superior and these inferior factors are also considered more significant. In this particular case, the difference in the rentable area ratios may be considered to have the least impact on value. Therefore, the analysis of Comparable B indicates that the subject should have a unit value greater than $71.38 per square foot of rentable area.

Comparable C has a unit price of $76.09 per square foot of rentable area. The location of the comparable is similar to that of the subject, but the comparable has a superior rentable area ratio. The expense ratio for the property is slightly higher than typical, resulting in a lower net income. Since a higher rentable area ratio usually has a greater effect on value than a higher expense ratio, Comparable C is superior to the subject and the value for the subject should be less than $76.09 per square foot of rentable area.

Comparable D indicates a unit price of $80.90 per square foot of rentable area. Because it is situated at the intersection of two major arterial highways, the property has a significantly superior location compared to that of the subject. The availability of parking is more limited. Comparable D has a higher occupancy rate than the stabilized occupancy rate that characterizes the market for this type of property. The superior location and higher occupancy outweigh the limited parking. Overall, this comparable is superior to the subject and an appropriate value for the subject would be less than $80.90 per square foot of rentable area.

Comparable E has an indicated unit price of $73.08 per square foot of rentable area. The location of the property on a major collector street is inferior to that of the subject. The property is similar to the subject in all other elements of comparison. Since Comparable E has an inferior location, the price of the subject should be greater than $73.08 per square foot of rentable area.

The value indications derived from the comparable sales are reconciled into a single value indication by arranging the five sales in an array relative to the subject.

Comparable	Price Per Square Foot	Overall Comparability
D	$80.90	superior
A	$77.93	superior
C	$76.09	superior
Subject	–	–
E	$73.08	inferior
B	$71.38	inferior

Comparables A, C, and D have unit values greater than that of the subject; Comparables B and E have unit values less than that of the subject. The lowest value indication in the first group is $76.09 per square foot of rentable area for Comparable C. The higher value indication in the second group was $73.08 per square foot of rentable area for Comparable E. Therefore, the *bracket* for the value of the subject is between $73.08 and $76.09 per square foot of rentable area. Comparable E is the property most similar to the subject and therefore may be accorded the greatest weight. Based on the indicated range of value and the weight placed on Comparable E, a single point estimate of $74.00 per square foot of rentable area may be concluded.

A total value indication for the subject property may then be calculated by multiplying the unit value of $74.00 per square foot of rentable area by the 31,800 square feet of rentable area, resulting in a value indication of $2,353,200, which may be rounded to $2,350,000.

In relative comparison analysis, reliable results can usually be obtained by bracketing the subject between comparables that are superior and inferior to it. If the comparables are either all superior or all inferior, only a lower or upper limit is set and no range of possible values for the subject can be defined. In this case, the only conclusion the appraiser can draw for the subject is either that its value is more than the highest comparable indication (if all that comparable's qualitative factors are inferior) or less than the lowest comparable indication (if all that comparable's qualitative factors are superior).[1] Obviously, the appraiser must search the market diligently to obtain and analyze sufficient pertinent data to bracket the value of the subject property. If the available comparable data do not bracket the subject's value, the appraiser should consider employing other analytical techniques to establish such a bracket. Quantitative adjustments to the comparables can often serve this purpose. An example illustrating the combined use of quantitative adjustments and qualitative analysis is provided later in the chapter.

A value indication derived with qualitative analysis will usually require more narrative explanation in an appraisal report than an indication derived with quantitative adjustments. In applying either technique, the appraiser must ensure that his or her reasoning is clear and adequately explained. The extent of narrative explanation required

---

1. While the example provided here was used to illustrate relative comparison analysis, a qualitative technique, it may also be solved statistically. The appraiser might rate each sale qualitatively as a "value explainer," expressing the ratings applied as whole numbers. Two such methods are shown below.

Method A					
Comparable	**Price/Sq.Ft.**	**x**	**Reliability Rating**	**=**	**Product**
D	$80.90		1		$80.90
A	$77.93		3		$233.79
C	$76.09		2		$152.18
Subject					
E	$73.08		5		$365.40
B	$71.38		4		$285.52
	Column totals		15		$1,117.79
	$1,117.79 divided by		15	=	$74.52
Indicated unit value = $74.50 (rounded)					

Method B					
Comparable	**Price/Sq.Ft.**	**x**	**Percentage Weighting**	**=**	**Product**
D	$80.90		5.0%		$4.05
A	$77.93		20.0%		$15.59
C	$76.09		15.0%		$11.41
Subject					
E	$73.08		35.0%		$25.58
B	$71.38		25.0%		$17.85
	Column totals		100.0%		$74.48

depends on the complexity of the property being appraised. The more complex the property, the more factors that must be considered.

Relative Comparison Analysis of an Apartment Complex

The subject property is a 468-unit garden apartment complex that was built nine years ago. The complex includes a total of 320 one-bedroom apartment units and 148 two-bedroom apartment units. It also has an exercise room, a swimming pool with a whirlpool bath, a tennis court, and a clubhouse. The larger units have fireplaces. None of the units have balconies. The property is in average physical condition. The effective gross income is $3,280,702 and the net operating income is $1,637,998, which is equivalent to an *NOI* per unit of $3,500.

The following sales were selected as comparables.

Sale 1 is a 436-unit garden apartment complex that was built nine years ago. The property is in excellent condition. Apartments feature dishwashers, garbage disposals, microwave ovens, laundry facilities, and cable TV. The larger units have fireplaces and cathedral ceilings, and all the units have patios or balconies. Indoor parking is available for residents. The location is more desirable than the subject's. Title to the property was conveyed 13 months ago for $22,000,000, or $50,459 per unit. Financing did not affect the sale price. The effective gross income was $3,401,608, which is equivalent to $7,802 per unit, and the effective gross income multiplier is 6.47. The net operating income was $2,005,615, which is equivalent to an NOI per unit of $4,600. The overall capitalization rate was 9.12%. The average monthly rent was $0.90 per square foot.

Sale 2 is a 58-unit garden apartment complex that was built 10 years ago. It is in fair condition. The property was sold eight months ago for $1,740,000, or $30,000 per unit. The net operating income was $165,300, which is equivalent to an *NOI* per unit of $2,850. The overall capitalization rate was 9.5%. Effective gross income was $321,763, which equates to $5,548 per unit, and the effective gross income multiplier is 5.41. At the time of sale, four units were vacant. According to the broker, the seller provided financing at market rates. The location is less desirable than the subject's.

Sale 3 is an 80-unit garden apartment complex that was built 14 years ago. The property is in fair condition. Title to the property was conveyed six months ago for $2,500,000, or $31,250 per unit. The net operating income at the time of the sale was $263,995, which is equivalent to an *NOI* per unit of $3,300 and a 10.56% overall capitalization rate. The effective gross income was $469,511, or $5,869 per unit. The indicated effective gross income multiplier is 5.32. The location is less desirable than the subject's.

Sale 4 is a 236-unit garden apartment complex that was built seven years ago. The property is in excellent condition. The apartments feature wall-to-wall carpeting, microwave ovens, frost-free refrigerators, dishwashers, garbage disposals, fireplaces in the larger units, patios or balconies, and monitored alarm systems. Title to the property was conveyed 21 months ago. The sale price was $9,250,000 or $39,195 per unit. The effective gross income multiplier is 5.40. The net operating income was $870,277, which is equivalent to an *NOI* per unit of $3,700 and an overall capitalization rate of 9.41%. The location is less desirable than the subject's.

	Summary of Apartment Building Comparables				
Sale	No. of Units	Sale Price	Sale Price per Unit	R_o	EGIM
1	436	$22,000,000	$50,459	9.12%	6.47
2	58	$ 1,740,000	$30,000	9.50%	5.41
3	80	$ 2,500,000	$31,250	10.56%	5.32
4	236	$ 9,250,000	$39,195	9.41%	5.40

Low: $30,000 per unit

High: $50,459 per unit

The appraiser considered nine elements of comparison in the qualitative analysis.

Real property rights conveyed. The leased fee interest was conveyed in each of the comparable sales and the leased fee in the subject is the interest being valued on the effective date of appraisal. The comparables and the subject are equivalent in this respect.

Financing. Financing did not affect the price of any of the sale properties. Typical financing is assumed in the sale of the subject. The comparables and subject are considered similar.

Conditions of sale. Each sale was an arm's-length transaction, so the comparables and the subject are similar in this regard as well.

Market conditions. Sales of larger garden apartments have picked up in the market area after last year's downturn. Sales 1, 2, and 3 were transacted below current market prices.

Economic characteristics. The *NOI*s per unit for Sales 3 and 4 are fairly close to that of the subject. Sale 1 has a considerably higher *NOI* per unit, while Sale 2 has a considerably lower *NOI* per unit.

Location. The subject has a less desirable location than Sale 1. The location of the subject is superior to that of Sales 2, 3, and 4.

Physical condition. The subject is in worse physical condition than Sales 1 and 4, but in better condition than Sales 2 and 3.

Size. Normally there is a negative correlation between building size and price per unit. The subject is larger than Sales 2, 3, and 4, and roughly equivalent in size to Sale 1.

Marketability. Sale 1 includes patios or balconies in each unit and available indoor parking for residents. By comparison, the subject is inferior. The rent structure and effective gross income of the subject are higher than the rents and incomes of Sales 2 and 3. Although Sale 4 also has balconies, the effective gross income per unit is somewhat lower than the subject's. Overall, the subject is superior to Sale 4.

The chart below shows the qualitative comparison of the sale properties to the subject.

	Qualitative Analysis			
Sale	1	2	3	4
No. of units	436	58	80	236
Sale price	$22,000,000	$1,740,000	$2,500,000	$9,250,000
Price per unit	$50,459	$30,000	$31,250	$39,195
Property rights conveyed	Leased fee	Leased fee	Leased fee	Leased fee
Financing	Market	Market	Market	Market
Conditions of sale	Arm's-length	Arm's-length	Arm's-length	Arm's-length
Market conditions	–	–	–	Similar
Economic characteristics	+	–	Similar	Similar
Location	+	–	–	–
Physical condition	+	–	–	+
Size	Similar	+	+	+
Marketability	+	–	–	–
Overall comparability	Superior (+++)	Highly Inferior (– – – –)	Inferior (– – –)	Similar (0)

Ranking Analysis

The value of the subject is bracketed in the ranking analysis shown below. The comparable sales are then ranked in ascending or descending order according to their desirability.

	Ranking Analysis	
Sale	Sale Price Per Unit	Overall Comparability
1	$50,459	+++
Subject		
4	$39,195	0
3	$31,250	– – –
2	$30,000	– – – –

Conclusion

The subject is most similar to Sales 1 and 4 in terms of location, size, income characteristics, and investor appeal. The most emphasis is placed on these comparables. The market value of the leased fee estate in the subject property falls at the lower end of the bracket since Sale 1 is superior to the subject whereas Sale 4 is fairly similar. The value of the subject is indicated by the sales comparison approach to be $40,000 per unit, or $18,700,000 (rounded).

$$468 \text{ units @ } \$40,000 \text{ per unit} = \$18,720,000$$

Combining Quantitative Adjustments and Qualitative Analysis

In everyday appraisal practice, available market data may allow the appraiser to make quantitative adjustments for some elements of comparison and to analyze qualitatively the factors that cannot be quantified. When these techniques are combined, they should be consistently applied for each element of comparison. In other words, the appraiser should not make a quantitative adjustment for change in market conditions for some comparables and perform a qualitative analysis of market conditions for others. Quantitative adjustments should be made first. Qualitative analysis is subsequently applied to an adjusted sale or unit price. The following combined application of quantitative adjustments and qualitative analysis makes use of paired data and relative comparison analyses.

Combined Analysis of a Warehouse

Quantitative Analysis

The property being appraised is a 15-year-old warehouse containing 25,000 square feet of gross building area and 2,500 square feet of finished office area. The ceiling height is 18 feet. The quality of construction is good and the building's condition is average.

The five comparable sales described below were used in the analysis. All of the comparables are warehouses located in the subject property's market area.

Comparable A was sold one year ago for $622,000. The seller provided advantageous financing that resulted in the buyer paying $63,000 more that if the buyer had paid cash. The property is a 28,000-sq.-ft. warehouse with an 18-ft. ceiling height and 2,250 square feet of finished office area. It was 14 years old. The quality of construction is good, but at the time of sale the warehouse exhibited excessive deferred maintenance. The buyer has since spent $35,000 to upgrade the property.

Comparable B was sold six months ago for $530,000 in a cash payment to the seller. This 27,000-sq.-ft. warehouse has 18-ft. ceilings and 2,200 square feet of finished office area. It was 13 years old. The quality of construction and condition are average.

Comparable C is a current sale transacted for $495,000. The buyer assumed an existing loan at below market rates. This favorable financing resulted in the buyer paying $9,000 more than he would have if the buyer had obtained market terms. This 22,000-sq.-ft. warehouse has 17-ft. ceilings and 3,000 square feet of finished office area. The property is 13 years old. The quality of construction is good and its condition is average.

This warehouse is subject to a long-term lease at below-market levels so its purchase price was set at $25,000 below market prices.

Comparable D was sold three months ago for $554,000. This 25,000-sq.-ft. warehouse has a 17-ft. ceiling height and 2,500 square feet of finished office area. It is 16 years old. The quality of construction is good and the condition is good to excellent.

Comparable E is a current sale for $626,000 paid in cash to the seller. This 26,000-sq.-ft. warehouse has 19-ft. ceilings and 2,100 square feet of finished office area. It is 16 years old. The quality of construction is good and its condition is average. The property is subject to a long-term lease that is above market levels. The purchase price of the warehouse was consequently set at $80,000 above market prices.

The quantitative adjustment procedure is described below and summarized in Table 19.3.

Comparables C and E were sold subject to long-term leases, so both require an adjustment for property rights conveyed. Comparable C requires an upward adjustment of $25,000 because it is leased at below-market contract rent. Comparable E requires a downward adjustment of $80,000 because it is leased at above-market contract rent.

Comparables A and C require adjustment for financing terms. The seller of Comparable A provided advantageous financing that resulted in the buyer paying $63,000 more than the buyer would have in a cash transaction. Therefore, a downward adjustment of $63,000 is made to Comparable A. The buyer of Comparable C assumed an existing, below-market loan. The buyer paid a $9,000 premium above the price that would have been paid under market terms, so a downward adjustment of $9,000 is made to Comparable C.

Because all the comparables were arm's-length transactions, none requires an adjustment for conditions of sale.

The sales occurred over a 12-month period. Properties in this market have been appreciating at 4% annually. Comparables A, B, and D require an upward adjustment for change in market conditions.

Comparable A suffered from excessive deferred maintenance. After purchase the buyer spent $35,000 upgrading the building to good condition. The subject property is in average condition. Therefore, Comparable A is adjusted upward by $35,000 to bring it in line with the subject's average condition.

Comparable D had no deferred maintenance and was in good to excellent condition. Therefore, it requires a downward adjustment of $10,000 to bring it in line with the subject's average condition.

After applying all known quantitative adjustments, the comparables indicate a value range from $20.02 to $23.23 per square foot.

Qualitative Analysis

The appraiser next considers qualitative differences between the subject and the comparable properties. Qualitative analysis of the nonquantifiable attributes of the comparable properties is shown in Table 19.4. All the comparables are of similar quality construction, but slight differences may be recognized by the market. The quality of Comparable B is average, so it is inferior to the subject's good quality.

Table 19.3 | Quantitative Adjustments

	Subject	Comp. A	Comp. B	Comp. C	Comp. D	Comp. E
Price		$622,000	$530,000	$495,000	$554,000	$626,000
Area in square feet	25,000	28,000	27,000	22,000	25,000	26,000
Ceiling height	18 ft.	18 ft.	18 ft.	17 ft.	17 ft.	19 ft.
Age	15 years	14 years	13 years	13 years	16 years	16 years
Construction quality	Good	Good	Average	Good	Good	Good
Property rights	Fee simple	Fee simple	Fee simple	Leased fee	Fee simple	Leased fee
Adjustment		0	0	+ $25,000	0	- $80,000
Adjusted price		$622,000	$530,000	$520,000	$554,000	$546,000
Financing terms	Cash	Carryback	Cash	Loan assumption	Cash	Cash
Adjustment		- $63,000	0	- $9,000	0	0
Adjusted price		$559,000	$530,000	$511,000	$554,000	$546,000
Conditions of sale	Arm's-length	Arm's-length	Arm's-length	Arm's-length	Arm's-length	Arm's-length
Market conditions	Current	One year	Six months	Current	Three months	Current
Adjustment	0	x 1.04	x 1.02	0	x 1.01	0
Adjusted price		$581,360	$540,600	$511,000	$559,540	$546,000
Deferred maintenance (condition)	Average	Excessive	Average	Average	None	Average
Adjustment		+ $35,000	0	0	- $10,000	0
Adjusted price		$616,360	$540,600	$511,000	$549,540	$546,000
Adjusted price per sq.ft.		$22.01	$20.02	$23.23	$21.98	$21.00

An adjustment for extra ceiling height cannot be isolated from an analysis of the differences in rent, vacancy, or expenses. However, all else being equal, extra ceiling height ought to contribute to value. Comparables C and D, with 17-ft. ceiling heights, are inferior to the subject, which has an 18-ft. ceiling height. Comparable E, with a 19-ft. ceiling height, is superior to the subject.

Newer warehouses generally sell for more than older warehouses. Comparables A, B, and C, which are newer than the subject, are probably superior to the subject; Comparables D and E, which are older, are probably inferior to the subject.

The comparables range in size from 22,000 square feet to 28,000 square feet and the size of the subject is regarded as similar in this market. This market does show a preference for industrial properties with a higher percentage of office area to total building area up to an optimal level. Therefore, Comparables A, B, and E, which each have about 8% of office area to total building area, are slightly inferior to the subject, which has 10% office area. Comparable C has a higher percentage of office area (about 14%), so it is slightly superior.

After qualitative analysis, the comparables are arrayed in ascending order according to their values per square foot. The array also shows how the comparable sales compare to the subject overall.

Comparable	Dollars Per Square Foot	Overall Comparability
B	> $20.02	inferior
E	> $21.00	inferior
D	> $21.98	inferior
A	$22.01	similar
C	< $23.23	superior

The comparables indicate a value greater than $21.98 per square foot, but less than $23.23 per square foot. The major emphasis falls at $22.00 per square foot. The value of the subject is estimated at $22.00 per square foot, or a total value of $550,000 (25,000 square feet x $22.00 per square foot).

Reconciliation

Reconciliation is the last phase of any valuation analysis in which two or more value indications have been derived from market data. In reconciliation, the appraiser summarizes and reviews the data and analyses that resulted in each of the value indications. These value indications are then resolved into a range of value or a single value indication, often called a *point estimate*. It is important that the appraiser consider the strengths and weaknesses of each value indication derived, examining the reliability and appropriateness of the market data compiled and the analytical techniques applied. It is also good practice to review the major elements of comparison for which no adjustments were made and to explain why no adjustments for these elements were required. The appraisal report should clearly communicate the reasoning by which the appraiser arrived at the value conclusion.

Table 19.4 **Qualitative Analysis**

	Subject	Comp. A	Comp. B	Comp. C	Comp. D	Comp. E
Adjusted price per sq.ft.		$22.01	$20.02	$23.23	$21.98	$21.00
Construction quality		Similar	–	Similar	Similar	Similar
Ceiling height		Similar	Similar	–	–	+
Age		+	+	+	–	–
Percentage of office area to total building area		–	–	+	Similar	–
Overall comparability		Similar	Inferior	Superior	Inferior	Inferior
Value indication		$22.01	>$20.02	<$23.23	>$21.98	>$21.00

In the sales comparison approach, reconciliation may involve *two levels* of analysis. The first level of analysis pertains to the derivation of a value indication from the adjusted prices of two or more comparables that are expressed in terms of a single unit of comparison. The reconciliation process at this level of analysis was demonstrated in the sample applications of quantitative adjustment and qualitative analysis. A second level of analysis is required when the appraiser derives two or more value indications that are expressed in different units of comparison. For example, value indications expressed in price per square foot and price per dwelling unit must be reconciled into a value range or a single value indication for the sales comparison approach.

Reconciliation is also required when value indications are derived using two or more approaches to value. At this final point in the valuation process, reconciliation results in the value estimate identified in the problem definition. Final reconciliation is discussed in Chapter 25.

Two related points should be stressed in any discussion of the reconciliation process. In arriving at a final value indication in the sales comparison approach, the appraiser must ensure that the value concluded is consistent with the purpose of the appraisal and the value indications derived from the other approaches to value. This is especially important in regard to the date of prospective value estimates. For example, an appraiser may seek market value estimates of an income-producing property at two different points in the future—e.g., upon project completion and upon stabilized occupancy. The only market data available, however, may pertain to comparable properties at or near stabilized occupancy. Typically, these data are appropriate only for an analysis of the market value of the subject property at the point of stabilized occupancy. Thus, the appraiser has to reconcile the prospective value indication based on these data with value indications derived from the other approaches for the corresponding date of stabilized occupancy. These data should *not* be used to derive a value indication for the date of completion unless other, truly comparable sales can be identified.

The appraiser must also consider any differences in the property rights appraised between the comparables and the subject property since the comparable sales may include the transfer of a leased fee estate. If the data are not properly analyzed, the value indication concluded in the sales comparison approach for the leased fee estate in the subject property upon the achievement of stabilized occupancy might be lower than the value for the fee simple estate. This value indication would not be compatible with the corresponding value indications derived from the cost and income approaches for the fee simple estate in the subject property unless adjustments have been made. Failure to recognize that the value indications may apply to different property rights would likely result in an incorrect value conclusion. Weighted mean analysis is a useful tool for reconciling several values into a single value estimate.

Key Concepts

- Both quantitative and qualitative techniques are employed in the sales comparison approach. Quantitative adjustment techniques include paired data analysis, grouped data analysis, statistical analysis, graphic analysis, trend analysis, capitalization of income differences, cost analysis, and secondary data analysis. Qualitative analysis includes relative comparison analysis, ranking analysis, and personal interviews.

- Quantitative adjustments may be applied to comparable prices as percentage or dollar amounts.

- In qualitative analysis comparables are identified as those that are superior overall to the subject and those that are inferior overall. This division helps bracket the probable value range of the subject.

- Quantitative and qualitative methodologies are often combined in practice. Quantitative adjustments are applied before qualitative analysis is undertaken.

- To help in the analysis of comparable sales, appraisers make use of data array and adjustment grids.

- As part of reconciliation, the appraiser checks to ensure that value indications are expressed in the same units of comparison and reflect estimates of the same property interests as of the same date.

Terms

bracketing	quantitative adjustment
date of value estimate	range of value
gross adjustment	ranking analysis
grouped data analysis	reconciliation
net adjustment	relative comparison analysis
paired data analysis	unit of comparison
point estimate	weighting
qualitative analysis	

CHAPTER TWENTY

The Income Capitalization Approach

I ncome-producing real estate is typically purchased as an investment, and from an investor's point of view earning power is the critical element affecting property value. One basic investment premise holds that the higher the earnings, the higher the value, provided the amount of risk remains constant. An investor who purchases income-producing real estate is essentially trading present dollars for the expectation of receiving future dollars. The income capitalization approach to value consists of methods, techniques, and mathematical procedures that an appraiser uses to analyze a property's capacity to generate benefits (i.e., usually the monetary benefits of income and reversion) and convert these benefits into an indication of present value.

The income capitalization approach is one of three traditional approaches that an appraiser may use in the valuation process. However, it is not an independent system of valuation unrelated to the other approaches. The valuation process as a whole is composed of integrated, interrelated, and inseparable techniques and procedures designed to produce a convincing and reliable estimate of value, usually market value.

The analysis of cost and sales data is often an integral part of the income capitalization approach, and capitalization techniques are frequently employed in the cost and sales comparison approaches. Capitalization techniques are commonly used to analyze and adjust sales data in the sales comparison approach; in the cost approach, obsolescence is often measured by capitalizing an estimated rent loss. The income capitalization approach is described here as part of the systematic valuation process, but the various methods, techniques, and procedures used in the approach are general-purpose analytical tools applicable in the valuation and evaluation of income-producing properties.

This chapter provides a broad overview of the income capitalization approach and discusses the rationale, methods, and history behind it. Chapters 21 through 24 continue this discussion with detailed explanations of the specific methods, techniques, and procedures used to project and capitalize future benefits.

Relationship to Value Influences and Appraisal Principles

The income capitalization approach is based on, and consistent with, the basic value influences and principles of real estate appraisal.

Anticipation and Change

The principle of anticipation is fundamental to the approach. Because value is created by the expectation of benefits to be derived in the future, value may be defined as the present worth of all rights to these future benefits. All income capitalization methods, techniques, and procedures attempt to consider anticipated future benefits and estimate their present value. This may involve either forecasting the anticipated future income or estimating a capitalization rate that implicitly reflects the anticipated pattern of change in income over time.

The approach must also consider how change affects the value of income-producing properties. To provide sound value indications, investors' expectations of changes in income levels, the expenses required to ensure income, and probable increases or decreases in property value must be carefully addressed and forecast. The defined income of a real estate investment may differ according to the type of investor. The ongoing securitization of real estate investment has brought new participants into the market. The income lines that real estate investment trusts (REITs) and pension funds look to are different from the net income on which more traditional investors have focused.[1]

The capitalization procedure used to value a property must reflect the fact that the actual change in income, expenses, and property values may be different than was originally anticipated by investors at the time of the appraisal. The more uncertainty there is about how these variables will change, the riskier the property investment. Investors expect to earn a higher rate of return on investments that are riskier. This should be reflected in the discount rate and capitalization rate estimated by the appraiser.

Supply and Demand

The principle of supply and demand and the related concept of competition are particularly relevant in forecasting future benefits and estimating rates of return in the income capitalization approach. Both income streams and rates of return are determined in the market. The rents charged by the owner of a motel, a shopping center, an office building, an apartment building, or any income-producing property usually do not vary greatly from those charged by owners of competing properties.

If the demand for a particular type of space exceeds the existing supply, owners may be able to increase rents. Vacancy rates may fall and developers may find new construction profitable. Property values may increase until supply and demand are in balance. On the other hand, if the demand for space is less than the existing supply, rents may decline and vacancy rates may increase. Therefore, to estimate rates of return and forecast future benefits, appraisers consider the demand for the particular type of property and how this demand is related to supply.

Substitution

The prices, rents, and rates of return for property tend to be set by the prevailing prices, rents, and rates of return for equally desirable substitute properties. The principle of substitution is market-oriented and provides the basis for estimating rents and expenses and calculating an appropriate discount rate or capitalization rate for the subject

---

1. For a discussion of how pension fund managers and other institutional investors analyze income and cash flow to property, see Chapter 28 on the securitization of real estate markets.

property. The principle of substitution may also be used to test the validity of the income capitalization approach and the reliability of the assumptions and data used in its application.

Balance

The principle of balance and related concepts are especially significant in applying the income capitalization approach. A good balance between the types and locations of income-producing properties creates and sustains value; an imbalance in efficient land use may result in a decline in value. Efficient land use is facilitated by good planning and zoning laws.

The concept of contribution suggests that a reasonable balance among the four agents of production in an income-producing property creates and sustains maximum profitability. If a property is overimproved or underimproved, its rate of profit may be adversely affected.

Externalities

Positive and negative external forces affect the value of income-producing property. Apartments and office buildings are subject to the same types of external forces (e.g., the availability and quality of public transportation and shopping facilities) that affect single-family residences. Similarly, commercial establishments are enhanced by attractive, spacious, accessible surroundings and damaged by unattractive, poorly maintained, dirty surroundings. The negative externalities imposed by high crime rates have affected all types of income-producing property in recent years. External conditions such as pollution, unattractive surroundings, and high crime rates can even affect the value of property used for factories involved in heavy industry.

Interests to Be Valued

As has often been stated, appraisers do not value real estate, they value property interests in real estate. The form of ownership, financial interest, and legal estate all must be considered to identify the real property being appraised.

Legal interests are discussed in depth in Chapter 7. Appraisers should recognize that the rights of ownership in income-producing real estate are not always held in fee simple by individual owners. An investor may hold title to real property rights as an individual, as a corporate shareholder (in a C corporation, an S corporation, or a limited liability corporation), or as a general or limited partner. In addition, an interest in real estate is often subject to mortgage financing, which further divides the real property rights into debt and equity interests. Finally, income-producing real estate is usually leased, which creates legal estates of the lessor's interest (i.e., the leased fee) and the lessee's interest (i.e., the leasehold). There are also hybrid situations involving partially leased buildings. An appraiser may be called upon to value the lessor's marketable interest, i.e., the fee simple subject to existing leases.

As the flowchart in Figure 20.1 illustrates, the appraiser follows a logical sequence to identify the real property rights being appraised. The three main components of real property rights are ownership entities, financial interests, and legal estates. In a typical market value appraisal, the appraiser values an ownership entity's financial interest in a legal estate. By properly identifying all three categories of rights, the appraiser pinpoints the specific real property rights to be valued.

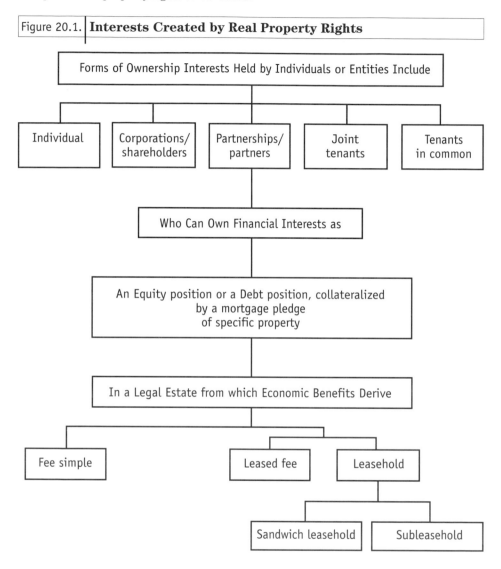

Figure 20.1. **Interests Created by Real Property Rights**

Market valuation assignments relating to income-producing real estate often concern 100% ownerships of equity interests in a leased fee estate. A 100% ownership includes all shareholders or partners in a real estate venture. A typical example is the valuation of an existing, multitenant office building for a prospective buyer. The real property rights to be valued may be free and clear of mortgage debt or they may be subject to specified financing terms. The scope of the assignment may require a value estimate of the equity interest alone or a total value including the mortgage. In the latter case, the final conclusion may be reported in cash, in terms equivalent to cash, or in other precisely revealed terms, depending on the nature of the assignment and applicable professional standards.

Appraisers do not only value fee simple, leased fee, and leasehold estates. They are often called upon to value real property rights complicated by other factors. For example, appraisers may value

- Minority shareholder or partnership interests
- Equity interests subject to various layers of debt, some of which may contribute to pre-tax cash flow and reversion
- Participation mortgages for lenders
- Master leasehold, sandwich leasehold, or subleasehold estates

Real property rights may be further affected by the specific requirements of the client, who may ask an appraiser to value a property subject to anticipated rezoning, planned renovation or rehabilitation, or the completion of construction. It is essential that the client and the appraiser begin with a clear understanding of the fundamentals of the appraisal assignment—i.e., the valuation of specified real property rights as of a specific date expressed in clearly defined terms.

Non-Realty Interests

Appraisers are often asked to value properties which include property components that are not "real property." For example, hotels include a significant amount of furniture, fixtures, and equipment which would often be classified as personal property.[2] When there is a business enterprise associated with the property (as in the case of a hotel), the price investors are willing to pay may also include a premium over the value of the real property for what is referred to as *business enterprise value*.

Business enterprise value is a value enhancement that results from items of intangible personal property such as marketing and management skill, an assembled work force, working capital, trade names, franchises, patents, trademarks, non-realty related contracts or leases, and some operating agreements. Going-concern value is the value created by a proven property operation with income sufficient to pay a fair return to all the agents of production. It consists of the total value of the real property; personal property such as furniture, fixtures and equipment; and intangible personal property, or the business enterprise. Properties with a business value component include hotels and motels, restaurants, bowling alleys, nursing homes, and other labor-intensive operations.

Market Value and Investment Value

The income capitalization approach is typically used in market value appraisals of income-producing property. The approach may also be used to estimate investment

---

2. Legal requirements stipulate that the assets of REITs be predominantly comprised of real property, from which the FF&E category of personal property is excluded. The percentage of assets other than real property which a REIT can hold is strictly limited. For this reason, REITs are effectively precluded from investing in certain kinds of hotel properties.

value, which is the value of a certain property use to a particular investor. Market value and investment value may coincide if the client's investment criteria are typical of investors in the market. In this case, the two value estimates may be the same number, but the two types of value are *not* interchangeable.

Market value is objective, impersonal, and detached; investment value is based on subjective, personal parameters. To estimate market value with the income capitalization approach, the appraiser must be certain that all the data and assumptions used are market-oriented and reflect the motivations of a typical investor who would be willing to purchase the property at the time of the appraisal. A particular investor may be willing to pay more than market value, if necessary, to acquire a property that satisfies investment objectives unique to that investor. Similarly, a particular investor may place a higher investment value on a property he or she already owns than the current price for which the property could be sold. The price a user-owner pays for a land parcel may differ significantly from the price paid by a speculator-investor.

This text discusses the income capitalization approach as it is applied to estimate the market value of a fee simple or leased fee interest. The conclusions reached reflect the use and analysis of market data; they should be consistent with the value indications reached in the other valuation approaches. The value indications from each of the approaches applied should reflect the same interest in the property.

Future Benefits

The benefits of owning specific rights in income-producing real estate include the right to receive all profits accruing to the real property over the holding period (i.e., the term of ownership) plus the proceeds from resale or reversion of the property at the termination of the investment. Various measures of future benefits are considered in the income capitalization approach. Commonly used measures include potential gross income, effective gross income, net operating income, pre-tax cash flow, and reversionary benefits.

Potential gross income (PGI) is the total potential income attributable to the real property at full occupancy before operating expenses are deducted. Potential gross income may refer to the level of rental income prevailing on the date of the appraisal or expected during the first full month or year of operation, or to the periodic income anticipated during the holding period.

Effective gross income (EGI) is the anticipated income from all operations of the real property adjusted for vacancy and collection losses. This adjustment covers losses incurred due to unoccupied space, turnover, and nonpayment of rent by tenants.

Net operating income (NOI) is the actual or anticipated net income remaining after all operating expenses are deducted from effective gross income, but before mortgage debt service and book depreciation are deducted. Net operating income is customarily expressed as an annual amount. In certain income capitalization applications, a single year's net operating income may represent a steady stream of fixed income that is expected to continue for a number of years. In other applications, the income may represent the starting level of a stream of income that is expected to change in a prescribed pattern over the years. Still other applications may require that net operating income be estimated for each year of the analysis.

Pre-tax cash flow is the portion of net operating income that remains after debt service is paid, but before ordinary income tax on operations is deducted. Like net operating income, a single year's pre-tax cash flow may represent a steady stream of fixed income, the starting level of a changing income stream, or the equity income for a particular year of the analysis. Pre-tax cash flow is also referred to as *equity dividend* or *before-tax cash flow*.

After-tax cash flow is the portion of pre-tax cash flow that remains after ordinary income tax on operations has been deducted.[3] The amount of ordinary income tax paid by the owner depends on the taxable income accruing from ownership of the property. This is affected by the amount of interest and depreciation that can be deducted from *NOI* in the calculation of taxable income.[4]

Reversion is a lump-sum benefit that an investor receives at the termination of an investment. The reversionary benefit may be calculated before or after deduction of the mortgage balance and income taxes. For example, the reversionary benefits for fee simple and leased fee estates are the expected net proceeds from resale of the properties at the end of the investment holding period (see Table 23.1). For a mortgagee or lender, reversion consists of the balance of the mortgage when it is paid off.

Reversionary benefits are usually estimated either as an anticipated dollar amount or as a relative change in value over the presumed holding period. A dollar estimate of the reversion might be based on a lessee's option to purchase the property at the end of the lease. Alternatively, the value of the reversion at the end of the holding period might be estimated by applying a capitalization rate to the income that a buyer might expect to receive at the time of resale. Reversionary benefits may or may not require separate measurement, depending on the purpose of the analysis and the method of capitalization employed.

Rates of Return

In applying the income capitalization approach, an appraiser assumes that the investor's ultimate objective is a total return that exceeds the amount invested. Therefore, the investor's expected return consists of 1) full recovery of the amount invested (i.e., the return *of* capital), and 2) a profit or reward (i.e., a return *on* capital).

Since the returns from real estate may be realized in a variety of forms, many rates, or measures of return, are used in capitalization. All rates of return can be categorized as either *income rates* or *yield rates*. The overall capitalization rate (R_O) and equity capitalization rate (R_E) (also called the *cash flow rate* or *cash on cash return*) are income rates. The interest rate (the rate of return on debt capital), discount rate (the rate used to convert future payments into present value), internal rate of return, and equity yield rate are yield rates.

---

3. After-tax cash flow is usually employed as a measure of investment value.
4. Certain categories of investments, e.g., REITs and pension funds, are tax-exempt. Individual shareholders and pensioners, however, are taxed on personal income.

Under certain conditions, the yield rate for a particular property may be numerically equivalent to the corresponding income rate; nevertheless, the rates are not conceptually the same nor are they interchangeable. An income rate is the ratio of one year's income to value;[5] a yield rate is applied to a series of individual incomes to obtain the present value of each.

In the income capitalization approach, both income rates and yield rates can be derived for, and applied to, any component of real property rights or the underlying physical real estate. For example, an appraiser may analyze total property income in terms of income to the land and income to the building or in terms of income to the mortgage and equity interests in the property. Similarly, an appraiser may seek the total investment yield or may analyze the separate yields to the land and the building or to the mortgage and the equity interests. Finally, an appraiser may want to know the value of the unencumbered fee simple, the leased fee, or the leasehold interest. (Practical examples of these applications and the relevant symbols, formulas, and procedures are presented in Chapters 21 through 23.)

Income Rates

An income rate expresses the relationship between one year's income and the corresponding capital value of a property. Several types of income rates are discussed below.

An overall capitalization rate (R_O) is an income rate for a total property that reflects the relationship between a single year's net operating income expectancy and the total property price or value; it is used to convert net operating income into an indication of overall property value. An overall capitalization rate is not a rate of return on capital or a full measure of investment performance. It may be more than, less than, or equal to the expected yield on the capital invested, depending on projected changes in income and value.

An equity capitalization rate (R_E) is an income rate that reflects the relationship between a single year's pre-tax cash flow expectancy and the equity investment. When used to capitalize the subject property's pre-tax cash flow into equity value, the equity capitalization rate is often referred to in the real estate market as the *cash on cash return* or *cash flow rate*. Like the overall capitalization rate, the equity capitalization rate is not a rate of return on capital; it may be more than, less than, or equal to the expected equity yield rate, depending on projected changes in income, value, and amortization of the loan.

Yield Rates

A yield rate is a rate of return on capital; it is usually expressed as a compound annual percentage rate. The yield rate considers all expected property benefits, including the proceeds from sale at the termination of the investment. The term *interest rate* usually refers to the yield rate for debt capital, not equity capital.

---

5. The rate is usually calculated with the income for the first year, although the income for the previous year may be used. In some cases the incomes for several years might be averaged to obtain a representative income figure.

A discount rate is a yield rate used to convert anticipated future payments or receipts into present value. The resulting present value represents the amount of capital to be invested so that the investor's expected yield equals the specified discount rate.

Internal rate of return (IRR), refers to the yield rate that is earned for a given capital investment over the period of ownership. The internal rate of return for an investment is the yield rate that equates the present value of the future benefits of the investment to the amount of capital invested. The internal rate of return applies to all expected benefits, including the proceeds from resale at the termination of the invest-ment. It can be used to measure the return on any capital investment, before or after income taxes.

An overall yield rate (Y_O) is a rate of return on the total capital invested. It takes into consideration changes in income over the investment holding period as well as the reversion at the end of the holding period. It does not, however, consider the effect of debt financing; it is calculated as if the property were purchased with no debt capital. The overall yield rate can be viewed as the combined yield on both the debt and equity capital. Conceptually it is a weighted average of the equity yield rate, which is discussed below, and the mortgage yield, or mortgage interest, rate.[6]

An equity yield rate (Y_E) is a rate of return on equity capital. It may be distinguished from a rate of return on debt capital, which is usually referred to as an *interest rate.* The equity yield rate is the equity investor's internal rate of return; it considers the effect of debt financing on the cash flow to the equity investor (equity dividend).

Leverage, the use of borrowed funds to increase the equity return, can enhance the equity yield rate over the overall yield rate. (Leverage is discussed in Chapter 23.)

Return on and Return of Capital

The notion that an investor anticipates realizing a complete recovery of invested capital plus a payment for the use of capital prevails in the real estate market just as it does in other markets. The term *return of capital* refers to the recovery of invested capital; the term *return on capital* refers to the additional amount received as compensation for use of the investor's capital until it is recaptured. Investors are concerned with both return of capital and return on capital. The rate of return on capital is analogous to the yield rate or the interest rate earned or expected.

In real estate investments, capital may be recaptured in many ways. (The term *recapture* was coined at a time when investors assumed that property values could only decline due to depreciation from physical or functional causes. Today appraisers use the term when some income provision must be made to compensate for the loss of invested capital.) Investment capital may be recaptured through annual income or it may be recaptured all or in part through resale of the property at the termination of the invest-ment. If the property value does not change between the time of the initial investment and the time the property is sold, the investor can recapture all the capital invested at its

6. In practice, the overall yield rate is not usually calculated by averaging the equity yield rate and the mortgage interest rate because the ratio of debt and equity changes each year as the loan is amortized and the property value changes.

sale. Thus the annual income can all be attributed to the return on capital. In this case, the indicated income rate—i.e., the overall capitalization rate—will equal the return on capital.

If, on the other hand, the property value is expected to decrease over time and the investor does not expect to recapture all of the original investment at the time of resale, some of the income stream must be used for the repayment of capital. In this case the rate of return on capital will be somewhat less than the indicated income rate (i.e., the overall capitalization rate in direct capitalization). The difference between the rate of return on capital and the indicated capitalization rate will be the rate of return of capital. The recapture rate is considered positive.

Finally, if the investor expects to receive more than the original investment at resale, the rate of return on capital is more than the indicated income rate; in this case the recapture rate appears to be negative because the annual income is not providing all of the expected return on capital.

In yield capitalization the distinction between the return on and the return of capital is always explicit. The discount rate estimated for cash flows yields a specified return on capital. Direct capitalization, on the other hand, uses income rates such as overall capitalization rates, which must implicitly allow for both the return on and return of capital. That is, when the capitalization rate is applied to the income of the subject property, the estimated present value must represent a price that would allow the investor to earn a market rate of return on, in addition to recapture of, the capital invested. Thus, the capitalization rate estimated and applied to value property must reflect the way that capital is expected to be recaptured.

Rate Estimation

Whether it is an income rate or a yield rate, the rate of return used to convert income into property value should represent the annual rate of return necessary to attract investment capital. This rate is influenced by many factors, including the degree of apparent risk, market attitudes toward future inflation, the prospective rates of return for alternative investments, the rates of return earned by comparable properties in the past, the supply of and demand for mortgage funds, and the availability of tax shelters. Because the rates of return used in the income capitalization approach represent *prospective* rates, not historical rates, the market's perception of risk and changes in purchasing power are particularly important. Generally, higher capitalization overall rates (R_Os) are associated with less desirable properties, and lower overall capitalization rates with more attractive properties.

The suitability of a particular rate of return cannot be proven with market evidence, but the rate estimated should be consistent with the data available. Rate estimation requires appraisal judgment and knowledge about prevailing market attitudes and economic indicators.

It is generally accepted that all investments are predicated on the expectation of receiving a return on capital that represents the *time value of money* with an appropriate adjustment for perceived risk. The concept of the time value of money underlies the accrual of interest on investments. The minimum rate of return for invested capital is sometimes referred to as the *safe*, *riskless*, or *relatively riskless* rate (e.g., the prevailing rate on insured savings accounts or guaranteed government bonds). Theoretically, the difference between the total rate of return on capital and the safe rate may be considered a premium to compensate the investor for risk, the burden of management, and the illiquidity of invested capital. Conceptually a discount rate may be developed with the *built-up method*, which involves adding together the four components in the rate, i.e., a basic safe or riskless rate plus adjustments for risk, illiquidity, and management.[7]

Risk

The anticipation of receiving future benefits creates value, but the possibility of losing future benefits detracts from value. Higher rewards are required in return for accepting higher risk. To a real estate investor, risk is the chance of incurring a financial loss and the uncertainty of realizing projected future benefits. Most investors try to avoid excessive risk; they prefer certainty to uncertainty and expect a reward in return for assuming a risk. Appraisers must recognize investors' attitudes in analyzing market evidence, projecting future benefits, and applying capitalization procedures. The appraiser must be satisfied that the income or yield rate used in capitalization is consistent with market evidence and reflects the level of risk associated with receiving the anticipated benefits.

Expected Inflation and Deflation

The amount of inflation or deflation expected affects the forecast of future benefits and the estimation of an appropriate income or yield rate. If inflation, the erosion of the purchasing power of currency, is anticipated, the desired nominal rate of return on invested capital will tend to increase to compensate for lost purchasing power. That is, the required nominal rate will increase to offset the expected inflation. It is the *real* rate of return that investors try to protect over time.

In theory, the total desired rate of return on capital includes any expected inflation rate. Therefore, the anticipated yield rate generally varies directly with the expected inflation rate. When discount rates that do not include a specific allowance for inflation are applied, the income streams and reversions calculated are expressed in constant, or uninflated, dollars.

Because the inflation rate and the yield rate tend to fluctuate together, there is no proof that a particular combination of rates provides the best reflection of current market attitudes. Nevertheless, the combination chosen must be consistent with general market

---

7. Traditionally, appraisal literature has not presented the built-up method as a viable method for deriving discount and yield rates. The sixth and seventh editions of *The Appraisal of Real Estate* stated that "because of the intangible character of the components, it [the built-up method] is not considered a valid procedure through which a specific rate may be derived." With the securitization of real estate investment and new methodologies to rate the risk associated with commercial real estate properties and portfolios, however, some analysts have called for a reconsideration of built-up rates.

A risk-rated discount rate may be assigned to securities with a comparable risk-rating. This risk-related rate can then be adjusted for illiquidity and management. An adjustment for illiquidity may be estimated based on the spread between yields on securities with short-term maturities and yields on securities with long-term maturities. An adjustment for management may be estimated by researching the fees charged by asset management organizations for handling investment portfolios. While the process is not simple, proponents stress that the data employed are market-driven. Critics contend that the methodology ascribes the risks and rewards of the security markets to real estate market investments. Interest-rate volatility is priced into the rates of security markets, but this is not so in real estate markets. See James E. Gibbons, "In Search of the Rate," *Real Estate Issues* (Fall/Winter 1992), 1-6.

expectations and the relationship or difference between the two rates must be plausible and supportable. In market value appraisals, the appraiser's objective is to simulate the expectations of a typical investor, not necessarily to make the most reliable prediction of yield and inflation rates.

Appraisers should be aware of the difference between inflation and appreciation in real value. Inflation is an increase in the volume of money and credit, a rise in the general level of prices, and the consequent erosion of purchasing power. Appreciation in real value results from an excess of demand over supply, which increases property values.

Inflation and appreciation have a similar effect on future dollars, but different effects on discount rates. Inflation tends to increase discount rates because investors require a higher nominal rate of return to offset the loss in value due to inflation. Appreciation will not affect the discount rate unless the risk associated with the property has changed. Inflation, however, may be accompanied by lower capitalization rates because these rates are applied to the income at the time of the appraisal, which has not increased due to inflation. When real estate is considered a hedge against inflation, the greater demand for real estate may exert downward pressure on capitalization rates. (This can be demonstrated by means of the property models discussed in Chapter 23.)

In oversupplied markets, real estate may not always keep up with inflation. This has become evident over the past decade as purchasing power and demand-pull pressure on the price of real estate failed to keep pace with cost-push inflation. In an inflationary environment, the value of real estate may tend to increase relative to the value of other investments such as stocks and bonds. Rents under annual leases can be adjusted upward periodically, while the interest and dividends paid on longer-term securities are more fixed. Although inflation does not create true value, certain properties seem to be better hedges against inflation than others. Thus, the outlook for inflation may affect property value.

An appraiser can account for the effects of inflation in capitalization by expressing future benefits in constant dollars, which are adjusted to reflect constant purchasing power, and by expressing the discount rate as a real, uninflated rate of return on capital. In practice, however, appraisers usually project income and expenses in unadjusted, inflated dollars and express the discount rate as a nominal, or apparent, rate of return on capital that includes an allowance for inflation.

Because lease terms often allow for inflation with expense pass-throughs and adjustments based on the Consumer Price Index (CPI), it is convenient and customary to project income and expenses in dollars as they are expected to occur, and not to convert the amounts into constant dollars. Unadjusted discount rates, rather than real rates of return, are used so that these rates can be compared with other rates quoted in the open market—e.g., mortgage interest rates and bond yield rates. Fixed-income securities like bonds do not respond to unexpected inflation in the same way real estate does because the interest rate and face value of securities are fixed at the time the bond is issued.

Any projected increases in income and property value due to inflation must be realistic. Property income ultimately depends on the supply and demand equation. In a cost-push inflationary spiral, purchasing power may fail to keep pace.

Projecting the income from real estate in nominal terms allows an analyst to consider whether or not the income potential of the property and the resale price will increase with inflation. The appraiser must be consistent and not discount inflated dollars at real, uninflated rates. When inflated nominal dollars are projected, the discount rate must also be a nominal discount rate that reflects the anticipated inflation.

Unexpected Inflation

A distinction must be made between expected inflation and unexpected inflation. Expected inflation refers to changes in price levels that are expected at the time the investment is made or the property is being appraised. As discussed above, anticipated inflation should be reflected in expected rates of return. However, actual inflation may differ from what was anticipated at the time the investment was made. Depending on how the investment responds to the actual change in price levels, its value may increase or decrease over time at a different rate than originally anticipated. If the return on the investment does not increase with unexpected inflation, the investor's real rate of return will be less than originally projected.

Investors sometimes include an additional risk premium in the rate of return required on investments in which the income steam may be compromised by unexpected inflation, e.g., office buildings under leases without escalation clauses or retail properties under leases without percentage rent increases. For many properties, however, it is reasonable to assume that the net operating income and resale value will reflect or adjust to unexpected inflation. Investors may not, therefore, require as great a premium in yield for the inflationary risk associated with real estate investments as they would for fixed-income investments like corporate bonds.

Income Capitalization Approach Methods

Two capitalization methods—direct capitalization and yield capitalization—are described below. These methods make use of different data provided by market participants (investors and brokers), are based on different measures of expected earnings, and include different assumptions concerning the relationship between expected earnings and value.

Direct Capitalization

Direct capitalization is a method used to convert an estimate of a single year's income expectancy into an indication of value in one direct step—either by dividing the income estimate by an appropriate income rate or by multiplying the income estimate by an appropriate income factor. The income expectancy considered is frequently the anticipated income for the following year. The rate or factor calculated represents the relationship between income and value observed in the market and is derived through comparable sales analysis. The income from a property, usually annual net operating income or pre-tax cash flow, is divided by its sale or equity price to obtain the income rate. A factor or multiplier can be derived by dividing the sale price of a property by its annual potential or effective gross income.

Direct capitalization is market-oriented. The appraiser analyzes market evidence and values property by inferring the assumptions of typical investors. Direct capitalization does not explicitly differentiate between the return on and return of capital because investor assumptions are not specified. However, it is implied that the calculated multiplier or rate will satisfy a typical investor and that the prospects for future monetary benefits, over and above the amount originally invested, are sufficiently attractive.

Direct capitalization may be applied to potential gross income, effective gross income, net operating income, or pre-tax cash flow (equity dividend). The income selected for capitalization depends on the purpose of the analysis and the data available.

Yield Capitalization

Yield capitalization is a method used to convert future benefits into present value by discounting each future benefit at an appropriate yield rate or by developing an overall rate that explicitly reflects the investment's income pattern, value change, and yield rate. Like direct capitalization, yield capitalization should reflect market behavior. The method is profit- or yield-oriented, simulating typical investor assumptions with formulas that calculate the present value of expected benefits assuming specified profit or yield requirements. To apply the method, the appraiser must understand market attitudes and expectations, which he or she directly investigates by talking to market participants.

The procedure used to convert periodic income and reversion into present value is called *discounting*; the required yield rate of return is called the *discount rate*. The discounting procedure presumes that the investor will receive a satisfactory return on the investment and complete recovery of the capital invested. The method is referred to as *yield capitalization* because it analyzes whether an investment property will produce the particular level of profit or yield required. Yield capitalization includes both the analysis of *property models* based on different income patterns and *discounted cash flow analysis*, in which a discount rate is used to calculate the present value of anticipated future cash flows.

Appraisers distinguish between contract rent and market rent in analyzing income. Typically, market rent is used to value a fee simple estate which is owner-occupied or vacant and pending lease-up. In the absence of contract rent, market rent serves as the benchmark for property income. If a leased fee estate is being valued, the appraiser considers contract rent for the existing leases and market rent for lease renewals. A property encumbered by a lease should be valued as a leased fee, even when the rent specified in the lease is at market levels. A number of analytical techniques and procedures can be used to value an entire property, specific property benefits, or partial interests in property. Present value can be calculated with or without considering the impact of financing and income taxes as long as the specific rights being appraised are clearly identified. The techniques and procedures selected are determined by the purpose of the analysis, the availability of data, and the market practices.

Direct Capitalization, Yield Capitalization, and Discounting Compared

Direct capitalization makes use of a single year's income and a market-derived factor or overall capitalization rate. Initially, the process appears rather simple. The practitioner need only estimate the income and the factor or overall capitalization rate. In contrast, the application of yield capitalization requires that the practitioner set forth explicit forecasts of income, expenses, and changes in vacancy levels and expenditures over the holding period. The net sale price of the property at the end of the holding period must also be estimated. The concluded yield rate is then applied to convert anticipated economic benefits into net present value.

Practitioners who use direct capitalization must recognize that while an overall capitalization rate is only applied to one characteristic of the property, i.e., to a single year's income, the overall capitalization rate is valid only if it accounts for all other characteristics of the property. For example, assume that annual increases of 3% are forecast in the net rent of a sale property over the holding period and annual increases of 2% are forecast in the net rent for the subject. Applying the sale property's 10% overall capitalization rate to the subject's income would represent a misapplication of the approach and overstate the subject's value.

As another example, consider a sale property which requires a major roof repair within the next three years and has been purchased on the basis of a 15% equity capitalization rate. Applying this rate to the subject property, which has a two-year-old roof that will not necessitate an expenditure from the replacement allowance, would also be a misapplication of the approach and an understatement of the subject's value.

In yield capitalization, the practitioner must draw specific conclusions about changes in net income, cash flow, and property value over the holding period. These conclusions are set forth in forecasts of future income streams and property reversion. The reader of the appraisal report can review the forecasts and examine each component of the future income stream and property value.

To estimate a market-oriented discount rate, market attitudes and expectations must be interpreted. In yield capitalization, specific investment goals for the return on and of invested capital can be considered. The property's projected income stream and reversion are capitalized into a present value by applying the investor's anticipated yield rate in the discounting procedure. Discounting can be performed with formulas and factors that are obtained from financial tables or calculated and applied with hand-held financial calculators or programmable computers. Various software programs for personal computers can also be used to discount cash flows.

In direct capitalization, the appraiser also draws conclusions about each of the income components of the property to estimate a valid overall capitalization rate, but in direct capitalization, the income stream is only for a single year. Thus, while direct capitalization does not require explicit estimates of future income, the capitalization rate must be extracted from comparable sales that reflect similar expectations regarding changes in income and property value. When the rate of change in the subject's value, the yield to the subject, or the factors affecting such rates differ from those of comparable properties, direct capitalization may be too simplistic a method for the valuation of the property.

Both direct capitalization and yield capitalization are market-derived and, when applied correctly, each should result in similar value indications for a subject property. In applying the income capitalization approach, the appraiser need not be limited to a single capitalization method. With adequate information and proper use, direct and yield capitalization methods should produce similar value indications.

Residual Techniques

Residual techniques are employed in the income capitalization approach so that physical value components (land and building), financial value components (mortgage and equity), or legal estates (leased fees and leaseholds) can be considered separately. Residual techniques presume that the value of a component or portion of the property is known or can be estimated. The income attributed to this component is then deducted from total property income to reveal the residual income, which is capitalized to estimate the value of the remaining portion of the property. Residual techniques can be used in both direct and yield capitalization. These techniques incorporate several assumptions; if the assumptions cannot be made, the techniques should not be applied. Limitations on the use of residual techniques are discussed in Chapter 22.

In Chapter 13 (Highest and Best Use Analysis), the land residual technique was introduced as a means to determine which land use maximizes the residual value of the land. In Chapter 22 (Direct Capitalization), the land residual technique will be explored in greater depth.

History of the Approach

To understand the development of the various methods, techniques, and procedures used in the income capitalization approach, it may be helpful to examine its history. The following discussion is divided into two time periods: the early years, when the theoretical bases for direct and yield capitalization were established, and the modern era, when specific techniques and procedures were developed and refined.[8]

Early Writings

The mathematical foundation for discounting can be traced to John Newton, who was among the first to provide a theory of compound interest, and Edmund Halley, the noted astronomer, who published the first present value tables in 1693. John Smart is credited with providing the first comprehensive set of tables and the first partial payment table in 1726. His book, *Tables of Interest and Annuities*, included tables identical to the present value and compound interest tables found in modern appraisal texts.

In 1811 William Inwood published tables that had originally appeared in the works of others, such as John Smart. Of particular significance to appraisers, Inwood used real estate valuation examples to illustrate the use of Smart's tables. Inwood's example postulated that the present value of an annuity was based on a single discount rate. Inwood's book also contained a table for calculating the present value of an income in perpetuity, which seems to mark the first time an author converted an interest rate into a coefficient. Inwood multiplied the coefficient by the investment's annual income, which was assumed to be perpetual, to calculate the current value of the investment. The Inwood premise has been used by real estate appraisers ever since.

In 1890 Alfred Marshall became the first economist to address valuation techniques specifically. He identified the interest rate as the link between income and value and offered the formula

---

8. See James H. Burton, *The Evolution of the Income Approach* (Chicago: American Institute of Real Estate Appraisers, 1982).

$$\text{Value} = \frac{\text{Income}}{\text{Interest rate}}$$

In the early 1900s Irving Fisher contributed to capitalization theory by analyzing the proposition that value is the present worth of future benefits. This concept is fundamental to modern appraisal theory and is recognized directly in discounted cash flow analysis. Thus, by the early 1900s the mathematical and conceptual foundations of direct and yield capitalization were established. In the years that followed, these concepts were applied in a manner consistent with prevailing investor attitudes and behavior.

Modern Era

Pre-1959

In the history of the income capitalization approach, two characteristics distinguish the years before 1959 from the periods that followed. First, prior to 1959 property was usually valued by dividing it into its land and improvement components. During this period the land and building residual techniques dominated appraisal practice. Their use reflected investors' concern with the physical components of property and the need to recapture the cost of depreciating improvements.

Second, before 1959 property value was estimated without considering financing. An all-cash market value transaction was assumed without recognizing that a purchaser might use borrowed funds. Although band-of-investment techniques were available to synthesize an overall capitalization rate from the required returns of debt and equity investors, capitalization was dominated by physical residual techniques.

Real estate investors at this time were concerned with the productive economic life of the improvements, not with investment attributes such as financing. Prices were relatively stable and the effects of physical deterioration were not obscured by inflation. Capital gains were not seen as a significant source of equity return. Loan-to-value ratios and interest rates were relatively low, and creative financing, variable interest rates, and lender participation were not common. Because real estate financing was predictable, its effect on value was of little concern.

1959 to Mid-1970s

The year 1959 is especially significant to the income capitalization approach and serves as a transitional point in appraisal history. With the publication of *The Ellwood Tables*, L. W. Ellwood signaled the shift from reliance on physical residual techniques to techniques based on the debt and equity components of real estate investment.

Ellwood's contribution to the income capitalization approach was monumental because his system allowed for the capitalization of a stream of cash flows and provided a basis for analyzing specific investment assumptions in the valuation process. Ellwood popularized the notion that the total value of a property should reflect both the value of the mortgage and the value of the equity and he included financing in his formula. He recognized that the property appreciation or depreciation reflected in the proceeds of resale or reversion was a potentially important benefit of real property investment. Ellwood's formula explicitly considered reversion and the effects of mortgage amortization. Ellwood also recognized that a finite, relatively short holding period was the proper framework for analysis and valuation. Although the Ellwood formula is essentially a way to solve a discounted cash flow problem, Ellwood simplified the discounting procedure by publishing tables of precalculated rates that could be combined into a representative overall capitalization rate. These tables were particularly useful before electronic calculators and personal computers became available.

In the 1960s many appraisers began to use investment component, or band-of-investment, techniques to synthesize overall capitalization rates. (For further discussion of band-of-investment techniques, see Chapter 22.) Soon many appraisers applied a band-of-investment technique that employed the loan constant and the equity capitalization rate as the appropriate returns to the lender and the equity investor. This technique, which is similar to one introduced by S. Edwin Kazdin in 1944, was especially significant during the 1970s and 1980s.

Ellwood techniques were popular at this time for several reasons. First, stable income streams became less common because inflation and real increases in property values began to overtake the effects of physical depreciation. Thus, capital gains became more significant. Second, investors were becoming increasingly sophisticated. They began to think in terms of leveraging and shorter holding periods, rather than the economic lives of properties, recapture rates, and long-term investments. During this period major appraisal organizations first recognized the effect of financing in their definitions of market value.

Mid-1970s to the Present

Since the mid-1970s, capitalization theory and practice have been influenced by inflation and recurring national recessions. Recent developments in the real estate market include

- The marketing of partial interests such as limited partnerships, joint ventures, and shares of real estate investment trusts (REITs)[9]
- Rapid increases in market rent levels until the mid 1980s, followed by declining rent levels in many metropolitan areas
- Use of complex participation mortgages, creative financing, and seller financing
- Fluctuating mortgage interest rates, which resulted in a preponderance of all-cash transactions in periods of high interest rates
- More foreign investment in U.S. real estate
- Numerous changes in tax laws, which have drastically changed the treatment of real estate relative to other investments
- Cycles of overbuilding, underbuilding, excess demand, and a lack of sufficient demand
- Creative leasing and tenant inducement packages offering free rent, lease buyout options, and substantial tenant improvement allowances

---

9. For a discussion of how the value of REITs is established, see Chapter 28, Securitization of Real Estate Investment Markets.

In recent years appraisers have focused on market participants' reactions to the dynamics of the market and relied on capitalization methods, techniques, and procedures to simulate investor decision making.

The methods that are most useful today include direct capitalization and yield capitalization employing DCF analysis. In many circumstances these methods best reflect the behavior of market participants. The availability of computers has also had a major effect on investment analysis and valuation. Computers process data quickly and can be used for statistical analysis, DCF analysis, and business accounting, as well as the storage of comparable sales data.

Appraisers do not always agree on which income valuation techniques are appropriate. There is ongoing debate on the relevance of traditional capitalization techniques and the validity of DCF analysis. However, market participants use both traditional techniques and DCF analysis, so both are valid and relevant tools for real property appraisers.

Key Concepts

- In the income capitalization approach, an appraiser analyzes a property's capacity to generate future benefits and capitalizes the income stream into an indication of present value. The principle of anticipation is fundamental to the approach. Techniques and procedures from this approach are used to analyze comparable sales data and to measure obsolescence in the cost approach.

- The three main components of property rights are ownership entities (individual, partnership, or corporation), financial interest (equity and debt), and legal estate (fee simple, leased fee, leasehold, sandwich, or subleasehold).

- A market value appraisal of income-producing property most often involves 100% ownership of equity interests (debt-free or subject to specific financing) in a leased fee estate. Appraisers also value minority shareholder or partnership interests, participation mortgages, equity positions subject to layers of debt, and various leasehold positions.

- Defined values other than market value may also have to be estimated, e.g., business value, going-concern value, investment value.

- An income capitalization analysis considers the following components of future property benefits: potential gross income (PGI), effective gross income (EGI), net operating income (NOI), pre-tax cash flow, after-tax cash flow, and the resale value or reversion.

- An investor's total expected return includes the return of capital (recapture of capital) and a return on capital (compensation for use of capital until recapture). Rates of return may be income rates (ratios of annual income to value that are used to convert income into value) or yield rates (rates of return on capital).

- Income rates include overall capitalization rates (R_O) and equity capitalization rates (R_E). Yield rates include interest rates, discount rates, internal rates of return (IRR), overall yield rates (Y_O) and equity yield rates (Y_E).

- The two methods of income capitalization are direct capitalization, in which a single year's income is divided by an income rate or multiplied by an income factor to reach an indication of value and yield capitalization, in which future benefits are converted into a value indication by discounting them at an appropriate yield rate (DCF analysis) or applying an overall rate that reflects the income pattern, value change, and yield rate.

- In direct capitalization, the overall capitalization rate applied to property income reflects both the return of and return on investment. In yield capitalization, the distinction between return on and return of capital is explicit.

- The rate of return on investment combines a safe rate with a premium to compensate the investor for risk, the burden of management, and the illiquidity of invested capital. The rate of return on capital may incorporate inflationary expectations and should reflect the competition for capital among alternative investments of comparable risk.

Terms

after-tax cash flow	interest rate
annuity	internal rate of return (IRR)
appreciation	investment value
built-up method	leverage
bundle of rights	market rent
business enterprise value	market value
capital recapture	net operating income (NOI)
capitalization rate	non-realty interests
cash flow rate	overall capitalization rate (R_O)
cash on cash rate	overall yield rate (Y_O)
contract rent	partial interest
cost-push inflation	potential gross income (PGI)
deflation	pre-tax cash flow
demand-pull inflation	real estate
direct capitalization	real estate investment trust (REIT)
discount rate	real property
discounted cash flow (DCF)	recapture rate
analysis	residual techniques
discounting	return of capital
effective gross income (EGI)	return on capital
equity capitalization rate (R_E)	reversion
equity yield rate (Y_E)	risk rating
future benefits	safe rate
going-concern value	securitization
income capitalization rate	time value of money
income rate	yield capitalization
inflation	yield rate (Y)

CHAPTER TWENTY-ONE

Income and Expense Estimates

To apply any capitalization procedure, a reliable estimate of income expectancy must be developed. Although some capitalization procedures are based on the actual level of income at the time of the appraisal rather than a projection of future income, an appraiser must still consider the future outlook. Failure to consider future income would contradict the principle of anticipation, which holds that value is the present worth of future benefits. Historical income and current income are significant, but the ultimate concern is the future. The earning history of a property is important only insofar as it is accepted by buyers as an indication of the future. Current income is a good starting point, but the direction and expected rate of income change are critical to the capitalization process.

Four types of income can be converted into value in the income capitalization approach: potential gross income (*PGI*), effective gross income (*EGI*), net operating income (*NOI*), and pre-tax cash flow (*PTCF*). Reliable projections of income are important because significant value differences can result when the same rate or factor is used to convert different income estimates into value. If, for example, a potential gross income multiplier of 6.0 is applied to potential gross income estimates of $50,000 and $55,000, values of $300,000 and $330,000 result. A $5,000 difference in potential gross income produces a $30,000 difference in value. Similarly, when an overall capitalization rate of 10.0% is applied to net operating income estimates of $35,000 and $40,000, values of $350,000 and $400,000 result. In this example a $5,000 difference in net operating income results in a $50,000 value difference. Thus, income forecasting is a sensitive and crucial part of income capitalization.

An appraiser may estimate income for a single year or series of years depending on the data available and the capitalization method employed. The analysis can be based on the actual level of income at the time of the appraisal, a forecast of income for the first year of the investment, a forecast of income over a specified holding period, or a stabilized, average annual income over a specific holding period. If a market value estimate is sought, the income forecast should reflect the expectations of market participants. In an assignment to estimate investment value, the appraiser may base the income forecasts on the specific ownership or management requirements of the investor.

If an investment in a partial interest—e.g., an equity interest in a fee simple or leased fee estate—is being valued, pre-tax cash flow is usually capitalized. The appraiser must deduct mortgage debt service from net operating income to calculate pre-tax cash flow. Sometimes debt service is based on an existing mortgage and the amount is specified; in other cases, debt service must be estimated based on the typical mortgage terms indicated by current market activity.

Lease Analysis

The income to various lease interests is generally derived through the conveyance and operation of leases. *A lease is a written document in which the rights to use and occupy land or structures are transferred by the owner to another for a specified period of time in return for a specified rent.* An appraiser begins to develop an income and expense forecast for investment real estate by studying all existing and proposed leases that apply to the subject property. These leases provide information on rent and other income and on the division of expenses between the landlord and the tenant.

If leases exist and the income estimate is based on the continuation of lease income, the appraiser examines lease provisions that could affect the quantity, quality, and durability of property income. The appraiser may either read the leases or rely on the client or another authorized party to disclose all pertinent lease provisions. The appraiser also analyzes the leases of competitive properties to estimate market rent and other forms of income. Because lease analysis is important, the characteristics of leases must be fully understood.

Lease Types

Although a lease can be drawn to fit any situation, most leases fall into one of several broad classifications: flat rental, graduated rental, revaluation, index, and percentage.[1] Leases may be applied on a *gross rental basis*, with the lessor paying all the operating expenses of the real estate, or on a *net rental basis*, with the tenant paying all expenses. Lease terms frequently fall between these extremes and specify the division of expenses between the lessor and the lessee. Leases can also be categorized by their terms of occupancy—e.g., month-to-month, short-term (of five years or less), or long-term (of more than five years).

Flat Rental Lease

A flat rental lease specifies a level of rent that continues throughout the duration of the lease. In a stable economy, this type of lease is typical and acceptable. In a changing economy, however, leases that are more responsive to fluctuating market conditions are preferred. When flat rental leases are used in inflationary periods, they tend to be short-term. Some assignments for the federal government require the appraiser to express the estimate of market rent on a "leveled" basis.

Graduated Rental Lease

Graduated rental leases provide for specified changes in the amount of rent at one or more points during the lease term. A step-up lease, which allows for smaller rent payments in the early years, can be advantageous to a tenant establishing a business in a new location. This type of lease can also be used to recognize tenant expenditures on a property that are effectively amortized during the early years of the lease. Long-term ground leases may include provisions for increasing the rent to reflect the expectation of future increases in property value and protect the purchasing power of the landlord's

---

1. Other lease types are defined in accounting practice, e.g., capital or financing leases and operating or service leases. These leases often involve equipment.

investment. Because property value is usually expected to increase, tenants are expected to pay commensurately higher rents.

Step-down leases are less common than step-up leases. They are generally used to reflect unusual circumstances associated with a particular property such as the likelihood of reduced tenant appeal in the future or capital recapture of interior improvements during the early years of a long-term lease.

Revaluation Lease

Revaluation leases provide for periodic rent adjustments based on revaluation of the real estate under prevailing market conditions. Although revaluation leases tend to be long-term, some are short-term with renewal option rents based on revaluation of the real estate when the option is exercised. When the parties to a lease cannot agree on the amount of the revaluation, revaluation through appraisal or arbitration may be stipulated in the lease.

Index Lease

Index leases are generally long-term leases that provide for periodic rent adjustment based on the change in a specific index such as a nationally published, cost-of-living index. The Consumer Price Index (CPI) is frequently the index selected.

Percentage Lease

In percentage leases some or all of the rent charged is based on a specified percentage of the volume of business, productivity, or use achieved by the tenant. Percentage leases may be short- or long-term and are most frequently used for retail properties. A straight percentage lease may have no minimum rent, but most specify a guaranteed *minimum rent* and an *overage rent*, which is a percentage, or graduated percentage, to be paid on sales that exceed a specified level, known as the *breakpoint*.

Lease Data

The data contained in a typical lease include

- Date of the lease
- Reference information, if the lease is recorded
- Legal description or other identification of the leased premises
- Name of lessor—i.e., owner or landlord
- Name of lessee—i.e., tenant
- Lease term
- Occupancy date
- Commencement date for rent payment
- Rent amount, including any percentage clause, graduation, escalation provisions, and payment terms
- Rent concessions, including any discounts or benefits
- Landlord's covenants—i.e., items such as taxes, insurance, and maintenance for which the owner or landlord is responsible

- Tenant's covenants—i.e., items such as taxes, insurance, maintenance, utilities, and cleaning expenses for which the tenant is responsible
- Right of assignment or right to sublet—i.e., whether the leasehold, or tenant's interest, may be assigned or sublet, under what conditions, and whether assignment relieves the initial tenant of future liability
- Option to renew, including the date of required notice, term of renewal, rent, and other renewal provisions
- Expense caps and expense stops, escalation rent, and expense recoveries
- Options to purchase
- Escape clauses, cancellation clauses, and kick-out clauses
- Continued occupancy contingency
- Security deposits, including advance rent, bond, or expenditures by the tenant for items such as leasehold improvements
- Casualty loss—i.e., whether the lease continues after a fire or other disaster and on what basis
- Lessee's improvements, including whether they can be removed when the lease expires and to whom they belong
- Noncompete and exclusive use clauses
- Condemnation, including the respective rights of the lessor and the lessee if all or any part of the property is appropriated by a public agency
- Revaluation clauses
- Special provisions

A sample form for analyzing a typical office lease is shown in Figure 21.1. Special attention should be paid to lease data on rent, rent concessions, the division of expenses, renewal options, escalation clauses, purchase options, escape clauses, and tenant improvements.

Rent

The amount of rent to be paid by the tenant is basic lease data. An appraiser considers rent from all sources, which may include base, or minimum, rent, contract rent, percentage rent, and escalation rent. The sources of rental income should be clearly identified.

Rent Concessions

When real estate markets are oversupplied, landlords may give tenants concessions such as free rent for a specified period of time or extra tenant improvements. In shopping center leases, retail store tenants are sometimes given rent credit for interior store improvements. All rent concessions result from market conditions and the relative negotiating strengths of the landlord and the tenant.

| Figure 21.1 | **Office Space Rental Worksheet** |

Building: _____

Lessor: _____

Lessee: _____

Premises: Floor _____ Rentable area _____ Usable area _____ Loss factor _____

Term: Commencement _____ Expiration _____

Base rent: _____ CPI _____

Graduations: _____

Escalations:

Real estate taxes _____

Operating expenses _____

Energy _____

Work letter (costs): _____

Special provisions (e.g., repainting, etc.): _____

Who pays:	Lessor	Lessee	Stop	Stop Amount per Sq. Ft.	Cap	Cap Amount per Sq. Ft.
Fixed expenses						
Real estate taxes	( )	( )	( )	( )	( )	( )
Property insurance	( )	( )	( )	( )	( )	( )
(Fire, storm, vandalism)						
Variable expenses						
Tenant electric	( )	( )	( )	( )	( )	( )
Building electric	( )	( )	( )	( )	( )	( )
Tenant HVAC	( )	( )	( )	( )	( )	( )
Building HVAC	( )	( )	( )	( )	( )	( )
Tenant space cleaning	( )	( )	( )	( )	( )	( )
(Janitorial service)						
Public space cleaning	( )	( )	( )	( )	( )	( )
(Janitorial service)						
Fuel	( )	( )	( )	( )	( )	( )
Repairs and maintenance						
Exterior	( )	( )	( )	( )	( )	( )
Interior	( )	( )	( )	( )	( )	( )
Management	( )	( )	( )	( )	( )	( )

Renewal options:

How many: _____ Years each _____

New rent: _____

New escalation (and base year): _____

New rentable area or loss factor: _____

New work letter: _____

Occupancy (or status) of building when lease was originally signed: _____

Comments: _____

Lessor/Lessee Division of Expenses

Most leases outline the obligations of the lessor and the lessee to pay for taxes, utilities, heat, repairs, and other expenses required to maintain and operate the leased property. The appraiser should identify the division of expenses in each lease analyzed and compare the rents and estimated rental value of the subject space to those of comparable space.

Renewal Options

Renewal options that allow a tenant to extend the lease term for one or more prescribed periods of time are frequently included in short- and long-term leases. A typical renewal option requires that the tenant provide advance notice of the intention to exercise the option and identifies the length of the renewal period or periods as well as the rent or method of determining the rent to be paid. The option rent may be set at the original rent or at a level determined when the lease was negotiated, or it may be calculated with an established procedure or formula when the option is exercised. Renewal options are binding on the lessor, but they allow the tenant to reach a decision in light of the circumstances prevailing at the time of renewal. Thus, they are generally considered favorable to the tenant, not the lessor.

Expense Cap and Expense Stop Clauses

Leases often include clauses setting an upper limit on the expenses that either the landlord or the tenant will pay. With an *expense cap*, operating expenses are borne by the tenant to a specified level above which the landlord picks up additional expenses. With an *expense stop*, the landlord meets operating expenses to a specified level above which increases in the operating expenses become the obligations of the tenant or lessee. Usually, the level of expenses incurred during the first year of the lease is specified as the level of the stop.

An expense cap limits the tenant's exposure to the risk of increasing expenses. One example of an expense cap is a landlord burden clause, which caps an anchor tenant's share of common area maintenance (CAM) expenses. The burden of the remaining expense is generally shifted to other mall tenants or sometimes to the owner.

An expense stop protects the landlord against unforeseen increases in expenses resulting from inflation or other factors. Expense stop clauses are often added to traditional gross or flat rental leases. In multitenanted retail or office buildings, increased expenses are usually prorated among the tenants in proportion to the area they occupy or on some other equitable basis. The prorated shares are then added to the tenants' rents; the expenses allocated to vacant space are normally paid by the owner.

Sometimes a single stop provision is used to cover all the expenses to be passed through to the tenants. Alternatively, an expense stop might be specified for individual expense items. For example, tax stop clauses provide that any increases in taxes over a specified level be passed on to the tenant.

Escalation Clauses

Escalation payments are frequently based on changes in a local wage rate or index such as the Consumer Price Index (CPI). In New York City, for example, the porter wage escalation formula is frequently used. Each one cent increase in the porter wage rate (i.e., the hourly wage paid to office workers who are members of the porters' union) produces a one to one and one-half cent increase in expense charges per square foot of space. An escalation clause helps the landlord offset increases in operating expenses, which are passed on to tenants on a pro rata basis. Some escalation clauses are drawn so broadly that the lease is almost applied on a net rental basis.

Expense Recovery Clauses

An expense recovery clause stipulates that all operating expenses paid by the landlord are recoverable from the tenant. In different parts of the country, expense recoveries are known as *reimburseables*, *billables*, or *pass-throughs*. Some of these items, e.g., common area maintenance (CAM) charges, may normally be considered under operating expenses, while others may be considered under replacement allowance. Recoverable expenses are deducted as expenses (or were already included as deductions in previous years), and recoveries are treated as separate revenue items in income and expense statements.

Expense recovery clauses are written into net rental leases. Double net leases contain expense recovery clauses for property taxes and insurance; triple net leases contain expense recovery clauses for property taxes, insurance and maintenance.[2] (Because the meaning of terms such as *net*, *double net*, and *triple net* varies in different parts of the country, appraisers should be aware of the terms used in the specific market.)

Purchase Options

Certain leases include a clause granting the lessee an option to purchase the leased property. In some cases this option must be exercised on the lease termination date or at some point or points during the lease term; in other cases this option may be available at any time. The option price may be fixed or it may change periodically based on an empirical formula or a depreciated book value. In build-to-suit situations, the option price may be the cost to construct plus the interest through the option period. A purchase option may only give the lessee the right to purchase the property or make an offer if an offer to purchase is made by a third party. This provision is referred to as a *right of first refusal*. A purchase option restricts marketability and, unless the property is being appraised in fee simple, the option price, if stated, may represent a limit on the market value of the leased fee estate.

Escape Clauses, Lease Cancellation Clauses, and Kick-Out Clauses

An escape clause permits a tenant to cancel a lease under circumstances that would not ordinarily be considered justification for lease cancellation. For example, a condemnation or casualty clause might allow the tenant to cancel the lease if the condemnation or casualty loss creates a serious obstacle to continued operations. A casualty clause may stipulate that the lessor be allowed a reasonable amount of time to make necessary repairs and provide for appropriate abatement of rent in the interim. A landlord might

---

2. James D. Vernor and Joseph Rabianski, *Shopping Center: Appraisal and Analysis* (Chicago: Appraisal Institute, 1993), 189 and 203-206 and Roland D. Nelson, "Expenses on a Triple-Net Lease," *The Appraisal Journal* (October 1991), 551-553.

include a demolition clause in a lease to preserve the prospects for sale or redevelopment of the site. This type of escape clause can affect rent levels and market value.

A kick-out clause written into a shopping center lease allows a lessee to cancel a long-term lease (five to ten years) if sales have not achieved a specified level after the first, second, or third year. Another type of kick-out clause allows the tenant to cancel the lease if the landlord fails to replace a departing anchor within a specified period of time. Kick-out clauses may create risk and warrant discount rate adjustments.

Continued Occupancy Clauses

Multitenanted properties may be subject to leases that condition the continued occupancy of one tenant on the occupancy of another tenant. An anchor tenant's decision to vacate during the lease term can precipitate the departure of other tenants as well. In appraising shopping centers, the probability of an anchor tenant leaving at or before expiration of the current lease must be carefully analyzed. This is true whether or not the satellite stores have leases conditioning their occupancy on the continued occupancy of the anchor tenant. Small stores are often unable to continue operation if the anchor leaves the center.

Tenant Improvements

Extensive tenant improvements can influence lease rent. When capital expenditures are made by the lessor, reimbursement may be accomplished through rent increases that amortize the lessor's expenditures over all or part of the lease period. If capital expenditures are made by the tenant, the lessor may lower the tenant's rent below market levels for all or part of the lease term.

Noncompete and Exclusive Use Clauses

Leases may contain a provision that prohibits both parties from operating a nearby business that competes with either party. For example, a tenant who sells sporting goods may agree not to open another, competing sporting goods facility near the shopping center. The value of the additional income resulting from a noncompete clause may be estimated and discounted for the term of the lease.

An exclusive use clause may be written into a lease by the landlord who wishes to control the retail mix of the shopping center. Such a clause may be also sought by the tenant who wants to achieve some degree of monopoly status.

Rent

The income to investment properties consists primarily of rent. Different types of rent affect the quality of property income, which is studied in the income capitalization approach to value. Several categories are used by appraisers to analyze rental income.

Contract rent is the actual rental income specified in a lease. It is the rent agreed on by the landlord and the tenant and may be higher, lower, or the same as market rent. Contract rent may be distinguished from *scheduled rent*, the contract rent due under existing leases.

Market rent is the rental income that a property would most probably com-

mand in the open market; it is indicated by the current rents paid and asked for comparable space as of the date of the appraisal. Market rent is sometimes referred to as *economic rent*.

In markets where concessions take the form of free rent, above-market tenant improvements, or atypical allowances, the true effective rent must be quantified. *Scheduled rent is the rental income specified in existing leases, adjusted for rental concessions, if appropriate; scheduled rent does not include percentage rent.* Effective rent is an analytical tool used as a common denominator to compare leases with different provisions and develop an estimate of market rent. One definition of effective rent follows: *Effective rent is the total of base rent, or minimum rent stipulated in a lease, over the specified lease term less rental concessions such as free rent, above-standard tenant improvements, moving allowances, lease buyouts, cash allowances, and other leasing incentives.* Effective rent may be estimated on the basis of rental income from existing leases at contract rates (gross leases in particular) or rental income from leases at market rates; it may be calculated either on a discounted basis, reflecting the time value of money, or on a simple, straight-line basis. (The two ways of estimating *effective rent* are discussed later in this chapter.)

Excess rent is the amount by which contract rent exceeds market rent at the time of the appraisal. Excess rent is created by a lease that is favorable to the lessor and may reflect unusual management or a lease that was negotiated in a stronger rental market. Excess rent can be expected to continue for the remainder of the lease but, due to the higher risk associated with the receipt of excess rent, it is often calculated separately and capitalized at a higher rate. Because excess rent is a result of the lease contract rather than the income potential of the underlying real property, the incremental value created by a lease premium is sometimes considered a non-realty, or business value, component of value.

Deficit rent is the amount by which market rent exceeds contract rent at the time of the appraisal. Deficit rent is created by a lease favorable to the tenant and may reflect uninformed parties, unusual management, or a lease executed in a weaker rental market.

Percentage rent is rental income received in accordance with the terms of a percentage clause in a lease. Percentage rent is typically derived from retail store tenants and based on a certain percentage of their retail sales. It is usually paid at the end of each year. The emergence of new competition in the area or the departure of an anchor tenant from a shopping center may reduce or eliminate anticipated percentage rent.

Overage rent is percentage rent paid over and above the guaranteed minimum rent or base rent. As mentioned previously, the specified level of sales at which a percentage clause is activated is called the *breakpoint*. This type of rent should not be confused with excess rent. Overage rent is a contract rent; it may be market rent, part market and part excess rent, or excess rent only.

To a certain extent, the interest being appraised determines how rents are analyzed and estimated. The valuation of fee simple interests in income-producing real estate is based on the market rent the property is capable of generating. To value proposed projects without actual leases, properties leased at market rent, and owner-occupied properties, only market rent estimates are used in the income capitalization approach.

To value a lessor's marketable interest in real estate, the leased fee, the appraiser generally must consider existing contract rent for leased space, which may or may not be at market levels, and market rent for vacant and owner-occupied space. When discounted cash flow analysis is used, future market rent estimates are also required to estimate income after existing leases expire. It should be emphasized that the discounting of contract rents does *not* necessarily result in a market value estimate of the fee simple interest.

To appraise the leased fee value of recently completed, income-producing properties that have not achieved stabilized occupancy, an appropriate vacancy and collection loss must be forecast. In appraising the fee simple value of a newly completed, 100% owner-occupied property, it may be appropriate to make a deduction in the forecast period for the owner-occupant to achieve 100% use and occupancy of the building (on analogy with the deduction for lease-up to stabilized occupancy in tenanted properties).

Appraisers usually estimate the market value of income-producing property in one of two ways. An appraiser can value a fee simple interest in property at the market rent the property is capable of generating and deduct the present value of the rent loss, calculated as market rent less contract rent. To use this technique the appraiser may extract capitalization rates or factors from comparable sales of fee simple real property interests, but such sales of multitenant buildings are rare. Therefore, the appraiser may need to analyze a number of property sales subject to leases to find properties that were sold with market rents or with rent structures that can be easily adjusted for market rent equivalency.

To apply the second technique, an appraiser values a leased fee property by estimating the existing contract rent for leased space and market rent for vacant and owner-occupied space. Because most real estate transactions reflect similar income characteristics, market-derived capitalization rates and factors may adequately reflect the estimated value of lessors' marketable interests. If adequate comparable data exist, rent loss analysis is unnecessary.

Rent analysis begins with study of the subject property's present rent schedule. By examining audits and leases and interviewing selected tenants during property inspection, an appraiser can verify the rent schedule. Further verification may be necessary if the owner's or manager's representation of the schedule is in doubt.

The sum of *scheduled*, current rents may be compared with previous totals using operating statements for the past several years. Statements of rents, including the rent paid under percentage leases or escalation clauses, should be examined for all building tenants. After analyzing the existing rent schedule for the subject property, the appraiser reduces all rents to a unit basis for comparison. All differences in rents within the property are described and explained. Then rental data for comparable space in the market are assembled so that market rents can be adjusted to an equivalent rent basis, if necessary, and reduced to a unit of comparison.

When a market rent estimate for the subject property is required, the appraiser gathers, compares, and adjusts comparable market data. The parties to each lease should be identified to ensure that the party held responsible for rent payments is actually a party to the lease or, by endorsement, the guarantor. It is also important to ascertain that the lease represents a freely negotiated, arm's-length transaction. A lease that does not meet these criteria, such as a lease to an owner-tenant, does not provide a reliable indication of the rental terms typical in the market.

The rents of comparable properties can provide a basis for estimating market rent for a subject property once they have been reduced to the same unit basis applied to the subject property. Comparable rents may be adjusted just as the transaction prices of comparable properties are adjusted in the sales comparison approach. Recent leases at the subject property may be a good indication of market rent, but lease renewals or extensions negotiated with existing tenants should be used with caution. Existing tenants may be willing to pay above-market rents to avoid relocating. Alternatively, a landlord may offer existing tenants lower rent to avoid vacancies and the expense of obtaining new tenants.

The elements of comparison considered in rental analysis are the real property rights being appraised, conditions of rental (i.e., arm's-length lease terms), market conditions, location, physical characteristics, economic characteristics stipulated in the lease, use of the property, and non-realty components. Rents for comparable properties are analyzed and adjusted for differences in these elements of comparison to develop a market rent estimate for the subject property.

The amount of data needed to support a market rent estimate for a subject property depends on the complexity of the appraisal problem, the availability of comparable rentals, and the extent to which the pattern of adjusted rent indications derived from the comparables differs from the income pattern of the subject property.

When sufficient, closely comparable rental data are not available, the appraiser should include data that require adjustment. First, the real property rights and conditions that affect the rent paid must be analyzed and adjustments must be made. Rentals that do not reflect arm's-length negotiations might have to be eliminated as comparables. Each rental is then analyzed to determine possible adjustment for market conditions. Economic conditions change and leases negotiated in the past may not reflect prevailing rents.

The stability of the location or changes in the market's attitude toward the property location might also affect income potential and therefore require adjustment. Physical differences such as the functionality of the building are then analyzed and adjustments are made for these differences. Next the appraiser examines the economic (i.e., income-producing) characteristics of the lease to determine who pays operating expenses and to make adjustments for any differences. Market rents might also have to be adjusted for the intended use of the subject property when it differs from that of the comparable. Finally, adjustments may be needed to account for differences in non-realty components, which can result in differences in the income of the properties. For example, the income of a hotel that is part of a national chain may be higher than that of a hotel that is not in a chain because of the franchise value associated with the name of the hotel rather than any difference in the income potential of the real property. If an appraiser uses proper judgment in making adjustments, a reasonably clear pattern of market rents should emerge.

Developing Income Estimates

To assess the earning power of a property, an appraiser must first analyze its net operating income expectancy. The appraiser estimates income and expenses after researching and analyzing 1) the income and expense history of the subject property; 2) income and expense histories of competitive properties; 3) recently signed leases, proposed leases, and asking rents for the subject and competitive properties; 4) actual vacancy levels for the subject and competitive properties; 5) management expenses for the subject and competitive properties; 6) published operating data; and 7) tax assessment policies and projected changes in utility and taxation rates.

Appraisers often present this information in tabular form to assist the reader of the report. Income and expenses are generally reported in annual or monthly dollar amounts and analyzed in terms of total dollar amounts, dollars and cents per unit of rentable area, or dollars and cents based on another unit of comparison. Table 21.1 summarizes a subject property's operating expense history, Table 21.2 presents comparable rental data, and Table 21.3 analyzes the operating expenses of comparable properties.

After thoroughly analyzing property and lease data for the subject and comparable properties, the appraiser develops a net operating income estimate for the subject property. If the appraiser is focusing on the benefits accruing to the investment before taxes, he or she also estimates the pre-tax cash flow. A sample outline for estimating net operating income is presented in Table 21.4. This estimate is developed from the gross income estimate. The specific items involved in the generation of income and the allocation of expenses may vary for different property types. Table 21.5 lists the key elements to investigate in developing income and expense estimates for various property types.

Potential Gross Income

Potential gross income is the total income attributable to a real property at 100% occupancy before operating expenses are deducted. Appraisers usually analyze potential gross income on an annual basis. Potential gross income comprises rent for all space in the property, rent from escalation clauses, and all other income to the real estate.

Scheduled Rent

Scheduled rent is the portion of potential gross income derived from the rent stipulated in the leases in effect on the date of the appraisal. Some appraisers refer to this income as *existing lease* or *contract income* or *rent*. Scheduled rent may or may not coincide with the rent that could currently be obtained in the local market if the space were vacant and available for leasing.

In calculating scheduled rent, an appraiser must adjust for rent concessions, discounts, or other benefits that may induce a prospective tenant to enter into a lease. These concessions, or offsets, usually take the form of rent-free months at the beginning of the lease term, but they may also be reflected in extra services or tenant benefits. Such benefits might include higher tenant improvement allowances, reduced expense or

Table 21.1 Subject Property Operating Expense History (Based on 435,146 rentable square feet)

	Year 1 Actual		Year 2 Actual		Year 3 Actual		Year 4 Budget	
	Dollars	Per Square Foot	Dollars	Per Square Foot	Dollars	Per Square Foot	Dollars	Per Square Foot
Fixed expenses								
Real estate taxes	$1,689,600	$3.88	$1,973,722	$4.54	$2,279,860	$5.24	$2,347,500	$5.39
Insurance	18,948	0.04	17,956	0.04	46,861	0.11	50,000	0.11
Variable expenses								
Electricity	$1,453,482	$3.34	$1,569,948	$3.61	$1,534,296	$3.53	$1,800,000	$4.14
Steam heat	575,599	1.32	519,203	1.19	525,646	1.21	619,190	1.42
Cleaning	848,260	1.95	797,455	1.83	935,544	2.15	990,000	2.28
Payroll	62,441	0.14	73,553	0.17	82,350	0.19	90,000	0.21
Repairs and maintenance	125,417	0.29	222,074	0.51	283,215	0.65	381,996	0.88
Water and sewer	19,638	0.05	23,444	0.05	16,958	0.04	33,600	0.08
Administrative, legal, and accounting	8,603	0.02	13,712	0.03	77,397	0.18	77,400	0.18
Management fees	33,240	0.08	36,105	0.08	36,643	0.08	38,400	0.09
Miscellaneous	22,492	0.05	511	0.001	3,862	0.01	3,600	0.01
Total operating expenses	$4,857,720	$11.16	$5,247,683	$12.05	$5,822,632	$13.39	$6,431,686	$14.79

Note. Figures have been rounded.

Table 21.2 | Actual Rentals of Competitive Office Buildings in Downtown CBD of Major U.S. City

I.D. Number	Location	Tenant	Commencement Date	Rentable Area in Square Feet	Term (in Years)	Rent per Square Foot	Leases Are Net Subject to Escalation	Work Letter/ Miscellaneous
1	180 Main Street	Law firm	7/1/97	11,600	15	$22.00*	Pro rata share of operating expenses and real estate taxes in excess of base year	$20.00 work letter 4 months free rent; one 5-year renewal option at $5.00 below market rent
		Oil company	8/15/97	15,600	10	23.00 (5 years) 26.50 (5 years)	Pro rata share of operating expenses and real estate taxes in excess of base year	Building standard; 6 months free rent; one, 5-year renewal option
		Stock brokerage company	9/1/98	15,600	10	29.00 (5 years) 41.50 (5 years)	Pro rata share of operating expenses and real estate taxes in excess of base year	Building standard; three, 5-year renewal options
		Accounting firm	7/1/98	31,200	10	28.00	Pro rata share of operating expenses and real estate taxes in excess of base year	Not available
2	33 Broad Street	Bank	7/1/97	25,000	10	8.00† 35.00‡ 22.00§	Pro rata share of operating expenses and real estate tax increases in excess of a $4.00 base for each	Building standard; 3 months free rent
		Computer services firm	7/1/98	10,000	10	25.00‖	Pro rata share of operating expenses and real estate tax increases in excess of a $5.00 base for each	$20.00 work letter
		Stock brokerage firm	7/1/97	10,200	10	26.50	Pro rata share of operating expenses and real estate tax increases in excess of a $4.00 base for each	$22.00 work letter plus $6.00 work letter for computer room; 3 months free rent; one, 5-year renewal option

Table 21.2 continued

I.D. Number	Location	Tenant	Commence-ment Date	Rentable Area in Square Feet	Term (in Years)	Rent per Square Foot	Leases Are Net Subject to Escalation	Work Letter/ Miscellaneous
3	One Exchange Place	Law firm	7/1/98	15,000	10	26.00	Pro rata share of operating expenses and real estate tax increases in excess of a $4.00 base for each	$22.00 work letter
4	101 Front Street	Accounting firm	1/1/98	25,000	3	22.00	Pro rata share of real estate taxes in excess of first full assessment; $.01 per square foot for each $.01 increase in the porter wage	Building standard
5	One Commercial Plaza	Bank	7/1/98	88,823#	20	27.10 (5 years) 30.81 (5 years) 35.65 (5 years) 40.93 (5 years)	25.0% of real estate taxes in excess of $2.85 per square foot**; 25.0% of operating expenses in excess of $3.42 per square foot	$25.00 work letter

* For 10 years, then $2.00 below market rent for 5 years; minimum rent set at $29.00

† Basement

‡ Ground floor

§ Floors 2 through 4

‖ For 7 years, then market rent for 3 years

Includes 4,600 square feet of retail space

** Tenant's contribution to real estate escalations is reduced 50% in Year 1, 40% in Year 2, 30% in Year 3, 20% in Year 4, and 10% in Year 5

Note. Base year is year of lease commencement.

Table 21.3 Analysis of Operating Expense Comparables (Per Square Foot)

Property I.D.	Subject Property Pro Forma	Comparable A 130 Main Street	Comparable B 110 Second Avenue	Comparable C 717 Fourth Avenue	Comparable D 133 Third Avenue	Comparable E One Commerce Plaza
Operating year	1999	1998	1998	1998	1998	1998
Year built	1992	1992	1981	1974	1977	1991
Rentable area in square feet	60,000	75,000	49,411	56,411	52,000	66,000
Operating Expenses						
Fixed expenses						
Real estate taxes	$ 3.50	$ 3.51	$ 3.48	$ 3.01	$ 3.47	$3.35
Insurance	0.11	0.06	0.09	0.10	0.17	0.09
Variable expenses						
Cleaning	$ 1.40	$ 1.61	$ 1.38	$ 1.27	$ 1.28	$1.30
Payroll, payroll taxes, and benefits	0.60	0.45	0.52	0.98	0.93	0.41
Electricity	2.50	3.03	2.47	2.31	2.25	2.45
HVAC	1.50	1.25	1.60	1.35	1.75	1.55
Repairs and maintenance	0.25	0.25	0.43	0.78	0.79	0.18
Water and sewer	0.04	0.02	0.02	0.02	0.03	0.04
Administrative and general	0.27	0.19	0.19	0.26	0.08	0.11
Management	0.30	0.25	0.20	0.40	0.35	0.30
Total operating expenses	$10.47	$10.62	$10.38	$10.48	$11.10	$9.78

Table 21.4	**Income and Expense Estimate**	
Potential gross income		
Scheduled rent*	$XXXX	
Escalation income	XXXX	
Percentage rent	XXXX	
Overage rent	XXXX	
Market rent†	XXXX	
Other income‡	<u>XXXX</u>	
Total potential gross income		$XXXX
Vacancy and collection loss		<u>-XXXX</u>
Effective gross income		$XXXX
Operating expenses		
Fixed	$XXXX	
Variable	XXXX	
Replacement allowance	<u>XXXX</u>	
Total operating expenses		<u>- XXXX</u>
Net operating income		$XXXX

* Contract rent from existing leases adjusted for rental concessions, if appropriate, results in an estimate of effective rent.

† Rent attributed to vacant space, lease renewals, and owner-occupied space;in fee simple valuation, rent attributable to the whole property; market rent, considering adjustment for rental concessions

‡ May include expense recoveries.

base rent escalations, below-market renewal options, tenant cancellation clauses, or building naming rights.[3]

Effective Rent

Effective rent may be defined as the total of base rent, or minimum rent stipulated in a lease, over the specified lease term less rental concessions (e.g., free rent, excessive tenant improvements, moving allowances, lease buyouts, cash allowances, and other leasing incentives). There are two conventional ways to calculate effective rent: as the average, annual rent net of rental concessions and as an annual rent that produces the same present value as the actual, annual rents net of rental concessions. While these two methods are considered interchangeable, they do not produce the same results.[4] There are additional options for the treatment of tenant improvement costs. Some practitioners

3. Kenneth Barnes, "Rental Concessions and Value," *The Appraisal Journal* (April 1986).

4. Because of the great diversity in lease provisions, a common denominator is needed to measure real rent. Effective rent can meet this need. Peter F. Korpacz and Mark I. Roth have demonstrated a present value method for calculating effective rent. In their method, the appraiser 1) applies a market-derived discount rate to the *actual rents* to be paid over the term of a lease (*actual rent* is *face rent* less *free rent*), 2) adjusts the present value for tenant improvements (i.e., the difference between *actual tenant improvements* and *market-standard tenant improvements*), and 3) converts the adjusted present value to *initial annual rent* by (a) deducting the present value of the rent derived from typical base rent increases (where rent increases are typical of the market), and (b) dividing the remaining present value by the present value factor for receiving $1.00 per year for the given lease term. See "Valuation Issues, Effective Rent," *Korpacz Real Estate Investor Survey*, vol. 6, no. 3 (Third Quarter 1993), 5-7.

Table 21.5 Characteristic Income and Expenses of Principal Property Types

Property Type	Lease & Income	Expenses	Non-realty Interest(s)
Warehouses & space in industrial parks	Medium- to long-term net lease; standard rent.	Tenants pay most operating expenses and sometimes property taxes, insurance, and exterior maintenance; landlord pays management fees; tenant improvement allowance provided by landlord; leasing commissions paid by landlord to agent or broker; tenant improvements and leasing commissions are typically treated as below-the-line items.	May or may not include business enterprise value.
Shopping Centers			May or may not include business enterprise value.
Major (anchor) tenants	Long-term net lease; minimum & percentage (overage) rent.	Tenants pay utilities, interior maintenance, & common area maintenance (such expense recoveries are prorated); tenants may share in advertising and management costs; tenant improvement allowance provided by landlord; leasing commissions paid by landlord to agent or broker; tenant improvements and leasing commissions are typically treated as below-the-line items.	
Smaller (local) tenants	Short- to medium-term net lease; mini-mum & percentage (overage) rent.	Same as above	
Hotels	Typically the property is not leased; income depends on average occupancy and daily room rates.	Owner pays operating expenses & fixed expenses; replace-ment allowance is treated as an above-the-line item; no tenant improvement allowance or leasing commissions.	Includes value of personal property & business enterprise value.
Multifamily Residential	One-year or less; semi-gross lease; standard rent.	Tenants pay own utility expenses; landlord pays property taxes, insurance, management, maintenance and common area maintenance; replacement allowance may be treated as an above-the-line item; no tenant improvement allowance or leasing commissions.	
Office Buildings	Medium- to long-term; base rent may be adjusted upward on an escalation basis according to an index or, for retail properties, as a percentage of sales.	Under a gross lease, tenants pay all operating expenses; under a net lease, tenants pay some or all expenses; under triple net leases, tenants pay property taxes, insurance & maintenance; leases contain provisions to pass through any increase in certain expenses, over a specified base amount and customarily on a per square foot basis. Tenant improvement allowance provided by landlord; leasing commissions paid by landlord to agent or broker; tenant improvements and leasing commissions are typically treated as below-the-line items.	

Note: The treatment of expenses described is typical of many markets, but not universal.

deduct all tenant improvements, while others deduct only the excess of actual tenant improvement costs over a market standard.

Escalation Income

Escalation income is derived from escalation clauses in leases. Escalation income may be additional charges to tenants for part or all of the increases in operating expenses or charges that result from exercising a specific escalation formula contained in an existing lease.

Percentage Rent

Percentage rent is typically derived from retail store tenants and set at a certain percentage of their sales. It can be paid either monthly or annually, and is usually paid in lieu of a fixed base or contract rent.

Overage Rent

Overage rent is estimated based on the percentage, or graduated percentage, payable on sales that exceed a specified level or breakpoint. This rent is usually paid in addition to a fixed base or contract rent.

Market Rent

Rent for vacant or owner-occupied space is usually estimated at market rent levels and distinguished from scheduled rent in the income estimate. In fee simple valuations, all rentable space is assumed to be leased at market rent; no rent attributable to specific leases is included in the income estimate. In developing market rent estimates, the appraiser assumes that property management is competent.

Other Income

Other income covers all income generated by the operation of the real property that is not derived directly from space rental. It includes income from services supplied to the tenants such as switchboard service, antenna connections, and garage space; income from coin-operated equipment and parking fees is also included. Because service-derived income may or may not be attributable to the real property, an appraiser might find it inappropriate to include this income in the property's potential gross income. The appraiser may treat other income as business income or as real property income, depending on its source.

Vacancy and Collection Loss

Vacancy and collection loss is an allowance for reductions in potential income attributable to vacancies, tenant turnover, and nonpayment of rent.

Annual rent collections are typically less than annual potential gross income, so an allowance for vacancy and collection loss is usually included in the appraisal of income-producing property. The allowance is usually estimated as a percentage of potential gross income, which varies depending on the type and characteristics of the physical property, the quality of its tenants, current and projected supply and demand relationships, and general and local economic conditions.

Published surveys of similar properties under similar conditions may indicate an appropriate percentage allowance for vacancy and collection loss. An appraiser should survey the local market to support the vacancy estimate, but his or her conclusion may differ from the current level indicated by primary or secondary data because it reflects typical investor expectations over the specific holding period assumed or projected in the income capitalization approach.

Effective Gross Income

Effective gross income is the anticipated income from all operations of the real property, i.e., potential gross income less the vacancy and collection loss allowance.

Operating Expenses

In the income capitalization approach, a comprehensive analysis of the annual expenses of property operation is essential whether the value indication is derived from estimated net operating income or pre-tax cash flow. *Operating expenses are the periodic expenditures necessary to maintain the real property and continue the production of the effective gross income.*

An operating statement that conforms to this definition of operating expenses is used for appraisal purposes; this statement may differ from a statement prepared for an owner or an accountant. Because operating statements are prepared on either a cash or accrual basis, the appraiser must know the accounting basis used in the operating statements for the property being appraised. Operating statements provide valuable factual data and can be used to identify trends in operating expenses.

Expenses may be recorded in categories selected by the property owner, or the records may follow a standard system of accounting established by an association of owners or by accounting firms that serve a particular segment of the management market. In any case an appraiser analyzes and reconstructs expense statements to develop a typical expense expectancy for the property on an annual accrual basis.

Operating expense estimates usually list fixed expenses, variable expenses, and a replacement allowance. These classifications have long been in use, but there are other valid systems that an appraiser can employ and various property types may require different formats.

Fixed Expenses

Fixed expenses are operating expenses that generally do not vary with occupancy and have to be paid whether the property is occupied or vacant. Real estate taxes and building insurance costs are typically considered fixed expenses. Although these expenses rarely remain constant, they generally do not fluctuate widely from year to year, do not vary in response to changing occupancy levels, and are not subject to management control. Therefore, an appraiser can usually identify a trend and legitimately estimate these expense items.

Tax data can be found in public records, and the assessor's office may provide information about projected changes in assessments or rates and their probable effect on future taxes. If a property is assessed unfairly, the real estate tax expense may need to be adjusted for the reconstructed operating statement used in the appraisal. If the subject property is subject to an unusually low assessment compared to other, similar properties or appears to deviate from the general pattern of taxation in the jurisdiction, the most probable amount and trend of future taxes must be thoroughly analyzed. Any past changes in the assessment of the subject property should be studied. If the assessment is low, the assessor may raise it sooner or later; if the figure is high, however, a reduction may not be easily obtained. In projecting real estate taxes, an appraiser tries to anticipate tax assessments based on past tax trends, present taxes, the municipality's future expenditures, and the perceptions of market participants.

For proposed properties or properties that are not currently assessed, appraisers can develop operating statement projections without including real estate taxes. The resulting estimate is net operating income before real estate taxes, but a provision for real estate taxes is included in the capitalization rate used to convert this net income into property value. For example, assume that real estate taxes are typically 2% of market value and net operating income after real estate taxes would normally be capitalized at 11% to derive a market value estimate for the subject property. In this case the estimated net operating income before real estate taxes could be capitalized at 13% (i.e., 11% + 2%) to derive a property value indication. Alternatively, the appraiser may choose to estimate real estate taxes for a proposed project based on building costs or the taxes paid by recently constructed, competitive properties.

An owner's operating expense statement may show the insurance premiums paid on a cash basis. If the premiums are not paid annually, they must be adjusted to an annual accrual basis before they are included in the reconstructed operating statement. Fire, extended coverage, and owner's liability insurance are typical insurance items; depending on the type of property, elevators, boilers, plate glass, or other items may also be insured. The appraiser must determine the amount of insurance and, if it is inadequate, adjust the annual cost to indicate appropriate coverage for the property.

Insurance on business inventory and other personal property is the occupant's responsibility and, therefore, should not be charged to the operation of the real estate. When questions concerning co-insurance or terms of coverage arise, an appraiser might need to obtain professional insurance counsel.

Variable Expenses

Variable expenses are operating expenses that generally vary with the level of occupancy or the extent of services provided. Individual expense items of this type may vary greatly from year to year, but similar types of property often reflect a reasonably consistent pattern of variable expenses in relation to gross income. Because fewer services are provided to the tenants of free-standing retail and industrial properties, these properties usually have a much lower ratio of expenses to gross income than apartment and office buildings.

Operating statements for large properties frequently list many types of variable expenses. Typical categories include

- Management charges
- Leasing fees
- Utilities—e.g., electricity, gas, water, and sewer
- Heat
- Air-conditioning
- General payroll
- Cleaning
- Maintenance and repair of structure
- Decorating
- Grounds and parking area maintenance
- Miscellaneous—e.g., security, supplies, rubbish removal, and exterminating

Management charges. Management charges are proper expenses of operation, whether management services are contracted or provided by the property owner. The expense of management is usually expressed as a percentage of effective gross income and conforms to the local pattern for such charges.[5]

The operation of multitenant properties requires a considerable amount of supervision, accounting, and other services. Larger properties may have on-site offices or apartments for resident managers and corresponding expenses for their maintenance and operation. Other management expenses may include the cost of telephone service, clerical help, legal or accounting services, printing and postage, and advertising. Management fees may occasionally be included among recoverable operating expenses.

In some markets, standard retail leases contain a provision for levying administrative charges as a percentage of common area maintenance charges. These charges are treated as a mark-up to the tenant and are distinct from, and unrelated to, the management fee.

Leasing commissions. Leasing commissions are paid to agents for negotiating and securing property leases. When these commissions are spread over the term of a lease or lease renewal, they are included in the operating statement. However, initial leasing commissions, which may be extensive in a new shopping center or other large development, are usually treated as part of the capital expenditure for developing the project. These initial leasing commissions are not included as periodic expenses. When a net income or pre-tax cash flow forecast is developed, leasing fees can be deducted in the year they are payable or spread over the lease term, depending on local practice. A blended rate can be developed to reflect leasing commission costs for both existing leases and new leases. This procedure is demonstrated later in a footnote to Table 21.8.

---

5. Actual property management should be distinguished from asset management. Large, investment-grade properties are often held as part of a portfolio which includes both securities and real estate. The managers of these portfolios make critical decisions concerning when to acquire a real estate asset, how to finance or when to refinance, and when to reposition a property in the market. Though their roles are distinct, the functions of a property manager and an asset manager may sometimes be intertwined. Asset management fees should not be included among the items enumerated as operating expenses for real property. *The Office Building: From Concept to Investment Reality*, John Robert White, ed. (Chicago: Counselors of Real Estate, Appraisal Institute, and Society of Industrial and Office REALTORS, 1993), 488-489, 529-530.

Utilities. Utility expenses for an existing property are usually projected based on an analysis of past charges and current trends. The subject property's utility requirements can be compared with known unit utility expenses for similar properties to estimate probable future utility expenses. Hours of tenant operation may prove to be significant in the analysis. For example, the number of nights per week that a shopping center is open and the hours of after-dark operation will directly affect electricity consumption, and may indirectly affect expenses for maintenance and garbage removal. In analyzing utility expenses, appraisers recognize local circumstances and the increasing cost of all types of energy.

Although the cost of *electricity* for leased space is frequently a tenant expense, and therefore not included in the operating expense statement, the owner may be responsible for lighting public areas and for the power needed to run elevators and other building equipment.

Gas. When used for heating and air-conditioning, gas can be a major expense item that is either paid by the tenant or reflected in the rent.

Water. The cost of water is a major consideration for industrial plants that use processes depending on water and for multifamily projects, in which the cost of sewer service is usually tied to the amount of water used. It is also an important consideration for laundries, restaurants, taverns, hotels, and similar operations. The leases for these properties may stipulate that the tenant pay this expense. If the owner typically pays for gas and water, these charges should be included in the expense statement.

Sewer. In municipalities with sewerage systems, a separate charge for use of the system may be paid by the tenant or the owner of the real estate. When the property owner is responsible, the total expense may be substantial, particularly for hotels, motels, recreation facilities, apartments, and office buildings.

Heat. The cost of heat is generally a tenant expense in single-tenant properties, industrial or retail properties, and apartment projects with individual heating units. It is a major expense item shown in operating statements for office buildings and many apartment properties. The fuel consumed may be coal, oil, gas, electricity, or public steam. Heating supplies, maintenance, and workers' wages are included in this expense category under certain accounting methods.

Public steam suppliers and gas companies maintain records of fuel consumption in terms of degree days from year to year. (One degree day is equal to the number of degrees, during a 24-hour day, that the mean temperature falls below 65° Fahrenheit, which is the base temperature in the United States.) An appraiser can use these records and fuel cost data to compare the property's heating expense for the most recent year or years with a typical year. Probable changes in the cost of the fuel used should be reflected in the appraiser's projection.

Air-conditioning. Air-conditioning expenses may be charged under the individual categories of electricity, water, payroll, and repairs, or heating and air-conditioning may be combined under the category of heating, ventilation, and air-conditioning (HVAC). The cost of air-conditioning varies substantially with local climatic conditions and the type of system installed. A projection of this expense may be based on typical unit charges for the community or the property type. Most office buildings and many apartment buildings have central HVAC systems and operating expenses are included in their annual statements. Most commercial properties and some apartment buildings have individual heating and air-conditioning units that are operated by the tenants. The maintenance and repair of these units, particularly in apartments, may continue to be the property owner's obligation.

General payroll. General payroll expenses include payments to all employees whose services are essential to property operation and management, but whose salaries are not included in other specific expense categories. In some areas the cost of custodial or janitorial service is based on union wage schedules; in others the charge is negotiated based on local custom and practice. If a custodian or manager occupies an apartment as partial payment for his or her services, the apartment's rental value may be included as income and an identical amount deducted as an expense. In certain properties additional expenses are incurred to pay the salaries of watchmen, doormen, porters, and elevator operators. Unemployment and social security taxes for employees may be included under general payroll expenses or listed in a separate expense category.

Cleaning. In office buildings the cost of cleaning is a major expense. It is usually estimated in terms of cents per square foot of rentable area, whether the work is done by payroll personnel or by an outside cleaning firm. This expense is equivalent to maid service or housekeeping in hotels and furnished apartments. In hotels and motels, cleaning expenses are attributed to the rooms department and may be estimated as a percentage of the department's gross income. The percentage established reflects the property's previous experience and industry standards. Cleaning may be an owner or tenant expense, depending on the property type and lease provisions.

Maintenance and repair of structure. Maintenance and repair expenses may cover roof repair, window caulking, tuckpointing, exterior painting, and the repair of heating, lighting, and plumbing equipment. Under triple net leases, maintenance fees are payable by the tenants. There may be a contract for elevator maintenance and repair, but because these contracts vary, the appraiser must determine any additional operating expense not covered by the maintenance contract. A contract that covers air-conditioning equipment, for example, would probably be included in the air-conditioning expense category.

Alterations may be considered capital expenditures and, therefore, are not included as a periodic expense under repair and maintenance. If the lessor makes alterations in the rented space, the expense may or may not be amortized by additional rental; in some cases the tenant may pay for alterations.

The total expense for property maintenance and repair is affected by the extent to which building component and equipment replacements are covered in the replacement allowance. If an extensive replacement allowance is included in the reconstructed operating statement, annual maintenance and repair expenses will be reduced. In any case, maintenance and repair expenses for the main portion of the building should always be listed in the maintenance and repair category.

Decorating. Decorating expenses may include the cost of interior painting, wallpapering, or wall cleaning in tenant or public areas. Lease provisions may stipulate that the owner is only responsible for decorating vacant space to attract new tenants. Decorating expenditures may vary with local practice and the supply and demand for space.

Grounds and parking area maintenance. The cost of maintaining grounds and parking areas can vary widely depending on the type of property and its total area. Hard-surfaced public parking areas with drains, lights, and marked car spaces are subject to intensive wear and can be costly to maintain. These expenses may be entirely or partly compensated with an increment added to the rents of tenants served by the facility. In this case both the added income and the added expenses are included in the appraiser's reconstructed operating statement.

Miscellaneous. Expenses for miscellaneous items vary with property type. If this expense category represents a significant percentage of effective gross income, however, it may be wise to explain individual expense items or reallocate them to specific categories.

Security. Certain types of buildings in some areas may require security provisions, the cost of which will vary according to the number of employees needed to control entry and exit and to circulate through the property. Maintenance and energy expenses may also be incurred if security provisions include electric alarm systems, closed circuit television, or flood lighting.

Supplies. The cost of cleaning materials and miscellaneous items not covered elsewhere may be included under supplies.

Rubbish removal and exterminating. Garbage and pest control services are usually contracted and their cost is included in the expense statement. The cost of snow removal may be substantial in northern states, particularly if properties have outdoor parking in addition to sidewalks and driveways.

Replacement Allowance

A replacement allowance provides for the periodic replacement of building components that wear out more rapidly than the building itself and must be replaced periodically during the building's useful life. These components may include

- Roof covering
- Carpeting
- Kitchen, bath, and laundry equipment
- Compressors, elevators, and boilers
- Specific structural items and equipment that have limited economic life expectancies
- Interior improvements to tenant space that are made periodically by the landlord, usually at lease renewal
- Sidewalks
- Driveways

- Parking areas
- Exterior painting

The annual allowance for each component is usually estimated as the anticipated cost of its replacement prorated over its total useful life, provided this does not exceed the total useful life of the structure. Some appraisers use simple averaging, while others prefer to show the actual cost and timing of these replacements. New elevators or other components that are expected to have useful lives that equal or exceed the remaining useful life of the structure do not require an allowance for replacement.

The scope of items to be covered in a replacement allowance is a matter of appraisal judgment based on market evidence; however, the extent of the replacement allowance is based on the annual repair and maintenance expenses of the property. Historical operating statements prepared on a cash basis may include periodic replacement expenses under repair and maintenance. If extensive provisions for replacement are made in the reconstructed operating statement, these charges may be duplicated unless the annual maintenance expense estimate is reduced.

In certain real estate markets, space is rented to a new tenant only after substantial interior improvements are made. If this work is performed at the landlord's expense and is required to achieve market rent, the expense of these improvements should be included in the reconstructed operating statement as part of the replacement allowance.

A total expense estimate that provides for all items of repair and replacement may exceed the actual expenditures shown in the owner's operating statements for recent years. This is particularly common when the building being appraised is relatively new and the owner has not set up a replacement allowance. In preparing a reconstructed operating statement for a typical year, an appraiser recognizes that replacements must be made eventually and that replacement costs affect operating expenses; these costs can be reflected in increased annual maintenance costs or, on an accrual basis, in an annual replacement allowance.

The appraiser must know whether or not a replacement allowance is included in an operating statement to derive a market capitalization rate for use in the income capitalization approach. It is essential that the income statements of comparable properties be compatible. Otherwise, adjustments will be required. A capitalization rate derived from a comparable sale property is valid only if it is applied to the subject property on the same basis. Consequently, a rate derived from a sale with an expense estimate that does not provide for a replacement allowance cannot be applied to an income estimate for a subject property that includes such an allowance.

Total Operating Expenses

Total operating expenses are the sum of fixed and variable expenses and the replacement allowance cited in the operating expense estimate.

Net Operating Income

Net operating income is the anticipated net income remaining after all operating expenses are deducted from effective gross income but before mortgage debt service and book depreciation are deducted.

Total Mortgage Debt Service

Total mortgage debt service is the periodic payment for interest on and retirement of the mortgage loan (principal). Mortgage debt service is deducted from net operating income to derive pre-tax cash flow, which is used in certain capitalization procedures. The definition of market value assumes financing terms compatible with those found in the market. Thus, in estimating market value, the mortgage debt service to be deducted from the net operating income must be based on market terms. In some cases the appraiser may be asked to estimate the value of the equity investor's position based on existing financing. Here the debt service would reflect the terms specified in the existing mortgage.

Pre-Tax Cash Flow

Pre-tax cash flow (equity dividend) is the income that remains after total mortgage debt service is deducted from net operating income. It is also referred to as *before-tax cash flow.*

Expense and Income Ratios

The ratio of total operating expense to effective gross income is the *operating expense ratio.* The complement of this ratio is the *net income ratio*—i.e., net operating income to effective gross income. These ratios tend to fall within limited ranges for specific categories of property. Experienced appraisers recognize appropriate ratios, so they can identify statements that deviate from typical patterns and require further analysis.

Nationwide studies of apartment and office building properties conducted by the Institute of Real Estate Management (IREM) and the Building Owners and Managers Association (BOMA) can often be used as general guides in selecting operating expense ratios. Similar studies are also available for hotels, industrial properties, and miniwarehouses. Sometimes local BOMA or IREM chapters, or real estate appraisal organizations and their chapters, conduct and publish studies of operating expenses that can be used as market indicators. Published studies are useful, but the appraiser must still develop operating expense ratios from comparable properties in the subject property's market or verify the applicability of published ratios to this market.

Exclusions from Reconstructed Operating Statements

The operating statements prepared for real estate owners typically list all expenditures made during a specific year. Owners' statements may include nonrecurring items that should not be included in an expense estimate intended to reflect typical annual expenses. They may also include items of business expense or costs associated with the specific circumstances of ownership.

A reconstructed operating statement represents an opinion of the probable future net operating income of an investment.[6] Certain items included in operating statements

---

6. Some practitioners use the term *pro forma* synonymously with *reconstructed operating statement.* Technically, a pro forma is a financial statement—e.g., a balance sheet or income statement used by a business. The term *reconstructed operating statement* is unique to appraisal practice. A reconstructed operating statement is developed to conform to the appraiser's definition of net operating income, which generally differs from the definition of income used by accountants. Thus a reconstructed operating statement drawn up by an appraiser will usually differ from a pro forma income statement prepared by an accountant.

prepared for property owners should be omitted in reconstructed operating statements prepared for appraisal purposes. These items include book depreciation, income tax, special corporation costs, and additions to capital.

Book Depreciation

The book depreciation for the improvements on a parcel of real estate is based on historical cost or another previously established figure which may have no relation to current market value. Moreover, book depreciation may be based on a formula designed for tax purposes. The capitalization method and procedure selected provide for the recapture of invested capital, so including depreciation in the operating expense statement would be redundant.

Income Tax

The amount of income tax varies with the type of property ownership—i.e., the property may be held by a corporation, a partnership, a public utility, or an individual. The income tax obligation of the ownership is not an operating expense of the property, but it is an expense to the ownership.

Special Corporation Costs

The expenses attributable to corporate operation also pertain to the type of ownership. Corporate expenses are not part of a reconstructed operating statement developed for appraisal purposes.

Additions to Capital

Expenditures for capital improvements do not recur annually and therefore should not be included in an estimate reflecting the typical annual expenses of operation. Capital improvements may enhance value by increasing the annual net operating income or economic life of the property, but the capital expenditure is not a periodic operating expense.

The exclusion of capital expenditures is specific to reconstructed operating statements, which are used to calculate net operating income. When cash flows are estimated for a discounted cash flow analysis, capital expenditures may be deducted from the net operating income in the year the expenditure is expected to occur. This is particularly important when the property's future net operating income is based on the assumption that the capital expenditure will be made. In this case, failure to account for the capital expenditure could result in an overstatement of value.

Sample One-Year Income Forecast

The property being appraised, ABC Apartments, is a 55-unit apartment project with a potential annual rent of $177,120 at 100% occupancy. Open parking is included in the rent. Additional income from coin-operated equipment averages about $1,380 per year, so the total, annual potential gross income at 100% occupancy is $178,500. Annual vacancy and collection loss is estimated at 4% and local management services are available for 5% of rent collections. The building superintendent receives an annual salary of $16,800, including fringe benefits.

Last year's tax bill was $17,875, but taxes are expected to be $18,700 by the end of this year. The owner carries $1 million in fire and extended coverage insurance and pays an annual premium of $1,567. The appraiser believes that this coverage should be increased to $1,200,000 (1.2 x $1,567 = $1,880). The additional expense for other insurance coverage is $770 per year.

The payroll to cover site maintenance and snow removal averages $5,900 per year. Trash removal costs $45 per month and miscellaneous supplies are estimated at $325 per year. Pest control costs are $65 per month and other miscellaneous expenditures are projected at $325 per year.

Building tenants pay their own utilities, including the gas and electricity for individual apartment heating and air-conditioning units. Based on the expenses of the comparables and anticipated rate changes, the electricity for public space is expected to cost $2,200 in the coming year. Expenses for other utilities, including water, consistently run about $1,000 each year.

Repair and maintenance expenses are $12,000 to $13,000 per year, including replacement expenditures. The appraiser anticipates that replacement expenses will increase, and the reconstructed operating statement should include a separate replacement allowance in addition to normal repair and maintenance expenses. Exterior painting, which is estimated to cost $4,650 in the present market, is scheduled to be done every three years.

Most of the apartments are rented on three-year leases, with a typical redecorating cost of $200 per apartment at lease renewal. Public space is minimal, and redecorating this space costs about $240 every third year. All the apartments have stoves, refrigerators, dishwashers, garbage disposals, and exhaust fans, so a replacement allowance of $1,300 per apartment is required. The economic lives of these items vary, but they are estimated to average 10 years. The replacement of carpeting costs the owner about $900 per unit, and the average economic life of carpeting is six years. The roof is considered to have a 20-year life and a replacement cost of $18,000.

The operating statement shown in Table 21.6 reflects these figures. The precision of each entry is set by the appraiser, but rounding to the closest $5 or $10 is well within the estimated accuracy of the data.

Sample Multiyear Income Forecast

In certain appraisals, such as those in which discounted cash flow analysis is used, the appraiser forecasts the expected future monetary benefits of the investment over the total projected holding period. The anticipated benefits may include the net operating income or the pre-tax cash flow for each year of the expected holding period plus the reversion—i.e., the resale price after the expenses of sale are deducted. (The owner's net sale proceeds from the property, sometimes called the *equity reversion*, is equal to this reversion minus any mortgage balance). The analysis that follows is based on a 10-year forecast of the future benefits from an office building investment. Both net operating

Table 21.6 | ABC Apartments: Reconstructed Operating Statement

Income

Potential gross annual income

Rents	11 units @ $2,880/yr.	$31,680	
	12 units @ $3,096/yr.	37,152	
	16 units @ $3,312/yr.	52,992	
	16 units @ $3,456/yr.	55,296	
		$177,120	
Other income		+ 1,380	
Total potential gross income @ 100% occupancy		$178,500	
Less vacancy and collection loss @ 4%		– 7,140	
Effective gross income			$171,360

Operating expenses

Fixed

Real estate taxes	$18,700	
Insurance		
Fire and extended coverage	1,880	
Other	+ 770	
Subtotal	$ 21,350	

Variable

Management ($171,360 x .05)	$ 8,570	
Superintendent	16,800	
Payroll	5,900	
Electricity	2,200	
Other utilities	1,000	
Repair and maintenance	12,500	
Exterior paint ($4,650/3)	1,550	
Interior decorating	3,750 *	
Miscellaneous		
Trash removal ($45 x 12)	540	
Pest control ($65 x 12)	780	
Supplies	325	
Other	325	
Subtotal	$ 54,240	

Replacement allowance

Kitchen and bath equipment ($1,300 x 55)/10	$ 7,150	
Carpeting ($900 x 55)/6	8,250	
Roof $18,000/20 yrs.	900	
Subtotal (9.5% of *EGI*)	$16,300	
Total operating expenses		–$91,888
Operating expense ratio ($91,888/$171,360) = 53.6%		
Net operating income†		$79,472
Net operating income ratio ($79,472/$171,360) = 46.4%		

---

* 55 units x $200 = $11,000; $11,000 + $240 = $11,240; $11,240/3 = $3,750 (rounded). This entry could be included under *replacement allowance*.

† For a one-year statement for an apartment property, no *tenant improvement allowance* or *leasing commissions* need be shown. In multiyear forecasts for retail centers and office buildings, estimates of these expenses are generally, though not universally, treated as "below-the-line" items, i.e., deductions appearing below the estimate of *NOI*. See James Vernor and Joseph Rabianski, *Shopping Center: Appraisal and Analysis*, pages 222-223 and 227 and John R. White, ed., *The Office Building: From Concept to Investment Reality*, Table 21-2, page 402, and Table 30-3, page 595. Both books are available from the Appraisal Institute.

income and pre-tax cash flow are estimated for each year. The proceeds from resale of the property at the end of the tenth year are also estimated.[7]

All the techniques discussed in this chapter are used to develop a net operating or pre-tax cash flow estimate for the first year of the forecast. Estimates for the other years are based on existing lease provisions and assumptions regarding lease renewals and growth rates applied to other income and operating expenses.

Property Analysis

The subject property is a 50,000-sq.-ft. site improved with a 50-year-old, 25-story office building in a secondary location north of the downtown commercial district. The rentable area totals 951,049 square feet of office and retail space. The retail space consists of 13,293 square feet of space and is covered by five leases. The building is fully occupied by 19 tenants under 21 leases. Many of the leases are old and will expire soon. The leases for approximately 58.4% of the building's rentable area will expire and be available for renewal or releasing in 1998 and 1999. The last existing lease will expire in 2017. Hence, all of the leases will roll over in 22 years. (Lease expiration and subsequent re-leasing is referred to as *lease rollover*.) The property's lease expiration profile is summarized in Table 21.7.

The current, average gross rent per square foot of rentable area is $8.57. Appraisers estimate current average market rents at $18 per square foot for office space and $25 per square foot for retail space. The weighted-average market rent is estimated to be $18.10 per square foot. Therefore, the market differential (i.e., the difference between potential gross income at market rent and existing contract rent) is $9.53 per square foot ($18.10 - $8.57), and the total actual rent is 47.35% of market rent. The market for office space is in balance and there is above-average demand for space in this building. Although the building is old, it has been remodeled and extensive capital expenditures have been made to improve its mechanical systems and maintain its competitive position. It is located in a good secondary area and is ideally suited to back office, computer, bookkeeping, or storage operations that require a large, contiguous space.

Rationale for the Forecast

The appraiser determines that investors in office buildings similar to the subject property typically forecast net operating incomes or pre-tax cash flows over a 10-year projected holding period. To establish a purchase price that will justify the risk inherent in the proposed investment, the forecast net operating incomes or pre-tax cash flows and the reversion are discounted at an appropriate yield rate.

To simulate typical investor analysis, an appraiser

1. Analyzes current income, establishes the market rent level for each tenant's space, and forecasts future income for each year of a 10-year period based on existing leases, probable lease renewal at market rent, and expected vacancy experience (In oversupplied commercial markets, *rent spikes* are sometimes used to allow

---

7. This example has been adapted from an article by Peter F. Korpacz and Mark I. Roth titled "Changing Emphasis in Appraisal Techniques: The Transition to Discounted Cash Flow," *The Appraisal Journal* (January 1983).

Table 21.7 | **Subject Property Lease Expiration Profile**

Year	No. of Expiring Leases	Rentable Area in Sq. Ft.	Percent of Total Area Available for Leasing (Cumulative)
1996	0	0	
1997	0	0	
1998	7	268,458	28.2
1999	6	286,706	58.4
2000	2	51,302	63.8
2001	2	22,730	66.2
2002	1	7,930	67.0
2003	1	45,979	71.8
2004-2005	0	0	71.8
2006	1	924	71.9
2007-2016	0	0	71.9
2017	1	267,020	100.0
Total	21	951,049	

market rents to catch up to levels that would have otherwise been achieved by annual inflationary increases in rents. Rent spikes are generally a function of demand.)

2. Forecasts other income, including income from escalation clauses contained in existing leases and assumed escalation provisions in new leases

3. Forecasts future property expenses after analyzing historical operating expenses, the experience of competitive properties, and the current budget for the property

4. Forecasts mortgage debt service based on existing or proposed financing terms

5. Estimates the net operating incomes (or pre-tax cash flows, when appropriate) to be generated by the property in each year of the forecast holding period

6. Estimates the reversionary benefits to be received at the end of the forecast holding period.

In a market value appraisal, these steps must be applied in a manner that reflects the thinking of market participants. In this sample application, the appraiser begins by assembling pertinent information on comparable office buildings in the same market as the subject property. To verify the data, the appraiser interviews one of the participants, usually the buyer, to determine the net operating income (or pre-tax cash flow) forecast assumptions associated with each comparable. Table 21.8, which lists information on Comparable 1, illustrates the type of detailed information that should be sought for each comparable.

Table 21.8	Comparable Data

Comparable No.
: 1

Address
: 110 Main St.
  Subject city, subject state

Date of sale
: June 1995

Sale price
: $60 million

Seller
: XYZ Investment Co.

Purchaser
: 110 Main Street Co.

Description
: A 32-story, multitenant office building that was built in 1969 and contains 748,701 square feet of area on floors that range in size from 8,100 square feet to 30,600 square feet situated on a 32,609-sq.-ft. plot

Comments
: The property was sold on an all-cash basis; the buyer expects above-average increases in net income.

Sale price per sq. ft.
: $80.14

Average scheduled rent per sq. ft. at sale date
: $12.44

Anticipated financial data for Year 1 (buyer's estimate):

Average market rent per square foot	$18.00
Average scheduled rent per square foot	$12.44
Fixed expenses per square foot	$ 2.67
Variable expenses per square foot	$ 4.79
Replacement allowance per square foot	$ 0.50
Net operating income per square foot	$ 4.98
Overall capitalization rate*	6.2%
Equity capitalization rate	6.2%

Anticipated 10-year yield (IRR)
: 13.5%

Purchaser's assumptions:

Market rent rate
: Averages $18 per square feet in Years 1 and 2, increasing 5% per year thereafter

Escalation income
: Typical total rent will closely approximate market rent rates

Expense increases
: Real estate taxes assumed to increase 2% per year; energy expenses assumed to increase 5% per year; other operating expenses assumed to increase 4% per year

Re-leasing
: All space assumed to be re-leased for successive 5-year terms

Vacancy
: 75% of space being re-leased assumed to be vacant for 3 months

Leasing commissions†
: Standard commission schedule payable in first year of lease

Interior improvements to tenant space
: $20.00 per square foot for new leases; $7.50 per square foot for renewal of existing leases

Resale
: Computed by applying a 10% overall capitalization rate to the net operating income in Year 11 after deducting 2.5% for selling expenses

---

* Because the property is not mortgaged, the equity capitalization rate is the same as the overall capitalization rate. The occupancy level for this building is 100%.

† It is imperative that the appraiser consider leasing commission costs for both new tenants and existing tenants as well as probable tenant renewal/turnover ratios. To account for these factors, the appraiser develops a blended rate by means of weighting. For example, if the tenant renewal ratio for a property is 70%, the leasing commission for existing tenants is 2.5%, and the leasing commission for new tenants is 6%, a blended rate can be developed as follows:

$$0.70 \times 0.025 = 0.0175$$
$$0.30 \times 0.06 \ = 0.018$$
$$\text{Blended rate} = 0.0355 \ (3.5\% \text{ rounded})$$

This blended rate is then applied to existing tenant leases as they expire.

Assumptions for the Subject Property

After gathering and analyzing data on local market conditions and the income and expense expectations of comparable properties, the appraiser makes some assumptions about the subject property.

Forecast Period

The forecasts are based on an assumed 10-year holding period commencing on the date of valuation. A 10-year forecast is typical in this market. This forecast considers the effects of re-leasing 71.9% of the building space; a lease for the other 28.1% of the building is held by one major tenant and does not expire until the year 2017. Income for the eleventh year of the investment is forecast to estimate the resale price of the property at the end of the 10-year projection period. The income for Year 11 of this forecast is the income for the first year of operation under the new owner.

Existing Rents

Contract rents and rent adjustments are forecast in light of existing leases and escalation provisions.

Escalation Income

Escalation income is calculated in accordance with the specific terms of existing leases. For anticipated new leases, escalation income is based on a pro rata share of the amount by which operating expenses and real estate taxes exceed these expenses in the base year. The base year is defined as the year of lease commencement. By local custom, escalation income is assumed to be collected in the year after it accrues.

Although specific escalation provisions vary, the appraiser's analysis reveals that prospective investors use a combination of escalation provisions which, taken together, increase tenant collections annually so that total collections in any given year do not lag far behind market rents.

Renewal Options

It is assumed that the renewal options contained in existing leases, all of which specify new contract rents or escalation provisions, will be exercised; the income specified under these renewals is incorporated into the forecast. One lease has a seven-year renewal option beginning in 1997 that specifies an annual rent that is less than the expected market rent for that year ($18.00 market rent compared with $13.00 contract rent). Other renewal options that do not specify contract rent or escalation provisions are also assumed to be exercised; in these cases market rental rates and new escalation provisions are applied.

Tenant Turnover

Approximately 35% of the space in the building is occupied by three major corporations that are likely to remain. It is assumed that this space will be re-leased to the existing tenants. Another 50% of the building is assumed to be re-leased to other existing tenants; the remaining 15% will be leased to new tenants. These assumptions are consistent with comparable sales data, given the character of the property and its tenants.

New Lease Terms

When the existing leases and any renewal options expire, all space is assumed to be re-leased for successive 10-year terms. In this market 10-year leases are customary for this type of space.

Market Rental Rates

The market rental rates applied to leasing activity are set forth below.

> Office space: For two years beginning January 1, 1996, rent will average $18 per square foot; the market rate is assumed to increase 5% per year thereafter.
>
> Retail space: For the year beginning on January 1, 1996, average rent will be $25 per square foot; the market rate is assumed to increase 5% per year.

The office rental rate assumptions are supported by an analysis of actual leases for office space in competitive buildings. Assumptions pertaining to rate increases are consistent with the assumptions made by the buyers of all but one of the comparable sales (see Table 21.9).

Vacancy and Collection Loss

Fifteen percent of the building space is being leased to new tenants and is assumed to remain vacant for an average of four months. The other 85% is assumed to be re-leased by existing tenants, so no vacancy is anticipated. The appraiser has considered the rent loss associated with vacancies by not accruing contract rent or escalation income for the space for a four-month period beginning at the expiration of each lease. Furthermore, an additional allowance for the underlying level of vacancy and collection loss for multi-tenant office buildings in this market is estimated at 0.5% of total gross revenue, as indicated by comparable sales data.

Real Estate Taxes and Insurance

Real estate taxes and insurance are estimated at $998,000, or $1.05 per square foot of rentable area, for the year ending in December 1996. The combined real estate tax and insurance expense is assumed to increase at a rate of 4% per year thereafter.

Management

Management fees are estimated at $75,000 for 1996 and are expected to increase 4.5% each subsequent year. Although the building is large, the small number of tenants and the significant leasing activity scheduled for the near term should attract competent management at this rate.

Leasing Commissions

To estimate leasing commissions, the appraiser applies a weighted-average leasing commission rate of 17.15% of the first year's base rent to all re-leasing activities. This estimate assumes that 35% of the space will be re-leased to the three major tenants at a commission rate of 14% of the first year's contract rent; 50% of the space will be re-leased to existing tenants at a commission rate of 14% of the first year's contract rent;

Table 21.9 **Analysis of Growth Rate Assumptions Derived from Office Building Data**

Sale No.	Date	Market Rent Growth Rates					Expense Growth Rates		
		1st Period		2nd Period			Variable		Real Estate Taxes
		%	No. of Years	%	No. of Years	Thereafter	Operating	Energy	and Insurance
1	9/95	0.0	2	—	—	5.0%	4.0%	5.0%	2.0%
2	9/95	4.0	—	—	—	4.0	4.5	4.5	3.0
3	6/95	0.0	2	4.0	2	5.0	4.5	5.0	3.0
4	7/94	0.0	3	—	—	5.0	4.0	4.0	4.0
5	3/95	0.0	2	4.0	2	5.0	4.0	5.0	4.0
6	3/95	0.0	3	—	—	5.0	4.0	4.0	4.0
7	4/94	5.0	—	—	—	5.0	5.0	5.0	4.0
8	4/94	0.0	2	—	—	5.0	4.5	4.5	4.0
9	7/94	5.0	—	—	—	5.0	5.0	6.0	5.0
10	10/94	0.0	3	—	—	5.0	4.0	5.0	4.0
11	8/95	0.0	2	4.0	2	5.0	4.0	4.0	5.0

and 15% of the space will be leased to new tenants at a commission rate of 35% of the first year's contract rent. Commissions are assumed to be paid in full upon occupancy and are deducted from income. This commission schedule is consistent with the typical rates obtained by local real estate brokers.

Variable Operating Expenses

Variable operating expenses, excluding leasing commissions and management which have been treated separately, are estimated to be $2,161,000 in 1996, or $2.27 per square foot of rentable area (see Table 21.10). The expense estimates are supported by an analysis of the recent operating histories of competitive buildings. The HVAC estimate is decreased from 1995 to 1996 because the building is being converted from steam to oil heat (see Table 21.10). Expenses for energy-related items are expected to increase 5% per year, and other expenses are estimated to increase 4.5% per year. These rate increases are based on the expense rate increase assumptions indicated by comparable sales. Expenses for tenant electricity and the cleaning of tenant space are not included because existing tenants pay for their own cleaning and electricity. This is not unusual in the leasing back of office space, and the market rent estimate of $18 per square foot is based on the assumption that future tenants will continue this practice.

Table 21.10 | **Estimate of Variable Operating Expenses for Subject Property***

	1995 Budget	**1996 Estimate**
HVAC	$ 500,000	$ 400,000 †
Payroll	154,000	175,000
Repairs and maintenance	385,000	440,000
Building electricity	600,000	660,000
Security	175,000	200,000
Cleaning public areas	25,000	30,000
Garbage collection	5,000	6,000
Administrative and general	185,000	200,000
Water and sewer	44,000	50,000
Total	$2,073,000	$2,161,000
Total per rentable sq. ft.	$2.18	$2.27

* Excluding management expenses and leasing commissions, which are estimated separately
† Reflects conversion to oil heat for part of year

Replacement Allowance

The replacement allowance consists of the cost of replacing building components that wear out over time. The cost to replace building improvements (e.g., roof and HVAC equipment) is forecast at $100,000 for Year 1, increasing 4.5% each following year.

Tenant Improvements

Tenant improvements consist of the cost of preparing tenant space. The forecast for the replacement allowance begins the third and fourth years out with seven leases expiring in 1998 and six leases in 1999 (see Table 21.7). All space being leased to new tenants is assumed to require decorating at a cost of $20.00 per square foot. Space being re-leased to existing tenants is assumed to incur decorating expenses of $7.50 per square foot.

Reversion

There are several ways to estimate a resale price. A capitalization rate can be applied to the appropriate income for the last year of the forecast or the year following the end of the forecast. In this case the resale price is forecast by applying a 10% overall capitalization rate to the net operating income for the year after the projection period (Year 11). The net operating income for Year 11 represents the projected income for Year 1 under the next owner. When an overall capitalization rate is used to estimate a resale price, it is sometimes referred to as a *terminal or residual capitalization rate* (R_N). The terminal or residual capitalization rate stands in contradistinction to the *going-in capitalization rate*, i.e., the overall capitalization rate found by dividing a property's net operating income for the first year after purchase by the present value of the property. The terminal or residual capitalization rate forecast is generally, though not necessarily, higher than the going-in capitalization rate. The terminal capitalization rate must reflect the reduction in the remaining economic life of the property and the greater risk associated with estimating *NOI* at the end of the holding period.[8] In this application sales expenses of 2.5% are deducted to arrive at the net resale price. (The balance of the mortgage could then be deducted to calculate the owner's net sale proceeds, or equity reversion.)

Forecast Results

Mathematical calculations based on the assumptions set forth in this sample application result in the forecast shown in Table 21.11. The future benefits are converted into a value indication for the subject property using an appropriate capitalization procedure.

This example demonstrates one method for forecasting future benefits, but this is not the only acceptable forecasting procedure. The rent levels, growth rates, expense levels, and other economic and financial information described here relate to the specific property being appraised and the real estate market under consideration. In market value appraisals, the forecasting of future benefits should be based on market-derived information. In assignments to estimate investment value, the appraiser has more latitude in interpreting market attitudes and specific investor preferences.

---

8. Footnote 10 in Chapter 23 references a discussion of the criteria for assessing the reasonableness of terminal capitalization rates.

Table 21.11 Income Estimates

	1996	1997	1998	1999	2000	2001	2002	2003	2004	2005	2006†
Income											
Contract and market rents*	$8,149,802	$8,149,802	$8,986,591	$12,645,178	$15,241,645	$16,035,714	$16,485,322	$17,432,668	$19,487,680	$20,291,478	$20,291,478
Escalation income	153,078	283,867	360,523	528,617	625,906	772,308	1,074,136	1,455,791	1,816,841	2,061,857	2,336,857
Vacancy and collection loss	(40,749)	(40,749)	(44,933)	(63,226)	(76,208)	(80,179)	(82,427)	(87,163)	(97,438)	(101,457)	(101,457)
Effective gross income	$8,262,131	$8,392,920	$9,302,181	$13,110,569	$15,791,343	$16,728,343	$17,477,031	$18,801,296	$21,207,083	$22,251,878	$22,526,878
Operating expenses											
Fixed expenses											
Real estate taxes	926,671	963,738	1,002,287	1,042,379	1,084,074	1,127,437	1,172,534	1,219,436	1,268,213	1,318,942	1,371,699
Insurance	71,329	74,182	77,149	80,235	83,445	86,783	90,254	93,864	97,619	101,523	105,584
Variable expenses											
HVAC	400,000	420,000	441,000	463,050	486,203	510,513	536,038	562,840	590,982	620,531	651,558
Payroll	175,000	182,875	191,104	199,704	208,691	218,082	227,896	238,151	248,868	260,067	271,770
Repair and maintenance	440,000	459,800	480,491	502,113	524,708	548,320	572,994	598,779	625,724	653,882	683,307
Electricity	660,000	693,000	727,650	764,033	802,234	842,346	884,463	928,686	975,121	1,023,877	1,075,070
Security	200,000	209,000	218,405	228,233	238,504	249,236	260,452	272,172	284,420	297,219	310,594
Cleaning	30,000	31,350	32,761	34,235	35,776	37,385	39,068	40,826	42,663	44,583	46,589
Garbage removal	6,000	6,270	6,552	6,847	7,155	7,477	7,814	8,165	8,533	8,917	9,318
Water/sewer	50,000	52,250	54,601	57,058	59,626	62,309	65,113	68,043	71,105	74,305	77,648
Administrative and general	200,000	209,000	218,405	228,233	238,504	249,236	260,452	272,172	284,420	297,219	310,594
Management	75,000	78,375	81,902	85,587	89,439	93,464	97,670	102,065	106,658	111,457	116,473
Replacement allowance	100,000	104,500	109,203	114,117	119,252	124,618	130,226	136,086	142,210	148,609	155,297‡
Total operating expenses	$3,334,000	$3,484,340	$3,641,510	$3,805,824	$3,977,611	$4,157,206	$4,344,974	$4,541,285	$4,746,536	$4,961,131	$5,185,501
Net operating income	$4,928,131	$4,908,580	$5,660,671	$9,304,745	$11,813,732	$12,571,137	$13,132,057	$14,260,011	$16,460,547	$17,290,747	$17,341,377
Tenant improvements	0	0	1,399,740	1,562,261	292,114	135,266	49,309	298,771	312,216	326,266	6,851
Leasing commissions	0	0	870,166	976,026	183,356	85,293	31,239	190,196	0	0	4,424
Net income from operations	$4,928,131	$4,908,580	$3,390,765	$6,766,458	$11,338,262	$12,350,578	$13,051,509	$13,771,044	$16,148,331	$16,964,481	$17,330,102

Resale price (based on NOI in 2006) $173,413,770
Less sales expenses @ 2.5%   -4,335,344
Net resale price $169,078,426

* Reflects added vacancy associated with lease rollovers, as discussed under vacancy and collection loss

† For calculation of residual value or reversion in 2005

‡ In some models, a replacement allowance is not deducted as an expense item in the NOI estimate for the last year of the forecast. The NOI estimate for that year (which comes to $17,496,674 without deduction of the replacement allowance) would be capitalized to arrive at the reversion. Whether or not it is appropriate to deduct a replacement allowance for that year is a function of the terminal or residual capitalization rate applied to the NOI.

Key Concepts

- In the income capitalization approach, four income streams are analyzed: potential gross income (*PGI*), effective gross income (*EGI*), net operating income (*NOI*), and pre-tax cash flow.

- An income and expense forecast begins with lease analysis. Lease types include gross rental, net rental, flat rental, graduated rental, revaluation, index, and percentage leases.

- Among the data examined in a lease analysis are the dates, terms, rents, rent concessions, lessor/lessee division of expenses, right to assign/sublet, renewal options, expense caps or stops, escalation clauses, expense recoveries, purchase options, escape clauses, kick-out clauses, advance rent or bonding, casualty loss provisions, continued occupancy clauses, tenant improvement specifications, noncompete and exclusive use clauses, and revaluation clauses.

- Fundamental categories of rent analyzed include contract rent, market rent, scheduled rent, effective rent, excess rent, deficit rent, percentage rent and overage rent.

- The market value of the leased fee interest in a property under leases that specify rent at market levels is based on market rent. The market value of the leased fee interest in a property under existing leases or contracts that specify rent at nonmarket levels is estimated by adjusting contract rents, under specified lease terms and conditions, to market levels. The market value of vacant and owner-occupied space in such properties is based on market rent.

- Income estimates are developed by analyzing information on the subject and competitive properties, i.e., individual income and expense histories, recent transactional data (signed leases, rents asked and offered), vacancy levels, and management expenses; published operating data, tax assessment policies, projected utility rates, and market expectations should also be investigated.

- The treatment of specific items in an income and expense estimate may vary depending on the property type and local market practices.

- An estimate of net operating income is derived by computing potential gross income (based on scheduled rent, effective rent, and categories of income such as escalation rent, percentage rent, market rent to vacant and owner-occupied space, and other income) and then deducting for vacancy and collection loss. From this remaining sum, the effective gross income, total operating expenses are deducted. Operating expenses comprise three categories: fixed expenses, variable expenses, and the replacement allowance.

- Pre-tax cash flow, which is used in certain income capitalization procedures, is derived by deducting mortgage debt service from net operating income.

- Operating expense ratios and net income ratios are used to identify income and expense statements that are not typical.

- A reconstructed operating statement reflects the probable future net operating income of an investment property. Book depreciation, income taxes, special corporation costs, and additions to capital are excluded from the reconstructed operating statements used for appraisal purposes.

- Estimates of future net operating income or pre-tax cash flow and the reversion are discounted to obtain an indication of the present value of the investment. Alternatively, an indication of the value of the reversionary benefit may be obtained by dividing the last year of projected income by a terminal or residual capitalization rate.

Terms

book depreciation	net income ratio
capital expenditures	net lease (triple net lease)
common area maintenance (CAM)	net operating income (NOI)
continued occupancy clause	net rental basis
contract rent	net sale proceeds (equity reversion)
deficit rent	noncompete clause
effective gross income (EGI)	non-realty interest
effective rent	operating expense ratio (OER)
escalation clause	operating expenses
escalation income	option to purchase
escape clause	option to renew
excess rent	overage rent
exclusive use clause	percentage lease
expense cap	percentage rent
expense recovery	potential gross income (PGI)
expense stop	pre-tax cash flow
fixed expenses	pro forma
flat rental lease	reconstructed operating statement
forecast	renewal option
going-in capitalization rate	rent spikes
graduated rental lease	rental concessions
gross lease	replacement allowance
gross rental basis	revaluation lease
index lease	right of first refusal
kick-out clause	scheduled rent
landlord burden clause	semi-gross lease
lease	step-up (step-down) lease
lease analysis	tenant improvement allowance
lease cancellation clause	terminal or residual capitalization
leasing commission	rate (R_N)
line item (above-the-line/	total mortgage debt service
below-the-line item)	total operating expenses
management charge	vacancy and collection loss
market rent	variable expenses
mortgage debt service	

CHAPTER TWENTY-TWO

Direct Capitalization

D irect capitalization is a method used in the income capitalization approach to convert a single year's income estimate into a value indication. This conversion is accomplished in one step, either by dividing the income estimate by an appropriate income rate or by multiplying it by an appropriate income factor.

In direct capitalization no precise allocation is made between the return on and the return of capital because the method does not usually specify investor assumptions or forecast the holding period, the pattern of income, or changes in the value of the original investment. A satisfactory rate of return for the investor and recapture of the capital invested are implicit in the rates or factors applied in direct capitalization because they are derived from similar investment properties with similar expectations as to holding period, pattern of income, and change in value. An appraiser must obtain this information directly from market participants.

Direct capitalization may be based on various income flows, such as potential gross income, effective gross income, net operating income, equity income, mortgage income, land income, building income, income to the landlord's leased fee position, and income to the tenant's leasehold position. This list is not all-inclusive. The income rates used in direct capitalization include the overall (property) capitalization rate (R_O); the mortgage capitalization rate (R_M); the equity capitalization, or equity dividend, rate (R_E); the land capitalization rate (R_L); the building capitalization rate (R_B); the capitalization rate for the leased fee position (R_{LF}); and the capitalization rate for the leasehold position (R_{LH}). Income factors include the potential gross income multiplier $(PGIM)$, the gross rent multiplier (GRM), the effective gross income multiplier $(EGIM)$, and the net income multiplier (the reciprocal of R_O).

Income rates and factors reflect the relationship between income and value and are derived from market data. It is essential that the properties used as comparables are similar to the property being appraised in terms of risk, income, expense, and physical and locational characteristics. Income multipliers and rates must be extracted from properties that reflect similar income-expense ratios, land value-to-building value ratios, risk characteristics, and expectations as to change in income and value over a typical investment holding period.

In addition to direct capitalization procedures in which a rate or factor is directly applied to the income estimate, physical, financial, economic,[1] and legal residual techniques may be used.

---

1. The economic residual technique is also known as the *property residual technique*. This rather dated term refers to an application of discounted cash flow analysis. No residual income is actually found by this technique, so the term may be misleading. This usage persists in DCF analysis as well, where the estimated reversion is sometimes referred to as *residual value* and the capitalization rate used to estimate it is called the *residual capitalization rate*.

Derivation of Overall Capitalization Rates

Any interest in real estate that has an income can be valued by direct capitalization, but the interest most commonly appraised is the fee simple estate, which includes all property rights in the real estate. The direct capitalization formula that applies to this type of valuation is

$$\text{Value} = \frac{\text{Net operating income}}{\text{Overall capitalization rate}}$$

Overall capitalization rates can be estimated with various techniques; the techniques used depend on the quantity and quality of data available.[2] Accepted techniques include 1) derivation from comparable sales, 2) derivation from effective gross income multipliers and net income ratios, 3) band of investment—mortgage and equity components, 4) band of investment—land and building components, 5) the debt coverage formula, and 6) yield capitalization techniques such as the general yield change formula, R_O = yield – change in income and value, and the Ellwood method.

Derivation from Comparable Sales

Deriving capitalization rates from comparable sales is the preferred technique when sufficient data on sales of similar, competitive properties are available. Data on each property's sale price, income, expenses, financing terms, and market conditions at the time of sale are needed. In addition, the appraiser must make certain that the net operating income of each comparable property is calculated and estimated in the same way that the net operating income of the subject property is estimated. *NOI* per square foot should also be considered in the analysis. Moreover, neither nonmarket financing terms nor different market conditions should have affected the prices of the comparables. If the objective of the appraisal is to value the fee simple interest, the comparable(s) analyzed must be leased at market rent or adjustment(s) will be necessary. If the value of the leased fee is being sought, the comparable(s) must be leased in the same manner as the subject property or again adjustment(s) will be required.

The overall level of risk associated with each comparable should be similar to that of the subject property. Risk can be analyzed by investigating the credit rating of the property's tenants, the stability of the property's income stream, and the property's upside/downside potential.

When these requirements are met, the appraiser can estimate an overall rate by dividing each property's net operating income by its sale price. Table 22.1 illustrates this procedure using data from four comparable sales. If all four transactions are equally reliable and comparable, the appraiser might conclude that an overall rate of 0.1320 to 0.1378 should be applied to the subject property. The final rate concluded depends on the appraiser's judgment as to how comparable each sale is to the subject property.

If there are differences between a comparable property and the subject property that could affect the overall capitalization rate concluded, the appraiser must account for

---

2. Surveys of overall capitalization rates based on the market expectations of lenders and owners are available, but such data should be rigorously scrutinized. Owners may understate the expected capitalization rate while lenders may overstate it.

these differences. In such cases the appraiser must decide whether the rate concluded for the subject property should be higher or lower than the rate indicated by a specific sale. Appraisal judgment is also needed to determine whether the rate selected for the

Table 22.1 **Derivation of Overall Capitalization Rates From Comparable Sales**

	Comparables			
	A	B	C	D
Price	$368,500	$425,000	$310,000	$500,000
Net operating income	$50,000	$56,100	$42,718	$68,600
Indicated R_0	0.1357	0.1320	0.1378	0.1372

subject should fall within the range established by the sales or, as in certain cases, be set above or below the range.

When rates derived from comparable sales are used, the overall capitalization rate is applied to the subject property in a manner consistent with its derivation. In other words, if the market-derived capitalization rates are based on the properties' net operating income expectancies for the first year, the capitalization rate for the subject property should be applied to its anticipated net operating income for the first year of operation. *To capitalize prospective income from a subject property, an analyst should not rely solely on retrospective capitalization rates from comparable sales.*[3]

The net income to be capitalized may be estimated before or after an annual allowance for replacements is considered (e.g., the allowance for furniture, fixtures, and equipment for hotel properties and replacement reserves for office properties).[4] Again, it is imperative that the appraiser analyze comparable sales and derive their capitalization rates in the same manner used to analyze the subject property and capitalize its income.

The examples that follow illustrate the importance of deriving and applying rates consistently. In the first example, the replacement allowance for the subject property is estimated at $2,500. The overall rate indicated by comparable sales in which a replacement allowance was not deducted as an operating expense was 0.0850. In the second example, the replacement allowance is deducted as an operating expense, and the indicated overall rate becomes 0.0825. In the first calculation, the allowance is not included as an expense item to be deducted from effective gross income, so the net operating income here is $2,500 higher than in the second calculation. The valuation conclusions produced by the two calculations are identical.

---

3. For more information on prospective value estimates, see Statement on Appraisal Standards No. 4 in the Uniform Standards of Professional Appraisal Practice.
4. In some markets, practitioners no longer deduct a replacement allowance as an above-the-line item in direct capitalization. Whenever this expense item is implicit in the capitalization rate, however, it should be included in the estimated net operating income to which the capitalization rate is applied.

Before Deducting Allowance for Replacements

Net operating income	$ 85,000
Overall rate	0.0850
Capitalization: $85,000/0.0850	$1,000,000

After Deducting Allowance for Replacements

Net operating income	$ 82,500
Overall rate	0.0825
Capitalization: $82,500/0.0825	$1,000,000

This simple technique for estimating overall capitalization rates is preferred and will produce a reliable indication of value by the income capitalization approach if three conditions are met.

1. Income and expenses must be estimated on the same basis for the subject property and all comparable properties.

2. Market expectations concerning resale prices and holding periods must be similar for all the properties.

3. The financing terms and market conditions that affect the comparables must be similar to those affecting the subject property or an adjustment must be made for any dissimilarities.

Derivation from Effective Gross Income Multipliers

Sometimes an overall capitalization rate cannot be derived directly because the stringent data requirements cannot be met, but reliable transaction data and *gross* income data can be obtained from several comparable sales. In such cases an effective gross income multiplier can be derived and used in conjunction with a net income ratio (*NIR*) to produce an overall capitalization rate. (The derivation of income multipliers is discussed later in this chapter.)

The net income ratio is the ratio of net operating income to effective gross income. Although effective gross income multipliers can be based on annual or monthly income, annual income is used unless otherwise specified. Monthly income is primarily used for single-family or small multifamily residential properties. Frequently an appraiser can obtain marketwide averages of operating expense ratios as well as the effective gross income multipliers indicated by comparable sales. If a comparable is truly comparable to the subject, it is appropriate to use the subject's net income ratio and the comparable's effective gross income multiplier to develop the rate.

The formula for deriving an overall capitalization rate from a net income ratio, which is the complement of the operating expense ratio (*NIR* = 1 − *OER*) and an effective gross income multiplier is

$$R_O = \frac{1 - OER}{EGIM}$$

Returning to Table 22.1, consider Comparable A, which was recently sold for $368,500. Assume the property's potential gross income is $85,106 and its effective gross income is $80,000. The operating expense ratio of the property is 37.5%, so its operating expenses are $30,000. The effective gross income multiplier is 4.6063 ($368,500/$80,000) and the net income ratio is 0.6250 (1 - 0.375). The overall capitalization rate extracted from the effective gross income multiplier of Comparable A is

$$R_O = \frac{0.625}{4.6063}$$
$$= 0.1357$$

After this calculation is performed for all the comparables, an estimated overall capitalization rate can be reconciled from the overall capitalization rate indications derived. The effective gross income multiplier is supportable if the property is sufficiently comparable to allow the direct derivation of an overall rate.

Band of Investment—Mortgage and Equity Components

Because most properties are purchased with debt and equity capital, the overall capitalization rate must satisfy the market return requirements of both investment positions. Lenders must anticipate receiving a competitive interest rate commensurate with the perceived risk of the investment or they will not make funds available. Lenders generally require that the loan principal be repaid through periodic amortization payments.[5] Similarly, equity investors must anticipate receiving a competitive equity cash return commensurate with the perceived risk or they will invest their funds elsewhere.

The capitalization rate for debt is called the *mortgage constant* (R_M). It is the ratio of the annual debt service to the principal amount of the mortgage loan.[6] If the loan is paid off more frequently (e.g., with monthly payments), the mortgage constant is calculated by multiplying each period's payment by the frequency of payment and then dividing this amount by the amount of the loan. For example, the annual constant for a monthly payment loan is obtained by multiplying the monthly payment by 12 and dividing the result by the amount of the loan. Of course, the same result can be obtained by multiplying the ratio of monthly payments to the mortgage amount (i.e., the monthly constant) by 12. It should be noted that the mortgage constant (R_M) is different from the mortgage yield rate (Y_M). The mortgage yield rate is the discount rate that equates the present value of the mortgage payments with the principal borrowed.

The mortgage constant is a function of the interest rate, the frequency of amortization, and the amortization term of the loan. It is the sum of the interest rate and the sinking fund factor. When the loan terms are known, the mortgage constant can be found in financial tables. An appraiser must take care to use a table that corresponds to the

---

5. Commercial banks often provide developers with short-term or interim financing, i.e., bullet loans that have an amortization of less than 15 years. Insurers may have to roll over loans that cannot be refinanced by paying the interest only.
6. The term *mortgage constant* may be a misnomer. After a payment is made, the balance on the mortgage is reduced. The ratio of debt service to the mortgage balance changes with each payment.

frequency of amortization (e.g., monthly, quarterly, annually). In everyday practice, however, appraisers generally use calculators or computer software to perform such operations.

The equity investor also seeks a systematic cash return. The rate used to capitalize equity income is called the *equity capitalization rate* (R_E). It is the ratio of annual pre-tax cash flow to the amount of equity investment. This rate is *not* a rate of return on capital. The equity capitalization rate may be more or less than the eventual equity yield rate (Y_E). For appraisal purposes, a property's equity capitalization rate is the anticipated cash flow to the equity investor, usually for the first year of the holding period.

The overall capitalization rate must satisfy both the mortgage constant require-ment of the lender and the pre-tax cash flow requirement of the equity investor. It is a composite rate, weighted in proportion to the total property investment represented by debt and equity. The overall capitalization rate is a weighted average of the mortgage constant (R_M) and equity dividend rate (R_E). The loan-to-value ratio (M) represents the loan or debt portion of the property investment; the equity ratio (E) may be expressed as ($1 - M$) where the sum of E and M is 1, i.e., 100%. Typical mortgage terms and conditions may be obtained by surveying lenders active in the market area. Equity capitalization rates are derived from comparable sales by dividing the pre-tax cash flow of each sale by the equity investment. The equity capitalization rate used to capitalize the subject property's pre-tax cash flow ultimately depends on the appraiser's judgment as to how individual investors perceive the relationship between market value and investment value.

When the mortgage constant and equity capitalization rates are known, an overall rate may be derived with the band-of-investment, or weighted-average, technique using these formulas.

Mortgage component $\quad M \times R_M =$

Equity component $\quad\;\; E \times R_E = +$ _____

$\qquad\qquad\qquad\qquad\quad R_O =$

To illustrate how the overall capitalization rate is calculated with the band-of-investment technique, assume that the following characteristics describe the subject property.

Available loan	75% ratio, 10.0% interest, 25-year amortization period (monthly payment), 0.1090 mortgage constant (R_M)
Equity capitalization rate	12.0% (derived from comparable sales)

The overall rate is calculated as follows:

$$
\begin{aligned}
R_O &= (0.75 \times 0.1090) + (0.25 \times 0.1200) \\
&= 0.0818 + 0.0300 \\
&= 0.1118
\end{aligned}
$$

Although this technique can be used to derive overall capitalization rates, appraisers should be extremely careful when using it for this purpose. The technique is only applicable when sufficient market data are available to extract equity capitalization rates and pre-tax cash flows are the primary investment criteria used by buyers and sellers. A capitalization rate used to estimate market value should be justified and supported by market data, but such data often are not available. When survey and opinion data about equity capitalization rates, available loan terms, and loan-to-value ratios must be substituted for market data, mortgage-equity techniques may be more appropriately used to test capitalization rates than to develop them. The mortgage yield rate (Y_M) should not be used in place of the mortgage constant (R_M), nor should an equity yield rate (Y_E) be substituted for an equity capitalization rate (R_E). The equity yield rate is discussed in Chapter 23.

Band of Investment—Land and Building Components

A band-of-investment formula can also be applied to the physical components of property—i.e., the land or site and the buildings. Just as weighted rates are developed for mortgage and equity components in mortgage-equity analysis, weighted rates for the land and buildings can be developed if accurate rates for these components can be estimated independently and the proportion of total property value represented by each component can be identified. The formula is

$$R_O = L \text{ x } R_L + B \text{ x } R_B$$

where L = land value as a percentage of total property value, R_L = land capitalization rate, B = building value as a percentage of total property value, and R_B = building capitalization rate.

Assume that the land represents 45% of the value of a property and the building represents the other 55%. The land capitalization rate derived from comparable sales data is 0.1025; the building capitalization rate is 0.1600. The indicated R_O is calculated as follows:

$$
\begin{aligned}
R_O \ &= \ (0.45 \text{ x } 0.1025) + (0.55 \text{ x } 0.1600) \\
&= \ 0.0461 + 0.0880 \\
&= \ 0.1341
\end{aligned}
$$

Land and building capitalization rates may be extracted by applying residual analysis to improved properties. (Land and building residual techniques are illustrated later.)

Debt Coverage Formula

In addition to the traditional terms of lending (i.e., the interest rate, loan-to-value ratio, amortization term, maturity, and payment period), real estate lenders sometimes use another constraining factor—the debt coverage ratio (DCR). This is the ratio of net operating income to annual debt service (I_M), or the payment that covers interest on and retirement of the outstanding principal of the mortgage loan.

$$DCR \ = \ \frac{NOI}{I_M}$$

The debt coverage ratio is frequently used by institutional lenders, who are generally fiduciaries. They manage and lend the money of others, including depositors and policyholders. Because of their fiduciary responsibility, institutional lenders are particularly sensitive to the safety of loan investments, especially the safety of principal. They are concerned with safety and profit and are anxious to avoid default and possible foreclosure. Consequently, when they underwrite loans on income-producing property, institutional lenders try to provide a cushion so that the borrower will more likely be able to meet the debt service obligations on the loan even if building income declines. The debt coverage ratio increases every time a mortgage payment is made, which is good for the lender. The method should only be applied, however, if the property is at stabilized occupancy.

To estimate an overall rate, the debt coverage ratio can be multiplied by the mortgage constant and the loan-to-value ratio.[7] Lenders refer to overall capitalization rates derived by this method as *in-house capitalization rates*. The formula is

$$R_O = DCR \text{ x } R_M \text{ x } M$$

For a property with net operating income of $50,000 and annual debt service of $43,264, the debt coverage ratio is calculated as

$$DCR = \frac{\$50,000}{\$43,264}$$
$$= 1.1557$$

If R_M equals 0.1565 and M is 0.75, R_O is estimated as

$$R_O = 1.1557 \text{ x } 0.1565 \text{ x } 0.75$$
$$= 0.1357$$

With this method lenders can use market data to check on the reasonableness of capitalization rates derived from comparables.

Residual Techniques

Residual techniques allow an appraiser to capitalize the income allocated to an investment component of unknown value once all investment components of known value have been satisfied. The physical, or land and building, residual techniques and the financial, or mortgage and equity, residual techniques are the primary residual techniques used in direct capitalization. Residual techniques are based on a number of assumptions and their application is only justified if the assumptions can be reasonably made.

Regardless of which known and unknown, or residual, components of the property are being analyzed, the appraiser starts with the value of the known item(s) and the net operating income. The appraiser

1. Applies an appropriate capitalization rate to the value of the known component to derive the annual income needed to support the investment in that component
2. Deducts the annual income needed to support the investment in the known

---

7. See Ronald E. Gettel, "Good Grief, *Another* Method of Selecting Capitalization Rates?!" *The Appraisal Journal* (January 1978).

component from the net operating income to derive the residual income available to support the investment in the unknown component

3. Capitalizes the residual income at a capitalization rate appropriate to the investment in the residual component to derive the present value of this component

4. Adds the values of the known component and the residual component to derive a value indication for the total property

Building Residual Technique

An appraiser who applies the building residual technique assumes that land or site value can be estimated independently. The technique is especially applicable when data on land values and long-term land leases are available to establish land capitalization rates. The appraiser applies the land capitalization rate to the known land value to obtain the amount of annual net income needed to support the land value. Then this amount is deducted from the net operating income to derive the residual income available to support the investment in the building(s). The appraiser capitalizes this residual income at the building capitalization rate to derive an indication of the present value of the building(s). Finally, the land value and the building value are added to derive an indication of total property value. The land and building capitalization rates derived from the market are then applied to the subject property. Sample calculations are shown below.

Estimated land value		$200,000
Net operating income	$85,500	
Land value x R_L ($200,000 x 0.09)	-18,000	
Residual income to building	$67,500	
Building value (capitalized: $67,500/0.15)		+450,000
Indicated property value		$650,000

To apply the building residual technique, the appraiser must obtain information on present land value, current net operating income, and land and building capitalization rates. This technique is simple, but its applicability and usefulness are extremely limited. Applicability is premised on the following assumptions regarding changes in the components of property value: 1) the value of the land will remain constant; 2) income will steadily decline; and 3) the value of the building and the value of the total property will decline in equal increments annually. The assumption that value and income will decline steadily is often inconsistent with market behavior.[8]

When the required data are available, the building residual technique can be used to value properties with improvements that have suffered substantial accrued depreciation. In fact, current reproduction or replacement cost minus the present value of the improvements provides an estimate of total accrued depreciation. In addition, the building residual technique directly measures the contribution of the improvements to total property value, so it can help an appraiser determine when demolition or major

---

8. The building residual technique does not necessarily reflect the way purchaser-investors regard investment real estate. It is also extremely difficult to apply when the income projection is less than the remaining economic life of the improvements, and the reversion consequently represents more than simply the value of the site. See William Kinnard, *Income Property Valuation: Principles and Techniques of Appraising Income-Producing Real Estate* (Lexington, Mass: Heath Lexington Books, 1971), 246.

renovation of property improvements is economically feasible or, if appropriate, help establish the tax basis for depreciation of the improvements.

Land Residual Technique

The land residual technique assumes that the value of the building(s) can be estimated separately. In land residual applications, an appraiser will often consider a new highest and best use assuming a building that does not exist. Thus, building value is usually estimated as the current cost to construct a new building that represents the highest and best use of the land or site.

The building capitalization rate is applied to the building value to obtain the amount of annual net income needed to support the value of the building. This amount is then deducted from net operating income to indicate the residual income available to support the investment in the land. The residual income is capitalized at the land capitalization rate to derive an indication of the value of the land. Finally, the building value is added to the land value to derive a total property value indication. As in the building residual technique, the land and building capitalization rates derived from the market are applied to the subject property. Sample calculations are shown below.

Estimated building value		$450,000
Net operating income	$85,500	
Building value x R_B ($450,000 x 0.15)	-67,500	
Residual income to land	$18,000	
Land value (capitalized: $18,000/0.09)		+200,000
Indicated property value		$650,000

The land residual technique allows an appraiser to estimate land values when recent data on land sales are not available. The technique can be applied to proposed construction to test the highest and best use of the land or site or to new structures that do not suffer from accrued depreciation. However, the land residual technique is not applicable when the cost to produce a new building is inconsistent with the amount of value such a building would contribute to property value.

Equity Residual Technique

To apply the equity residual technique, an appraiser deducts annual debt service from net operating income to obtain the residual income for the equity interest. An appraiser who uses this technique assumes that mortgage loan terms can be obtained from the market and that the dollar amount of the debt can be estimated. The residual equity income is then capitalized into value with a market-derived equity capitalization rate as shown below. This technique is especially useful for appraising the fee simple interest in a newly constructed property or the equity interest in a property subject to a specific mortgage.

Mortgage amount		$375,000
Mortgage interest rate	10.0%	
Mortgage amortization term	25 yrs.	

Monthly amortization payment
   ($375,000 x 0.0090870) $3,408

Net operating income		$ 60,000
Mortgage x R_M ($375,000 x 0.10904)		-40,890
Residual income to equity		$ 19,110
Equity value		
(capitalized: $19,110/0.09)		+212,333
Indicated property value		$587,333

Mortgage Residual Technique

When the mortgage residual technique is applied, the amount of available equity is the known component and the mortgage amount or value is unknown. The income needed to satisfy the equity component at the equity capitalization rate is deducted from the net operating income to obtain the residual income to the mortgage component. The residual mortgage income is then capitalized into value at the mortgage capitalization rate. Sample calculations are demonstrated below.

Available equity		$140,000
Net operating income	$60,000	
Equity x R_E ($140,000 x 0.09)	-12,600	
Residual income to mortgage	$47,400	
Mortgage value		
(capitalized: $47,400/0.1264)		+375,000
Indicated property value		$515,000

The mortgage residual technique assumes that the amount of funds the equity investor is willing to invest in the property has already been determined and that he or she requires a specified equity dividend rate from the property. This implies that the loan amount depends on the residual cash flow available for mortgage debt service and the mortgage constant.

As with any capitalization method, residual techniques should only be used to estimate market value when they reflect market behavior. The importance of this point is especially apparent in the case of the mortgage residual technique because lenders are generally unwilling to make a loan unless net operating income exceeds the mortgage debt service by a specified amount. Thus, the mortgage amount implied may not reflect the behavior of lenders.

It should also be noted that once the loan is made, the lender has the legal right to receive the agreed-upon debt service. Any residual cash flow goes to the equity investor. Thus, the mortgage residual technique would not normally be appropriate for estimating the value of a property subject to a specific mortgage.

Gross Income Multipliers

Gross income multipliers are used to compare the income-producing characteristics of properties. A potential or effective gross income stream may be converted into a lump-sum capital value by applying the relevant gross income multiplier. This method of capitalization is mathematically related to direct capitalization since rates are the reciprocals of multipliers or factors (e.g., an overall capitalization rate is the reciprocal of a net income multiplier). Therefore, it is appropriate to discuss the derivation and use of multipliers under direct capitalization.

To derive a gross income multiplier from market data, sales of properties that were rented at the time of sale or were anticipated to be rented within a short time must be available. The ratio of the sale price of a property to its annual gross income *at the time of sale* or projected over the first year of ownership is the gross income multiplier.

Appraisers who attempt to derive and apply gross income multipliers for valuation purposes must be careful for several reasons. First, the properties analyzed must be comparable to the subject property and to one another in terms of physical, locational, and investment characteristics. Properties with similar or even identical multipliers can have very different operating expense ratios and, therefore, not be comparable for valuation purposes.

Second, the term *gross income multiplier* is used because some of the gross income from a property or type of property may come from sources other than rental. A *gross rent multiplier* applies to rental income only.

Third, the appraiser must use similar income data to derive the multiplier for each transaction. The sale price can be divided by either the potential or effective gross income, but the data and measure must be used consistently throughout the analysis to produce reliable results. Different income measures may be used in different valuation studies and appraisals, however. The income measure selected is dictated by the availability of market data and the purpose of the analysis.

To illustrate the difference between different gross income multipliers, the following calculations are made using data from Comparable A, which were presented in Table 22.1 and the subsequent discussion.

$$\text{Potential gross income multiplier} = \frac{\text{sale price}}{\text{potential gross income}}$$

$$= \frac{\$368,500}{\$85,106}$$

$$= 4.3299^*$$

$$\text{Effective gross income multiplier} = \frac{\text{sale price}}{\text{effective gross income}}$$

$$= \frac{\$368,500}{\$80,000}$$

$$= 4.6063^*$$

* In actual practice, multipliers are typically rounded to one or two decimal places.

After the gross income multiplier is derived from comparable market data, it must be applied on the same basis it was derived. In other words, an income multiplier based on effective gross income can only be applied to the effective gross income of the subject property; an income multiplier based on potential gross income can only be applied to the potential gross income of the subject property. The timing of income also must be comparable. If sales are analyzed using next year's income expectation, the multiplier derived must be applied to next year's income expectation for the subject property.

Key Concepts

- Direct capitalization is used to convert an estimate of a single year's income expectancy into an indication of value in one step, either by dividing the income estimate by an appropriate rate or multiplying it by an appropriate factor. Direct capitalization does not distinguish between the return on and return of capital.

- The two formulas basic to direct capitalization are:

  Value = income/ rate   Income multiplier = 1/rate.

- Various income flows may be analyzed in direct capitalization, e.g., net operating income, equity income, mortgage income, land income, building income, income to the leased fee, and income to the leasehold. The appropriate capitalization rate is applied to the income flow: R_O is used with NOI; R_E with equity income; R_M with mortgage income; R_L with land income; R_B with building income; R_{LF} with income to the leased fee; and R_{LH} with income to the leasehold.

- Potential gross income, effective gross income, and gross rent may be capitalized by applying the appropriate income factor, i.e., potential gross income multiplier ($PGIM$), effective gross income multiplier ($EGIM$), or gross rent multiplier (GRM).

- Overall capitalization rates may be derived from comparable sales, effective gross income multipliers and operating expense ratios, band-of-investment or weighted-average techniques (based on mortgage and equity components with R_M and R_E or land and building components with R_L and R_B), and debt coverage ratios (DCRs).

- Residual techniques allow an appraiser to capitalize the income allocated to an investment component of unknown value after other investment components of known value have been satisfied. They can be applied to the physical components of a property (land and building) or the financial components of a property (mortgage and equity). Residual techniques are based on specific assumptions. If these assumptions are unreasonable, application of the residual technique is not justified. The usefulness of the building residual and mortgage residual techniques is extremely limited.

- The application of income multipliers is also a direct capitalization procedure. In developing an income or rent multiplier, it is essential that the income or rent of the properties used to derive the multiplier are comparable to that of the subject and that the specific multiplier derived be applied to the same income base.

Terms

band of investment

building capitalization rate (R_B)

building residual technique

debt coverage ratio (DCR or

   NOI/I_M)

debt service (I_M)

direct capitalization

effective gross income

effective gross income multiplier

   ($EGIM$)

equity capitalization rate (R_E)

equity ratio (1-*M*)
equity residual technique
gross income
gross income multiplier (*GIM*)
gross rent
gross rent multiplier (*GRM*)
land capitalization rate (R_L)
land residual technique
land value-to-building value ratio
loan-to-value ratio (*M*)
mortgage constant (R_M)
mortgage residual technique
net income ratio (*NIR*)
   (*NOI/EGI* or 1-*OER*)

net operating income (*NOI*)
operating expense ratio (*OER*)
   (1 - *NIR*)
overall capitalization rate (R_O)
potential gross income
potential gross income multiplier
   (*PGIM*)
pre-tax cash flow
replacement allowance
residual technique
weighted average

CHAPTER TWENTY-THREE

Yield Capitalization— Theory and Basic Applications

Yield capitalization is used to convert future benefits into present value by applying an appropriate yield rate. To select an appropriate yield rate for a market value appraisal, an appraiser analyzes market evidence of the yields anticipated by typical investors. When investment value is sought, the yield rate used should reflect the individual investor's requirements, which may differ from the requirements typical of investors in the market.

To perform yield capitalization, an appraiser 1) selects an appropriate holding period; 2) forecasts all future cash flows or cash flow patterns; 3) chooses an appropriate yield, or discount, rate; and 4) converts future benefits into present value by discounting each annual future benefit or by developing an overall rate that reflects the income pattern, value change, and yield rate. The application of capitalization rates that reflect an appropriate yield rate, the use of present value factors, and discounted cash flow analysis are all yield capitalization procedures. Mortgage-equity formulas and yield rate or value change formulas may be used to derive overall capitalization rates. Like direct capitalization, yield capitalization may also employ residual techniques.

To apply the discounting procedure, the appraiser must be familiar with income patterns, capital return concepts, the mathematics of discounting, investor requirements or assumptions (i.e., holding period, anticipated market growth, and inflation), and the appropriateness of discount rates. Yield capitalization may be appropriate when direct capitalization cannot be applied because the property data available do not describe sufficiently comparable properties.

The Nature of Annuities

Although the word *annuity* means an annual income, it is used to refer to a program or contract specifying regular payments of stipulated amounts. Payments need not be annual, but the interval between payments must be regular. An annuity can be level, increasing, or decreasing, but the amounts must be scheduled and predictable. Income characterized as an annuity is expected at regular intervals and in predictable amounts. Obviously real estate income or rental income can have the characteristics of an annuity. Monthly mortgage payments are perhaps the best example of an annuity.

The pattern of income expected from a real estate investment may be regular or irregular. Various capitalization techniques can be applied to different patterns of income streams.

Discounting

Periodic income and reversions are converted into present value through discounting, a procedure based on the assumption that benefits received in the future are worth less than the same benefits received today. The return on an investment compensates the investor for foregoing present benefits (i.e., the immediate use of capital) and accepting future benefits and risks. This return is usually called *interest* by lenders and *yield* by equity investors. The discounting procedure includes the assumption that the return of capital will be accomplished through periodic income, the reversion, or a combination of the two.

An investor seeks a total return that exceeds the amount invested. The present value of a prospective benefit must be less than its expected future value. A future payment is discounted to present value by calculating the amount that, if invested today, would grow with compound interest at a satisfactory rate to equal the future payment. In other words, discounting is the reciprocal of the growth of compound interest. The standard formula for discounting future value to present value is

$$\text{Present value} = \frac{\text{Future value}}{(1 + i)^n}$$

where i is the rate of return on capital per period that will satisfy the investor and n is the number of periods that the payment will be deferred.[1] The two examples that follow illustrate applications of the discounting formula.

Problem 1. *What is the present value of $115 due one year hence discounted at 15% per year?* To solve this problem, the amount that should be invested now to grow to $115 with compound interest at the rate of 15% per year must be calculated.

$$\text{Present value} = \$115/1.15^1 = \$100$$

Problem 2. *What is the present value of $1,000 due in three years discounted at 10% per year?* This problem can be solved by calculating the amount that should be invested now to grow to $1,000 in three years with compound interest at 10% per year.

$$\text{Present value} = \$1,000/1.10^3 = \$751.31$$

If a series of future payments is expected, each payment is discounted with the standard formula, and the present value of the payments is the sum of all the present values. This standard discounting procedure is the foundation for all yield capitalization techniques.

The amount deposited or received can be in the form of a single lump sum, a series of periodic installments such as rental income, or a combination of both. When amounts are compounded or discounted, the rate used is the effective interest rate; on an annual basis, this rate is identical to the *nominal interest rate*. If amounts are compounded or discounted more often than annually (e.g., semiannually or monthly), the nominal

---

1. To calculate the accrual of interest (compounding), the periodic payment needed to amortize a loan, or the present value of future income (discounting), the financial professions make use of six compound interest factors known as the *six functions of $1*. The formula used to calculate the *present value of $1* is the fourth function of $1 ($1/S^n$), which is the reciprocal of the first function of $1 ($S^n$) or *future value of $1*. For formulas, tables, and sample applications of the financial functions, see Appendix C.

interest rate is divided by the number of compounding or discounting periods. For example, a nominal rate of 12% is an effective rate of 6% for semiannual conversion periods, or an effective rate of 1% for monthly conversions. Standard tables of factors or preprogrammed financial calculators can be used to facilitate the application of factors, but the user must select the appropriate conversion frequency (i.e., monthly, quarterly, or annually).

Each precomputed factor and yield capitalization formula has specific, built-in investment assumptions that are implied when the table is used or the factor is calculated. Therefore, the appraiser must identify the assumptions applicable to the subject property and use the factor table and capitalization formula that correspond to these assumptions. Thus, to apply compounding or discounting procedures, the appraiser must know the basic formulas, how the various factors relate to one another, and how they may be used or combined to simplify income capitalization.

Tables and factors allow appraisers to solve many arithmetic problems that are fundamental to the valuation process, thus they are useful in applying capitalization techniques. However, in the final analysis, a value estimate reflects the appraiser's judgment based on appropriate research of the subject property and the market.

Discounted Cash Flow Analysis

Discounted cash flow (DCF) analysis can be used both to estimate present value and to extract a discount rate from a comparable sale. In DCF analysis the quantity, variability, timing, and duration of cash flows are specified. *Cash flow* refers to the periodic income attributable to the interests in real property. Each cash flow is discounted to present value and all the present values are totaled to obtain the value of the real property interest being appraised. The future value of that interest, the reversion, is forecast at the end of the projection period (i.e., the holding period or remaining economic life) and is also discounted. The cash flows discounted with the DCF formula may be the net operating income to the entire property or the cash flows to specific interests—e.g., the (pre-tax) cash flows to the equity interest (equity dividends) or debt service for the mortgage interest.

The DCF formula is a yield formula expressed as

$$PV = \frac{CF_1}{1+Y} + \frac{CF_2}{(1+Y)^2} + \frac{CF_3}{(1+Y)^3} + \ldots + \frac{CF^n}{(1+Y)^n}$$

where PV = present value; CF = the cash flow for the period specified; Y = the appropriate periodic yield, or discount, rate; and n = the number of periods in the projection.[2]

With the DCF formula an appraiser can discount each payment of income separately and add all the present values together to obtain the net present value of the property interest being appraised. The formula treats the reversion as a cash flow that can be valued separately from the income stream. The formula can be used to estimate

---

2. The above formula represents the comprehensive equation that describes the mathematical operations performed to discount a series of cash flows. The discounting of forecast cash flows, however, is not generally done by means of this equation. Instead, practitioners rely on discounting factors and calculators into which these factors are programmed.

total property value (V_O), loan value (V_M), equity value (V_E), leased fee value (V_{LF}), leasehold value (V_{LH}), or any other interest in real property.

When a series of periodic incomes varies in an irregular pattern, the basic DCF formula is used in its analysis and valuation. Any series of periodic incomes, with or without a reversion, can be valued with the basic formula. Formulas for valuing level annuities and increasing and decreasing annuities, which are introduced later in this chapter, are merely shortcuts to be used in these special situations.

Estimation of a Yield Rate for Discounting

The estimation of a yield rate is critical to DCF analysis. To select an appropriate rate an appraiser must verify and interpret the attitudes and expectations of market participants, including buyers, sellers, advisers, and brokers. Although the actual yield on an investment cannot be calculated until the investment is sold, an investor may set a target yield for the investment before or during ownership. Historical yield rates derived from comparable sales may be relevant, but they reflect past, not future, benefits in the mind of the investor and may not be reliable indicators of current yield. Therefore, the estimation of yield rates for discounting cash flows should focus on the prospective or forecast yield rates anticipated by typical buyers and sellers of comparable investments. An appraiser can verify investor assumptions directly, by interviewing the parties to comparable sales transactions, or indirectly, by estimating the income expectancy and likely reversion for a comparable property and deriving a prospective yield rate.

The appraiser narrows the range of indicated yield rates and selects an appropriate rate by comparing the physical, economic, financial, and risk characteristics of the comparable properties with the property being appraised and assessing the competition for capital in other financial markets. In some situations there may be reason to select a yield rate above or below the indicated range. The final estimation of a yield rate requires judgment, just as an the appraiser uses judgment to select an overall rate or equity capitalization rate from the range indicated by comparable sales. In selecting a yield rate, the appraiser should analyze current conditions in capital and real estate markets and the actions, perceptions, and expectations of real estate investors.

Different Rates

Yield rates are primarily a function of perceived risks. Different portions of forecast future income may have different levels of risk and, therefore, different yield rates.[3] In lease valuation, for example, one rate might be applied to discount the series of net rental incomes stipulated in the lease and a different rate might be applied to discount the reversion. One rate reflects the creditworthiness of the tenant as well as the benefits, constraints, and limitations of the lease contract, while the other is subject to free, open-market conditions. The decision to apply a single yield rate to all benefits or to apply different rates to different benefits should be based on investors' actions in the market. It

---

3. When future events that could profoundly impact the income-producing potential of a property may or may not occur, probability analysis may be appropriate. Probability analysis is frequently required when properties are subject to potential environmental hazards and compliance with environmental regulations is pending. For example, a site may require an undetermined level of environmental remediation; such remediation may or may not be completed within a given time frame; or the environmental regulation(s) governing such remediation may be modified. In such situations, probability analysis can assist an appraiser in developing a yield rate. See Chapter 27.

may be prudent for an appraiser to check a bond rating service such as Moody's for the specific rating of the company leasing a property. Typically, long-term leases are underwritten on this basis.

Income Stream Patterns

After specifying the amount, timing, and duration of the cash flows to the property interest being appraised, the appraiser should identify the pattern that the income stream is expected to follow during the projection period. These patterns may be grouped into the following basic categories—variable annuity, level annuity, and increasing or decreasing annuity.

Variable Annuity: Nonsystematic Change

A variable annuity is an income stream in which payment amounts may vary each period. To value a variable annuity, the present value of each income payment is calculated separately and these values are totaled to obtain the present value of the entire income stream. This procedure is discounted cash flow analysis.

     Any income stream can be valued as if it were a variable annuity. Level annuities and annuities that change systematically are special cases which can also be handled with special formulas that reflect the systematic pattern of the income stream. These shortcut formulas can save time and effort in certain cases, but valuing an income stream as a variable annuity with a calculator or computer program may be just as easy.

Level Annuity

A level annuity is an income stream in which the amount of each payment is the same; it is a level, unchanging flow of income over time. The payments in a level annuity are equally spaced and regularly scheduled. There are two types of level annuities: ordinary annuities and annuities payable in advance.

Ordinary Annuity

An ordinary annuity, which is the most common type of level annuity, is distinguished by income payments that are received at the *end* of each period. Standard fixed-payment mortgage loans, many corporate and government bonds, endowment policies, and certain lease arrangements are ordinary annuities.

Annuity Payable in Advance

An annuity payable in advance is a level annuity in which the payments are received at the *beginning* of each period. A lease that requires payments at the beginning of each month creates an annuity payable in advance.

Increasing or Decreasing Annuity

An income stream that is expected to change in a systematic pattern is either an increasing annuity or a decreasing annuity. Three basic patterns of systematic change are reflected in 1) step-up and step-down annuities, 2) straight-line (constant-amount) change per period annuities, and 3) exponential-curve (constant-ratio) change per period annuities.

Step-Up and Step-Down Annuities

A step-up or step-down annuity is usually created by a lease contract that calls for a succession of level annuities of different amounts to be paid in different periods of the lease term. For example, a lease might call for monthly payments of $500 for the first three years, $750 for the next four years, and $1,200 for the next six years. Over the 13-year term of the lease, there are three successive level annuities—one for three years, one for four years, and one for six years.

Straight-Line (Constant-Amount) Change per Period Annuity

An income stream that increases or decreases by a fixed amount each period fits the pattern of a straight-line (constant-amount) change per period annuity. These income streams are also called *straight-line increasing* or *straight-line decreasing annuities*. For example, a property may have an estimated first-year net operating income of $100,000 that is forecast to increase by $7,000 per year. Thus, the second year's net operating income will be $107,000, the third year's net operating income will be $114,000, and so forth. Similarly, the income stream of a straight-line decreasing annuity is expected to decrease by a constant amount each period.

Exponential-Curve (Constant-Ratio) Change per Period Annuity

An income stream with an exponential-curve (constant-ratio) change per period is also referred to as an *exponential annuity*. This type of income stream increases or decreases at a constant ratio and, therefore, the increases or decreases are compounded. For example, a property with an estimated first-year pre-tax cash flow of $100,000 that is forecast to increase 7% per year over each preceding year's cash flow will have a pre-tax cash flow in the second year of $107,000 ($100,000 x 1.07). However, the third year's pre-tax cash flow will be $114,490 ($107,000 x 1.07) and the fourth year's cash flow will be $122,504 ($114,490 x 1.07).

Reversion

As mentioned previously, income-producing properties typically provide two types of financial benefits—periodic income and the future value obtained from sale of the property or reversion of the property interest at the end of the holding period. The length of the holding period usually may be determined by reviewing the property's lease expiration date(s). The length of the holding period and the discount rate are interactive. Generally, the longer the holding period, the greater the risk and the higher the discount rate. This future cash flow is called a *reversion* because it represents the anticipated return of a capital sum at the end of the investment.

A single property may include one or more property interests that have their own streams of periodic benefits and reversions. For example, a property may have an equity interest with pre-tax cash flow, or equity dividend, as the periodic benefit and the equity reversion (i.e., property reversion minus the mortgage balance at loan maturity or property resale) as the reversionary benefit. The same property could have a mortgage with debt service as the periodic benefit and the mortgage balance (called a *balloon payment*) as the reversionary interest. A single property also comprises both building and land components. In situations involving long-term ground leases where the objective is to value the leasehold estate in the building, annual ground rent should be deducted before capitalizing *NOI*. Table 23.1 shows several possible investment positions in an income-producing property and identifies the income streams and reversions associated with each interest.

Table 23.1	Summary of Incomes and Reversions Associated with Various Real Property Interests in Income-Producing Property

Real Property Interest	Income	Reversion
Fee simple	Net operating income	Net proceeds of resale
Mortgagee (lender's position)	Mortgage debt service	Balance if paid prior to maturity, or balloon payment if paid at maturity
Equity	Cash flow (equity dividend)	Net equity proceeds of resale
Leased fee	Net operating income based on contract rents	Property reversion or net proceeds of resale of leased fee estate
Leasehold	Rental advantage when contract rent is below market rent; rental disadvantage when contract rent is above market rent	None if held to end of lease or net proceeds of resale of leasehold estate

The reversion is often a major portion of the total benefit to be received from an investment in income-producing property. If the investor's capital is not recaptured through some combination of cash flow and reversion proceeds, the effective rate of return *on* the investment will always be negative or zero. For certain investments, *all* capital recapture is accomplished through the reversion, indicating higher risk; for other investment properties, part of the recapture is provided by the reversion and part is provided by the investment's income stream. For those properties in which the net present value of the reversion exceeds the net present value of the income stream, a higher discount rate should be applied to reflect the additional risk associated with the investment.

To judge how much of the return of an investment will be provided by the reversion, an appraiser acknowledges that three general situations could result from the original investment. First, the property may increase in value over the holding period. Second, the property's value may not change—i.e., the value of the property at the end of the holding period or remaining economic life may be equal to its value at the beginning of the period. Third, the property may decline in value over the period being analyzed. Because these possible outcomes affect the potential yield of the investment and the amount of income considered acceptable, the appraiser must ascertain market expectations as to the change, if any, that will occur in the original investment or the property value over the holding period. (For leveraged investments, equity build-up may also occur through periodic debt service payments that include amortization.)

When a property is expected to be sold, the appraiser projects the reversion amount as the net proceeds of resale. The term *net proceeds of resale* refers to the net difference between the transaction price and the selling expenses, which may include brokerage commissions, legal fees, closing costs, transfer taxes, and possibly penalties for the prepayment of debt. The costs of repairs, capital improvements, and environmental remediation may also have to be deducted from the transaction price if such costs are incurred by the purchaser.

An appraiser establishes the likely value of the reversion in light of the expectations of investors in the market for the type of property being appraised. The appraiser may ask: Do investors expect a change in the value of this type of property in this particular locale? By how much will values change and in which direction? The appraiser analyzes and interprets the market and estimates the value of the future reversion based on the direction and the amount or percentage of change that investors expect. The use of personal computers and software to perform lease-by-lease analysis allows appraisers to make more accurate forecasts of future cash flows, which are the basis for the reversion estimate.

Discounting Models

The present value of any pattern of increasing, level, or decreasing income or of any irregular income can be calculated with DCF analysis. Specific valuation models, or formulas, categorized as either income models or property models have been developed for application to corresponding patterns of projected benefits. Income models are based on fewer assumptions than DCF analysis and require fewer data inputs. When these models fit investor thinking, they may be applied as shortcuts in place of more detailed DCF analysis.

Income models can be applied only to a stream of income including a reversion. The present value of an expected reversion or any other benefit not already included in the income stream must be added to obtain the investment's total present value. When a property model is used, an income stream and a reversion are valued in one operation. Other present value models employ mortgage-equity concepts and discounted cash flow analysis; these are discussed in Chapter 24.

Income Models

Valuation models can be applied to the following patterns of income: variable or irregular income, level income, straight-line (constant-amount) change per period income, and exponential-curve (constant-ratio) change per period income.

Variable or Irregular Income

As mentioned previously, the present value of an uneven stream of income is the sum of the discounted benefits treated as a series of separate payments or reversions. This model simply totals all present values using the standard discounting formula. The routine can be applied as a property valuation model as well as an income valuation model because it can be adapted to include the final reversion as part of the final cash flow expected at the end of the last, or nth, period.

Level Income

When a lease provides for a level stream of income or when income can be projected at a stabilized level, one or more capitalization procedures may be appropriate depending on the investor's assumptions with respect to capital recovery. Capitalization can be accomplished using capitalization in perpetuity, the Inwood premise, or the Hoskold premise.

Capitalization in perpetuity. Capitalization in perpetuity can be considered a property valuation model or an income valuation model. If, for example, a property is expected to generate level net operating income for a finite period of time and then be resold for the original purchase price, the property could be valued with capitalization in perpetuity simply by dividing the expected periodic income by an appropriate discount rate. In this model the discount rate and the overall capitalization rate are the same because the original investment is presumed to be recovered at the termination of the investment.

The Inwood premise. The Inwood premise applies to income that is an ordinary level annuity. It holds that the present value of a stream of income is based on a single discount rate. Each installment of income is discounted with a single discount rate, and the total discounted values of the installments are accumulated to obtain the present value of the income stream. The present value of a series of $1 payments can be found in compound interest tables for a given rate and a given period of time. It is assumed that the income will be sufficient to return all investment capital to the investor and to pay the specified return on the investment.

In most mortgages the amount of interest declines gradually over the holding period and is calculated as a specified percentage of the unrecaptured capital. Any excess over the required interest payment is considered a return of capital and reduces the amount of capital remaining in the investment. Because the installments are always the same amount, the principal portion of the payments increases by the same amounts that the interest portion of the payments decreases. It is also valid, but not customary, to see the interest payments as constant, always amounting to the specified return on the original investment, with any excess over the required, fixed-interest payments credited to a hypothetical sinking fund that grows with interest at the same rate to repay the original investment.

An Inwood capitalization rate can be constructed by adding the interest rate to a sinking fund factor $(1/S_{\overline{n}|})$ that is based on the same interest rate and duration as the income stream.[4]

---

4. A sinking fund factor is used to calculate the amount per period that will grow, with compound interest, to $1. The *sinking fund factor* $(1/S_{\overline{n}|})$ is the third function of $1 and the reciprocal of the second function of $1, the *future value of $1 per period*, which is also known as the *sinking fund accumulation factor*.

The resulting capitalization rate is simply the reciprocal of the ordinary level annuity (present value of $1 per period) factor found in financial tables. Thus, the Inwood premise is consistent with the use of compound interest tables to calculate the present value of the income stream.

The Inwood premise applies only to a level stream of income. Therefore, the present value of any expected reversion or other benefit not included in the income stream must be added to obtain the total present value of the investment. For example, assume that the *NOI* of a property is $10,000 per year for five years. What is the value of the property assuming an overall yield rate (Y_O) of 10% under the Inwood premise?

Solution 1

Apply the *PV* of $1 per period (ordinary level annuity) factor to the *NOI*:

$$3.79079 \times \$10,000 = \$37,908 \text{ (rounded)}$$

Solution 2

Use the general yield capitalization formula[5] for a level income with a percentage change in value:

$$R_O = Y_O - \Delta_O \, 1/S_{\overline{n}|}$$

Because there is no reversion, the property will lose 100% of its value. Δ_O is thus -1.0 and the yield capitalization formula becomes:

$$R_O = Y_O + 1/S_{\overline{n}|}$$

This equation represents the Inwood premise. By substituting the data given in the example, we may arrive at R_O:

$$R_O = 0.10 + 0.163797$$
$$R_O = 0.263797$$

The value of the property may be estimated using the basic valuation formula.

$$V_O = NOI/R_O$$
$$= \$10,000/0.263797$$
$$= \$37,908 \text{ (rounded)}$$

Note that the sinking fund factor ($1/S_{\overline{n}|}$) is based on a 10% discount rate, which implies that a portion of the *NOI* could be reinvested at 10% to replace the investment. It can be said that Y_O represents the return *on* capital and $1/S_{\overline{n}|}$ represents the return *of* capital.

The Inwood premise assumes a constant rate of return on capital each year with the return of capital being reinvested in a sinking fund at the same yield rate as Y_O. The amount accumulated in this sinking fund can be used to replace the asset at the end of its economic life. Using the assumptions applied in the preceding example, the *NOI* for the first year may be allocated as follows:

NOI	$10,000.00
Return on capital (10% of $37,908)	$ 3,790.80
Return of capital	$ 6,209.20

---

5. The general yield capitalization formula, which is discussed in the subsequent section on property models, appears in the modified notation: $R = Y - \Delta a$ where R is the capitalization rate, Y is the yield rate, Δ is the total relative change in income and value, and a is the annualizer, which under the Inwood premise is a sinking fund factor.

If the return of capital ($6,209.20) is placed in a sinking fund earning 10%, the fund will accumulate to $37,908 over five years. The sinking fund accumulation factor (future value of $1 per period),[6] $S_{\overline{n}|}$, is applied to the return of capital: $6.1051 \times \$6,209.20 = \$37,908$. This is the exact amount required to replace the asset.

The Hoskold premise. The Hoskold premise differs from the Inwood premise in that it employs two separate interest rates: a speculative rate, representing a fair rate of return on capital commensurate with the risks involved, and a safe rate for a sinking fund, designed to return all the invested capital to the investor in a lump sum at the termination of the investment.

In contrast to the Inwood premise, the Hoskold premise assumes that the portion of NOI needed to recover or replace capital (the return of capital) is reinvested at a "safe rate" (e.g., the prevailing rate for insured savings accounts or government bonds), which is lower than the "speculative" yield rate (Y_O) used to value the other portion of NOI. Like the Inwood premise, the Hoskold technique was designed to be applied when the asset value of the investment decreases to zero over the holding period. However, Hoskold assumed that funds would have to be set aside at a lower, safe rate to replace the asset at the end of the holding period. Hoskold suggested that this technique might be appropriate for valuing wasting assets such as a mine where the value is reduced to zero as minerals are extracted; thus funds have to be set aside to invest in a new mine once the minerals are totally depleted (the reversion equals zero).

Using the same NOI, yield, and term set forth in the previous example, assume that a portion of NOI has to be set aside at a 5% safe rate to allow for the recovery of capital at the end of every five years. All other assumptions remain the same. This problem may be solved with the same yield capitalization formula applied in the Inwood calculation, but the sinking fund factor $(1/S_{\overline{n}|})$ is based on the safe rate of 5% rather than the yield rate of 10%. Thus, the overall rate is calculated as follows:

$$R_O = Y_O + 1/S_{\overline{n}|}$$
$$= 0.10 + 0.180975$$
$$= 0.280975$$

Because the sinking fund factor $(1/S_{\overline{n}|})$ is calculated at a 5% rate rather than the 10% rate, the capitalization rate is higher and the value is lower. The value is calculated as:

$$V_O = NOI/R_O$$
$$= \$10,000/0.280975$$
$$= \$35,590 \text{ (rounded)}$$

The lower value is a result of setting aside the portion of NOI earning 5% to allow for the recovery of capital ($35,590) at the end of five years. The income allocation for the first year can be shown as follows:

NOI	$10,000
Return on capital (10% of $35,590)	3,559
Return of capital	$ 6,441

---

6. The *sinking fund accumulation factor,* also known as the *future value of $1 per period factor,* is the second function of $1.

To find the future value of $6,441 at 5% for five years, apply the sinking fund accumulation factor (future value of $1 per period), $S_{\overline{n}|}$, to the return of capital: 5.525631 x $6,441.00 = $35,590. The result is the exact amount required to recover the capital invested.

The Hoskold premise has become less popular and rarely reflects the thinking of real estate investors. It is now considered appropriate only for certain types of investments, e.g., in calculating the replacement reserves for leasing equipment or personal property. A Hoskold capitalization rate can be easily constructed by adding the speculative rate to the sinking fund factor for the safe rate, e.g., the prevailing rate for insured savings accounts or government bonds.

Straight-Line (Constant-Amount) Change per Period in Income

When income is expected to increase or decrease by a fixed amount per period, the periodic income over time can be graphically portrayed as a straight line. Hence the term *straight-line* is used to describe this type of income pattern.

The formula for valuing straight-line income patterns[7] should not be confused with direct capitalization with straight-line recapture. Although direct capitalization with straight-line recapture may be seen as a model for valuing a particular income stream, the procedure can also be applied to properties in which the expected change in value is commensurate with the expected change in income. Therefore, direct capitalization with straight-line recapture and related concepts are discussed with property models later in this chapter. Again, the formula applies to income streams only. Special tables of present value factors based on the formula are available.[8]

Exponential-Curve (Constant-Ratio) Change per Period in Income

In the absence of lease-by-lease analysis, sometimes the best way to reflect market expectations is to project income to change at a constant rate. In soft markets, no growth or slowly accelerating rates of growth are often projected for the first few years of cash flow. In active markets, more rapidly accelerating rates of growth may be projected for the first few years of cash flow. Portrayed graphically, this type of income stream follows an exponential curve[9] rather than a straight line.

---

7. To obtain the present value of an annuity that has a starting income of d at the end of the first period and increases h dollars per period for n periods, the following equation is used:

$$\text{Present value} = (d + hn)a_n - \frac{h(n - a_n)}{i}$$

where a_n is the present value of $1 per period at a rate of i for n periods. In the formula, h is positive for increases and negative for decreases. The formula is not generally applied to estimate the present value of an annuity that increases in a straight-line pattern. It is presented here only to illustrate the mathematical operations performed.

8. See James J. Mason, MAI, ed. and comp., *American Institute of Real Estate Appraisers Financial Tables*, rev. ed. (Chicago: American Institute of Real Estate Appraisers, 1982), Table No. 5, Ordinary Annuities Changing in Constant Amount.

9. To obtain the present value of an annuity that starts at $1 at the end of the first period and increases each period thereafter at a rate of x for n periods, the following equation is used:

$$\text{Present value} = \frac{1 - (1 + x)^n /(1 + i)^n}{i - x}$$

where i is the annual discount rate and x is the ratio of the increase in income for any period to the income for the previous period. The formula for calculating the present value of a stream of income that declines at a constant rate is similar, but the sign of x is reversed to indicate a negative rate of change. Thus, the formula for calculating the present value of an annuity starting at $1 and declining thereafter at a rate of x may be rewritten as

$$\text{Present value} = \frac{1 - (1 - x)^n /(1 + i)^n}{i + x}$$

These formulas are not generally applied to estimate the present value of an annuity that increases or decreases in an exponential curve pattern. They are presented here only to illustrate the mathematical operations performed.

Property Models

When both value and income changes are expected to follow a regular or predictable pattern, one of the yield capitalization models for property valuation may be applicable. The common yield capitalization models employ a capitalization rate, R, which is also used in direct capitalization. There is a difference, however, between direct capitalization and yield capitalization. In direct capitalization R is derived directly from market data, without directly addressing the expected rate of return on capital or the means of recapture; in yield capitalization R cannot be determined without taking into account the income pattern, the anticipated rate of return on capital, and the timing of recapture. This does not mean that yield capitalization procedures are not market-oriented. On the contrary, for some property types yield capitalization procedures may represent the most realistic simulation of decision making in the marketplace.

Real estate investors are greatly influenced by expectations of change in the value of a property. When an investor looks forward to property appreciation as a component of the eventual investment yield, he or she is anticipating that the total yield rate will be higher than the expected rate of income—i.e., the overall capitalization rate. The total yield rate is a complete measure of performance that includes any property appreciation. The formula for this relationship is:

$$Y = R + A$$

where Y is the yield rate, R is the capitalization rate, and A is the adjustment rate that reflects the total change or growth in income and value.

Thus, the capitalization rate for an appreciating property equals the total yield rate minus an adjustment for expected growth ($R = Y - A$). Similarly, the capitalization rate for a depreciating property can be seen as the yield rate plus an adjustment for expected loss, e.g., $R = Y - (-A)$ or $R = Y + A$.

Because A is often expressed as a function of the total relative change in property income and value, the Greek letter delta (Δ) is used to denote it. To calculate A it is usually necessary to multiply Δ by a conversion factor such as an annual sinking fund factor or an annual recapture rate to convert the total relative change in income and value into an appropriate periodic rate of change. The symbol for the annualizer is a. The general formula for R may be expressed as

$$R = Y - \Delta a$$

where R is the capitalization rate, Y is the yield rate, Δ is the total relative change in income and value, and a is the annualizer or conversion factor.

This general formula for the capitalization rate can be adapted for use with typical income/value patterns for the property as a whole or for any property components. In the general formula, R, Y, and Δ apply to the total property and are expressed without subscripts. However, if there is a possibility of confusing the total property with any of its components, subscripts should be used for clarification. Once the appropriate capitalization rate has been determined, an indication of property value can be obtained by applying the following universal valuation formula:

$$\text{Value} = \frac{\text{Income}}{\text{Cap rate}} \quad \text{or} \quad V = \frac{I}{R}$$

Level Income

Level income with no change in value. When both income and value are expected to remain unchanged, a property may be valued by capitalization in perpetuity, which was explained in the discussion of income models. According to the general formula, $R = Y - \Delta a$, the capitalization rate (R) becomes the yield rate (Y) when there is no change in value because Δ equals zero.

Level income with change in value. When level income with a change in value is projected over a period of n years, the general formula for R can be adapted by substituting the sinking fund factor for rate Y over n years in place of the conversion factor (a). For example, consider a commercial property that will generate a stable *NOI* of $25,000 per year for the next 8 years. Total property appreciation of 40% is expected during this 8-year period. The appraiser is asked to value the property to yield 15%. To solve this problem, the formula $R = Y - \Delta a$ is used with the sinking fund factor for 15% over 8 years as a. According to the tables, the sinking fund factor is 0.072850, so R is calculated as follows.

$$R = 0.15 - (0.40 \times 0.072850) = 0.12086$$
$$\text{Value} = NOI/R$$
$$\text{Value} = \$25,000/0.12086 = \$206,851$$

Property models used in solving for value manipulate a given set of market data to determine other unknowns. For example, in the problem above only the *NOI* and rate of change or appreciation in property value are known. While DCF analysis may be used as proof of the solution, it is not feasible to apply DCF analysis to solve the problem because only the rate of appreciation is known from the market, not future value or present value, which are interdependent.

Straight-Line (Constant-Amount) Changes in Income and Value

When income and value are expected to increase or decrease by fixed amounts per period according to the standard, straight-line pattern, property value can be estimated using direct capitalization with straight-line recapture. The general formula for the capitalization rate (R) can be adapted for use with the standard, straight-line income/value pattern by using the straight-line recapture rate as the conversion factor (a). The straight-line recapture rate is simply the reciprocal of the projection period. For example, if income is projected over a period of 25 years, the annual, straight-line recapture rate is 1/25, or 4%. Depreciation of 100% would indicate that the projection period is equal to the property's remaining economic life. The concept of a limited remaining economic life does not apply to appreciating properties, but 100% appreciation would indicate a projection period equal to the amount of time required for the property to double in value.

Classic straight-line recapture. The straight-line capitalization procedure has historically been used to value wasting or waning assets, i.e., investments whose income is declining as their asset base wanes. This classic procedure has limited applicability due to its underlying assumptions, but it should be thoroughly understood to ensure its proper use. The classic straight-line procedure presumes that capital is recaptured in equal amounts during the economic life of the investment and that net income always consists of a fixed amount that represents the return of capital plus a declining return on the capital remaining in the investment. Total income, therefore, diminishes until the asset is worthless and all capital has been recovered.

The presumption that value and income will decline steadily is frequently inconsistent with market behavior; nevertheless, the procedure has important uses. Straight-line recapture is appropriate whenever the projection of income and value in an investment corresponds with the assumptions implicit in the procedure. Classic straight-line recapture is most easily understood when it is applied to an investment in a wasting asset such as a perishable structure, a stand of timber, or a mineral deposit. The procedure is not appropriate for valuing an investment in land or another asset that can sustain value indefinitely.

For example, consider an investment in a partial interest in real estate such as a leasehold in which all improvements must be written off during the term of the lease. Assume that $50,000 is invested in a 10-year leasehold to earn 8% per year as a yield on capital. What flow of income to the investor would be required to return the entire amount of the investment on a straight-line basis during the 10-year period and, in addition, yield 8% per year to the investor?

Yearly recapture would, of course, be one-tenth of $50,000, or $5,000. The investor is entitled to a return on unrecaptured capital amounting to 8% of $50,000 in the first year, 8% of $45,000 in the second year, 8% of $40,000 in the third year, and so forth. (See Table 23.2.) The income flow starts at $9,000 the first year and drops $400 each year after that. The total income payable at the end of the tenth and final year would be $5,400, of which $5,000 would be the last installment of the return of capital and the other $400 would be the interest due on the capital remaining in the investment during the tenth year. Thus the investor achieves 100% capital recovery plus an 8% return on the outstanding capital, assuming nonlevel income.

Table 23.2	**Periodic Return of and Return on Capital**			
End of Year	**Invested Capital**	**Return of Capital**	**Return on Capital at 8%**	**Total Return**
0	$50,000	—	—	—
1	45,000	$5,000	$4,000	$9,000
2	40,000	5,000	3,600	8,600
3	35,000	5,000	3,200	8,200
4	30,000	5,000	2,800	7,800
5	25,000	5,000	2,400	7,400
6	20,000	5,000	2,000	7,000
7	15,000	5,000	1,600	6,600
8	10,000	5,000	1,200	6,200
9	5,000	5,000	800	5,800
10	0	5,000	400	5,400

Note that the recapture rate amounts to 10% of the original investment and is simply the reciprocal of the economic life. Also, all income is presumed to be payable at the end of each year and the yields are always computed at the end of the year on the amount of capital outstanding during the year. Based on the starting income, the capitalization rate in this example would be $9,000/$50,000, or 18%. The 18% capitalization rate could also be calculated by adding the 10% recapture rate to the 8% yield rate.

The straight-line capitalization procedure reflects some useful mathematical relationships.

First period return on investment = original value x yield rate
Periodic change in value = original value x periodic rate of change
Periodic change in income = periodic change in value x yield rate

When the decline in income and value reflects these relationships, the periodic rate of change is the recapture rate and the reciprocal of the recapture rate is the economic life.

Expanded straight-line concept. The traditional concept of straight-line recapture can be expanded to remove some of its theoretical constraints and facilitate a broader range of practical applications. The assumption of a predictable decline in income can be expanded to include any predictable change, which allows the appraiser to consider growing assets as well as wasting assets. Presuming a predictable rate of change within the foreseeable future can also eliminate the need to consider the full economic life of a property. Although there are significant theoretical differences, the expanded straight-line concept corresponds mathematically to classic straight-line recapture.

Under both the expanded and classic straight-line concepts, changes in value and income are presumed to occur on a straight-line basis. The basic requirements for a satisfactory return on, and complete recovery of, invested capital are also preserved. The expanded concept does not presume, however, that capital is recaptured in annual installments throughout the economic life of a property. Rather, the property could be resold for a predictable amount at some point during its economic life, thereby providing for partial or complete return of the invested capital at the time of resale.

The straight-line capitalization rate is simply a combination of the yield rate and the straight-line rate of change, which is expressed in the general formula $R = Y - \Delta a$, where Δ is the relative change in value in n periods and a is $1/n$. For example, consider a leasehold that will produce NOI of $19,000 the first year. This NOI is expected to decline thereafter in the standard straight-line pattern and value is expected to fall 25% in 10 years. The anticipated income pattern must match up with the lease contract. To appraise the leasehold to yield 12%, use the formula $R_{LH} = Y_{LH} - \Delta_{LH}a$, where the subscript LH denotes the leasehold.

$$R_{LH} = 0.12 - (-0.25 \times 0.1) = 0.145$$
$$\text{Value} = NOI/R$$
$$\text{Value} = \$19,000/0.145 = \$131,034$$

The classic and expanded straight-line concepts are popular because they are simple and do not require the use of compound interest tables. However, straight-line concepts have theoretical and practical limitations. The straight-line premise is not always a realistic reflection of investor expectations of changing income and value.

Exponential-Curve (Constant-Ratio) Changes in Income and Value

When both income and value are expected to change at a constant ratio, the capitalization rate can be determined without tables using the general formula

$$R = Y - \Delta a$$

where Δa is the relative change in value and income for one period. Thus, Δa can be replaced with the periodic compound rate of change (CR). The formula then becomes

$$R = Y - CR$$

where Y is the yield rate per period and CR is the rate of change per period. An expected loss is treated as a negative rate of change, and the formula becomes

$$R = Y - (-CR)$$

or

$$R = Y + CR$$

If both income and value are expected to change at the same rate, the capitalization rate is expected to remain constant. Thus this pattern of growth or decline is sometimes referred to as the *frozen cap rate* pattern. For example, assume an income-producing property is expected to produce *NOI* of $50,000 for the first year. Thereafter both *NOI* and value are expected to grow at a constant ratio of 2% per year. In other words, 2% is the expected ratio of the increase in income for any year to the income for the previous year; the ratio of the increase in value for any year to the value for the previous year is also 2%. To appraise the property to yield 11%, the formula is $R_O = Y_O - CR_O$

$$R_O = 0.11 - 0.02 = 0.09$$
$$\text{Value} = \$50,000/0.09 = \$555,556$$

The elements in the above equation can be transposed so that:

$$Y_O = R_O + CR_O$$

The overall yield rate, therefore, is equal to the overall capitalization rate plus the time adjustment, provided the rate of appreciation indicated by the sales comparison approach is anticipated to continue at the same rate into the foreseeable future. Property models based on an exponential pattern of change in income and value often reflect the thinking of investors in the market.

Variable or Irregular Income and Value Changes

When income and value are not expected to follow a regular pattern of change, the present value of a property can be obtained by applying the standard discounting formula separately to each projected benefit, including the final reversion. This is often done by discounted cash flow analysis rather than an income or property model.

To illustrate a variable or irregular pattern of change in income, the reader is referred to the income estimate for the office building that was developed in Chapter 21. The projected *NOI* and reversion are shown in Table 21.11. It is assumed that a typical buyer projects income for a 10-year holding period. Net operating income for Year 11 is projected to estimate the resale price of the property. The reversion is calculated by applying a 10% capitalization rate to the *NOI* for Year 11. Care should be taken to note variations in *NOI* subsequent to Year 11, which may warrant use of a different capitalization rate or different annual income to calculate the reversion.

The value of the property can be estimated by calculating the present value of the *NOI* for each year of the 10-year holding period and adding the present value of the cash flow from the sale of the property in Year 11 (the net resale price). Suppose the typical investor requires an overall yield rate (Y_O) of 13%. At a 13% discount rate, the present value of the *NOI* and reversion is $95,882,893 (see Table 23.3). This means that the investor would expect to earn a 13% rate of return if $95,882,893 is paid for the property.

Table 23.3 | **Discounting of Income Streams and Reversion for Office Building**

Year	NOI*	PV of $1 factor (13%)	Discounted Value
1996	$4,928,131	0.884956	$4,361,179
1997	$4,908,580	0.783147	$3,844,140
1998	$5,660,671	0.693050	$3,923,128
1999	$9,304,745	0.613319	$5,706,777
2000	$11,813,732	0.542760	$6,412,021
2001	$12,571,137	0.480319	$6,038,156
2002	$13,132,057	0.425061	$5,581,925
2003	$14,260,011	0.376160	$5,364,046
2004	$16,460,547	0.332885	$5,479,469
2005	$17,290,747	0.294588	$5,093,647
			$51,804,488

Reversion (based on *NOI* in 2006) $173,413,770
Less sales expenses @ 2.5%   -4,335,344
                                      $169,078,426

Discounted at 0.294588 $49,808,426
Value of office building as of January 1, 1996 $101,612,963

* *NOIs from Table 21.11.*

Although property value was estimated by discounting the projected cash flow for each year rather than by applying a formula to develop an overall capitalization rate, an overall capitalization rate is implied in the solution. In this case the overall capitalization rate (R_O) for Year 1 is 4.8% ($4,928,131/$101,612,963). This overall capitalization rate is considerably lower than the 10% capitalization rate applied to the estimated *NOI* for Year 11 to estimate the resale price. The difference is attributable to the fact that the *NOI* for Year 1 in this example is relatively low due to the impact of existing leases. The overall capitalization rate of 4.8% implied by a value estimate of $101,612,963 was calculated using only the *NOI* for Year 1. In this example, many of the existing leases specify a contract rate that is below market rate. As these leases are renewed at market levels during the 10-year holding period, the *NOI* is projected to increase. By the end of the holding period, most of the leases will have been renewed. Thus, the projected increase in *NOI* from Year 11 onward should closely parallel changes in the market rental rate, and the 10% capitalization rate used to estimate the resale price would reflect this assumption.

For example, if *NOI* is projected to increase 5% per year from Year 11 onward and the discount rate is still assumed to be 13%, then the exponential-curve property model discussed earlier in this chapter, which implies a capitalization rate of 10%, would be appropriate. In addition, all else being equal, *terminal capitalization rates* (R_Ns) are usually, though not necessarily, higher than first-year capitalization rates. This is due to the reduction in the remaining economic life of the property over the forecast period (as the property loses its competitive position in the market) and the increased risk associated with projecting income several years into the future.[10] Recapture requirements for older properties are generally also higher because of shorter remaining economic lives and greater associated risk.

The estimated present value of the property, $101,612,963 in this example, reflects the projected increase in *NOI* due to lease renewals and increases in the market rental rate and the estimated resale price. The resulting value estimate for the property is high relative to the *NOI* for the first year, which explains the relatively low overall capitalization rate of 4.8%. Although many investors base their purchase decisions on the total expected yield (discount rate), most have minimum first-year return requirements (capitalization rate).

The long-term projections of income and expenses developed by appraisers will almost always differ from actual property income and expenses. However, rather than attempt to forecast the peaks and troughs that will occur during an anticipated holding period, appraisers simulate how market participants expect the property to perform.

The preceding example illustrates the need to consider carefully the anticipated pattern of *NOI* when selecting an overall capitalization rate to be used in direct capitalization or a property model for yield capitalization. Capitalization rates can differ significantly for properties with different patterns of *NOI* beyond the first year and different resale potential. The absence of a regular income pattern does not necessarily mean that detailed DCF analysis is the only method that should be considered. The appraiser may discover that one of the standard valuation models can be adjusted to compensate for a deviation from the regular income pattern or that a special valuation model can be devised to solve the problem at hand.

---

10. See D. Richard Wincott, "Terminal Capitalization Rates and Reasonableness," *The Appraisal Journal* (April 1991), 253-260. If, over the holding period, a substantial capital expenditure is allocated for the refurbishment or renovation of an aging property, R_N may equal or be less than R_O. Such a relationship between R_N and R_O is also likely when current income exceeds market levels.

Mortgage Interests

The purchase and ownership of real property often involves debt capital secured with the real estate as collateral. Appraisers use mortgage information in the form of dollar amounts and rates or factors, depending on the data available, to value income-producing properties. Mortgage information may include 1) the monthly or periodic payments and annual debt service on a level-payment, fully amortized loan; 2) the accompanying partial payment factors and annual constants (R_M); and 3) the balance outstanding (B) on an amortized loan at any time before it is fully amortized, expressed as a dollar amount or a percentage of the original loan amount. The percentage or proportion of the principal amount paid off before full amortization (P) must also be calculated, especially if mortgage-equity analysis is used.

Mortgage investments have a great impact on real property value and equity yield rates. Because yield is a significant consideration in the lender's decision to invest in a mortgage interest in real estate, the lender's yield must be understood and often calculated. In the absence of points and any participation or accrual feature, the lender's yield equals the interest rate.

Types of Mortgage Loans

A mortgage is a legal document pledging a described property as security or collateral for the repayment of a loan under certain terms and conditions. There are various types of mortgage loans and many are identified by their repayment characteristics—e.g., interest only, direct reduction, variable rate, and equity participation mortgages.

An interest-only mortgage is a nonamortizing loan in which the lender receives interest only during the term of the loan and recovers the principal in a lump sum at the time of maturity.

A direct reduction mortgage is a mortgage loan that is repaid in periodic, usually equal, installments that include repayment of part of the principal and the interest due on the unpaid balance. Although the payments are level, the amount of principal and interest varies with each payment. In the most common type of direct reduction mortgage, the interest component decreases with each payment while the principal or amortization component increases.

An adjustable variable-rate mortgage is a mortgage with an interest rate that may move up or down following a specified schedule or in accordance with the movements of a standard or index to which the interest rate is tied.

A wraparound mortgage is a mortgage that is subordinate to, but inclusive of, any existing mortgage(s) on a property. Usually, a third-party lender refinances the property, assuming the existing mortgage and its debt service which are wrapped around a new, junior mortgage. A wraparound lender gives the borrower the difference between the outstanding balance on the existing mortgage(s) and the face amount of the new mortgage. Wraparound mortgages became widespread in periods of high mortgage rates and appreciating property values, but have generally fallen into disuse with declining mortgage rates.

A participation mortgage is a mortgage in which the lender receives a share of the income and sometimes the reversion from a property on which the lender has made a loan. Lenders may opt for this type of arrangement either as a hedge against inflation or as a means of increasing their total yield on the loan.

A shared appreciation mortgage is a mortgage in which the borrower receives assistance in the form of capital when buying the real property in return for a portion of the property's future appreciation in value.

A convertible mortgage is a mortgage in which the lender may choose to take an equity interest in the real estate in lieu of cash amortization payments by the borrower. In this way the mortgage interests of the lender may be converted into equity ownership at specified times during the life of the mortgage.

A graduated-payment mortgage is a mortgage designed to aid borrowers by matching mortgage payments to projected increases in income; the periodic payments start out low and gradually increase. Because the borrower's payments in the early years of the loan are not sufficient to pay the entire interest due or to amortize the mortgage, the borrower actually borrows the difference between the payments and the current interest due.

A zero-coupon mortgage is a debt secured by real estate with interest payments accruing rather than being paid by the borrower; in some circumstances, a rate of interest may be imputed—e.g., for income taxation.

A reverse annuity mortgage (RAM) is a negative amortization mortgage which allows owners to use some or all of the equity they have accumulated in their property as retirement income while retaining ownership of the property. Typically, the loan increases as more money is borrowed and unpaid interest on the outstanding balance accumulates up to an agreed-upon amount, which is generally scheduled to coincide with the sale of the property.

Mortgage Components

Periodic (Monthly) Payment

The monthly payment factor for a fully amortized, monthly payment loan with equal payments is the direct reduction loan factor, or monthly constant, for the loan, given the interest rate and amortization term. Thus, the monthly payment factor for a 30-year, fully amortized, level monthly payment loan at 15.5% interest is 0.013045. This number can be obtained from a direct reduction loan table or by solving for the monthly payment (PMT) on a preprogrammed financial calculator, given the number of periods (n), the interest rate (i), and the principal loan amount.

If the loan had an initial principal amount of $160,000, the monthly payment required to amortize the principal over 30 years and provide interest at the nominal rate of 15.5% on the outstanding balance each month would be

$$\$160,000 \times 0.013045 = \$2,087.20$$

Annual Debt Service and Loan Constant

Cash flows are typically converted to an annual basis for real property valuation, so it is useful to calculate the amount of annual debt service as well as the monthly payments. For the 30-year, fully amortized, level monthly payment loan of $160,000 at a 15.5% interest rate, the annual debt service is

$$\$2,087.20 \times 12 = \$25,046.40$$

The annual loan constant is simply the ratio of annual debt service to the loan principal. (The annual loan constant, often called the *mortgage constant*, describes a rate although it is actually the annual debt service per dollar of mortgage loan outstanding, which may be expressed as a dollar amount.) The annual loan constant is expressed as R_M to signify that it is a capitalization rate for the loan or debt portion of the real property investment. For the loan mentioned, the annual loan constant can be calculated as follows:

$$R_M = \frac{\text{Annual debt service}}{\text{Loan principal}}$$

$$= \frac{\$\,25,046.40}{\$160,000.00}$$

$$= 0.156540$$

The annual loan constant can also be obtained when the amount of the loan principal is not known. In this case the monthly payment factor is simply multiplied by 12.

$$R_M = \text{monthly payment factor} \times 12$$
$$= 0.013045 \times 12$$
$$= 0.156540$$

Although these figures are rounded to the nearest cent, in actual practice most loan constants are rounded up to make sure that the loan will be repaid during the stated amortization period.

Outstanding Balance

Properties are frequently sold, or loans may be refinanced, before the loan on the property is fully amortized. Furthermore, loans often mature before the completion of loan amortization. In such cases there is an outstanding balance or balloon payment due on the note; from the lender's point of view, this is the loan or debt reversion to the lender.

The outstanding balance (B) on any level-payment, amortized loan is the present value of the debt service over the *remaining* amortization period discounted at the interest rate. Thus, at the end of 10 years, the balance for the 30-year note discussed above would be the present value of 20 years of remaining payments. The balance is calculated by multiplying the monthly payment by the present value of $1 per period factor (monthly) for 20 years at the interest rate. The balloon payment, or future value, may be calculated.

$$B = \$2{,}087.20 \times 73.861752$$
$$= \$154{,}164.25$$

Similarly, the outstanding balance at the end of 18 years would be equal to the monthly payment times the present value of $1 per period factor (monthly) for 12 years at the interest rate.

$$B = \$2{,}087.20 \times 65.222881$$
$$= \$136{,}133.20$$

The outstanding balance on a loan can also be expressed as a percentage of the original principal. This is useful, and sometimes necessary, if dollar amounts are not given or are unavailable. For a 10-year projection with 20 years remaining on the note, the outstanding balance is

$$B = \frac{\$154{,}164.25}{\$160{,}000.00}$$
$$= 0.963527$$

For an 18-year projection with 12 years remaining on the note, the balance is

$$B = \frac{\$136{,}133.20}{\$160{,}000.00}$$
$$= 0.850833$$

A percentage balance can also be calculated as the *ratio* of the present value of $1 per period factor for the remaining term of the loan at the specified interest rate divided by the present value of $1 per period factor for the full term of the loan at the interest rate. This can be expressed as

$$B = \frac{PV \ 1/P \text{ remaining term}}{PV \ 1/P \text{ full term}}$$

In the case of the 30-year, 15.5% loan, the balance for a 10-year projection with 20 years remaining is calculated as

$$B = \frac{73.861752}{76.656729}$$
$$= 0.963539$$

For an 18-year projection with 12 years remaining, the balance would be

$$B = \frac{65.222881}{76.656729}$$
$$= 0.850844$$

These results are similar to those obtained using dollar amounts.

Percentage of Loan Paid Off

It is often necessary to calculate the percentage of the loan paid off before full amortization over the projection period, especially in Ellwood mortgage-equity analysis. The percentage of the loan paid off is expressed as P and is most readily calculated as the complement of B.

$$P = 1 - B$$

For the 30-year note, P is calculated as follows:

$$
\begin{aligned}
P_{10} &= 1 - 0.963539 \\
&= 0.036461 \\
P_{18} &= 1 - 0.850844 \\
&= 0.149156
\end{aligned}
$$

The percentage of the loan paid off prior to full amortization over the projection period (P) can also be calculated directly. There are many different procedures for this operation and they are not all presented here. Calculator users are advised to consult their manuals on the AMORT function.

The simplest, most direct procedure is to calculate P as the *ratio* of the sinking fund factor for the full term (monthly) divided by the sinking fund factor for the projection period (monthly).

$$P = \frac{1/S_{\overline{n}|}}{1/S_{\overline{n}|P}}$$

For the 30-year monthly payment note at 15.5%, the calculations are

$$
\begin{aligned}
P_{10} &= \frac{0.000129}{0.003524} \\
&= 0.036606 \\
P_{18} &= \frac{0.000129}{0.000862} \\
&= 0.149652
\end{aligned}
$$

Any differences are due to rounding.

Lender's Yield

The monetary benefits that accrue to the lender are similar to the benefits received by the equity owner—i.e., periodic income from debt service and the reversion represented by the outstanding principal paid off prior to or at maturity. In calculating the lender's yield, discounting formulas must be applied.

To illustrate how the lender's yield on a mortgage loan investment is calculated, consider a mortgage loan with the following characteristics.

Loan amount	$100,000
Interest rate	13.5%
Term	25 years
Payment	Monthly
Balance in five years	$96,544
Points	3
Other costs	Borrower to pay all other costs

If the mortgage runs full term, the yield can be obtained using a calculator.

$$n \quad = \quad 300$$
$$PMT = \$1,165.65$$
$$PV \quad = \quad \$97,000 \ (\$100,000 \text{ less 3 points, or } \$3,000)^*$$
$$i \quad = \quad 13.97\%$$

* Each point is equal to 1% of the loan amount: $100,000 x 0.01 = $1,000.

The lender's yield is greater than the nominal interest rate because of the points paid by the borrower. In effect, the lender only loaned $97,000 ($100,000 - $3,000) but receives a stream of debt service payments based on $100,000. If the mortgage is paid off in five years, the lender's yield is calculated with these figures.

$$n \quad = \quad 60$$
$$PMT = \$1,165.65$$
$$PV \quad = \quad \$97,000$$
$$FV \quad = \quad \$96,544$$
$$i \quad = \quad 14.36\%$$

If there were no points in either of these examples, the yield to the lender would be 13.5% in each case. Points or any other monetary payments that reduce the lender's investment are important considerations in calculating the lender's yield. The lender's yield may be supplemented through the syndication process.

In some depressed markets, lenders may find that the property securing the loan has declined in value to the point that the loan balance exceeds the property's value. In this case there is no longer any equity interest in the property, and the value of the loan may often be calculated based on the actual cash flows to the property rather than the cash flows projected when the loan contract was obtained. To do otherwise would be to estimate the value of the mortgage interest as greater than the value of the property.

Equity Interests

The equity in real property is the owner's interest after all claims and liens have been satisfied. An equity interest, like a mortgage loan, represents a financial interest in real property.

Equity ownership in real property can be legally accomplished in many ways—e.g., as an individual owner, joint owner, partner, or shareholder in a corporation. The legal form of equity ownership does not affect property value in most appraisal assignments. However, an appraiser is sometimes called upon to estimate the value of a specific legal form of equity interest.

For example, an appraiser may be asked to value a limited partner's equity interest in a partnership which was created solely to make the individual the legal owner of certain limited rights in the real property. Partial interests are often valued at less than their pro rata share of ownership, especially if the holder of the partial interest does not have any voice in the management or control of the asset. An assignment to value a limited partnership interest may be undertaken to appraise assets for estate tax purposes or for sale or purchase decisions.

Because the equity side of the real estate market dominates sales activity, appraisers must thoroughly understand the benefits that accrue to equity owners and know how equity yield is calculated.

Benefits of Equity Ownership

Equity owners look for two kinds of benefits: income, usually on an annual basis, and reversion at the end of the ownership period. Income is the annual cash flow before or after taxes; the reversion is the pre- or after-tax equity proceeds of resale after any outstanding mortgage balance and all selling expenses have been paid. Any refinancing benefits taken during the ownership period are usually viewed as a form of early reversion. In investment analysis assignments, the sum of all benefits received over the ownership period is analyzed in comparison to the equity invested to reveal the equity yield rate. In valuation assignments an equity yield rate is applied to the forecast benefits to produce a present value conclusion. If the market value of the equity interest is sought, the equity yield rate can be derived from the market.

Equity Yield Rate

For the investor the prime measures of investment performance are the equity yield rate and the first-year dividend, usually expressed as the equity capitalization rate (or equity dividend rate), and, to a lesser extent, the price per square foot. An investor may compare the expected equity yield on a real property investment with the yields on alternative investments with commensurate risk (e.g., stocks and bonds) and with a lender's yield on mortgages secured by similar real property. Usually the equity investor will seek a higher yield than the lender because the lender has a more secure position. The lender can foreclose the mortgage and take title to the real property if the mortgage terms are not fulfilled.

The equity yield rate (Y_E) must be distinguished from the equity capitalization rate (R_E). The equity yield rate is a rate of return *on* equity capital; the equity capitalization rate simply reflects the relationship between one year's equity income or cash flow and equity capital (cash on cash). The equity yield rate is a full measure of investment performance, but the equity capitalization rate is not. The equity capitalization rate is *not* a rate of return on capital. It may be more or less than the eventual equity yield on the capital invested, depending on future changes in equity income and equity value. Although it cannot be considered a full measure of performance, the equity capitalization rate is useful and important. In certain markets and at certain times, it is the preferred measure of investment performance.

Derivation of the Equity Yield Rate

To estimate equity yield rates, appraisers must do market research. This research can take many forms and may include one or more of the following analyses.

- Direct comparison with equity yield rates extracted from recent comparable sales; these equity yield rates are retrospective, however, and the appraiser's focus must always be prospective. (For an example, see the two-variable algebraic method of rate extraction described in Appendix C.)

- Verification of the prospective equity yields considered by market participants, particularly buyers, in recent or anticipated sales.

- Comparison with the equity yield rates achieved in alternative investments of comparable risk such as stocks and bonds.

- Review of published investor surveys, which can provide guidelines for appraisers.

Appropriate equity yield rates vary with property characteristics. To develop an equity yield rate from recent comparable sales, an appraiser analyzes the forecast benefits of equity ownership in relation to the equity capital invested. This process will be covered in the next chapter.

The equity capitalization rate (R_E) should *not* be confused with the equity yield rate (Y_E). A further word of caution is in order. Band-of-investment techniques in which equity capitalization rates are loaded/unloaded for equity buildup and appreciation/depreciation are inappropriate for the estimation of equity yield rates.

Leverage

The term *leverage* refers to how borrowed funds increase or decrease the equity return free and clear. Leverage was at one time used almost exclusively to analyze equity capitalization rates in relation to overall and mortgage capitalization rates. Leverage may also be considered in analyzing the relationship between equity yield rates and overall yield rates. In other words, how does the use of borrowed funds enhance the equity yield rate over the overall yield rate? In both cases, the underlying principles are the same. (See Table 23.4 and the example that follows.) The leverage an investor obtains by using borrowed funds to finance an investment is attended by risk. The investor seeks compensation for this risk by requiring a higher equity yield rate.

Table 23.4 | **Types of Leverage**

Using equity capitalization rates	Using equity yield rates
If $R_O > R_M$, then $R_E > R_O$: leverage is positive	If $Y_O > Y_M$, then $Y_E > Y_O$: leverage is positive
If $R_O = R_M$, then $R_E = R_O$: leverage is neutral	If $Y_O = Y_M$, then $Y_E = Y_O$: leverage is neutral
If $R_O < R_M$, then $R_E < R_O$: leverage is negative	If $Y_O < Y_M$, then $Y_E < Y_O$: leverage is negative

In analyzing cash flows, positive leverage is indicated when the overall capitalization rate is greater than the mortgage capitalization rate. The difference between the two rates directly benefits the equity owner, so the equity capitalization rate is higher than it would be if there were no mortgage.

For example, assume a property was sold for $100,000 and analysis of the transaction indicates a net operating income of $10,000, an equity investment of $25,000, and a mortgage of $75,000 payable in annual installments of $7,125.00. The indicated capitalization rates are:

Overall (R_O)	10.0%
Mortgage (R_M)	9.5%
Equity (R_E)	11.5%

The leverage is positive because the mortgage capitalization rate is less than the overall capitalization rate and the equity capitalization rate is greater than the overall capitalization rate. If there were no mortgage, the equity capitalization rate would be 10.0%, the same as the overall capitalization rate.

When the overall capitalization rate exceeds the mortgage capitalization rate, positive leverage results. Similarly, when the overall yield rate exceeds the mortgage yield rate, positive leverage is indicated and the equity yield rate must exceed the overall yield rate. However, if the overall capitalization rate is less than the mortgage capitalization rate or the overall yield rate is less than the mortgage yield rate, negative leverage results. The leverage is neutral when the overall rate, the mortgage capitalization rate, and the equity capitalization rate are equal.[11]

The analysis of leverage is important because positive or negative leverage can affect the level of risk associated with a real property investment and the yield required to satisfy an investor willing to assume the risk. The use of leverage tends to magnify fluctuations in cash flow and enhanced variability translates into risk. If property performance falls below expectations and periods of insufficient cash flow are protracted, the investor may become strapped for cash to service the debt on the property. If market conditions become illiquid, the investor may be unable to command a price for the property that allows for repayment of the debt.

Proportionate increases in loan-to-value ratios produce ever wider spreads between equity capitalization rates whether leverage is positive or negative. For example, a property that carries a 12% interest-only mortgage has a R_O of 0.15. Leverage therefore is positive. Consider the change in R_E as the loan-to-value ratio increases from 40% to 60% and from 60% to 80%.

$$R_E = R_O + (R_O - R_M)[M/(1 - M)]$$

At a 40% loan-to-value ratio, the equity capitalization rate is 0.1699.

---

11. Cash flows include both the periodic income to the real property and the reversion. Thus, investors can lever periodic income and/or the reversion. Leverage on income may be negative (i.e., $Y_E < Y_O < Y_M$) while leverage on the reversion is positive (i.e., $Y_E > Y_O > Y_M$). In such a situation, the appraiser should compare the equity yield rate (Y_E) and overall yield rate (Y_O) instead of the equity capitalization rate (R_E) and overall capitalization rate (R_O).

$$R_E = 0.15 + (0.15 - 0.12)[0.4/(1 - 0.4)]$$
$$R_E = 0.15 + (0.03)[0.4/(0.6)] = 0.1699$$

At a 60% loan-to-value ratio, the equity capitalization rate is 0.195.

$$R_E = 0.15 + (0.15 - 0.12)[0.6/(1 - 0.6)]$$
$$R_E = 0.15 + (0.03)[0.6/(0.4)] = 0.195$$

At an 80% loan-to-value ratio, the equity capitalization rate is 0.27.

$$R_E = 0.15 + (0.15 - 0.12)[0.8/(1 - 0.8)]$$
$$R_E = 0.15 + (0.03)[0.8/(0.2)] = 0.27$$

The same holds true when leverage is negative. Assume this property with the 12% interest-only mortgage has an 0.11 overall capitalization rate. Now consider the change in R_E as the loan-to-value ratio increases from 40% to 60% and from 60% to 80%.

$$R_E = R_O + (R_O - R_M)[M/(1 - M)]$$

At a 40% loan-to-value ratio, the equity capitalization rate is 0.143.

$$R_E = 0.11 + (0.11 - 0.12)[0.4/(1 - 0.4)]$$
$$R_E = 0.15 + (-0.01)[0.4/(0.6)] = 0.143$$

At a 60% loan-to-value ratio, the equity capitalization rate is 0.135.

$$R_E = 0.11 + (0.11 - 0.12)[0.6/(1 - 0.6)]$$
$$R_E = 0.15 + (-0.01)[0.6/(0.4)] = 0.135$$

At an 80% loan-to-value ratio, the equity capitalization rate is 0.11.

$$R_E = 0.11 + (0.11 - 0.12)[0.8/(1 - 0.8)]$$
$$R_E = 0.15 + (-0.01)[0.8/(0.2)] = 0.11$$

Often negative leverage on early cash flows suggests the need to achieve a greater equity yield rate. Conversely, positive leverage on early cash flows may reduce the equity yield rate required. On an equity yield basis, positive leverage is expected due to the greater risk associated with the equity interest as compared to the more secure mortgage interest. If negative leverage is anticipated based on equity yield, the equity buyer may consider the investment to be inappropriate.

Key Concepts

- Yield capitalization is used to convert future benefits, typically a periodic income stream and reversion, into present value by discounting each future benefit at an appropriate yield rate or by applying an overall rate that explicitly reflects the investment's income pattern, change in value, and yield rate.

- In yield capitalization, an appraiser 1) selects an appropriate holding period; 2) forecasts all future cash flows or cash flow patterns; 3) selects the appropriate yield rate or discount rate; and 4) converts future benefits into present value by discounting each annual future benefit or applying an overall rate that reflects the income pattern, value change, and yield rate ($R_O = Y - \Delta a$).

- Discounted cash flow (DCF) analysis, a yield capitalization procedure that has gained widespread acceptance, specifies the quantity, variability, timing, and duration of a property's cash flows and reversion.

- Rental income is similar to an annuity. Real estate income streams may conform to the pattern of a variable annuity, a level annuity, or a regularly increasing or decreasing annuity reflecting either 1) levels of step-up/step-down change, 2) straight-line change per period, or 3) exponential-curve change per period.

- The reversion often represents a major portion of the benefits provided by income-producing property. Proceeds of resale are the net difference between the transaction price and total sale expenses.

- Specific valuation formulas, called *income* and *property models*, have been developed to project patterns of benefits. Income models may describe variable or irregular income patterns, level income patterns, straight-line change per period income, and exponential-curve change per period income. Property models may describe properties with level income and unchanging value, properties with income and value that are increasing or decreasing in straight-line amounts, properties with income and value that are increasing or decreasing in an exponential-curve or constant-ratio pattern, and properties with income and value changes that do not follow a regular pattern.

- A mortgage is a legal document pledging a described property as security or collateral for the repayment of a loan under certain terms and conditions. Mortgages are distinguished by their repayment characteristics, i.e., interest-only, direct reduction, adjustable- or variable-rate, wraparound, participation, shared appreciation, convertible, graduated-payment, and zero-coupon mortgages.

- Equity in real estate is the owner's interest after all claims and liens are satisfied. Two benefits are received by an equity owner: income and the proceeds of resale.

- An equity yield rate (Y_E) is the rate of return on equity capital. It considers the effect of financing on the investor's rate of return. Y_E should not be confused with the equity capitalization rate (R_E), which is the ratio between one year's equity income and equity capital. The overall yield rate (Y_O) is the rate of return on the total invested capital, both debt and equity, through income and proceeds of resale. It does not consider the effects of financing.

- Leverage refers to how borrowed funds increase or decrease the equity return free and clear. Whether the leverage is positive, neutral, or negative depends on the characteristic relationship between R_E and R_O/R_M and/or Y_E and Y_O/Y_M.

Terms

adjustable- or variable-rate
   mortgage (ARM/VRM)

amortization

annual debt service

annualizer or conversion factor (a)

annuity payable in advance

balance outstanding (B)

balloon payment

capitalization in perpetuity

cash flow

compounding

compound interest

conversion factor or annualizer (a)

convertible mortgage

debt service

delta (Δ)

direct reduction mortgage

discounted cash flow (DCF) analysis

discounting

effective interest rate

equity

equity yield rate (Y_E)

exponential-curve (constant-ratio)
   change per period

graduated-payment mortgage

Hoskold premise

income model

increasing or decreasing annuity

interest-only mortgage

Inwood premise

lender's yield

level annuity

leverage

loan constant

mortgage

mortgage constant (R_M)

mortgage yield rate (Y_M)

nominal interest rate

ordinary annuity

outstanding balance (B)

overall capitalization rate (R_O)

overall yield rate (Y_O)

participation mortgage

percentage of the loan paid off (P)

periodic (monthly) payment factor

principal

proceeds of resale

property model

reverse annuity mortgage

reversion

shared appreciation mortgage

sinking fund accumulation factor
   $(S_{\overline{n}|})$

sinking fund factor $(1/S_{\overline{n}|})$

six functions of $1

step-up or step-down annuity

straight-line (constant-amount)
   change per period

terminal capitalization rate (R_N)

variable annuity

wraparound mortgage

yield capitalization

zero-coupon mortgage

CHAPTER TWENTY-FOUR

Discounted Cash Flow Analysis and Special Applications in Income Capitalization

D iscounted cash flow (DCF) analysis is appropriate for any pattern of regular or irregular income.[1] In many markets DCF analysis is the technique preferred by investors. Advanced computer technology makes DCF analysis a practical tool for everyday appraisal work. The specialized yield capitalization formula formerly used for DCF analysis has been replaced by the use of computerized programs.[2]

Applicability of DCF Analysis

Generally, DCF analysis is used to solve for present value given the rate of return or to solve for the rate of return given the purchase price. In typical appraisal work, the appraiser begins by developing detailed spreadsheets with computer software. These spreadsheets show itemized incomes, expenses, and cash flows year by year, or occasionally month by month, over the presumed period of ownership. The cash flows, including the net resale price, are then discounted at a required rate of return to derive an indication of present value. In this way the appraiser can account for all cash flows in and out of the real property interest being appraised and the timing of these cash flows so that the time value of money is properly recognized in the analysis.

Critics point out that projections not warranted by market evidence can result in unsupported market values and that the results of the analysis can be subtly affected by minor leaning. These problems, like the problems associated with the Ellwood formula, reflect misuse by individual appraisers; they do not undermine the soundness of the technique. Other critics object to the uncertainty of projecting financial results five or 10 years into the future and cite this as a reason for not using or relying on the DCF technique. However, this argument ignores the reality of the real estate marketplace.

1. Statement on Appraisal Standards No. 2 of the Uniform Standards of Professional Appraisal Practice addresses criteria for proper DCF analysis as well as unacceptable practices.
2. The past six editions of *The Appraisal of Real Estate* presented the formula for mortgage-equity analysis, which L.W. Ellwood introduced in 1959 and expanded thereafter. In the 1960s and 1970s, the Ellwood technique had a profound impact on the application of the income capitalization approach. The most significant contribution of the Ellwood formula was the expression of overall and equity yield rates as a function of the property's mix of debt and equity financing. When overall income was projected to change in a known pattern, *J-* and *K-*factors could be used with the equation. Ellwood developed the income stabilization factors known as *J-factors* to convert variable income streams changing on a curvilinear basis into their level equivalents. *K-factors*, widely used in financial and engineering disciplines, were adapted to stabilize income streams changing at a constant ratio into their level equivalents. During the 1960s and 1970s, the Ellwood equation gained widespread acceptance among appraisers.

It has been demonstrated that the Ellwood method of calculating an overall capitalization rate represents a special case of discounted cash flow valuation; every critical point of analysis done with Ellwood can be accomplished by means of DCF analysis. The advent of computers and spreadsheet programs in the 1980s has contributed to the accessibility and convenience of DCF analysis and to the demise of the Ellwood method. See Wayne Kelly, Donald R. Epley, and Phillip Mitchell, "A Requiem for Ellwood," *The Appraisal Journal* (July 1995), 284-290. Readers interested in reviewing Ellwood mortgage-equity analysis may consult Appendix C.

Investors do make forecasts and rely on DCF analysis, particularly in regard to investment-grade, multitenanted properties such as shopping centers and office buildings.

In keeping with the principle of anticipation, forecasting is the essence of valuation. Hence, forecasting must be approached in the same way that all market data extractions are accomplished—i.e., with diligent research and careful verification. Discounted cash flow analysis can only provide accurate results if the forecasts developed are based on accurate, reliable information. Rather than attempt to forecast peaks and troughs over the holding period, a level of precision that is virtually impossible to achieve, appraisers reflect market expectations as to how the subject property will perform over a reasonably long time frame. For example, an appraiser may assume that inflation-driven expense items will increase at an average annual rate of X% over the next Y years.

Forecasting

In making forecasts an appraiser employs the same procedure applied by investors who use DCF analysis in their decision making. The procedural steps typically include forecasting income, vacancy, operating and capital expenses, and pre-tax cash flow over ownership periods of five to 15 years. In some markets, 10 years is cited as an average or standard period of ownership; in others, the forecast period may be shorter or longer. When appropriate, debt service and after-tax cash flow may also be forecast. The residual income from the sale of the property at the end of the forecast period is also estimated.

Typical forecast categories to be addressed in DCF analysis include:

- Current market rental rates and expected rate changes
- Existing base rents and contractual base rent adjustments
- Renewal options
- Existing and anticipated expense recovery (escalation) provisions
- Re-leasing assumptions including new lease terms, vacancy loss and sometimes free rent at existing lease expirations, tenant space preparation costs, and leasing commissions
- Tenant turnover
- Operating expenses
- Reversion and any selling or transaction costs
- Changes in inflation (Consumer Price Index)
- Discount rate(s)
- Business cycle—i.e., the state of the economy and economic trends
- Monetary cycle—i.e., the expansion or contraction of the money supply

Applications

The two DCF analyses that follow concern a shopping center and an office building. The first example provides an overview of the procedures used to forecast and discount cash flows into value. The second example presents more detailed market research of cash flow assumptions and a more complicated valuation procedure.

Shopping Center Example

The property being appraised is a strip shopping center consisting of five units of 2,000 square feet each. Market rents are currently $8.00 per square foot per year and are increasing at a compound rate of 4% per year. The landlord is responsible only for real estate taxes and exterior maintenance; tenants are responsible for all other expenses.

Taxes are currently $7,000 per year. The tax assessor reviews and reassesses properties every three years. The subject property was reviewed one year ago and taxes are expected to increase by about $800 with each subsequent review.

General exterior maintenance, including cleanup and landscaping, costs $100 per month; this expense is expected to increase each year by $10 per month. The roof should be replaced during the second year at a cost of $12,500, but no other exterior repairs or replacements are expected during the projection period.

Management fees, which include lease-up costs, are set at 5% of the rents collected plus 5% of the repair and maintenance expense negotiated. No vacancy or collection loss is anticipated.

The lease on Store A will run for two more years at a rent of $825 per month. The tenant will re-lease at market rent when the lease expires. Store B has a 10-year lease with six years remaining. The rent is currently $1,223 per month and will increase at a rate of 5% per year or one-half the change in the Consumer Price Index (CPI), whichever is greater. The CPI is expected to increase 4% per year over the next five years. Stores C, D, and E were recently leased for 10 years. These leases and all new leases are set at market rent with provisions to keep the rents at market rates throughout the projection period.

The net resale price of the property in five years is expected to be approximately $657,000 (*NOI* for Year 6 capitalized at 12% minus 3% sales expense). The appraiser has determined that a discount rate of 15% is proper and is using the five-year discounted cash flow analysis shown in Table 24.1 to estimate the value of the owner's interest—i.e., the leased fee estate.

Office Building Example

An appraiser has been engaged to estimate the current market value of the leased fee interest in a property 1) on an all-cash basis (free and clear of existing financing) and 2) subject to two existing mortgages. The property being appraised is a 45,000-sq.-ft. site improved with a four-year-old, three-story suburban office building in a desirable location several miles from a major city. The property has 11,000 square feet of rentable office space and 4,000 square feet of retail space. Leases are held by three tenants: RKM Insurance Corporation, ABC Appraisal Company, and BMI Computer Center. The effective date of the value estimate is July 1, 1996.

Leases

The insurance corporation's lease, which covers 5,000 square feet of rentable area, was signed four years ago and expires on June 30 of Year 6 of the DCF analysis. The base rent is set at $18.00 per square foot through December 31 of Year 3 of the DCF analysis and $20.00 per square foot thereafter. There are no renewal options.

Table 24.1 **Five-Year DCF Analysis of a Shopping Center**

	Year 1	Year 2	Year 3	Year 4	Year 5	Year 6
Income						
Store A	$ 9,900	$9,900	$17,306	$17,999	$18,718	$19,467
Store B	14,676	15,410	16,180	16,989	17,839	18,730
Store C	16,000	16,640	17,306	17,999	18,718	19,467
Store D	16,000	16,640	17,306	17,999	18,718	19,467
Store E	16,000	16,640	17,306	17,999	18,718	19,467
Total	$72,576	$75,230	$85,404	$88,985	$92,711	$96,598
Expenses						
Taxes	$ 7,000	$ 7,000	$ 7,800	$ 7,800	$ 7,800	$ 8,600
Maintenance	1,200	1,320	1,440	1,560	1,680	1,800
Management	3,689	4,453	4,342	4,527	4,720	4,920
Replacement	0	12,500	0	0	0	0
Total	$11,889	$25,273	$13,582	$13,887	$14,200	$15,320
NOI	$60,687	$49,957	$71,822	$75,098	$78,511	$81,278

Present Value of Income Stream

Cash Flow		PV of $1 @ 15%		Present Value
$60,687	X	0.869565	=	$ 52,771
$49,957	X	0.756144	=	$ 37,775
$71,822	X	0.657516	=	$ 47,224
$75,098	X	0.571753	=	$ 42,938
$78,511	X	0.497177	=	$ 39,034
Subtotal			=	$219,742

Present Value of Net Resale Price
(Year 6 *NOI* capitalized at 12% less 3% sales expense)

$657,000	X	0.497177	=	$326,645
Total present value				$546,387

The tenant also pays:

- A pro rata share of any increases in real estate taxes that exceed $1.50 per square foot
- A pro rata share of total energy-related expenses
- A pro rata share of all other operating expenses that exceed $1.50 per square foot plus a 15% administrative charge that is applied to all expenses

The lease held by ABC Appraisal Company covers 6,000 square feet of rentable area. It was signed recently and expires on March 31 of Year 7 of the DCF analysis. The base rent is $24.50 per square foot and there are no renewal options. In addition to base rent, the tenant pays:

- A pro rata share of any increases in real estate taxes that exceed $2.05 per square foot
- A pro rata share of all energy expenses that exceed $2.50 per square foot
- A pro rata share of all increases in other operating expenses that exceed $2.60 per square foot

BMI Computer Center leases 4,000 square feet of ground floor retail space. The lease is one year old and expires on December 31 of Year 8 of the DCF analysis. Base rent is $23.00 per square foot until December 31 of Year 4 of the DCF analysis; thereafter it is $26.00 per square foot. This tenant pays percentage rent based on 6% of sales in excess of $600,000. Sales for the current year totaled $468,000 and are forecast to increase 7% per year. In addition, the tenant pays:

- A pro rata share of all increases in real estate taxes that exceed $1.75 per square foot
- Thirty percent of all increases in energy expenses that exceed $2.20 per square foot
- Thirty percent of all increases in other operating expenses that exceed $2.35 per square foot

Other Revenue

Parking revenue is expected to be $15,000 per year for the next two years, increasing 5% per year thereafter.

Property Expenses

Property expenses for Year 1 of the DCF analysis are forecast as follows:

Real estate taxes	$2.05 per square foot
Utility-related expenses	$2.50 per square foot
Other operating expenses	$2.60 per square foot
Replacement allowance	$0.10 per square foot (not inflated)
Management expense	2.5% of effective gross revenue

In this market neither management expense nor replacement allowance are reimbursed by the tenants.

Mortgage Information

The two mortgages on the property are summarized below. The terms are the same as those in effect on the date of value.

First mortgage

Outstanding balance	$1,100,000
Annual interest rate	11.25%, payable monthly
Amortization term	32 years
Payments	Level payment, self-amortizing

Second mortgage

Outstanding balance	$250,000
Annual interest rate	13.5% for Years 1 and 2, 14% thereafter; payable monthly
Amortization term	25 years
Payments	Interest only for Years 1 and 2; level payment, self-amortizing for balance of term

Miscellaneous assumptions

Leasing commissions	For a new tenant, 3% of base rent per year payable in the first year of the lease; for a renewal tenant, 1.5% per year
Tenant turnover	The RKM Insurance Corporation is expected to move out when its lease expires; the other tenants are expected to re-lease their space
Lease terms	All new leases will have four-year terms
Tenant improvement costs	For a new tenant, $15.00 per square foot; for an existing tenant, $5.00 per square foot in Year 1 dollars
Growth rate	6%
Selling expense at resale	2.5%

Market research

Eight recent sales of competitive office buildings have been researched and verified. The information derived from the sales is summarized in Tables 24.2 and 24.3.

The comparable sales are analyzed to extract capitalization rates, discount rates, growth rates, and other pertinent information. The appraiser has formed the following conclusions.

Forecast period	10 years
Market rent	$24.50 per square foot
Market rent growth rate	6% per year
Vacancy and collection loss	3.0% + 3 months vacancy at rollover
Expense growth rates	
Real estate taxes	5.0%
Utility costs	8.0%
Other operating expenses	6.0%
Overall capitalization rate for calculating reversion	11.0%
Discount rates	
Free and clear of financing	13.0%
Subject to existing financing	14.0%

Based on these investment assumptions, a 10-year cash-flow forecast is prepared for the subject property (see Table 24.4). The present value of the subject is estimated free and clear in Table 24.5 and subject to existing financing in Table 24.6.

Table 24.2 | Comparable Office Building Sales

Sale	Rentable Area (Sq. Ft.)	Sale Price	Sale Price per Sq. Ft.	Equity	Mortgage Amount	Mortgage Interest Rate	NIR*	EGIM†	First Year Cash Flow Rate	First Year Overall Rate	Forecast Equity IRR‡	Forecast Period (Years)
1	16,000	$2,464,000	$154.00	$1,000,000	$1,464,000	10.50%	45.5%	6.0	6.50%	7.58%	13.8%	10
2	23,000	$3,500,000	$152.17	$1,250,000	$1,500,000 (1st) $750,000 (2nd)	12.00% 13.25%	52.5%	7.5	2.10%	7.00%	14.0%	11
3	12,500	$1,950,000	$156.00	$1,500,000	$450,000	9.00%	60.0%	8.0	5.50%	7.50%	13.8%	10
4	25,000	$4,050,000	$162.00	$1,500,000	$1,500,000 (1st) $1,050,000 (2nd)	11.50% 13.50%	50.5%	7.0	4.30%	7.21%	14.5%	10
5	16,000	$2,550,000	$159.38	$2,550,000	0	-	55.0%	7.7	7.14%	7.14%	13.0%	5
6	15,000	$2,265,000	$151.00	$1,500,000	$765,000	9.50%	48.0%	7.5	6.20%	6.40%	14.0%	10
7	9,000	$1,575,000	$175.00	$1,575,000	0	-	43.0%	5.0	8.60%	8.60%	13.0%	10
8	35,000	$5,075,000	$145.00	$1,600,000	$3,000,000 (1st) $475,000 (2nd)	12.50% 14.0%	65.0%	7.5	3.00%	8.67%	14.0%	10

The data presented above are retrospective and may not be relevant in cases where they differ from the prospective expectations of the market.
* NIR = net operating income/effective gross revenue
† EGIM = effective gross income multiplier; sale price/effective gross income
‡ IRR = prospective internal rate of return or discount rate

Table 24.3 Analysis of Cash Flow Assumptions for Comparable Office Building Sales

Sale	Market Rent Growth Rate	Expense Growth Rate			Resale Price (R_o)	Vacancy	Terms of New Leases (Years)	Re-Leasing Escalation Provisions		
		R. E. Taxes	Utility Items	Other Operating Expenses				R. E. Taxes	Utility Items	Other Operating Expenses
1	6.0%	5.0%	8.0%	8.0%	11.0%	3 months plus 2.0%	3	*	*	*
2	5.5%	5.0%	10.0%	6.0%	11.0%	3 months plus 3.0%	5	*	*	*
3	6.0%	4.5%	7.5%	6.0%	12.0%	5.0%	5	*	*	*
4	6.0%	5.0%	8.0%	7.0%	10.5%	3 months plus 3.0%	3	*	*	*
5	5.5%	5.0%	8.0%	6.0%	12.0%	4 months plus 2.0%	3	*	*	*
6	6.5%	6.0%	8.5%	6.0%	10.5%	3 months plus 3.0%	3	*	*	*
7	6.0%	5.0%	7.5%	5.0%	11.0%	3 months plus 3.0%	5	*	*	*
8	6.0%	4.5%	9.0%	6.0%	11.0%	2 months plus 2.5%	5	*	*	*

Data on these eight comparables are presented for purposes of illustration. The date of sale for each property is not cited, but this information would be critical in assessing the usefulness of the data.
* Pro rata share of increases over base year—i.e., year in which lease commences

Table 24.4 Cash Flow Forecast for Subject Office Building

For the Years Ending	Year 1 Jun 1997	Year 2 Jun 1998	Year 3 Jun 1999	Year 4 Jun 2000	Year 5 Jun 2001	Year 6 Jun 2002	Year 7 Jun 2003	Year 8 Jun 2004	Year 9 Jun 2005	Year 10 Jun 2006	Year 11 Jun 2007
Potential gross revenue											
Base rental revenue	$329,000	$329,000	$334,000	$345,000	$351,000	$351,000	$440,149	$507,969	$529,647	$529,647	$577,539
Absorption & turnover vacancy	0	0	0	0	0	0	(43,442)	0	0	0	(120,659)
Scheduled base rental revenue	$329,000	$329,000	$334,000	$345,000	$351,000	$351,000	$396,707	$507,969	$529,647	$529,647	$456,880
Expense reimbursement revenue	30,549	37,310	45,210	53,640	62,631	72,226	54,084	44,261	44,515	56,659	49,279
Parking revenue	15,000	15,000	15,750	16,538	17,364	18,233	19,144	20,101	21,107	22,162	23,270
Total potential gross revenue	$374,549	$381,549	$394,960	$415,178	$430,995	$441,459	$469,935	$572,331	$595,269	$608,468	$529,429
General vacancy	(11,236)	(11,439)	(11,849)	(12,455)	(12,930)	(13,244)	0	(17,170)	(17,858)	(18,254)	0
Effective gross revenue	$363,313	$369,871	$383,111	$402,723	$418,065	$428,215	$469,935	$555,161	$577,411	$590,214	$529,429
Operating expenses											
Real estate taxes	30,750	32,287	33,902	35,597	37,377	39,246	41,208	43,268	45,432	47,703	50,089
Utilities	37,500	40,500	43,740	47,239	51,018	55,100	59,508	64,268	69,410	74,963	80,960
Other operating expenses	39,000	41,340	43,820	46,450	49,237	52,191	55,322	58,642	62,160	65,890	69,843
Management	9,083	9,247	9,578	10,068	10,452	10,705	11,748	13,879	14,435	14,755	13,236
Total operating expenses	$116,333	$123,374	$131,040	$139,354	$148,084	$157,242	$167,786	$180,057	$191,437	$203,311	$214,128
Net operating income	$246,980	$246,497	$252,071	$263,369	$269,981	$270,973	$302,149	$375,104	$385,974	$386,903	$315,301
Debt service											
Interest payments	157,312	156,870	157,553	156,823	156,002	155,077	154,035	152,862	151,539	150,050	0
Principal payments	3,725	4,166	5,847	6,576	7,398	8,322	9,364	10,538	11,860	13,350	0
Total debt service	$161,037	$161,036	$163,400	$163,399	$163,400	$163,399	$163,399	$163,400	$163,399	$163,400	$0
Leasing & capital costs											
Tenant improvements	0	0	0	0	0	0	105,000	20,000	0	0	75,000
Leasing commissions	0	0	0	0	0	0	33,363	8,841	0	0	26,325
Replacement reserves	1,500	1,500	1,500	1,500	1,500	1,500	1,500	1,500	1,500	1,500	1,500
Total leasing & capital costs	$1,500	$1,500	$1,500	$1,500	$1,500	$1,500	$139,863	$30,341	$1,500	$1,500	$102,825
Net income after debt service	$84,443	$83,961	$87,171	$98,470	$105,081	$106,074	$(1,113)	$181,363	$221,075	$222,003	$212,476

| Table 24.5 | **Prospective Present Value—Free and Clear of Financing: Cash Flow Before Debt Service Plus Property Resale Discounted Annually (End-point on Cash Flow & Resale) Over a 10-Year Period** |

Analysis Period	For Year Ending	Annual Cash Flow*	PV of Cash Flow @ 13.00%
Year 1	June 1997	$245,480	$217,239
Year 2	June 1998	244,997	191,869
Year 3	June 1999	250,571	173,658
Year 4	June 2000	261,869	160,609
Year 5	June 2001	268,481	145,721
Year 6	June 2002	269,473	129,433
Year 7	June 2003	162,286	68,981
Year 8	June 2004	344,763	129,686
Year 9	June 2005	384,474	127,986
Year 10	June 2006	385,403	113,535
Total cash flow		$2,817,797	$1,458,717
Property resale @ 11% cap rate[†]		$2,794,714	823,290
Total property present value			$2,282,007
Rounded to thousands			$2,282,000
Per square foot			$152.13

Percentage value distribution

Assured income	0.5065
Prospective income	0.1327
Prospective property resale	0.3608
	1.0000

* Annual cash flow=annual *NOI* less total leasing and capital costs
† Net operating income for Year 10 ($315,301) capitalized at 11%, less 2.5% selling expense

Table 24.6	**Prospective Present Value Subject to Existing Financing: Cash Flow After Debt Service Plus Property Resale Discounted Annually (End-point on Cash Flow & Resale) Over a 10-year Period**

Analysis Period	For Year Ending	Annual Cash Flow*	PV of Cash Flow @ 14.00%
Year 1	June 1997	$84,443	$74,073
Year 2	June 1998	83,961	64,605
Year 3	June 1999	87,171	58,838
Year 4	June 2000	98,470	58,302
Year 5	June 2001	105,081	54,576
Year 6	June 2002	106,074	48,326
Year 7	June 2003	(1,113)	(445)
Year 8	June 2004	181,363	63,578
Year 9	June 2005	221,075	67,983
Year 10	June 2006	222,003	59,884
Total cash flow		$1,188,528	$549,720
Property resale @ 11% cap rate†		$1,525,862	411,592
Value of equity interest			$961,312
Rounded to thousands			$961,000
Per square foot			$64.06
Value of equity interest			$961,312
Debt balance as of July 1996		$1,350,000‡	1,350,000
Total leveraged present value			$2,311,312
Rounded to thousands			$2,311,000
Per square foot			$154.0875

* Annual cash flow after debt service but before income tax
† Proceeds from resale of property
‡ First mortgage plus second mortgage ($1,100,000 + $250,000)

Several observations can be made from this example. First, note that the yield rate used to discount the property on an all-cash (free-and-clear) basis is lower than the rate used to value the property subject to existing financing. The yield rate generally increases when financing is involved, which may be attributed to the impact of leverage. The discount rate is not *significantly* higher (14% versus 13%) because the existing loans are only about 54% of the property value. The value estimates are fairly close under the different assumptions, although the value is still slightly higher when estimated subject to existing financing.[3]

Second, consider the overall rate implied by each estimated value. For example, on a free-and-clear basis, the implied overall capitalization rate is about 10.8% ($246,980/$2,282,000). To check the reasonableness of the value estimated with the discounted cash flow analysis, this overall rate could be compared to the overall rates derived from comparable sales, if available.

Third, note that the implied overall capitalization rate (10.8%) is less than the overall capitalization rate or terminal capitalization rate used to estimate the resale price, which was assumed to be 11%.[4] Higher capitalization rates are often used to estimate a future resale price because more risk is associated with income estimated at the end of the investment holding period. The relationship between these two capitalization rates appears to be reasonable.

DCF Models: Net Present Value and the Internal Rate of Return

Net present value (*NPV*) and the internal rate of return (*IRR*) are two models widely used for measuring investment performance and developing decision-making criteria. Both models are based on discounted cash flow analysis. *Net present value is the difference between the present value of all positive cash flows and the present value of all negative cash flows, or capital outlays.* When the net present value of the positive cash flows is greater than the net present value of the negative cash flows or capital outlays, an investment is deemed viable. If the reverse relationship exists, the investment is not considered feasible.[5]

A net present value of zero indicates that the present value of all positive cash flows equals the present value of all negative cash flows or capital outlays. *The rate of discount that makes the net present value of an investment equal zero is the internal rate of return (IRR).* In other words, the *IRR* discounts all returns from an investment, including returns from its termination, to a net present value equal to the original investment.[6]

---

3. In theory the total value of the real estate should not increase when subject to market rate debt financing. Any apparent premium due to favorable financing does not increase the value of the real property; it only increases the price an investor would be willing to pay to buy the property subject to the existing loan.

4. An overall capitalization rate used to estimate the resale price of an investment is usually referred to as a *terminal* or *residual capitalization rate*. (See Chapters 21 and 23.)

5. Net present value does not explicitly consider the time value of money nor does it adequately deal with the problem of risk. Each is implicit in the discount rate. *NPV* is discussed at greater length in Chapter 27.

6. Practitioners often use the terms *yield rate* and *IRR* interchangeably. The yield rate or *IRR* is the discount rate which equates the present value of all expected future cash flows with the initial investment.

Limitations and Pitfalls of the *IRR*

The *IRR* has limitations and appraisers may encounter pitfalls in its use. By understand-ing these shortcomings, practitioners can avoid wasted effort and false conclusions. The search for a single *IRR* within a plausible range is not always successful. Unusual combinations of cash flows may produce strange results and more than one *IRR* or no *IRR* may be indicated.

More Than One IRR

Consider a real estate investment with the cash flows set forth in Table 24.7. Assuming that the investor borrows $10,000 and pays 10% interest only, with the principal to be repaid in a lump sum at the end of 10 years, the investor's net cash flows can be tabu-lated.

Table 24.7	Net Cash Flow			
Year	Cash Flow Before Loan/Interest	Loan	Interest	Net Cash Flow
0	-$12,300*	$10,000	$0	-$2,300
1	$2,000	0	-$1,000	$1,000
2	$2,000	0	-$1,000	$1,000
3	$2,000	0	-$1,000	$1,000
4	$2,000	0	-$1,000	$1,000
5	$1,000	0	-$1,000	0
6	$1,000	0	-$1,000	0
7	$1,000	0	-$1,000	0
8	$1,000	0	-$1,000	0
9	$1,000	0	-$1,000	0
10	$9,000†	-$10,000	-$1,000	-$2,000

* Initial cash outlay
† Income and proceeds from sale

The *IRR* for the net cash flows after financing can be obtained through graphic analysis. Net present values are calculated for even discount rates between 0% and 24% and plotted on a graph. Table 24.8 and Figure 24.1 indicate not one, but two, *IRR*s. With a computer the two *IRR*s are calculated as 4.50839% and 18.3931%.

Multiple rates like these are interesting from a theoretical point of view, but it is difficult to accept more than one *IRR* as a useful measure of performance. In real estate investment analysis, the presence of more than one *IRR* usually suggests that some other measure of performance would be more appropriate or that the cash flows or time frame should be adjusted to permit a more meaningful analysis. Close examination of the example presented here reveals some characteristics of the *IRR* that may not be apparent in more typical examples.

Table 24.8	**Table of Net Present Values**

Discount Rate	Net Present Value
0	-$300
2	-$133
4	-$21
6	$48
8	$86
10	$99
12	$93
14	$74
16	$45
18	$8
20	-$34
22	-$80
24	-$128

Figure 24.1	**Graphic Solution to Example**

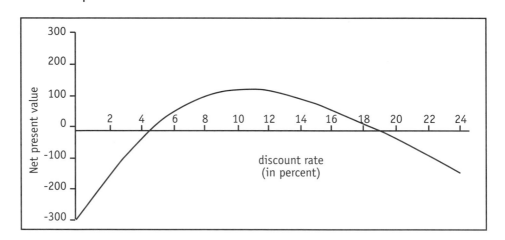

Negative Net Present Value at Zero Rate of Return

The cumulative value of the net cash flows in Table 24.7 is negative. Negative net cash flows total $4,300, while positive net cash flows total $4,000. Therefore, the net present value—i.e., the difference between the present value of expected benefits, or positive cash flows, and the present value of capital outlays, or negative cash flows—with no discounting or at a zero discount rate is -$300 (see graph). This should be a warning sign to the analyst. Whenever the total capital invested over a period of time is equal to or more than the total income for the same period, the *IRR* should be viewed with suspicion.

Under these conditions, the *IRR* cannot be positive unless the mixture of positive and negative cash flows over time is such that the net present value increases with increases in the discount rate until the net present value reaches zero. This phenomenon can be seen in the preceding example. This type of reverse discounting is mathematically valid, but it is contrary to the practical notion of reducing net present value by increasing the discount rate. It is not surprising that the *IRR* in such cases is difficult to comprehend and of questionable practical use.

Negative *IRR*

If the net present value of an investment at a 0% rate of return is negative, a negative *IRR* may be indicated. A negative *IRR* may be interpreted as a rate of loss, but the *IRR* is generally understood to be a positive rate of return. Any prospective rate of loss will normally discourage capital investment.

The concept of a negative *IRR* has theoretical, as well as practical, limitations. A glance at the *IRR* equation reveals that a negative *IRR* of 100% or more has no meaning because it involves division by zero or powers of a negative number.

Little or No Equity

Because the *IRR* is a measure of the return on invested capital, it cannot be used to measure the performance of opportunities that require no investment of capital. Some investments can be "financed out"—i.e., financed with loans that cover 100% or more of the capital required. If the projected net cash flows are all positive, there is no *IRR*. Obviously, no discount rate can make a series of exclusively positive benefits equal zero.

The same rationale can be applied to investments that call for very low equity or a very small down payment in relation to expected returns. For example, a profit of $1 on an investment of $1 amounts to a 100% rate of return; a return of $100 on an investment of $1 indicates a 10,000% rate of return. When the investment is very small, slight changes in income can cause astronomical changes in the rate of return or rate of loss. The *IRR* is an impractical yardstick for such investments.

However, the *IRR* can be a valuable indicator in analyzing investments that are 100% financed at the start and then expected to operate at a loss for a period of time. In these arrangements, the early negative cash flows may represent a significant investment of equity capital and the prospective *IRR* may be the best measure of performance. It may also be useful to compare the prospective *IRR* before financing with an interest rate that reflects the cost of capital. The difference can be used as a measure of prospective leverage.

Reinvestment Concepts

The *IRR* is an *internal* rate of return on the capital *within* an investment. No consideration is given to the rate of return on reinvested capital after it has been withdrawn from the investment. The income from a real estate investment may be reinvested in another project at another rate of return, stored in a vault, or spent, but the *IRR* is not affected. Thus, no assumptions about a reinvestment rate are needed to understand and use the *IRR*.

Although reinvestment rates are not relevant to the *IRR*, some analysts choose to envision the reinvestment of income at a rate equal to the *IRR*. This assumption is implied if the objective is to measure the total return on a fixed capital sum over a fixed period of time and the fruits of reinvestment are not otherwise taken into account. This is a popular premise, but it can be misleading.

It is correct to assume that if all the dollars withdrawn from a project are reinvested at the same *IRR*, the final composite rate of return will be equal to the *IRR* of the investment. It is also correct to assume that if all the dollars withdrawn from a project are reinvested at a rate of return that is not equal to the *IRR*, the final composite rate of return will not be equal to the *IRR* of the investment. It does not follow, however, that the final composite rate of return on invested and reinvested dollars must equal the original *IRR* of the investment.

If an investor wants to find the *IRR* associated with a *capital sum* at work over a period of time, the reinvestment of income must be considered. If, on the other hand, the objective is to find the *IRR* associated with a *particular property*, the reinvestment of income may be irrelevant. Therefore, unless instructed otherwise by a client, an appraiser need not address reinvestment assumptions when valuing property on the basis of an *IRR*.

An *IRR* is an independent, informative statistic that reflects the amount of earnings for each dollar invested over a specific unit of time for a particular set of cash flows. It can be applied to a single property or to an entire investment portfolio. If an overall *IRR* that reflects the combined results of project earnings and reinvestment is sought, the reinvestment cash flows can be incorporated into the analysis. In short, there is no automatic or implicit assumption in the *IRR* regarding reinvestment. The *IRR* can, however, accommodate reinvestment assumptions by including the expected costs and benefits of reinvestment in the projection of cash flows if so desired.

Reinvestment assumptions are sometimes made to prevent multiple *IRR*s such as those found in the preceding example. If it is assumed that all income is reinvested at a known rate and withdrawn in a lump sum at the termination of the investment, there can be only one overall *IRR* that represents the combined results of project earnings and reinvestment.

IRR Before Taxes Versus *IRR* After Taxes

The *IRR* is generally seen as a measure of an investment's ultimate net financial performance after all expenses, including income taxes, have been paid. It is a convention among real estate analysts, however, to analyze property on a *pre-tax* basis. The *IRR* can be used to measure profit before income taxes. In fact, the *IRR* is applicable to any level of financial return; it is a general-purpose comparative measure with no arbitrary restrictions.

Comparing the after-tax performance of one investment opportunity to the after-tax performance of another is only one of its many applications. As mentioned earlier, the *IRR* before financing for a particular investment can be compared to the *IRR* after financing to assess the effects of leverage produced by borrowing. Similarly, the *IRR* before taxes can be compared to the *IRR* after taxes to determine the impact of taxation and any tax-shelter benefits. Although the *IRR* is not restricted to a particular use, there is considerable debate regarding its proper use in the analysis of real estate investments.

Arguments in Favor of the *IRR* Before Income Taxes

Income taxes depend on the tax bracket of the individual investor as well as the earning power of the real estate. Therefore, many analysts feel that the *IRR* before taxes is a better measure of intrinsic performance because it is not dependent on outside influences. This argument is often raised when market value is sought and the tax bracket of the investor is not known.

The market for real estate investments is influenced, to some extent, by decision makers who are tax-exempt or do not pay income taxes directly (e.g., charitable foundations, pension funds, real estate investment trusts). Consequently, the *IRR* before taxes is more meaningful in comparisons that involve this segment of the market.

The *IRR* before taxes also has the advantage of simplicity. Projecting cash flow before taxes is less complicated and less subject to error because many calculations are eliminated. Including assumptions regarding tax brackets and allowable deductions introduces more uncertainties and weakens the credibility of the forecast. Furthermore, yields on stocks, bonds, and mortgages are reported in terms of a rate of return before income taxes. Real estate must compete for capital with these alternative investment opportunities, so the *IRR* before income taxes provides a logical basis of comparison.

Arguments in Favor of the *IRR* After Income Taxes

Tax shelter was once a major attraction for real estate investors. Some analysts argue that any yardstick that does not reflect the full effect of taxes and tax-shelter benefits is deficient. (For a discussion of how the Tax Reform Act of 1986 has affected tax shelters, see Chapter 27.)

The fact that income taxes vary with the tax bracket of the investor may be seen to encourage, rather than discourage, the use of the *IRR* after taxes. The tax bracket of the investor is an important variable that cannot be ignored in any complete analysis. If an estimate of market value is sought and the investor's tax bracket is unknown, the analyst can simulate the decision-making process of a typical investor by using a typical tax rate.

Computer models are readily available and can be used to produce detailed after-tax cash flow analyses. The required calculations can be automated without significant effort or expense. However, the appraiser or analyst must know the assumptions of the analysis, especially the manner in which the program calculates taxes. Similarly, the reported yields on stocks, bonds, and mortgages can easily be converted to reveal equivalent yields after taxes for purposes of comparison. The yields reported for tax-exempt municipal bonds need not be converted at all, but can be compared directly to the *IRR* after taxes.

Clearly, there are valid arguments for using either the *IRR* before taxes or the *IRR* after taxes. The *IRR* selected depends on the application and the objective of the analysis.

Conclusion

The *IRR* can be as important to the real estate investor as the interest rate is to the mortgage lender; in fact, the two measures are equivalent. The interest rate on a mortgage is the same as the mortgagee's yield, or the *IRR*. The *IRR* is not a meaningful measure of all investments and, even when it is meaningful, it is not the only possible criterion. It is, however, a fundamental and pure measure of the financial performance of a particular investment. In general, the *IRR* is an extremely valuable analytical tool if the decision maker understands its attributes and limitations and has access to complementary or alternative analytical techniques.

Other Measures of Performance

Popular alternative measures of financial performance or profitability include the payback period, the profitability index or cost/benefit ratio, the net present value or dollar reward, and the time-weighted rate, which are discussed in Chapter 27. *These yardsticks do not measure performance or profit on the same scale or under the same assumptions as the IRR.* Their usefulness depends on the situation and the preferences of the user. Neither the *IRR* nor any alternative measure is superior in all situations. The two measures described below represent specific modifications of the *IRR*.

IRR with Reinvestment

This variation of the *IRR* was mentioned in the discussion of reinvestment concepts. It assumes that all income from a project can be immediately reinvested at a specified rate and left to grow at that rate until the end of the investment holding period. The combined results of the investment's earnings and reinvestment are then reflected in one overall rate of return. The *IRR* with reinvestment traces the presumed total performance of a capital sum at work in more than one investment, rather than the performance of a single real estate project. This measure can also be used to prevent multiple solutions to the *IRR* equation. The *IRR* with reinvestment is often called the adjusted or modified *IRR* (*AIRR* or *MIRR*). The formula for the *MIRR* appears in Appendix C.

IRR with a Specified Borrowing Rate

The *IRR* with a specified borrowing rate is another variation of the *IRR* that can be used to prevent multiple rates. It is sometimes called *the IRR for investment* or *financial management rate of return* (FMRR). The *IRR* for investment or *FMRR* specifies an interest rate for the borrowed funds needed during the period when the investment is producing negative cash flows; thus it prevents the use of the *IRR* as a borrowing rate. Stipulating a fixed borrowing rate modifies the cash flows as well as the *IRR* and prevents the possibility of more than one *IRR*. Like the *IRR* with reinvestment (*AIRR* or *MIRR*), the *IRR* with a specified borrowing rate (*FMRR*) is a measure of the performance of a capital sum, not the returns generated exclusively by a real estate investment.

Business Enterprise Value

Business enterprise value is a value enhancement that results from items of intangible personal property such as marketing and management skill, an assembled work force, working capital, trade names, franchises, patents, trademarks, non-realty related contracts/leases, and some operating agreements. The reporting requirements of USPAP as well as certain assignments, such as appraisals for tax appeals or eminent domain, require that value be allocated among its various components, i.e., real estate, FF&E, business enterprise, and other intangibles. There are divergent methods of estimating business enterprise value and no single technique is universally accepted. The general principles followed by appraisers in making this determination are discussed below.

In estimating business enterprise value and determining whether the business enterprise makes a contribution to the going concern, the central issue is net operating income. How much *NOI* is required to support the investment in real estate? If any residual income exists, how much is required to support other personal and/or intangible property components? As an example, consider a property with the following net operating income characteristics.

Total *NOI* to the going concern (overall property)	$320,000
NOI attributable to the real estate	$270,000
Residual income to the business enterprise	$50,000
Capitalization rate for the real estate	13.0%
Overall capitalization rate for the going concern (from sales extraction)	14.0%
Indicated value of the going concern $320,000/0.14	$2,285,700 (rounded)
Indicated value of the real estate $270,000/0.13	$2,076,900 (rounded)
Contributory value of the business enterprise	$208,800
Capitalization rate imputed to the business enterprise ($50,000/$208,800)	23.9%

In some instances, it may be necessary to further allocate income among items of personalty, e.g., FF&E are commonly considered in the appraisal of hotels, motels, nursing homes, and other similar operations.

The above example provides a rudimentary procedure for deriving business enterprise value. It is not always easy to differentiate income to the real estate from income to the business enterprise or other intangibles. Included among the items generally associated with the business enterprise are management fees, performance incentives, franchise fees, and certain contracts that may either enhance or limit revenue in comparison to market norms.

The concept of business enterprise value is a very real issue that confronts practitioners daily. It is also highly controversial. As the body of knowledge relating to this issue expands, techniques currently in development may achieve greater definition and acceptance. A word of caution is in order regarding any attempt to estimate a property's business enterprise value. Although business enterprise components may be associated with certain properties, the specific property operation may be such that the net operating income generated is only sufficient to support the real estate component. Consequently there may be no supportable business enterprise value. Extreme care must be taken by the appraiser in making business value determinations.

Appraisal of Proposed and Problem Properties

Over the past three decades, all aspects of the real estate industry have undergone change. Real estate developments have become larger, the design of structures has evolved, and property values have greatly increased. Mortgage lending has also grown more complicated. Not all of these changes have been advantageous. Bad underwriting precipitated the failure of a significant number of lenders and resulted in the S&L crisis of the late 1980s.

Appraisers have to deal with increasingly complicated valuation problems. The basic theory, concepts, and principles of valuation have remained the same, but the application of the basics has become more complex. Appraisal work is facilitated by the availability of additional tools such as calculators, computers, and statistical methods. Discounted cash flow analysis has become widespread, but the technique itself is not new. Marketability analysis, which is now universally recognized as important in the valuation of property, has long been in the purview of appraisers.

The following section discusses the application of valuation fundamentals to the appraisal of proposed and problem properties. Excluded from this discussion are properties that are not sold or rented to multiple end users, i.e., single-family residences, small multifamily residences, owner-occupied properties, and special-use properties.

Proposed properties may be defined as properties slated for planned improvements which will change the use and/or functional utility. Proposed properties include new development projects and existing properties that are to be renovated. *Problem properties* encompass several categories. One type of problem property is a property that has not achieved the level of utility for which it was designed and consequently is a financial failure, e.g., a strip shopping center that did not meet a breakeven occupancy level and thus has not generated the necessary cash flow to pay debt service or provide a return on the investment. A second kind of problem property is a project that remains partially completed. A third type is a development that carries high risk because of its size or complexity, e.g., a timeshare resort project, a large mixed-use development.

Characteristics of Proposed and Problem Properties

To value a proposed or problem property, the appraiser often must estimate value at multiple points in time, i.e., as the property exists, upon completion or at a given phase of construction, and upon achievement of a stabilized condition. As applied to these properties, the basic components of the valuation process include:

1. The estimation of separate values at different points on the development timeline
2. A marketability study upon which the appraisal is based, and
3. An estimation of the entrepreneurial profit made in the project

The analysis of proposed and problem properties is usually undertaken to facilitate decision making by assessing the property's economic feasibility.

The determination of economic feasibility requires a market value estimate of the property as currently existing (its "as is" value) and a value estimate at a prospective time—i.e., upon completion of some phase of construction, achievement of a stabilized condition, or both. *Stabilized condition* or *stabilization* indicates that the property has reached the level of utility for which it was designed or planned. For rental projects, this means stabilized occupancy; for projects in which units are to be sold to multiple end users, also called *for sale properties*, it means sellout. For a subdivision in which the lots have been improved for sale to end users, who intend to build homes for their own use or for sale to other users, stabilization occurs when all the improved subdivision lots are sold. For a residential subdivision in which homes have been developed by a builder for sale to multiple end users, it means sellout of all the subdivision homes.

It is essential to recognize that the values of a property as is, upon completion of construction, and upon stabilization are not concurrent; they occur at different times on the development timeline. An appraiser who fails to remember this may lose sight of predictable changes in market conditions and make erroneous assumptions in feasibility analysis and value estimation.

A marketability study is critical to the valuation of proposed and problem properties because it provides the foundation for most of the assumptions an appraiser must make in valuing the property—e.g., probable tenant or buyer characteristics, pricing or a price range appropriate for the market, absorption rate.

All four agents of production are generally included in the cost to develop a proposed or problem property into a viable project. Entrepreneurial profit may be considered the defining component because it remains a consideration in all phases of a development project. An entrepreneur will only develop a proposed or problem property if an entrepreneurial profit can be earned. If some or all of the improvements on a problem property are completed, an entrepreneur will purchase that property only if an entrepreneurial profit can be earned by creating value through construction, conversion, renovation, and marketing the real estate product. Sufficient market demand must clearly exist. Entrepreneurial profit is the reward to the developer for creating value despite the risks and effort involved. The development phase includes both constructing (converting or renovating) and marketing the proposed product up to the achievement of its planned end use or stabilized condition, i.e., sellout or stabilized occupancy.

Basic Concepts

Marketability Studies

In a marketability study, the appraiser investigates how a particular property will be absorbed, sold, or leased under current or anticipated market conditions; a market study or analysis of the general class of property should be included. A marketability study is property-specific. It should identify the characteristics of the subject's market and quantify their effect on the value of the property.

The development of a property usually entails both a construction (conversion or renovation) phase and a marketing phase. The marketability study must describe the demand and supply situation under current market conditions (for the estimate of "as is" value) as well as the demand and supply situation over the planned construction period (for the value upon completion) and the marketing period (for the estimate of value upon stabilization). In other words, a marketability study for a property must focus on each point on the development timeline for which a value is to be estimated. The demand and supply analysis must investigate market conditions, both current and future, to determine the absorption rate and other factors that will affect value during the marketing period.

One common deficiency in the valuation of proposed or problem properties is inadequate analysis of the demand and supply situation from the date of the appraisal through the marketing phase. A market study that only concerns itself with current market conditions will produce unsupported value estimates if the property is a proposed improvement and/or must be marketed to achieve a stabilized condition. Even when an appraiser estimates the value of a property as if completed or stabilized on the date of the appraisal, the marketability study must include a forecast of demand and supply through the expected marketing phase to project the likely absorption period for the property.

The highest and best use analysis of a property must incorporate the findings of the marketability study and include analysis of the four tests of highest and best use—physical possibility, legal permissibility, economic feasibility, and maximum productivity. The highest and best use analysis for proposed or problem properties should include consideration of:

- The existing property
- The property upon completion of construction (conversion or renovation)
- The property upon stabilization, i.e., at stabilized occupancy for a rental property (if not at stabilized occupancy upon completion of construction) and at sellout for a property consisting of units to be sold to multiple end users.

A marketability study is founded on analysis of the four factors of value—utility, scarcity, desire, and effective purchasing power. The interaction of these four factors will determine the marketability of a property. Utility and scarcity are supply-side factors, while desire and effective purchasing power are demand-side factors. A marketability study must answer the following questions:

- Who will the end users be—i.e., buyers or tenants?
- What are the characteristics of the expected end users? (age, family size, space needs, and preferences as to facilities and amenities)
- Does the utility of the improvements, whether proposed or existing, satisfy the requirements of the intended market?
- What is the demand for the proposed property that is to be marketed?
  - How many end users would want the property? (desire)
  - How many potential users can afford it? (effective purchasing power)
  - What share of demand is the property likely to capture? (capture rate)
- What is the supply of competitive properties that will be marketed?

— How many competitive units currently exist?

— How many competitive units are under construction?

— How many competitive units are planned?

• What is the estimated absorption rate for the proposed property to be marketed?

• Are there alternative uses for the property that would provide a higher return on the investment?

— What are the relative risks associated with the alternative uses?

An appraiser must be careful not to misinterpret data. For example, the absorption rate experienced by competitive projects is sometimes incorrectly assumed to indicate the absorption rate for the subject when it is actually an indication of demand. Consider an appraiser who is analyzing a proposed residential subdivision and finds three competitive subdivisions in the subject's market area. Over the past year, these subdivisions have had average sales rates of three lots per month, five lots per month, and seven lots per month. Simply using five lots per month, the average sales rate for the three competitive subdivisions, as the estimated absorption rate for the subject would most likely be incorrect. The total lot sales for the three competitive subdivisions can, however, be used as an indication of the total historic *demand* for similarly developed residential lots in the subject's market area—i.e., 15 lots per month is the demand for this type of real estate product. The appraiser should study additional market factors, including growth patterns and the development of new competitive subdivisions, to support the estimate of total demand over the subject's marketing period.

The subject's marketing period can be determined by analyzing the supply of competitive residential subdivision lots in the market area, including the subject and all other proposed and existing subdivisions. Assuming that the three existing subdivisions mentioned above continue to sell off lots during the subject's marketing period, that another proposed subdivision will be added to the competition in the subject's market during this period, and that total demand is 15 lots per month, the average absorption rate for the five subdivisions will be three lots per month. The appraiser can then determine whether the subject's absorption rate will be the same as, higher than, or lower than the average rate. The reasoning for the rate chosen should be explained in the appraiser's conclusion.

If a marketability study prepared by another party is being used in the valuation, the appraiser must recognize that this study represents secondary data. The appraiser should carefully review the study to determine its validity and whether it can be used.

The Four Agents of Production

Traditional economic theory holds that four agents of production are combined to create real estate and real estate value is based on the costs to develop a property. In other words, a finished real estate product is created by combining land, labor, capital, and entrepreneurship. This concept is fundamental to the cost approach, and it may also be applied to the analysis of any proposed or problem property. By analyzing these four major components, the appraiser can logically break down the total cost to develop a property. A well-supported value estimate can be derived through systematic analysis of each of these components, their interrelationships, and their relationship to the property as a whole.

The first thing an entrepreneur generally considers in developing a proposed property is the cost of acquiring the land. The cost of a vacant site or parcel of raw land is the cost of acquisition. In analyzing a problem property, the appraiser may modify the concept of the land component to include land and existing improvements as of the date the property was purchased or the date of appraisal. In either case, the appraiser anticipates that improvements will be added and the property will be marketed to tenants or multiple end users.

The labor component comprises all direct and indirect costs required to construct and market the product. Direct costs include not only the wages paid to individuals, but also the cost of materials used in construction. Indirect costs consist of permit fees, marketing expenses, taxes, overhead, maintenance after construction is completed, the cost of project coordination or supervision, and financing costs that are not included in the rate of return to the lender over the development period.

The cost of capital is the return on both the borrowed capital and the equity capital invested in the project; it is usually represented by the discount rate applied in DCF analysis. This discount rate is the property yield rate that satisfies the return requirement for the equity investment, considering the risks, the type of development, and the time it takes to construct and market the property. The discount rate used in DCF analysis is best obtained from market data.

A weighted average of the interest rate on the loan and the rate of return on the equity may not be the correct discount rate. Weighted-average rates are only applicable when the loan-to-value ratio remains constant over the discounting period, e.g., an interest-only loan which keeps the loan-to-value ratio constant. In some cases, a development loan is an interest-only loan. Lot or unit releases, however, are generally phased so that the amount of each release is more than a pro rata share of the total loan, which results in a decreasing loan-to-value ratio. The discount rate used in DCF analysis should always be tested for reasonableness. Proposed properties and problem properties involve more risk. The discount rates applied in DCF analyses of these properties should be higher than discount rates applied to income properties that have achieved a stabilized condition.

Entrepreneurial profit is generally the component given the least attention in the analysis of a proposed property. Entrepreneurial profit should not be confused with builder's profit, which is paid to a contractor to construct the improvements. The accounting concept of entrepreneurial profit equates it with the net residual value after the property has been sold and all tangible costs have been paid. This residual, however, reflects more than entrepreneurial profit since it usually includes the return on equity capital.

To the appraiser, entrepreneurial profit represents the cost to produce or create a real estate project in addition to the cost of equity capital. No legitimate developer will undertake to construct and market a property without anticipating receipt of a profit in addition to a return on the equity investment. A purchaser who acquires a rental property at stabilized occupancy anticipates a rate of return on his or her equity investment. The purchaser is not creating value, only maintaining value through proper management of the property. A developer, on the other hand, has not only invested equity in a development, but also time and expertise. Accordingly, entrepreneurial profit is the reward the entrepreneur receives for creating and marketing a real estate product.

The cost of day-to-day project coordination or supervision should not generally be included in entrepreneurial profit since this cost is recognized as part of the labor component and is typically paid regardless of whether the project succeeds or not. Only in small-scale projects requiring part-time supervision or minimal supervision by the developer may it sometimes be appropriate to include the cost of project supervision in entrepreneurial profit. Entrepreneurial profit is the last agent of production to be paid out of the income from sales or rents, thus it is not realized if the project fails. In the valuation of proposed and problem properties, the appraiser must account for entrepreneurial profit or the value conclusion will be overstated.

Entrepreneurial profit is earned as units are sold or leased. In DCF analysis, entrepreneurial profit is entered as a line item in the various periods when it is anticipated. If it is not treated as a line item in DCF analysis, entrepreneurial profit can be included in the discount rate. A discount rate that incorporates entrepreneurial profit will be significantly higher than a discount rate applied in a DCF analysis where this profit is deducted as a line item.

The appraiser should ascertain whether the profit estimated is reasonable, as both a percentage of gross sales or costs and as a dollar amount. The profit estimate should reflect what the typical entrepreneur in the market would require to develop the type of property being valued. Unlike permit fees, engineering fees, or interest on capital, entrepreneurial profit is a cost that is realized only as the project passes certain milestones. Therefore, when estimating the value of a proposed or problem property as existing or upon completion of construction (conversion or renovation), it is essential to identify and estimate the entrepreneurial profit that has not yet been realized.

Generalized Inventory of Costs in Proposed and Problem Properties

The four agents of production may also apply to the delineation of costs within a generalized inventory, which can be used to develop value estimates as of the three points in time typically required for proposed and problem properties. Usually, the "as is" value estimate for a proposed property reflects only the land value. The "as is" value estimate for a problem property, however, normally includes some improvements, which may or may not be complete. If construction of more improvements is required to achieve the property's planned use, the cost inventory shown in Table 24.9 may be modified by substituting "land and existing improvements" for "land." If the problem property requires no further improvements, the "as is" value of the property would be the value indicated after the construction phase. An alternative inventory may be developed for situations in which no improvements are to be added to the property and, consequently, no construction phase is included. In this case, the inventory would proceed from "land and existing improvements," which indicate the "as is" value, to the costs incurred during the marketing phase.

Table 24.9	**Generalized Cost Inventory**

Value of a proposed property prior to construction
>   Land value = value of proposed property as existing or "as is"

Value of a proposed property upon completion of construction
>   Value of land and improvement(s) = land value plus costs incurred
>   during the construction phase

Construction-phase costs include:
> Labor costs during construction
>> Building and infrastructure
>> Site improvements
>> Taxes and insurance
>> Engineering and architecture
>> Appraisal
>> Legal and accounting
>> Contractor's overhead and profit
>> Developer's overhead and supervision
> Capital costs during construction
>> Fees and interest on borrowed funds
>> Return on equity funds
> Entrepreneurial profit realized, if any, during construction
> Less depreciation, if applicable

Value of a proposed property at stabilization, i.e., sellout or stabilized occupancy
>   Value of land and improvement(s) = land value plus costs incurred over
>   the construction and marketing phases

Marketing-phase costs include:
> Labor costs during marketing
>> Marketing costs, i.e., sales commissions, advertising, etc.
>> Project maintenance during marketing
>> General and administrative overhead
>> Taxes and insurance
>> Legal and accounting
>> Developer's overhead and supervision
> Capital costs during marketing
>> Fees and interest on borrowed funds
>> Return on equity funds
> Entrepreneurial profit realized during marketing
> Less depreciation, if applicable

Note: A non-realty component of value may be included in the cost approach, but it must be clearly identified as a separate component. Separate value indications must be concluded for the realty and non-realty components.

Development Timeline

Appraisals of proposed and problem properties are typically used to assist in decisions concerning economic feasibility and loan underwriting, which require market value estimates at different stages of product development. Two of the agents of production, labor and capital, are expended over intervals on the development timeline. Entrepreneurial profit is usually realized during the marketing phase. Entrepreneurial profit is not usually *received* until the other three agents of production have been compensated, but it may be accounted for as it is realized, i.e., as each unit of the project is sold off.

To arrive at the required estimates of market value, an appraiser must use a dynamic valuation model, deducting expenditures and performing discounting at the appropriate points on the development timeline. A static valuation model that treats "as is" value and prospective values as simultaneous events cannot properly account for the phasing of expenditures and discounting. A static valuation model will also distort the analysis of economic feasibility. Although a project may be economically feasible under current market conditions, these conditions are not static. The project could be deemed unfeasible under prospective market conditions. Therefore, economic feasibility should be determined based on a comparison of costs and value at project stabilization, by which time all costs of production will have been accounted for.

Figure 24.2 represents a development timeline for a proposed subdivision. The timeline illustrates the phases in which the four agents of production are paid. Similar timelines can be graphed for other types of proposed and problem properties. For a problem property, the graph usually starts at some point in the construction phase, i.e., after Point A, and the contributions of the cost components may vary. A timeline graph can also illustrate the costs that have been incurred up to the completion of construction. It must be emphasized, however, that the vertical axis represents cost, not value.

Economic Feasibility Analysis

Economic feasibility analysis is defined as an analysis undertaken to investigate whether a project will fulfill the objectives of the investor. The profitability of a specific real estate project is thus analyzed in terms of the criteria of a specific market or investor. Alternatively, the term may be defined as an investment's ability to produce sufficient revenue to pay all expenses and charges and to provide a reasonable return on and recapture of the money invested.[7] Economic feasibility is indicated when the market value or gross sellout of a project upon achievement of a stabilized condition equals or exceeds all costs of production, including entrepreneurial profit. *Market value* applies to a planned rental property; *gross sellout* applies to a project that will be developed as multiple units to be sold to multiple users.

The costs graphed in Figure 24.2 indicate that this proposed subdivision would be economically feasible if the total sale prices of the aggregate lots equal or exceed the costs at Point C. If the gross sellout of all lots amounts to less than the costs at Point C, then the project is not economically feasible. On the graph, the proposed property

---

7. *The Dictionary of Real Estate Appraisal*, 3d. ed. (Chicago: Appraisal Institute, 1993). The terms *feasibility analysis, economic feasibility analysis,* and *financial feasibility analysis* are used interchangeably. See also Stephen Fanning, MAI, Terry Grissom, MAI, PhD, and Thomas Pearson, MAI, PhD, *Market Analysis for Valuation Appraisals* (Chicago: Appraisal Institute, 1994), 190, fn. 1.

Figure 24.2 | **Subdivision Development Cost-Timeline Graph**

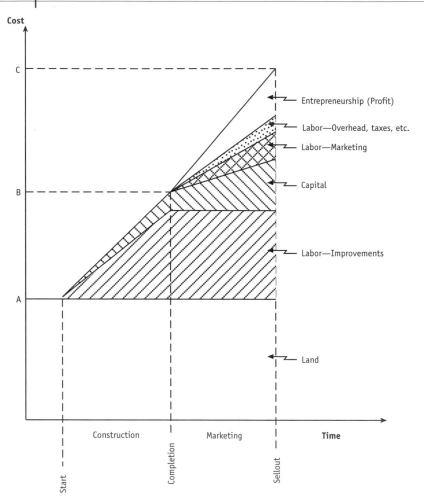

achieves its maximum market value at Point B, i.e., upon completion of construction. After that time, the market value of the aggregate unsold lots declines as the lots are sold off. Eventually, sellout (stabilization) occurs and the market value declines to zero. It is essential that clients, especially lenders, understand these relationships.

Other Issues in the Appraisal of Proposed and Problem Properties

Ownership Rights

The ownership rights in proposed and problem properties are not usually fee simple interests. Thus, to value these properties, the appraiser must correctly identify the ownership rights in both the subject and comparable properties. The ownership rights in most new subdivisions and condominium projects are encumbered by deed restrictions which ensure the use and maintenance of common areas for the good of all owners. If the maintenance fees are far above or below the market standard, the value of the units may be affected. Deed restrictions that limit the use of the individual units may penalize the value of the units in relation to competitive properties. Failure to identify the ownership rights in the subject property correctly usually results in a poorly supported, and often inaccurate, value conclusion. The issue of property rights has caused many problem properties to fail.

Property Descriptions at Multiple Points on Development Timeline

An appraisal must include a complete and accurate description of the subject property at each stage of development for which a value estimate is concluded. For a typical proposed property, this means the property must be described as it exists ("as is"), as expected upon completion of construction, and as anticipated when a stabilized condition is achieved, i.e., sellout or stabilized occupancy. In some cases, completion of construction and stabilization may occur at the same or nearly the same point in time. Each description should be based on appropriate plans and specifications, which should be identified. If the subject property is part of a larger project, e.g., the first phase of a multiple-phase subdivision, the larger project should also be described. When applicable, the description should include information on the economic characteristics of the property, e.g., occupancy level and rents. The existing condition and depreciated items should be noted. In essence, all factors affecting value that are considered in the valuation analysis should be included in the appraisal report in the section where the subject property is described.

Identification of Primary and Secondary Data

All data presented in the appraisal report should be identified as either primary or secondary data. Primary data are data collected and generated by the appraiser, while secondary data are collected and generated by others. Often secondary data are of a general nature, e.g., the data compiled in national survey reports. Secondary data should be used only as additional support for primary data, and only when they pertain to the same type and class of property as the subject. For example, overall capitalization rates or discount rates from a national survey of institutional-class properties should not be reported as the primary support for the overall capitalization or discount rates used in the valuation of small local properties or older properties.

Data Analysis

All income and expense projections used in the valuation of the subject property must be supported by analysis of market data. Market rental data are analyzed using the same process applied to market sales data in the sales comparison approach, and the analysis should be just as thorough. When rental histories are available, past income and expense data relating to the subject property should be analyzed and reported.

Consistency Among Approaches and Comparables

The value indications derived from each of the three approaches should be consistent with one another and with the purpose of the appraisal. Each value indication should specify the status or condition of the property, i.e., "as is," upon completion of construction, or upon achievement of stabilized occupancy. If the market data available are not comparable, the data should not be used to derive a market value indication. For example, if the subject of the appraisal assignment is an office building or retail center that has not leased up to stabilized occupancy, market sales of similar properties that were sold at stabilized occupancy would be inappropriate comparables for estimating the value of the subject property "as is." These sales could be used, however, to value the subject property at stabilized occupancy.

Valuation Approaches

Whenever possible, all three approaches should be used to derive the market value of the subject at stabilized occupancy. Then a DCF analysis based on the indications of market value at stabilized occupancy may be performed to derive the market values of the property "as is" and upon completion of construction. In this way all costs, including entrepreneurial profit, can be properly accounted for.

The market value of an income-producing property that is not at stabilized occupancy should not be estimated simply by deducting the value of the rent loss over the marketing period from the value at stabilization. This method is only appropriate when the occupancy level of the property has nearly stabilized and no entrepreneurial profit remains to be realized. It is incorrect to deduct the "rent loss" only and to overlook the cost of capital, entrepreneurial profit, and the operating and marketing expenses incurred over the remainder of the marketing phase. This methodology would likely overstate the value of the subject property.

Rental Loss During Lease-up

The construction of proposed multitenant properties is often completed before all rentable space can be leased up. When a building is completed, it may have no tenants or be partially leased up. The appraiser should account for the impact of the rent lost while the building is moving toward stabilized occupancy.

Several techniques may be used to estimate the impact of rent loss on property value. The first discounts the net income loss during lease-up, which is then deducted from the value of the property at stabilized occupancy. For example, it has been projected that it will take 12 months to find a tenant for a single-tenant property. The property has an estimated net operating income of $10,000 per month and a value of $1,000,000 at stabilized occupancy. Applying an annual discount rate of 14% calculated at a monthly frequency (11.137355) to the $10,000 *NOI* produces a present value for the 12-month rental loss of $111,374, which can be rounded to $111,000. Deducting this amount from the $1,000,000 value of the property at stabilized occupancy results in a $889,000 value indication for the property upon completion of construction and as yet unleased. In a situation involving a multitenanted property that is expected to lease up in a straight-line pattern from 0% occupancy to a stabilized occupancy of 90% over 12 months, the loss of monthly income may be proportionally allocated over the 12 months.

A second technique incorporates the loss of rental income into the income and expenses projected in the DCF analysis during the lease-up period and beyond, thereby building the impact of the rent loss directly into the value conclusion. Because DCF analysis precisely identifies income and expenses during lease-up, this is generally the best way of addressing rental loss in complex multitenanted buildings. The activity, conventions, and expectations of the local market affect the assumptions about the normal marketing time and the appropriate discount rate used in DCF analysis as well as the method for deriving the value of the net rental loss. Two DCF analyses may be conducted: one using projected cash flows based on anticipated lease-up to stabilized occupancy and a second with projected cash flows as though stabilized occupancy had occurred on the date of the value estimate. Since the cash flows are almost certain to incur little risk, a safe rate is generally applied for discounting. The difference between the two discounted cash flows, or *shortfall,* may then be applied as an adjustment to the values derived in the cost and sales comparison approaches.

There are other ways to approximate the present value of the rental loss. Note that over a 12-month period, the average net income received for income beginning at $0 and growing to $10,000 would be one half of that range, or $5,000. The present value of $5,000 per month for 12 months at 14% is $55,687 ($5,000 x 11.137355). Alternatively, each of the monthly incomes of $10,000 may be discounted from one month to 12 months, or for an average of six months. $10,000 per month discounted for six months at 14% ($10,000 x 5.762427) produces a present value of $57,624. The $1,937 difference ($57,624 - $55,687) is inconsequential for a property valued at $1,000,000. Thus, an approximate rental loss of $56,000 may be deducted from the $1,000,000 value upon stabilization to arrive at a $944,000 indicated value upon completion of construction and still unleased.

The techniques described above can also be applied to vacant, existing buildings that may require an extended lease-up period.

Additional Considerations

The appraisal of a problem property is sometimes complicated by other circumstances surrounding the property—e.g., the stigma of failure, adverse market conditions, the need to rehabilitate the existing improvements, required changes in rents or prices, additional construction and marketing costs to ensure the success of the project, and the amount of anticipated entrepreneurial profit. The appraiser must understand why a project failed in order to determine whether the proposed rehabilitation of the property will succeed. Usually a marketability study is the key to appraising this kind of property. An adequate description of the property being appraised and analysis of the property, both as existing and subject to the proposed improvement(s) and marketing program, must be set forth in the appraisal report.

Sample Valuation of a Proposed Property

An appraisal is being sought to estimate the value of a proposed subdivision upon completion of all infrastructure, but prior to the sale of any lots. The subdivision consists of 54 lots, each of which is approximately 15,000 square feet in size and has full utilities. Based on analysis of the market data and the marketability study, the appraiser has made the following assumptions and projections. The average sale price per lot is $35,000, which will not change over the marketing period. The absorption rate is nine lots per quarter. Marketing costs are estimated at 6% of gross sales revenue and legal and closing costs at 2% of the gross sales price. Real estate taxes are $350 per lot per year and the subdivision was completed at the end of the last tax year. Annual overhead and maintenance expenses will run $100 for each lot in the inventory and project supervision will be $12,000 per quarter. Anticipated entrepreneurial profit during the marketing phase is estimated at 12% of gross sales revenue. A DCF analysis of the proposed subdivision is shown in Table 24.10. The resulting value indication is $1,283,000, which is approximately 68% of the gross sellout of $1,890,000.

The Appraisal of Partial Interests

Real property refers to the interests, benefits, and rights that are inherent in the ownership of tangible real estate. The bundle of rights with which the ownership of real estate is endowed may be held *in toto* (i.e., a fee simple estate) or may be divided.[8] Common examples of partial interests created by the economic division of the bundle of rights in real property include leased fee interests, leasehold interests, and economic syndications.

Leased Fee and Leasehold Interests

Leases divide property into leased fee and leasehold ownership estates. The rights that pertain to the leased fee and leasehold estates are specified by the lease contract and body of law governing leases. Lease contracts vary considerably and can give rise to a variety of appraisal situations, even when the properties to which they apply are physically similar.

When a property is subject to one or more leases, an analysis of lease terms is performed as part of its appraisal. A lease contract specifies the obligations of each party to the lease and identifies the economic relationships to which the parties have agreed. The party who owns the property subject to the lease is the *landlord* and the owner's interests are called the *leased fee estate*. The party who receives the right to use the property is the *tenant* and the tenant's interests are called the *leasehold estate*.

An appraiser considers many factors in analyzing the quantity, quality, and durability of the economic benefits created by a lease. What is the term of the lease? What is the likelihood that the tenant will be able to meet all the rental payments on time? Are there "rents" to be paid in a form other than cash, e.g., as services provided by the tenant? Are the various stipulations in the lease typical of the market, or do they create special advantages or disadvantages for the parties? Is either the leased fee interest or the leasehold interest transferable, or does the lease prohibit transfer? Is the lease written in a manner that will accommodate reasonable change over time, or may it eventually become cumbersome to the parties? Does rent include participation in the earnings or activities of the tenant? What obligations are specified in the lease for the owner of the leased fee?

---

8. In common parlance, appraisers refer to "the property appraised," "the subject property," or "the property that was personally inspected." But in the language of the law, the term *property* applies only to the ownership of rights, either as an entire bundle or as a partial interest. Appraisers must clearly define whether the entirety of interests or a partial interest in the real estate is being valued.

Table 24.10 | **Value Indication for Subdivision at Completion of Construction**

Quarter	1	2	3	4	5	6	Total
Beginning inventory of units	54	45	36	27	18	9	
Number of units sold	9	9	9	9	9	9	54
Ending inventory of units	45	36	27	18	9	0	0
Cumulative no. of units sold	9	18	27	36	45	54	54
Average price/unit ($)	35,000	35,000	35,000	35,000	35,000	35,000	
Gross sales income ($)	315,000	315,000	315,000	315,000	315,000	315,000	1,890,000
Expenses ($)							
Marketing costs (6%)	18,900	18,900	18,900	18,900	18,900	18,900	113,400
Legal/closing costs (2%)	6,300	6,300	6,300	6,300	6,300	6,300	37,800
Real estate taxes ($350/lot/yr.)	4,331	3,544	2,756	1,969	1,181	394	14,175
Overhead/maint. ($100/yr.)	1,238	1,012	788	562	338	112	4,050
Supervision ($48,000/yr.)	12,000	12,000	12,000	12,000	12,000	12,000	72,000
Total expenses ($)	42,769	41,756	40,744	39,731	38,719	37,706	241,425
Entrepreneurial profit at 12% ($)	37,800	37,800	37,800	37,800	37,800	37,800	226,800
Net cash flow	234,431	235,444	236,456	237,469	238,481	239,494	1,421,775
Present value	227,603	221,928	216,391	210,988	205,716	200,572	1,283,198
Discount rate	12.00%						
Value at completion	$1,283,198						
Rounded	$1,283,000						

The appraiser cannot simply assume that each of the estates created by the lease has a market value. Many leases create no separate value for the tenant. When the tenant in place cannot or will not pay the rent, the market value of the leased fee estate may be reduced to an amount less than the market value of a comparable property that is unleased or one leased to a more reliable tenant at below-market terms. If a lease prohibits the transfer of interests, it will have no market value at all. Thus, the valuation of a property subject to a lease requires additional study beyond the analysis of the real estate itself.

Like any economic division of property, leases create multiple estates and each party may have rights pertaining to both realty and non-realty components. It is essential, therefore, that the appraiser distinguish between those rights (and values) that involve the real estate and those that are solely contractual. Generally, the rights associated with real estate contracts are fairly standardized for given property types and particular locales, so they are usually consistent with the market requirements and expectations associated with the real estate. Contractual provisions that are not standard often involve non-realty rights, which should be separately identified in the appraisal.

For example, a lease may stipulate that the tenant pay a rent that is higher than market rent. If the tenant is considered sufficiently strong to sustain the burden of this *excess rent* (i.e., the amount by which contract rent exceeds market rent), the value of the property may be higher than the market value of the real estate alone. Any incremental increases in value must be carefully explained and the higher risk associated with excess rent should be properly analyzed. Any value ascribed to the excess rent must be identified as value attributable to the contract, not the market value of the real estate itself. Similarly, if a lease provides the tenant with an economic advantage, it must be recognized that the market value of the property is not that of the leased fee alone, but must be divided between the leased fee and leasehold positions. In both of these situations, the market value of the real estate itself does not change. Rather, it is the economic interests associated with the positions created by the lease contract that are affected.

Chapter 21 discusses types of leases, lease provisions, income and expense analysis, and the basic procedures used to value leased fee estates. The following applications relate to the analysis and valuation of interests held by tenants. The most common tenant-held interests are simple leasehold interests and sandwich leasehold interests. Such interests are created by contracts and each is valued by analyzing the economic division effected by the contract.

A leasehold estate may have market value if the rent specified in the lease contract is less than the market rent paid for the particular real estate. Even if the tenant's interest is nontransferable, the tenant may have an economic advantage which reflects a non-realty (contractual) benefit.[9] For this advantage to have market value, however, the tenant's interest must be transferable. In valuing the tenant's interest, the appraiser analyzes any marginal economic advantage associated with the leasehold position, and also investigates any other elements of the lease the market may consider. In such situations, the appraiser must ultimately measure the tenant's net economic advantage.

---

9. The leasehold interest acquires some value by virtue of occupancy even if contract rent and market rent are the same.

The following application illustrates the valuation of a leasehold interest created by a long-term lease that gives the tenant a rent advantage. All other elements of the lease are consistent with lease provisions typical of the market.

Sample Leasehold Valuation

Given:
Rents are to be paid at the beginning of each year.

Contract rent:	$12,000 per year
Market rent:	$14,000 per year
Lease term:	20 years

The rent margin is expected to remain constant over the remaining lease term. The discount rate in the market for comparable leasehold interests is 15% annually.

Procedure:
Leasehold advantage
$14,000 - $12,000 = $2,000 per year
Present value factor of $1 per period, at 15% for 19 years = 6.198231

Present value of initial payment	$2,000
Present value of additional 19 payments ($2,000 x 6.198231)	12,396
Present value of leasehold	$14,396

The market value of the leased fee interest is known to be $125,000. It would be inaccurate to assume that the unencumbered fee simple (the total ownership interest in the absence of any lease) would be $139,396 ($125,000 + $14,396). The provisions of the lease contract may encumber either the economic interest in the leased fee or in the leasehold, and each must be considered individually. The unencumbered fee may indeed be worth $139,396, but a simple summation (or, alternatively, subtraction of the value of the leasehold interest from the overall property value to arrive at the value of the leased fee interest) is incorrect and a violation of Standards Rule 1-4 (c) of the Uniform Standards of Professional Appraisal Practice.

Another special lease situation results when a tenant in place subleases all or part of the leased space to a subtenant. The original lessee (the leasehold holder) becomes the holder of a sandwich leasehold, and a new tenant relationship is created. Although such situations are common and increasingly upheld by the courts, a sublease may affect all the parties, including the owner of the leased fee interest. It is necessary to distinguish between the value of the real estate as an unencumbered fee which remains unchanged and the value of the economic positions created by the lease contracts.

A tenant under a sublease may not have any of the rights of the holder of the leasehold under the original lease contract. It is also possible that the holder of the sandwich leasehold position may offer various economic benefits to induce the new tenant to sublease the property. Thus, the contract between the holder of the sandwich leasehold interest and the tenant under the sublease may contain provisions that go beyond, but do not violate, the provisions of the original lease. Attempts to value individual lease interests by summation or subtraction can produce even more inaccurate results when applied to sandwich and subleasehold interests than when applied to leased fee and leasehold interests.

The following sets of computations summarize the arithmetic procedures used to value sandwich and subleasehold interests. They relate to the same property described in the previous example.

Sample Valuation of Sandwich and Subleasehold Interests

Given:
Rents are paid at the beginning of each year.

Rent specified in base lease	$12,000 per year
Rent specified in sublease	$13,000 per year
Rent obtainable in the market	$14,000 per year
Lease terms (sandwich and subleasehold positions)	20 years

The rent margins are expected to remain constant over the remaining lease terms.

Discount rates:

Sandwich leasehold position	13%
Subleasehold position	18%

Procedure for valuing the sandwich leasehold position

Advantage to sandwich leasehold:		
Rent received under sublease	$13,000	
Rent paid to leased fee	12,000	
Advantage	$ 1,000	
Present value of initial payment		$1,000
Present value of additional 19 payments = present value of $1 per period, at 13% for 19 payments = 6.937969		
($1,000 x 6.937969)		6,938
Present value of sandwich leasehold		$7,938

Procedure for valuing subleasehold position

Advantage to subleasehold:		
Market rent	$14,000	
Rent paid under sublease	13,000	
Advantage	$ 1,000	
Present value of initial payment		$1,000
Present value of additional 19 payments = present value of $1 per period, at 18% for 19 payments = 5.316241		
($1,000 x 5.316241)		5,316
Present value of subleasehold		$6,316

As previously stated, there is no reason to expect that the sum of the two interests in this example should equal the estimated value of the leasehold interest unencumbered by a sublease (e.g., the $14,396 figure derived in the previous example). The terms of the sublease may require that rent under the sublease exceed market rent. This excess rent imposes a burden on the subleasehold tenant which may not be sustainable, resulting in instability for both the sandwich leasehold and leased fee positions. Caution must be exercised in ascribing value to any subleasehold position, especially one encumbered by excess rent. Many subtenants go into bankruptcy and leave store space vacant, so the sandwich leaseholder must assume the rent burden and the attendant risk to the leased fee owner increases. This is particularly problematic when related properties are also owned by the leased fee holder, e.g., multiple stores in a shopping center.

Economic Syndications

Increasingly, real estate investment trusts (REITs) and other securitized investment vehicles are making use of a special economic division of interests involving the revenue streams of income-producing property. The purchase of real estate has typically been financed with a 75% mortgage and a 25% equity payment. More recently, up to 100% of the acquisition cost of certain investment-grade properties is being funded through investment *tranches*. Each tranche, or layer, represents a specified portion of the earnings of the property and/or a portion of the proceeds from its resale. Each has its own associated risk and market-required rate of return.

Under current market practice, securities analysts make use of spreadsheet models to separate out income and expense items and break down expected net revenue streams for income-producing properties. A risk analysis is then performed, and each defined investment tranche, or group of revenues, is assigned an investment rating. This process is analogous to lease analysis in that a series of "sandwich positions" may be created by the investment contract. As with leases, the focus of economic analysis is on the contract positions. The underlying real estate is the backdrop for the analysis, not the central consideration.

In analyzing securitized investment vehicles, appraisers must distinguish between the value of the real estate and the value attributable to the non-real estate component, i.e., the investment contract. In many situations, portfolio considerations enter into the selection of the discount rates that are applied to various investment positions. For example, the analyst may pick a discount rate because a specified grouping of properties allows achievement of a desired concentration or diversification, has highly regarded ownership, sells on specified investment exchanges, or because the portfolio manager has a proven record of success.

Appraisers can contribute their knowledge of and expertise in real estate markets to help those involved in securitization understand the fundamental economics underlying the contractual arrangements. In reporting the results of a valuation of a property subject to securitization, appraisers must fully disclose the facts and circumstances of the situation, identify the indicators used to analyze realty and non-realty components, and clearly distinguish between realty and non-realty values. The securitization of real estate is discussed in greater depth in Chapter 28.

Key Concepts

- Discounted cash flow (DCF) analysis is a procedure in which a discount rate is applied to a set of projected income streams and a reversion to determine whether the investment property will produce a required yield. Given the rate of return, DCF analysis can be used to solve for the present value of the property. If the property's purchase price is known, DCF analysis can be applied to find the rate of return.

- Forecasts typically include data on potential gross income, vacancy and collection losses, effective gross income, operating expenses, net operating income, debt service (where appropriate), pre- and after-tax cash flow over the holding period, and residual income from the sale of the property at the end of the forecast period.

- Net present value (*NPV*) and the internal rate of return (*IRR*) are two widely used models for measuring investment performance.

- Net present value (*NPV*) is the difference between the present value of all positive cash flows and the present value of all negative cash flows or capital outlays.

- The internal rate of return (*IRR*) is the rate of discount that makes the net present value of an investment equal to zero. The *IRR* discounts all cash flows from an investment to a net present value equal to the original investment.

- The *IRR* has notable limitations. Unusual combinations of cash flows may produce more than one *IRR*. The *IRR* must be viewed with suspicion when net cash flows to an investment at a zero rate of return have a negative cumulative value. A negative *IRR* may be interpreted as a rate of loss, but is theoretically meaningless. Moreover, as a measure of return on invested capital, the *IRR* is not valid for investments that are "financed out" and require little or no equity capital.

- Reinvestment concepts may be incorporated into *IRR* analysis. The adjusted or modified *IRR* (*AIRR* or *MIRR*) is an *IRR* with reinvestment. The financial management rate of return (*FMRR*) is an *IRR* with a specified borrowing rate. The effect of taxation on investment performance can be measured by comparing the *IRR* before taxes with the *IRR* after taxes.

- Highly comparable properties within the same use category that are operated differently may generate divergent net incomes. Overall value is allocated among the real estate and business enterprise components.

- The appraisal of proposed and problem properties generally requires multiple values for different points on the development timeline, a marketability study upon which to base the appraisal, and an accounting of the entrepreneurial profit made in the project.

- In developing an inventory of costs for proposed and problem properties, an appraiser considers the costs of the four agents of production—land, labor, capital, and entrepreneurship. Specific labor/capital costs and entrepreneurial profit are phased over construction and marketing periods at the points when they are to be compensated.

- The economic or financial feasibility of proposed and problem properties is indicated when the market value (of planned rental properties) or gross sellout value (of multiple units for multiple end users)upon stabilization equals or exceeds all costs of production, including entrepreneurial profit.

- Partial interests created by the economic division of the bundle of rights in real property through lease contracts include leased fee, leasehold, sandwich leasehold, and subleasehold interests as well as economic syndications. The appraiser must consider the reliability of the tenant, the term and transferability of the lease, and the contractual rights and contract rents stipulated in the lease.

Terms

allocation of value

"as is" value

business enterprise value

contract rent

discounted cash flow (DCF)
      analysis

economic feasibility analysis

excess rent

feasibility analysis

financial feasibility analysis

forecasting

four agents of production

gross sellout

internal rate of return (*IRR*)

leased fee interest

leasehold interest

marketability study

market rent

market value

net present value (*NPV*)

partial interest

problem property

proposed property

prospective value

real estate investment trust (REIT)

sandwich leasehold interest

securitization

subleasehold interest

syndication

tranche

value "as is"

value upon achievement of stabilized
      occupancy/condition

value upon completion of
      construction

CHAPTER TWENTY-FIVE

Reconciling Value Indications

A n appraisal is performed to answer a client's question about real estate. The
question usually relates to property value and to answer it the appraiser follows
the valuation process. In the course of this process, the appraiser identifies,
gathers, and analyzes general and specific data; determines the property's highest and
best use; and applies the sales comparison, income capitalization, and cost approaches.
The extent of analysis performed is determined by the client's question and the available
data.

Usually more than one approach is applied, and each approach typically results in a
different indication of value. Thus, if two or more approaches are used, the appraiser
must reconcile at least two value indications. Moreover, several value indications may be
derived in a single approach. In the sales comparison approach, for example, the analysis
of each comparable sale produces an adjusted sale price, which is an indication of value.
When the sales are considered together, the various units of comparison may also
produce different value indications—e.g., apartment properties may be analyzed in terms
of price per dwelling, price per room, price per square foot of gross building area (*GBA*),
or price per square foot of rentable area. In an analysis of income, different indications of
value may result from applying gross income multipliers to income streams, directly
capitalizing net income, and discounting income (cash flows).

The appraiser often resolves multiple value indications derived within a single
approach as part of the application of the approach. At times, however, an appraiser may
choose to resolve these differences after reviewing the entire appraisal. In either case,
the integrity of each approach is maintained. Resolving the differences among various
value indications is called reconciliation. *Reconciliation is the analysis of alternative
conclusions to arrive at a final value estimate.*

Review

To prepare for reconciliation the appraiser reviews the entire appraisal, making sure that
the data available and the analytical techniques, assumptions, and logic applied have led
to consistent judgments. Data are reviewed to ensure that they are authentic, pertinent,
and sufficient. The value definition, the identified property rights, and the qualifying
conditions imposed are carefully reconsidered to ascertain whether the procedures used
in the analysis specifically address each of these items. The appraiser should examine the
differences in the conclusions derived from the various approaches, apply tests of
reasonableness to these primary conclusions, and resolve any inconsistencies.

For example, is the effective age of the property used in the cost approach
consistent with the physical condition reported? Is the same physical condition used as

the basis for adjustments to rent comparables, expense comparables, and sales comparables in the income and sales comparison approaches? Are the results of all the approaches consistent with the appraiser's determination of highest and best use? Do the indications derived from the approaches applied reflect the same defined value? For example, a value indication derived from income capitalization that is higher than an indication based on the cost approach may or may not include a non-realty or business enterprise value component.

All mathematical calculations should be checked, preferably by someone other than the person who performed them originally; significant errors can lead to incorrect value indications, but even minor errors can diminish the client's confidence in the appraisal. Finally, the logic employed throughout the valuation process should be scrutinized. Do the approaches and methods applied consider all the available data and systematically lead to meaningful conclusions that relate directly to the intended use(s) of the appraisal? Does the appraisal provide the information required to solve the client's problem? For example, if the client wants to establish a depreciation basis to compute federal income tax, does the appraisal allocate separate values to the improvements and the land? A client who contemplates remodeling will want information on the costs and benefits of this plan. The client seeking insurance coverage needs a well-supported insurable value estimate that is consistent with the carrier's definition. If the client is considering whether to accept an offer to purchase, the appraiser must adequately analyze the terms of the proposed contract.

Relationship to the Valuation Process

Resolving the varying results of the valuation procedures applied may depend on recognizing differences in data, techniques, and judgment. Subtle differences in the intended uses of the appraisal or in the interests being appraised may also be significant. For example, if an appraiser is estimating the market value of a proposed office tower both 1) as completed and at stabilized income and 2) as completed but unoccupied, the value contribution of stabilized occupancy must be carefully considered in each approach applied.

In all appraisals, but particularly in appraisals required for litigation, the definition of the appraised value should be reexamined in reconciliation. Does the client-specified definition call for the value to be expressed in cash equivalent financing or in simple cash? Does it indicate the most probable price or the highest price available in the open market? Does it specify that the value be commensurate with all the uses to which the property is physically, legally, and economically adaptable, or merely the highest and best use?

Appraisers may also need to answer questions that relate to the potential users of property. Can the investment value of a property to the owner of an adjacent plot be reasonably reconciled with an estimate of the property's market value to a typical purchaser? Can the intrinsic value of a new office property be reasonably reconciled with an estimate of its market value for a mortgagee who is contemplating foreclosure? Must an opinion of the insurable value of a property be reconciled with the market value contribution of the insurable improvements?

Relationship to the Market

Appraisers should keep in mind that an appraisal client seeking a professional opinion will want to know the basis for that opinion. The final value estimate represents the application of the appraiser's judgment to mathematical results. The appraiser should employ the quantity of data that market participants would consider appropriate to solve the appraisal problem at hand. These data should be applied consistently in the specific approach(es) relevant to the appraisal problem. The valuation process is a collection of available analytical tools from which an appraiser selects those appropriate to the assignment.

Approaches that are not of primary importance in a specific assignment may nevertheless be useful in reconciliation. In some cases, for example, the appraiser may omit the cost approach but, in reconciliation, consider the difference between 1) the sum of the reproduction cost new and the land value, and 2) the final opinion of market value. A discussion of the property depreciation is often instructive.

All estimates used in the approaches to value must be consistent with market perceptions. The appraisal conclusion should reflect market value and the data analyzed should support the appraiser's final value opinion, but data alone do not produce a value estimate. By combining data analysis with professional training and experience, the appraiser is able to exercise professional judgment and form a sound value opinion. Sometimes an appraiser may offer substantive, albeit subjective, judgments when precise market information is not available. The effect of these judgments must be evaluated in the reconciliation process. When an appraisal assignment calls for an estimate of market value but market data are scarce, the opinion of an impartial appraiser who has pertinent training and experience may be relied upon.

Reconciliation Criteria

Reviewing an appraisal helps substantiate its accuracy, its consistency, and the logic leading to the value indications. An appraiser relies more on professional experience, expertise, and judgment in reconciliation than in any other part of the valuation process. In reconciliation an appraiser considers and evaluates varying value indications to arrive at a final value estimate. The appraiser weighs the relative significance, applicability, and defensibility of each value indication and relies most heavily on the approach that is most appropriate to the nature of the appraisal.

Reconciliation requires appraisal judgment and a careful, logical analysis of the procedures that lead to each value indication. Appropriateness, accuracy, and quantity of evidence are the criteria with which an appraiser forms a meaningful, defensible final value estimate. These criteria are used to analyze multiple value indications within each approach and to reconcile the indications produced by the different approaches into a final estimate of defined value.

Appropriateness

Using the criterion of appropriateness, an appraiser judges how pertinent each approach is to the intended use of the appraisal. The appropriateness of an approach is usually directly related to property type and market viability. For example, an appraisal to estimate the market value of a 30-year-old community shopping center will ordinarily employ procedures associated with the income capitalization approach—e.g., the derivation of a gross rent multiplier, net income capitalization, or the discounting of cash flows. The cost approach might not be useful in valuing obsolete improvements, but it may be applied to estimate land value and determine, through an analysis of highest and best use, whether demolition of all or part of an improvement is appropriate. The sales comparison approach can be used to obtain value indications through analysis of physical units of comparison.

Although the final value estimate is based on the approaches that are most applicable, the final value opinion need not be identical to the value produced by the most applicable approach. If two approaches are applicable, the final estimate of value may be closer to one value indication than to the other. For example, the value indication derived from the income capitalization approach may be lower than the value indication derived from the sales comparison approach. If market participants are primarily interested in income-earning potential, the final estimate may be closer to the conclusion from income capitalization than the conclusion from sales comparison. If the property were an owner-occupied dwelling, the sales comparison approach would likely be of primary relevance.

The criterion of appropriateness is also used to judge the relevance of each comparable property and each significant adjustment made in an approach. The appraiser asks whether this comparable property is a valid and reliable indicator of the value of the subject property. Is it similar in terms of physical characteristics and location? Was it developed, rented, or sold in the same market? Are the characteristics of the transaction similar to those expected for the subject property? In some cases the appraiser may ask: Are the expenses of the comparables appropriate indicators of the expenses of the appraised property? Are the estimates of accrued depreciation in the appraised improvements justified by the comparison of comparable costs and comparable sales?

Accuracy

The accuracy of an appraisal is measured by the appraiser's confidence in the correctness of the data and the adjustments made to each comparable property analyzed in the approaches applied. For example, how confident is the appraiser of the adjustments to each cost comparable, each sale comparable, and each rent comparable? Similarly, how reliable are the data supporting estimates of depreciation and cost, estimates of income and expenses, and the capitalization rate selected? An appraiser may have more confidence in the accuracy of the data and calculations used in one approach than on another.

The number of comparable properties, the number of adjustments, and the gross and net dollar amounts of adjustments may suggest the relative accuracy of a particular approach. If a large number of comparable properties are available for one approach and seem to conform to a reasonably close pattern of market activity, greater accuracy may be indicated and the appraiser may place more reliance on this approach. For example, if there are many rental properties competitive with the appraised property, an appraiser may be able to extract current income, expense, and capitalization rate data from these properties and attribute greater accuracy and confidence to the income capitalization approach. If the appraiser finds several recently developed properties similar to the subject of the appraisal, comparable data supporting land values and development costs may inspire confidence in the cost approach. Recent sales of similar properties may provide the necessary data to estimate accurate unit values by sales comparison.

If one or two comparable properties require fewer total adjustments than the other comparables studied within an approach, an appraiser may attribute greater accuracy and give more weight to the value indications obtained from these comparables, particularly if the magnitude of the adjustments is approximately the same. Although the number of adjustments made to the comparable properties may be similar, the gross dollar amount of the total adjustments might vary considerably. For example, in the sales comparison approach an appraiser may analyze five comparable properties that each require several adjustments. However, the gross dollar amount of adjustments for one comparable property may total 15% of the sale price, while the gross dollar adjustment for each of the other four properties may be less than 5% of the sale price. If the sales are similar otherwise, less accuracy will probably be attributed to the comparable properties that require large adjustments.

In some cases, however, one large adjustment may be more accurate and supportable in the market than many smaller adjustments. For example, an appraiser may find abundant market evidence in a community to indicate the amount of value diminution caused by an atypical vacancy rate in one of the comparable buildings. Even though a large adjustment is required, the appraiser might impute greater accuracy to this sale because it is otherwise very similar and reliable market evidence is available to support the adjustment.

Usually the magnitude of net adjustments is a less reliable indicator of accuracy. The net adjustment is calculated by totaling the positive and negative adjustments and subtracting the smaller amount from the larger amount. A net adjustment figure may be misleading because one cannot assume that any inaccuracies in the positive and negative adjustments will cancel each other out. For example, if a comparable property is 20% superior to the subject in some characteristics and 20% inferior in others, the net adjustment is zero but the gross adjustment is 40%. Another comparable may require several adjustments, all positive or all negative, resulting in a net adjustment of 6%. This property may well be a more accurate indicator of the subject's value than the comparable with the 0% net adjustment. Several adjustments that are all positive or all negative may be more correct and produce a smaller total gross adjustment than a combination of positive and negative adjustments.

Even when they are supported by comparable data, adjustments reflect human judgment; small inaccuracies can be compounded when several adjustments are added or multiplied. For this reason, the precise arithmetic conclusion derived from adjusted data should support, rather than control, the appraiser's judgment.

Quantity of Evidence

Appropriateness and accuracy affect the *quality* and relevance of the value indication derived from a comparable or an approach. Although these criteria are considered separately in reconciliation, both must be studied in relation to the *quantity* of evidence provided by a particular comparable or approach. Even data that meet the criteria of appropriateness and accuracy can be weakened by a scarcity of evidence.

To illustrate the importance of the quantity of evidence, consider an appraiser who is attempting to extract an overall capitalization rate from three comparable sales. The properties are considered appropriate in terms of their physical and locational characteristics and the similarity of the transactions. The available data for each sale are verified and considered reliable, and it appears that each comparable could produce an accurate indication of value. However, the available data for one comparable include a detailed capital budget and operating statement of the property's expenses and income for the preceding three years. The data on the two other comparables are less detailed. Only total gross and net income data for three years are available for one comparable; for the other, detailed data are available for only one year. Because more data are available for the first comparable, the appraiser will have greater confidence in the value indication obtained from it than the indications obtained from the other two sales. In statistical terms, the confidence interval in which the true value lies may be narrowed by the additional data.

Regardless of the quantity of evidence available, the responsibility of the appraiser goes beyond the manipulation of numbers. It is the appraiser's duty to provide a value estimate consistent with the definition of value used in the assignment.

Finally, although the evidence from comparable sales may be accurate and appropriate, these data relate to events that took place before the effective date of the appraisal. Improved property sales, land sales, rentals, expenses, construction and development costs, and vacancy and absorption rates all reflect the past. These data are relevant only insofar as they help the appraiser estimate the future anticipated benefits of the property and the present value of these benefits. Market data are important, but they must help, not hamstring, the appraiser's analyses.

Final Value Estimate

In an appraisal report the final value estimate may be stated as a single figure, a range of values, or both. Traditionally a value estimate is reported as a single dollar amount called a *point estimate*. This figure is the appraiser's best estimate of the value of the property. A point estimate is required for many purposes—e.g., real estate taxation; calculating depreciation deductions for federal income tax; estimating compensation in casualty, liability, and condemnation cases; determining value-based rent; and making property transfer decisions. In other words, because of legal requirements, many clients expect a point estimate of value.

A point estimate should be rounded to reflect the degree of precision associated with the particular value estimate; however, even a rounded figure may imply greater precision than is warranted. Because an appraised value is an estimate, it implies a range in which the property value may fall. That value range usually reflects the range of conclusions derived from two or more approaches, but the final value opinion need not fall within this range. For example, an appraiser may report a value estimate of $9,400,000 to represent a result drawn from two approaches with preliminary conclusions of $9,390,000 and $9,380,000. In this case the conclusion of $9,400,000 is not statistically derived. It is outside the range indicated by the two approaches, but it reflects the market value of the property based on the two approaches. In addition to the point value estimate, the appraiser might report the value range as "between $9,300,000 and $9,400,000."

Sometimes an appraiser may deliberately avoid stating a single point estimate and report a range of value. By reporting a range, the appraiser indicates that the value lies somewhere within the range—i.e., that the value is no lower than the low end and no higher than the high end of the range. A wide range is of no use to a client; a narrow range may imply precision that is not warranted. When provided with a value range, a client is likely to see the extreme that suits his or her purpose as a virtual guarantee. Accordingly, most appraisers choose to report their final value conclusions as single figures.

Aside from a range of value, an appraiser may report a *probability range* to suggest the confidence level or optimism or pessimism associated with the value estimate. The evidence considered in each approach should allow for such variation. For example, an appraiser may consider a more aggressive and a less aggressive market rent schedule for a proposed shopping center. Different capitalization rates may be applied to the two income streams as well as different discount rates and gross income multipliers. Any value differences resulting from the higher and lower projected rents in the income approach should also be related to different levels of risk-related entrepreneurial profit in the cost approach.

An appraisal results in an opinion of value. Although it is an impartial, expert, and reasoned conclusion formed by a trained professional based on an analysis of all relevant evidence, it remains an opinion. If it is an opinion of market value, it represents the appraiser's perception of the most likely, most probable price available in an arm's-length transaction for the appraised interest subject to the qualifying conditions imposed.

Key Concepts

- In reconciliation, alternative value conclusions are analyzed to arrive at a final value estimate.

- The appraiser uses reconciliation criteria to form a meaningful, defensible final value conclusion. The appraiser considers the appropriateness of the approaches, the accuracy of the data and calculations, and the quantity or sufficiency of evidence presented relative to the specific appraisal problem.

- In reconciliation, the appraiser reviews the entire appraisal to check for inconsistencies among the approaches applied (comparables used and adjustments calculated), the highest and best use conclusions upon which each approach is based, the defined value estimated in each approach, and the real property interests being appraised.

- The approaches and methods employed should be appropriate to the intended use of appraisal, i.e., the problem the client is seeking to solve. The reasonableness of assumptions, judgments, and conclusions must be established.
- The final value estimate, which should be rounded, may be stated as a single figure (point estimate), a range of value, or both, i.e., a single figure within a range.

Terms

accuracy	probability range
appropriateness	quantity of evidence
confidence interval	range of value
final value estimate	reasonableness
gross adjustment	reconciliation
net adjustment	reconciliation criteria
point estimate	rounding

CHAPTER TWENTY-SIX

The Appraisal Report

An appraisal report leads the reader from the definition of the appraisal problem through analysis and relevant descriptive data to a specific conclusion. The appraiser must present all facts, reasoning, and conclusions clearly and succinctly. The length, type, and content of appraisal reports are dictated by the intended user, regulatory requirements, the courts, the type of property being appraised, and the nature of the problem.

Every appraisal report is prepared to answer a particular question and provide specific information needed by an intended user. Some common appraisal questions are: What is the market value of the property? What is the highest and best use of the land as though vacant and the property as improved? What is the value of the part taken in condemnation? What is the damage or benefit to the remainder of the property as a result of the taking?

Appraisal Institute Standards for Written Reports

Each analysis, opinion, or conclusion that results from an appraisal must be communicated in a manner that is meaningful to the intended user and will not be misleading to this user or to the public. To ensure the quality of appraisal reports, professional appraisal organizations have set minimum standards for the facts, descriptions, and statements of work and purpose to be included in all types of appraisal reports.

All members of the Appraisal Institute are required to conduct their professional appraisal activities in compliance with the requirements of the Standards of Professional Appraisal Practice, which include both the Uniform Standards of Professional Appraisal Practice (USPAP) and two supplemental standards.

The Preamble to the Uniform Standards states, "It is essential that a professional appraiser arrive at and communicate his or her analyses, opinions, and advice in a manner that will be meaningful to the client and will not be misleading in the marketplace." The 10 standards and the accompanying statements and advisory opinions are augmented by the guide notes and the supplemental standards, which are applicable only to members of the Appraisal Institute. (See Appendix A.)

The Uniform Standards of Professional Appraisal Practice (USPAP) address the minimum requirements for all written and oral reports as well as the responsibility of the review appraiser. Standards Rule 2-1 states that each written or oral real property appraisal report must:

(a) clearly and accurately set forth the appraisal in a manner that will not be misleading;

(b) contain sufficient information to enable the person(s) who are expected to receive or rely on the report to understand it properly;

(c) clearly and accurately disclose any extraordinary assumption or limiting condition that directly affects the appraisal and indicate its impact on value.

Standards Rule 2-2 requires that each written appraisal report be prepared under one of the following three options and prominently state which option is being used: self-contained report, summary report, or restricted report. Standards Rule 2-2 (a) requires that each self-contained appraisal report:

(i) identify and describe the real estate being appraised;

(ii) state the real property interest being appraised;

(iii) state the purpose and intended use of the appraisal;

(iv) define the value to be estimated;

(v) state the effective date of the appraisal and the date of the report;

(vi) state the extent of the process of collecting, confirming, and reporting data;

(vii) state all assumptions and limiting conditions that affect the analyses, opinions, and conclusions;

(viii) describe the information considered, the appraisal procedures followed, and the reasoning that supports the analyses, opinions, and conclusions;

(ix) describe the appraiser's opinion of the highest and best use of the real estate being appraised, when such an opinion is necessary and appropriate;

(x) explain and support the exclusion of any of the usual valuation approaches;

(xi) describe any additional information that may be appropriate to show compliance with, or clearly identify and explain permitted departures from the requirements of Standard 1; and

(xii) include a signed certification in accordance with Standards Rule 2-3. (For members of the Appraisal Institute, the certification must also conform to the Supplemental Standards rules.)

Standards Rule 2-2 (b) and (c) set forth the requirements for summary and restricted appraisal reports. The essential difference between the three reporting options is the level of detail required in certain areas of presentation. Figure 26.1 compares the reporting options and indicates which elements may be abbreviated in summary and restricted reports. Note the use of the terms "describe," "summarize," and "state" to specify the level of detail required. The Standards are revised periodically, so practitioners are advised to refer to the most current revision of USPAP for more detailed explanation.

Figure 26.1 | Comparison of Report Types

Self-Contained	Summary	Restricted
i. Identify and describe the real estate being appraised.	i. Identify and provide a summary description of the real estate being appraised.	i. Identify the real estate being appraised.
ii. State the real property interest being appraised.	ii. State the real property interest being appraised.	ii. State the real property interest being appraised.
iii. State the purpose and intended use of the appraisal.	iii. State the purpose and intended use of the appraisal.	iii. State the purpose and intended use of the appraisal.
iv. Define the value to be estimated.	iv. Define the value to be estimated.	iv. State and reference a definition of the value to be estimated.
v. State the effective date of the appraisal and the date of the report.	v. State the effective date of the appraisal and the date of the report.	v. State the effective date of the appraisal and the date of the report.
vi. State the extent of the process of collecting, confirming, and reporting data.	vi. Summarize the extend of the process of collecting, confirming, and reporting data.	vi. Describe the extent of the process of collecting, confirming, and reporting data.
vii. State all assumptions and limiting conditions that affect the analysis, opinions, and conclusions.	vii. State all assumptions and limiting conditions that affect the analyses, opinions, and conclusions.	vii. State all assumptions and limiting conditions that affect the analyses, opinions, and conclusions.
viii. Describe the information considered, the appraisal procedures followed, and the reasoning that supports the analyses, opinions, and conclusions.	viii. Summarize the information considered, the appraisal procedures followed, and the reasoning that supports the analyses, opinions, and conclusions.	viii. State the appraisal procedures followed. State the value conclusions and reference the existence of specific file information in support of the conclusion.
ix. Describe the appraiser's opinion of the highest and best use of the real estate, when such an opinion is necessary and appropriate.	ix. Summarize the appraiser's opinion of the highest and best use of the real estate, when such an opinion is necessary and appropriate.	ix. State the appraiser's opinion of the highest and best use of the real estate, when such an opinion is necessary and appropriate.
x. Explain and support the exclusion of any of the usual valuation approaches.	x. Explain and support the exclusion of any of the usual valuation approaches.	x. State the exclusion of any of the usual valuation approaches.
xi. Describe any additional information that may be appropriate to show compliance with, or clearly identify and explain permitted departures from, the specific guidelines of Standard 1.	xi. Summarize any additional information that may be appropriate to show compliance with, or clearly identify and explain permitted departures from, the requirements of Standard 1.	xi. Include a prominent use restriction that limits reliance on the report to the client and warns that the report cannot be understood properly without additional information in the work file of the appraiser; and clearly identify and explain any permitted departures from the requirements of Standard 1.
xii. Include a signed certification in accordance with Standards Rule 2-3.	xii. Include a signed certification in accordance with Standards Rule 2-3.	xii. Include a signed certification in accordance with Standards Rule 2-3.

Note: No comment sections are included in this chart; the chart is prepared for discussion purposes only.

Types of Appraisals and Types of Reports

The Uniform Standards of Professional Appraisal Practice provides for two types of appraisals: complete appraisals and limited appraisals. The distinction between complete and limited appraisals depends on the amount of work performed in the collection and analysis of data. A limited appraisal represents something less than, or different from, the work that would otherwise be required by the specific guidelines; consequently, the Departure Provision is invoked by the appraiser. If an appraisal is less than complete, this fact must be clearly disclosed. The report of a limited appraisal must contain a prominent section that clearly identifies the extent of the appraisal process performed and the departures taken.[1]

The three reporting formats may be employed to communicate either a complete or limited appraisal. The Uniform Standards require that both the type of appraisal and the format be prominently identified in the report.

An appraisal report may be oral or written. Written communications which are prepared in the three reporting options include form and narrative reports. Usually a report is presented in the manner requested by the intended user. However, when a client asks for something less than a self-contained report, i.e., the appraiser's opinion without detailed documentation, the appraiser must still undertake the analysis required for a complete appraisal, if this is the type of appraisal being performed. In this case all material, data, and working papers used to prepare the report are kept in the appraiser's permanent file. Although the appraiser may never need to provide written substantiation for the opinion submitted in abbreviated form, he or she may be asked to explain or defend the opinion at a later time. The extent of file documentation depends on the type of report prepared.

Oral Reports

An appraiser may make an oral report when the circumstances or the needs of the intended user do not permit or warrant a written report. Expert testimony, whether presented in deposition or in court, is considered an oral report. Many oral reports are not made under oath; they are communicated to the intended user in person or by telephone. Standards Rule 2-4 states that, to the extent that it is possible and appropriate, oral reports must address the substantive matters set forth in Standards Rule 2-2 (b). Each oral report should include a property description and the facts, assumptions, conditions, and reasoning on which the conclusion is based. After communicating an oral report, the appraiser should keep on file all notes and data relating to the assignment and a complete memorandum on the analysis, conclusion, and opinion.

Form Reports

The form report is probably the most common format for reports that are not self-contained. A form report may be classified as a summary or restricted report depending

---

1. The comment to Standards Rule 2-2 (a) (xi) states, "When the Departure Provision is invoked, the assignment is deemed to be a Limited Appraisal. Use of the term Limited Appraisal makes it clear that the assignment involved something less than, or different from the work required by the specific guidelines [of USPAP]. The report of a Limited Appraisal must contain a prominent section that clearly identifies the extent of the appraisal process performed and the departures taken."

on the level of detail and the quantity of supporting documentation. Form reports generally meet the needs of financial institutions, insurance companies, and government agencies. Form reports are required for the purchase and sale of most existing mortgages on residential properties in the secondary mortgage market created by government agencies and private organizations. Because these intended users review many appraisals, using a standard report form is both efficient and convenient. When a form is used, those responsible for reviewing the appraisal know exactly where to find each category or item of data in the report. By completing the form, the appraiser ensures that no item required by the reviewer is overlooked. Figure 26.2 shows a Uniform Residential Appraisal Report form.

Form reports prepared by Appraisal Institute members must meet the reporting requirements of the Appraisal Institute. Certain forms do not contain a certification statement that complies with these standards. Therefore, Appraisal Institute members must attach supplemental material when these forms are used. Guide Note 3 to the Standards of Professional Appraisal Practice addresses the use of form reports in the appraisal of residential property. Forms are increasingly being used for appraisals of both residential and nonresidential properties, e.g., apartment, commercial, and industrial properties.[2] Current market trends indicate that the use of form reports for all kinds of properties is likely to continue.

The methodology employed in a valuation is determined by the nature of the specific appraisal problem. If a report form seems too rigid and does not provide for the inclusion of all data that the appraiser believes to be pertinent, the relevant information and comments should be added as a supplement.

The appraiser should make sure that the completed form report is consistent in its description of the property being appraised and provides all the data indicated by the categories listed. If the highest and best use of the property does not conform to the use for which the form is appropriate, the form should not be used unless it is appropriately qualified. The properties and neighborhoods compared should be as similar as possible and all appropriate adjustments should be made. Data must be presented in a clear and comprehensible manner and all form reports should include a proper certification and statement of limiting conditions.

A form appraisal report is unacceptable if the appraiser fails to 1) consider the purpose of the report, the value definition, and the assumptions and conditions inherent in the report; 2) question the intended user about any underwriting criteria that conflict with proper appraisal practice; and 3) review the report before signing it.

Narrative Reports

As mentioned previously, Standards Rule 2-2 recognizes three reporting options. These three options offer a full range of report types. At one end of the spectrum is the self-contained appraisal report, which includes detailed descriptions of the data, reasoning,

---

2. For an in-depth discussion of appraisal form reports, see the following guidebooks from the Communicating the Appraisal series by Arlen C. Mills and Dorothy Z. Mills: *The Uniform Residential Appraisal Report*, 2d ed. (Chicago: Appraisal Institute, 1994); *The Individual Condominium Unit Appraisal Report*, 2d ed. (Chicago: Appraisal Institute, 1995); and *The Small Residential Income Property Appraisal Report*, 2d ed. (Chicago: Appraisal Institute, 1995).

| Figure 26.2 | **Uniform Residential Appraisal Report Form** |

Property Description — **UNIFORM RESIDENTIAL APPRAISAL REPORT** — File No. _____

<table>
<tr><td colspan="4">Property Address</td><td>City</td><td>State</td><td>Zip Code</td></tr>
<tr><td colspan="4">Legal Description</td><td colspan="3">County</td></tr>
<tr><td colspan="4">Assessor's Parcel No.</td><td>Tax Year</td><td>R.E. Taxes $</td><td>Special Assessments $</td></tr>
<tr><td colspan="2">Borrower</td><td colspan="2">Current Owner</td><td colspan="3">Occupant ☐ Owner ☐ Tenant ☐ Vacant</td></tr>
<tr><td colspan="3">Property rights appraised ☐ Fee Simple ☐ Leasehold</td><td colspan="4">Project Type ☐ PUD ☐ Condominium (HUD/VA only) HOA$ _____ /Mo.</td></tr>
<tr><td colspan="4">Neighborhood or Project Name</td><td colspan="2">Map Reference</td><td>Census Tract</td></tr>
<tr><td colspan="2">Sales Price $</td><td colspan="2">Date of Sale</td><td colspan="3">Description and $ amount of loan charges/concessions to be paid by seller</td></tr>
<tr><td colspan="2">Lender/Client</td><td colspan="5">Address</td></tr>
<tr><td colspan="2">Appraiser</td><td colspan="5">Address</td></tr>
</table>

(SUBJECT)

Location	☐ Urban	☐ Suburban	☐ Rural
Built up	☐ Over 75%	☐ 25-75%	☐ Under 25%
Growth rate	☐ Rapid	☐ Stable	☐ Slow
Property values	☐ Increasing	☐ Stable	☐ Declining
Demand/supply	☐ Shortage	☐ In balance	☐ Over supply
Marketing time	☐ Under 3 mos.	☐ 3-6 mos.	☐ Over 6 mos.

Predominant occupancy ☐ Owner ☐ Tenant ☐ Vacant (0-5%) ☐ Vacant (over 5%)

Single family housing	PRICE $(000)	AGE (yrs)
Low		
High		
Predominant		

Present land use %	
One family	___
2-4 family	___
Multi-family	___
Commercial	___
( )	

Land use change ☐ Not likely ☐ Likely ☐ In process
To: _____

(NEIGHBORHOOD)

Note: Race and the racial composition of the neighborhood are not appraisal factors.

Neighborhood boundaries and characteristics: _____

Factors that affect the marketability of the properties in the neighborhood (proximity to employment and amenities, employment stability, appeal to market, etc.): _____

Market conditions in the subject neighborhood (including support for the above conclusions related to the trend of property values, demand/supply, and marketing time...such as data on competitive properties for sale in the neighborhood, description of the prevalence of sales and financing concessions, etc.): _____

(PUD)

Project information for PUDs (If applicable) — Is the developer/builder in control of the Home Owners' Association (HOA)? ☐ Yes ☐ No
Approximate total number of units in the subject project _____ . Approximate total number of units for sale in the subject project _____ .
Describe common elements and recreational facilities:

(SITE)

Dimensions _____	Topography _____
Site area _____ Corner Lot ☐ Yes ☐ No	Size _____
Specific zoning classification and description _____	Shape _____
Zoning compliance ☐ Legal ☐ Legal nonconforming (Grandfathered use) ☐ Illegal ☐ No zoning	Drainage _____
Highest & best use as improved: ☐ Present use ☐ Other use (explain)	View _____

Utilities	Public	Other	Off-site improvements	Type	Public	Private	
Electricity	☐	____	Street	____	☐	☐	Landscaping ____
Gas	☐	____	Curb/gutter	____	☐	☐	Driveway Surface ____
Water	☐	____	Sidewalk	____	☐	☐	Apparent easements ____
Sanitary sewer	☐	____	Street lights	____	☐	☐	FEMA Special Flood Hazard Area ☐ Yes ☐ No
Storm sewer	☐	____	Alley	____	☐	☐	FEMA Zone ____ Map Date ____
							FEMA Map No. ____

Comments (apparent adverse easements, encroachments, special assessments, slide areas, illegal or nonconforming zoning use, etc.): _____

(DESCRIPTION OF IMPROVEMENTS)

GENERAL DESCRIPTION	EXTERIOR DESCRIPTION	FOUNDATION	BASEMENT	INSULATION
No. of Units ____	Foundation ____	Slab ____	Area Sq. Ft. ____	Roof ____ ☐
No. of Stories ____	Exterior Walls ____	Crawl Space ____	% Finished ____	Ceiling ____ ☐
Type (Det./Att.) ____	Roof Surface ____	Basement ____	Ceiling ____	Walls ____ ☐
Design (Style) ____	Gutters & Dwnspts. ____	Sump Pump ____	Walls ____	Floor ____ ☐
Existing/Proposed ____	Window Type ____	Dampness ____	Floor ____	None ____ ☐
Age (Yrs.) ____	Storm/Screens ____	Settlement ____	Outside Entry ____	Unknown ____ ☐
Effective Age (Yrs.) ____	Manufactured House ____	Infestation ____		

ROOMS	Foyer	Living	Dining	Kitchen	Den	Family Rm.	Rec. Rm.	Bedrooms	# Baths	Laundry	Other	Area Sq. Ft.
Basement												
Level 1												
Level 2												

Finished area **above** grade contains: _____ Rooms; _____ Bedroom(s); _____ Bath(s); _____ Square Feet of Gross Living Area

INTERIOR	Materials/Condition	HEATING	KITCHEN EQUIP.	ATTIC	AMENITIES	CAR STORAGE
Floors	____	Type ____	Refrigerator ☐	None ☐	Fireplace(s) # __ ☐	None ☐
Walls	____	Fuel ____	Range/Oven ☐	Stairs ☐	Patio ____ ☐	Garage _ # of cars
Trim/Finish	____	Condition ____	Disposal ☐	Drop Stair ☐	Deck ____ ☐	Attached ____
Bath Floor	____	**COOLING**	Dishwasher ☐	Scuttle ☐	Porch ____ ☐	Detached ____
Bath Wainscot	____	Central ____	Fan/Hood ☐	Floor ☐	Fence ____ ☐	Built-In ____
Doors	____	Other ____	Microwave ☐	Heated ☐	Pool ____ ☐	Carport ____
		Condition ____	Washer/Dryer ☐	Finished ☐		Driveway ____

Additional features (special energy efficient items, etc.): _____

(COMMENTS)

Condition of the improvements, depreciation (physical, functional, and external), repairs needed, quality of construction, remodeling/additions, etc.: _____

Adverse environmental conditions (such as, but not limited to, hazardous wastes, toxic substances, etc.) present in the improvements, on the site, or in the immediate vicinity of the subject property: _____

Valuation Section   **UNIFORM RESIDENTIAL APPRAISAL REPORT**   File No. _____

COST APPROACH

ESTIMATED SITE VALUE .... = $ _____

ESTIMATED REPRODUCTION COST-NEW OF IMPROVEMENTS:

Dwelling _____ Sq. Ft. @ $ _____ = $ _____

_____ Sq. Ft. @ $ _____ = _____

  = _____

Garage/Carport _____ Sq. Ft. @ $ _____ = _____

Total Estimated Cost New .... = $ _____

Less   Physical | Functional | External

Depreciation _____ = $ _____

Depreciated Value of Improvements .... = $ _____

"As-is" Value of Site Improvements .... = $ _____

INDICATED VALUE BY COST APPROACH   = $ _____

Comments on Cost Approach (such as, source of cost estimate, site value, square foot calculation and, for HUD, VA, and FmHA, the estimated remaining economic life of the property): _____

SALES COMPARISON ANALYSIS

ITEM	SUBJECT	COMPARABLE NO. 1		COMPARABLE NO. 2		COMPARABLE NO. 3	
Address							
Proximity to Subject							
Sales Price	$	$		$		$	
Price/Gross Liv. Area	$ ☑	$ ☑		$ ☑		$ ☑	
Data and/or Verification Sources							
VALUE ADJUSTMENTS	DESCRIPTION	DESCRIPTION	+ (−) $Adjustment	DESCRIPTION	+ (−) $Adjustment	DESCRIPTION	+ (−) $Adjustment
Sales or Financing Concessions							
Date of Sale/Time							
Location							
Leasehold/Fee Simple							
Site							
View							
Design and Appeal							
Quality of Construction							
Age							
Condition							
Above Grade Room Count	Total Bdrms Baths	Total Bdrms Baths		Total Bdrms Baths		Total Bdrms Baths	
Gross Living Area	Sq. Ft.	Sq. Ft.		Sq. Ft.		Sq. Ft.	
Basement & Finished Rooms Below Grade							
Functional Utility							
Heating/Cooling							
Energy Efficient Items							
Garage/Carport							
Porch, Patio, Deck, Fireplace(s), etc.							
Fence, Pool, etc.							
Net Adj. (total)		☐ + ☐ −	$	☐ + ☐ −	$	☐ + ☐ −	$
Adjusted Sales Price of Comparable			$		$		$

Comments on Sales Comparison (including the subject property's compatibility to the neighborhood, etc.): _____

ITEM	SUBJECT	COMPARABLE NO. 1	COMPARABLE NO. 2	COMPARABLE NO. 3
Date, Price and Data Source for prior sales within year of appraisal				

Analysis of any current agreement of sale, option, or listing of the subject property and analysis of any prior sales of subject and comparables within one year of the date of appraisal:

RECONCILIATION

INDICATED VALUE BY SALES COMPARISON APPROACH .... $ _____

INDICATED VALUE BY INCOME APPROACH (If Applicable) Estimated Market Rent $ _____ /Mo. x Gross Rent Multiplier _____ = $ _____

This appraisal is made ☐ "as is" ☐ subject to the repairs, alterations, inspections, or conditions listed below ☐ subject to completion per plans and specifications.

Conditions of Appraisal: _____

Final Reconciliation: _____

The purpose of this appraisal is to estimate the market value of the real property that is the subject of this report, based on the above conditions and the certification, contingent and limiting conditions, and market value definition that are stated in the attached Freddie Mac Form 439/Fannie Mae Form 1004B (Revised_____).
**I (WE) ESTIMATE THE MARKET VALUE, AS DEFINED, OF THE REAL PROPERTY THAT IS THE SUBJECT OF THIS REPORT, AS OF _____
(WHICH IS THE DATE OF INSPECTION AND THE EFFECTIVE DATE OF THIS REPORT) TO BE $_____ .**

APPRAISER: **SUPERVISORY APPRAISER (ONLY IF REQUIRED):**

Signature _____   Signature _____   ☐ Did ☐ Did Not

Name _____   Name _____   Inspect Property

Date Report Signed _____   Date Report Signed _____

State Certification # _____ State   State Certification # _____ State

Or State License # _____ State   Or State License # _____ State

Freddie Mac Form 70   6-93   PAGE 2 OF 2   Fannie Mae Form 1004   6-93 and analyses used to arrive at the value conclusion. At the other end of the spectrum is the restricted report, which contains virtually none of this information. In the middle of the range is the summary appraisal report, which contains some, but not all, of the descriptive information. All three types of reports must contain certain elements (see Figure 26.1).

By prior agreement with the intended user, an appraiser may submit the results of an appraisal in a summary or restricted report. Although these reports are abbreviated, they still must conform to the Uniform Standards. The Departure Provision of the Standards specifies which elements of the appraisal report may be omitted under certain circumstances and which may not. Although the discussion of some topics may be less extensive in a summary or restricted report, the report must contain sufficient information to lead the reader to the appraiser's conclusions. As in the case of an oral report, the appraiser who prepares a summary or restricted report must keep all notes and data on file with a complete synopsis of the analysis, conclusions, and value opinion.

Self-Contained Reports

A self-contained appraisal report gives an appraiser the opportunity to support and explain his or her opinions and conclusions fully and to convince the reader of the soundness of the final value estimate. Self-contained reports often provide the best means for appraisers to fulfill their obligations to their clients. Because this type of report is the most common and most complete, this chapter focuses primarily on the self-contained report.

The objectives of a self-contained appraisal report are to answer in writing the intended user's questions and to substantiate those answers with facts, reasoning, and conclusions. To achieve these objectives and be most useful to the intended user, an appraisal report must guide the reader to the appraiser's conclusions by presenting adequate, pertinent supporting data and logical analysis.

A self-contained report summarizes the factual data and the appraisal methods and techniques that the appraiser has applied within the framework of the valuation process to arrive at a value estimate or another conclusion. This type of report reflects the appraiser's ability to interpret relevant data and select appropriate procedures to estimate a specifically defined value.

In preparing an appraisal report, the appraiser should keep descriptions separate from analysis and interpretation. Factual and descriptive data are usually presented in early sections of the report so that subsequent analysis and interpretation may refer to these facts and indicate how they influence the final value estimate. Repetition and unnecessary duplication should be avoided, but the presentation of data may depend on the nature and length of the report.

Because the appraiser may not be present when a report is reviewed or examined, the report is the appraiser's representative; a good report creates a favorable impression of the appraiser's professional competence. The following suggestions may help appraisers improve the impression created by their reports.

- The paper, cover, and binding used should be of good quality.

- Advances in computer technology enable appraisers to print high-quality reports in the office. The size and style of the type used should be attractive and readable. Graphic illustrations such as photographs and charts should be carefully prepared. The style of headings and subheadings should be appropriate to the subject matter.

- Ideally, illustrations should be integrated with in the text or presented on pages that face the material being discussed. For example, a photograph of the subject property may be placed on the page facing the identification of the property. A neighborhood map could be included on a page facing the neighborhood description to show the location of the subject property. Charts and graphs should be presented where they are discussed. Illustrations that are not directly related to the report should be placed in the addenda.

- The contents of a report should be presented in clearly labeled sections that are identified in the table of contents.

Self-Contained Report Format

A self-contained appraisal report should be designed for the convenience of the reader, who may be the intended user or another person to whom the report is submitted. Readers may scan rather than study a self-contained report, so it is wise to organize the report in a manner that readily discloses the property description, the essential analysis of the problem, and the value conclusion.

A well-prepared report will have more than thorough research, logical organization, and sound reasoning. These basic attributes are enhanced by good composition, a fluid writing style, and clear expression. The use of technical jargon and slang should be avoided. To communicate with the reader effectively, the contents of the report should be set forth as succinctly as possible.

General Outline

Self-contained appraisal reports may vary in content and organization, but they all contain certain elements. Essentially, a self-contained appraisal report follows the order of the valuation process.

Most self-contained reports have four major parts. The contents of each section may be formally divided with subheadings or presented in a continuous narrative. In either case, the major divisions of the report should be identified with individual headings and be separated from one another. The four basic parts of a report are the introduction, the premises of the appraisal, the presentation of data, and the analysis of data and conclusions. Many reports have a fifth section, the addenda, which includes supplemental information and illustrative material that would interrupt the text. The organization of narrative reports varies, but the following outline can be used as a general guide.

Part One—Introduction

Title page

Letter of transmittal

Table of contents

Certification of value

Summary of important conclusions

Part Two—Premises of the Appraisal

Identification of type of appraisal and report format

Assumptions and limiting conditions

Purpose and use of the appraisal

Definition of value and date of value estimate

Property rights appraised

Scope of the appraisal

Part Three—Presentation of Data

Identification of the property, legal description

Identification of any personal property or other items that are
    not real property

Area, city, neighborhood, and location data

Site data

Description of improvements

Zoning

Taxes and assessment data

History, including prior sales and current offers or listings

Marketability study, if appropriate

Part Four—Analysis of Data and Conclusions

Highest and best use of the land as though vacant

Highest and best use of the property as improved

Site value

Cost approach

Sales comparison approach

Income capitalization approach

Reconciliation and final value estimate

Estimate of marketing period

Qualifications of the appraiser

Addenda

Detailed legal description, if not included in the presentation of data

Detailed statistical data

Leases or lease summaries

Other appropriate information

Secondary exhibits

The arrangement of items in this outline is flexible and can be adapted to almost any appraisal assignment and any type of real property. In practice, an appraiser would adapt this outline to the particular requirements of the assignment and to suit his or her personal preference. Some types of property may require unique treatment within or in addition to the basic framework presented here.

Part One—Introduction

Title page. The title page lists the property address, the date of value, and the name and address of the intended user. The name and address of the person authorizing the report may also be included.

Letter of transmittal. The letter of transmittal formally presents the appraisal report to the person for whom the appraisal was prepared. It should be drafted in proper business style and be as brief as the character and nature of the assignment permit. A suitable letter of transmittal may include these elements:

- Date of letter and salutation
- Street address of the property and a brief description, if necessary
- Statement identifying the interest in the property being appraised
- Statement that the property inspection and all necessary investigation and analyses were made by the appraiser
- Reference that the letter is accompanied by an appraisal report and identification of the type of appraisal and report format
- Effective date of the appraisal
- Value estimate
- Any extraordinary assumptions and limiting conditions
- Appraiser's signature

Table of contents. The various sections of the report are customarily listed in order in the table of contents. The major divisions of the report and any subheadings used in the report should be shown here.

Certification of value. The certification of value may follow the final value estimate or be combined with it. The signature of the appraiser, the date, and a seal, if appropriate, may then be added. The certification states that the appraiser has personally conducted the appraisal in an objective manner.

According to Standards Rule 2-3 and the Supplemental Standards rules, the certification must be similar in content to the following:

I certify that, to the best of my knowledge and belief:

- the statements of fact contained in this report are true and correct.

- the reported analyses, opinions, and conclusions are limited only by the reported assumptions and limiting conditions, and are my personal, unbiased professional analyses, opinions, and conclusions.

- I have no (or the specified) present or prospective interest in the property that is the subject of this report, and I have no (or the specified) personal interest or bias with respect to the parties involved.

- my compensation is not contingent upon the reporting of a predetermined value or direction in value that favors the cause of the client, the amount of the value estimate, the attainment of a stipulated result, or the occurrence of a subsequent event.

- my analyses, opinions, and conclusions were developed, and this report has been prepared, in conformity with the Uniform Standards of Professional Appraisal Practice.

- I have (or have not) made a personal inspection of the property that is the subject of this report. (If more than one person signs the report, this certification must clearly specify which individuals did and which individuals did not make a personal inspection of the appraised property.)

- no one provided significant professional assistance to the person signing this report. (If there are exceptions, the name of each individual providing significant professional assistance must be stated.)

- the reported analyses, opinions, and conclusions were developed, and this report has been prepared, in conformity with the requirements of the Code of Professional Ethics and the Standards of Professional Appraisal Practice of the Appraisal Institute.

- the use of this report is subject to the requirements of the Appraisal Institute relating to review by its duly authorized representatives.

One of the following statements must be included in any report prepared by a designated member of the Appraisal Institute:

Either

As of the date of this report, I (or Designated Member's name or Designated Members' names) have/has completed the requirements of the continuing education program of the Appraisal Institute.

or

As of the date of this report, I (or Designated Member's name or Designated Members' names) have not/has not completed the requirements of the continuing education program of the Appraisal Institute.

Whether the certificate is included in the transmittal letter or presented on a separate, signed page, certification is important because it establishes the appraiser's position, thereby protecting both the appraiser's integrity and the validity of the appraisal.

Summary of important conclusions. When an appraisal report is long and complicated, a summary of the major points and important conclusions in the report may be useful. Such a statement is convenient for readers of the report and allows the appraiser to stress the major points considered in reaching the final estimate. The following list indicates the type of material that is frequently included in a summary; however, all of the items do not apply to every appraisal assignment.

- Brief identification of the property
- Identification of the type of appraisal and report format
- Any special assumptions and conclusions
- Determinations of the highest and best use of the land as though vacant and the property as improved
- Age of improvements
- Estimate of site value
- Value indication from the cost approach
- Value indication from the sales comparison approach
- Value indication from the income capitalization approach
- Final estimate of defined value
- Allocation of value between the land and the improvements, between the leased fee and the leasehold estates, or between real and personal property

An appraiser may use a different type of summary for longer or more complex reports. In many appraisal reports a summary is omitted, particularly if the letter of transmittal briefly discusses the major conclusions set forth in the report.

Part Two—Premises of the Appraisal

Identification of type of appraisal and report format. The type of appraisal (i.e., limited or complete) and the report format (i.e., self-contained, summary, or restricted) must be stated.

Assumptions and limiting conditions. Assumptions and limiting conditions may be stated in the letter of transmittal, but they are usually included as separate pages in the report. These statements are used to protect the appraiser and to inform and protect the client and other users of the report. Appropriate standard conditions are an important part of a report and should be stated clearly. The general assumptions typically found in an appraisal report deal with issues such as legal and title considerations, liens and encumbrances, property management, information furnished by others (e.g., engineering studies, surveys), concealment of hazardous substances on the property, and compliance with zoning regulations and local, state, and federal laws.

Some typical general assumptions and limiting conditions are listed below as they might appear in an appraisal report.

This appraisal report has been made with the following general assumptions:

1. No responsibility is assumed for the legal description provided or for matters pertaining to legal or title considerations. Title to the property is assumed to be good and marketable unless otherwise stated.

2. The property is appraised free and clear of any or all liens or encumbrances unless otherwise stated.

3. Responsible ownership and competent property management are assumed.

4. The information furnished by others is believed to be reliable, but no warranty is given for its accuracy.

5. All engineering studies are assumed to be correct. The plot plans and illustrative material in this report are included only to help the reader visualize the property.

6. It is assumed that there are no hidden or unapparent conditions of the property, subsoil, or structures that render it more or less valuable. No responsibility is assumed for such conditions or for obtaining the engineering studies that may be required to discover them.

7. It is assumed that the property is in full compliance with all applicable federal, state, and local environmental regulations and laws unless the lack of compliance is stated, described, and considered in the appraisal report.

8. It is assumed that the property conforms to all applicable zoning and use regulations and restrictions unless a nonconformity has been identified, described and considered in the appraisal report.

9. It is assumed that all required licenses, certificates of occupancy, consents, and other legislative or administrative authority from any local, state, or national government or private entity or organization have been or can be obtained or renewed for any use on which the value estimate contained in this report is based.

10. It is assumed that the use of the land and improvements is confined within the boundaries or property lines of the property described and that there is no encroachment or trespass unless noted in the report.

11. Unless otherwise stated in this report, the existence of hazardous materials, which may or may not be present on the property, was not observed by the appraiser. The appraiser has no knowledge of the existence of such materials on or in the property. The appraiser, however, is not qualified to detect such substances. The presence of substances such as asbestos, urea-formaldehyde foam insulation, and other potentially hazardous materials may affect the value of the property. The value estimated is predicated on the assumption that there is no

such material on or in the property that would cause a loss in value. No responsibility is assumed for such conditions or for any expertise or engineering knowledge required to discover them. The intended user is urged to retain an expert in this field, if desired.

This appraisal report has been made with the following general limiting conditions:

1. Any allocation of the total value estimated in this report between the land and the improvements applies only under the stated program of utilization. The separate values allocated to the land and buildings must not be used in conjunction with any other appraisal and are invalid if so used.

2. Possession of this report, or a copy thereof, does not carry with it the right of publication.

3. The appraiser, by reason of this appraisal, is not required to give further consultation or testimony or to be in attendance in court with reference to the property in question unless arrangements have been previously made.

4. Neither all nor any part of the contents of this report (especially any conclusions as to value, the identity of the appraiser, or the firm with which the appraiser is connected) shall be disseminated to the public through advertising, public relations, news, sales, or other media without the prior written consent and approval of the appraiser.

An appraisal report might contain these additional assumptions and limiting conditions.

1. Any value estimates provided in the report apply to the entire property, and any proration or division of the total into fractional interests will invalidate the value estimate, unless such proration or division of interests has been set forth in the report.

2. Only preliminary plans and specifications were available for use in the preparation of this appraisal; the analysis, therefore, is subject to a review of the final plans and specifications when available.

3. Any proposed improvements are assumed to have been completed unless otherwise stipulated; any construction is assumed to conform with the building plans referenced in the report.

4. The appraiser assumes that the reader or user of this report has been provided with copies of available building plans and all leases and amendments, if any, that encumber the property.

5. No legal description or survey was furnished, so the appraiser used the county tax plat to ascertain the physical dimensions and acreage of the property. Should a survey prove this information to be inaccurate, it may be necessary for this appraisal to be adjusted.

6. The forecasts, projections, or operating estimates contained herein are based on current market conditions, anticipated short-term supply and demand factors, and a continued stable economy. These forecasts are, therefore, subject to changes with future conditions.

7. The Americans with Disabilities Act (ADA) became effective January 26, 1992. The appraiser has not made a specific compliance survey or analysis of the property to determine whether or not it is in conformity with the various detailed requirements of ADA. It is possible that a compliance survey of the property and a detailed analysis of the requirements of the ADA would reveal that the property is not in compliance with one or more of the requirements of the act. If so, this fact could have a negative impact upon the value of the property. Since the appraiser has no direct evidence relating to this issue, possible noncompliance with the requirements of ADA was not considered in estimating the value of the property.

In addition, any departure from the guidelines in Standard 1 must be clearly disclosed. An appraisal in which the Departure Provision is involved is a limited appraisal.

Purpose and use of the appraisal. The purpose of an appraisal report is the question for which the intended user seeks an answer. The intended use of the appraisal must also be stated.

Definition of value and date of value estimate. An acceptable definition of the value being appraised is included in the report to eliminate any confusion in the mind of the intended user or another reader of the report. (Acceptable definitions of various types of value are cited in Chapter 2.)

An appraisal assignment may call for an estimate of current value or an estimate of value as of some point in the past. It is essential to report the date as of which the value conclusion is applicable. When an estimate of value as of a future date is requested by a client, special care and analysis are required. The report must clearly identify the future date of the value estimate and include a statement of qualifying assumptions and limiting conditions appropriate to the terms of the assignment.

Property rights appraised. In identifying the subject property, the appraiser must state and should define the particular rights or interests being valued. This is particularly important in appraisals of partial interests in property, limited rights such as surface or mineral rights, fee simple estates subject to long-term leases, and leasehold interests. Other encumbrances such as easements, mortgages, and special occupancy or use requirements should also be identified and explained in relation to the defined value to be estimated.

Scope of the appraisal. A clear and accurate description of the scope of the appraisal is desirable to protect third parties whose reliance on the appraisal may be affected. The term *scope of the appraisal* refers to the extent of the process of collecting, confirming, and reporting data. The standards clearly impose a responsibility on the appraiser to determine the extent of the work and the report required in relation to the significance of the appraisal problem. By describing the scope of the appraisal the appraiser signifies his or her acceptance of this responsibility.

Part Three—Presentation of Data

Identification of the property. The subject property is identified so that it cannot be confused with any other parcel of real estate. This can be achieved by including a full legal description of the property in the report. When a copy of the official plat or an assessment map is used, the appraiser may refer to it at this point and present it on a facing or following page. If the official plat is unavailable, the appraiser can describe the property by name, specifying the side of the street on which the property fronts, the street address, and the lot and block number. A photograph of the subject property on a facing page can enhance this section of the report. *Personal property and other items that are not real property should be identified.*

Area, city, neighborhood, and location data. All facts about a city and its surroundings that the appraiser considers pertinent to the appraisal problem should be included in the area data. (Different types of data, their appropriate uses in relation to various classifications of property and specific appraisal problems, and their degrees of influence are discussed in Chapters 8 and 9.) An appraiser weighs and considers all pertinent factors in data analysis, but the report should discuss only those data that are found to be significant to the problem at hand. Both positive and negative aspects of the area should be discussed. If the appraiser only provides data in support of either positive or negative factors, the report will be misleading.

If a considerable amount of supporting statistical data—e.g., population figures, cost of living indexes, family income figures—is needed, the appraiser may choose to incorporate these data into the body of the report or present them in tabular form on facing pages and reference them in the discussion. A separate section for area data is not needed in many reports; area data are often combined with neighborhood data.

Area data that may be significant to an appraisal report include

- Distance and direction from employment centers
- Public transportation
- Road patterns, road layout, and street widths
- Adequacy of utilities and street improvements
- Proximity to shopping
- Proximity to schools
- Proximity to parks and recreational areas
- Proximity to sources of nuisances
- Police and fire protection
- Rubbish collection
- Trends in the neighborhood or district
- Population trends
- Percentage of home ownership

- Types of employment and wage levels
- Conformity of development
- Vacancy and rent levels
- Restrictions and zoning
- New construction activity
- Percentage of vacant land
- Changing land use
- Level of taxes
- Adequacy of street parking and off-street parking
- Type and amount of street traffic
- Type and amount of pedestrian traffic
- Proximity to expressways, tollroads, and airports
- Rail connections and service for freight
- Concentration of advertising by retail merchants
- Other beneficial or detrimental influences

The amount of neighborhood and location data required depends on the appraisal assignment and the intended user. For example, when an appraisal is prepared for an out-of-town client who is unfamiliar with the property and the community, it may be wise to include more community and neighborhood data than would be needed by a local client. If the appraisal concerns an important business property that derives its income from the purchasing power of the surrounding area, the appraiser should provide a detailed description of the neighborhood and discuss how the population and its purchasing power affect the value of the subject property.

An appraiser should also note the presence of special amenities or detrimental conditions in the neighborhood and provide reasons or data to support any conclusions about these factors. For example, if the appraiser states that the area is growing, actual growth figures or building projections should be included in the report. If a report states that a neighborhood is in decline due to abnormal deterioration or poor maintenance, the appraiser might refer to specific properties that exhibit these detrimental conditions or use photographs to illustrate this conclusion.

Area and neighborhood data form the background against which a property is considered. The data are significant to the extent that they affect property value. This section of the appraisal is incomplete if the trends indicated by the data are not analyzed. The appraiser applies professional experience and judgment to interpret how relevant data affect the marketability of the subject property. Without interpretation, city and neighborhood data lose their significance; proper analysis of data is needed to establish the potential of the property being appraised.

In studying neighborhood trends, appraisers must abide by the provisions of fair lending laws and regulations. Analyses should never be based on assumptions or unsupported premises about neighborhood decline and a property's effective age or remaining useful life.

Site data. Pertinent facts about the subject site belong in the site data section. Site data may include descriptions of the property's frontage, depth, site area, and shape; soil and subsoil conditions; easements and restrictions; utilities; and any improvements that benefit or harm the site. The appraiser should offer a conclusion as to the utility or adaptability of the site for existing or proposed improvements.

Description of improvements. In the description of improvements section, all building and improvement data relevant to the appraisal problem are presented and discussed. Although an appraiser considers and processes much data in the course of an appraisal, only significant property characteristics that influence the value conclusion are presented in the report. These characteristics may include

- Actual and effective building age and building size
- Number and size of units
- Structural and construction details
- Mechanical equipment
- Physical condition
- Functional utility or inutility

Property information may be supported with drawings, photographs, floor plans, and elevations. If the description of structural details and mechanical equipment is long, an outline may be used in the body of the report with emphasis on the important items.

Zoning. Zoning data are either included in the land description section of the appraisal report or presented in a separate section. When they are significant, zoning and private restrictions should be discussed in detail. The appraiser should provide sufficient data to help the reader understand the limitations that zoning regulations place on the use or development of the site. If appropriate, the appraiser may explore the possibility of a zoning change. Other existing public and private restrictions such as floodplain regulations, scenic easements, and wetland restrictions should be discussed and their effect on the utility and value of the property described.

Taxes and assessment data. Current assessed values and ad valorem tax rates should be reported and a calculation of the current annual tax load of the subject property should be included. Existing assessment trends or prospective changes in tax rates should be analyzed. It may be appropriate to discuss the tax assessment or tax load on the subject in relation to the taxes on other properties, particularly if the difference is significant.

History. Any recent sale of the subject property should be discussed as well as any other sales transacted within the past three years. For properties other than single-family residences, recent changes in the property's operating profile should be considered along with any offers to purchase. Historical property data may include information on original assemblage, acquisition, or construction costs; expenditures for capital additions or modernization; financial data or transfers of ownership; casualty loss experience; history and type of occupancy; reputation or prestige; and any other facts that may pertain to or affect the computations, estimates, or conclusions presented in the report. An appraiser should also investigate the previous history of ownership and use of the property for possible environmental problems.

Marketability study. In the appraisal of income-producing properties such as office buildings, shopping centers, and apartment buildings, a marketability study may be performed to find out how the subject property fits into the overall market in terms of rent levels and absorption rates. A marketability study is usually directly related to the conclusions presented in the appraisal report. Such a study may examine the specific real estate market or submarket, the supply of existing properties (e.g., inventory of space, construction trends, vacancy patterns, and absorption rates), the demand forecast (e.g., projected expansion or shrinkage), the current balance of supply and demand, and competitive rent levels.

Part Four—Analysis of Data and Conclusions

Highest and best use should be expressed in terms of the property's most probable and profitable use. Typically, four criteria—physical possibility, legal permissibility, financial feasibility (market support), and maximum productivity—are discussed in relation to the subject property. Land use patterns in the area, zoning regulations, and the profitability of existing or proposed improvements should be discussed. (For more information on how an appraiser determines highest and best use, see Chapter 13.)

Highest and best use of the land as though vacant. Land is generally appraised as though vacant and available for development to its highest and best use. The highest and best use on which the appraiser based the value estimate of the land as though vacant should be clearly stated in the report. The character and amount of data presented and analyzed in this section are dictated by the purpose of the appraisal.

Highest and best use of the property as improved. To determine the highest and best use of a property as improved, an appraiser discusses whether or not the removal and replacement of the existing improvements are economically warranted on the date of the appraisal. If the existing improvement is to be retained, the property's highest and best use is based on how the entire property should be used to maximize its benefits or the income it produces. An appraiser may suggest a possible course of action such as rehabilitation, improved maintenance, or better property management.

Site value. In the site value section of an appraisal report, market data are presented along with an analysis of the data and reasoning that lead to the land value estimate. The factors that influence land value should be presented in a clear and precise manner. The narrative should lead the reader to the land value estimate.

Approaches to value. An appraiser develops the approaches applicable to the assignment and derives indications of value. For each approach used, factual data and the analysis and reasoning leading to the value indication are presented.

Many intended users are not familiar with the mechanics of the three approaches to value, so the appraiser may want to briefly explain the procedures applied. The extent of explanation required depends on the circumstances of the appraisal. Simple statements that describe what is included in each of the three approaches can help the reader understand the report.

For example, the approaches could be described as follows.

In the sales comparison approach, the subject property is compared to similar properties that have been sold recently or for which listing prices or offers are known. Data from generally comparable properties are used and comparisons are made to demonstrate a probable price at which the subject property would be sold if offered on the market.

In the cost approach, an estimated reproduction or replacement cost of the building and land improvements as of the date of appraisal is developed together with an estimate of the losses in value that have taken place due to wear and tear, design and plan deficiencies, or neighborhood influences. To the depreciated building cost estimate, entrepreneurial profit and the estimated value of the land are added. The total represents the value indicated by the cost approach.

In the income capitalization approach, the current rental income to the property is calculated and deductions are made for vacancy and collection loss and expenses. The prospective net operating income of the property is then estimated. To support this estimate, operating statements for the subject property in previous years and for comparable properties are reviewed along with available operating cost estimates. An applicable capitalization method and appropriate capitalization rates are developed and used in computations that lead to an indication of value.

The three approaches are seldom completely independent. An appraisal is composed of a number of integrated, interrelated, and inseparable procedures that have a common objective—a convincing, reliable estimate of value.

Reconciliation of value indications. The reconciliation of value indications should lead the reader logically to the final estimate of value. The final estimate of defined value may be stated in many ways. The following is a simple example.

As a result of my investigation and analysis, it is my opinion that the market value of the identified interest in the property, on July 20, 1996 is:

FOUR HUNDRED THOUSAND DOLLARS

($400,000)

Note that the date on which the value opinion is applicable may differ from the date of the letter of transmittal.

When the appraiser chooses to allocate the value estimate among property components, a breakdown may be presented after the final value estimate.

. . . which may be allocated as follows:

Land	$ 80,000
Improvements	300,000
Personal property and other items	+ 20,000
Total	$400,000

Marketing time. Many clients, including most financial institutions, require that appraisals consider the "reasonable marketing period" for the property at the concluded value. Advisory Opinion 7 of USPAP states,

> since marketing time occurs after the effective date of the market value estimate and the marketing time estimate is related to, yet apart from the appraisal process, it is appropriate for the section of the appraisal report that discusses this issue and its implications to appear toward the end of the report after the market value conclusion. The request to estimate a reasonable marketing time exceeds the normal information required for the conduct of the appraisal process, and should be treated separately from that process.

Qualifications of the appraiser. The appraiser's qualifications are usually included in the report as evidence of the appraiser's competence to perform the assignment. These qualifications may include facts concerning

- Professional experience
- Educational background and training
- Business, professional, and academic affiliations and activities
- Clients for whom the appraiser has rendered professional services, the types of properties appraised, and the nature of the appraisal assignments undertaken

The use of qualifications is so widespread that many appraisers find it expedient to insert a printed statement of their qualifications in each appraisal report. Of course, the appraiser's qualifications must be presented accurately and in a manner that is not misleading.

Addenda

Depending on the size and complexity of the appraisal assignment, addenda may be included to present information that would interrupt the narrative portions of the report. The following list indicates items that might be included in the addenda, if they have not already been incorporated into the body of the report:

- Plot plan
- Plans and elevations of buildings
- Photographs of properties referred to in the report
- City, neighborhood, and other maps
- Charts and graphs
- Historical income and expense data

- Building specifications
- Detailed estimates of the reproduction or replacement costs of buildings
- Sales and listing data
- Leases and lease abstracts
- Marketability analysis data (e.g., information on construction trends, vacancy trends, and competitive rent levels)

Key Concepts

- The intended use of an appraisal report is to lead the reader from the definition of the appraisal problem through the analysis of relevant data to a specific conclusion.
- Appraisal Institute members are required to conduct their professional appraisal activities in compliance with the Standards of Professional Appraisal Practice, which include the Uniform Standards of Professional Appraisal Practice (USPAP), guide notes, and two supplemental standards. Standards Rules 2-1 through 2-5 of USPAP deal with reporting requirements.
- Each report or communication concerning the results of an appraisal must 1) clearly and accurately set forth the appraisal in a manner that is not misleading, 2) contain sufficient information to enable the person(s) who will rely on the report to understand it properly, and 3) clearly and accurately disclose any extraordinary assumption or limiting condition that directly affects the appraisal and indicate its impact on value.
- Appraisal reports may be oral (e.g., expert testimony) or written (e.g., any of the three reporting formats specified in USPAP). Reports may also be submitted on the forms used by government agencies, insurance companies, and financial institutions. Guide Note 3 addresses the use of form reports for residential appraisals. Form reports must meet specific requirements.
- Regardless of how a report is conveyed, all data and notes as well as a summary of the analysis and conclusions should be kept in the appraiser's file.
- USPAP provides for two types of appraisals (limited appraisals under the departure provision and complete appraisals) and three reporting formats (restricted, summary, and self-contained). The type of report and the reporting format must always be identified. When a client requests a complete appraisal but specifies that the appraiser's opinion be communicated without detailed documentation (e.g., in a summary or restricted report), the appraiser must still undertake a complete analysis.
- A self-contained report generally has four parts and an addenda. The *introduction* contains a letter of transmittal, title page, table of contents, certification of value, and summary of important conclusions. The *premises of the appraisal* identify the type of appraisal, report format, assumptions and limiting conditions, the purpose and use, scope of the appraisal, and the definition and date of value. The *presentation of the data* section includes the property's legal description, identification of personal or non-realty items, and data on the neighborhood, site,

improvements, zoning, taxes, assessments, prior owners, and marketability. The *analysis of the data and conclusions* presents the highest and best use conclusion(s), land value, value indications derived from the approaches applied, a final reconciled value conclusion, the estimated marketing period, and the qualifications of the appraiser. The *addenda* may include legal documentation, statistical data, lease data or summaries, and other appropriate information.

Terms

appraisal report	narrative report
certification of value	oral report
complete appraisal	restricted report
departure provision	self-contained report
form report	summary report
letter of transmittal	Uniform Residential Appraisal
limited appraisal	Report (URAR) form

CHAPTER TWENTY-SEVEN

Consulting

R eal estate appraisals may involve valuation, consulting (analysis or evaluation), or both. In valuation assignments a specific type of value is sought for the defined rights in an identified property as of a given date. In consulting assignments valuation techniques are frequently used, but the objective is not to value a particular property. Instead, the focus is on decision making and providing advice for a client. Consulting may be either general or specific in nature. A consulting assignment may include both valuation and consulting services, each of which is covered by the Appraisal Institute's Code of Professional Ethics and Standards of Professional Appraisal Practice.

Specific consulting assignments may include any or all of the following: highest and best use studies, market studies, marketability studies, pricing and rent projection studies, absorption analyses, feasibility studies, other analytical studies with a specific objective, and studies that provide support for litigation. In more general assignments, practitioners provide clients with unbiased advice regarding real estate decisions. This advice may help clients set goals, establish an analytical framework for real estate investment, or finalize real estate decisions.

Many real estate valuation assignments call for consulting services. In conducting a market value appraisal required for mortgage loan purposes, an appraiser may also provide data and advice that can be used to structure the specific terms of the mortgage.

Buyers and sellers who wish to establish a market-based price for transaction purposes are usually interested in other market facts as well—e.g., high and low market price indicators, the frequency of offers and sales, and the average market exposure of properties before sale. This information can help investors finalize their decisions.

Although valuation and consulting are closely associated, consulting has long been considered to be distinct from the appraisal function. Traditionally professional real estate organizations have conferred a special designation on members who demonstrate the training and experience required to perform analytical assignments.[1]

Relationship of Consulting to Valuation

Valuation studies are primarily microeconomic analyses because they focus on valuing identified interests in specified real estate as of a given date. Broad economic trends and forces are considered, but the valuer concentrates on a specific parcel or parcels of real estate.

---

1. Holders of the MAI and SREA designations are qualified to perform evaluation and analysis assignments. These designations were conferred by the American Institute of Real Estate Appraisers and the Society of Real Estate Appraisers, which merged in 1991 to form the Appraisal Institute. The Counselors of Real Estate (formerly the American Society of Real Estate Counselors, or ASREC), was founded to enhance the quality of advice on real estate matters available to the public. This group confers the CRE (Counselor of Real Estate) designation.

Consulting, on the other hand, may include macroeconomic analyses, microeconomic analyses, or a combination of both. It may relate to broad market categories or to a given parcel or parcels of real estate. Valuation assignments always include the identification and definition of one or more types of value. In consulting assignments, the nature and scope of the services being performed must be explained, but a particular type of value may not be specified because a value estimate may not be sought. Appraisers must clearly distinguish between valuation and consulting assignments to avoid confusion and possible misunderstanding.

Market Value and Investment Value

When the word *value* is applied to real estate, it must be qualified. The statement "The value of your property is $150,000" is not specific enough to be meaningful to real estate professionals. If, however, an appraiser says, "Your property is estimated to have a market value of $150,000" an explicit meaning is conveyed. Of necessity, appraisers refer to market value, insurable value, liquidation value, and other precisely identified and defined types of value.Consulting assignments frequently call for estimates of market value or investment value as well as associated analyses that will enable a client to make one or more real estate decisions. Just as appraisers must distinguish between valuation and consulting assignments, they must also distinguish between market value and investment value.

Market value can be called "the value in the marketplace." Investment value is the specific value of goods or services to a particular investor (or class of investors) based on individual investment requirements. Market value and investment value are different concepts; the values estimated for each may or may not be numerically equal depending on the circumstances. Moreover, market value estimates are commonly made without reference to investment value, but investment value estimates are frequently accompanied by a market value estimate to facilitate decision making.

Market value estimates assume no specific buyer or seller. Rather, the appraiser considers a hypothetical transaction in which both the buyer and the seller have the understanding, perceptions, and motivations that are typical of the market for the property or interests being valued. Appraisers must distinguish between their own knowledge, perceptions, and attitudes and those of the market or markets for the property in question. The special requirements of a given client are irrelevant to a market value estimate.

In contrast, the goals of a specific investor are directly related to investment value, which reflects the advantages or disadvantages of a particular property or real estate situation to that investor. An appraiser may be asked to analyze a series of investment opportunities or possible business decisions and evaluate them in terms of their benefits to a given client. Even decisions involving a single parcel of real estate may require the evaluation of other possible decisions and an analysis of how each possibility may affect the decision being considered.

For example, an appraiser may be asked to consider whether a parcel of land that is adjacent to the client's industrial property is worth $500,000, the price being asked by its owner. Market analysis indicates that the property is overpriced in comparison with other properties and that its market value is $400,000. However, the client's successful business must be expanded and it will have to be relocated if the additional land is not acquired. If the existing operation is moved, disruption of business and other factors will create a loss of more than $100,000. Because this loss exceeds the difference between the property's market value and its asking price, it might be concluded that the property has an investment value of $500,000 or more to the client in question.

Each voluntary purchase or sale of real estate is based on an investment value decision made by the parties to the transaction. Thus, the market is made up of transactions in which willing participants make investment decisions.

The transaction price of a property varies with the bargaining strength and motivation of buyers and sellers and with the number of opportunities available to these market participants. Ultimately, a property's market price reflects the interaction of those who create market supply and demand. Depending on the circumstances of the buyer and the seller in each case, the transaction price at a given moment can be expected to fluctuate above or below the property's market value at perfect market equilibrium. Sellers are normally expected to accept a price that equals or exceeds investment value, while buyers will pay a price that does not exceed investment value. Market value estimates synthesize these transactions without considering any particular buyer or seller.

The field of real estate consulting is diverse, so the remainder of this chapter focuses on some of the techniques used by investors, developers, lenders, and real estate professionals to estimate investment value. Although these techniques can be applied in various types of valuation assignments, they are especially useful in providing clients with specific advice for real estate decision making.

Common Measures of Investment Performance

Great strides have been made in the field of real estate consulting since the 1950s. The analytical tools used in consulting now generally parallel the techniques used in other investment fields. However, some measures of investment performance are particularly applicable to real estate. These measures are not individually perfect, but as a collection of tools they have proven effectiveness. They reflect a common market understanding and are useful in typical real estate applications.

It is beyond the scope of this text to explore all analytical techniques, but a basic understanding of the most common measures of investment performance is considered essential to both valuation and consulting.

Simple Ratios

For many years investors have used simple ratio relationships to compare and evaluate the returns from investment properties. One of the most common relationships is the overall rate of return, which is the ratio between the net earnings of a given parcel of investment real estate and the price or value of that parcel. It is expressed as R in the formula

$$R = \frac{I}{V}$$

Other formulas employ simple gross income or net income multipliers. In these formulas the price or value of a property is expressed as a multiple of its potential gross or effective gross earnings, or as a multiple of its net earnings. This multiple is the reciprocal of the overall rate.

Each of these measures can be an effective tool of comparison when applied to very similar properties. Comparing the gross incomes of investments reflects differences among properties to a degree, but measures of investment performance that relate to net income produce better results.

Unfortunately, simple measures of investment performance incorporate many factors that may require specific analysis in a consulting assignment. For example, if an overall rate is used alone, future changes in net incomes, terminal investment values, financing structures, the effects of income taxes, and other elements that may be crucial to a particular property decision are not considered. The overall rate may reflect the combined effect of these and other factors but, in its simple form, it does not consider these factors individually. Therefore, the overall rate and related simple measures of comparison can be misunderstood or misapplied in some situations.

Payback Period

As a measure of investment return, the payback period is seldom used alone; it is commonly employed in conjunction with other measures. *The payback period is defined as the length of time required for the stream of net cash flows produced by an investment to equal the original cash outlay.* The breakeven point is reached when the investment's cumulative income is equal to its cumulative loss. The payback period can be calculated from either before- or after-tax cash flows, so the type of cash flow selected should be identified. The equation for payback period may be expressed as follows:

$$PB = \frac{\text{Equity capital outlay}}{\text{Annual net equity cash flows}}$$

This measure of performance is used by investors who simply want to know how long it will take them to recapture the dollars they have invested. In theory an investment with a payback period of three years would be preferable to one with a payback period of five years, all else being equal. Similarly, an investment that will return the investor's capital in six years would be unacceptable to an investor who seeks investment payback within four years.

For an equity investment that is expected to produce equal cash flows, the payback period is simply the reciprocal of the equity capitalization, or equity dividend, rate.

$$PB = \frac{1}{R_E}$$

If annual equity cash flows are not expected to be equal over the payback period, the equity cash flows for each year must be added until the sum equals or exceeds the equity capital outlay; this point indicates the year in which payback occurs.

Although the payback period is simple and easily understood, it has a number of drawbacks. First, it measures the amount of time over which invested money will be returned to the investor, but it does not consider the time value of the money invested. A five-year investment payback for a $100,000 investment that pays $10,000 in Year 1 and $90,000 in Year 5 is not distinguished from the payback for a $100,000 investment that pays $90,000 in Year 1 and $10,000 in Year 5. The time value of money allows the first investment to use an additional $80,000 (i.e., the difference between the $90,000 paid in the second investment and the $10,000 paid in the first investment) from the second year through the fifth.[2] Another shortcoming of the payback period is that it does not consider the effect of any gain or loss of invested capital beyond the breakeven point and does not specifically account for investment risks. An investment with a three-year payback may be far riskier than another investment with a five-year payback, but the shorter period generally appears preferable. Thus this measure of performance should only be used to compare investments with similar investment characteristics or in conjunction with other performance measures in carefully weighted applications.

Investment Proceeds per Dollar Invested

Investment proceeds per dollar invested is a simple relationship calculated as the anticipated total proceeds returned to the investment position divided by the amount invested. The resulting index or multiple provides a crude measure of investment performance that is not time-weighted. It is sometimes used to compare very similar investments over similar time periods.

Profitability Index

Although measuring the investment proceeds per dollar invested is too imprecise for general use, a refinement of this technique is commonly applied. *A profitability index (PI), or benefit/cost ratio, is defined as the present value of the anticipated investment returns (benefit) divided by the present value of the capital outlay (cost).* The formula is

$$PI = \frac{\text{Present value of anticipated investment returns}}{\text{Present value of capital outlay}}$$

This measure employs a desired minimum rate of return or a satisfactory yield rate. The present value of the anticipated investment returns and the present value of the capital outlay are calculated using the desired rate as the discount rate. If, for example, the present value of the capital outlay discounted at 10% is $12,300 and the present value of the benefits is $12,399, the profitability index, based on a satisfactory yield rate of 10%, is $12,399/$12,300 = 1.008.

---

2. A more sophisticated, but less popular, measure is the discounted payback period, which recognizes the time value of money at a stipulated rate of return. In this context the payback period is the amount of time required for the discounted benefits to equal the discounted costs.

A profitability index greater than 1.0 indicates that the investment is profitable and acceptable in light of the chosen discount rate. A profitability index of less than 1.0 indicates that the investment cannot generate the desired rate of return and is not acceptable. A profitability index of exactly 1.0 indicates that the opportunity is just satisfactory in terms of the desired rate of return and, coincidentally, the chosen discount rate is equal to the anticipated *IRR*. The discount rate used to compute the profitability index may represent a minimum desired rate, the cost of capital, or a rate that is considered acceptable in light of the risks involved.

This refined measure of investment performance considers the time value of money, which is not considered in calculating the proceeds per dollar invested. A profitability index is particularly useful in comparing investments that have different capital outlay requirements, different time frames for receiving income or other investment returns, and different risk characteristics.

A profitability index is commonly used in conjunction with other measures, particularly net present value. When combined, these measures provide special insights into the investments under consideration. Like all other measures of investment performance, a profitability index is *not* generally used alone in making investment decisions. A common rule of thumb for investors is that the profitability index of an investment should be at least 1.0—i.e., the present value of the benefits divided by the capital outlay should be equal to or greater than one.

Net Present Value

Net present value (dollar reward) is defined as the difference between the present value of all expected benefits, or positive cash flows, and the present value of capital outlays, or negative cash flows. Net present value (*NPV*) is simply the present value of anticipated investment returns *minus* the present value of the capital outlay. This measure, like a profitability index, is based on a desired rate of return. It is computed using the desired rate as a discount rate and the result is viewed as an absolute dollar reward. The reward (or penalty) is expressed in total dollars, not as a ratio. The formula is

$$NPV = CF_0 + \frac{CF_1}{(1 + i)} + \frac{CF_2}{(1 + i)^2} \quad \ldots \quad + \frac{CF_n}{(1 + i)^n} - CO$$

where i is the applicable discount rate and n is the number of periods in the analysis. This formula calculates the difference between the present value of all investment returns and the amount of the original capital investment. The dollar reward is simply *NPV* at a stipulated discount rate. A positive *NPV* indicates a reward; a negative *NPV* indicates a penalty. An *NPV* of zero indicates that the chosen discount rate coincides with the *IRR*.

A number of decision rules can be established for applying the *NPV*. For example, assume that a property with an anticipated present value of $1,100,000 for all investment returns over a 10-year holding period can be purchased for $1,000,000. If one investor's *NPV* goal is zero, this investment exceeds that criterion. It also meets a second investor's goal for an *NPV* of $100,000, but it would not qualify if the goal were $150,000.

Net present value does consider the time value of money and different discount rates can be applied to different investments to account for general risk differences. However, this method cannot handle different required capital outlays. It cannot differentiate between an *NPV* of $100,000 on a $1,000,000 capital outlay and the same *NPV* on a $500,000 capital outlay. Therefore, this technique is best used in conjunction with other measures.

Time-Weighted Rate

A *time-weighted rate is technically an average of all actual, instantaneous rates over a period of time*. It is similar to the rate of growth for capital invested in a mutual fund in which all dividend income is automatically reinvested. The time-weighted rate, which is also known as the *unit-method rate* or the *share-accounting rate*, is used primarily to measure the performance of a portfolio manager, not the performance of the portfolio itself.

Discounted Cash Flow

Discounted cash flow (DCF) analysis provides appraisers and other investment analysts with the most detailed, precise means of considering the amounts and timing of investment cash inflows and outflows over the life of an investment. With this procedure any series of cash inflows and outflows over any specified time frame at any rate of return can be analyzed and the present value of the investment's anticipated performance can be measured.

In discounted cash flow analysis, compound interest measurements are used to convert future dollars into their present value equivalents. Because dollars to be received in the future are worth less than current dollars, successive cash inflows and outflows are discounted at a selected rate to their present value as of a given date. The sum of the present values of future positive and negative cash flows represents the DCF value indication at a given discount rate. Different rates may be used to reflect differences in investment risks.

Given similar data, DCF calculations may produce the same results as other income comparison methods. However, methods that are less precise may produce different results because they do not consider the explicit details considered in DCF analysis. Discounted cash flow techniques may be applied to cash flows before or after income taxes. The results of DCF analysis can then be used as the present value component (*PV*) in comparisons made with profitability indexes or net present value methods.

Discounted cash flow techniques can be applied on either a constant-dollar or nominal-dollar basis. If constant dollars are used, they are discounted with rates that do not include an allowance for inflation. Consequently, investment performance is measured without considering the effects of inflation. More often, nominal or actual dollars are measured for the cash inflows and outflows anticipated. In this case the discount rate applied contains a component that accounts for inflation. However, because the rate of inflation is an element of risk, a specific analysis of future inflation rates or components of inflation is not usually included in the discount rate, although this may be done in more detailed analyses.

For income streams that extend over many years, such as those stipulated in long-term leases, DCF is commonly performed for terms of five, 10, or 15 years. Although these terms may be shorter than the term of a given property lease, they offer two principal advantages. First, buyers and sellers in many markets develop their expectations of future price changes over short or medium-length terms. Thus, the appraiser can establish market expectations regarding the terminal values of the investment and factor these expectations into income analysis time frames that are consistent with market thinking and behavior. Second, the mathematics of compound interest are data-specific and precise, but they sometimes lead to conclusions that are difficult to accept.

Consider, for example, the following table which shows the amounts to which $100,000 will grow at 10% interest compounded annually over various investment periods.

Years	Future Value
10	$259,374
20	$672,750
30	$1,744,940
40	$4,525,926
50	$11,739,085
75	$127,189,537

Although these figures are accurate and a 10% rate of growth may well represent market thinking for a given property, many people cannot accept the implication that the property *must* have a value of more than $127 million in 75 years. Therefore, an appraiser may determine that the market is acting as though it considers a 10% growth rate appropriate over the income projection period, but conclude that the market is not actually considering the effect produced by that growth rate over an extremely long time frame.

Although DCF analysis can be applied to historical investment results, it is usually applied to future expectations. Therefore, DCF analysis frequently involves forecasting cash inflows and outflows. In valuation assignments, the analyst applies the anticipations of the marketplace; in performing DCF analysis in evaluation assignments, different investment scenarios are presumed to test the subjective judgments of the appraiser or others.

Discounted cash flow techniques are precise, persuasive, and time-sensitive. They can be applied to different income patterns and risk situations. They reduce the number of assumptions required for a given analysis and explicitly consider both advantageous and disadvantageous investment expectations.

Discounted cash flow techniques have some disadvantages, however. They are based on forecast estimates and the analyst must consider and have access to historical data. The precision of DCF techniques can suggest greater accuracy than is warranted and the rates applied in discounting may be highly subjective.

Analysts and other users of DCF techniques should recognize that all analytical techniques are based on combinations of implicit and explicit assumptions. Some practitioners will defend the use of the overall capitalization rate in place of DCF analysis with the reasoning that property income and property value, the two components of an overall capitalization rate, are more knowable and less speculative. In situations in which the property being analyzed is to be sold immediately, the overall capitalization rate may be mathematically valid. However, future cash flows, risks, and terminal sale prices all affect the value of the investment property. The use of an overall capitalization rate does not obviate consideration of these factors. It simply leaves them unstated. Similarly, the specific identification of such items in DCF analysis should not be interpreted as a statement of fact, but as an estimate or forecast of future possibilities.

Internal Rate of Return

The internal rate of return (*IRR*), which is discussed in Chapter 24 in the context of yield analysis, expands on present value calculations and techniques. It represents a special case among investment performance measures. *The IRR is simply defined as that rate of discount that produces a profitability index of one and a net present value of zero.* Measured separately, the *IRR* is the discount rate at which the present value of all net investment returns, including any return of capital from disposal of the investment, exactly equals the capital outlay for the investment.

In other words, the *IRR* calculation is a DCF analysis solved backwards—i.e., all cash inflows and outflows are analyzed to find what discount rate can be applied to make them exactly equivalent to the original capital outlay. Thus, the *IRR* considers all positive and negative cash flows from the inception of the investment to its termination and reflects the indicated return *on* the investment in addition to the return *of* the investment.

The *IRR* concept and method are also referred to as *yield analysis*. Although the term is imprecise and appears in different contexts, the *IRR* is considered a prominent example of yield analysis.

As mentioned in Chapter 24, the reinvestment presumption is a controversial aspect of *IRR* analysis. The presumption that money received from the investment before its termination is actually reinvested is not essential to the *IRR* concept. Nevertheless, mathematical consistency can be demonstrated between the results of such an analysis and the presumption that these funds are reinvested at the same rate of interest as the *IRR*. This controversy, and other weaknesses in the *IRR*, have led to the development of alternative measures such as the financial management rate of return (*FMRR*), the adjusted internal rate of return (*AIRR*), and the modified internal rate of return (*MIRR*). These methods were created to address other factors or to compensate for the reinvestment consideration.

Calculating an *IRR* is an iterative process. A successive series of calculations is made to establish a range for the *IRR* and this range is refined to the required degree of precision. These calculations can be facilitated with financial calculators and computers, but they can also be done manually. Because many variables are usually involved, no formula can calculate the *IRR* in a single step.

Despite its precision and persuasiveness, the *IRR* has many weaknesses, which are analyzed in Chapter 24. These weaknesses are reviewed below.

More than one IRR. In some situations it is possible that more than one number will mathematically satisfy the *IRR* definition. Although this is somewhat unusual, appraisers are cautioned against the unqualified use of *IRR* measures and concepts.

Discounting of negative cash flows. Standard *IRR* and DCF methods discount both positive and negative cash flows at the applicable discount rate. Some investors argue that different risks are attributable to these cash flows and that this methodology does not make financial sense.

Disparity with NPV. The *IRR* of an investment may vary considerably from the *NPV* for that investment. To illustrate, consider the following data for a one-year investment.

	Required Capital	Net Receipt at Year End
Investment A	$20,000	$24,000
Investment B	30,000	35,100

The *IRR* calculated for Investment A is 20% and the *IRR* for Investment B is 17%. For an investor who requires a 10% yield, the net present values for each investment are calculated as follows:

$$\text{Investment A: } \$24,000 \times 0.909091 - 20,000 = \$1,818$$

$$\text{Investment B: } \$35,100 \times 0.909091 - 30,000 = \$1,909$$

Both techniques are based on compound interest, but these calculations reveal that Investment B, the larger investment, produces a higher *NPV*, while Investment A, the smaller investment, has a higher *IRR*.

No recognition of differences in capital outlays. A primary weakness of the *IRR* is that it does not account for differences in the amount of capital outlay required for the various properties under consideration. It presumes that all capital amounts have both the opportunity *and the obligation* to earn a return at the same rate as the calculated *IRR*. Consequently, the *IRR* is less effective when it is applied to investments that have very different capital requirements. In these cases the profitability index is used in conjunction with the *IRR*. In the example presented above, the *PI* (present value of the investment at year end divided by capital invested) for Investment A ($21,818/ $20,000) is 1.09, while the *PI* for Investment B ($31,909/$30,000) is 1.06. Although the *PI* supports the *IRR* indication in this case, it is possible that the higher the *IRR* becomes, the lower the corresponding *PI*.

Although the *IRR* is of substantial importance in the analysis of investment properties, it has been subject to abuse. When properly applied and interpreted, however, this measure may be given significant weight in analyzing and comparing investment alternatives. Because the *IRR* normally deals with unknown factors in the future, the forecast data required in its estimation should never be misinterpreted as predictive. The *IRR* can be of particular value to decision makers when the likelihoods and risks associated with each component of data in the analysis can be fully assessed. Like other measures of investment performance, the *IRR* should be used in conjunction with other techniques and considerations.

The "Correct" Investment Performance Measure

No single investment performance measure is the best or most appropriate in all situations. Each has its advantages and disadvantages and all are more effective when used in conjunction with other measures. Under certain circumstances one or more of these measures should be given greater weight, but the analyst must always recognize the individual limitations of each measure.

Omitting one or more of these measures in making a given real estate decision does not indicate the likely failure of that investment; similarly, applying appropriate measures is no guarantee of success. All decisions are made under conditions of uncertainty, but the measures of investment performance discussed here represent valuable tools that allow appraisers and investors to weigh the facts, exercise sound judgment, and make reasoned decisions. They also provide a framework for implementing an investment program and monitoring investment decisions once they are made.

Judgment is the ability to draw on information and individual experience to make better decisions. As used in valuation and consulting assignments, investment performance measures are not panaceas, but aids that can be useful in developing, considering, and explaining investment decisions and judgments.

Consulting Services

Appraisers are asked to perform consulting services because they have the market knowledge and experience needed to help clients solve real estate problems. Just as the valuation process is a time-honored approach to conducting real estate valuations, an appropriate problem-solving process is needed to perform consulting assignments.

Most, if not all, of the techniques used in valuation studies are also applicable to the analyses performed in consulting. However, a consulting assignment may not require any valuation or it may use one or more valuations as part of a broader analysis. In addition, consulting frequently involves consideration of the specific needs and objectives of the client, not the generalized, composite market perspective that characterizes market value assignments.

Although the tools common to valuation and consulting may be used differently in each type of assignment, appraisers must at all times maintain their objectivity and support their findings with facts extracted from competent research. By their nature, consulting assignments are often more subjective than valuation assignments. Therefore, a practitioner who undertakes a consulting assignment must identify and evaluate both facts and judgments and then relate his or her findings to the financial decisions under consideration.

In the remainder of this chapter, essential consulting services and elements common to typical consulting assignments are reviewed. Risk analysis is a fundamental part of any type of decision making. The analytical tools employed include the investment performance measures previously discussed and other techniques. Consulting studies commonly focus on specific analyses of the income tax consequences of investments, but there are many other types of studies that appraisers may be asked to perform. Appraisers may be retained to provide real estate counseling services in conjunction with their valuations or consulting work. Each of these activities is briefly discussed.

Risk Analysis

The concepts of risk and uncertainty are fundamental to real estate consulting and other forms of investment analysis. Frequently, the results of valuation analyses and many investment performance measures used in consulting are viewed as point estimates—i.e., single parameter estimates. Real estate professionals typically regard point estimates as the most probable numbers, not the only possible numbers. Recognizing and dealing with other possibilities is a major function of risk analysis.

Risk is defined as the probability that foreseen events will not occur. An appraiser may identify the most probable amounts and timing of cash flows and then analyze both the probability that the cash flow forecasts are correct as stated and the risk that they are not. If the appraiser is absolutely certain that the exact amounts forecast will be realized, there is no risk.

Uncertainty is the probability that unforeseen events will occur. With the supplementary concept of uncertainty, an appraiser can analyze the range of probabilities that certain events will happen and also allow for the possibility that unforeseen events will occur. These two considerations form the basis for risk analysis.

Most analysts who consider the investment implications of future cash flow opportunities do not expect their forecasts to be realized exactly as they have anticipated. Appraisers avoid predictions, even in valuation assignments; instead they make forecasts. Thus when a single figure is used in an analysis, it is usually considered the point of central tendency or the most probable number within a range of possible numbers.

In some situations, however, appraisers deal with exact figures—e.g., contract rents, purchase prices, mortgage terms, calculated units of comparison, and other historical data. A distinction must be made between a number that represents a fact and a number that reflects a future estimate. If a practitioner does not understand an estimated or forecast number in terms of its range of possibilities and associated probabilities, he or she may seriously misjudge investment risks or fail to consider other uncertainties.

A number of methods have been developed to analyze the risk and uncertainty of real estate investments directly. None of these methods offers any special insight into the future, but each provides an opportunity to analyze the factors upon which the success or failure of an investment is contingent and to deal with the expected consequences.

Probability Analysis

Probability is the relative likelihood that a specified event will occur. Although the concept is usually associated with games of chance, the concept of probability is basic to life. As people grow and learn, they translate their experiences into intuitive probabilities. Thus people carry umbrellas on cloudy days, stop at red lights, avoid harmful foods, and generally act in accordance with the probability of possible future outcomes.

The same processes are applicable to real estate consulting. Based on past experience and other factors, judgments can be made about the foreseeable future. Various possibilities are identified and their relative probabilities are assessed. Probability, the relative frequency of an expected occurrence, is linked to risk, the identification of events that are unlikely to occur, in the framework of risk analysis.

Ranges of probability can be determined with at least four methods. First, observation and analysis of past events may indicate patterns or measures of relative frequency. Second, probability may be determined through controlled experiment and observation, which is the method applied in scientific investigations. In real estate applications, survey research methods may be employed. Third, theoretical distributions may be used to establish probability. For example, an appraiser may infer that the rates of return on a particular type of real estate investment will fall within a given range because of a theoretical relationship between these rates and the rates of return obtainable in other capital markets. Fourth, probability ranges can be based on subjective judgment. When ranges of probability are determined in this way, they should be tested and all judgments should be evaluated.

Some analysts avoid identifying several possible outcomes (e.g., for cash flow amounts or resale prices) and the probabilities associated with each because the process seems too indefinite. However, when the process is conducted properly, the limitations of a single point estimate are overcome. In fact, risk analysis facilitates judgments and investment decision making.

Some prominent risk analysis methods are briefly described here. These methods may not be applied in every consulting assignment, but each is applicable in specific circumstances. Occasionally two or more of these methods are used together to confirm or contrast their conclusions and provide another basis for making investment decisions.

Utility Functions

Utility functions are subjective weights that are assigned to possible investment outcomes to reflect a particular investor's relative preference for each. According to this concept, an investor who believes in taking risks would give a higher ranking of personal utility to a riskier investment than would an investor with a more conservative investment outlook.

Although utility functions are very subjective, they do offer a quantitative means of analyzing differences between investment options. For example, assume that an investor has two real estate investment alternatives. The first is a relatively conservative investment that is judged to have a 60% chance of developing an *NPV* of $20,000 and a 40% chance of producing an *NPV* of $10,000. The second investment has an 80% chance of earning a $40,000 *NPV* for the same capital outlay, but a 20% chance of suffering a $10,000 loss.

Different investors may view these outcomes and probabilities in different ways. If an investor is particularly interested in the opportunity to earn a $40,000 *NPV*, he or she may be willing to accept the risk of loss associated with the second investment. In this case the investor may assign the utility functions shown below to calculate the total utility of each investment. In the example, the utility functions assigned range between –30 and +200.

	Possible Outcomes	Utility Function	Probability	Utility x Probability
First investment	$20,000	125	0.60	75
	10,000	90	0.40	36
Total utility				111
Second investment	$40,000	200	0.80	160
	−10,000	-30	0.20	− 6
Total utility				154

The second investment, with a total utility measure of 154, would be selected over the first investment, which has a total utility measure of 111. However, another investor may be unable or unwilling to deal with the possibility of loss. This investor would assign a different set of utility functions to the risks associated with each investment and would probably prefer the first investment.

Debt Coverage Ratio

The debt coverage ratio (DCR) is a risk measure that is commonly used in mortgage loan situations. It can be useful in structuring a mortgage or deed of trust and in testing the relative degree of safety associated with a given set of loan terms.

A debt coverage ratio is measured as the ratio of a property's net operating income to its annual debt service. The DCR for a property with debt service of $800,000 and a net operating income of $1,000,000 would be calculated as

$$DCR = \frac{\text{Net operating income}}{\text{Annual debt service}} = \frac{\$1,000,000}{\$800,000} = 1.25$$

If the lender's risk measurement criterion precluded any loan with a DCR of less than 1.25 as being too risky, the property in this example would be marginally acceptable.

The DCR is commonly used in simple feasibility analyses. If a builder or developer knows that a DCR of 1.25 would probably apply to the project being undertaken, he or she might develop an estimate of the most probable NOI that the property could produce and calculate the amount of debt service required to obtain a ratio of 1.25. Then the allowable mortgage could be determined on the basis of that debt service. If the amount were sufficient, the developer could proceed with the proposed project.

To illustrate another use of the DCR, assume that an 80% mortgage is available for a particular type of development and that the applicable mortgage constant is 0.12. If the required DCR is 1.3, the overall rate necessary to warrant the loan would be

$$R_O = M \times R_M \times DCR$$
$$= 0.80 \times 0.12 \times 1.3$$
$$= 0.1248$$

With further calculations, the pre-tax cash flow rate can be found.

Overall rate:	1.00	0.1248
Mortgage portion:	0.80 × 0.12 =	0.0960
Equity portion:	0.20	0.0288

The indicated pre-tax cash flow rate is 0.0288/0.20 = 0.1440. Thus, given the details and requirements of the loan, the equity position must be capable of producing income at a pre-tax cash flow rate of 14.4% to make the investment's risk acceptable to the lender.

Debt service coverage requirements vary for different lenders at different times. To use the ratio effectively, a reasonably accurate estimate of net operating income must be presumed. Although the *DCR* is simple to use, it does not measure the amount of risk associated with the borrower. However, because *DCR*s establish a standard ratio of risk between property income and debt service, they are commonly used for mortgage underwriting purposes.

Payback Period

The payback period discussed previously can also be used as a simple risk measurement. Its use varies in different situations, but in any application the payback period indicates the amount of time that investment money will be exposed to the risks inherent in a given investment.

If the economy is moving from a recession into a period of anticipated continuous growth, investors may be more willing to expose their real estate investments to longer periods of risk because they anticipate that longer terms will allow them to take advantage of the growth cycle. Conversely, when economic problems are expected, investors may desire shorter payback periods to avoid the adverse conditions of a downward business cycle.

In managing investment portfolios that may include real estate, it is possible to commit funds for discrete time periods. Thus, the payback period may also be used to help determine exactly when to enter into and exit from a given investment.

Upside/Downside Potential

Considering the upside and downside potentials of an investment is a general analytical tool for comparing investment risk. To apply this method to alternative properties or investment concepts, the analyst first quantifies the best and worst anticipations for the investments being analyzed and then forms general conclusions regarding the risks associated with each.

No single analytical procedure characterizes this method of risk analysis. Commonly, a series of possible DCF outcomes under alternative hypotheses or situations are presumed; then the best outcomes are compared with one another and the worst outcomes are compared with one another. This method also identifies the factors that create downside situations and recommends possible steps to avoid these factors or mitigate their effect.

An analysis of upside/downside potential does not provide any absolute measure of risk, but it does avoid the pitfalls of single point estimates and can be especially useful in developing hypothetical outcomes for risk analysis and investment planning.

Expected Values

The use of expected values, which are determined with probabilities, was illustrated in the example of utility functions. The concept is simple. A series of possibilities is defined for each investment decision under consideration and the probability of each is assessed. P indicates the probability of various investment outcomes. Every investment outcome is multiplied by a weighted probability and the sum of these figures indicates the expected value of that investment. This procedure is shown below.

	Investment A			Investment B		
	NPV	P	Expected Value	NPV	P	Expected Value
Best case	$600,000	0.30	$180,000	$500,000	0.40	$200,000
Most probable case	500,000	0.60	300,000	450,000	0.40	180,000
Worst case	200,000	0.10	20,000	400,000	0.20	80,000
		1.00	$500,000		1.00	$460,000

Given these data, Investment A has a higher expected value than Investment B. Note, however, that the method also allows the analyst to identify other important risk factors, such as the possibility that Investment A may realize an *NPV* of only $200,000. If the investor has established a target *NPV* of at least $350,000, the risk of Investment A would be considered higher than the risk of Investment B because there is no probability of a lower *NPV* in the latter investment.

Monte Carlo Simulation

To perform a Monte Carlo simulation, the practitioner constructs an analytical model in which all the elements of the investment are assigned probabilities. These various elements are then integrated into a larger theoretical population. By repeatedly sampling from this group, the range of possible outcomes and the "values" that each of the underlying assumptions produces can be determined.

For example, a simple DCF model can be used to identify high, low, and best case possibilities for each income and expense item and the associated probabilities. Monte Carlo simulation can then be applied to sample the possibilities repeatedly as though they existed in a very large population of occurrences. The expected values are totaled and a probability distribution for the outcomes is indicated.

This method enhances the utility of risk analysis because it lets the practitioner see the range of consequences associated with different combinations of possible outcomes and weigh their expected values. The method is particularly valuable because it can be used to identify extreme possible outcomes so that extremes of risk can be properly considered.

As its name suggests, Monte Carlo simulation is based on gaming studies. It is frequently used in development analysis and other large-scale real estate decision-making situations. It is especially effective in consulting work because the consequences of various alternatives can be tested against their expected outcomes and the associated probabilities.

Risk-Adjusted Discount Rates

Risk-adjusted discount rates are frequently used in financial analysis; they are also applicable in some real estate valuations and consulting work. Generally an analyst capitalizes income with a discount rate that reflects all the elements of risk associated with the income stream. However, in some situations the specific analysis of one or more risk factors may warrant a special adjustment to the discount rate used.

For example, consider a real estate developer who seeks a return of 18% on his development activities. This developer generally rejects projects that extend beyond five years to avoid the risk of a future downswing in the business cycle. Accordingly, if the developer were attracted to an opportunity that extended beyond five years, the additional *term risk*—i.e., the risk associated with the extra time—would be offset by adjusting the discount rate applied to the periods after the fifth year.

It is mathematically possible to develop a single discount rate to cover multiple-term, multiple-risk situations. However, when direct market evidence is available to support risk-adjusted rates in individual situations, these rates are more representative of market behavior and their direct application is more appropriate than the use of an indirect, synthesized discount rate.

Risk-adjusted discount rates may be used in at least two ways. When market research indicates that they are supportable and produce reliable results, risk-adjusted discount rates are used in valuation applications to incorporate market information directly into risk analysis. In consulting work, these rates help adjust financial analyses for perceived risks by identifying outcomes that directly reflect the risk factors used in adjusting the discount rate.

Other Analytical Methods

So far this chapter has focused on measures of real estate investment performance and methods of risk analysis. Like the broader field of financial analysis, real estate consulting abounds with analytical tools and methods. A survey of some important techniques follows.

Sampling

Appraisers rarely have access to all available information for use in their analyses. Even when an appraiser has conducted extensive research, sample information frequently must be used. Therefore, the principles and implications of sampling should be understood by all appraisers.

Appraisers frequently must deal with incomplete information due to time and cost limitations. Research involves the collection of both specific data and sample data for analytical purposes. The data used by appraisers are seldom *random samples*. To establish a framework for selecting and drawing a random sampling, strict requirements must be met. More often, appraisers deal with *judgment samples*, i.e., sample data which are selected on the basis of personal judgment and thought to constitute a representative group. While certain statistical tests used with random samples cannot be applied to judgment samples, in many circumstances judgment samples can produce superior results. For example, data selected from five shopping centers by an experienced analyst may be more comparable to the subject shopping center than a random sampling of data from a broader array of shopping centers.

The use of sample data has both strengths and weaknesses. Samples are generally cheaper and more readily obtained than complete data; selected samples are sometimes more indicative than a broader survey. Samples are easily tabulated, lend themselves to cross-referencing, and provide a foundation for statistical inference, including probability studies. Often, samples may be the only source of data available. On the other hand, sampling must be conducted carefully and the data must be properly interpreted. If not, the results can be inaccurate and misleading, more expensive than they are worth, or less reliable than they appear. Sampling requires special training and understanding; many people misunderstand or mistrust samples for a variety of reasons.

Whether or not the appraiser conducts formal sampling, the extent to which sample data have been used should be considered in the analytical process. The risks associated with identified sample data and the uncertainties associated with other potential data must be considered.

Data samples may be particularly important when other data are scarce or when the available data are less applicable due to market changes. Sampling may be the only way to obtain some types of data. Samples are particularly important in quantifying market demand; defining market characteristics; identifying market attitudes, perceptions, motivation, and understanding; analyzing market behavior; and interpreting market activities and intentions.

Sensitivity Analysis

Sensitivity analysis, which is applied in both valuations and consulting work, is performed by entering one or more variables at a time into an analytical model to determine the model's sensitivity to each change. Factors that cause greater changes in the results are considered more sensitive and, therefore, pose greater risk to the expected outcome.

For example, assume that a property has an estimated *NOI* expectancy of $200,000. It is possible that the *NOI* could be as much as 10% less, or only $180,000. A 75% mortgage is available for the property with a debt service constant of 13%. The equity capitalization, or equity dividend, rate is most probably 10%, but it may range up to 11%. The analyst wants to know which variable is more sensitive, a 10% change in the *NOI* or a 10% change in the equity capitalization rate. The calculations are shown below.

	$200,000 *NOI*	$180,000 *NOI*
0.75 mortgage x 0.13 constant	0.0975	0.0975
0.25 equity x 0.10 cap rate	0.0250	0.0250
Indicated overall rate	0.1225	0.1225
Indicated value (NOI/R_o)	$1,632,653	$1,469,388

	$200,000 *NOI*	$180,000 *NOI*
0.75 mortgage x 0.13 constant	0.0975	0.0975
0.25 equity x 0.11 cap rate	0.0275	0.0275
Indicated overall rate	0.1250	0.1250
Indicated value (NOI/R_o)	$1,600,000	$1,440,000

This sensitivity test indicates that a 10% change in the *NOI* is substantially more significant than a 10% change in the equity capitalization rate. The largest resulting change for the discount rate was approximately $32,500 ($1,632,653 - $1,600,000), compared with a maximum change of more than $163,000 ($1,632,653 - $1,469,388) for the *NOI*.

Sensitivity tests can be applied to virtually any element in the analysis that is subject to change. The results of sensitivity analysis facilitate decisions regarding the need for further data, the ranges and consequences of risk factors, and the steps that should be taken to implement these decisions.

Network Analysis

Network analysis is commonly used as a management tool to schedule and conduct project activities. In real estate consulting, network analysis allows an appraiser to outline the steps to be followed in implementing real estate decisions, to identify critical variables and contingencies, and to deal with the risks and uncertainties associated with given decisions.

Project Evaluation and Review Technique (PERT) charts[3] illustrate how network analyses are conducted. Simple flow charts can also be used to show the orderly processing of decisions and to indicate the critical timing aspects involved. Large-scale analyses may rely on computer programs, which are available even for small computers, but network analysis can also be applied with manual computations.

Rating Grids

Rating grids have many applications and can be used in many different ways. A "most appropriate" investment alternative is selected by assigning arbitrary weights to the factors considered in a given decision and then totaling the weights for each alternative. For example, assume that three people are given the responsibility to select a site for a new building. They consult an appraiser who identifies seven factors that are important to the decision and locates three properties from which the choice must be made. Each factor is to be judged on a scale of one to 10; a rating of 10 is extremely good and a rating of one is unacceptable. The analysis is represented by the following grid.

Factor	Alternative 1			Alternative 2			Alternative 3		
	Joe	Sam	Ann	Joe	Sam	Ann	Joe	Sam	Ann
Lot size	8	7	7	5	4	6	6	5	4
Exposure	3	3	4	9	7	7	5	6	7
Quality of area	6	7	6	8	6	7	5	6	4
Traffic conditions	8	6	8	7	5	6	3	5	4
Price	4	7	5	7	6	6	9	9	8
Utilities	6	6	7	6	7	6	8	9	8
Distance to homes	3	8	8	9	6	3	6	5	4
Totals	38	44	45	51	41	41	42	45	39

---

3. PERT charts were originally developed for the U.S. Navy to facilitate scheduling and cost control of projects in which timing and costs are uncertain.

A grid such as this can be very helpful to those who must reach a specific real estate decision. In an actual application, decision makers may center their discussion on individual preferences, the various weights assigned to individual factors, and the adequacy of the original list of factors. As the grid shows, each individual favors a different alternative, so it is unlikely that any choice can be made without further discussion.

Linear Programming

Linear programming is a complex type of mathematical analysis which is concerned with optimizing the allocation of resources. An equation in linear form is developed and the various resources are subjected to linear inequality constraints.

The optimization model designates certain values as constants and then tests for one or more investment-decision variables. For example, one application may identify dollar returns and capital outlay requirements at varying times as constants and test for the present value of the investment in dollars. Another model could be constructed to solve for the minimum cost of an annuity to produce a desired minimum result.

Linear programming provides an opportunity to deal with two or more projects simultaneously; thus, it is especially effective in making portfolio investment decisions. The optimization technique is a unique way to consider risk-return relationships and to analyze the diversification of opportunities. Due to the complexity of linear programming, however, a computer is required.

Regression Analysis

With the increased accessibility and capability of small computers, regression analysis has become an important tool for all types of financial analyses. It is particularly useful and applicable to real estate studies. Regression analysis may be used for explanatory purposes, to make predictions or forecasts, or for a combination of these activities. Regression identifies the possible relationships between or among variables to provide a better understanding of the underlying data.

Simple regression analysis measures the relationship between an independent variable and a dependent variable with the equation

$$Y_C = a + bX$$

where Y_C is the forecast value, a is a constant, b is a multiplier or coefficient, and X is the value of an independent variable. Thus the equation states that for the independent variable, X, the expected value of the Y variable to which it is being related is Y_C.

Regression analysis does not necessarily imply or attempt to quantify causative relationships. Rather, it reveals the apparent relationships between the values of different variables and their tendency to vary regularly with one another. When strong relationships are found, measuring these relationships can help explain one or more of the variables and forecast their values.

When more than one independent variable is involved in the analysis, multiple regression is used. For multiple regression analysis, the simple regression equation is expanded by adding terms for subsequent independent variables. The equation becomes

$$Y_C = a + b_1 X_1 + b_2 X_2 + \ldots + b_n X_n$$

This equation uses the same symbols as the basic equation, but each independent variable and its associated multiplier or coefficient are identified with an appropriate numerical subscript.

Regression analysis takes a number of mathematical forms, but it is relatively simple to perform even with a small computer. Care should be exercised in entering the data and interpreting the results; both require special consideration. Computer applications also allow practitioners to analyze situations in which the relationships among variables are best expressed graphically with some type of curved line.

Regression is an important tool in real estate valuation, particularly when a large number of properties or a large quantity of data is being considered. It is equally applicable to a broad range of market and property analyses in real estate consulting. Regression analysis is often used in forecasting, but its explanatory powers should not be overlooked. It may, for example, be used to identify the factors to be analyzed, explain their significance, and avoid duplication in weighting two variables that are closely associated.

Geographic Information Systems (GIS)

Geographic Information Systems (GIS) technology facilitates the addition of geographic reference data to individual items in real estate databases. Desktop and larger computers can make use of this information to map or model the spatial referents and represent the spatial relationships among the data points. Equally important, spreadsheets or tabular grids can be produced in written formats which allow a better understanding of these relationships.

While GIS applications are still in an embryonic stage, the creative uses of GIS are rapidly growing in the real estate field as the accessibility of various types of data increases and the development of computer programs expands. Data from public sources at local, state, and national levels are readily available and, in most cases, less expensive than the cost of undertaking one's own research. By combining public data with other data available from proprietary sources, the information an appraiser can assemble and map is greatly enhanced and analytical functions previously regarded as technically unfeasible or too costly are well within the appraiser's capabilities. To date, attention has largely focused on the mapping capabilities of GIS, but this new technology should also help expand opportunities for data analysis and promote greater understanding of the results of such analysis.

GIS can integrate digital maps with point- or area-specific data to answer basic questions such as:

1. What is found in a specific location?
2. Where within a given area is a specific feature, activity, or event located?
3. What changes have occurred in an area over a given period of time?
4. What type of spatial patterns characterize a given area?
5. What impact will a specific change have on the area?

The data used to generate such maps are typically found in computer databases that include referents to a specific point on the earth's surface (i.e., latitude and longitude) and/or a specific area (e.g., city, zip code area, census tract).

Given sufficient information, the system can quickly pinpoint properties with very specific characteristics. For example, the system can identify the locations of all parcels of vacant land in a given county that have the following characteristics:

- Contain 40 or more acres

- Meet specific soil suitability standards

- Are equipped with municipal water and sewer lines

- Are zoned for residential use

- Have an elementary school within a one-half mile radius and are adjacent to neighborhoods where median home value exceeds $150,000

The dramatic increase in the use of GIS equipment is the result of three factors: 1) the decline in the price of high-powered personal computers, 2) improvements in GIS software, and 3) expansion of commercially available geo-referenced data. In the 1990 census, data were gathered and reported with reference to a computer-based digital street map of the entire United States. Topologically Integrated Geographic Encoding and Referencing (TIGER) datafiles are commercially available to GIS users; the system will continue to provide a wealth of information as new data are released.

Highly accurate digital base maps for most areas of the United States are also available at reasonable prices from the United States Geological Survey (USGS). Many local governments sell geo-referenced digital data on individual parcels that are compiled from assessment data and public record information. Data vendors will continue to expand the amount of commercially available data compatible with GIS.

Studies Undertaken in Consulting

Real estate appraisers are frequently asked to provide both valuation and consulting services for use in real estate decision making. The decisions being contemplated may involve the acquisition or disposition of real estate, the development or redevelopment potential of a property, or financial management and planning alternatives.

The specific services performed for a client must be tailored to the individual circumstances and meet established professional standards. The range of possible services is nearly infinite, but some typical studies undertaken in consulting work are discussed below. Each study may be conducted independently or as a component of a more detailed investment analysis.

Feasibility Studies

Feasibility studies are performed to test the ability of various investment scenarios to meet explicit investment objectives. Scenarios that meet the objectives are feasible, while those that do not are infeasible.

Feasibility studies are frequently confused with highest and best use studies. Highest and best use studies, which are also commonly undertaken in consulting work, seek to determine the optimum use or uses for a specified parcel of real estate. The use that produces the highest net return is considered the highest and best use. Feasibility studies focus on specific investment objectives and analyze all contributing and limiting factors to determine whether a given combination of factors meets the minimum objectives established by the decision makers.

Highest and best use studies center on a property and its use. Feasibility studies are concerned not only with a property and its selected use, but also with an investment alternative and the objectives of a given client. The business interests or motivations of a particular client may lead to real estate decisions that appear to defy highest and best use determinations, but meet the standards established by the feasibility criteria. Even when common uses are being considered, a given investment alternative may be feasible for one investor and infeasible for another.

These distinctions demonstrate that feasibility studies involve both objective analysis and the subjective interpretation of findings in light of a particular client's circumstances. In providing consulting services, appraisers must help clients distinguish among facts, estimates, and subjective factors and weigh the results of analyses and the anticipated consequences of the real estate decision. Virtually any analytical tool may be used in a feasibility study, but DCF analysis is the technique most commonly applied. A proper feasibility study provides for analysis at several points to test the internal consistency and findings of the study and to facilitate the application of the decision-making guidelines established to determine feasibility.

For example, an appraiser who is assessing the feasibility of a developer's plans for a subdivision could devise a test to monitor cumulative positive and negative cash flows. If the developer has established that the development must at no time have a negative cash flow of more than $200,000, the appraiser can determine the possibility and associated probability of the negative cash flow exceeding this limit and report that the plan is infeasible if an excess appears likely. Feasibility analysis may also identify crucial variables which by themselves indicate that a planned investment is impracticable.

Market Studies

Market studies relate to the general market conditions of supply, demand, and pricing or to the demographics of specific areas or property types. They are generally considered macroeconomic studies and often focus on housing conditions in a given sector of a community, a region, or the nation as a whole. Market studies may include analyses of construction and absorption trends, pricing and price changes, construction types and locations, or other factors relating to housing.

The studies may reveal or explain facts and behavior regarding property types, investor activities, or other matters of market concern. Market studies pertaining to the activities of mortgage lenders and borrowers, the construction of various types of buildings, and the preferences of investors are particularly common.

Marketability Studies

Marketability studies are microeconomic studies that focus on the marketability of a given property or class of properties. Usually the appraiser must identify one or more market segments in which the property would generate market demand and all the factors related to that demand.

Such studies are especially useful in determining highest and best use and testing specific development proposals. In either case a marketability study can provide a client with the information needed to judge the source or sources of likely demand, the timing of this demand, the amount of money that would probably be spent by each demand component, and the property's ability to capture the available demand.

Marketability studies are commonly undertaken to project the tenant composition of planned retail facilities or to improve the tenant mix in existing facilities. They are fundamental to an economic understanding of how potential demand is translated into effective demand and the risks involved in achieving cash flow objectives.

Studies of marketability often provide the basis for development decisions considering single-family subdivisions, multifamily projects, and residential condominiums. In fact, these studies are useful whenever time and money are available to conduct a detailed analysis of demand factors and to adapt the proposed plans to the findings.

Cost-Benefit Studies

Cost-benefit studies can be conducted on a macroeconomic or microeconomic basis. For example, a community may require a cost-benefit study to determine the economic benefits that would most likely result from a new public project such as an expressway or a sewage treatment plant. The cost-benefit study would focus on the relationship between the benefits created and the costs associated with the project to determine whether the benefits warrant the costs.

Developers also use cost-benefit studies, particularly when they are called upon to install major items that properly belong to the infrastructure. Such work clearly goes beyond direct project requirements, so developers must look to the future to recapture the extra dollars invested. A cost-benefit study can establish the relative worth of such expenditures in relation to the benefits.

Pricing and Rent Projection Studies

Pricing and rent projection studies may be components of marketability studies or the subject of separate studies. These analyses are frequently conducted to establish sales and marketing strategies for real estate projects and to facilitate decisions involving property management and investment.

International Valuation

As American investors expand their overseas activities, appraisers based in the United States are increasingly called upon to prepare appraisal reports in foreign countries for American clients. Domestic investors are accustomed to receiving comprehensive appraisal reports that include discussion of subjects such as local market dynamics, the analysis of comparable sales, and the supportability of market rent estimates. While the thought process and level of analysis undertaken by valuation experts in the United Kingdom and other European countries may be comparable to the efforts of appraisers in the United States, their reports often do not contain the same level of documentation.

To ensure the correct analysis of data in overseas markets, American appraisers usually find it necessary to consult with local appraisers. Although the same principles are applied in valuation assignments throughout the world, local customs and institutions vary significantly. For example, in many of the countries of Eastern Europe and the former Soviet Union, the definition of property rights is still evolving. Ownership may mean "the right to use" rather than possession of the full bundle of rights and interests associated with real property. In some Latin American countries, actual transaction prices may not be recorded because of high transfer taxes, or sale records may not be maintained in a single location. The American appraiser should be aware of the impact of local leasing practices, which may affect the selection of an appropriate valuation technique. In countries where office space is rented under long-term net leases, direct capitalization may be more appropriate than discounted cash flow analysis. In many European countries (e.g., France), sales commissions are often factored in at the beginning, not the end, of the holding period.

Most businesspeople overseas have a working knowledge of English as a second language, so language does not generally pose a problem. While security can be a concern in some countries, American appraisers on assignment abroad can generally expect a warm reception from their foreign colleagues, who recognize the advanced state of valuation practice in the United States and are eager to learn our valuation techniques.

Other Real Estate Studies

Other types of real estate studies include economic base studies, consumer profile studies, absorption studies, land-use strategy studies, and studies of other economic characteristics. Many of these analyses call for special skills and training on the part of the real estate appraiser and some require the services of other professionals. Most real estate appraisers possess a variety of skills and many are qualified by their experience and training to provide a range of real estate services.

Income Taxes and Real Estate Consulting

Federal and state income taxation affects all types of investments. Real estate has long been the subject of special provisions under various income tax codes and rulings and these provisions influence investors' decisions regarding different real estate types and locations, the prices they will pay, and the structuring of legal ownership to obtain every available advantage.

Income tax codes have historically provided real estate investors with the advantages of tax shelter, the deduction of expenses, income tax deferral, leverage, and the conversion of ordinary income into capital gains.

Tax shelter. To encourage investment in real estate, income tax laws have long allowed some investors to shelter all or part of the income produced by a real estate investment from income taxes. Surplus benefits that exceed the income produced by a given investment could also be credited toward the income produced by other investments, thereby multiplying the benefits produced by the tax-sheltered real estate.

The deduction of passive activity losses, yet another type of tax-sheltered investment, was disallowed by the Tax Reform Act of 1986. Passive activity is an arrangement in which the individual who receives the income has no material participation in the enterprise—i.e., no regular, continuous, or substantial involvement in the business operation. The "at risk" rule of the Tax Reform Act of 1986 allows the deduction of losses only to the extent that the financial resources of the operation are at risk. In other words, the deduction cannot exceed the amount of the investment. Moreover, deductions are reduced and eventually eliminated as the investor's income increases. A ceiling on deductions is placed on taxable income of $150,000 or more.

Deduction of expenses. Specified operating expenses and depreciation allowances, which reduce the income tax liability of a given real estate investment, qualify as deductions from taxable income.

Income tax deferral. The tax laws provide a means to shift the time frames in which income taxes must be filed and paid. This provision allows investors to structure their investments to take advantage of special timing and reduce their total income tax liability. However, the Tax Reform Act of 1986 strongly recommends that investors adhere to the calendar year for income tax reporting purposes.

Leverage. Leverage is important to virtually all types of investors. In real estate investments leverage is considered both before and after income taxes. Under the old tax laws, some cash flow situations that looked particularly onerous before income taxes could be structured to provide attractive after-tax cash flows.

Conversion of ordinary income into capital gains. The treatment of capital gains as qualifying income items once permitted taxpayers in high income brackets to state the returns from profits on real estate investments at the time of sale and obtain lower marginal tax rates for these returns. Due to the differences among tax brackets, this provision was a major consideration in the income tax structuring of investments. The Tax Reform Act of 1986 eliminated this treatment of capital gains from real estate and other investments. Now capital gains are taxed like income, but filed under a separate classification.

In the 1980s federal income taxes were subject to frequent and sweeping changes. There was strong public support for income tax simplification and the revision of federal and state income taxes as a means to reduce the public debt.

In real estate consulting, the fundamental economics of a real estate investment must be distinguished from the marginal benefits that may accrue as a result of income tax advantages, investment structuring schemes, favored financing plans, or other programs that manipulate the specific circumstances of a given situation. Fundamental economic laws and relationships remain operative in all business cycles and investment situations. Although the marginal benefits associated with specific investment circumstances are important, the value of these benefits depends on the underlying economics of the real estate operation to which they pertain. The importance of marginal benefits to a real estate investment should not be overstated.

In consulting assignments appraisers must understand how federal and state income taxes influence real estate investments, especially when specific client needs are involved and general market data reflect the effects of income tax provisions.

Counseling as an Extension of Consulting

Real estate counseling is defined by the Counselors of Real Estate (formerly the American Society of Real Estate Counselors of the National Association of Realtors[R], or ASREC) as

> Providing competent, disinterested, and unbiased advice, professional guidance, and sound judgment on diversified problems in the broad field of real estate involving any or all segments of the business such as merchandising, leasing, management, planning, financing, appraising, court testimony, and other similar services. Counseling may involve the utilization of any or all of these functions.

Unlike appraisers, counselors may go beyond consulting or advising a client and directly represent the client's interests. The Code of Professional Ethics and Standards of Professional Appraisal Practice of the Appraisal Institute distinguish between appraisal assignments and the ancillary services that go beyond appraising; these documents set forth the procedures to be followed by appraisers in such situations. ASREC has similar ethical and performance standards to guide practitioners in the field of real estate counseling.

Counseling assignments cover a variety of real estate situations; counseling services can be provided in all real estate fields and in an unlimited range of situations. Counseling services may include appraising just as appraisers may counsel clients within the scope of consulting assignments. Appraisers may offer advice on real estate economics and the components and consequences of the economic decisions a client must make.

When counseling clients as part of real estate consulting, appraisers base their advice on supportable facts and conclusions. The typical result of a consulting assignment is a letter or report that summarizes the appraiser's facts, data, analyses, and conclusions and confirms any advice that has been rendered orally. A report for consulting work not only establishes the appraiser's services on a professional basis, but also provides direct communication that can prevent misunderstandings and give the client a framework within which to apply the appraiser's findings and advice.

Key Concepts

- Appraisal services include valuation, consulting, and assignments involving both. While a property valuation may be included in a consulting assignment, the focus of consulting is typically to assist clients in decision making.

- The distinction between market value and investment value is fundamental to consulting. Market value reflects the value of a good or service to the hypothetical or typical market participant. Investment value relates the specific value of property, goods, or services to the individual investment requirements of a particular investor (or class of investors).

- Measures of investment performance are analytical tools used to evaluate investments. No single measure is always the most appropriate and each has its limitations. Used in combination, however, such measures can provide valuable insights.

- Common measures of investment performance include simple ratios, payback period (or breakeven point), investment proceeds per dollar invested, profitability index (or benefit/cost ratio), net present value (or dollar reward), time-weighted value (or unit-method rates/share-accounting rates), discounted cash flow analysis (discounting forecast cash flows), and the internal rate of return (yield analysis).

- Risk analysis employs quantitative techniques to measure the probability that various scenarios will occur. Techniques include utility functions, debt coverage ratio (DCR), payback period, upside/downside potential, expected values, Monte Carlo simulation, and risk-adjusted discount rates.

- Consulting draws on other analytical methods, e.g., sampling (random samples/ judgment samples), sensitivity analysis, network analysis, rating grids, linear programming, regression analysis, and the mapping and modeling of spatial data (GIS).

- Consulting assignments include feasibility studies, highest and best use studies, market studies, marketability studies, cost-benefit studies, pricing and rent projection studies, international valuations, and other studies (such as economic bases analyses, consumer profile studies, absorption analyses, and land-use strategy studies).

- The fundamental economics of a real estate investment must be distinguished from the marginal benefits that may accrue as a result of income tax advantages or investment structuring. The Tax Reform Act of 1986 curtailed tax shelter benefits and the treatment of capital gains as ordinary income.

- Real estate counseling is defined by the Counselors of Real Estate and recognized by the Appraisal Institute's Code of Professional Ethics and Standards of Professional Appraisal Practice. Counseling involves services that are often associated with consulting and are beyond the scope of appraising. Appraisers who provide these services are advised to prepare a report summarizing the data, analyses, and conclusions presented and any advice rendered.

Terms

absorption study	feasibility study
analysis	financial management rate of
"at risk" rule	return (*FMRR*)
breakeven point	Geographic Information
capital gain	Systems (GIS)
consulting	highest and best use study
cost-benefit study	internal rate of return (*IRR*)
counseling	international valuation
debt coverage ratio (DCR)	investment proceeds per dollar
discounted cash flow (DCF)	invested
analysis	investment value
expected values	linear programming
evaluation	marketability study

market equilibrium
market study
market value
measures of investment
    performance
Monte Carlo simulation
net present value (*NPV*)
network analysis
passive activity loss
payback period
point estimate
pricing or rent projection study
probability (*P*)
probability analysis
profitability index (*PI*)
rating grid
regression analysis
reinvestment presumption

rent projection or pricing study
risk-adjusted discount rate
risk analysis
sampling (random sample/
    judgment sample)
sensitivity analysis
Tax Reform Act of 1986
tax shelter
time-weighted rate
Topographically Integrated
    Geographic Encoding and
    Referencing (TIGER) datafiles
transaction price
uncertainty
upside/downside potential
utility functions
yield analysis

CHAPTER TWENTY-EIGHT

Securitization of Real Estate Investment Markets

F or many years appraisers and those involved in the investment field have debated the degree to which returns on real estate may be analogous with, or even directly parallel to, yields on other forms of investment, most notably real estate securities. Historically, real estate appraisal has focused on individual properties and the specific market in which each property competes. More recently, however, interests in real estate have been pooled into securities, which are sold directly in the securities market as investment packages. By the 1990s, real estate securitization has achieved especially high levels, creating significant changes for the real estate industry and real estate professionals.

The central appraisal issue arising from the securitization of real estate is the nature of the entity being valued. The distinction between *real estate*, the tangible physical entity, and *real property*, the intangible bundle of rights, interests, and benefits inherent in the ownership of real estate, is fundamental to appraisal. *Partial interests* are created by the separation of rights from this bundle. A further distinction, however, must be drawn to understand real estate securitization.

Securities are marketable investment instruments which convey partial ownerships in specified property (stocks) or establish debt obligations specified in the security (bonds). Debt securities may involve simple promises made in good faith or may be collateralized by property which the investor claims as guarantee of repayment in the event that the original debt is not repaid.

By dividing a single property into a series of ownerships through partnership, corporation, or trust entities, securities create opportunity and allow more investors to be involved. Since risk can be diffused through a greater number of smaller investments, securities reduce the risk to the individual investor. Securitization usually ensures professional portfolio management as well as professional management of the assets that are securitized. Securitization also expands liquidity, which may not otherwise exist for the investments.

The laws of some states once made little or no distinction between real estate and securities. In other states, however, the laws have tacitly acknowledged this distinction by recognizing the special attributes of real estate (e.g., immobility) which set it apart from stocks, bonds, and other investment vehicles. Until recently, regulations governing the securities industry also made this distinction. Just as questions have arisen about realty and non-realty components of property value, new attention has focused on the basic nature of real estate. As new investment vehicles proliferate, appraisers will want to know when to value the individual real estate and when to reflect any differences attributable to the ownership vehicle, within which the property is grouped with other properties.

Many real estate analysts distinguish between markets for *real estate ownership* and *real estate space*. Although appraisers frequently value property ownership interests that are less than the ownership of a fee simple *estate*, the most common appraisal assignment is to estimate the market value of a fee simple ownership interest. Appraisers also study markets for real estate space, identifying supply and demand relationships and tracking the activity of market participants to develop value estimates consistent with the definition of market value. The specific form of ownership may or may not be relevant to the final value conclusion.

In the analysis of real estate securities, however, the form of ownership of the given security becomes a principal consideration beyond the underlying real estate. Moreover, the value conclusion for a real estate security is unlikely to reflect the market value of the underlying real estate as though held in fee simple ownership. Rather, it will depend on the pricing of individual or aggregate shares in the particular security. Pricing is set by the market itself and reflects the outcome of the competition for capital.

Many factors account for the securitization of investment in real estate. It would be incorrect, and perhaps even misleading, to single out one factor or a set of factors as the principal reason for this ongoing development. It is a complex story which dates back at least 35 years and is still unfolding. Among the factors that have played a more significant role in the securitization of real estate are extensive reform of the income tax laws, the growing significance of the regulation of real estate as an element of national fiscal policy, and the creation of "new" investment vehicles such as limited partnerships and real estate investment trusts (REITs). The enthusiastic response of the financial markets to these new investment vehicles has played a role in securitization as have structural changes in the banking, lending, and investment systems.

The Evolution of Securitization

The 1960s and 1970s

Although legislation providing for the establishment and operation of real estate investment trusts (REITs) was enacted in 1960,[1] the securitization of real estate investment made little progress until the following decade. The initial market reaction to the sale of groups of properties through REITs was mixed and the success of early securitization was limited, in part because of changing tax laws. The potential markets for REITs considered investor payout requirements and the limitations on financial leverage set by the tax laws to be onerous.

The creation of REITs did serve to introduce the notion that a variety of investment vehicles might be available, provided appropriate laws and income tax provisions were in place, and that an investor or entity might gain advantages by holding groups of properties in a single investment package rather than owning several properties individually. Investments that required large capital outlays could be packaged so that a number of investors could buy as a group what none of them could afford to buy individually.

---

1. Donald J. Valachi, "REITs: A Historical Perspective," *The Appraisal Journal* (July 1977), 449-455.

Although both equity and mortgage REITs were created in the 1960s, only real estate equity attracted much early REIT investment. Many limited partnerships were also developed within a quasi-securitized framework during this period.

Securitization received broader attention in the 1970s, with the continued growth of REITs and the incipient activity of pension fund managers and other institutional investors. The Employee Retirement Income Security Act (ERISA) of 1974 was landmark legislation, permitting the diversification of pension fund investment which extended to real estate (see Chapter 6, fn. 5).

By the 1970s a problem recognized by appraisers a decade before had become a heated issue, i.e., when should securitized real estate investment be considered real estate and when should it be regarded as a security? Sponsors of securitized investments in real estate could effectively demonstrate that the aggregate price of the shares in a real estate security often exceeded the value of the underlying real estate. Many fund managers argued that appraisers' valuations of these properties were incorrect. They asserted that the efficiencies of the securities markets exceeded those of the real estate markets. To them, the proof was undeniable. Scant recognition was paid to the real issue — the difference between the appraisers' focus on the market value of property under fee simple ownership and the concern of those dealing with securities, which was the pricing of individual or aggregate shares in a security whose value was directly related to the ownership vehicle.

During the 1970s, the controversy continued, relevant laws were drafted, and capital flowed into securitized real estate investment. However, run-away inflation from the mid-1970s to the early 1980s and three economic recessions (1969-1970, 1974-1976, and 1980-1982) repeatedly diverted attention from the newly developing investment vehicles. Eventually, in the face of pressing market need and the increasing potential for market abuse, the appraisal community responded by defining *investment value* as a concept to be distinguished from market value and by identifying the difference between an estate in fee simple ownership and an estate held in a series of ownerships defined by a given security. While a particular parcel of real estate was considered to have only one market value, interests created by a security in the same property could take on a variety of values depending, not simply on the value of the real estate, but on the structure and market acceptance of the ownership vehicle. Appraisers were cautioned to estimate the values of fee simple estates, to make full and proper disclosure if securities issues were involved, and to identify any differences between the fee simple value and the values indicated from the sale of securities as premiums or discounts attributable to the ownership vehicle.

The entry of pension fund managers and other institutional investors into the real estate securities field during the 1970s precipitated a structural change in capital market financing for real estate. A secondary mortgage market developed for packages of single-family VA and FHA mortgages. With the evolution of private mortgage insurers, this secondary market expanded into securities issues backed by mortgages on other residential properties.

Despite strong investor support for the secondary market in securities backed by single-family mortgages, no secondary mortgage market existed for nonresidential, commercial-grade real estate. Of the funds available for investment from large institutions, relatively few were invested in real estate. The notion of increasing the share of real estate investment within a portfolio was controversial. Against this backdrop, pension fund managers with real estate expertise began investing in *open-end funds*, sponsored by insurance companies. Somewhat like a mutual fund, an open-end fund sells and redeems its shares continually; the number of shares in an open-end fund is fluid and the ownership of shares is transferable.

The 1980s and 1990s

In response to the adverse economic conditions of the mid 1970s and changes in the investment system, two new vehicles for securitized real estate investment were developed in the early 1980s: the *closed-end fund* and the *direct or separate account*.[2] A closed-end fund has a fixed number of shares in identified real estate assets. (Many REITs are closed-end funds.) The direct or separate account is more akin to a revolving fund for a single investor, such as a pension fund. Investment funds can be selectively placed into or withdrawn from a direct account. These vehicles are administered by insurance companies, which have traditionally had far more real estate experience than other large-scale investors. Of more recent origin is the *commingled account*, an account created for a group of outside investors who pool their funds for real estate investment.

Although securitized real estate investment and REITs, in particular, had already seen some expansion, the Tax Reform Act of 1986 gave securitization further impetus. By removing many of the special income tax benefits that real estate investments had enjoyed, the Tax Reform Act paved the way for the widespread use of securitized investment vehicles in real estate. In a short time, the trading of mortgage-backed securities (CMOs) and other investment vehicles increased on the public exchanges. (The Tax Reform Act of 1986 had an adverse effect on many limited partnerships in real estate, taking away the tax benefits which they had conferred.)

The problems afflicting many savings and loans institutions in the late 1980s further accelerated the pace of securitization which took off after 1992. The Resolution Trust Corporation (RTC) was established in 1989 to dispose of the vast real estate assets held by failed S&Ls. In much the same way as collateralized mortgage obligations (CMOs) were developed in the late 1980s for mortgages on residential properties, the RTC created special classes of securitized instruments for mortgages on commercial properties, which were sold off through investment bankers, mostly to nontraditional mortgage investors. These investment instruments are known as *commercial mortgage backed securities* (CMBSs).

CMOs represent pools of mortgages on residential property, which is a fairly standardized product. Because they have gained market acceptance and can produce a performance record to substantiate their assessed risk, CMOs generally achieve the highest-quality, AAA risk rating. The dissimilarities among commercial property, however, makes the risk rating of CMBSs more difficult. (CMBSs do not normally receive a AAA rating and are heavily collateralized.) The establishment of a guarantee fund for CMBS

---

2. Nancy L. Lashine and Gail Lee, "The Four Quadrant Manager," *Pension Real Estate Quarterly* (Spring 1995), 14-18.

issues by the RTC was a breakthrough that initially secured CMBSs and gave them market credibility. This not only helped facilitate the risk rating of CMBSs by the rating agencies, but also opened the door for the creation of other securities collateralized by real estate components.

In the creation of CMBS vehicles, the traditional role of the real estate appraiser has largely been bypassed. In valuations of improved commercial properties, particularly investment-grade real estate, appraisers had for more than two decades included likely sales proceeds (or "terminal" values) as part of their income and risk analyses. For CMBS securities, however, real estate appraisals are often not procured. Instead, a more traditional securities analysis is done on immediate cash flows, investment risks, and associated investment characteristics. On the basis of these analyses, rating firms assign an investment classification and portfolios of securities are marketed. These portfolios are backed by real estate representing diverse locations, property types, and risks.

The securitization of real estate investment, which the RTC helped set into motion, closely links the pricing of real estate securities to that of other capital assets since publicly traded securities are continuously being repriced relative to non-real estate investment alternatives in the capital markets.[3] Although an appraisal may be required for purposes of underwriting or rating a securitized real estate asset in an initial public offering (IPO), thereafter the pricing of the securitized asset is established in the over-the-counter market where most real estate securities are traded (with the exception of REITs). Market makers knowledgeable about who is selling and who is buying put deals together and rapidly adjust pricing to changes in interest rates. A market maker stands to earn the difference between what is being asked and what is being bid.

Increased regulation of real estate lending, a consequence of the S&L crisis, further encouraged securitization by limiting the activity of traditional lenders. The imposition of strict regulatory guidelines severely curtailed the ability of S&Ls to lend on commercial real estate and served to refocus their lending activity on home loans. Stringent guidelines requiring substantially greater capital reserves for real estate investments were also imposed on other traditional real estate lenders such as commercial banks and life insurance companies. The effect of regulation was to make real estate debt a less attractive investment for these traditional providers of capital.

The Four-Quadrant Capital Market

In 1993 and 1994, Wall Street began refinancing much of the capital shortfall in public markets, both in debt and equity investment. Recently, it has become customary to speak of a four-quadrant capital market represented by public debt and equity investment and private debt and equity investment. The most common vehicles for capital in the public real estate equity investment market are public offerings of real estate investment trusts

---

3. Charles H. Wurtzebach, "The Four Quadrants: A New Real Estate Investment Paradigm for Pension Funds," *Pension Real Estate Quarterly* (Spring 1995), 20-22. The value of REITs and other securitized assets is set in the open market and reported daily on the stock exchanges. The Securities and Exchange Commission (SEC) does not require that the valuation of REITs be based on the value of the real estate assets the REIT owns. REITs are subject to general SEC regulations that apply to the setting up and trading of public securities on the exchanges, i.e., standard disclosure, public offerings, and payback. The value of the real estate assets listed in the prospectus of a REIT is established by accounting, not appraisal, procedures. The performance of REITs is linked to cash flow management; their value is also affected by the leverage the REIT wields.

(REITs) and publicly traded shares in real estate operating companies (REOCs).[4] In the public real estate debt investment market, the most common investment vehicles are pools of commercial mortgage backed securities (CMBSs) and CMOs. The private real estate equity investment market, which has long been the mainstay of private and institutional investment, includes individuals, partnerships, corporations, pension funds, and insurance companies for their own accounts. This market attracts capital via direct (separate) accounts, commingled accounts, and private REITs. The private real estate debt investment market comprises commercial mortgages originated by banks and other private lenders.

The pricing of asset shares in the two public quadrants of the real estate capital market reflects continuous transactions and is directly linked to non-real estate investment alternatives. Pricing in the two private quadrants can readily be linked to the capital markets as well.[5]

| Figure 28.1 | **The Four-Quadrant Investment Capital Market for Real Estate** |

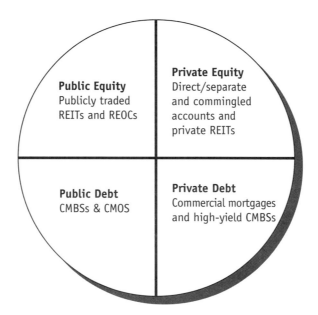

Public Equity
Publicly traded
REITs and REOCs

Private Equity
Direct/separate
and commingled
accounts and
private REITs

Public Debt
CMBSs & CMOS

Private Debt
Commercial mortgages
and high-yield CMBSs

---

4. Real estate operating companies (REOCs) differ from REITs in two respects: REOCs do not enjoy the tax pass-through of REITs and are not required to pay back 95% of income to shareholders.
5. The pricing mechanism is not the only characteristic that differentiates asset shares from real estate, the value of which is derived through appraisal methods. The definitions of *net income* and *cash flow* used by pension fund managers and other institutional investors also differ widely from appraisal usage. The income line for a REIT is the cash thrown off by funds from operations (FFOs), computed by adjusting the net operating income for nonoperating income and expenses, which include items attributable to the business enterprise rather than the real estate per se. Pension funds, which often use REITs as investment vehicles, need to ensure a stable distributable cash flow to sponsors of, or investors in, the plan. (The dividend averages 7% to 8% on the investment). Distributable cash flow is calculated on the basis of a weighted-average applied to the FFO. The structure of pension funds, therefore, allows volatility to be shifted from the income component to the capital component.
   Another measure of property return is the NCREIF Classic Property Index (until recently, the Russell-NCREIF Property Index), which tracks the performance of properties that are acquired on behalf of tax-exempt institutions in all-cash, unleveraged transactions and are held under a fiduciary or trusteeship arrangement. The total return for a property calculated by the NCREIF Classic Property Index represents a composite of the income return and capital appreciation return. The formulas used by the NCREIF Index to calculate the periodic rate of return over the holding period differ substantially from the methodology applied by appraisers to analyze period-to-period change in value.

Table 28.1 shows a breakdown of the principal sources of real estate capital among non-institutional and institutional investment. The latter includes vehicles such as REITs and CMBSs.

Table 28.1	**Capital Sources for Real Estate Investment***		
	1993	**1994**	**1995**
Non-institutional			
Individuals, partnerships, not-for-profit organizations & corporations	$1.836 trillion	$1.8 trillion	$1.86 trillion
Institutional	$1.174 trillion	$1.2 trillion	$1.22 trillion
Commercial banks	$ 425.7 billion	$ 382.4 billion	$ 397 billion
Life insurance companies	$ 288.7 billion	$ 283.8 billion	$ 252 billion
Pension funds	$ 179.4 billion	$ 159.45 billion	$ 135.6 billion
Foreign investors	$ 150.2 billion	$ 128.66 billion	$ 153.3 billion
Savings associations	$ 114.4 billion	$ 136.7 billion	$ 135.8 billion
REITs	$ 15.6 billion	$ 33.3 billion	$ 58.4 billion
Private CMBSs	n/a	n/a	$ 57.8 billion
Other	n/a	$ 56.8 billion	$ 33.8 billion

Breakdown of Institutional Investment into Equity and Debt

	Equity	Debt	Equity	Debt	Equity	Debt
Commercial banks	$ 29.4	$ 396.3	$ 16.83	$ 365.6	$ 5.67	$ 391.41
Life insurance companies	$ 50.6	$ 238.1	$ 54.2	$ 229.6	$49.95	$ 202.19
Pension funds	$120.0	$ 59.4	$128.95	$ 30.5	$100.52	$ 35.1
Foreign investors	$ 35.2	$ 114.96	$ 28.61	$100.05	$ 29.0	$ 124.32
Savings associations	$ 12.6	$ 101.8	$ 8.46	$ 128.3	$ 2.92	$ 132.92
REITs	$ 11.0	$ 4.57	$ 25.61	$ 7.7	$ 43.48	$ 14.92
Private CMBSs	n/a		n/a			$ 57.82
Other	n/a		$ 56.8			$ 33.87

* Based on data appearing in *Emerging Trends in Real Estate, 1994, 1995, and 1996* published by Equitable Real Estate Investment Management, Inc. and Real Estate Research Corporation.

Security vs. Real Estate

Although public market pricing has some advantages, investor-driven pricing does not necessarily reflect the value of the underlying real estate asset. There is wide variation among real estate securities, depending on the structure of the particular investment vehicle. For example, REITs may be subject to stringent requirements as to the dividends paid to investors (expectations of higher dividends influence pricing) or to legal restrictions limiting the amount of property that can be sold in any given year. REITs can also employ investment leverage which increases the potential return on the investment, but creates possible difficulties for the investment in market downturns.

One of the newer real estate investment securities vehicles divides real estate interests into a series of layers called *tranches*. Property investments have long been divided into equity and mortgage layers, sometimes even into a series of mortgage layers. In the 1960s, L. W. Ellwood and others showed that the typical fee simple estate was purchased with a combination of equity and mortgage funds and that analysis of the income to each of these layers represented a valid approach to appraisal. The modern tranche goes well beyond this concept, but the mathematical processes used in investment analysis still apply.

One type of real estate tranche is collateralized by a portion of the expected cash flows from an income-producing property.[6] This kind of tranche can be illustrated with the following example, which involves a single property although the principle demonstrated also applies to pools of real estate holdings within a single securities package. The property in question was acquired without mortgage financing. The securities packager is marketing four simple tranches, each of which corresponds to 25% of the expected cash flows to the property (see Figure 28.2, right-hand column).

Figure 28.2	**Traditional Fee Simple and Modern Securities "Tranche" Views of Cash Flow Levels (Assume Net Operating Income)**

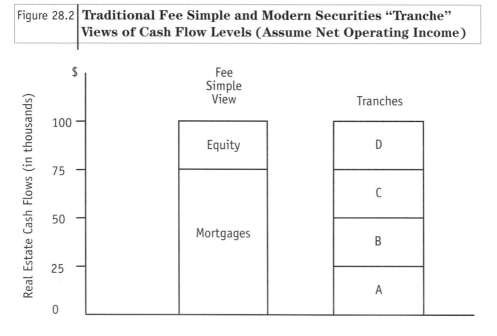

The chart is intended to illustrate the breakdown of cash flows to the equity/mortgage components and the four tranches. It does not reflect the respective values of these positions. The value of the equity and mortgage components is not necessarily the same as that of the four tranches.

6. In the late 1980s, CMOs were the first real estate securities to make use of the idea of *tranches*. Packages of conventional-term (i.e., 30-year) mortgages were typically divided into three tranches: the return to the first tranche came from the payment of mortgage interest for the first ten years; the return to the second tranche came from payment on the mortgage principal also for the first ten years; the return to the remaining or residual tranche was from the remaining payment on interest and principal beyond the first ten years. CBMSs have extended the use of tranches to portions of expected cash flows. The sponsors of real estate securities have shown great ingenuity in developing applications of this investment vehicle.

The return to investors holding securities in Tranche A is paid from the bottom 25% of expected cash flows, which presumably bears the lowest risk. The return to investors holding securities in Tranche B is paid from the next 25% of cash flows. The return to investors holding Tranche C and D securities is paid from the upper 50% of expected cash flows, which are riskier. If there is a 25% reduction in cash flows, Tranche D receives no income. If there is a 50% reduction in cash flows, Tranches D and C receive no income. Thus, risk proceeds from Tranche A, the least risky, to Tranche D, the most risky.

From the viewpoint of a securities packager, the risk of fluctuations in net income to a single property can be offset by combining properties with diverse characteristics and locations into investment pools. Thus, securities in Tranche A may be structured for investors who seek stability, risk avoidance, and dependable returns on their investment. Similarly, securities in Tranches C and D may be structured for investors who are seeking higher yields and growth potential and tolerate higher risks.

Because tranche-type investment vehicles offer many advantages that are not found in traditional real estate investments, they have had special appeal in the capital markets, where they have both expanded the source of funds for real estate equity capital and replaced many of the traditional sources of real estate mortgage capital. In the above example, Tranche D may be loosely equated with what appraisers have traditionally considered the equity position, i.e., the top 25% of the risk. However, the equity interest in a fee simple estate has typically been an investment in one, single-location property, most probably 80% encumbered by a mortgage. A tranche-type investment vehicle may represent a fractional interest in the cash flows attributable to this equity position but, depending on its structure, it may include similar interests in hundreds or even thousands of other properties. The investment characteristics of the tranche positions and the specific tranches may differ widely from those of a single property held as a fee simple estate.

Besides the structure of a tranche-type security, other considerations may influence its value, e.g., the past success of the investment sponsor in the market, the proven ability of the sponsor at portfolio management, the grouping of properties to achieve a specified concentration or diversification, the market pricing structure for a particular security or class of securities, and other non-real estate factors.

Conclusion

At present it is unlikely that real estate appraisers will be called upon to estimate the value of real estate securities. In a variety of situations, however, real estate appraisers are required to distinguish between real estate and non-real estate values, such as those created by real estate securities. Because of the significant differences between risk analyses for securities and the underlying real estate, appraisers must distinguish between indicators used to analyze securities and real estate (e.g., investment yields or capitalization rates), clearly distinguish between real estate and non-real estate values, and make full disclosure of the facts and circumstances in any appraisal involving property subject to real estate securitization.

It remains to be seen what impact significant market downturns will have on many of the new investment vehicles.[7] There is hope that securitization will make ownership of real estate assets available to many investors who previously could not afford to invest, who lack the requisite skill at asset management, who want to avoid the illiquidity of real estate, or who prefer the efficiencies of more organized capital markets. To date, no standards for real estate securities analysis have been developed. Although standards are evolving, particularly in the accounting arena, many real estate securities are marketed without detailed real estate analysis. Thus, direct comparison between investment returns and securities pricing may be extremely misleading. It is not improbable that the Securities and Exchange Commission may eventually step in to ensure clear differentiation between the value of underlying assets and the premium attributable to the investment vehicle.

Greater involvement by those with appraisal skills and experience can help correct pricing distortions and provide long-range stability for real estate securitization. Because the framework for pricing securities differs significantly from the valuation of the underlying real estate based on market dynamics, there is potential for investor uncertainty, market instability, and market abuse. An important new role for appraisers could arise in the area of real estate securitization. Ultimately, the need for competent, property-specific appraisal information may make their expertise increasingly vital.

Key Concepts

- Over the past 35 years, real estate securitization has gained considerable momentum. In analyzing real estate securities, the form of ownership becomes a principal consideration. The value of a real estate security is unlikely to be the same as the market value of the real estate in fee simple ownership. Rather, the value will depend on market pricing of the shares in the security.

- Structural changes in the capital market financing of real estate have resulted in the development of a four-quadrant market with sectors for public equity (REITS and REOCs), public debt (CMBSs and CMOs), private equity (direct and commingled accounts and REITs), and private debt (commercial mortgages and high-yield CMBSs). Real estate securities often partition expected cash flows from a real estate portfolio into layers known as *tranches*, which are tailored to meet specific income or growth requirements.

---

7. As interest rates bottomed out in 1993, mortgage refinancing peaked. CMO tranches paid from mortgage interest saw a rapid repricing downward, which resulted in billions of dollars in losses. When interest rates rebounded the following year, the cash flow into CMO tranches that are paid from mortgage principal began to dry up and the pricing of these tranches declined. These developments have made investors wary of interest-only and principal-only tranches.

Terms

closed-end fund

collateralized mortgage
    obligation (CMO)

commercial mortgage backed
    security (CMBS)

commingled account

direct or separate account

distributable cash flow

Employee Retirement Income
    Security Act (ERISA) of 1974

four-quadrant capital market

funds from operations (FFOs)

initial public offering (IPO)

market maker

NCREIF Classic Property Index

open-end fund

partial interest

real estate investment trust (REIT)

real estate operating company
    (REOC)

Resolution Trust Corporation (RTC)

risk rating

secondary market in commercial
    mortgages

Securities and Exchange
    Commission (SEC)

securitization

Tax Reform Act of 1986

tranche

CHAPTER TWENTY-NINE

Appraisal Review

I n many fields the final work product is subject to examination by inspectors or controllers. Appraisal review procedures may be likened to a quality control or auditing function. The appraisers in an office may review the work of one another before submitting it to their staff managers or to clients. In an appraisal review, many elements of the appraisal and appraisal report may be scrutinized. To meet the defined objectives of the review, the reviewer may examine the data, reasoning, analyses, and conclusions developed by the appraiser. Historically, most appraisal reviews were undertaken to determine the reliability of the value conclusion and the adequacy of the supporting evidence provided. Over time, the scope of appraisal reviews has expanded and many reviewers focus on elements other than the value estimate.

Appraisal reviews are performed by appraisers, clients, and other users of appraisal services. The type and extent of a review may vary with the training of the reviewer, the specific needs of the client, and other circumstances. Many reviews are performed by clients who deal with a large volume of appraisal reports—e.g., regulatory agencies and revenue offices, agencies exercising the power of eminent domain or acquiring rights-of-way, land management agencies, and quasi-governmental entities that insure mortgages. Private lending organizations and intermediaries such as thrift institutions, commercial banks, insurance companies, mortgage bankers, pension fund managers, investment trusts, and asset-based lenders all conduct some type of appraisal reviews.

Review appraisers also serve the corporate and private sectors by facilitating decisions pertaining to the buying, selling, and leasing of property as well as decisions relating to the management of properties as fixed assets. Often review appraisers are hired on a fee basis to assess the validity of an appraisal prepared by another appraiser.

A review appraiser is an appraiser who examines the reports of other appraisers to determine whether their conclusions are consistent with the data reported and other generally known information.[1] In performing this function, the review appraiser interprets and critiques the methods and procedures applied in a valuation analysis.

Like those who prepare appraisals, those who review appraisals must disclose the nature and extent of their work and carefully detail the contingent or limiting conditions under which their work is performed. For example, a review appraiser may be asked to analyze an appraisal report to ascertain what specific information the report contains regarding the need for rehabilitation prior to the sale of the property. The review should state that the scope of the review was limited to this stated purpose and included no other.

---

1. *The Dictionary of Real Estate Appraisal,* 3d ed. (Chicago: Appraisal Institute, 1993).

Purpose of Appraisal Review

One of the primary functions of an appraisal review is to provide a test of reasonableness for the user of an appraisal report, who may have questions about the data, reasoning, analyses, and conclusions presented in the report. The reasonableness of the assumptions and limiting conditions is also considered.

Appraisal reviews are tests of appropriateness. The methodology and techniques employed in the appraisal are considered in terms of their appropriateness to the appraisal problem. A review appraiser checks for consistency and mathematical accuracy throughout the report. Because appraisal reports are not standardized products, review appraisers must determine whether the data have been analyzed in a logical fashion and whether the conclusions are consistent with the data presented. Inconsistencies arising from the use of nonstandardized reporting formats also require interpretation and verification.

Appraisal reviews are often conducted to enhance the client's confidence in an appraisal. The review appraiser determines whether the appraiser has examined all relevant economic indicators, considered all elements of comparison, and applied all available techniques consistent with the appraisal problem.

Appraisal reviews contribute to the risk management procedures of lending organizations. A review appraiser may attempt to identify the trends referred to in an appraisal report or use sensitivity analysis to assess the degree of risk involved in a business decision. Appraisal reviews are also important in litigation. An appraiser may be asked to testify regarding the work of another appraiser. More limited reviews may be required to extract historical information from an appraisal or to help a client determine if a formal, technical review is needed. In some instances, arbitrators may present appraisal reviews for consideration in lieu of formal litigation.

The appraisal review process can raise appraisers' level of professionalism, encouraging them to produce uniform, high-quality reports. Appraisal reviews can also promote career advancement insofar as they may be part of the screening process used to establish clients' lists of approved and recommended appraisers. General administrative reviews may be conducted by appraisers or nonappraisers to determine whether the appraisal report under review has met the requirements of a client. (The distinction between technical reviews and administrative reviews is discussed later.)

Client Review Requirements

Appraisal review requirements vary depending on the client. The review requirements of lenders may be tailored to their specific policies and procedures, which include compliance with the requirements of federal agencies. Mortgage insurers have unique appraisal requirements, as do federal and quasi-federal agencies that conduct appraisal reviews as a normal part of their audit procedures. State and local governmental agencies such as highway departments conduct reviews in conjunction with the acquisition of rights-of-way and have specific appraisal requirements for condemnation proceedings. Many corporations and private organizations such as relocation companies perform appraisal review services.

If an appraiser accepts an assignment to conduct a third-party review of an appraisal prepared by another appraiser, it may be wise for the review appraiser to inform the client of the different levels of appraisal reviews available and to recommend the type of review appropriate to the client's needs. Again, the review appraiser should clearly disclose the nature and extent of the review performed to preclude any misunderstanding or abuse of the review comments.

Reviewing Process

An appraisal review differs from an appraisal. The function of the review appraiser is not to appraise the subject property, but to examine the contents of the appraisal report and form an opinion as to its adequacy and appropriateness. In some instances a review appraiser may be called upon to form an opinion of property value based on the information contained in the appraisal report. When this occurs, the review appraiser "changes hats," becomes an appraiser, and is subject to all the requirements that apply to making an appraisal.

Usually a review appraiser identifies and judges the reasoning and logic that underlies another appraiser's work, but does not substitute his or her own judgment for the judgment of that appraiser. The reviewer appraiser's task is to analyze the total work product of the appraiser in an impartial and objective manner.

Although appraisal reviews are performed for a variety of reasons, many are routine assignments. As indicated previously, appraisal reviews are regularly conducted for government agencies involved in takings for public projects and for financial entities that use property as collateral for mortgage loans. Review assignments can have serious consequences, and appraisal reviews based on investigative work may have civil, or even criminal, implications.

In the past 60 years, real estate appraisal has evolved from an occupation filled with seasoned generalists into a highly technical discipline practiced by computer-literate specialists. In the past, only the client reviewed an appraisal report and, since many clients were nonprofessionals, many appraisal reports were inadequately reviewed. Today appraisal reviews are increasingly necessary because the complexity of the appraisal process has increased; both the vocabulary and methodology of appraisal have become more technical. Greater specialization and accountability have resulted from the globalization of capital markets and the popularity of investment-grade real estate. Regulators scrutinize appraisal reports and carry out other audit functions designed to protect the public interest. These developments have created a need for qualified review appraisers, formal appraisal review procedures, and formal appraisal management policies.

The appraisal reports prepared by practitioners outside of North America have historically been less comprehensive than those prepared by North American appraisers. As international standards take hold, the reports prepared by appraisers in other countries will become more comprehensive and the appraisal review function will likely expand as well.

Appraisal Management

Establishing a sound appraisal management policy makes good business sense for any financial institution or government agency. The proper valuation of real estate used as loan collateral is essential. A solid value basis is needed both to secure the loan or asset and to provide a reliable source of repayment. Appraisal review procedures and practices must be specified.

A good appraisal management policy can help standardize the criteria used to evaluate property performance and measure risk. Good appraisal management reflects an institution's commitment to operate in a safe and sound manner.

Appraisal services must meet the lending policies and investment guidelines of the institutions and agencies served. Before an assignment is accepted, the appraiser and the client should reach a mutual understanding. This will foster the client's confidence in the appraiser and make the review process go smoothly.

Many institutional investors have learned that the data contained in an appraisal report may well represent the most current and complete information available on the market position of a property and its likely ability to compete in the future. Client demands and expectations place an added burden on appraisers and have led to the proliferation of many new types of appraisal reports and reviews by those who seek information on risk, property management, the feasibility of alternative investments, and other issues not directly related to a value estimate.

The development of an appraisal management policy begins with a review of existing policies on loans and investments. The policy established must direct managers to work closely with appraisers to ensure that appraisal problems are properly defined and that appropriate appraisal data, techniques, and methods are employed.

An appraisal management policy should reflect regulatory obligations, mandate due diligence, ensure conformance to professional standards, and establish criteria for a thorough review process. In addition, the policy should specify why and when appraisals are required and how to implement appraisals once they are initiated.

Developing an Appraisal Policy

Whether appraisal review is performed as a stand-alone function or as an adjunct to the preparation of appraisals and appraisal reports, it is important that written policies and procedures be developed to guide the review function. In areas of business that rarely call for appraisal reviews, this requirement is less important. When formal reviews are regularly performed, however, written policies and procedures are critical. The responsibilities involved in developing, implementing, and maintaining an appraisal policy include:

- Development of a set of written policies and procedures to be communicated to all employees
- Maintenance of independent control over the actual appraisal process
- Approval of all appraisals utilized
- Maintenance of files documenting the review of all appraisals governed by the policy

- Assurance that all appraisals are prepared according to accepted standards of professional appraisal practice and in compliance with regulatory requirements

Among the issues to be addressed in the formation of an appraisal policy are definitions of value, the qualifications of staff members, selection of outside fee appraisers, acceptable appraisal practices, appraisal review procedures, specific appraisal guidelines, appraisal update requirements, and procedures to ensure quality control and compliance with standards.

Specific considerations include:

- The type of appraisal reports the institution requires—i.e., self-contained, summary, or restricted reports
- The standards of practice that appraisers must follow and the minimum content and documentation requirements that must be met
- The types of value sought in appraisal reports prepared for the institution
- Identification of the appraisers authorized to prepare appraisals on behalf of the institution— i.e., appraiser selection procedures
- The procedures for commissioning appraisals and the manager to whom this task will be delegated
- The type of information to be furnished to appraisers
- Identification of the managers who will monitor the work flow to ensure that the objectives of the assignment are understood, the work is submitted on time, and the product is of good quality
- Appraisal review policies and procedures
- Identification of those responsible for determining if the appraisals obtained are acceptable to the institution
- Procedures to identify appraisals that may be too dated to be reliable
- The procedures to be followed when market conditions are changing rapidly, the plans or specifications of a proposed property have been altered, or the appraised property no longer matches the original real estate interest

Appraiser Guidelines

Management is responsible for selecting both staff appraisers and contractual fee appraisers. The criteria for selecting appraisers depend on the size of the institution or agency, its location, and the institution's current and anticipated involvement in real estate transactions. The appraisal function must remain independent of the other functions of the agency. In banks and thrift institutions, the appraisal function must be totally separate from lending and collection functions. The appraisal staff should have no financial or personal interest in the collateral appraised.

The appraisers selected should demonstrate the competence required to perform appraisals according to accepted standards and regulations. They must be qualified to perform the assignments they are given, and their experience should be commensurate with the complexity of their assignments. The hiring guidelines established should apply to both staff appraisers and appraisers retained on a contractual fee basis.

To evaluate an appraiser's professional qualifications, management should consider the appraiser's education, training, type of experience, license or certification, and membership in professional appraisal organizations. A review of recent appraisal reports completed by the appraiser and a check of client references may be useful in the selection process.

The hiring of appraisers should be guided by the needs of the institution or agency and the character of the targeted market, the types of properties appraised, and the complexity of the anticipated assignments.

Appraisal Report Content

Each appraisal report prepared for a lending institution should 1) contain sufficient information to enable management to determine reasonable loan amounts, 2) support classification of the specified assets as collateral for a real estate loan, and 3) help determine other terms of credit. The practices and procedures described below reflect accepted appraisal standards and are appropriate for most institutions:

- Appraisals should be prepared according to accepted standards and meet the reporting requirements set forth in the written appraisal guidelines of the institution. All appraisers approved by the institution should be provided with a copy of these guidelines.
- Each appraisal should be sufficiently current to ensure that any change in market conditions is unlikely to reduce the collateral value of the property.
- An appraisal should specify the value of the identified property rights in the real estate involved in the transaction or being offered as security. All other values or interests appraised must be clearly labeled and separately valued—e.g., the value of chattels, the value of financing terms, the value of the business component of the property, the value of furniture, furnishings, and equipment.
- Appraisal reports must contain adequate information on current and anticipated market conditions and their likely impact on value. The scope of the market information provided will depend on the property type, the credit or investment arrangement, and the financial considerations involved in the contemplated transaction.
- The appraiser must be aware of, understand, and correctly employ the recognized methods and techniques required to arrive at a creditable appraisal.

Appraisals that do not conform to standards can usually be identified in the appraisal review process. A review appraiser who does not possess the requisite real estate experience, education, and training will not perform a satisfactory review.

Customized Criteria

Each institution should develop its own appraisal specifications to ensure that the appraisal reports it uses contain sufficient information to evaluate potential underwriting risks prudently. Many short-term and interim-term lenders require information that may not be included in standard appraisal reports. Such specific needs do not always represent extraordinary requirements. The institution may simply need an appraisal that focuses on meaningful value issues such as appropriate market analysis or provides substantiation for the key assumptions on which the appraisal is based. Most institutions develop customized criteria which may include the following:

- Formal market studies for specialized property types such as lodging facilities or congregate care centers (The need for such studies must be communicated to the appraiser.)
- Alternative valuation scenarios to estimate liquidation value or disposition value for purposes of internal risk management.
- Reminders to ensure that appraisers comply with accepted requirements—e.g., state if the site is located in a FEMA flood hazard zone; specify the known presence of hazardous materials, toxic waste, or seismic fault lines; stipulate that the appraisal meets the accepted Uniform Standards.

Appraiser Selection

An institution or agency should only retain appraisers who consistently provide a satisfactory work product, apply accepted appraisal methods and techniques, and, above all, demonstrate good judgment. Appraisers and appraisal firms should provide prospective employers with a summary of their professional qualifications, the resumes of their principal staff members, and client references. Prospective appraisers may be asked to submit samples of completed reports as part of the selection process. Sample reports should represent the appraiser's best efforts. Permission must be granted by the client before reports are distributed or the appraiser runs the risk of violating confidentiality.

From the prospective employer's perspective, former clients are a good source of information. Some lenders and agencies send performance ratings to an appraiser's former clients to gather information on the overall expertise of the appraiser, the timeliness and quality of the reports submitted, and the client's satisfaction with the services provided.

Real estate lenders and other clients are ill-advised to select appraisers solely because they will perform assignments for the lowest fee. An institution may eventually pay for such shortsightedness with loan losses, higher asset management costs, or overly committed reserves. Clients who rely on poor appraisal reports may make bad investment decisions or risk monetary losses. Problems typically result from

- Selection of the appraiser who charges the lowest fee
- Selection of the appraiser who can provide the quickest turnaround even if the time frame is unrealistic
- Retention of an appraiser who lacks expertise in valuing the specific property type or has little understanding of the market
- Use of appraisals that are not prepared in accordance with accepted standards
- Failure to provide specific guidelines to the appraiser retained

- Lack of communication—i.e., the client's failure to communicate potential problems to the appraiser or the appraiser's failure to inform the client of critical problems in the assignment.

Clients should demand well-reasoned appraisal analyses based on substantiated assumptions and presented in well-organized appraisal reports. They should also be willing to pay fees that are commensurate with the scope and quality of the work performed.

To ensure quality control, independent valuation consultants may be called upon to do periodic spot checks of the appraisal reports on file. This procedure should include a field inspection of sample properties, especially high-priced, "market- sensitive" properties. A representative sample of more typical appraisal reports should also be reviewed. Spot checks serve to verify the sound judgment of the appraiser and the review appraiser and test whether the value conclusions presented have been properly supported and documented.

Because it is the institution or agency that ultimately relies on the appraisal reports prepared, contracts with appraisers should be negotiated directly. Federally regulated lenders require that appraisal reports be prepared by appraisers who are selected by and directly under contract to the lender. Entities with a vested interest in the outcome of an appraisal should not be assigned responsibility for procuring appraisals for the institution or agency.

When clients retain an appraiser, it is recommended that they utilize an engagement letter. While this may not be required, an engagement letter generally makes sound business sense. The letter describes the nature and scope of the assignment, the client's specifications and guidelines, and the definition(s) of the value(s) to be estimated. The agreed-upon fee and delivery date for the report should also be stated.

Any extraordinary services to be performed should be fully described in the engagement letter. Use of an engagement letter helps formalize the contract and ensures that the nature of the assignment is clearly understood by all parties.

Review Procedures

Advisory Opinion 6 to USPAP distinguishes between two categories of appraisal reviews: technical reviews and administrative reviews. A *technical review* is performed by an appraiser in accordance with Standard 3 of the Uniform Standards to form an opinion as to whether the analyses, opinions, and conclusions in the report under review are appropriate and reasonable. An *administrative review* is performed by a client or user of appraisal services to exercise due diligence in making a business decision (e.g., underwriting, purchase, sale). On occasion an appraiser may perform an administrative review to assist a client with these functions. An appraiser or consultant may become a user of the appraisal, particularly when the report contains information that might not be available from other sources.

An administrative review is sometimes called a *compliance review*. While the outline provided by Standard 3 may be helpful to the parties who perform administrative reviews, they are not bound to observe Standard 3 as is the appraiser who conducts a technical review.[2]

Before an appraisal is submitted to a review appraiser for a technical review, another person may conduct a compliance review to check the calculations and determine whether the appraisal report complies with basic content specifications. If any discrepancies or omissions of items specified in the appraisal contract are found during the compliance review, the review appraiser should determine how significant the errors are and whether the omissions are justified.

Whether or not a compliance review is performed, the review appraiser who conducts a technical review renders a written opinion as to whether to accept, reject, or modify the conclusions contained in the report. In drafting this opinion, the review appraiser generally follows the procedures described below.

The review appraiser first checks the appraisal file on the subject property or project. The file will reveal the purpose of the appraisal, the scope of the assignment, and the contractual obligations under which the appraisal was performed and the results of the appraisal analysis were presented in the appraisal report. Many review appraisers then do a preliminary reading of the entire appraisal report to get an overall impression.

This initial perusal may suggest several intermediate courses of action. For example, the review appraiser may recommend that additional market data be obtained, that specific pages be corrected for the compliance review, that interviews be scheduled with people familiar with the property (including the appraiser), or that opinions be obtained from experts in disciplines such as timber cruising, building demolition, property management, environmental hazards, or real estate law. If the review appraiser has received more than one appraisal report on the same property, he or she may compare the reports at this point to uncover any inconsistencies. The review appraiser then analyzes the contents of the appraisal report, focusing on specific questions such as:

- Are the data compiled by the appraiser of adequate quality and quantity?
- Are the limiting conditions imposed by the appraiser both required and reasonable? (Too many limiting conditions may diminish the usefulness of a report.)
- If more than one appraiser has worked on an assignment, are their methodologies consistent?
- If the highest and best use of the property is rehabilitation, what level of rehabilitation has been suggested?
- If the purpose of the appraisal is to provide an estimate of value to determine the amount of a mortgage loan, does the report satisfy the requirements of the appropriate regulatory agency?
- If the report is subject to litigation, is the supporting evidence admissible in court?

2. Administrative reviews are performed by lawyers, accountants, loan underwriters, bank examiners, corporate decision-makers, and appraisers. Individuals involved in administrative reviews may or may not have the competence or requisite information to perform an appraisal. After completing the administrative review, however, the reviewer will understand the strengths and weaknesses of the information leading to the value estimate in the report under review. With this and other information, this individual should be in a position to make decisions on issues such as whether or not to pursue litigation; what book value to establish for an asset; whether to apply conservative or aggressive underwriting guidelines; and whether to make or accept an offer to purchase. (USPAP, Advisory Opinion 6, 1995) While the Uniform Standards do not prohibit an appraiser from performing an administrative review, the review will be considered a technical review and becomes subject to Standard 3 if the appraiser makes a judgment concerning the analysis or conclusions in the appraisal. (ASB State Advisory Bulletin, July 1993.)

When a field review is needed, the review appraiser conducts a thorough field inspection. In some offices most reports are subject to a desk review, and field inspections are performed only for a representative sampling. A field inspection is a quality control procedure. A field review may be undertaken to augment the data reported by the appraiser or to resolve discrepancies between the facts or assumptions reported by two appraisers who have arrived at divergent market value estimates for the same property. Supplementary information can often be obtained or clarified by telephone or letter. Some offices do not routinely conduct field reviews, while others do field reviews of every appraisal report submitted. The extent of the review required may be determined by the relative importance of the investment decision contemplated by the client.

The review appraiser must clearly distinguish between a difference of opinion with the appraiser who prepared the report and an objective review of the report itself. The review appraiser determines whether the data and analyses in the appraiser's report support the opinion reached. When a review appraiser makes a judgment or forms an opinion concerning the analysis or conclusions in the appraisal, his or her conduct is governed by Standard 3 of the Uniform Standards.[3]

It may sometimes be difficult to distinguish between a technical review and an administrative review. When an administrative review is performed by an appraiser, it is possible that the appraiser's comments may be misconstrued as resulting from a technical review. This is especially likely when the review appraiser has strong or special appraisal qualifications. The administrative reviewer, therefore, should carefully explain that the scope of the work is not that of an exhaustive technical review. The administrative reviewer should state any limitations that may apply to the review.

In addition to reviewing appraisal reports, review appraisers have other responsibilities. For example, they often clarify client guidelines for an appraisal, assess the qualifications of appraisers and decide which appraisers to retain, or serve as liaisons between clients and appraisers. Review appraisers may monitor the progress of appraisers on assignments to ensure that reports are timely and comply with regulations.

Review Report Format

Although there is no standard format for review reports, each review report will contain certain items, including: identification of the appraiser; specification of the property rights appraised, the purpose and date of the appraisal, and the defined value; statement of the qualifying conditions and assumptions on which the appraisal is based; the report conclusion(s); and the opinions, conclusions, and recommendations of the review appraiser.[4] The review should be dated and signed. The review appraiser prepares an impartial review report and keeps the opinion of value and the judgment of the appraiser confidential. Review appraisers should always operate in accordance with the Uniform Standards of Professional Appraisal Practice promulgated by the Appraisal Foundation.

---

3. The comment to Standards Rule 3-1 states "An opinion of a different estimate of value from that in the report under review...may be expressed, provided the review appraiser satisfies the requirements of Standard 1; identifies and sets forth any additional data relied upon and the reasoning and basis for the different estimate of value; and clearly identifies and discloses all assumptions and limitations connected with the different estimate of value to avoid confusion in the marketplace."
4. Standards Rule 3-2 addresses the requirements an appraiser must meet in reporting an appraisal review.

Relationship Between the Appraiser and the Review Appraiser

Role of the Appraiser

The professional appraiser is accountable for his or her valuation and should be available to answer the client's questions after the report has been submitted. Although it is not the appraiser's responsibility to educate the client about appraisal theory, the appraiser must be certain that the client understands the content of the appraisal report.

An appraisal should be performed independently of all parties who have a vested interest in the proposed transaction—e.g., buyers, sellers, borrowers, lenders, brokers. The appraiser is a neutral agent with the ethical responsibility to develop an objective value conclusion. A well-reasoned appraisal provides market data that will assist the client, whether he or she is a purchaser, a seller, a borrower, or a lender.

As mentioned previously, lending institutions that commission appraisals should separate the appraisal function from the lending function. This separation creates a buffer between the lending officer, who has a vested interest in making a loan, and the appraiser, who must conduct an impartial valuation. Such a separation also assures the client that the appraisal conclusion has not been influenced by coercion.

Appraisers enhance their image and standing in the real estate community when they communicate well and promote good working relationships with clients. Clients should be encouraged to provide all information required by the appraiser. Full disclosure of pertinent data allows the appraiser to begin an assignment confidently and not waste time puzzling through incomplete data.

Role of the Reviewer

The qualifications of a professional review appraiser include appropriate education, training, and experience. Under Standard 3 of the Uniform Standards, the Competency Provision applies to the appraiser performing a technical review as well as to the appraiser who prepared the report under review. Review appraisers should possess the same level of education and skill as the appraisers who carry out assignments for the institution. Review appraisers who do not have extensive experience should attend appraisal courses to increase their knowledge to appropriate levels. For example, a review appraiser who reviews reports on income-producing or investment properties should have successfully completed courses on income capitalization. A varied appraisal background will obviously increase the qualifications of a review appraiser.

Like other appraisers, review appraisers are accountable for their decisions. They must do their work with fairness, objectivity, and an open, receptive attitude. Review appraisers need both analytical ability and mature judgment, but they should refrain from adopting a superior attitude in their role as overseer. Most professional review appraisers have appraisal experience and are as competent as the appraisers whose work they review. Nevertheless, it is entirely appropriate for an appraiser to inquire into the professional credentials of the review appraiser before accepting an assignment, just as a client would review the appraiser's credentials.

Training and Experience of Review Appraisers

The desired minimum educational qualifications for a review appraiser are

- Academic training in appraisal techniques
- Successful completion of appropriate appraisal courses
- Membership in a recognized appraisal association that has strict testing and standards requirements
- Active participation in a continuing education program

The desired minimum level of experience should include

- Several years of specialized appraisal experience in the review appraiser's field of employment
- Court experience if the review appraiser examines appraisals for condemnation purposes
- Administrative experience in the reviewer's field of employment to ensure a full understanding of the purpose and use of the appraisal

The desired minimum level of competence includes

- Adherence to professional ethics and standards of professional practice
- A good professional reputation and unquestionable integrity
- Analytical ability and mature judgment
- Objectivity and fairness

Limitations of Appraisal Reviews

The role of the review appraiser is not universally understood. An appraiser is sometimes asked to act as a review appraiser without clearly understanding what services he or she is expected to provide.

The distinction between an appraisal review and a second opinion of value is critical. An appraisal review does not lead to an alternative value conclusion. The review appraiser may disagree with the value estimate or the analytical process presented in the report, and he or she may even recommend that another appraisal be commissioned. Nevertheless, the review appraiser should not offer, nor be required to offer, a second opinion of value. The review appraiser must distinguish between the review process and appraisal process. Once a review appraiser suggests an alternative opinion of value, he or she has assumed the role of an appraiser and is no longer acting as a review appraiser.[5] To preclude any confusion concerning these different functions in the minds of market participants, appraisers who review appraisal reports should not sign the appraisal reports under review.[6]

---

5. See the comment to Standards Rule 3-1 quoted in footnote 3.
6. The comment to Standard 3 states, "Reviewing is a distinctly different function from that addressed in Standards Rule 2-5. In accordance with Standards Rule 2-5, any appraiser who signs the appraisal report accepts full responsibility for the appraisal and the appraisal report. To avoid confusion between these two functions, review appraisers should not sign the report under review unless they intend to take the responsibility of a cosigner."

Guidelines for Review Appraisers

Review appraisers should follow the guidelines in Standards Rule 3-1, which are paraphrased below:

1. Identify the report under review, the real estate and real property rights being appraised, the effective date of the opinion in the report, and the date of the review.
2. Explain the extent of the review process that was conducted.
3. Form an opinion as to the completeness of the report in light of standards requirements.
4. Form an opinion as to the adequacy and relevance of the data and the appropriateness of any adjustments applied to the data. The review appraiser must determine whether the data support the appraiser's judgment.
5. Form an opinion as to the appropriateness of the methods and techniques employed in the appraisal and, if they are considered inappropriate, explain why.
6. Form an opinion as to the soundness and appropriateness of the analyses, opinions, and conclusions in the report under review and explain the reasons for any disagreement with these conclusions.

Review appraisers have an obligation to their clients or employers to be conscientious and exercise due diligence. The review appraiser should assume that the appraisal under review was performed competently and is acceptable unless the review process proves otherwise.

The following practices constitute serious misrepresentations or deficiencies in an appraisal review:

- Analyzing only parts of an appraisal report and identifying this analysis as an appraisal review without reporting on the total work product.
- Refuting data in the original report without verifying that such data are inaccurate.
- Criticizing the methodology applied in the appraisal without fully explaining why it is improper.
- Using an appraisal prepared at a different time as a yardstick for judging the appraisal report under review.
- Using hindsight in reviewing an appraisal. Reviews should be based on the market activity and perspective at the time of the analysis. Subsequent events should not be used to refute the report unless, at the time of the appraisal, they seemed certain to occur.
- Ignoring or altering the definition of the appraisal problem stated in the report.
- Ignoring or altering any limiting conditions or special assumptions of the appraisal report without demonstrating why the assumptions are blatantly invalid.
- Overemphasizing the significance of minor errors in data, calculations, or word processing that the report may contain.

- Substituting the review appraiser's own judgment for that of the appraiser when the appraiser's original conclusion was a reasonable one.
- Submitting an unprofessional review, report, or other communication that contains subjective or pejorative comments.

Review appraisers violate rules of fairness and objectivity when they level undue criticism against an appraisal report. If an appraisal review contains factual errors or substitutes a review appraiser's judgment for that of the appraiser, it may result in a breach of ethics regardless of the significance of the assignment. Ethics violations can cause serious harm to others.

At the outset of a review assignment, the review appraiser must understand the consequences of approving or rejecting the appraisal. Review appraisers are often required to examine the formats of appraisals as well as the valuation techniques and conclusions presented. The appraisal review document should clearly identify what has been reviewed and comment on all significant aspects of the appraisal that affect the value conclusion.

Communication with the Appraiser

If questions arise regarding an appraisal, the review appraiser may communicate his or her concerns to the appraiser who prepared the report. The appraiser should be prepared to defend the methodology applied, the comparables selected, and the key assumptions made and be willing to discuss them with the client or review appraiser. Without feedback, appraisers cannot know how their performance compares with that of their peers. For maximum effectiveness, the review appraiser's concerns should be communicated in a fair and objective manner. The review appraiser should distinguish between major deficiencies in the report and minor errors, and present his or her comments in a tactful manner.

Types of Appraisal Review

The type of appraisal review performed varies with the scope or nature of the assignment, the requirements of the client, and the complexity of the property appraised. The distinction between a technical and an administrative review, which was discussed earlier, involves the purpose of the review and the observance of Standard 3. A review appraiser performing a technical review forms an opinion of the appropriateness and reasonableness of the appraisal and is governed by Standard 3. A review appraiser performing an administrative review exercises due diligence in the context of a business decision and is not bound by the requirements of Standard 3.

There are two basic types of review procedures: desk reviews and field reviews. Both represent acceptable procedures for checking the thoroughness and consistency of appraisals, but the desk review is more common.

Desk Review

A desk review is completed without a field inspection and is usually limited by the data presented in the report. The data in the appraisal report may or may not be independently confirmed and additional market data are typically not researched. The review appraiser often uses a customized checklist. Mathematical calculations are checked; the appraiser's methodology is reviewed for appropriateness; and the appraisal is reviewed to ascertain that it was completed in accordance with the client's guidelines, appraisal policy requirements, regulatory requirements, and the Uniform Standards of Professional Appraisal Practice.

The thoroughness of desk reviews varies greatly. Seven levels of analysis are described below.

Level 1. The report is merely scanned.

Level 2. The mathematical calculations are checked and the data are examined for reasonableness.

Level 3. Selected pertinent sections of the report are read.

Level 4. The appraisal is checked to ascertain that the methodology is appropriate.

Level 5. The entire report is read thoroughly.

Level 6. Limited confirmation of market data is attempted.

Level 7. Full confirmation of market data is attempted.

Field Review

In addition to the tasks performed in a desk review, a field review may include:

- Inspection of the exteriors of comparable properties
- Limited verification of select market data
- Full verification of market data
- Independent research to gather additional market data
- Verification of electronic spreadsheet software, including the integrity of formulas and the accuracy of the data
- Verification of computer software used in lease-by-lease analysis and the data input

Many variations exist in desk reviews, field reviews, and combinations of the two. Review policies should be flexible enough to allow review appraisers to exercise due diligence in each case. The extent of the review process will vary with the needs of the client and the level of confidence the client has in the skill and expertise of the appraiser. The extent of the review is usually a function of the complexity of the property and the transaction value involved.

A special type of technical review is applied to the investment portfolios of lending institutions. This type of review may be undertaken to test the validity of previous appraisal reports. Usually an independent appraiser is retained as a consultant to review a sample of the appraisal reports pertaining to the investments in the portfolio. Quality control checks may also be performed by the staff of a professional appraisal firm or lending institution to monitor the quality of appraisal reports and the daily performance of appraisers. Appraisers are sometimes called upon to review appraisals as independent, third-party arbitrators in value disputes.

Preliminary and Formal Appraisal Reviews

A preliminary review addresses the thoroughness of the appraisal report and its adherence to performance requirements regarding format, methodology, consistency, and reasonableness. The review appraiser may use a checklist to help determine whether the appraisal report is complete and conforms to the criteria of the client.

Using a checklist helps the review appraiser systematize the review process, ensure that no section is inadvertently overlooked, and assess whether the appraisal report conforms to client requirements. The basic premises and facts that the review appraiser notes on the checklist assist in evaluating the report's internal consistency. The list may also help the review appraiser relate the appraisal to market conditions and check its reasonableness in terms of externalities.

Strict adherence to a checklist can be overdone, however, and shortchange the qualitative aspects of the report. The checklist does not determine the acceptability of the appraisal report; it is merely a tool to help systematize the review process. Like appraisal formats, appraisal review checklists vary. No single review checklist is universally accepted. Most need to be tailored to the specific criteria of the institution, agency, or corporation that will use them.

The extent of the review depends on the quality and thoroughness of the appraisal. The review appraiser need not duplicate work that has been adequately performed in the appraisal. If the appraisal is well researched and well documented, little additional work may be required of the review appraiser. If additional data are required, the review appraiser's work may be almost as involved as a complete appraisal. When the review appraiser believes additional data or a different valuation technique is required, the matter should be discussed with the appraiser prior to completion of the review appraisal assignment.

The Review Appraiser's File

The review appraiser's file on a completed assignment should contain:

- A copy of the appraisal report
- A copy of the review document
- The field notes and working papers of the review appraiser
- Copies of final computer runs used to check calculations
- The names and phone numbers of all persons interviewed during the course of the review process—e.g., appraisers, brokers, investors.

Items Targeted for Review

An appraisal report should convey the appraiser's confidence in the solution to the appraisal problem. A poorly written report will not be convincing to the review appraiser. It is unnerving for a review appraiser to read a report that contains tantalizing hints about market conditions or investment risk, but never really addresses the problem head on. If the review appraiser is forced to read between the lines, he or she may lose confidence in the value conclusion and order another appraisal report for confirmation. Appraising is problem solving, and the review appraiser expects a clear-cut solution.

Review appraisers should look for incongruities. Is a claim made too often, too emphatically, or in too facile a manner? Is an issue being avoided? Are there implicit rather than explicit references to a potential problem? Inconsistencies within an appraisal—e.g., discrepancies between the data and analyses—detract from a report and erode confidence in its conclusions. The use of jargon and elaborate graphics may appear authoritative, but the review appraiser will not be taken in by overly technical terms and fancy printouts.

Appropriate Emphasis

To provide a useful service, the appraiser must offer guidance and not ignore obvious problems. Too often the critical part of a report lacks essential analysis. For example, an appraiser who is valuing a property under an older, uneconomic use in a growth area may fail to consider that the land might have a higher value if developed to an alternative use. In this case appropriate emphasis has obviously not been given to the analysis of the highest and best use of the land as though vacant.

The rationale an appraiser uses in arriving at a solution to the appraisal problem should be straightforward and supportable. Because the analysis employed should reflect the way active market participants would approach the problem, the use of esoteric techniques not recognized by market participants should be avoided

Competency Issues

Risk Analysis

Risk factors must be directly addressed. All real estate, particularly investment-grade property, involves potential risks, which must be analyzed and weighed against the risks associated with alternative investments.

Bases for Decision Making

Appraisers must thoroughly investigate the motivation of market participants. Whether a single-family residence in suburbia or a trophy office building in the CBD is being valued, the appraiser must identify who market participants are, what motivates them, and why. Without this knowledge, the analysis and the value conclusion are meaningless.

Often appraisers do not have complete information about a sale or a lease. They may fail to ask the right questions or interview the right people. Some may proceed with the analysis without alerting the client to the limitations imposed by incomplete data.

In the appraisal of a property that is being purchased, the appraiser should include the current transaction price. For a newly constructed property, the appraiser should provide a cost analysis. In either case any variance between the market data and the concluded value should be explained. When a transaction price differs from the concluded value, the difference may be due to the poor negotiating skills of one party, duress, or the inordinate market influence wielded by a limited number of suppliers. A cost analysis at odds with the concluded value may reflect an overimprovement or an underimprovement.

An appraisal report on an existing, income-producing property should reconcile differences between the revenue and expense history of the subject property and the revenue and expense projections used in the appraisal analysis. The client should not have to surmise how the appraiser arrived at the revenue and expense projection for the subject or how it correlates with the past performance of the property. The appraisal report should present this information clearly, explaining where and why the projection differs from the property's recorded history. An appraiser may choose to synthesize much of the property's financial history in the text of the report, but it is wise to include a complete copy of the historical data provided by the client in the addenda.

Common Deficiencies

Most of the problems that review appraisers find in appraisal reports may be attributed to deficiencies in one or more of the areas listed below.

Analysis and Reasoning

- Inadequate analysis and reasoning, reliance on old market data, and discrepancies between the data presented in the report and key assumptions deemed essential to the final value conclusion. An appraiser may fail to strike a balance between aggressive, upside assumptions and conservative, downside assumptions.
- Inadequate highest and best use analysis in situations in which the highest and best use conclusion is critical to the value estimate.
- Failure to present both the negative and positive attributes of the subject property or to identify negative and positive influences on property value and marketability. If an appraiser soft-pedals negative features and overstates positive features, the review appraiser is forced to read between the lines for clues about the actual situation.
- Overreliance on historical trends and scant attention to current conditions, which may differ significantly. For example, rental growth figures for the past 10 years may show an overall 10% increase per year while rates for the past three years show a decline of 2% per year, which is considered a more meaningful figure.
- Inadequate explanation of a wide discrepancy between a current or recent transaction price and the value the appraiser concluded.
- Misinterpretation of data.
- Representation of conditions or circumstances that are not factual which, in combination with other appraisal considerations, render the appraisal hypothetical. For example, an appraiser may state: "Assuming the zoning change is approved, the highest and best use of the property will be a high-rise office building." The valuation is thereby conditioned upon a change in zoning, but the likelihood of rezoning has not be established. The resulting valuation is purely hypothetical and misleading even though the report contains an appropriate limiting condition.

replacement reserves and to fail to recognize regional variations in revenues and expenses.

- Failure to clarify whether gross rents or net rents were derived from the analysis of comparable rental properties.
- Failure to cross-check a value indication obtained through computer analysis with an indication obtained directly from the cost approach or the sales comparison approach. Tests of reasonableness must be applied to detect errors in the data input. Cross-checking is also needed to detect errors lurking in the program.
- Inconsistencies in the reported data and inconsistencies between the analyses and conclusions. The appraiser must recognize the interdependency of the three approaches. An appraisal assignment comprises a variety of interrelated and inseparable procedures directed at a common objective — a reliable and convincing value estimate.
- Failure to keep in touch with rapidly changing market conditions, transaction data, and market behavior.
- Inadequate analysis of the profile of potential tenants or buyers. Such analysis is particularly important in the appraisal of complex projects and projects proposed for construction or rehabilitation.
- Failure to estimate the available supply—i.e., the total amount of unoccupied square footage in the specific property market—which provides the basis for forecasting market absorption.
- A meaningless boilerplate reconciliation of the value indications derived.
- The use of obsolete valuation techniques which are probably unknown to the investors whose actions they purportedly simulate.

Data Collection and Investigation

- Inadequate research or documentation.
- Overreliance on data provided by the owner or developer of the intended project without cross-checking the data against other viable data or undertaking an independent investigation.
- Failure to question an assumption about the likelihood of a zoning change or to provide appropriate verification of the reasonableness of such an assumption.
- Reliance on insufficient transaction data in a given market. If the market is characterized by little sales activity, the appraiser should describe market conditions and explain the reasons for the scarity of data.
- Failure to confirm a sales transaction by at least one of the parties involved. Confirming a sale can verify transaction data, provide information on the purchaser's motivation, and offer additional information on the reuse or redevelopment of the property purchased.
- Failure to identify potential environmental problems or hazardous waste evident during site inspection. Hazardous substances may be indicated by the presence of chemical drums, underground storage tanks, nearby transmission lines, deteriorat-

ing basement insulation, and evidence of sludge, paints, chemical residues, and oil spills.

Vocabulary and Syntax

- Lack of clarity and conciseness. Reports may be adversely affected by the excessive use of legalese, appraisalese, or other jargon; hackneyed or arcane language; and the passive voice.
- Excess verbiage in reports, redundancies, and vague or general statements.
- Overuse of hedge words such as *appear*, *seem*, *likely*, and *probably*, which leave the review appraiser in doubt about the true meaning of an otherwise declarative statement.

Standards Issues

- Failure to meet the minimum requirements of the Uniform Standards of Professional Appraisal Practice.
- Identification of reports as self-contained when they do not comply with the requirements for self-contained reports.
- Failure to clearly identify the property rights being appraised.
- In the appraisal of subdivision developments and condominium projects, failure to distinguish between the aggregate retail value of the individual components of the property and the market value of the entire property.
- In appraisals of the "as is" value of a project being built or rehabilitated, intentional vagueness regarding the work that has been done and work that remains to be completed.
- Submission of an incompetent work product. Appraisers are sometimes reluctant to turn down an assignment on a complex or special-purpose property, such as a lodging or health care facility, which requires specialized knowledge or experience. They may overestimate their own professional capabilities and violate the Competency Provision.

Unacceptable Practices in the Preparation of Residential Form Reports

The following list specifies practices that are considered unacceptable by Fannie Mae, the Federal National Mortgage Association.

- Inclusion of inaccurate data on the subject site and improvements, comparable sales, or the neighborhood.
- Failure to consider negative factors affecting the subject property and neighborhood or adverse influences in proximity to the property.
- Use of data from comparable properties that the appraiser has not personally inspected or at least seen.
- Selection and use of inappropriate comparables or use of comparables that are physically or locationally dissimilar to the subject property.

- Use of data provided by parties with a financial interest in the sale or financing of the subject property without independently verifying them with a disinterested source. For example, it would be inappropriate for an appraiser to use comparable sales data provided by the real estate broker who is handling the sale of the subject property unless the appraiser verifies the accuracy of the data. The appraiser must consult a disinterested source and independently investigate whether the comparables provided are the best ones available.

- Adjustments applied to comparable sales that do not reflect the market's perception of the effect on value produced by the differences between the subject and the comparables. Appraisers must make adjustments when they are clearly indicated.

- A value conclusion developed on the basis of the race, ethnicity, or religion of the prospective owners or occupants of the subject property or the current owners or occupants of properties near the subject.

- A value conclusion that is not supported by available market data.

The most common errors found in form reports are described below.

- Errors in mathematical calculations.

- Inadequate explanation of atypical factors, adjustments, or analyses.

- Incorrect identification of the type of property under appraisal—e.g., single-family detached or attached, condominium, or planned unit development (PUD).

- Lines left blank on the completed form. Lines should be marked "n/a" to indicate that data are not available or that the entry does not apply to the subject property. An empty line creates the impression that the item was inadvertently overlooked.

- Inconsistencies involving trend indicators, adjustments for market conditions, or estimates of marketing time.

- Discrepancies between the photographs of the subject property and the physical description provided in the form.

- Meaningless statements in the "comments" sections of the form.

- No explanation as to why large gross or net adjustments were made to the comparables and inconsistencies among the adjustments to the comparables.

- No reasonable reconciliation of the wide range of values indicated by the adjusted sale prices of the comparables or the values derived in the various approaches employed.

- Discrepancies between the factual data provided on the front of the form and the valuation analysis described on the back.

- Selection of dated or distant comparables or comparable sales that do not bracket the subject's value. Comparables should reflect a sampling of representative sales that are priced both higher and lower than the subject. The rationale for the selection of comparables must be explained.

- Failure to recognize and adjust for functional problems evident in the floor plan sketch of the subject.

- Inconsistencies between the information reported by the appraiser (e.g., replacement costs, land values, sales data, and comparable adjustments) and similar information reported by other appraisers for similar properties in similar neighborhoods.

Adherence to Standards Rules

Review appraisers retained to perform technical reviews should be aware that their activities are subject to Standards Rule 3-1 of the Uniform Standards. After forming an opinion as to the adequacy and appropriateness of the report being reviewed, the review appraiser must prepare a separate report or memorandum setting forth the results of the review process and disclosing the precise nature of the work undertaken. In reporting the results of an appraisal review, review appraisers are subject to Standards Rule 3-2 of the Uniform Standards. This requirement can be met in three different ways:

1. A separate report or letter
2. A checklist form prepared and signed by the reviewer and attached to the report under review
3. A stamped imprint on the original appraisal report, signed by the review appraiser, which briefly indicates the extent of the review and references the file memorandum in which the review process is outlined (This procedure separates the review function from the actual signing.)

Standards Rule 2-5 of the Uniform Standards states:

An appraiser who signs a real property appraisal report prepared by another in any capacity accepts full responsibility for the appraisal and the contents of the appraisal report.

This rule is directed at the employer or supervisor who reviews and signs an appraisal report prepared by an employee or contractor. The employer or supervisor is as liable for the content and conclusions in the report as the individual who prepared the appraisal report. Furthermore, insertion of a conditional clause next to the signature of the employer or supervisor does not exempt that individual from adherence to the standards.

Assumptions and Limiting Conditions

The review document should contain a statement of assumptions and limiting conditions similar in content to the following:

1. This review report is based on data and information contained in the appraisal report that is the subject of this review and on additional information from appropriate sources.
2. It is assumed that the data and information are factual and accurate.
3. The review appraiser reserves the right to consider any additional data or information that may subsequently become available and to revise the opinions and conclusions in this report if such data and information indicate the need for such a change.

4. All of the assumptions and limiting conditions contained in the appraisal report that is the subject of this review are also conditions of this review unless otherwise stated.

Certification

The review appraiser's report must contain a statement of certification similar in content to the certification required under Standards Rule 3-2, which appears below.

I certify that, to the best of my knowledge and belief:

— the facts and data reported by the review appraiser and used in the review process are true and correct.

— the analyses, opinions, and conclusions in this review report are limited only by the assumptions and limiting conditions stated in this review report, and are my personal, unbiased professional analyses, opinions, and conclusions.

— I have no (or the specified) present or prospective interest in the property that is the subject of this report and I have no (or the specified) personal interest or bias with respect to the parties involved.

— my compensation is not contingent on an action or event resulting from the analyses, opinions, or conclusions in, or the use of, this review report.

— my analyses, opinions, and conclusions were developed and this review report was prepared in conformity with the requirements of the Uniform Standards of Professional Appraisal Practice.

— I did not (did) personally inspect the subject property of the report under review.

— no one provided significant professional assistance to the person signing this review report. (If there are exceptions, the name of each individual providing significant professional assistance must be stated.)

Key Concepts

- A review appraiser examines the reports of other appraisers to determine whether their conclusions are consistent with the data reported and other generally known information. To form an alternative conclusion of value is not the function of an appraisal review.

- A technical review is conducted by an appraiser in accordance with Standard 3 of USPAP to form an opinion as to whether the analyses, opinions, and conclusions in the report under review are appropriate and reasonable. An administrative review (or compliance review) may be conducted by either an appraiser or a nonappraiser (e.g., user of appraisal services) to ascertain whether due diligence has been exercised and to determine if the appraiser whose report is under review has met the requirements of the client (e.g., lender, pension fund or portfolio manager, regulatory agency, or quasi-governmental mortgage underwriting agency).

- Lending institutions and governmental agencies often establish appraisal management policies which outline when appraisal reports are required, how appraisers are selected, and the procedures and criteria for reviewing appraisal reports.

- A desk review is completed without the benefit of a field inspection and is limited to the data in the report. A field review includes inspection of the subject and comparables (generally only the exterior, but sometimes the interior as well).

- A review appraiser may use a checklist to systematize the preliminary review process. A formal review is more extensive. If the appraisal report is well re-searched and well documented, a formal review will not duplicate the work of the appraiser who prepared the report.

- Like appraisal reports, appraisal reviews should contain a statement of assumptions and limiting conditions and a certification statement.

- Items typically targeted for review include emphasis (Was sufficient attention given to the market and highest and best use analyses?), competency (Do the economic forecast and risk analysis provide a basis for decision making?), soundness of the analysis or reasoning, and quality of the product. Problems can arise from poor communication with the client, failure to disclose all assumptions and limiting conditions, inconsistencies in the application of the approaches or the reconcilia-tion of value indications, inadequate research effort (data collection and investiga-tion), and possible violations of standards.

Terms

administrative review	formal review
competency provision	preliminary review
compliance review	review
desk review	review appraiser
due diligence	self-contained appraisal report
field review	technical review

Professional Practice
and Law

T he body of knowledge that comprises the discipline of appraisal is the foundation of professional practice. In solving most appraisal problems, however, the final conclusions depend to a great extent on the ability, judgment, and integrity of individual appraisers. To form a sound conclusion, relevant data must be available and the appraiser must be committed to finding and analyzing the data; a valid analysis also depends on the skillful application of appraisal techniques. Because appraisal is an inexact science, appraisers must reach their conclusions in an impartial, objective manner, without bias or any desire to accommodate their own interests or the interests of their clients. Professional appraisers have the requisite knowledge and the ability to apply it capably and objectively.

A profession is distinguished from a trade or service industry by a combination of the following factors:

- High standards of competence in a specialized field
- A distinct body of knowledge that is continually augmented by the contributions of members and can be imparted to future generations
- A code of ethics or standards of practice and members who are willing to be regulated by peer review

The Appraisal Institute was formed for three purposes.

1. To establish criteria for selecting and recognizing individuals with real estate valuation skills who were committed to competent and ethical practice
2. To develop a system of education to train new appraisers and sharpen the skills of practicing appraisers
3. To formulate a code of professional ethics and standards of professional conduct to guide real estate appraisers and serve as a model for other practitioners

The heart of the Appraisal Institute's commitment to professionalism is contained in the six canons of the Code of Professional Ethics and in the Standards of Professional Appraisal Practice, which include the Uniform Standards of Professional Appraisal Practice, the Supplemental Standards, and the Guide Notes.

Canon 1

A Member must refrain from conduct that is detrimental to the Appraisal Institute, the appraisal profession and the public.

Canon 2

A Member must assist the Appraisal Institute in carrying out its responsibilities to the users of appraisal services and the public.

Canon 3

In the performance of an assignment, a Member must develop and communicate each analysis and opinion without being misleading, without bias for the client's interest and without accommodation of his or her own interests.

Canon 4

A Member must not violate the confidential nature of the appraiser-client relationship.

Canon 5

A Member must use care to avoid advertising or solicitations that are misleading or otherwise contrary to the public interest.

Canon 6

A Member must comply with the requirements of the Standards of Professional Appraisal Practice.

Standard 1

In developing a real property appraisal, an appraiser must be aware of, understand, and correctly employ those recognized methods and techniques that are necessary to produce a credible appraisal.

Standard 2

In reporting the results of a real property appraisal an appraiser must communicate each analysis, opinion, and conclusion in a manner that is not misleading.

Standard 3

In reviewing an appraisal and reporting the results of that review, an appraiser must form an opinion as to the adequacy and appropriateness of the report being reviewed and must clearly disclose the nature of the review process undertaken.

Standard 4

In performing real estate or real property consulting services, an appraiser must be aware of, understand, and correctly employ those recognized methods and techniques that are necessary to produce a credible result.

Standard 5

In reporting the results of a real estate or real property consulting service, an appraiser must communicate each analysis, opinion, and conclusion in a manner that is not misleading.

Standard 6

In developing a mass appraisal, an appraiser must be aware of, understand, and correctly employ those generally accepted methods and techniques necessary to produce and communicate credible appraisals.

Standard 7

In developing a personal property appraisal, an appraiser must be aware of, understand, and correctly employ those recognized methods and techniques that are necessary to produce a credible appraisal.

Standard 8

In reporting the results of a personal property appraisal, an appraiser must communicate each analysis, opinion, and conclusion in a manner that is not misleading.

Standard 9

In developing a business appraisal, an appraiser must be aware of, understand, and correctly employ those recognized methods and techniques that are necessary to produce a credible appraisal.

Standard 10

In reporting the results of a business or intangible asset appraisal an appraiser must communicate each analysis, opinion, and conclusion in a manner that is not misleading.

Standards 7 through 10 will not be enforced by the Appraisal Institute. Two supplemental standards follow. These standards apply only to members of the Appraisal Institute.

Supplemental Standard 1

The form of certification used by a Member in a written report must include

1. A statement indicating compliance with the Code of Professional Ethics and Standards of Professional Appraisal Practice; and
2. A statement advising the client and third parties of the Appraisal Institute's right to review the report; and
3. A statement indicating the current status of the Designated Member under the Appraisal Institute's continuing education program.

Supplemental Standard 2

The Appraisal Standards Board of the Appraisal Foundation added an Ethics Provision to the Uniform Standards of Professional Appraisal Practice on December 4, 1989. The language in this Ethics Provision is very broad and the Appraisal

Institute has interpreted this Ethics Provision to apply to appraisal conduct only. The Appraisal Institute has an existing Code of Professional Ethics that is adequate to carry out the intent of the Ethics Provision. Therefore, the Appraisal Institute will enforce its own Code of Professional Ethics under its existing enforcement procedures as the proper means of enforcing the Ethics Provision of the Uniform Standards of Professional Appraisal Practice.

USPAP Definitions

The following definitions are taken from the Uniform Standards of Professional Appraisal Practice (USPAP), 1996 edition.

Appraisal: (noun) the act or process of estimating value; an estimate of value. (adjective) of or pertaining to appraising and related functions, e.g., appraisal practice, appraisal services.

Complete Appraisal: the act or process of estimating value or an estimate of value performed without invoking the Departure Provision.

Limited Appraisal: the act or process of estimating value or an estimate of value performed under and resulting from invoking the Departure Provision.

Appraisal Practice: the work or services performed by appraisers, defined by three terms in these standards: appraisal, review, and consulting.

Comment: These three terms are intentionally generic, and not mutually exclusive. For example, an estimate of value may be required as part of a review or consulting service. The use of other nomenclature by an appraiser (e.g., analysis, counseling, evaluation, study, submission, valuation) does not exempt an appraiser from adherence to these standards.

Binding Requirement: all or part of a standards rule of USPAP from which departure is not permitted. (See Departure Provision)

Business Assets: tangible and intangible resources that are employed by a business enterprise in its operations.

Business Enterprise: a commercial, industrial or service organization pursuing an economic activity.

Business Equity: the interests, benefits, and rights inherent in the ownership of a business enterprise or a part thereof in any form (including but not necessarily limited to capital stock, partnership interests, cooperatives, sole proprietorships, options, and warrants).

Cash Flow Analysis: a study of the anticipated movement of cash into or out of an investment.

Client: any party for whom an appraiser performs a service.

Consulting: the act or process of providing information, analysis of real estate data, and recommendations or conclusions on diversified problems in real estate, other than estimating value.

Feasibility Analysis: a study of the cost-benefit relationship of an economic endeavor.

Intangible Property (Intangible Assets): nonphysical assets, including but not limited to franchises, trademarks, patents, copyrights, goodwill, equities, mineral rights, securities, and contracts, as distinguished from physical assets such as facilities and equipment.

Investment Analysis: a study that reflects the relationship between acquisition price and anticipated future benefits of a real estate investment.

Market Analysis: a study of real estate market conditions for a specific type of property.

Market Value: market value is the major focus of most real property appraisal assignments. Both economic and legal definitions of market value have been developed and refined. A current economic definition agreed upon by agencies that regulate federal financial institutions in the United States of America is:

> The most probable price which a property should bring in a competitive and open market under all conditions requisite to a fair sale, the buyer and seller each acting prudently and knowledgeably, and assuming the price is not affected by undue stimulus. Implicit in this definition is the consummation of a sale as of a specified date and the passing of title from seller to buyer under conditions whereby:
>
> 1. buyer and seller are typically motivated;
>
> 2. both parties are well informed or well advised, and acting in what they consider their best interests;
>
> 3. a reasonable time is allowed for exposure in the open market;
>
> 4. payment is made in terms of cash in United States dollars or in terms of financial arrangements comparable thereto; and
>
> 5. the price represents the normal consideration for the property sold unaffected by special or creative financing or sales concessions granted by anyone associated with the sale.
>
> Substitution of another currency for *United States dollars* in the fourth condition is appropriate in other countries or in reports addressed to clients from other countries.
>
> Persons performing appraisal services that may be subject to litigation are cautioned to seek the exact legal definition of market value in the jurisdiction in which the services are being performed.
>
> *Please Note:* The definition of Market Value has been published in this section of USPAP as an example only.

Mass Appraisal: the process of valuing a universe of properties as of a given date utilizing standard methodology, employing common data, and allowing for statistical testing.

Mass Appraisal Model: a mathematical expression of how supply and demand factors interact in a market.

Personal Property: identifiable portable and tangible objects which are considered by the general public as being "personal," e.g., furnishings, artwork, antiques, gems and jewelry, collectibles, machinery and equipment; all property that is not classified as real estate.

Real Estate: an identified parcel or tract of land, including improvements, if any.

Real Property: the interests, benefits, and rights inherent in the ownership of real estate.

> *Comment:* In some jurisdictions, the terms *real estate* and *real property* have the same legal meaning. The separate definitions recognize the traditional distinction between the two concepts in appraisal theory.

Report: any communication, written or oral, of an appraisal, review, or consulting service that is transmitted to the client upon completion of an assignment.

> *Comment:* Most reports are written and most clients mandate written reports. Oral report guidelines (See Ethics Provision: Record Keeping) are included to cover court testimony and other oral communications of an appraisal, review or consulting service.

> The types of written reports listed below apply to real property appraisals:

> *Self-Contained Appraisal Report:* a written report prepared under Standards Rule 2-2(a) of a Complete or Limited Appraisal performed under Standard 1.

> *Summary Appraisal Report:* a written report prepared under Standards Rule 2-2(b) of a Complete or Limited Appraisal performed under Standard 1.

> *Restricted Appraisal Report:* a written report prepared under Standards Rule 2-2(c) of a Complete or Limited Appraisal performed under Standard 1.

Review: the act or process of critically studying a report prepared by another.

Signature: personalized evidence indicating authentication of the work performed by the appraiser and the acceptance of the responsibility for content, analyses, and the conclusions in the report.

> *Comment:* A signature can be represented by a handwritten mark, a digitized image controlled by a personalized identification number, or other media, where the appraiser has sole personalized control of affixing the signature.

Specific Guideline: all or part of a standards rule of USPAP from which departure is permitted under certain limited conditions. (See Departure Provision)

Federal Legislation Affecting the Appraisal Profession*

Existing Legislation, Regulations, and Banking/Examining Circulars†	Areas of Appraisal Affected	Government Agencies Subject to Specific Legislation
Uniform Relocation Assistance and Real Properties Acquisition Act of 1970 (Public Law 91-646, Titles II & III) Amended in the **Surface Transportation Bill** (1987)‡	Just compensation for displaced owners and tenants affected by land acquisitions for federally funded projects	**Department of Agriculture; Department of the Interior— National Park Service; Department of Transportation (DOT)** (A total of 14 agencies are affected.)
R-41 Memoranda Series (1977-1987) The R-41 Memoranda Series was superseded by CEBA (see below)	Appraisals of properties under federally insured mortgages	**Federal Home Loan Bank Board** (independent agency)
12 CFR 7.3025 "Other Real Estate Owned" (8/28/79) Amended 3/28/84	Appraisals done for commercial banks	**Office of Comptroller of the Currency (OCC) (Treasury Department)**
Examining Circular 234 "Troubled Real Estate Loans" (10/30/85) and **Supplement No. 1 "Guidelines for Troubled Real Estate Loans Clarified"** (7/10/87)	Appraisals done for commercial banks	**Office of Comptroller of the Currency (OCC) (Treasury Department)**
Internal Revenue Service Regulation Section 1.170A-13 (1986)	Reporting requirements established for appraisals done for income tax purposes (specifically dealing with charitable contributions)	**Internal Revenue Service (Treasury Department)**
Competitive Equality Banking Act of 1987 (CEBA) (Public Law 100-86) CEBA was the foundation for FIRREA§	Appraisals done for the five Federal Financial Institutions Regulatory Agencies (FFIRAs) Brought appraisals for S&Ls under the same policies and procedures as those for commercial banks	**Office of Thrift Supervision** (OTS) (since 1989) and **Office of Comptroller of the Currency (OCC),** both under the **Treasury Department;** the **Federal Reserve Board;** the **Federal Deposit Insurance Corporation (FDIC);** and the **National Credit Union Administration** (The last three are independent agencies.)

For further insights on the development of appraisal legislation, see Alison K. Bailey Seas, "Evolution of Appraisal Reform and Regulation in the United States," *The Appraisal Journal* (January 1994), 26-46.

*The **Federal Interagency Real Property Appraisal Committee** (FIRPAC) is made up of various federal agencies with an interest in appraisal issues. FIRPAC, which is headed by OMB, was established to develop and revise Circular A-129. It includes many agencies not bound by FIRREA. FIRPAC is currently drawing up uniform standards for appraisals submitted to federal agencies.

†Appraisal policies and procedures may also be established by means other than regulatory legislation. Memoranda and banking or examining circulars and executive orders are noteworthy examples. Several federal agencies (OCC, FDIC, OTS) issue circulars that specify the definition of value they require, e.g., fair value, net realizable value (see 12 CFR 7.3024 and the two other banking/examining circulars cited in this chart and the final note on the next page). Also note Executive Order 12630.

‡Uniform appraisal standards for land acquisition, developed in the Yellow Book of 1973, were revised and published as *Uniform Appraisal Standards for Federal Land Acquisitions* by the Interagency Land Acquisition Conference (Washington, D.C.: U.S. Government Printing Office, 1992).

§In response to **CEBA,** the Federal Home Loan Bank Board (FHLBB) adopted **Regulation 563.17-1a** and **Statement of Policy 563-1b** (12/12/87).

Existing Legislation, Regulations, and Banking/Examining Circulars[†]	Areas of Appraisal Affected	Government Agencies Subject to Specific Legislation
Banking Circular 225 "Guidelines for Real Estate Appraisal Policies and Review Procedures" (12/7/87) and **"Clarification of Guidelines for Real Estate Appraisal Policies and Review Procedures"** (9/8/88)	Appraisals done for commercial banks	**Federal Reserve Board, Federal Deposit Insurance Corporation (FDIC),** and the **Office of Comptroller of the Currency (OCC)**
Executive Order 12630 (1988) (Current legislation to codify this executive order is pending.)	Requires all agencies to determine whether an action will result in a taking.	**All federal agencies**
Federal Land Exchange Facilitation Act of 1988 (Public Law 101-17)	Valuation of parcels involved in exchanges between federal agencies or federal and state agencies	**Department of Agriculture— U.S. Forestry Service; Department of the Interior—Bureaus of Land Management** (public land) and **Mines**
Circular A-129 of 1988	Appraisals done for any federal credit agency under the Office of Management and Budget (OMB) (Does not apply to land acquisition agencies; mandates hiring of certified appraisers.)	**Office of Management and Budget (OMB)** (an executive agency)
Financial Institutions Reform, Recovery, and Enforcement Act of 1989 (FIRREA) (Public Law 101-73, Title XI) (8/8/89) Each of the five FFIRAs plus the RTC was directed to draft preliminary and final rules (within a year) to give substance to this legislation[‖] Title XI was amended 11/27/91; executive approval is pending.	Appraisals done for the five Federal Financial Institutions Regulatory Agencies (FFIRAs) Appraisals for all federal and state S&Ls and banking institutions	**Office of Thrift Supervision (OTS)** [superseding the **FHLBB**] and **Office of Comptroller of the Currency (OCC)** both under **Treasury;** the **Federal Reserve Board;** the **Federal Deposit Insurance Corporation (FDIC);** the **National Credit Union Administration** (The last three are independent agencies.); and the **Resolution Trust Corporation (RTC),** a quasi-independent agency set up to oversee the liquidation of insolvent S&Ls (The RTC became defunct in 1995.)

[‖] Pursuant to FIRREA, banking/examining circulars were issued by the federal banking agencies. The dates when these circulars were published are shown below; all became effective between 8/9/90 and 9/21/90:

Office of Comptroller of the Currency, 12 CFR Part 34, Subpart C "Real Estate Appraisals" (8/24/90)
Federal Reserve Board, 12 CFR Parts 208 and 225 (7/28/90)
Federal Deposit Insurance Corporation, 12 CFR Part 323 (8/20/90)
Resolution Trust Corporation, 12 CFR Part 1608 (8/22/90)
Office of Thrift Supervision, 12 CFR Parts 506, 545, 563, 564, 571 (8/23/90)
National Credit Union Administration, 12 CFR Parts 701, 722, 741 (7/25/90)

State Legislation Regulating the Licensing and Certification of Appraisers

State	Year Enacted	State	Year Enacted
Alabama	5/90	Montana	1991
Alaska	6/90	Nebraska	4/94
Arizona	1990	Nevada	6/89
Arkansas	1991	New Hampshire	4/90
California	8/90	New Jersey	3/91
Colorado	6/90	New Mexico	4/93
Connecticut	1988	New York	6/90
Delaware	7/89	North Carolina	7/89
District of Columbia	3/90	North Dakota	4/91
Florida	1992	Ohio	7/89
Georgia	4/90	Oklahoma	5/94
Hawaii	1990	Oregon	3/91
Idaho	1994	Pennsylvania	7/90
Illinois	1989	Puerto Rico	1991
Indiana	1991	Rhode Island	7/90
Iowa	6/89	South Carolina	3/91
Kansas	4/94	South Dakota	2/90
Kentucky	4/90	Tennessee	3/94
Louisiana	6/95	Texas	1991
Maine	4/90	Utah	3/94
Maryland	5/90	Vermont	6/90
Massachusetts	1991	Virginia	4/90
Michigan	5/94	Virgin Islands	11/91
Minnesota	5/89	Washington	5/89
Mississippi	4/90	West Virginia	3/90
Missouri	4/90	Wisconsin	1990
		Wyoming	2/89

Based on *Appraisal Institute State Law Summaries* (Chicago 1996), which contains summaries of specific legislation and regulations relating to the licensure and certification of real estate appraisers in each state. A breakdown of the type of state appraiser regulations is also included. (Some states mandate licensing or certification for all appraisals; others require licensing or certification only for federally related transactions.) *Appraisal Institute State Law Summaries* is updated annually to reflect the numerous amendments to the laws enacted each year as well as any new regulations promulgated by the licensure boards in each state. The publication also includes information on the categories of trainee types, continuing education and renewal requirements, fees, exemptions, temporary practice, reciprocity, regulatory boards, and the names, phone numbers, and addresses of contact persons.

Environmental Legislation Affecting Appraisal

The **Comprehensive Environmental Response, Compensation, and Liability Act of 1980 (CERCLA)** provides for the establishment of a superfund to expedite the cleanup of contaminated sites. Under CERCLA, liability is adjudicated on a "strict, joint, several, and retroactive" basis. While the method(s) of determining the risk or environmental liability associated with a site are not defined by federal law, a procedure known as an **environmental property assessment (EPRA)** is commonly conducted at commercial and industrial sites to identify potential environmental concerns prior to the transfer of a property.

The **Superfund Amendments and Reauthorization Act of 1986 (SARA)** exempts third parties who acquired real property after the disposal or placement of hazardous materials, provided such defendants at the time of acquisition made "all appropriate inquiry into the previous ownership and uses of the property consistent with good commercial or customary practice in an effort to minimize liability."

Reform provisions in recent EPA policy statements clearly delineate the circumstances under which owners and lenders may be liable for environmental cleanup costs, specify the steps owners and buyers must take to fulfill CERCLA's due diligence requirements, and extend current tax laws involving the cost recovery of environmental cleanup expenses to cover cleanup costs as deductible repairs.

In addition to **CERCLA** and **SARA,** legislation with a significant impact on real estate appraisal includes the following:

- The Resource Conservation and Recovery Act (RCRA) of 1976, amended on various occasions over the subsequent decade, provided for the control of hazardous waste and the regulation of underground storage tanks.

- The Clean Water Act (CWA) of 1977, amended in 1987, expanded previous legislation aimed at regulating the discharge of pollutants and set goals for water quality improvement. Section 404 of CWA authorized the U.S. Army Corps of Engineers to issue dredge and fill permits for wetlands.

- The Endangered Species Act (ESA) of 1973, amended in 1988, prohibited development in habitats of endangered species, e.g., the snaildarter, furbish lousewort (Pedicularis furbishiae) or gopher turtle.

- The Toxic Substances Control Act (TSCA) of 1976, variously amended over the subsequent decade, provided for the regulation of polychlorinated biphenyls (PCBs) and the removal of asbestos.

- The Clean Air Act (CAA) of 1963, variously amended during the 1960s and 1970s and substantially expanded in 1990, provided for the establishment of air quality standards and the regulation of hazardous air pollutants.

- The Federal Insecticide, Fungicide, and Rodenticide Act (FIFRA) of 1972, amended in 1988, provided for the registration, storage, transport, and disposal of pesticides.

- The Safe Drinking Water Act (SDWA) of 1974, amended in 1988, set limits on the concentration of lead in drinking water (a result of lead piping commonly used in construction for many years) and regulated wells and water treatment plants.

- The National Flood Insurance Act (NFIA) of 1968, broadened by the Flood Disaster Protection Act (FDPA) of 1973, set up the National Flood Insurance Program (NFIP) and Federal Emergency Management Agency (FEMA). FEMA issues directives on where and where not to build in coastal and floodplain areas. Appraisers must report whether a property is located in a flood hazard area. They should also investigate the availability and cost of flood insurance, which is generally required for mortgagors of floodplain properties.

- The North American Wetlands Conservation Act, enacted in 1989, expanded on previous legislation (e.g., the Emergency Wetlands Resources Act of 1986) to protect and conserve North American wetland ecosystems and the waterfowl, migratory birds, fish, and wildlife that depend on such habitat. Efforts by the federal government to acquire property rights (in fee simple and under easement) were broadened. An executive order issued by President Bush in August 1991 articulated the goal of "no net wetland loss." When development adversely impacts wetlands, the developer must restore or enhance other wetlands to take the place of those adversely impacted.

The Private Property Rights Act (H.R. 925) approved in the House of Representatives and the Omnibus Property Rights Act (S. 605) proposed in the Senate in 1995 were both pending at the time of publication. The former would govern cases of regulatory takings and provide compensation for private property owners whose property value declines as a result of government actions. This House-approved act would only apply to regulatory actions pertaining to wetlands, endangered species, and water rights. The Senate-proposed act would be broader in scope and require the federal government to compensate property owners if federal regulatory action reduces the value of their property by one-third. This act would also require agencies to perform a takings impact analysis of regulations to help ensure that the regulatory alternative selected minimizes the taking of private property.

APPRAISAL INSTITUTE®

PROPERTY OBSERVATION CHECKLIST

LIMITED SCOPE ANALYSIS

The Property Observation Checklist is a limited scope analysis voluntarily prepared by the appraiser during the normal course of his/her inspection of the subject property in the preparation of a real estate appraisal. In completing the checklist, only visual observations are recorded. The intent of the checklist is to identify possible environmental factors that could be observable by a non-environmental professional. The appraiser did not search title, interview the current or prior owners, or do any research beyond that normally associated with the appraisal process, unless otherwise stated.

The user of this checklist is reminded that all responses to the questions are provided by an appraiser who is not an environmental professional and is not specifically trained or qualified to identify potential environmental problems; therefore, it should be used only to assist the appraiser's client in determining whether an environmental professional is required. The checklist was not developed for use with single-family residential or agricultural properties.

The appraiser is not liable for the lack of detection or identification of possible environmental factors. The appraisal report and/or the Property Observation Checklist must not be considered under any circumstances to be an environmental site assessment of the property as would be performed by an environmental professional.

GENERAL INSTRUCTIONS

The appraiser should distinguish, as appropriate, between the physical presence of possible environmental factors and the economic effect such factors may have in the marketplace or on the value estimate. In completing the checklist, the appraiser should attach reports, photographs, interview records, notes, public records, etc., as documentation for specific observations. The instructions for each section of the checklist specify the kinds of documentation required.

If, for any reason, this checklist is prepared as a stand-alone document, it must be accompanied by an attached statement of limiting conditions and certification of the appraiser's qualifications.

TERMINOLOGY AND APPRAISAL STANDARDS

The following checklist terms appear in *The Dictionary of Real Estate Appraisal*, Third Edition (Chicago: Appraisal Institute, 1993) and are specifically referenced in the Property Observation Checklist: *adjoining properties; environmental professional; environmental site assessment;* and *pits, ponds, or lagoons.* Please refer to *The Dictionary of Real Estate Appraisal*, Third Edition, for discussions of these terms.

Please refer to Guide Note 8, "The Consideration of Hazardous Substances in the Appraisal Process," *Guide Notes to the Standards of Professional Appraisal Practice* (Chicago: Appraisal Institute, 1995); Advisory Opinion G-9, "Responsibility of Appraisers Concerning Toxic or Hazardous Substances Contamination," *Uniform Standards of Professional Appraisal Practice* (Washington, D.C.: The Appraisal Foundation, 1995 ed.); and other appropriate statements in the professional standards documents for additional information.

SECTION 1 Extent of Appraiser's Inspection of the Property

Describe the appraiser's on-site inspection of the subject property and, as applicable, the adjoining properties:

_____

_____

_____

_____

SECTION 2 Possible Environmental Factors Observed by the Appraiser

Indicate below if any of the following possible environmental factors were observed during the appraiser's visual inspection(s) of the subject property and, as applicable, the adjoining properties. A written description of possible environmental factors should be provided for all questions where "Yes" is checked.

1. Did the appraiser observe an indication of current or past industrial/manufacturing use on the subject property or adjoining properties?

   ○ Yes   ○ No   **If observed, describe below:**

_____

_____

2. Did the appraiser observe any containers, storage drums, or disposal devices not labeled or identified as to contents or use on the subject property?

   ○ Yes   ○ No   **If observed, describe below:**

_____

_____

3. Did the appraiser observe any stained soil or distressed vegetation on the subject property?

   ○ Yes   ○ No   **If observed, describe below:**

_____

_____

4. Did the appraiser observe any pits, ponds, or lagoons on the subject property?

   ○ Yes   ○ No   **If observed, describe below:**

_____

_____

5. Did the appraiser observe any evidence of above-ground or underground storage tanks (e.g., tanks, vent pipes, etc.) on the subject property?

   ○ Yes   ○ No   **If observed, describe below:**

_____

_____

6. Did the appraiser observe any flooring, drains, or walls associated with the subject property that are stained or that emit unusual odors?

○ Yes   ○ No   **If observed, describe below:**

_____

_____

7. Did the appraiser observe any water being discharged on or from the subject property?

○ Yes   ○ No   **If observed, describe below:**

_____

_____

8. Did the appraiser observe any indication of dumping, burying, or burning on the subject property?

○ Yes   ○ No   **If observed, describe below:**

_____

_____

9. Did the appraiser observe any chipped, blistered, or peeled paint on the subject property?

○ Yes   ○ No   **If observed, describe below:**

_____

_____

10. Did the appraiser observe any sprayed-on insulation, pipe wrapping, duct wrapping, etc., on the subject property?

○ Yes   ○ No   **If observed, describe below:**

_____

_____

11. Did the appraiser observe any transmission towers (electrical, microwave, etc.) on the subject property or adjoining properties?

○ Yes   ○ No   **If observed, describe below:**

_____

_____

12. Did the appraiser observe any coastal areas, rivers, streams, springs, lakes, swamps, marshes, or watercourses on the subject property or adjoining properties?

○ Yes   ○ No   **If observed, describe below:**

_____

_____

13. Did the appraiser observe any other factors that might indicate the need for investigation(s) by an environmental professional?

○ Yes   ○ No   **If observed, describe below:**

_____

_____

SECTION 3   Possible Environmental Factors Reported by Others

Indicate below if in completing this assignment the appraiser was informed—verbally or in writing—of any information concerning possible environmental factors reported by others. "Others" may include the client, the property owner, the property owner's agent, or any other person conveying such information. Documentation should be provided for all instances where "Yes" is checked. If the information was presented verbally, then a written description of the source and circumstance of the communication should be attached to this checklist and/or the appraisal report. Copies of printed reports provided to the appraiser should be attached to this checklist and/or the appraisal report.

14. Has the appraiser been informed about federal- or state-maintained records indicating that environmentally sensitive sites are located on the subject property or adjoining properties?

    ○ Yes   ○ No   **If yes, provide documentation.**

15. Has the appraiser been informed about past or current violations (e.g., liens, government notifications, etc.) of environmental laws concerning the subject property?

    ○ Yes   ○ No   **If yes, provide documentation.**

16. Has the appraiser been informed about past or current environmental lawsuits or administrative proceedings concerning the subject property?

    ○ Yes   ○ No   **If yes, provide documentation.**

17. Has the appraiser been informed about past or current tests for lead-based paint or other lead hazards on the subject property?

    ○ Yes   ○ No   **If yes, provide documentation.**

18. Has the appraiser been informed about past or current tests for asbestos-containing materials on the subject property?

    ○ Yes   ○ No   **If yes, provide documentation.**

19. Has the appraiser been informed about past or current tests for radon on the subject property?

    ○ Yes   ○ No   **If yes, provide documentation.**

20. Has the appraiser been informed about past or current tests for soil or groundwater contamination on the subject property?

    ○ Yes   ○ No   **If yes, provide documentation.**

21. Has the appraiser been informed about other professional environmental site assessment(s) of the subject property?

    ○ Yes   ○ No   **If yes, provide documentation.**

Signature

Name

Date Checklist Signed

State Certification or State License #   State

4 of 4

Mathematics in Appraising

Appraisers use a wide variety of mathematical techniques ranging from simple arithmetic and algebraic formulas to the statistical techniques of multiple regression analysis. Addition, subtraction, multiplication, and division can be done manually or with a simple calculator, but more sophisticated calculators may be needed to solve algebraic formulas and to perform linear regression analyses. Computers are required for nearly all stepwise multiple regression analyses.

With the general availability of calculators and computers, the use of sophisticated techniques is increasing in appraisal practice. This section provides a review of the mathematical procedures and terminology used by appraisers. Familiar processes are illustrated and the rules that apply to each process are discussed.

Basic Arithmetic for Data Processing

Data collected in the market are analyzed in the valuation process to derive an estimate of value. These data may include building dimensions, population figures, reproduction and replacement costs, rents, and sale prices. Processing these data ultimately leads to conclusions and final value estimates, which are expressed numerically. The mathematical relationships represented by rates and factors are usually stated as decimals rather than fractions.

Rates

Rates are percentages expressed in terms of a specific time period. For example,

$8 interest per year on $100 principal = 8% interest per year
$0.50 interest per month on $100 = 0.005 or 0.5% interest per month

A rate reflects the relationship between one quantity and another. In the first example, the 8% rate relates the $8 of interest returned to the $100 of principal invested. In appraising, an unknown capital amount can be determined when only the rate and the amount of annual return are known.

Reciprocals

The reciprocal of a number is 1 divided by that number. For example, the reciprocal of 4 is ¼, which may be expressed as 0.25. When two numbers have a reciprocal relationship, 1 divided by either number equals the other number. Reciprocal relationships exist between some financial factors. For example, the present value of $1 per period factor and the partial payment factor are reciprocals. These annual factors in the 10% tables for 10 periods are 6.144567 and 0.162745, respectively. Because they are reciprocals,

$$\frac{1}{6.144567} = 0.162745$$

and

$$\frac{1}{0.162745} = 6.144567$$

When a reciprocal relationship exists, multiplication by one of the numbers is equivalent to division by the other.

Factors

Factors are the reciprocals of rates and may be used to express relationships between income and capital value. Using I, R, and V to represent income, rate, and value, and F to represent a factor, the relationships may be expressed as

$$I = V \times R \qquad I = \frac{V}{F}$$

$$R = \frac{I}{V} \qquad F = \frac{V}{I}$$

$$V = \frac{I}{R} \qquad V = I \times F$$

These relationships, which are commonly referred to as IRV and VIF, may be shown as follows.

$$\frac{I}{R \mid V} \quad \text{and} \quad \frac{V}{I \mid F}$$

The formula for any single component is represented by the horizontal or vertical relationship of the remaining two components as one multiplied by, or divided by, the other.

Basic Statistics

Statistics can be applied to interpret available data and to support a value conclusion. In the language of statistics, a *population* is defined as all the items in a specific category. If, for example, the category is houses in Chicago, the population consists of all the houses in Chicago. However, data pertaining to an entire population are rarely available and conclusions often must be developed from incomplete data.

Using statistical concepts, conclusions about a population can be derived and evaluated from sample data. A *sample* is part of a population; the quality of conclusions based on a sample will vary with the quality and extent of the sample.

One item in a population is called a *variate*. In appraising, statistics can be used to identify the attributes of the typical variate in a population. When observations about a population can be measured, the analysis may be quantitative; when these observations cannot be measured, the analysis is qualitative—i.e., it reflects the attributes of the population.

A variate is *discrete* when it can assume a limited number of values on a measuring scale and *continuous* when it can assume an infinite number of values. A typical population of attributes for house types might include one-story, two-story, and split-level houses. It is usually impractical to display or identify a population of variates because there are many.

One common problem in statistics is how to describe a population in universally understandable terms. For example, how does one describe all the houses in a community that have sold in the past year without describing each sale individually? One possible solution is to use a single number called a *parameter* to describe the whole population. When one parameter is used to describe a population, it is called an *aggregate,* which is the sum of all the variates. For example, all the house sales in a community in a given year can be described by the total dollar amount of all the sales. In statistical language this is written as

$$\Sigma = \text{sigma or sum of}$$
$$X = \text{variate}$$
$$\Sigma X = \text{aggregate (summation of the variates)}$$

Measures of Central Tendency

Three common statistical measures are the mean, the median, and the mode. All three measure central tendency and are used to identify the typical variate in a population or sample. Measures that refer to a population are called *parameters,* while similar measures in a sample are called *statistics.*

The *mean,* which is commonly called the *average,* is by far the most commonly used parameter. It is obtained by dividing the sum of all the variates in a population by the number of variates. In real estate appraising, the mean may represent an average sale price, an average number of days on the market, an average apartment rent, or an average cost per square foot.

When the mean is used to describe a population, it can be distorted by extreme variates. Consider the following list of 36 house sales in a neighborhood. From these figures, the mean of the population can be calculated. (The list indicates the median and the mode of the population, which are discussed next.)

$72,000
74,600
76,000
77,200
78,000
79,000
79,800
79,800

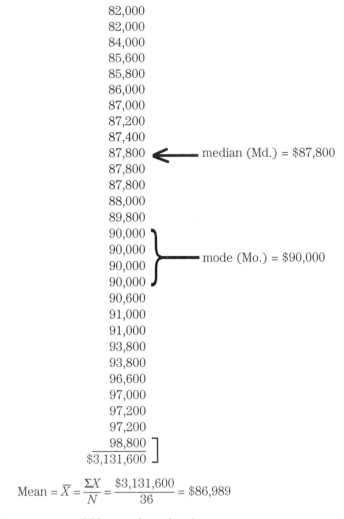

$$\text{Mean} = \overline{X} = \frac{\Sigma X}{N} = \frac{\$3,131,600}{36} = \$86,989$$

where ΣX = sum of the variates and N = number of variates.

The same procedure can be performed with grouped data. To group the data, the frequency (f) with which a given sale price occurs must be identified and its contribution must be effectively weighted. Given the same data, identical results are produced.

X	f	fX
$72,000	1	$72,000
74,600	1	74,600
76,000	1	76,000
77,200	1	77,200
78,000	1	78,000
79,000	1	79,000
79,800	2	159,600
82,000	2	164,000

84,000	1	84,000
85,600	1	85,600
85,800	1	85,800
86,000	1	86,000
87,000	1	87,000
87,200	1	87,200
87,400	1	87,400
87,800	3	263,400
88,000	1	88,000
89,800	1	89,800
90,000	4	360,000
90,600	1	90,600
91,000	2	182,000
93,800	2	187,600
96,600	1	96,600
97,000	1	97,000
97,200	2	194,400
98,800	1	98,800
98,800	$N = 36$	$fX =$ $3,131,600

$$\text{Mean} = \overline{X} = \frac{fX}{N} = \frac{\$3,131,600}{36} = \$86,989$$

The average, or mean, price in this example might not accurately represent the population of houses that have been sold at prices outside the indicated range.

The *median* is another measure used to describe a population, a sample, or an average variate. The median divides the variates of a population or sample into equal halves. To find the median, the variates are arranged in numerical order like the list of sale prices in the example. If the total number of variates is odd, the median is the middle variate. If the total number of variates is even, as in the example, the median is the arithmetic mean of the two middle variates.

In the list of 36 house sales, the middle two variates are $87,800 and $87,800. The mean of these two variates is $87,800, which is the median of the 36 sales. The same number of sales occur above the median as below it.

Like the median and the mean, the *mode* is a parameter used to describe the typical variate of a population. The mode is the variate or attribute that appears most frequently in a population. Of the 36 house sales, four were sold at $90,000. No other sale price occurs with this frequency, so the mode in this sample is $90,000. If two variates occur with equal frequency, both are modes and the sample is bimodal.

To illustrate, consider the following population of the types of condominium apartments available in a nine-unit complex.

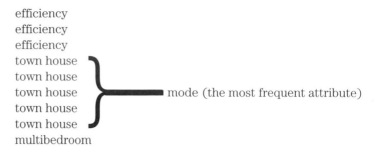

efficiency
efficiency
efficiency
town house
town house
town house — mode (the most frequent attribute)
town house
town house
multibedroom

One of the problems in using statistics is selecting the appropriate measure of central tendency to describe a population. The following numbers could be used to describe the 36 variates in the group of house sales.

$$\overline{X} = \$86{,}989 \text{ (the mean of all the sales)}$$
$$\text{Md.} = \$87{,}800 \text{ (the median of the sales)}$$
$$\text{Mo.} = \$90{,}000 \text{ (the mode of the sales)}$$

The mean is often used to describe a sample or population because this measure is widely understood and amenable to further statistical analysis.

Measures of Variation

The parameters of mean, median, and mode are used to describe the central tendencies of a population. Other sets of parameters can provide more information about the population being described. *Measures of variation,* or *measures of dispersion,* describe the disparity among the values of the variates that make up the population. They indicate the degree of uniformity among the variates and reflect the quality of the data as a basis for a conclusion.

Range

One way to measure the disparity between the variates is with a *range* (R). The range is the difference between the highest and the lowest variates.

$$R = \text{maximum variate minus minimum variate}$$

The range for the 36 house sales is calculated as

$$R = \$98{,}800 - \$72{,}000 = \$26{,}800$$

As a measure of variation, the range has limited usefulness because it considers only the variation between the highest and lowest values, not the variation in the remaining values. Furthermore, a range does not lend itself to further statistical analysis.

Average Deviation

Another parameter used to measure the variation in a population is the average deviation, which is also known as the *average absolute deviation* because positive and negative signs are ignored. The average deviation is a measure of how much the actual values of a population or sample deviate from the mean. It is the mean of the sum of the absolute differences of each of the variates from the mean of the variates.

The average deviation of the 36 sales can be calculated from ungrouped or grouped data.

Ungrouped Data	
X Sale Price	$\|X - \bar{X}\|$ **Absolute Deviation Between** **Each Variate and the** **Mean Sale Price of $86,989**
$72,000	$14,989
74,600	12,389
76,000	10,989
77,200	9,789
78,000	8,989
79,000	7,989
79,800	7,189
79,800	7,189
82,000	4,989
82,000	4,989
84,000	2,989
85,600	1,389
85,800	1,189
86,000	989
87,000	11
87,200	211
87,400	411
87,800	811
87,800	811
87,800	811
88,000	1,011
89,800	2,811
90,000	3,011
90,000	3,011
90,000	3,011
90,000	3,011
90,600	3,611
91,000	4,011
91,000	4,011
93,800	6,811
93,800	6,811
96,600	9,611
97,000	10,011
97,200	10,211
97,200	10,211
98,800	11,811
$3,131,600 Total of sale prices	$192,088 Total deviation from mean $\Sigma\|X - \bar{X}\|$

	Grouped Data		
X	|X − X̄|	f	f|X − X̄|
$72,000	$14,989	1	$14,989
74,600	12,389	1	12,389
76,000	10,989	1	10,989
77,200	9,789	1	9,789
78,000	8,989	1	8,989
79,000	7,989	1	7,989
79,800	7,189	2	14,378
82,000	4,989	2	9,978
84,000	2,989	1	2,989
85,600	1,389	1	1,389
85,800	1,189	1	1,189
86,000	989	1	989
87,000	11	1	11
87,200	211	1	211
87,400	411	1	411
87,800	811	3	2,433
88,000	1,011	1	1,011
89,800	2,811	1	2,811
90,000	3,011	4	12,044
90,600	3,611	1	3,611
91,000	4,011	2	8,022
93,800	6,811	2	13,622
96,600	9,611	1	9,611
97,000	10,011	1	10,011
97,200	10,211	2	20,422
98,800	11,811	1	11,811
		36	$192,088 Total deviation from mean Σf|X − X̄|

$$\text{A.D. (ungrouped data)} = \frac{\Sigma |X - \overline{X}|}{n} = \frac{\$192,088}{36} = \$5,336$$

$$\text{A.D. (grouped data)} = \frac{\Sigma f |X - \overline{X}|}{n} = \frac{\$192,088}{36} = \$5,336$$

A.D. = average deviation

Σ = sum of

f = frequency

X = observed value

| | = aggregation (ignore whether the difference is positive or negative)

n = number of observations in sample

$\overline{X}$ = mean of sample

These calculations indicate that the average deviation of the individual values in the population from the mean is $5,336, or about 6%. This relatively small variation suggests that the mean is an acceptable representation of the population.

Like the range, the average deviation does not lend itself to further statistical calculations.

Standard Deviation

The standard deviation is a way to describe a sample or a population that lends itself to further mathematical treatment. When this measure is used, the rules of probability can be applied to draw inferences from samples concerning the attributes of the population. The square of the difference between each observation and the mean of the observations is used in lieu of the absolute deviation. In this way the effects of extreme variance from the mean are magnified.

In the example the mean house sale price is $86,989; for an $82,000 sale, the standard deviation is $4,989 squared, or $24,890,121.

When the standard deviation of an entire population is being calculated, it is symbolized by the lowercase sigma (σ). The formula may be expressed verbally as follows: *The standard deviation of a population is the square root of the sum of the squared differences between each observation and the mean of all the observations in the population, divided by the number of observations in the population.*

When the standard deviation of a sample of a population is being calculated, it is symbolized by the lowercase letter *s*. Expressed verbally, the formula is: *The standard deviation of a sample is the square root of the sum of the squared differences between each observation and the mean of all the observations in the sample, divided by the number of observations in the sample minus one.*

One is subtracted from the number of observations in a sample to adjust for the one degree of freedom that is lost when the mean is calculated. (See the discussion of simple linear regression analysis that is presented later in this appendix.) A set of data starts with as many degrees of freedom as there are observations; each time a statistic is calculated directly from the data, one degree of freedom is lost.

Formulas for calculating the standard deviations follow.

For a population:

$$\text{Ungrouped} \qquad\qquad \text{Grouped}$$

$$\sigma = \sqrt{\frac{\Sigma(X - \bar{X})^2}{N}} \qquad\qquad \sigma = \sqrt{\frac{\Sigma f\,(X - \bar{X})^2}{N}}$$

For a sample:

$$\text{Ungrouped} \qquad\qquad \text{Grouped}$$

$$s = \sqrt{\frac{\Sigma(X - \bar{X})^2}{n - 1}} \qquad\qquad s = \sqrt{\frac{\Sigma f\,(X - \bar{X})^2}{n - 1}}$$

Samples are typically used in real estate appraising, so the second formula is usually applicable. The standard deviation for the 36 house sales as grouped data is calculated in Table B.1.

The standard deviation is a useful way to describe the dispersion of a population or sample. It indicates how well the mean represents the whole sample or population by describing a standard measure of variation. The standard deviation is used and understood in many disciplines and it can be calculated easily with an

| Table B.1 | Standard Deviation for 36 House Sales | | | |

X	f	(X − X̄)	(X − X̄)²	f(X − X̄)²
$72,000	1	$14,989	$224,670,000	$224,670,000
74,600	1	12,389	153,487,000	153,487,000
76,000	1	10,989	120,758,000	120,758,000
77,200	1	9,789	95,824,500	95,824,500
78,000	1	8,989	80,802,100	80,802,100
79,000	1	7,989	63,824,100	63,824,100
79,800	2	7,189	51,681,700	103,363,000
82,000	2	4,989	24,890,100	49,780,200
84,000	1	2,989	8,934,120	8,934,120
85,600	1	1,389	1,929,320	1,929,320
85,800	1	1,189	1,413,720	1,413,720
86,000	1	989	978,121	978,121
87,000	1	11	121	121
87,200	1	211	44,521	44,521
87,400	1	411	168,921	168,921
87,800	3	811	657,721	1,973,160
88,000	1	1,011	1,022,120	1,022,120
89,800	1	2,811	7,901,720	7,901,720
90,000	4	3,011	9,066,120	36,264,500
90,600	1	3,611	13,039,300	13,039,300
91,000	2	4,011	16,088,100	32,176,200
93,800	2	6,811	46,389,700	92,779,400
96,600	1	9,611	92,371,300	92,371,300
97,000	1	10,011	100,220,000	100,220,000
97,200	2	10,211	104,265,000	208,530,000
98,800	1	11,811	139,500,000	139,500,000
				$1,631,755,444
				Rounded $1,631,760,000

electronic calculator. It will undoubtedly be more widely used by appraisers in the future.

The standard deviation can also indicate what percentage of the sample of a population may be expected to fall within selected ranges of *confidence intervals*. (Confidence levels are discussed later in this appendix.) Approximately 68.26% of the sample or population will generally fall within plus or minus one standard deviation from the mean, provided the data meet the tests of normal distribution, which are explained later. Many types of real estate data conform to the pattern of a normal distribution when they are developed with appropriate sampling techniques.

Assuming this is a normal distribution, 68.26% of the house sales in the population will fall between $80,161 ($86,989 - $6,828) and $93,817 ($86,989 + $6,828). Approximately 95.44% of the sales should fall within two standard deviations from the mean and approximately 99.74% should fall within three standard deviations from the mean.

Because the standard deviation lends itself to further mathematical calculations, it can be used for analytical purposes as well as to describe a population.

$$s = \sqrt{\frac{\Sigma f (X - \overline{X})^2}{n - 1}}$$

Mean: $86,989

$$s = \sqrt{\frac{\$1,631,760,000}{36 - 1}}$$

$$s = \sqrt{\$46,621,714}$$

$$s = \$6,828$$

Statistical Inference

Statistical inference is based on the assumption that past market actions provide a valid basis for forecasting present or future market actions. In the example, past sale prices are used to estimate current sale prices. The same technique can be used to forecast rents, costs, depreciation, and other amounts using the rules of probability.

A normal curve is produced when a normal distribution is plotted on a graph to illustrate a distribution of data. Although the original data may not be normally distributed, the results of repeated random samples may approximate a normal distribution. Sales are often treated as though they were normally distributed in competitive, open-market situations.

A normal curve often takes the form of a bell curve. One major characteristic of a bell curve is its symmetry. Both halves of the curve have the same shape and contain the same number of observations. The mean, median, and mode are the same value and fall at the midpoint, or apex, of the curve.

Figure B.1 is a bell curve that illustrates the 36 house sales. It shows that 68.26% of the observations will fall within the range of the mean, plus or minus one standard deviation; 95.44% will fall within plus or minus two standard deviations; and 99.74% will fall within plus or minus three standard deviations. The figure depicts an analysis of the probable population distribution for the 36 sales, assuming a normal distribution.

Under the bell curve, the ranges for one, two, and three standard deviations are shown. The percentage of the population that will fall within a given distance from the mean or within any specified range can be calculated. For example, the percentage of sales included within a range of $91,989 to $81,989 (i.e., the mean of $86,989 plus or minus $5,000) may be estimated by calculating the Z value for this range with the formula presented below and then consulting a table of areas under the normal curve for the calculated value of Z.

Z = the deviation of X from the mean measured in standard deviations

$$Z = \frac{X - \text{mean}}{\text{standard deviation}}$$

$$Z = \frac{\$91,989 - \$86,989}{\$6,828} = 0.73$$

This formula shows that $91,989 and $81,989 each deviate from the mean of $86,989 by 0.73 standard deviations.

Figure B.1 | **Area Under the Normal Curve for 36 House Sales**

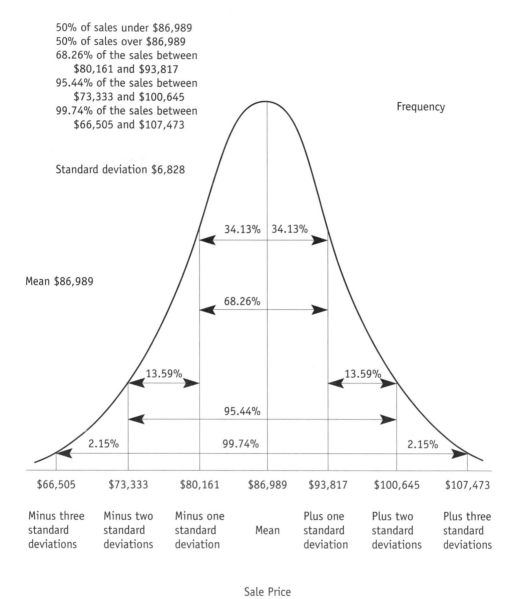

50% of sales under $86,989
50% of sales over $86,989
68.26% of the sales between
$80,161 and $93,817
95.44% of the sales between
$73,333 and $100,645
99.74% of the sales between
$66,505 and $107,473

Standard deviation $6,828

Frequency

34.13% 34.13%

Mean $86,989

68.26%

13.59%   13.59%

95.44%

2.15%   99.74%   2.15%

$66,505	$73,333	$80,161	$86,989	$93,817	$100,645	$107,473
Minus three standard deviations	Minus two standard deviations	Minus one standard deviation	Mean	Plus one standard deviation	Plus two standard deviations	Plus three standard deviations

Sale Price

Source: Joseph Lambert, PhD

The percentage of sales within this Z range of plus or minus 0.73 standard deviations can be found by locating 0.7 in the Z column of Table B.2 and then looking across the top of the table for the next digit—i.e., 0.03. The table indicates that 26.73% of the sales fall between $86,989 and $91,989 or between $86,989 and $81,989; therefore, 53.46% of the sales will fall between $91,989 and $81,989.

Table B.2 | **Areas Under the Normal Curve**

Z	.00	.01	.02	.03	.04	.05	.06	.07	.08	.09
0.0	0.0000	0.0040	0.0080	0.0120	0.0160	0.0199	0.0239	0.0279	0.0319	0.0359
0.1	0.0398	0.0438	0.0478	0.0517	0.0557	0.0596	0.0636	0.0675	0.0714	0.0753
0.2	0.0793	0.0832	0.0871	0.0910	0.0948	0.0987	0.1026	0.1064	0.1103	0.1141
0.3	0.1179	0.1217	0.1255	0.1293	0.1331	0.1368	0.1406	0.1443	0.1480	0.1517
0.4	0.1554	0.1591	0.1628	0.1664	0.1700	0.1736	0.1772	0.1808	0.1844	0.1879
0.5	0.1915	0.1950	0.1985	0.2019	0.2054	0.2088	0.2123	0.2157	0.2190	0.2224
0.6	0.2257	0.2291	0.2324	0.2357	0.2389	0.2422	0.2454	0.2486	0.2517	0.2549
0.7	0.2580	0.2611	0.2642	0.2673	0.2704	0.2734	0.2764	0.2794	0.2823	0.2852
0.8	0.2881	0.2910	0.2939	0.2967	0.2995	0.3023	0.3051	0.3078	0.3106	0.3133
0.9	0.3159	0.3186	0.3212	0.3238	0.3264	0.3289	0.3315	0.3340	0.3365	0.3389
1.0	0.3413	0.3438	0.3461	0.3485	0.3508	0.3531	0.3554	0.3577	0.3599	0.3621
1.1	0.3643	0.3665	0.3686	0.3708	0.3729	0.3749	0.3770	0.3790	0.3810	0.3830
1.2	0.3849	0.3869	0.3888	0.3907	0.3925	0.3944	0.3962	0.3980	0.3997	0.4015
1.3	0.4032	0.4049	0.4066	0.4082	0.4099	0.4115	0.4131	0.4147	0.4162	0.4177
1.4	0.4192	0.4207	0.4222	0.4236	0.4251	0.4265	0.4279	0.4292	0.4306	0.4319
1.5	0.4332	0.4345	0.4357	0.4370	0.4382	0.4394	0.4406	0.4418	0.4429	0.4441
1.6	0.4452	0.4463	0.4474	0.4484	0.4495	0.4505	0.4515	0.4525	0.4535	0.4545
1.7	0.4554	0.4564	0.4573	0.4582	0.4591	0.4599	0.4608	0.4616	0.4625	0.4633
1.8	0.4641	0.4649	0.4656	0.4664	0.4671	0.4678	0.4686	0.4693	0.4699	0.4706
1.9	0.4713	0.4719	0.4726	0.4732	0.4738	0.4744	0.4750	0.4756	0.4761	0.4767
2.0	0.4772	0.4778	0.4783	0.4788	0.4793	0.4798	0.4803	0.4808	0.4812	0.4817
2.1	0.4821	0.4826	0.4830	0.4834	0.4838	0.4842	0.4846	0.4850	0.4854	0.4857
2.2	0.4861	0.4864	0.4868	0.4871	0.4875	0.4878	0.4881	0.4884	0.4887	0.4890
2.3	0.4893	0.4896	0.4898	0.4901	0.4904	0.4906	0.4909	0.4911	0.4913	0.4916
2.4	0.4918	0.4920	0.4922	0.4925	0.4927	0.4929	0.4931	0.4932	0.4934	0.4936
2.5	0.4938	0.4940	0.4941	0.4943	0.4945	0.4946	0.4948	0.4949	0.4951	0.4952
2.6	0.4953	0.4955	0.4956	0.4957	0.4959	0.4960	0.4961	0.4962	0.4963	0.4964
2.7	0.4965	0.4966	0.4967	0.4968	0.4969	0.4970	0.4971	0.4972	0.4973	0.4974
2.8	0.4974	0.4975	0.4976	0.4977	0.4977	0.4978	0.4979	0.4979	0.4980	0.4981
2.9	0.4981	0.4982	0.4982	0.4983	0.4984	0.4984	0.4985	0.4985	0.4986	0.4986
3.0	0.4987	0.4987	0.4987	0.4988	0.4988	0.4989	0.4989	0.4989	0.4990	0.4990

The probability of a randomly selected sale falling within a given range can also be determined with the Z value. Using the sample of 36 house sales, which has a mean of \$86,989 and a standard deviation of \$6,828, the probability of a randomly selected sale falling between \$86,989 and \$88,989 is calculated as follows:

$$Z = \frac{X - \text{mean}}{\text{standard deviation}} = \frac{\$88,989 - \$86,989}{\$6,828} = 0.29$$

The table of areas under the normal curve, Table B.2, shows that a Z value of 0.29 corresponds to 0.1141. This indicates that there is an 11.41% chance that the sale will fall within \$2,000 above the mean. Because the curve of a normal distribution is symmetrical, there is the same probability that a sale will fall within $2,000 below the mean.

Probability a sale will fall between $88,989 and $86,989	11.41%
Probability a sale will fall between $84,989 and $86,989	11.41%
Probability a sale will fall between $84,989 and $88,989	22.82%

If the range in this example is expanded to $4,000 plus or minus the mean of $86,989—i.e., between $82,989 and $90,989—the probability of a randomly selected sale falling within this range is increased.

$$Z = \frac{X - \text{mean}}{\text{standard deviation}} = \frac{\$90,989 - \$86,989}{\$6,828} = 0.59$$

According to Table B.2, 0.59 = 0.2224.

Probability a sale will fall between $90,989 and $86,989	22.24%
Probability a sale will fall between $82,989 and $86,989	22.24%
Probability a sale will fall between $82,989 and $90,989	44.48%

In these examples the range being tested has been equally distributed above and below the mean sale price. However, the probability of a randomly selected sale falling within any selected range in the population can also be tested. For example, the probability of a sale falling between $80,000 and $100,000 can be calculated as follows:

$$Z \text{ area}^1 = \frac{X^1 - \text{mean}}{\text{standard deviation}} = \frac{\$80,000 - \$86,989}{\$6,828} = 1.02$$

$$Z \text{ area}^2 = \frac{X^2 - \text{mean}}{\text{standard deviation}} = \frac{\$100,000 - \$86,989}{\$6,828} = 1.91$$

A Z value of 1.02 in Table B.2 indicates a probability of	0.3461
A Z value of 1.91 in Table B.2 indicates a probability of	0.4719
Probability	0.8180

There is an 81.8% chance that a randomly selected sale in this sample will fall between $80,000 and $100,000.

Confidence Level

Using statistical inference and the laws of probability for a normal distribution, the previous examples have shown how confidence intervals can be constructed for a sample when normally distributed data have been assumed or approximated. These calculations may be valuable in loan administration, housing development, appraising, and other decision-making situations involving real estate.

The examples have illustrated that, with 36 sales as a sample, an appraiser can state with a 95% degree of confidence that any sale randomly selected from the population will fall between $73,333 and $100,645. Similarly, there is a 68% level of confidence that a given sale will fall between $80,161 and $93,817.

These measures may be meaningful when used in conjunction with other statistical conclusions. However, they depend on how accurately the estimated mean represents the true population mean, so some confidence in the reliability of the mean must be established. Regardless of the size of the population, there is a specific sample size that will permit a certain level of confidence in the estimated mean.

For the 36 house sales, the standard deviation for price has been calculated as $6,828. The arithmetic mean is $86,989, or approximately $87,000. If an appraiser wants to be 95% certain that the true mean is within $1,000 of the estimated mean of $86,989—i.e., between $86,000 and $88,000—the necessary sample size can be calculated with the following formula:

$$n = \frac{z^2 s^2}{e^2}$$

$$n = \frac{(1.96)^2 \ (\$6,828)^2}{(\$1,000)^2} = 179 \text{ sales}$$

where n = sample size required
   z = Z statistic at 95% confidence level
   s = standard deviation of the sample
   e = required maximum difference in the mean

Thus, with a sample of 179 sales, the required level of confidence could be met. Similarly, for a confidence interval of not more than $1,500, the calculations would be

$$n = \frac{(1.96)^2 \ (\$6,828)^2}{(\$1,500)^2} = 80 \text{ sales}$$

Using the original sample of 36 sales, an appraiser may want to know the limits within which the true population mean may fall at a 95% confidence level. By substitution

$$e^2 = \frac{z^2 s^2}{n}$$

and

$$e^2 = \frac{(1.96)^2 \ (\$6,828)^2}{36} = \$4,975,041$$

$$e = \sqrt{\$4,975,041} = \$2,230$$

Thus, the appraiser can be 95% certain that the true population mean falls between $84,759 and $89,219.

Although calculations such as these may not seem to be directly related to day-to-day appraising, professional appraisers have a continuing interest in obtaining adequate data and understanding the markets in which they appraise. Statistical calculations can be useful in quantifying change and performing the neighborhood analyses that are essential to value estimation. Many appraisers routinely analyze the inferences that can be drawn from measures such as the standard deviations of raw and adjusted sale or rental data. These calculations are also applied in appraisal review, loan underwriting, and other analyses.

Regression Analysis

Regression analysis is another technique used by appraisers to analyze market data. It can be applied to estimate value and to isolate and test the significance of specific value determinants.

Simple Linear Regression Analysis

To estimate a probable sale price in the market, it is seldom sufficient to develop a sample of sales, calculate the standard deviation, and base an estimate on this evidence. In most cases the range of values at the confidence level required is too broad to be useful. However, the accuracy of an estimate can be substantially increased by considering one or more characteristics of the sale properties in addition to their sale prices.

In simple linear regression analysis, one independent variable, or property characteristic, is used to reflect a relationship that changes on a straight-line basis. In other words, a change in the independent variable is reflected in the same proportion in the dependent variable, which is unknown. The basic regression equation is

$$Y_C = a + bX$$

where Y_C is the predicted value of the dependent variable; a is the constant; b is the coefficient, or multiplier, for the independent variable; and X is the value of the variable. If, for example, the independent variable is the square foot area of a building and the dependent variable is its sale price, the simple linear regression equation $Y_C = 10,000 + 45X$ means that the sale price of the building is predicted to be $10,000 plus $45 times its square foot area.

To find the constant, a, the data for this regression must be graphed. Increasing square foot areas are indicated along the horizontal axis of the graph and increasing sale prices are indicated along the vertical axis. Then a number of sales are plotted on the graph and a line that evenly divides these points is drawn. This is the regression line, and its slope is the b coefficient. The point on the vertical axis of the graph at which the regression begins is the intercept, or the constant symbolized as a. In other words, this is a base value that represents all positive and negative factors that are *not* explained by the equation and to which the coefficients, or adjustment factors, are added.

Another important statistic that results from a simple linear regression is the coefficient of determination, r^2. This statistic represents the approximate percentage of variation in the dependent variable, which is explained by the equation and is one measure of the efficacy of the regression. When a regression is performed on an electronic, handheld calculator, the coefficient of determination given is unadjusted for degrees of freedom (i.e., the number of observations minus the number of variables). This adjustment should be applied to the resulting coefficient of determination:

$$r^2_{adj} = 1 - (1 - r^2)\ (n - 1/n - 2)$$

The standard error of the estimate is another measure of how well the regression fits. It is expressed as S_{yx} and represents the remaining dispersion in the data after the regression equation is applied. The equation for arriving at the standard error of the estimate is:

$$S_{yx} = S_y\ \sqrt{1 - r^2}$$

The b coefficient also has a t value. The t value is the coefficient expressed as a ratio to its standard deviation; it is a measure of the significance of the coefficient. The precise degree of significance represented by a particular t value depends on several factors and must be calculated. As a general rule, however, coefficients with t values greater than 2 are usually significant at a reasonably high confidence level.

Simple regression analysis is particularly useful when one element is overwhelmingly important in determining a property's sale price. Furthermore, this technique allows appraisers to analyze the relationships between real estate values and the significance of their various components.

Example of Simple Linear Regression

Using the 36 house sales analyzed earlier, simple linear regression can be used to demonstrate the apparent relationship between the sale price of a property and its living area in square feet. The gross living area (GLA) of each of the 36 houses is shown in Table B.3. Most appraisers would only analyze properties with the same approximate square foot area as the subject property and disregard the other sales.

The appraiser is valuing a 1,375-sq.-ft. dwelling, so Sales 1, 2, and 3 are most similar in terms of size. Their prices are reported as $57.53, $64.14, and $55.95 per square foot, respectively. The other sales may provide a clue to the "right answer," but they do little to resolve the discrepancy between these figures. Adjustments could be made for other differences in the properties, but complications would develop if multiple adjustments produced overlapping effects.

Sales 1, 2, and 3 indicate a price range of $55.95 to $64.14 per square foot; when these figures are applied to the 1,375-sq.-ft. area of the subject property, a value range of $76,931 to $88,192 is indicated. (These figures would be rounded in the appraiser's report.) The remaining market information cannot be used effectively in traditional appraisal analysis except perhaps to reinforce the appraiser's judgment.

With simple linear regression, however, more of the market data can be analyzed. To apply the formula $Y_c = a + bX$, the 36 sales were analyzed with a calculator and produced the following figures.

a = $49,261

b = $22.59

r = 0.6599 (simple correlation coeffiient)

r^2 = 0.4354

Table B.3	Comparable Sales Data Set for Simple Regression Analysis

Sale	GLA in Square Feet	Sale Price	Price per Square Foot GLA
1	1,321	$76,000	$57.53
2	1,372	88,000	64.14
3	1,394	78,000	55.95
4	1,403	74,600	53.17
5	1,457	85,800	58.89
6	1,472	87,400	59.38
7	1,475	84,000	56.95
8	1,479	85,600	57.88
9	1,503	72,000	47.90
10	1,512	77,200	51.06
11	1,515	82,000	54.13
12	1,535	79,000	51.47
13	1,535	87,800	57.20
14	1,577	91,000	57.70
15	1,613	90,000	55.80
16	1,640	79,800	48.66
17	1,666	91,000	54.62
18	1,681	79,800	47.47
19	1,697	87,200	51.38
20	1,703	87,000	51.09
21	1,706	89,800	52.64
22	1,709	90,600	53.01
23	1,709	93,800	54.89
24	1,720	93,800	54.53
25	1,732	82,000	47.34
26	1,749	97,200	55.57
27	1,771	97,200	54.88
28	1,777	86,000	48.40
29	1,939	87,800	45.28
30	1,939	90,000	46.42
31	1,939	90,000	46.42
32	1,939	90,000	46.42
33	1,939	96,600	49.82
34	1,940	87,800	45.26
35	2,014	98,800	49.06
36	2,065	97,000	46.97

$$r^2_{adj} = 1 - (1 - 0.4354)(36 - 1)/(36 - 2)$$
$$= 0.4188 \text{ (adjusted coefficient of determination)}$$

Thus, for the 1,375-sq.-ft. property being appraised,

$$Y_c = \$49,261 + \$22.59 \text{ x } 1,375$$
$$= \$80,322, \text{ or } \$58.42 \text{ per square foot}$$

The 36 sales are plotted on the graph shown in Figure B.2 and the calculated regression line is indicated. The graph also shows the standard error of the estimate,

Figure B.2 | Plot of Sales, Regression Line, and Standard Error for 36 Sales

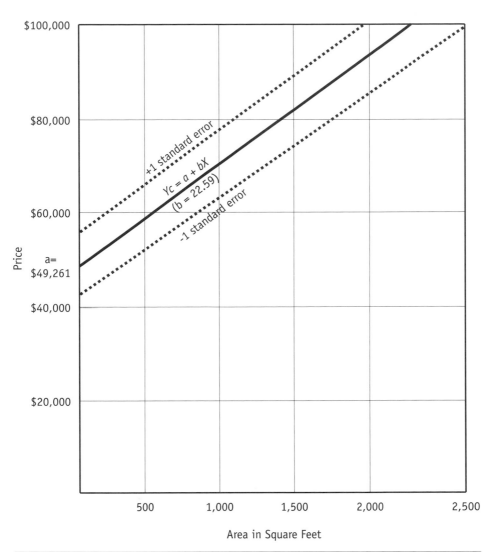

Source: Joseph Lambert, PhD

which allows the appraiser to construct confidence intervals around the regression line. The calculations in this example produce a standard error estimate of $5,205. When this figure is applied to the property being appraised, the appraiser can state that 36 sales in the market support an estimate of $80,300 for the appraised property, based only on a comparison of their square foot area. Moreover, at a 68% confidence level, the market price should fall between $80,300 ± $5,205—i.e., from $75,095 to $85,505. At a 95% confidence level, the price should fall between $80,300 ± 2 x $5,205, or from $69,890 to $90,710.

Although other statistical measures such as the standard error of the forecast (*sf*) may be used, most appraisers would consider this analysis to be sufficient and reasonably representative of most single-family market situations. Although a more refined analysis of these data could be performed, this example illustrates a simple application of a regression technique. The standard error of the forecast for the appraised property could be calculated as follows:

$$Sf = S_{yx} \sqrt{1 + \frac{1}{n} + \frac{(X_K - \overline{X})^2}{(X - \overline{X})^2}}$$

$$Sf = 5{,}205 \sqrt{1 + \frac{1}{36} + \frac{(1{,}720\text{-}1{,}670)^2}{1{,}469{,}045}}$$

$$Sf = 5{,}281$$

Applying this adjustment to the standard error makes only a small change because the measure of value (i.e., square footage) of the subject property is quite close to the mean square footage of the sample data. The greater the difference between the appraised property and the mean of the sample in regard to any property attribute, the more this distortion affects the standard error as a measure of variation in the regression prediction.

Multiple Regression Analysis

Multiple regression analysis is performed with the same basic methods as simple linear regression, but the analysis is expanded to include more than one independent variable. Some handheld calculators are preprogrammed or can be programmed to perform regressions using two or three independent variables, but multiple regressions are generally performed on a computer. Stepwise regression is an improvement on the standard regression procedure because variables can be added or removed from the regression equation depending on their degree of explanatory power. This type of regression produces an optimum combination of variables by retaining only the most significant.

Curvilinear Regression Analysis

Most appraisal data do not reflect straight-line relationships, but appraisers often deal with short segments of a curve so tools such as linear regression and correlation can be used. However, inferences can be distorted when linearity is assumed for data that are clearly curvilinear. Fortunately, many sets of curvilinear data may also be transformed rather easily and processed as if they were linear.

Financial Formulas

Basic Formulas

Symbols

I	=	income
R	=	capitalization rate
V	=	value
M	=	mortgage ratio
DCR	–	debt coverage ratio
F	=	capitalization factor (multiplier)
GIM	=	gross income multiplier
EGIM	=	effective gross income multiplier
NIR	=	net income ratio

Subscript:
- O = overall property
- M = mortgage
- E = equity
- L = land
- B = building

Basic Income/Cap Rate/Value Formulas

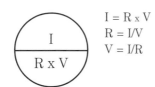

$$I = R \times V$$
$$R = I/V$$
$$V = I/R$$

Basic Value/Income/Factor Formulas

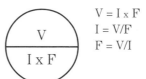

$$V = I \times F$$
$$I = V/F$$
$$F = V/I$$

Adaptations for Mortgage/Equity Components

Band of investment (using ratios)
$$R_O = M \times R_M + [(1 - M) \times R_E]$$
$$R_E = (R_O - M \times R_M)/(1 - M)$$

Equity residual
$$V_O = [(I_O - V_M \times R_M)/R_E] + V_M$$
$$R_E = (I_O - V_M \times R_M)/V_E$$

Cap Rate/Factor Relationships

$$R = 1/F$$
$$R_O = NIR/GIM$$
$$R_O = NIR/EGIM$$

Note. NIR may relate to scheduled gross or effective gross income; care should be taken to ensure consistency.

Mortgage residual
$$V_O = [(I_O - V_E \times R_E)/R_M] + V_E$$

Debt coverage ratio
$$R_O = DCR \times M \times R_M$$
$$DCR = R/(M \times R_M)$$
$$M = R/(DCR \times R_M)$$

Adaptations for Land/Building Components

Land residual
$$V_O = [(I_O - V_B \times R_B)/R_L] + V_B$$
$$R_L = (I_O - V_B \times R_B)/V_L$$

Building residual
$$V_O = [(I_O - V_L \times R_L)/R_B] + V_L$$
$$R_B = (I_O - V_L \times R_L)/V_B$$

Symbols

PV = present value	Subscript:
CF = cash flow	n = projection periods
Y = yield rate	O = overall property
R = capitalization rate	I = income
Δ = change	
a = annualizer	
$1/S_{\overline{n}}$ = sinking fund factor	
$1/n$ = 1/projection period	
CR = compound rate of change	
V = value	

Discounted Cash Flows/Present Value (DCF/PV)

$$PV = \frac{CF_1}{1 + Y} + \frac{CF_2}{(1 + Y)^2} + \frac{CF_3}{(1 + Y)^3} + ... + \frac{CF_n}{(1 + Y)^n}$$

Basic Cap Rate/Yield Rate/Value Change Formulas

$$R = Y - \Delta a$$
$$Y = R + \Delta a$$
$$\Delta a = Y - R$$
$$\Delta = (Y - R)/a$$

Adaptations for Common Income/Value Patterns

Pattern	Premise	Cap Rate (R)	Yield Rate (Y)	Value Change (Δ)
Perpetuity	$\Delta = 0$	$R = Y$	$Y = R$	
Level annuity*	$a = 1/S_{\overline{n}}$	$R = Y - \Delta 1/S_{\overline{n}}$	$Y = R + \Delta 1/S_{\overline{n}}$	$\Delta = (Y - R)/1/S_{\overline{n}}$
Straight-line change	$a = 1/n$	$R = Y - \Delta 1/n$	$Y = R + \Delta 1/n$	$\Delta = (Y - R)/1/n$
Exponential change	$\Delta_o a = CR$	$R_o = Y_o - CR$	$Y_o = R_o + CR$	$\Delta_o = (1 + CR)^n - 1$

*Inwood premise: $1/S_{\overline{n}}$ at Y rate; Hoskold premise: $1/S_{\overline{n}}$ at safe rate

Straight-Line Change* in Income	Straight-Line Change* in Value	Compound Rate of Change
$\$\Delta_I = V \times \Delta 1/n \times Y$	$\$\Delta 1/n = \$\Delta_I/Y$	$CR = \sqrt[n]{FV/PV} - 1$
$\Delta_I = (Y \times \Delta 1/n)/(Y - \Delta 1/n)$	$\Delta 1/n = (Y \times \Delta_I)/(Y + \Delta_I)$	$CR = Y_0 - R_0$

* In these formulas Δ_I is the ratio of one year's change in income to the first year's income.

Table Relationships

The following formulas may be used to convert the annual constant (R_M) for a monthly payment loan to the corresponding monthly functions.

Function for Monthly Frequency	Formula
Amount of $1	$S^n = R_M/(R_M - I)$
Amount of $1 per month	$S_{\overline{n}} = 12/(R_M - I)$
Sinking fund factor	$1/S_{\overline{n}} = (R_M - I)/12$
Present value of $1	$1/S_{\overline{n}} = (R_M - I)/R_M$
Present value of $1 per month	$a_{\overline{n}} = 12/R_M$
Partial payment	$1/a_{\overline{n}} = R_M/12$

In these formulas, I = nominal interest rate.

Present Value of Increasing/Decreasing Annuities

Straight-line changes. To obtain the present value of an annuity that has a starting income of d at the end of the first period and *increases* h *dollars* per period for n periods:

$$PV = (d + hn)\, a_{\overline{n}} - \frac{h(n - a_{\overline{n}})}{i}$$

To obtain the present value of an annuity that has a starting income of d at the end of the first period and *decreases* h dollars per period for n periods, simply make h negative in the formula.

Exponential-curve (constant-ratio) changes.

To obtain the present value of an annuity that starts at $1 at the end of the first period and *increases each period* thereafter at the rate x for n periods:

$$PV = \frac{1 - (1 + x)^n/(1 + i)^n}{i - x}$$

Where i is the periodic discount rate and x is the ratio between the increase in income for any period and the income for the previous period.

To obtain the present value of an annuity that starts at $1 at the end of the first period and *decreases each period* thereafter at rate x, simply make x negative in the formula.

Symbols

r = basic capitalization rate
Y = yield rate
M = mortgage ratio
C = mortgage coefficient
P = ratio paid off—mortgage
$1/S_{\overline{n}|}$ = sinking fund factor
R = capitalization rate
$S_{\overline{n}|}$ = future value of \$1 per period
Δ = change
J = J factor (changing income)
n = projection period
NOI = net operating income
B = mortgage balance
I = nominal interest rate

Subscript:
E = Equity
M = mortgage
P = projection
O = overall property
I = income
1 = 1st mortgage
2 = 2nd mortgage

Mortgage/Equity Formulas

Basic Capitalization Rate (r)

$r = Y_E - MC$
$r = Y_E - (M_1 C_1 + M_2 + C_2)$

$C = Y_E + P1/S_{\overline{n}|} - R_M$
$P = (R_M - I)/(R_{MP} - I)$
$P = 1/S_{\overline{n}|} \times S_{\overline{n}|} P$

Capitalization Rates (R)

Level income

$R = Y_E - MC - \Delta1/S_{\overline{n}|}$

$R = r - \Delta1/S_{\overline{n}|}$

J-factor changing income

$R_O = \dfrac{Y_E - MC - \Delta_O 1/S_{\overline{n}|}}{1 + \Delta_I J}$

$R_O = \dfrac{r - \Delta_O 1/S_{\overline{n}|}}{1 + \Delta_I J}$

Required Change in Value (Δ)

Level income

$\Delta = \dfrac{r - R}{1/S_{\overline{n}|}}$

$\Delta = \dfrac{Y_E - MC - R}{1/S_{\overline{n}|}}$

J-factor changing income

$\Delta_O = \dfrac{r - R_O(1 + \Delta_I J)}{1/S_{\overline{n}|}}$

$*\Delta_O = \dfrac{r - R_O}{R_O J + 1/S_{\overline{n}|}}$

Note. For multiple mortgage situations, insert M and C for each mortgage.

*This formula assumes value and income change at the same ratio.

Equity yield (Y_E)

Level income

$Y_E = R_E + \Delta_E 1/S_{\overline{n}|}$

J-factor changing income

$Y_E = R_E + \Delta_E 1/S_{\overline{n}|} + \left[\dfrac{R_O \Delta_I}{1 - M}\right] J$

Change in equity

$$\Delta_E = (\Delta_O + MP)/(1 - M) \text{ or}$$
$$\Delta_E = [V_O(1 + \Delta_O) - B - V_E]/V_E$$

Assumed mortgage situation

Level income

$$V_O = \frac{NOI + BC}{Y_E - \Delta_O 1/S_{\overline{n}|}}$$

J-factor changing income

$$V_O = \frac{NOI(1 + \Delta_I J) + BC}{Y_E - \Delta_O 1/S_{\overline{n}|}}$$

Mortgage/Equity Without Algebra Format

Loan ratio x annual constant	= _____
Equity ratio x equity yield rate	= + _____
Loan ratio x paid off loan ratio x SFF	= − _____
Basic rate (r)	= _____
+ Dep *or* − App x SFF	= ± _____
Cap rate (R)	= _____

Note. SFF is sinking fund factor at equity yield rate for projection period. Dep/App is the change in value from depreciation or appreciation during the projection period.

Symbols

PV = present value
NPV = net present value
CF = cash flow
  i = discount rate (in NPV formula)
  n = projection period
IRR = internal rate of return
  PI = profitability index
MIRR = modified internal rate of return
FVCFj = future value of a series of cash flows
  i = reinvestment rate (in MIRR formula)

Subscript:
0 = at time zero
1 = end of 1st period
2 = end of 2nd period
3 = end of 3rd period
n = end period of series

Net Present Value (NPV)

$$NPV = CF_0 + \frac{CF_1}{1 + i} + \frac{CF_2}{(1 + i)^2} + \frac{CF_3}{(1 + i)^3} + \dots + \frac{CF_n}{(1 + i)^n}$$

Internal Rate of Return (IRR)

Where NPV = 0; IRR = i

Profitability Index (PI)

$$PI = PV/CF_0$$

Modified Internal Rate of Return (MIRR)

$$\text{MIRR} = \sqrt[n]{\frac{\text{FVCF}_j}{\text{CF}_0}} - 1$$

$$\text{MIRR} = \sqrt[n]{\frac{\text{CF}_1(1 + i)^{n-1} + \text{CF}_2(1 + i)^{n-2} + \text{CF}_3(1 + i)^{n-3} + \dots + \text{CF}_n}{\text{CF}_0}} - 1$$

Note. In these formulas individual CFs may be positive or negative for *PV* and *NPV* solutions; however, CF$_0$ is treated as a positive value for *PI* and *MIRR* solutions.

Mortgage-Equity Analysis

L. W. Ellwood was the first to organize, develop, and promulgate the use of mortgage-equity analysis in yield capitalization for real property valuation. He theorized that mortgage money plays a major role in determining real property prices and values. Ellwood saw real property investments as a combination of two components—debt and equity—and held that the return requirements of both components must be satisfied through income, reversion, or a combination of the two. Thus, Ellwood developed an approach for estimating property value that made explicit assumptions as to what a mortgage lender and an equity investor would expect from the property.

In general mortgage-equity analysis involves estimating the value of a property on the basis of both mortgage and equity return requirements. The value of the equity interest in the property is found by discounting the pre-tax cash flows available to the equity investor. The equity yield rate (Y_E) is used as the discount rate. The total value of the property is equal to the present value of the equity position plus the value of the mortgage. This is true whether the value is found using discounted cash flow analysis or yield capitalization formulas that have been developed for mortgage-equity analysis.

Applications

Mortgage-equity analysis can facilitate the valuation process in many ways. It may be used 1) to compose overall rates, 2) to analyze and test the capitalization rates obtained with other capitalization techniques, 3) as an investment analysis tool to test the values indicated by the sales comparison and cost approaches, and 4) to analyze a capitalization rate graphically.

Given a set of assumptions concerning the *NOI,* mortgage (amount, rate, and term), reversion (rate of appreciation or depreciation), equity yield rate, and projection period, mortgage-equity analysis may be employed to estimate the present value of the equity and to arrive at the total property value. The following example illustrates a general approach to mortgage-equity analysis.

Given:

Annual NOI (level)	$25,000
Projection period	10 years
Loan amount	$168,000
Loan terms*	
Interest rate	9%
Amortization term	
(monthly payments)	25 years
Estimated reversion	$201,600
Equity yield rate	15%

* Contract terms are at current market rates

Using these assumptions, cash flow to the equity investor can be projected as follows:

Annual Cash Flow from Operations—Years 1-10

Annual net operating income	$25,000
Annual debt service	16,918
Pre-tax cash flow	$8,082

Cash Flow from Reversion—Year 10

Estimated resale price	$201,600
Mortgage balance	139,002
Cash flow from reversion	$62,598

Using the present value factor for a 15% yield rate and a 10-year holding period, we may calculate the present value of the cash flows to the equity investor as follows:

Years	Cash Flow	Present Value Factor	Present Value
1-10	$8,082	5.018769*	$40,562
10	$62,598	0.247185†	15,473
Present value of equity			$56,035

* Ordinary level annuity (present value of $1 per period) factor
† Reversion (present value of $1) factor

The total property value can now be found by adding the present value of the equity to the present value of the loan.[1]

Present value of the equity	$56,035
Present value of the loan	168,000
Total value	$224,035

---

1. Because the loan is assumed to be at current market rates, the face amount of the loan is equal to the value of the loan to the lender.

This example illustrates a fairly straightforward application of mortgage-equity analysis. The present value of the equity was easily calculated by discounting the dollar estimates of the cash flows. The assumptions in this example were simplified in several ways. First, the income was assumed to be level. In a more complex situation, income may be expected to change over the holding period. Second, the loan amount was specified in dollars.[2] If the loan amount were assumed to be based on a loan-to-value ratio, the dollar amount of the loan would depend on the property value being calculated. In such a case the cash flows to the equity investor could not be specified in dollars and discounted as they were in the example. Third, the resale price was specified in dollars.[3] Investors often assume that property values will change by a spfcified percentage amount over the holding period (see Chapter 21). Thus the resale price depends on the property value being calculated. Finally, in the preceding example the total property value is greater than the loan amount. If the opposite were true, the value of the loan could *not* exceed the combined debt and equity interests in the property.

When either the loan amount or the resale price depends on the value of the property, the cash flows cannot be projected in dollar amounts and discounted. An alternative procedure must be used to solve for the present value. One such alternative is to use a yield capitalization formula that has been developed to solve this type of problem.[4] This is what L. W. Ellwood did when he developed the Ellwood equation, which is illustrated in the following section.

Mortgage-Equity Formula

The general mortgage-equity formula is:

$$R_O = \frac{Y_E - M(Y_E + P\ 1/S_n - R_M) - \Delta_O\ 1/S_n}{1 + \Delta_I\ J}$$

where:

R_O = overall capitalization rate
Y_E = equity yield rate
M = loan-to-value ratio
P = percentage of loan paid off
$1/S_n$ = sinking fund factor at the equity yield rate
R_M = mortgage capitalization rate or mortgage constant
Δ_O = change in total property value
Δ_I = total ratio change in income
J = J factor (This symbol is discussed later in this chapter.)

---

2. This might be the case if the property were being valued subject to an existing loan. Such a situation is illustrated later in this chapter. Alternatively, the dollar amount may have resulted from a separate calculation of the maximum amount that could be borrowed to meet a minimum debt coverage ratio.

3. This situation might occur if there is a purchase option in a lease that the appraiser believes will be exercised. Alternatively, a dollar estimate may be the result of a separate estimate of the resale price calculated by applying a capitalization rate to the income at the end of the holding period.

4. A computer can be programmed to handle this type of valuation problem. For a discussion of this proceudure, see Jeffrey D. Fisher, "Using Circular Reference in Spreadsheets to Estimate Value," *The Quarterly Byte*, vol. 5, no. 4, fourth quarter 1989.

The part of the formula represented as: $Y_E - M(Y_E + P\ 1/S_n - R_M)$ can be referred to as the *basic capitalization rate* (r), which satisfies the lender's requirement and adjusts for amortization. It also satisfies the investor's equity yield requirement before any adjustment is made for income and value changes. Therefore, the basic rate starts with an investor's yield requirement and adjusts it to reflect the effect of financing. The resulting basic capitalization rate is a building block from which an overall capitalization rate can be developed with additional assumptions.

If level income and no change in property value are anticipated, the basic rate will be identical to the overall capitalization rate. The last part of the numerator, Δ_O $1/S_n$, allows the appraiser to adjust the basic rate to reflect an expected change in overall property value. If the value change is positive, referred to as property *appreciation,* the overall capitalization rate is reduced to reflect this anticipated monetary benefit; if the change is negative, referred to as *depreciation,* the overall capitalization rate is increased.

Finally, the denominator, $1 + \Delta_I J$, accounts for any change in income. The J factor is always positive. Thus, if the change in income is positive, the denominator will be greater than one and the overall rate will be reduced. If the change in income is negative, the overall rate will be increased. For level-income applications, $\Delta = 0$, so the denominator is $1 + 0$, or 1.

Akerson Format

The mortgage-equity procedure developed by Charles B. Akerson substitutes an arithmetic format for the algebraic equation in the Ellwood formula.[5] This format is applicable to level-income situations; when modified with the J or K factor, it can also be applied to changing-income situations.

The Akerson format for level income situations is

Loan ratio x annual constant	= _____
Equity ratio x equity yield rate	= + _____
Loan ratio x % paid off in projection period x $1/S_n$	= − _____
Basic rate (r)	= _____
+ dep *or* − app x $1/S_n$	= ± _____
Overall capitalization rate	= _____

where $1/S_n$ is the sinking fund factor at the equity yield rate for the projection period and dep/app denotes the change in value from property depreciation or appreciation during the projection period.

Level-Income Applications

Mortgage-equity analysis can be used to value real property investments with level income streams or variable income streams converted to level equivalents using overall capitalization rates and residual techniques.

---

5. The format was first presented by Charles B. Akerson in "Ellwood without Algebra," *The Appraisal Journal* (July 1970).

Use of Overall Capitalization Rates

In the simplest application of the mortgage-equity formula and the Akerson format, a level income and a stable or changing overall property value are assumed. The following example illustrates the application of the mortgage-equity formula using an overall capitalization rate applied to a level flow of income.

NOI (level)	$25,000
Projection period	10 years
Loan terms	
Interest rate	9%
Amortization term (monthly payments)	25 years
Loan-to-value ratio	75%
Property value change	20% gain
Equity yield rate	15%

The overall rate is calculated as follows:

$$R_O = \frac{Y_E - M\ (Y_E + P1/S_n - R_M) - D_O\ 1/S_n}{1 + \Delta_I\ J}$$

$$R_O = \frac{0.15 - 0.75\ (0.15 + 0.1726 \times 0.04925 - 0.1007) - (0.20 \times 0.04925)}{1 + 0 \times J}$$

$$R_O = \frac{0.15 - 0.75\ (0.057801) - 0.009850}{1}$$

$$R_O = \frac{0.15 - 0.043350 - 0.009850}{1}$$

$$R_O = \frac{0.096800}{1}$$

$$R_O = 0.0968\ \text{(rounded)}$$

The capitalized value of the investment is $25,000/0.0968 = $258,264

Using the same data and assumptions, an identical value can be derived by applying the Akerson format.

0.75 x 0.100704	=	0.075528
0.25 x 0.15	= +	0.037500
−0.75 x 0.172608 x 0.049252	= −	0.006376
Basic rate (r)	=	0.106652
0.20 x −0.049252	= −	0.009850
R_O	=	0.098602

The capitalized value is $25,000/0.0986 = $258,264

The answer derived in this example is virtually the same as the answer that would be derived using DCF analysis. In fact, it is possible to check the answer found with the Ellwood formula by discounting the implied cash flows. (This is true because the dollar amount of the loan and resale price are approximately the same in both examples. That is, the implied amount of the loan is 75% of $224,014, or approximately $168,000 and the implied resale price is 90% of $224,014, or approximately $201,600. It is important to realize, however, that this was not known until the problem was solved. The examples were designed to produce the same answer to demonstrate that both problems are based on the same concepts of discounted cash flow analysis.)

Use of Residual Techniques

Land and building residual techniques can be applied with land and building capitalization rates based on mortgage-equity procedures. The general mortgage-equity formula or the Akerson format is applied to derive a basic rate, which is used to develop land and building capitalization rates.

For example, assume that a commercial property is expected to produce level annual income of $15,000 per year over a 10-year term. Mortgage financing is available at a 75% loan-to-value ratio, and monthly payments at 11% interest are made over an amortization term of 25 years. The land is currently valued at $65,000 and is forecast to have a value of $78,000 at the end of the projection period, indicating a 20% positive change in land value. The building is expected to have no value at the end of the projection period and the equity yield rate is 15%.

The first step in valuing this property is to derive the basic rate (r) using the Ellwood Formula.

$$r = Y_E - M(Y_E + P\ 1/S_n - R_M)$$
$$= 0.15 - 0.75\ (0.15 + 0.137678 \times 0.049252 - 0.117614)$$
$$= 0.15 - 0.029375$$
$$= 0.120625$$

The Akerson format can also be used to derive the basic rate.

0.75 x 0.117614	=	0.088211
0.25 x 0.15	=	0.037500
0.75 x 0.137678 x 0.049252	=	– 0.005086
Basic capitalization rate (r)	=	0.120625

Next, the land and building capitalization rates are calculated. To solve for the land capitalization rate, R_L, the calculations are

$$R_L = r - \Delta_L\ 1/S_n$$
$$= 0.120625 - (0.20 \times 0.049252)$$
$$= 0.120625 - 0.009850$$
$$= 0.110775$$

The building capitalization rate, R_B, is calculated as follows:

$$R_B = r - \Delta_B\ 1/S_n$$
$$= 0.120625 - (-1.0 \times 0.049252)$$
$$= 0.120625 + 0.049252$$
$$= 0.169877$$

These rates can be used to value the property with the building residual technique.

NOI	$15,000
Land income	
$(V_L \times R_L) = \$65,000 \times 0.110775$	7,200
Residual income attributable to building	$7,800
Capitalized value of building	
$(I_B \div R_B) = \$7,800/0.169877$	$45,916
Plus land value	+ 65,000
Indicated property value	$110,916

When the rates are used in the land residual technique, a similar property value is indicated.

NOI	$15,000
Building income	
$(V_B \times R_B) = \$46,000 \times 0.169877$	7,814
Residual income attributable to land	$7,186
Capitalized value of land	
$(I_L - R_L) = \$7,186/0.110775$	$64,870
Plus building value	+ 46,000
Indicated total property value	$110,870

Changing-Income Applications

The general mortgage-equity formula can be applied to income streams that are forecast to change on a curvilinear or exponential-curve (constant-ratio) basis by using a J factor for curvilinear change or a K factor for constant-ratio change. The J factor, used in the stabilizer $(1 + \Delta_I J)$, may be obtained from precomputed tables or calculated with the J-factor formula.[6] The K factor, an income adjuster or stabilizer used to convert a changing income stream into its level equivalent, can be calculated with the K-factor formula.[7]

Use of the J factor

The J-factor formula for curvilinear income reflects an income stream that changes from time zero in relation to a sinking fund accumulation curve. The formula is

$$J = 1/S_n \times \left[\frac{n}{1 - 1/(1 + Y)^n} - \frac{1}{Y} \right]$$

where:

$1/S_n$ = sinking fund factor at equity yield rate
n = projection period
Y = equity yield rate

6. James J. Mason, ed., comp., *American Institute of Real Estate Appraisers Financial Tables*, rev. ed. (Chicago: American Institute of Real Estate Appraisers, with tables computed by Financial Publishing Company, 1982) 461-473.

7. Charles B. Akerson, *Capitalization Theory and Techniques: Study Guide* (Chicago: American Institute of Real Estate Appraisers, with tables computed by Financial Publishing Company, 1984) T-91 to T-96.

Consider the facts set forth in the level annuity example, but assume a 20% increase in income. Note that the J factor is applied to the income in *the year prior to the first year* of the holding period.

$$R_O = \frac{0.15 - 0.75\,(0.15 + 0.172608 \times 0.049252 - 0.100704) - (0.20 \times 0.049252)}{1 + (0.20 \times 0.3259)}$$

$$= \frac{0.15 - 0.043348 - 0.009850}{1 + 0.0652}$$

$$= \frac{0.096802}{1.0652}$$

$$= 0.09088$$

The capitalized value is $25,000/0.09088 = $275,088

The net operating incomes for the projection period that are implied by the curvilinear J-factor premise are calculated in the following table.

Period	1st Year Adjustment*		S_n		Periodic Adjustment		Base NOI[†]		NOI
1	$246.26	X	1/1.000000	=	$246	+	$25,000	=	$25,246
2	$246.26	X	1/0.465116	=	$529	+	$25,000	=	$25,529
3	$246.26	X	1/0.287977	=	$855	+	$25,000	=	$25,855
4	$246.26	X	1/0.200265	=	$1,230	+	$25,000	=	$26,230
5	$246.26	X	1/0.148316	=	$1,660	+	$25,000	=	$26,660
6	$246.26	X	1/0.114237	=	$2,156	+	$25,000	=	$27,156
7	$246.26	X	1/0.090360	=	$2,725	+	$25,000	=	$27,725
8	$246.26	X	1/0.072850	=	$3,380	+	$25,000	=	$28,380
9	$246.26	X	1/0.059574	=	$4,134	+	$25,000	=	$29,134
10	$246.26	X	1/0.049252	=	$5,000	+	$25,000	=	$30,000

*This adjustment was derived by multiplying the NOI ($25,000) by the assumed increase in the NOI (20%); the resulting figure ($5,000) was then multiplied by the sinking fund factor for the anticipated 15% equity yield rate over the 10-year projection period (1/S_n = 0.049252).

† The base NOI is the income for the year prior to the beginning of the projection period.

Mathematical proof of the example is provided below.

Valuation of Equity

Period	NOI		Debt Service		Cash to Equity		PVF at 15%		PV
1	$25,246	–	$20,772	=	$4,474	x	0.869565	=	$3,890
2	$25,529	–	$20,772	=	$4,757	x	0.756144	=	$3,597
3	$25,855	–	$20,772	=	$5,083	x	0.657516	=	$3,342
4	$26,230	–	$20,772	=	$5,458	x	0.571753	=	$3,121
5	$26,660	–	$20,772	=	$5,888	x	0.497177	=	$2,927
6	$27,156	–	$20,772	=	$6,384	x	0.432328	=	$2,760
7	$27,725	–	$20,772	=	$6,953	x	0.375937	=	$2,614
8	$28,380	–	$20,772	=	$7,608	x	0.326902	=	$2,487
9	$29,134	–	$20,772	=	$8,362	x	0.284262	=	$2,377
10	$30,000	–	$20,772	=	$9,228	x	0.247185	=	$2,281

$159,400* x 0.247185 = $39,401

Value of equity at 15% = $68,797

Check: $275,088 x 0.25 = $68,772

---

* The reversion is calculated as follows:

Resale ($275,088 x 1.20)	$330,106
Loan balance ($275,088 x 0.75)(1 – 0.1726)	170,706
Equity proceeds	$159,400

Use of the K factor

The K-factor formula, which is applied to income that changes on an exponential-curve (constant-ratio) basis, is expressed as

$$K = \frac{1 - (1 + C)^n / S^n}{(Y - C)a_n}$$

where:

K = factor
C = constant-ratio change in income
S^n = future value factor
Y = equity yield rate
a_n = present value factor for ordinary level annuity

When the general mortgage-equity formula is used to derive an overall capitalization rate applicable to an income expected to change on a constant-ratio basis, K is substituted for the denominator $(1 + \Delta_I J)$. The following example is based on the same property used for the level-income and J-factor examples, but assumes that NOI will increase by 2% per year, on a compound basis.

This property can be valued using the K factor in the mortgage-equity formula.

$$R_O = \frac{Y_E - M(Y_E + P \, 1/S_n - R_M) - \Delta_O \, 1/S_n}{K}$$

$$= \frac{0.15 - 0.75(0.15 + 0.172608 \times 0.049252 - 0.100704) - (0.20 \times 0.049252)}{1.070877}$$

$$= 0.090395$$

The capitalized value of the investment is $25,000/0.090395=$276,564

Note that the indicated values based on the J-factor and K-factor premises are very close, i.e., $275,088 and $276,564. The indicated value based on a level-income assumption is much lower, i.e., $238,264. This is because all of the yield has to occur on resale, not in increased income.

Based on the income data below, J factor and K factor income patterns are plotted on the graph in Figure C.1. Both examples assume a 20% increase in overall property value. In the J factor example, income is projected to increase by 20%. In the K factor example, income is projected to increase at a constant ratio of 2% per year. Under the J factor assumption, the value of the property is $275,088 and the R_o is 9.088%. Under the K factor assumption, the value of the property is $276,569, and the R_o is 9.039%.

Table C.1 **J-Factor Income Pattern and K-Factor Income Pattern**

	J Factor	K Factor
Year 1	$25,246	$25,000
Year 2	$25,529	$25,500
Year 3	$25,855	$26,010
Year 4	$26,230	$26,530
Year 5	$26,660	$27,060
Year 6	$27,156	$27,602
Year 7	$27,725	$28,154
Year 8	$28,380	$28,717
Year 9	$29,134	$29,291
Year 10	$30,000	$29,877

| Figure C.1 | **J-Factor and K-Factor Income Pattern Curves** |

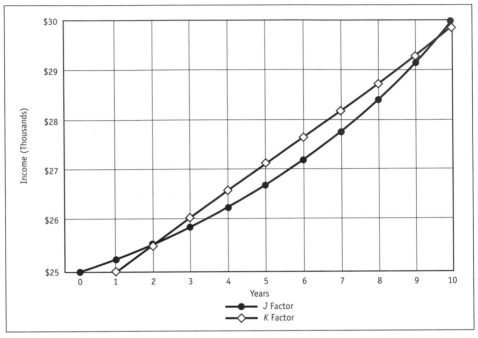

Courtesy of David C. Lennhoff

Solving for Equity Yield

Given an actual or proposed equity sale price and a forecast of equity benefits, an equity yield rate can be estimated. When level income is forecast, a formula is used. The calculations can be performed by iteration or with the financial functions of a calculator. When income is expected to change on a curvilinear basis or a constant-ratio basis, formulas must be used to solve for the yield. A calculator cannot be used to solve the problem conveniently, and the iteration technique is too time-consuming.

Level-Income Example

Consider a property that is purchased for $250,000. The net operating income is forecast to remain level at $35,000 per year and the buyer believes that property value will decline 15% over a five-year ownership period. The mortgage amount is $200,000 and monthly payments are at 10% interest with an amortization term of 20 years. The investment forecast is outlined below.

Purchase		Holding Period	
Sale price	$250,000	NOI	$35,000
Mortgage	200,000	Debt service	23,161*
Equity	$50,000	Pre-tax cash flow	$11,839

Resale After 5 Years

Sale price	$212,500
Mortgage balance	$179,605†
Equity reversion	$32,895
Original equity	$50,000
Equity change	-$17,105

* $200,000 x 0.115803 mortgage constant
† Unamortized portion of $200,000 mortgage at end of 5-year projection period.

$$R_E \text{ (equity capitalization rate)} = \frac{\$11,839}{\$50,000} = 0.236780$$

$$E \text{ (equity change)} = \frac{-\$17,105}{\$50,000} = -0.342100$$

The equity yield rate may now be computed through iteration or by using the formula and interpolation. Iteration is performed using the formula

$$Y_E = R_E + \Delta_E \, 1/S_n$$

Because the sinking fund factor for 5 years at the Y_E rate cannot be identified without knowing Y_E, a trial-and-error procedure must be used to develop Y_E. Without discounting, the 34.21% equity decline over the five-year holding period would subtract 6.84% each year from the equity capitalization rate of 23.67%. Consequently, Y_E will be less than 23.67% and more than 16.83% (23.67% – 6.84%).

The first computation is performed with a Y_E of 18%. When the correct equity yield rate is applied, the equation will balance.

Estimated Y_E	R_E	+	Δ_E	x	$1/S_n$	=	Indicated Y_E
0.1800	0.2368	+	(-0.3425)	x	0.139778	=	0.1889
0.2000	0.2368	+	(-0.3425)	x	0.134380	=	0.1908
0.1900	0.2368	+	(-0.3425)	x	0.137050	=	0.1899

Therefore, $Y_E = 0.1900$, or 19.0%

This procedure for computing Y_E is correct because Y_E is defined as the rate that makes the present value of the future equity benefits equal to the original equity. The future benefits in this case are the pre-tax cash flow of $11,839 per year for five years and the equity reversion of $32,895 at the end of the five-year period.

If Y_E is 19%, the present value of the two benefits can be computed.

$$\$11,839 \text{ x } 3.057635 = \$36,199$$
$$\$32,895 \text{ x } 0.419049 = \underline{13,785}$$
$$\$49,984$$

Thus, the equity yield rate has been proven to be 19.0%. Precision to 0.03% represents a level of accuracy in keeping with current practice and the normal requirements of the calculation. This example is based on level income, but the same procedure can be applied to changing income streams by incorporating J and K factors into the formula.

J-Factor Premise Example

Consider the information set forth in the previous example, but assume that income is expected to decline 15% according to the J-factor premise.

$$R_O = \$35{,}000/\$250{,}000 = 0.14, \qquad M = \$200{,}000/\$250{,}000 = 0.80$$

$$Y_E = R_E + \frac{\Delta_E}{S_n} + \frac{R_O \Delta_I}{1 - M} J$$

Try 15%,

$$0.2368 + {-}0.3421 \times 0.1483 + \frac{0.14 \text{ x} - 0.15}{0.2} \text{ x } 0.4861 = 0.135$$

Try 12%,

$$0.2368 + {-}0.3421 \times 0.1574 + \frac{0.14 \text{ x} - 0.15}{0.2} \text{ x } 0.5077 = 0.130$$

Try 13%,

$$0.2368 + {-}0.3421 \times 0.1543 + \frac{0.14 \text{ x} - 0.15}{0.2} \text{ x } 0.5004 = 0.131472$$

Therefore, $Y_E = 13.15\%$ (rounded)

K-Factor Premise Example

Consider the same information, but assume that income is expected to decrease at a compound rate of 3% per year, indicating a constant-ratio change in income.

$$Y_E = R_E + \Delta_E \, 1/S_n + \frac{R_O (K - 1)}{1 - M}$$

Try 13%,

$$0.2368 + {-}0.3421 \times 0.1543 + \frac{0.14 \text{ x } 0.9487 - 1}{0.2} = 0.148$$

Try 15%,

$$0.2368 + {-}0.3421 \times 0.1483 + \frac{0.14 \text{ x } 0.9497 - 1}{0.2} = 0.151$$

Therefore, $Y_E = 15.1\%$

Rate Analysis

Rate analysis allows an appraiser to test the reasonableness of the value conclusions derived through the application of overall capitalization rates. Once an overall capitalization rate has been developed with mortgage-equity analysis or another technique, its reliability and consistency with market expectations of equity yield and value change can be tested using Ellwood graphic analysis.

To create a graph for rate analysis, the appraiser chooses equity yield rates that cover a realistic range of rates expected and demanded by investors. It is often wise to include a rate that is at the low end of the range of market acceptance as well as a rate at the high end of the range. For the analysis to be useful to the client, the range of yield rates chosen should be in line with investors' perceptions of the market.

In most real estate investments, there is no assurance that the investment can be liquidated at the convenience of the equity investor or on the terms dictated by the investor. For example, in the early 1990s most liquidity evaporated from the market. Moreover, in negotiating a purchase price, the prospects for profit within a plausible range of possibilities may be greater than the chance of achieving a specific equity yield rate, which cannot be determined until the property is resold. However, the appraiser's value judgments can easily be subjected to realistic tests. The appraiser should ask the following questions.

- What resale prices correspond to various yield levels?
- Can the property suffer some loss in value and still produce an acceptable profit?
- How sensitive is the equity yield rate to possible fluctuations in value?
- What percentage of the investor's return is derived from annual cash flows, and what percentage comes from the reversion? (Reversion is generally considered riskier.)
- What prospective equity yield rates can be inferred from the overall capitalization rates found in the marketplace?

Many of these questions focus on the relationship between the change in property value and the equity yield rate. The unknown variable in rate analysis is the change in property value (Δ_0). The formula for the required change in property value in a level-income application is:

$$\Delta_0 = \frac{r - R_0}{1/S_n}$$

Level-Income Example

Consider an investment that will generate stable income and has an overall capitalization rate of 10%. The purchase can be financed with a 75% loan at 10% interest amortized over 25 years with level monthly payments. If the investment is held for 10 years, what levels of depreciation or appreciation should be expected with equity yield rates of 9%, 12%, and 15%?

To solve this problem the appraiser must first find the basic rate (r) and the sinking fund factor for each equity yield rate. The Ellwood Tables are the source of the figures listed below.

Y_E	r	$1/S_n$
9%	0.096658	0.065820
12%	0.105185	0.056984
15%	0.113584	0.049252

When the difference between r and the overall rate (R_O) is divided by the corresponding sinking fund factor, the result is the expected change in property value. If r is greater than R_O, a value increase is indicated; if r is less than R_O, value loss is indicated. Analysis of the 10% overall capitalization rate is shown below.

$$Y_E = \frac{r - R_O}{1/S_n}$$

9%	−0.0508 (5.1% depreciation)
12%	0.0910 (9.1% appreciation)
15%	0.2758 (27.6% appreciation)

The formula produces answers consistent with the notion that a loss is negative and a gain is positive. In some texts the numerator in this formula is expressed as $R_O - r$. Use of this formula results in a change of sign—i.e., positive answers indicate depreciation and negative answers indicate appreciation.

J-Factor Premise

A similar analysis can be performed when income is presumed to change commensurately with value according to the J-factor premise. In this case the expected change in overall property value is calculated by dividing $(r - R_O)$ by $(R_O J + 1/S_n)$.

Graphic Rate Analysis

Various systems have been developed to employ mortgage-equity concepts in graphic rate analysis. The graphic analysis of capitalization rates is a helpful analytical tool used by practicing appraisers and investment analysts. Rate analysis in graphic or tabular form is particularly useful in interpreting market data. Although analyzing a market-oriented overall capitalization rate cannot reveal a property's eventual equity yield rate or resale price, the analysis can reveal combinations of Y_E and Δ_O implicit in the overall rate. Thus, an appraiser can use rate analysis to decide whether a particular combination of Y_E and Δ_O is consistent with market behavior.

The accompanying figures illustrate two types of graphic analysis. Figure C.2 shows Ellwood-style graphic analysis, with time on the horizontal axis and the percentage change in property value on the vertical axis. Figure C.3 illustrates another type of graphic analysis with the equity yield rate on the horizontal axis and the percentage change in value on the vertical axis. Graphs like these can be constructed manually by plotting three or more key points and connecting the points with a smooth curve; they can also be constructed using a computer.

The graph in Figure C.2 shows change in value and income under the J-factor premise with respect to time for equity yield rates of 5%, 10%, 15%, 20%, and 25%. It is assumed that $R_O = 0.11, I = 0.125, R_M = 0.135, M = 0.7$, and $\Delta_O = \Delta_I$.

Figure C.2 | **Ellwood-style Graphic Analysis**

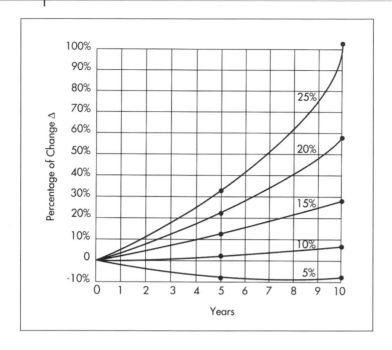

Figure C.3 | **Alternative Graphic Analysis**

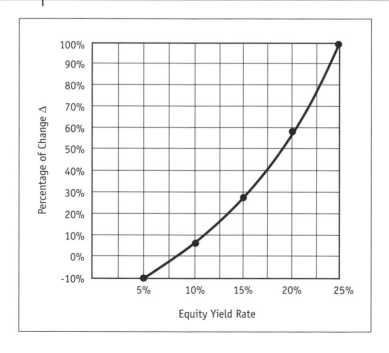

The graph in Figure C.3 shows the change in value and income under the J-factor premise for equity yield rates ranging from 5% to 25% over a 10-year holding period. Again, it is assumed that $R_O = 0.11$, $I = 0.125$, $R_M = 0.135$, $M = 0.7$, and $\Delta_O = \Delta_I$.

After a graph is created, it must be interpreted by the appraiser. Usually the appraiser determines the range of property value changes (Δ_O) anticipated by the market and then forms an opinion as to the reasonableness of the overall capitalization rate. If the value changes are in line with the expectations of market participants and there is nothing unusual about the subject property, the overall rate being tested may be reasonable. If the value changes are not within the range expected by the marketplace, the overall capitalization rate should either be considered unreasonable and in need of further analysis or must be explained and accounted for.

Rate Extraction

Rate extraction is a technique that allows an appraiser to infer the market's expectation of yield and change in property value from a market-oriented overall capitalization rate. The key is to determine what assumptions about the yield rate and the change in property value are consistent with the overall capitalization rates derived from comparable sales. Although an analyst cannot identify a specific yield rate or change in value using this approach, he or she can determine what change in property value is needed to produce a given yield rate. That is, for each assumed yield rate, there is only one assumption about the change in property value that can be used with that rate to obtain the overall capitalization rate implied by comparable sales.

The following example illustrates this technique. The subject property is an apartment complex. Data on three comparable properties are given.

Factual Data on Three Apartment Complexes

	Sale 1	Sale 2	Sale 3
Number of units	240	48	148
Sale price	$4,678,000	$811,000	$3,467,000
Cash down payment	$1,300,000	$462,145	$1,370,000
Gross income	$594,540	$126,240	$507,120
NOI	$368,600	$71,500	$293,400

Comparative Factors

	Sale 1	Sale 2	Sale 3
Price per unit	$19,492	$16,896	$23,426
Gross income per unit			
Annually	$2,477	$2,638	$3,426
Monthly	$206	$219	$285
Gross income multiplier (GIM)	7.870	6.420	6.830
Overall capitalization rate (R_O)	0.079	0.088	0.085
Loan-to-value ratio (M)	0.722	0.430	0.605
Mortgage constant (R_M)	0.107	0.127	0.136
Percent paid off (P)	−0.125	0.016	0.032
Equity capitalization rate (R_E)	0.006	0.059	0.006
Debt coverage ratio (DCR)	1.021	1.610	1.030

Using the mortgage-equity J-factor formula, pairs of Y_E and Δ_O can be extracted for each comparable sale. The formula for change in income and value is

$$\Delta_{O=I} = \frac{Y_E - M\ (Y_E + P\ 1/S_n - R_M) - R_O}{R_O\ J + 1/S_n}$$

The overall rate for each of the sales can be used in this formula to solve for the combinations of Y_E and Δ_O that would produce that overall capitalization rate. These data are shown in the table below.

Calculated Required Changes for the Three Sales
(Five-Year Projection)

	% $\Delta_{O = I}$		
%Y_E	Sale 1	Sale 2	Sale 3
10	19.9	10.7	16.1
12	23.2	16.8	20.8
14	26.7	23.3	25.7
16	30.5	30.3	31.0
18	34.5	37.8	36.6
20	38.8	45.8	42.7
22	43.4	54.3	49.1
24	48.3	63.4	55.9
26	53.7	73.2	63.2
28	59.0	83.4	70.9
30	64.9	94.6	79.2

Note that the rate of change in propety value is assumed to equal the rate of change in income. This reflects the appraiser's belief that this assumption is consistent with market perceptions. The relationship between equity yield and change in value and income can now be graphed (see Figure C.4).

Figure C.4 | **Graphic Illustration of the Relationship Between Equity Yield and Total Change in Value and Income**

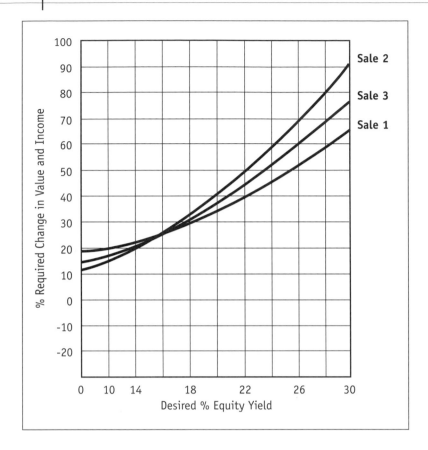

Once the graph is completed, the appraiser can draw certain conclusions. If the sales used accurately reflect market perceptions, every pair of equity yield rate and change in property value is a perfect pair. When the figures are inserted into the mortgage-equity formula to derive an overall capitalization rate, the resulting value estimate will be market-oriented.

In this case any pair of Y_E and Δ_O that does not coincide with the lines on the graph is not market-oriented. The lines have different slopes and cross at some point because each sale has a different loan-to-value ratio (M). Furthermore, because of the differences in the loan-to-value ratios, we would expect some variation in the yield rate that equity investors would require for each of the sales. For example, Sale 1 had the highest loan-to-value ratio and, therefore, probably had the highest required yield rate because of its greater risk. The curves indicate reasonable assumptions about yield rates and changes in value that are consistent with the prices paid for comparable sales and the manner in which they were financed.

The graph can also be used to reflect the most likely pair of Y_E and Δ_O for developing an overall capitalization rate. By verifying current investor perceptions of the yield anticipated for the type of property being appraised, the appraiser can determine the necessary property value change. Then, with the mortgage-equity formula, the overall capitalization rate can be calculated. This overall rate will reflect typical investor assumptions for both yield and change in property value.

Compound Interest (Future Value of $1)

This factor reflects the amount to which an investment or deposit will grow in a given number of time periods, including the accumulation of interest at the effective rate per period. It is also known as the *amount of one.*

$$S = (1 + i)^n$$

Where: S^n = future value factor

         i = effective rate of interest

         n = number of compounding periods

and $S^n = (e)^{in}$ for continuous compounding

Where: S^n = future value factor

         i = nominal rate of interest

         n = number of years

         e = 2.718282

This factor is used to solve problems dealing with compound growth.

Example 1

What is the future value of $10,000 assuming interest at 6% compounded annually for 10 years?

$$\$10,000 \times 1.790848 = \$17,908.48$$

Example 2

What is the future value of $10,000 assuming interest at 6% compounded annually for 10 years and 7 months?

$$\$10,000 \times 1.790848 \times 1.035000 = \$18,535.28$$

This calculation assumes simple interest for any time that is less than one conversion period.

Example 3

A property is sold for $135,000, but five years previously it was sold for $100,000. What is the trend in its sale price expressed as a monthly compound rate of growth?

$$\$135,000 \div \$100,000 = 1.350000 \text{ (future value factor)}$$

Scan the table of future value factors, monthly frequency, for 1.350000 at five years. The closest match is found at a 6% nominal rate, so the monthly rate of growth is approximately 0.5%.

Example 4

How long would it take prices to double if a 6% rate of inflation is assumed?

$$2.00 \div 1.00 = 2.000000 \text{ (future value factor)}$$

Scan the table of future value factors at 6% nominal interest for 2.000000. Assuming annual frequency, the target is between the factors for 11 and 12 years. Visual interpolation indicates an answer of slightly less than 12 years. Mathematical straight-line interpolation produces an answer of 11.9 years.

$$(2.000000 - 1.898299)/(2.012196 - 1.898299) + 11 = 11.9 \text{ years}$$

When money is invested or deposited at the beginning of a period in an account that bears interest at a fixed rate, it grows according to the interest rate and the number of compounding (conversion) periods that it remains in the account. To illustrate how and why this growth occurs, consider an investment of $1.00, a nominal interest rate of 10% with annual compounding, and an investment holding period of five years.

Original investment	$1.00
Interest, first year at 10%	0.10
Accumulation, end of 1 year	$1.10
Interest, second year at 10%	0.11
Accumulation, end of 2 years	$1.21
Interest, third year at 10%	0.121
Accumulation, end of 3 years	$1.331
Interest, fourth year at 10%	0.1331
Accumulation, end of 4 years	$1.4641
Interest, fifth year at 10%	0.14641
Accumulation, end of 5 years	$1.61051

One dollar grows to $1.61051 in five years with interest at 10%, so the future value of $1 factor at 10% annually for five years is 1.610510; $1,000 would grow 1,000 times this amount to $1,610.51 over the same five years at the same 10% annual rate. When interest is not collected or withdrawn as it is earned, it is added to the capital amount and additional interest accumulates in subsequent periods. This process is called *compounding*.

The results of compounding can be calculated with the formula $(1 + i)^n$, where n is the number of compounding periods and i is the interest rate per period.

n			
1	$1.10 \times 1 = 1.10^1$	=	1.10
2	$1.10 \times 1.10 = 1.10^2$	=	1.21
3	$1.10 \times 1.10 \times 1.10 = 1.10^3$	=	1.331
4	$1.10 \times 1.10 \times 1.10 \times 1.10 = 1.10^4$	=	1.461
5	$1.10 \times 1.10 \times 1.10 \times 1.10 \times 1.10 = 1.10^5$	=	1.61051

Thus, the factors in this table, the amount of one or the future value of $1, reflect the growth of $1.00 accumulating at interest for the number of compounding periods shown at the left and right sides of each page of tables. For example, the 10% annual column reveals a factor of 2.593742 for 10 periods. This means that $1.00 deposited at 10% interest compounded annually for 10 years will grow to $1.00 x 2.593742, or just over $2.59. In other words, $1.10^{10} = 2.593742$. The factors for seven and eight years indicate that $1.00 (or any investment earning 10% per year) will double in value in approximately 7.5 years. Similarly, an investment of $10,000 made 10 years ago, earning no periodic income during the 10-year holding period, must be liquidated in the current market at $10,000 x 2.593742, or $2.5,937.42, to realize a 10% return on the original investment.

This factor reflects the growth of the original deposit measured from the *beginning deposit period.* Thus, at the end of the first period at a rate of 10%, the original $1.00 has grown to $1.10 and the factor is 1.100000, as shown above.

Reversion Factors (Present Value of $1)

This factor is the present value of $1 to be collected at a given future time discounted at the effective interest rate for the number of periods between now and the date of collection. It is the reciprocal of the corresponding compound interest factor.

$$1/S^n = \frac{1}{(1 + i)^n}$$

Where: $1/S^n$ – present value factor

  i = effective rate of interest

  n = number of compounding periods

and $1/S^n = \frac{1}{(e)^{in}}$ for continuous compounding

Where: $1/S^n$ = present value factor

  i = nominal rate of interest

  n = number of years

  $e = 2.718282$

This table is used to solve problems that involve compound discounting.

Example 1

What is the present value of $10,000 to be received in 10 years, assuming an interest rate of 6% and annual compounding?

$$\$10,000 \times 0.558395 = \$5,583.95$$

Example 2

What is the present value of $10,000 to be received in 10 years and 7 months, assuming an interest rate of 6% and annual compounding?

$$\$10,000 \times 0.558395 \times 0.966184 = \$5,395.12$$

This calculation assumes simple interest for any time that is less than one conversion period.

Example 3

Assuming a 6% rate and annual compounding, what is the present value of the following cash flows: $1,000 in one year, $2,000 in two years, and $3,000 in three years?

Cash Flows		Present Value Factor		Present Value
$1,000	X	0.943396	=	$943.40
2,000	X	0.889996	=	1,779.99
3,000	X	0.839619	=	2,518.86
Present value				$5,242.25

Example 4

A property is sold for $100,000, but five years previously it was sold for $135,000. What is the depreciation in its sale price expressed as a monthly compound rate?

$$\$100,000/\$135,000 = 0.740741 \text{ (present value factor)}$$

Scan the tables of present value factors, monthly frequency, for 0.740741 at five years. The closest match is found at 6% nominal rate, so the monthly rate is approximately 0.5%.

Example 5

How long will it take $1.00 to be worth $0.50 assuming a 6% rate of inflation?

$$0.50/1.00 = 0.500000 \text{ (present value factor)}$$

Scan the tables of present value factors at 6% nominal interest for 0.500000. Assuming annual frequency, the target is between the factors for 11 and 12 years. Visual interpolation indicates an answer of slightly less than 12 years. Mathematical straight-line interpolation produces an answer of 11.9 years.

$$(0.526788 - 0.500000)/(0.526788 - 0.496969) + 11 = 11.9 \text{ years}$$

As demonstrated in the discussion of future value, $1.00 compounded annually at 10% will grow to $1.610151 in five years. Accordingly, the amount that will grow to $1.00 in five years is $1.00 divided by 1.61051, or $0.62092. In the 10% table, the present value of $1 factor for five years is 0.620921. In other words, $1.00 to be collected five years from today has a present value of $0.620921 when discounted at 10% per year. And $10,000 to be collected five years from today, discounted at the same 10% annual rate, has a present value of $10,000 x 0.620921, or $6,209.21. The $10,000 sum to be received in five years is a *reversion*.

Ordinary Level Annuity
(Present Value of $1 per Period)

This factor represents the present value of a series of future installments or payments of $1 per period for a given number of periods discounted at an effective interest rate. It is commonly referred to as the *Inwood coefficient.*

$$a_{\overline{n}|} = \frac{1 - 1/S^n}{i}$$

Where: $a_{\overline{n}|}$ = level annuity factor

$1/S^n$ = present value factor

i = rate of interest yield

This table is used in solving problems that deal with the compound discounting of cash flows that are level or effectively level.

Example 1

What is the present value of an ordinary annuity of $1,000 per month for 10 years, assuming an interest rate of 6%?

$$\$1,000 \times 90.073453 = \$90,073.45$$

Assuming payments are made in advance, the *PV* of this annuity would be

$$\$1,000 \times 90.073453 \times 1.005000 = \$90,523.82$$

or

$$\$1,000 \times 90.073453/0.995025 = \$90,523.81$$

Example 2

What is the present value of an ordinary annuity of $1,000 per month for 10 years and 7 months, assuming an interest rate of 6%?

$1,000 x 90.073453	= $90,073.45
$1,000 x 6.862074 x 0.549633* =	3,771.62
	$93,845.07

* Reversion factor for 120 months

Assuming payments in advance, the *PV* of this annuity would be

$$\$93,845.07 \times 1.005000 = \$94,314.30$$

or

$$\$93,845.07/0.995025 = \$94,314.28$$

Example 3

Assuming a 6% annual discount rate, what is the present value of an ordinary annuity consisting of the following cash flows: $1,000 per year for five years, then $2,000 per year for five years, and then $3,000 per year for five years?

$1,000 x 4.212364 =	$ 4,212.36
2,000 x (7.360087 – 4.21 2364) =	6,295.45
3,000 x (9.71 2249 – 7.360087) =	7,056.49
	$17,564.30

Assuming payments are made in advance, the *PV* of this annuity would be

$$\$17,564.30 \times 1.060000 = \$18,618.16$$

or

$$\$17,564.30/0.943396 = \$18,618.16$$

Example 4

If a 10-year ordinary level annuity of $1,000 per month has a present value of $90,000, what is the indicated interest or yield rate?

$$\$90,000/\$1,000 = 90.000000 \text{ (present value factor)}$$

Scan the ordinary level annuity tables at 10 years, monthly frequency, for 90.000000. The closest match is a 6% nominal rate.

Finding the present value of a future income stream is a discounting procedure in which future payments are treated as a series of reversions. The present value of a series of future receipts may be quickly ascertained using the precomputed present value of $1 per period factors for the selected discount rate provided the receipts are all equal in amount, equally spaced over time, and receivable at the end of each period.

If, for example, 10% per year is a fair rate of interest or discount, it would be justifiable to pay $0.909091 (i.e., the annual present value of $1 at 10%) for the right to receive $1.00 one year from today. Assuming that the cost of this right is $0.909091, the $1.00 received at the end of the year could be divided between principal and interest as follows.

Return of principal	$0.90909
Interest on principal for one year @ 10%	0.09091
Total received	$1.00000

If approximately $0.091 is the present value of the right to receive $1.00 of income one year from today at 10% interest, the present value of the right to receive $1.00 two years from today is less. According to the present value formula, the present value of $1.00 to he received two years from today is $0.826446. The present value of $1.00 payable at the end of two years can be confirmed with these calculations.

Return on principal	$0.82645*
Interest for first year at 10% on $0.82645	0.08264
	$0.90909
Interest for second year at 10% on $0.90909	0.09091
Total principal repayment + interest received	$1.00000

*Present value factor, 0.826446 x $1.00 = $0.82645 (rounded).

Similarly, the present value of the right to receive $1.00 at the end of three years is $0.751315, at the end of four years it is $0.683013, and at the end of the fifth year it is $0.620921. The present value of these rights to receive income at one-year intervals for five years is accumulated as the present value of $1.00 per year. This is known as the *compound interest valuation premise,* also referred to as the *ordinary annuity factor.* Therefore, the sum of the five individual rights to receive $1.00 each year, payable at the end of the year, for five years is $3.790787 (i.e., the 10% annual present value of $1 per period factor for five years).

Sum of Individual Present Values of $1.00

Payable at the End of the Period

Present value of $1.00 due in 1 year	$0.909091*
Present value of $1.00 due in 2 years	0.826446*
Present value of $1.00 due in 3 years	0.751315*
Present value of $1.00 due in 4 years	0.683013*
Present value of $1.00 due in 5 years	0.620921*
Total present value of $1.00 per year for 5 years	$3.790786**

* 10% present value of $1 factor.
**10% present value of $1 per period factor is 3.790787; the difference is due to rounding.

The present value of $1 per period table for five annual discounting periods (n = 5) gives a factor that represents the total of the present values of a series of periodic amounts of $1.00, payable at the end of each period. The calculation presented above is unnecessary because multiplying $1.00 by the factor for the present value of $1 per year for five years produces the same present value ($1.00 x 3.790787 = $3.790787).

For appraisal purposes, the present value of $1 per period factor may be multiplied by a periodic income with the characteristics of an ordinary annuity to derive the present value of the right to receive that income stream. The future payments of income provide for recapture of, and interest on, this present value. Present value factors are multipliers and perform the same function as capitalization rates.

The 10% ordinary annuity factor for five years, 3.790787, represents the present value of each $1.00 of annual end-of-year collection based on a nominal annual discount rate of 10%. Tables and formulas for semiannual, quarterly, and monthly payments are also available. The ordinary annuity factor for semiannual payments in the 10% nominal annual rate table is 7.721735. If payment continues for five years, each $1.00 of semiannual payment represents $10.00 received, but reflects only $7.72 of the discounted present value of monthly payments for five years. In the table for a 10% nominal rate, the monthly factor is 47.065369, indicating that the present value of an ordinary annuity income stream of 60 monthly payments of $1.00 each discounted at a nominal rate of 10% is 47.065369 x $1.00, or about $47.065.

Based on a 10% nominal rate, semiannual payments would involve an effective rate of 5%. In the 5% annuity table, the factor for 10 periods is 7.721735; this is the same factor shown in the 10% semiannual table for a five-year period. Thus, when tables are not available at the effective rate, annuity factors for more frequent payment periods can be derived using nominal annual rate tables. Preprogrammed financial calculators can be used to facilitate these calculations.

In computing the present value of an annuity income stream, it may be desirable to assume that periodic payments are made at the beginning rather than the end of each payment period. The present value of an annuity payable in advance is equal to the present value of an ordinary annuity in arrears multiplied by the base (i.e., 1 plus the effective interest rate for the discounting period: $1 + i$). Thus, the present value of semiannual payments in advance over a five-year period discounted at a nominal rate of 10% becomes $1.00 x 7.721735 x 1.05 = $8.107822, or $8.11, compared to $7.72 as computed for payments received at the end of each payment period.

Ordinary Annuities Changing in Constant Amounts

Present Value of Annual Payments Starting at $1 and Changing in Constant Amounts

$$PVF = (1 + hn)a_{\overline{n}|} - \frac{h(n - a_{\overline{n}|})}{i}$$

Where: PVF = present value factor

h^* = annual increase or decrease after 1st year

n = number of years

$a_{\overline{n}|}$ = PVF for ordinary level annuity

i = rate of interest yield

*h is positive for an increase and negative for a decrease

This table is used to solve problems dealing with the compound discounting of cash flows that are best represented by a straight-line pattern of change.

Example 1

Assuming a 15% interest or yield rate, what is the present value of an ordinary annuity consisting of 10 annual cash flows that start at $10,000 and increase $1,000 per year?

$$\$10,000 \text{ x } 6.7167 = \$67,167$$

Assuming payments are made in advance, the PV of this annuity would be

$$\$67,167 \text{ x } 1.150000 = \$77,242$$

or

$$\$67,167/0.869565 = \$77,242$$

Example 2

Assuming a 15% interest or yield rate, what is the present value of an ordinary annuity consisting of 10 annual cash flows that start at $10,000 and increase $300 per year?

$$\$10,000 \times (5.3584 + 5.6979)/2 = \$55,282$$

or

$$\$10,000 \times (5.018769 + 16.979477 \times 0.03) = \$55,281.53$$

Example 3

There are five years remaining on a lease that provides a level income of $1,000 per year. During this period inflation will cause purchasing power to decline an average of 10% per year (on a straight-line basis). What is the value of the income expressed in constant dollars and discounted at 6%?

$$\$1,000 \times (.90 \times 4.212364 - 7.934549 \times 0.10) = \$2,997.67$$

Proof:

Year	Income	x	Inflation Factor	x	PVF @ 6%	=	Value
1	$1,000	X	0.90	X	0.943396	=	$849.06
2	1,000	X	0.80	X	0.889996	=	712.00
3	1,000	X	0.70	X	0.839619	=	587.73
4	1,000	X	0.60	X	0.792094	=	475.26
5	1,000	X	0.50	X	0.747258	=	373.63
							$2,997.68

This table is similar to the ordinary level annuity table, but the annual receipts are converted into constant dollar amounts. For instance, assume that the amount to be received one year from today is $10,000, additional future receipts are expected to increase $1,000 per year for the next nine years, and 15% per year is a fair rate of interest. According to the 15% annual present value of $1 factor, it would be justifiable to pay $67,167 for the right to receive $10,000 one year from today and nine additional payments growing at $1,000 per year for nine additional years. The table indicates that the factor to be applied to the initial receipt is 6.7167.

Proof:

Year	Income	x	Present Value Factor	=	Present Value
1	$10,000	X	0.869565	=	$8,695.65
2	11,000	X	0.756144	=	8,317.58
3	12,000	X	0.657516	=	7,890.19
4	13,000	X	0.571753	=	7,432.79
5	14,000	X	0.497177	=	6,960.48
6	15,000	X	0.432328	=	6,484.92
7	16,000	X	0.375937	=	6,014.99
8	17,000	X	0.326902	=	5,557.33
9	18,000	X	0.284262	=	5,116.72
10	19,000	X	0.247185	=	4,696.52
	Present value				$67,167.17

$$\frac{\text{Present Value}}{\text{Initial receipt}} = \text{Factor}$$

$$\frac{\$67,167.17}{\$10,000.00} = 6.7167$$

Ordinary Annuities Changing in Constant Ratio

Present Value of Annual Payments Starting at $1 and Changing in Constant Ratio

$$PVF = \frac{1 - (1 + x)^n/(1 + i)^n}{i - x}$$

Where: PVF = present value factor

x* = constant ratio change in income

n = number of years

i = rate of interest or yield

* x is positive for an increase and negative for a decrease

This table is used to solve problems dealing with the compound discounting of cash flows that are best represented by an exponential-curve pattern of change.

Example 1

Assuming a 15% interest or yield rate, what is the present value of an ordinary annuity consisting of 10 annual cash flows that start at $10,000 and increase 10% per year compounded?

$10,000 x 7.1773 = $71,773

Assuming payments are made in advance, the *PV* of this annuity would be

$71,773 x 1.150000 = $82,539

$71,773/0.869565 = $82,539

Example 2

Assuming a 15% interest or yield rate, what is the present value of an ordinary annuity consisting of 10 annual cash flows that start at $10,000 and decrease 3% per year compounded?

$10,000 x 4.5429 = $45,429

Example 3

There are five years remaining on a lease that provides a level income of $1,000 per year. During this period inflation will cause purchasing power to decline 10% per year on a compound basis. What is the value of the income expressed in constant dollars and discounted at 6%?

$1,000 x 0.90 x 3.4922 = $3,142.98

Proof:

Year	Income	x	Inflation Factor	x	PVF @ 6%	=	Value
1	$1,000	x	0.900000	x	0.943396	=	$849.06
2	1,000	x	0.810000	x	0.889996	=	720.90
3	1,000	x	0.729000	x	0.839619	=	612.08
4	1,000	x	0.656100	x	0.792094	=	516.69
5	1,000	x	0.590490	x	0.747258	=	441.25
							$3,142.98

Sinking Fund Factors

Periodic Payment to Grow to $1

This factor represents the level periodic investment or deposit required to accumulate to $1 in a given number of periods including interest at the effective rate. It is commonly known as the *amortization rate* and is the reciprocal of the corresponding sinking fund accumulation factor.

$$1/S_{\overline{n}|} = \frac{i}{S^n - 1}$$

Where: $1/S_{\overline{n}|}$ = sinking fund factor

i = effective rate of interest

n = number of compounding periods

S^n = future value factor

This table is used to solve problems that involve calculating required sinking fund deposits or providing for the change in capital value in investment situations where the income or payments are level.

Example 1

Assuming a 6% interest rate, what monthly, end-of-period deposit would be required to yield $10,000 in 10 years?

$$\$10,000 \times 0.006102 = \$61.02$$

Assuming deposits are made at the beginning of the period, what amount would be required?

$$\$10,000 \times 0.006102/1.005 = \$60.72$$

Example 2

Assuming a 6% interest rate, what monthly, end-of-period deposit would be required to yield $10,000 in 10 years and 7 months?

$$\$10,000/(1/0.006102 + 1.819397*/0.140729) = \$56.56$$

* future value factor for 120 months

Assuming deposits are made at the beginning of the period, what amount would be required?

$$\$56.56/1.005 = \$56.28$$

Example 3

What is the annual constant for a direct reduction loan at 12% interest with monthly payments for 25 years?

$$0.12 + 12 \times 0.000532 = 0.126384$$

In actual practice, loan payments are rounded up to the nearest penny. Published tables of annual constants reflect this practice. In a typical table of annual constants, factors are calculated for each $1,000 of loan, so the sinking fund factor is rounded up to the fifth decimal place. On this basis, the constant for a 12%, 25-year loan would be

$$0.12 + 12 \times 0.000540 = 0.126480$$

Example 4

Assuming a 12% interest or yield rate, what monthly payment would provide for interest and 40% amortization of a $100,000 loan in 10 years?

$$\$100,000 \times (0.12/12 + 0.4 \times 0.004347) = \$1,173.88$$

Example 5

A property has an anticipated net operating income of $10,000 per year for the next five years. The trend in prices indicates a 15% increase in value over this period of time. What is the calculated value of the property assuming a 12% yield rate?

$$\$10,000/(0.12 - 0.15 \times 0.157410) = \$103,747$$

When deposits are made at the end of each compounding period, sinking fund factors reflect the fractional portion of $1.00 that must be deposited periodically at a specified interest rate to accumulate to $1.00 by the end of the series of deposits.

If $10,000 is to be accumulated over a 10-year period and annual deposits are compounded at 10% interest, the factor shown on the 10-year line of the annual column in the 10% sinking fund table indicates that each annual deposit must amount to $10,000 x 0.062745, or $627.45.

Sinking Fund Accumulation Factors

Future Value of Periodic Payments of $1

This factor represents the total accumulation of principal and interest on a series of deposits or installments of $1 per period for a given number of periods with interest at the effective rate per period. It is also known as the *amount of one per period*. It is the reciprocal of the corresponding sinking factor.

$$S_{\overline{n}|} = \frac{S^n - 1}{i}$$

Where: $S_{\overline{n}|}$ = sinking fund accumulation factor

i = effective rate of interest

S^n = future value factor

This table is used to solve problems that involve the growth of sinking funds or the calculation of capital recovery in investment situations where the income or payments are level.

Example 1

Assuming a 6% nominal interest rate, how much money would be accumulated if deposits of $100 were made at the end of each month for a period of 10 years?

$$\$100 \times 163.879347 = \$16,387.93$$

Assuming the deposits were at the beginning of each month, how much money would be accumulated?

$$\$16,387.93 \times 1.005 = \$16,469.87$$

Example 2

Assuming a 6% nominal interest rate, how much money would be accumulated if deposits of $100 were made at the end of each month for a period of 10 years and 7 months?

$$\$100 \times (163.879347 + 7.105879 \times 1.819397^*) = \$17,680.78$$

* Future value factor for 120 months

or

$$\$100 \times (7.105879 + 163.879347 \times 1.035529^*) = \$17,680.77$$

* Future value factor for 7 months

Example 3

Assuming a 6% nominal interest rate and daily compounding, how much money would be accumulated in a Keogh Retirement Plan if deposits of $1,200 were made at the end of each year for 10 years?

$$\$1,200 \times 13.294699 = \$15,953.64$$

Assuming the deposits were made at the beginning of each year, how much money would be accumulated?

$$\$15,953.64 \times 1.061831 = \$16,940.07$$

Example 4

Given a $100,000 loan with monthly payments of $908.71 including nominal interest at 10%, how much will be paid off in 10 years?

$$[\$908.71 - (\$100,000 \times 0.10/12)] \times 204.844979 = \$15,440.53$$

Sinking fund accumulation factors are similar to the future value of $1 (amount of one) factors except that deposits are periodic (in a series) and are assumed to be made at the *end* of the first compounding period and at the *end* of each period thereafter. Thus, the initial deposit, which is made at the end of the first period, has earned no interest and the factor for this period is 1.000000.

If compounding at 10% per year for 10 years is assumed, a factor of 15.937425 reveals that a series of 10 deposits of $1.00 each made at the end of each year for 10 years will accumulate to $1.00 x 15.937425, or almost $15.94.

Direct Reduction Loan Factors

Monthly Payment and Annual Constant per $1 of Loan

Payment: $$1/a_{\overline{n}|} = \frac{i}{1 - 1/S^n}$$

Annual constant: $R_M = 12/a_{\overline{n}|}$

Where: $1/a_{\overline{n}|}$ = direct reduction loan factor

$1/S^n$ = present value factor

i = effective rate of interest

R_M = annual constant

Part paid off: $$P = \frac{R_M - 12i}{R_{MP} - 12i}$$

Where: R_M = actual annual constant

R_{MP} = annual constant for projection period

i = effective rate of interest

This table is used to solve problems dealing with monthly payment, direct reduction loans. Payments and constants for quarterly, semiannual and annual payment loans can be obtained by calculating the reciprocals of the present value of $1 per period factors.

Example 1

What is the level monthly payment and annual debt service for a direct reduction loan of $100,000, assuming nominal interest at 10% and full amortization over 25 years?

$$\$100,000 \times 0.0090870 = \qquad \$908.70^*$$
$$\$100,000 \times 0.1090441 = \$10,904.41^*$$

* In actual practice, the payment would be rounded up to $908.71 and the debt service would be $908.71 x 12 = $10,904.52.

Example 2

How much of the loan in Example 1 would be paid off in 10 years?

$$\$100,000 \text{ x } 0.1544 = \$15,440$$

or

$$\$100,000 \text{ x } [(\$10,904.52/\$100,000 - 0.10)/(0.1585809 - 0.10)] = \$15,440.52$$

Example 3

What discounted price would achieve a 14% yield for this loan?
Assuming full term:

$$\$10,904.41/0.1444513 = \$75,488.49$$

Assuming a 10-year call:

$$\$10,904.52/0.1863197 = \$58,525.86$$
$$(\$100,000 - \$15,440.53) \text{ x } 0.248603* = \underline{21,021.74}$$
$$\$79,547.60$$

* Present value for 120 months

Example 4

What is the level monthly payment and annual debt service for a direct reduction
loan of $100,000, assuming nominal interest at 10% and full amortization over 25
years and 7 months?

$$\$100,000/(1/0.0090870 + 0.082940*/0.1476586) = \$904.09$$
$$\$904.09 \text{ x } 12 = \$10,849.08$$

* Present value factor for 300 months

Example 5

How much of the loan in Example 4 would be paid off in 10 years?

$$\$100,000 \text{ x } [(\$10,849.08/\$100,000 - 0.10)/(0.1585809 - 0.10)] = \$14,494.14$$

These factors, which are known as *mortgage constants for loan amortiza-*
tion, reflect the amount of ordinary annuity payment that $1.00 will purchase. They
indicate the periodic payment that will extinguish the debt and pay interest on the
declining balance of the debt over the life of the payments. The mortgage constant
may be expressed in terms of the periodic payments. A mortgage constant related to
a monthly payment is the ratio of the monthly payment amount to the original
amount of the loan. Whether payments are monthly, semiannual or annual, the
mortgage constant is usually expressed in terms of the total payments in one year as
a percentage of the original loan amount. This is called the *annual constant* and is
represented by the symbol R_M. As the loan is paid off and the outstanding balance is
reduced, a new annual mortgage constant can be calculated as the ratio of total

annual payments to the unpaid balance of the loan at that time.

A loan of $10,000 to be amortized in 10 annual end-of-year payments at a mortgage interest rate of 10% would require level annual payments of $10,000 x 0.162745, the 10% direct reduction annual factor for 10 years. If monthly payments were made at 10% over 10 years, the amount of each payment would be $132.15 (i.e., $10,000 x 0.013215). The annual mortgage constant in this case would be 0.158580, or 12 x 0.013215.

Direct reduction factors consist of the interest rate plus the sinking fund factor at the specific point in time. They are reciprocals of the corresponding ordinary level-annuity factors.

J Factors

Adjustment Factors for Changes in Income

Ellwood: $J = 1/S_{\overline{n}|}[n/(1 - 1/S^n) - (1/Y_E)]$

Straight-line: $J = (1/n - 1/S_{\overline{n}|})/Y_E$

Where: J = factor

$1/S_{\overline{n}|}$ = SFF at equity yield rate for projection period

n = projection period

$1/S^n$ = reversion factor at Y_E for projection period

Y_E = equity yield rate

This table is used to solve mortgage/equity problems that involve changing income. The factors can be substituted in any of the J-factor changing income formulas that solve for overall rates, change in property values, or equity yield rates.

The Ellwood-premise J factors reflect curvilinear income that changes from time zero in relation to a sinking fund accumulation curve; the straight-line premise J factors describe income changing in equal annual amounts after the first year.

In the following examples, the change in both income and value is + 25% in five years and the mortgage terms are 70% ratio at 12% nominal interest with a 25-year term. The desired equity yield rate is 18%.

$$C = Y_E + P\ 1/S_{\overline{n}|} - R_M$$
$$C = 0.18 + 0.0435 \times 0.139778 - 0.1263869$$
$$C = 0.0596934, \text{ or } 0.0597$$

Example 1

Assuming the income of a property at time zero is $10,000, what is its calculated value using the Ellwood premise?

$$R_O = (Y_E - MC - \Delta_O\ 1/\ S_{\overline{n}|})/ (1 + \Delta_1 J)$$
$$R_O = (0.18 - 0.70 \times 0.0597 - 0.25 \times 0.139778)/(1 + 0.25 \times 0.4651)$$
$$R_O = 0.092509$$
$$V_O = I_O/R_O$$
$$V_O = \$10,000/0.092509$$
$$V_O = \$108,098$$

Proof:

$$\text{Debt service} = \$108,098 \times 0.70 \quad = \$75,668$$
$$\$75,668 \times 0.1263869 = \$9,563$$
$$\text{Reversion} = \$108,098 \times 1.25 - \$75,668 \times (1 - 0.0435) = \$62,746$$
$$\text{Equity} = \$108,098 \times 0.30 \quad = \$32,429$$

Time	Income	−	Debt Service	=	Cash to Equity	x PVF @ 18%	=	Value
1	$10,349	−	$9,563	=	$786	x 0.847458	=	$666
2	10,762	−	9,563	=	1,199	x 0.718184	=	861
3	11,248	−	9,563	=	1,685	x 0.608631	=	1,026
4	11,823	−	9,563	=	2,260	x 0.515789	=	1,166
5	12,500	−	9,563	=	2,937	x 0.437109	=	1,284
Reversion					62,746	x 0.437109	=	27,427
Total equity								$32,430

Example 2

Assuming the income of the property at the end of Year One is $10,000, what is its calculated value using the straight-line premise:

$$R_O = (Y_E - MC - \Delta_O \, 1/S_{\overline{n}|})/(1 + \Delta_1 J)$$
$$R_O = (0.18 - 0.70 \times 0.0597 - 0.25 \times 0.139778)/(1 + 0.25 \times 0.3346)$$
$$R_O = 0.095294$$
$$V_O = I_O/R_O$$
$$V_O = \$10,000/0.095294$$
$$V_O = \$104,938$$

Proof:

$$\text{Debt service} = \$104,938 \times 0.70 = \$73,457$$
$$\$73,457 \times 0.1263869 = \$9,284$$
$$\text{Reversion} = \$104,938 \times 1.25 - \$73,457 \times (1 - 0.0435)$$
$$= \$60,911$$
$$\text{Equity} = \$104,938 \times 0.30 = \$31,481$$

Time	Income	−	Debt Service	=	Cash to Equity	x PVF @ 18%	=	Value
1	$10,000	−	$9,284	=	$716	x 0.847458	=	$607
2	10,500	−	9,284	=	1,216	x 0.718184	=	873
3	11,000	−	9,284	=	1,716	x 0.608631	=	1,044
4	11,500	−	9,284	=	2,216	x 0.515789	=	1,143
5	12,000	−	9,284	=	2,716	x 0.437109	=	1,187
Reversion					60,911	x 0.437109	=	26,625
Total equity								$31,479

If the income were expected to change by + 25% in five years and the yield rate were 16%, the J factor would be 0.4790 under the Ellwood (sinking fund) premise and 0.3412 on a straight-line basis. The appropriate factor would be inserted into the mortgage-equity formula.

Interrelationships Among the Tables

Note that mathematical relationships exist among the formulas for the various tables. These relationships can be useful in understanding the tables and solving appraisal problems. For example, appraisers should know that the factors in the ordinary level annuity and direct reduction loan tables are reciprocals; the factors in the ordinary level annuity table can be used as multipliers instead of using the direct-reduction loan factors as divisors.

Reciprocals

Reciprocals are numbers divided into 1. Thus, the reciprocal of 10 is 1/10 and the reciprocal of 0.5 is 1/0.5. The factors in some of the tables are reciprocals of those in other tables. This is indicated by their formulas.

Future value of $1 and reversion factors

$$S^n \text{ and } \frac{1}{S^n}$$

The reversion factor at 12% for 10 years with annual compounding is 0.321973, which is the reciprocal of the future value of $1 factor.

$$0.321973 = \frac{1}{3.105848}$$

Sinking fund accumulations and sinking fund factors

$$S_{\overline{n}|} \text{ and } \frac{1}{S_{\overline{n}|}}$$

The sinking factor at 12% for 10 years with annual compounding is 0.056984, which is the reciprocal of the sinking fund accumulation factor.

$$0.056984 = \frac{1}{17.548735}$$

Ordinary level annuity and direct reduction loan factors

$$a_{\overline{n}|} \text{ and } \frac{1}{a_{\overline{n}|}}$$

The direct-reduction loan factor at 12% for 10 years with annual compounding is 0.176984, which is the reciprocal of the ordinary level annuity factor.

$$0.056984 = \frac{1}{17.548735}$$

$$0.176984 = \frac{1}{5.650223}$$

Summations

Ordinary level annuity factors

An ordinary level annuity factor represents the sum of the reversion factors for all periods up to and including the period being considered. For example, the ordinary level annuity factor for five years at 12% with annual compounding is 3.604776, which is the sum of all the reversion factors for Years One through Five.

$$0.892887$$
$$0.797194$$
$$0.711780$$
$$0.635518$$
$$\underline{0.567427}$$
$$3.604776$$

Direct reduction loan factors

A direct reduction loan factor represents the sum of the interest, yield, or discount rate stated at the top of the table and the sinking fund factor. For example, the direct reduction loan factor at 12% for 10 years with monthly compounding is 0.1721651, which is the sum of 0.12 plus the monthly sinking fund factor of 0.0043471 times 12 (0.12 + 0.0521651 = 0.1721651).

Conversely, the sinking fund factor can be obtained by subtracting the interest rate from the direct reduction loan factor. The sinking fund factor at 12% for 10 years with monthly compounding is 0.1721651 – 0.12 = 0.0521651. In addition, the interest rate can be obtained by subtracting the sinking fund factor from the direct reduction loan factor. Given a mortgage constant of 0.1721651 with monthly compounding for 10 years, the interest rate is 0.1721651 – 0.0521651 = 0.12000, or 12.0%.

Bibliography

Selected Readings and Information Sources

Books

Abrams, Charles. *The Language of Cities: A Glossary of Terms.* New York: Viking Penguin, Inc., 1971.

Akerson, Charles B. *The Appraiser's Workbook.* 2d ed. Chicago: Appraisal Institute, 1996.

———. *Capitalization Theory and Techniques: Study Guide.* Rev. ed. Chicago: American Institute of Real Estate Appraisers, 1984.

Albritton, Harold D. *Controversies in Real Property Valuation: A Commentary.* Chicago: American Institute of Real Estate Appraisers, 1982.

Alexander, Ian. *Office Location and Public Policy.* New York: Chancer Press, 1979.

American Association of State Highway Officials. *Acquisitions for Right of Way.* Washington, D.C., 1962.

American Institute of Real Estate Appraisers. *The Appraisal of Rural Property.* Chicago, 1983.

———. *Appraisal Thought: A 50-Year Beginning.* Chicago, 1982.

———. *Forecasting: Market Determinants Affecting Cash Flows and Reversions.* Research Series Report 4. Chicago, 1989.

———. *Readings in the Income Capitalization Approach to Real Property Valuation, Volume II.* Chicago, 1985.

———. *Readings in Market Research for Real Estate.* Chicago, 1985.

———. *Readings in Real Property Valuation Principles, Volume II.* Chicago, 1985.

———. *Real Estate Market Analysis and Appraisal.* Research Series Report 3. Chicago, 1988.

Andrews, Richard B. *Urban Land Economics and Public Policy.* New York: Free Press, 1971.

Andrews, Richard N. L. *Land in America.* Lexington, Mass.: D. C. Heath, 1979.

Appraisal Institute. *Appraising Residential Properties.* 2d ed. Chicago, 1992.

———. *The Dictionary of Real Estate Appraisal.* 3d ed. Chicago, 1993.

Arnold, Alvin L. and Jack Kusnet. *The Arnold Encyclopedia of Real Estate.* Boston: Warren, Gorham & Lamont, Inc., 1978.

Babcock, Frederick M. *The Valuation of Real Estate.* New York: McGraw-Hill, 1932.

Barlowe, Raleigh. *Land Resource Economics.* 4th ed. Englewood Cliffs, N. J.: Prentice-Hall, 1986.

Bierman, Harold Jr., and Seymour Smidt. *The Capital Budgeting Decision.* 6th ed. New York: Macmillan, 1984.

Bish, Robert L. and Hugh O. Nourse. *Urban Economics and Policy Analysis.* New York: McGraw-Hill, 1975.

Bloom, George F., Arthur M. Weimer, and Jeffrey D. Fisher. *Real Estate.* 8th ed. New York: Wiley, 1982.

Bongiorno, Benedetto and Robert R. Garland. *Real Estate Accounting and Reporting Manual.* Boston: Warren, Gorham & Lamont, Inc., 1983.

Bonright, James C. *The Valuation of Property.* Vol. 1. New York: McGraw-Hill, 1937.

Brueggeman, William B., Jeffrey D. Fisher, and Leo D. Stone. *Real Estate Finance.* 8th ed. Homewood, Ill.: Irwin, 1989

Burton, James H. *Evolution of the Income Approach.* Chicago: American Institute of Real Estate Appraisers, 1982.

Byrne, Therese E. *A Guide to Real Estate Information Sources.* Therese E. Byrne, 1980.

Carn, Neil, Joseph Rabianski, Maury Seldin, and Ron Racster. *Real Estate Market Analysis: Applications and Techniques.* Englewood Cliffs, N.J.: Prentice-Hall, 1988.

Cartwright, John M. *Glossary of Real Estate Law.* Rochester, N.Y.: The Lawyers Co-Operative Publishing Co., 1972.

Clapp, John M. *Handbook for Real Estate Market Analysis.* Englewood Cliffs, N.J.: Prentice-Hall, 1987.

Colangelo, Robert V. and Ronald D. Miller. *Environmental Site Assessments and Their Impact on Property Value.* Chicago: Appraisal Institute, 1995.

Conroy, Kathleen. *Valuing the Timeshare Property.* Chicago: American Institute of Real Estate Appraisers, 1981.

Counselors of Real Estate (American Society of Real Estate Counselors). *Real Estate Counseling.* 2d ed. Chicago, 1988.

Davies, Pearl Janet. *Real Estate in American History.* Washington, D.C.: Public Affairs Press, 1958.

Desmond, Glenn M. and Richard E. Kelley. *Business Valuation Handbook.* Llano, Calif: Valuation Press, 1988.

Dilmore, Gene. *Quantitative Techniques in Real Estate Counseling.* Lexington, Mass.: D. C. Heath, 1981.

Dombal, Robert W. *Appraising Condominiums: Suggested Data Analysis Techniques.* Chicago: American Institute of Real Estate Appraisers, 1981.

Eaton, James D. *Real Estate Valuation in Litigation.* 2d ed. Chicago: Appraisal Institute, 1995.

Fanning, Stephen F., Terry V. Grissom, and Thomas D. Pearson, *Market Analysis for Valuation Appraisals.* Chicago: Appraisal Institute, 1994.

Financial Accounting Standards Board. FASB Statement No. 66, *Accounting for Sales of Real Estate,* and FASB Statement No. 67, *Accounting for Costs and Initial Rental Operations of Real Estate Projects.* Norwalk, Conn.: FASB, 1982.

Fisher, Clifford E., Jr., *Mathematics for Real Estate Appraisers.* Chicago: Appraisal Institute, 1996.

_____. *Rates and Ratios Used in the Income Capitalization Approach.* Chicago: Appraisal Institute, 1995.

Friedman, Jack P. et al. *Dictionary of Real Estate Terms.* New York: Barron, 1987.

Friedman, Edith J., ed. *Encyclopedia of Real Estate Appraising.* 3d ed. Englewood Cliffs, N.J.: Prentice-Hall, 1978.

Gibbons, James E. *Appraising in a Changing Economy: Collected Writings of James E. Gibbons.* Chicago: American Institute of Real Estate Appraisers, 1982.

Gimmy, Arthur E. and Michael G. Boehm. *Elderly Housing: A Guide to Appraisal, Market Analysis, Development and Financing.* Chicago: American Institute of Real Estate Appraisers, 1988.

Gimmy, Arthur E. and Brian B. Woodworth. *Fitness, Racquet Sports, and Spa Projects: A Guide to Appraisal, Development, and Financing.* Chicago: American Institute of Real Estate Appraisers, 1989.

Gimmy, Arthur E. and Martin E. Benson. *Golf Courses and Country Clubs: A Guide to Appraisal, Market Analysis, and Financing.* Chicago: Appraisal Institute, 1992.

Graaskamp, James A. *Graaskamp on Real Estate.* Stephen P. Jarchot, ed. Washington, D.C.: Urban Land Institute, 1991.

Graaskamp, James A. *A Guide to Feasibility Analysis.* Chicago: Society of Real Estate Appraisers, 1970.

Greer, Gaylon E. *The Real Estate Investment Decision.* Lexington, Mass.: D. C. Heath, 1979.

Gross, Jerome S., comp. *Webster's New World Illustrated Encyclopedia Dictionary of Real Estate.* 3d ed. New York: Prentice-Hall, 1987.

Haggett, Peter. *Locational Analysis in Human Geography.* New York: St. Martin's, 1965.

Harris, Cyril M. *Dictionary of Architecture and Construction.* New York: McGraw-Hill, 1975.

Harrison, Frank E. *Appraising the Tough Ones: Creative Ways to Value Complex Residential Properties.* Chicago: Appraisal Institute, 1996.

Harrison, Henry S. *Houses—The Illustrated Guide to Construction, Design & Systems.* Rev. ed. Chicago: Realtors^R National Marketing Institute, 1990.

Heilbroner, Robert L. *The Worldly Philosophers.* Rev. ed. New York: Simon and Schuster, 1964.

Himstreet, William C. *Communicating the Appraisal: The Narrative Report.* Chicago: American Institute of Real Estate Appraisers, 1988.

Hoover, Edgar M. *The Location of Economic Activity.* New York: McGraw-Hill, 1963.

Institute on Planning, Zoning, and Eminent Domain. *Proceedings.* Albany, N. Y.: Matthew Bender. Series began in 1959.

International Association of Assessing Officers. *Property Appraisal and Assessment Administration.* Chicago, 1990.

————. *Property Assessment Valuation.* Chicago, 1977.

Jevons, W. Stanley. *The Theory of Political Economy.* 5th ed. New York: Augustus M. Kelley, 1965.

Kahn, Sanders A. and Frederick E. Case. *Real Estate Appraisal and Investment.* 2d ed. New York: Ronald Press, 1977.

Keating, David Michael. *The Valuation of Wetlands.* Chicago: Appraisal Institute, 1995

Keune, Russell V., ed. *The Historic Preservation Yearbook.* Bethesda, Md.: Adler and Adler, 1984.

Kinnard, William N., Jr. *Income Property Valuation: Principles and Techniques of Appraising Income-Producing Real Estate.* Lexington, Mass.: D. C. Heath, 1971.

Kinnard, William N., Jr., ed. *1984 Real Estate Valuation Colloquium: A Redefinition of Real Estate Appraisal Precepts and Practices.* Boston: Oelgeschlager, Gunn & Hain and Lincoln Institute of Land Policy, 1986.

Kinnard, William N., Jr. and Byrl N. Boyce. *Appraising Real Property.* Lexington, Mass: D. C. Heath, 1984.

Kinnard, William N., Jr., Stephen D. Messner, and Byrl N. Boyce. *Industrial Real Estate.* 4th ed. Washington, D.C.: Society of Industrial Realtors®, 1979.

Klink, James J. *Real Estate Accounting and Reporting: A Guide for Developers, Investors and Lenders.* New York: John Wiley & Sons, Inc., 1980.

Kratovil, Robert and Raymond J. Werner. *Real Estate Law.* 8th ed. Englewood Cliffs, N.J.: Prentice-Hall, 1983.

Levine, Mark Lee. *Real Estate Appraisers' Liability.* New York: Clark Boardman Callaghan, 1991.

Love, Terrence L., *The Guide to Appraisal Office Policies and Procedures.* Chicago: Appraisal Institute, 1991.

Lovell, Douglas D. and Robert S. Martin. *Subdivision Analysis.* Chicago: Appraisal Institute, 1993.

Mason, James J., ed. and comp. *AIREA Financial Tables.* Chicago: American Institute of Real Estate Appraisers, 1981.

R.S. Means, Inc. *Means Illustrated Construction Dictionary.* New unabr. ed. Kingston, Mass.: R.S. Means, Inc., 1991.

Mills, Arlen C. and Dorothy Z. *Communicating the Appraisal: The Uniform Residential Appraisal Report.* 2d ed. Chicago: Appraisal Institute, 1994.

Minnerly, W. Lee. *Electronic Data Interchange (EDI) and the Appraisal Office.* Chicago: Appraisal Institute, 1996

National Cooperative Highway Research Program. *Reports*. Washington, D.C.: National Academy of Sciences Highway Research Board, 1966-1979.

North, Lincoln W. *The Concept of Highest and Best Use*. Winnipeg, Manitoba: Appraisal Institute of Canada, 1981.

Noyes, C. Reinold. *The Institution of Property*. London: Longmans, Green and Company, 1936.

Olin, Harold B., John L. Schmidt, and Walter H.Lewis. *Construction—Principles, Materials & Methods*. 4th ed. Chicago: Institute of Financial Education and Interstate Printers and Publishers, 1980.

O'Mara, Paul W. *Residential Development Handbook*. Washington, D.C.: Urban Land Institute, 1978.

Perin, Constance. *Everything in Its Place: Social Order and Land Use in America*. Princeton, N.J.: Princeton University Press, 1977.

Ratcliff, Richard U. *Modern Real Estate Valuation: Theory and Application*. Madison, Wis.: Democrat Press, 1965.

_____. *Urban Land Economics*. New York: Greenwood, 1972.

Rayburn, William B. and Dennis S. Tosh. *Fair Lending and the Appraiser*. Chicago: Apprasial Institute, 1996.

Reilly, John W. *The Language of Real Estate*. 3d ed. Chicago: Real Estate Education Co., 1989.

Reynolds, Judith. *Historic Properties: Preservation and the Valuation Process*. 2d ed. Chicago: Appraisal Institute, 1996.

Ring, Alfred A. and James H. Boykin. *The Valuation of Real Estate*. 3d ed. Englewood Cliffs, N.J.: Prentice-Hall, 1986.

Ring, Alfred A. and Jerome Dasso. *Real Estate Principles and Practices*. 10th ed. Englewood Cliffs, N.J.: Prentice-Hall, 1985.

Roca, Ruben A. *Market Research for Shopping Centers*. New York: International Council of Shopping Centers, 1980.

Rohan, Patrick J. and Melvin A. Reskin. *Condemnation Procedures and Techniques; Forms*. Albany, N.Y.: Matthew Bender, 1968 (looseleaf service).

Roll, Eric. *A History of Economic Thought*. 3d ed. Englewood Cliffs, N.J.: Prentice-Hall, 1964.

Rosenberg, Jerry M. *Dictionary of Banking and Finance*. New York: John Wiley & Sons, Inc., 1982.

Rushmore, Stephen. *Hotels and Motels: A Guide to Market Analysis and Valuations*. Chicago: Appraisal Institute, 1992.

Sackman, Julius L. and Patrick J. Rohan. *Nichols' Law of Eminent Domain*. 3d rev. ed. Albany, N.Y.: Matthew Bender, 1973 (looseleaf service).

Sahling, Leonard. *Real Estate Economics Special Report*. "Rent or Buy: A Market Analysis." New York: Merrill Lynch, June 1990.

Samuelson, Paul A. and William D. Nordhaus. *Economics*. 13th ed. New York: McGraw-Hill, 1989.

Schmutz, George L. *The Appraisal Process*. North Hollywood, Calif.: the author, 1941.

_____. *Condemnation Appraisal Handbook,* rev. and enl. by Edwin M. Rams. Englewood Cliffs, N.J.: Prentice-Hall, 1963.

Schwanke, Dean. *Smart Buildings and Technology—Enhanced Real Estate, Volume I.* Washington, D.C.: Urban Land Institute, 1976.

Seldin, Maury and James H. Boykin. *Real Estate Analyses.* Homewood, Ill.: American Society of Real Estate Counselors and Dow Jones-Irwin, 1990.

Shenkel, William M. *Modern Real Estate Appraisal.* New York: McGraw-Hill, 1978.

Shlaes, Jared. *Real Estate Counseling in a Plain Brown Wrapper.* Chicago: Counselors of Real Estate, 1992.

Sirmans, C.F. and Austin J. Jaffe. *The Complete Real Estate Investment Handbook: A Professional Investment Strategy.* 4th ed. New York: Prentice-Hall, 1988.

Smith, Halbert C. and Jerry D. Beloit. *Real Estate Appraisal.* 2d ed. Columbus, Ohio: Century VII Publishing Company, 1987.

Smith, Halbert C., Carl J. Tschappat, and Ronald L. Racster. *Real Estate and Urban Development.* 3d ed. Homewood, Ill.: Richard D. Irwin, 1981.

Talamo, John, J.D. *The Real Estate Dictionary.* Boston: Laventhal & Horwath/Financial Publishing Co., 1984.

United States Department of Commerce, Bureau of Census. *Statistical Abstract of the United States, 1990.* Washington, D.C.: U.S. Government Printing Office, 1990.

Urban Land Institute. *Shopping Center Development Handbook.* Washington, D.C.: ULI, 1985.

Vane, Howard R. and John L. Thompson. *Monetarism-Theory, Evidency and Policy.* New York: Halsted, 1979.

Ventrolo, William L. and Martha R. Williams. *Fundamentals of Real Estate Appraisal.* 5th ed. Chicago: Real Estate Education Co., 1990.

Vernor, James D. and Joseph Rabianski. *Shopping Center Appraisal and Analysis.* Chicago: Appraisal Institute, 1992.

Weinberg, Norman, Paul J. Colletti, William A. Colavito, and Frank A. Melchior. *Guide to the New York Real Estate Salespersons Course.* New York: John Wiley & Sons, Inc., 1983.

Wendt, Paul F. *Real Estate Appraisal Review and Outlook.* Athens: University of Georgia Press, 1974.

West, Bill W. and Richard L. Dickinson. *Street Talk in Real Estate.* Alameda/Sacramento, Calif.: Unique Pub., 1987.

White, John R., ed. *The Office Building From Concept to Investment Reality.* Chicago: Counselors of Real Estate, Appraisal Institute, and Society of Industrial and Office Realtors® Educational Fund, 1993.

White, John Robert. *Real Estate Valuing, Counseling, Forecasting: Selected Writings of John Robert White.* Chicago: American Institute of Real Estate Appraisers, 1984.

Witherspoon, Robert E., Jon P. Abbett, and Robert M. Gladstone. *Mixed-Use Developments: New Ways of Land Use.* Washington, D.C.: Urban Land Institute, 1976.

Wolf, Peter. *Land in America: Its Value, Use, and Control.* New York: Pantheon, 1981.

Dictionaries and Sources of Information on Computers

Arck Publications, Inc. *Small Business Computers.* Arck Publications, Inc., 1984

Dum, Mary. *The Computerized Appraisal Office.* Chicago: Appraisal Institute, 1996.

Freedman, Alan. *Electronic Computer Glossary.* Point Pleasant, Penn.: The Computer Language Co., 1993.

Microsoft Press. *Microsoft Press Computer Dictionary.* Redmond, Wash.: Microsoft Corporation, 1991.

Nader, Jonar. *Prentice-Hall's Illustrated Dictionary of Computing.* Englewood Cliffs, N.J.: Prentice-Hall, 1992.

Pfaffenberger, Bryan. *Que's Computer User's Dictionary.* Carmel, Ind.: Que Corporation, 1990.

Prentice-Hall. *Webster's New World Dictionary of Computing.* Englewood Cliffs, N.J.: Prentice-Hall, 1992

Building Cost Manuals

Boeckh Building Valuation Manual. Milwaukee: Thompson Publishing Corp., 1979. 3 vols.

Vol. 1—*Residential and Agricultural;* Vol. 2—*Commercial;* Vol. 3—*Industrial and Institutional.* Uses 1979 cost database and includes a wide variety of building models. Built up from unit-in-place costs converted to cost per square foot of floor or ground area. *Boeckh Building Cost Modifier* is published bimonthly for updating with current modifiers.

Building Construction Cost Data. Duxbury, Mass.: Robert Snow Means Co., annual.

Lists average unit prices on many building construction items for use in engineering estimates. Components arranged according to uniform system adopted by the American Institute of Architects, Associated General Contractors, and Construction Specifications Institute.

Dodge Building Cost Calculator & Valuation Guide. New York: McGraw-Hill Information Systems Co. (looseleaf service, quarterly supplements).

Lists building costs for common types and sizes of buildings. Local cost modifiers and historical local cost index tables included. Formerly *Dow Building Cost Calculator.*

Marshall Valuation Service. Los Angeles: Marshall and Swift Publication Co. (looseleaf service, monthly supplements).

Cost data for determining replacement costs of buildings and other improvements in the United States and Canada. Includes current cost multipliers and local modifiers.

Residential Cost Handbook. Los Angeles: Marshall and Swift Publication Co. (looseleaf service, quarterly supplements).

Presents square-foot method and segregated-cost method. Local modifiers and cost-trend modifiers included.

Sources of Operating Costs and Ratios

Only a few published sources are cited below. Attention is directed to the first item listed.

Robert Morris Associates. *Sources of Composite Financial Data—A Bibliography.* 3d ed. Philadelphia, 1971.

An annotated list of 98 nongovernment sources, arranged in manufacturing, wholesaling, retail, and service categories. Subject index to specific businesses. Publishers' names and addresses included for each citation.

Building Owners and Managers Association International. *Downtown and Suburban Office Building Experience Exchange Report.* Washington, D.C.

Published annually since 1920. Includes analysis of expenses and income quoted in cents per square foot as well as national, regional, and selected city averages.

Dun & Bradstreet, Inc. *Key Business Ratios in 125 Lines.* New York.

Published annually. Contains balance sheet and profit-and-loss ratios.

Institute of Real Estate Management. *Income/Expense Analysis: Apartments, Condominiums & Cooperatives.* Chicago.

Published annually since 1954. Data arranged by building type, then by national, regional, metropolitan, and selected city groupings. Operating costs listed per room, per square foot, etc. Formerly *Apartment Building Experience Exchange.*

_____. *Income/Expense Analysis: Suburban Office Buildings.* Chicago.

Published annually since 1976. Data analyzed on the basis of gross area and gross and net rentable office areas. Includes dollar-per-square-foot calculations; national, regional, and metropolitan comparisons; and detailed analyses for selected cities.

National Institute of Real Estate Brokers. *Percentage Leases.* 13th ed. Chicago, 1973.

Based on reports of 3,100 leases for 97 retail and service categories in seven U.S. regions. Data broken down by type of operation, area, center, and building. Regional and store averages given for average minimum rent, rent per square foot, average gross leasable areas, and sales per square foot.

National Retail Merchants Association, Controllers' Congress. *Department Store and Specialty Store Merchandising and Operating Results.* New York.

Published annually since 1925. Merchandise classification base used since 1969 edition (1968 data). Includes geographical analysis by Federal Reserve districts. Known as the "MOR" report.

_____. *Financial and Operating Results of Department and Specialty Stores.* New York.

Published annually since 1963. Data arranged by sales volume category. Known as the "FOR" report.

Pannell Kerr Forster. *Clubs in Town & Country.* Houston.

Published annually since 1953. Lists income-expense data and operating ratios for city and country clubs. Geographical data broken down into four U.S. regions.

_____. *Trends in the Hotel Industry.* Houston.

Published annually since 1937. Lists income-expense data and operating ratios for transient and resort hotels and motels. Geographical data broken down into five U.S. regions.

Urban Land Institute. *Dollars and Cents of Shopping Centers.* Washington, D.C., 1990.

First issued in 1961 and revised every three years. Includes income and expense data for neighborhood, community, and regional centers as well as statistics for specific tenant types.

Periodicals

American Council of Life Insurance Digest. American Council of Life Insurance, Washington, D.C.

American Right of Way Proceedings. American Right of Way Association, Los Angeles.
Annual. Papers presented at national seminars.

Appraisal Institute Magazine. Appraisal Institute of Canada, Winnipeg, Manitoba.
Quarterly. General and technical articles on appraisal and expropriation in Canada. Includes information on institute programs, news, etc.

The Appraisal Journal. Appraisal Institute, Chicago.
Quarterly. Oldest periodical in the appraisal field, published since 1932. Includes technical articles on all phases of real property appraisal and regular feature on legal decisions. Bibliographies for 1932-1969, 1970-1980, and 1980-1987 are available.

Appraiser News In Brief. Appraisal Institute, Chicago.
Published eight times a year. News bulletin covering current events and trends in appraisal practice.

Buildings. Stamats Communications, Inc., Cedar Rapids, Iowa.
Monthly. Journal of building construction and management.

Crittenden Report. Crittenden Institute. See also *Income Property Rates* and *Real Estate Finance* from Crittenden Publishing, Inc., Novato, California.

Editor and Publisher Market Guide. Editor and Publisher, New York.
Annual. Standardized market data for more than 1,500 areas in the United States and Canada, including population estimates for trading areas. List of principal industries, transportation, climate, chain store outlets, etc.

Emerging Trends in Real Estate. Real Estate Research Corp., Atlanta, Georgia and New York.
Annual.

Forum 500 Forecast. American Council of Life Insurance, Washington, D.C.

Income Property Rates. Crittenden Publishing, Inc., Novato, California.
Weekly. Rates and terms on funding for income properties.

Journal of the American Real Estate and Urban Economics Association. Bloomington, Indiana.
Quarterly. Focuses on research and scholarly studies of current and emerging real estate issues.

Journal of the American Society of Farm Managers and Rural Appraisers. Denver.
Semiannual. Includes appraisal articles.

Journal of Property Management. Institute of Real Estate Management, Chicago.
Bimonthly. Covers a broad range of property investment and management issues.

Journal of Real Estate Literature. American Real Estate Society, Cleveland, Ohio.
Semiannual. Contains review articles, case studies, doctoral dissertations, and reviews of technical literature, data sets, computer applications, and software.

Journal of Real Estate Portfolio Management. American Real Estate Society, Cleveland, Ohio.
Semiannual. Contains the results of applied research on real estate investment and portfolio management.

Journal of Real Estate Research. American Real Estate Society, Cleveland, Ohio.
> Quarterly. Publishes the results of applied research on real estate development, finance, investment, management, market analysis, marketing, and valuation.

Just Compensation. Sherman Oaks, California.
> Monthly. Reports on condemnation cases.

Land Economics. University of Wisconsin, Madison.
> Quarterly. Journal devoted to the study of economics and social institutes. Includes reports on university research and trends in land utilization. Frequently publishes articles on developments in other countries.

MarketSource. Appraisal Institute, Chicago.
> Quarterly. Published since 1991. Data on key rates, economic trends, and real estate financing and market conditions.

The following periodicals on debenture and equity investment are published by Moody's Investors Service, Inc., New York.

Moody's Bank and Finance News Reports.
> Twice weekly.

Moody's Bond Record.
> Monthly.

Moody's Commercial Paper Record.
> Monthly.

Moody's Dividend Record.
> Twice weekly.

Moody's Handbook of Common Stocks.
> Quarterly.

Moody's Handbook of Over-the-Counter Stocks.
> Quarterly.

Moody's Industrials.
> Twice weekly.

Moody's Investors Fact Sheets.
> Irregular.

Moody's Municipals and Governments.
> Twice weekly.

Moody's Over-the-Counter Industrials.
> Weekly.

Moody's Public Utilities.
> Twice weekly.

Moody's Transportation.
> Twice weekly.

National Real Estate Review. National Association of Realtors,® Washington, D.C.
   Annual. Includes information on office, industrial, retail, multifamily, and hotel real estate.

NCREIF Real Estate Performance Report. National Council of Real Estate Investment
   Fiduciaries, which maintains the NCREIF Classic Property Index (formerly the Russell-
   NCREIF Property Index).
   Quarterly. Tracks the performance of properties acquired on behalf of tax-exempt institutions, on an unleveraged basis, and held in fiduciary trusts. The index is calculated on the
   basis of four different rates of return (total return, income return, capital appreciation
   return, and annual/annualized return).

Pension Real Estate Quarterly. Pension Real Estate Association, Glastonbury, Connecticut.

Property Tax Journal. International Association of Assessing Officers, Chicago.
   Quarterly. Includes articles on property taxation and assessment administration.

Real Estate Capital Markets. Institutional Research, Inc., Walnut Creek, California.
   Quarterly. Contains articles and information on the financial markets and the availability,
   cost, and flow of capital.

Real Estate Finance. Crittenden Publishing, Inc., Novato, California.
   Weekly. Real estate finance information.

Real Estate Information Standards: 1995. Joint Task Force of the National Association of
   Real Estate Investment Managers (NAREIM), the National Council of Real Estate Investment Fiduciaries (NCREIF), and the Pension Real Estate Association (PREA).
   Includes standards for investment and asset information, valuation information, and
   performance measurement as well as the NCREIF market value accounting policy manual
   and appendices on terminology, computation methodology, prior initiatives and existing
   regulations, and reference source contacts.

Real Estate Investor Survey. Peter Korpacz, Frederick, Maryland.
   Quarterly. Survey of a cross-section of the major participants in real estate equity markets.

Real Estate Issues. American Society of Real Estate Counselors, Chicago.
   Semiannual.

Real Estate Law Journal. Warren, Gorham and Lamont, Inc., Boston.
   Quarterly. Publishes articles on legal issues and reviews current litigation of concern to real
   estate professionals.

Real Estate Market Forecast. Landauer Real Estate Counselors, New York.
   Annual.

Real Estate Report. Real Estate Research Corp., Atlanta, Georgia and New York.
   Quarterly.

Right of Way. American Right of Way Association, Los Angeles.
   Bimonthly. Articles on all phases of right-of-way activity—e.g., condemnation, negotiation,
   pipelines, electric power transmission lines, and highways. Includes association news.

Small Business Reporter. Bank of America, San Francisco.
   Irregular. Each issue devoted to a specific type of small business—e.g, coin-operated
   laundries, greeting card shops, restaurants.

The following periodicals on debenture and equity investment are published by Standard and Poor's Corporation, New York.

Standard and Poor's Bond Guide.
Monthly.

Standard and Poor's Bond Record.
Twice weekly.

Standard and Poor's Commercial Paper Ratings Guide.
Monthly.

Standard and Poor's Daily Stock Price Record: American Exchange.
Quarterly.

Standard and Poor's Daily Stock Price Record: N.Y. Stock Exchange.
Quarterly.

Standard and Poor's Daily Stock Price Record: Over-the-Counter Exchange.
Quarterly.

Standard and Poor's Dividend Record.
Daily and quarterly.

Standard and Poor's Earnings Forecaster.
Weekly.

Standard and Poor's Outlook.
Weekly.

Standard and Poor's Registered Bond Interest Record.
Weekly.

Standard and Poor's Stock Guide.
Monthly.

Standard and Poor's Stock Summary.
Monthly.

Survey of Buying Power. Sales Management, New York.
Annual. Includes population totals and characteristics and income and consumption data presented in national, regional, metropolitan area, county, and city categories. Separate section for Canadian information. Population estimates between decennial censuses.

Survey of Current Business. U.S. Bureau of Economic Analysis, U.S. Department of Commerce, Washington, D.C.
Monthly. Includes statistical and price data. Biennial supplement, *Business Statistics.*

Valuation. American Society of Appraisers, Washington, D.C.
Three issues per year. Articles on real property valuation and the appraisal of personal and intangible property. Includes society news.

Valuation Insights & Perspectives, Appraisal Institute, Chicago.
Published quarterly. Provides timely, practical information and ideas to assist real estate appraisers in conducting their businesses effectively.

Index

absorption studies, 602, 629

abstracts of title, 226, 629

accelerated cost recovery system (ACRS), 158

accessibility and site analysis, 235-236

accrued depreciation, 365fn
See also depreciation

accuracy, as reconciliation criterion, 604-605

active market, 68

actual age, 367, 369, 375

adaptive use movement, 292-293

addenda in appraisal reports, 632-633

adequacy and functional utility, 282-283

adjustable variable-rate mortgages, 548

adjustment grid, 178

adjustments
in sales comparison approach, 414-415, 419-420
sequence of, 420-422
See also dollar adjustments; gross adjustments; net adjustments; percentage adjustments; quantitative adjustments

administrative review, 686

ad valorem taxes, 165-166

Advisory Opinion 9, 199-200

after-tax cash flow, 455

age. *See* actual age; effective age

age and life relationships, 367-369

age-life method, 369, 374-378, 383-385

agents of production, 29

agricultural districts, 211-212

agricultural land, 237-238

agricultural properties
buildings on, 291-292
and market analysis, 75
and plottage, 230

air-conditioning systems, 264
in commercial buildings, 286
as variable expense, 493-494

air rights, 144-145, 148

Akerson, Charles B., 749

alarm systems, 266-267

allocation
and land valuation, 89, 326

amenities. *See* public amenities

Americans with Disabilities Act (ADA), 225, 285

annual debt service, 550

annual loan constant. *See* mortgage constants

annuities
and yield capitalization, 529

annuities payable in advance, 533

anticipation, 35
and land valuation, 321

apartment districts, 204-205

apartment hotels. *See* hotels

apartment houses
relative comparison analysis of, 437-440
and sample one-year income forecast, 498-499

appraisal
definition of, 11
discipline of, 7-10
foundations of, 35-52